Lecture Notes in Computer Science 3872

Commenced Publication in 1973
Founding and Former Series Editors:
Gerhard Goos, Juris Hartmanis, and Jan van Leeuwen

T0180230

Horst Bunke   A. Lawrence Spitz (Eds.)

Document Analysis Systems VII

7th International Workshop, DAS 2006
Nelson, New Zealand, February 13-15, 2006
Proceedings

 Springer

Volume Editors

Horst Bunke
University of Bern
Department of Computer Science
Neubrückstr. 10, 3012 Bern, Switzerland
E-mail: bunke@iam.unibe.ch

A. Lawrence Spitz
DocRec Ltd
34 Strathaven Place, Atawhai, Nelson 7001, New Zealand
E-mail: spitz@docrec.com

Library of Congress Control Number: 2005939178

CR Subject Classification (1998): I.5, H.3, I.4, I.7, J.1, J.2

LNCS Sublibrary: SL 6 – Image Processing, Computer Vision, Pattern Recognition, and Graphics

ISSN   0302-9743
ISBN-10   3-540-32140-3 Springer Berlin Heidelberg New York
ISBN-13   978-3-540-32140-8 Springer Berlin Heidelberg New York

Springer is a part of Springer Science+Business Media

springeronline.com

© Springer-Verlag Berlin Heidelberg 2006
Printed in Germany

Typesetting: Camera-ready by author, data conversion by Scientific Publishing Services, Chennai, India
Printed on acid-free paper   SPIN: 11669487   06/3142   5 4 3 2 1 0

Preface

DAS 2006 is the Seventh International Association for Pattern Recognition Workshop on Document Analysis Systems and was held in Nelson, New Zealand. DAS 2006 built on the tradition of past workshops held in Kaiserslautern, Germany (1994), Malvern, PA (1996), Nagano, Japan (1998), Rio de Janeiro, Brazil (2000), Princeton, NJ (2002), and Florence, Italy (2004). The goal of this meeting was to bring together those who have designed systems, or systems components, to solve real-world problems in document analysis.

Document analysis systems is inherently an interdisciplinary field encompassing such diverse disciplines as image processing, pattern recognition, document structure and natural language processing. DAS 2006 attempted to bring these disciplines together and to provide interactions between systems developers, suppliers and end users.

We received 78 papers from 19 countries. Each submission was reviewed by three reviewers. In addition to the Program Committee members, 42 other reviewers helped in this process. From those submissions and their reviews, we went through the difficult and sometimes painful process of ranking papers for acceptance or rejection. In the end we accepted 33 papers for oral presentation and 22 for presentation at poster sessions.

We, the Co-chairmen of DAS 2006, wish to express our gratitude to all of our colleagues who have reviewed the papers submitted for this conference.

We are proud to have brought two distinguished speakers to Nelson for keynote addresses: Ian Witten of the University of Waikato, the father of the New Zealand Digital Library, and James Fruchterman, a pioneer in modern commercial optical character recognition and currently CEO of Benetech.

We owe a special debt of gratitude to Marcus Liwicki of the University of Bern for his tireless work at maintaining the website, managing the flow of papers and reviews into the ConfMan system and assembling the proceedings for publication by Springer. He was ably assisted by Andreas Schlapbach.

We are fortunate that Siemens, Hitachi and Humanware provided DAS with financial support, and we thank them for doing so. Additionally, following the DAS tradition, the organizers of DAS 2004 have passed on the surplus from running that workshop for our use.

But ultimately it is the collection of authors who submitted papers to DAS to whom we owe the greatest gratitude. It is on them and their high-quality submissions that the success of DAS 2006 relies.

February 2006

Horst Bunke and Larry Spitz
Program Chairs
DAS 2006

Organization

DAS 2006 was organized by DocRec Ltd.

Executive Committee

Conference Chairs: Larry Spitz (DocRec Ltd, New Zealand)
                                    Horst Bunke (University of Bern, Switzerland)

Program Committee

Apostolos Antonacopoulos (UK)
Henry Baird (USA)
Thomas Breuel (Germany)
Horst Bunke (Switzerland)
Andreas Dengel (Germany)
David Doermann (USA)
Andrew Downton (UK)
Michael Fairhurst (UK)
Hiromichi Fujisawa (Japan)
Venugopal Govindaraju (USA)
Tin Kam Ho (USA)
Jianying Hu (USA)
Rolf Ingold (Switzerland)
Rangachar Kasturi (USA)
Koichi Kise (Japan)
Seong-Whan Lee (Korea)
Daniel Lopresti (USA)
Raghavan Manmatha (USA)
Simone Marinai (Italy)
Udo Miletzki (Germany)
Yasuaki Nakano (Japan)
Larry Spitz (New Zealand)
Karl Tombre (France)

Referees

Stefan Agne
Andrew Bagdanov
Ardhendu Behera
Koustav Bhattacharya
Alain Biem

Jean-Luc Blöchle
Matthew Boonstra
Jakob Brendel
Joshua Candamo
Farzin Deravi

Faisal Farooq
Gunnar Grimnes
Richard Guest
Sanaul Hoque
Gareth Howells
Jonathan Hull
Masakazu Iwamura
Stefan Jaeger
Thomas Kieninger
Malte Kiesel
Bertin Klein
Dar-Shyang Lee
Hansheng Lei
Jian Liang
Rainer Lindwurm
Vasant Manohar
Dalila Mekhaldi

David Mihalcik
Tristan Miller
Pranab Mohanty
Sunita Nayak
Shinichiro Omachi
Christoph Pesch
Maurizio Rigamonti
Thomas Roth-Berghofer
Sven Schwarz
Karthik Sridharan
Seiichi Uchida
Himanshu Vajaria
Ludger van Elst
Shankar Vembu
Alan Yang

Sponsoring Institutions

Siemens AG, Munich, Germany
HumanWare Group, Christchurch, New Zealand
Hitachi Central Research Laboratory, Tokyo, Japan

Scientific Sponsors

DocRec Ltd, Atawhai, Nelson, New Zealand
University of Bern, Switzerland
International Association for Pattern Recognition

Table of Contents

Session 1: Digital Libraries

Retrieval from Document Image Collections 1
A. Balasubramanian, Million Meshesha, C. V. Jawahar

A Semi-Automatic Adaptive OCR for Digital Libraries 13
Sachin Rawat, K. S. Sesh Kumar, Million Meshesha, Indraneel Deb Sikdar, A. Balasubramanian, C. V. Jawahar

Session 2: Image Processing

Contribution to the Discrimination of the Medieval Manuscript Texts: Application in the Palaeography 25
Ikram Moalla, Frank Lebourgeois, Hubert Emptoz, Adel M. Alimi

Restoring Ink Bleed-Through Degraded Document Images Using a Recursive Unsupervised Classification Technique 38
Drira Fadoua, Frank Lebourgeois, Hubert Emptoz

Networked Document Imaging with Normalization and Optimization 50
Hirobumi Nishida

Gray-Scale Thinning Algorithm Using Local Min/Max Operations 62
Kyoung Min Kim, Buhm Lee, Nam Sup Choi, Gwan Hee Kang, Joong Jo Park, Ching Y. Suen

Session 3: Handwriting 1

Automated Scoring of Handwritten Essays Based on Latent Semantic Analysis 71
Sargur Srihari, Rohini Srihari, Pavithra Babu, Harish Srinivasan

Aligning Transcripts to Automatically Segmented Handwritten Manuscripts 84
Jamie Rothfeder, R. Manmatha, Toni M. Rath

Virtual Example Synthesis Based on PCA for Off-Line Handwritten Character Recognition 96
Hidetoshi Miyao, Minoru Maruyama

Extraction of Handwritten Text from Carbon Copy Medical Form Images 106
Robert Milewski, Venu Govindaraju

Session 4: Document Structure and Format

Document Logical Structure Analysis Based on Perceptive Cycles 118
 Yves Rangoni, Abdel Belaïd

A System for Converting PDF Documents into Structured XML Format . 130
 Hervé Déjean, Jean-Luc Meunier

XCDF: A Canonical and Structured Document Format 142
 Jean-Luc Bloechle, Maurizio Rigamonti, Karim Hadjar, Denis Lalanne,
 Rolf Ingold

Structural Analysis of Mathematical Formulae with Verification Based
on Formula Description Grammar 154
 Seiichi Toyota, Seiichi Uchida, Masakazu Suzuki

Session 5: Tables

Notes on Contemporary Table Recognition 166
 David W. Embley, Daniel Lopresti, George Nagy

Handwritten Artefact Identification Method for Table Interpretation
with Little Use of Previous Knowledge 179
 Luiz Antônio Pereira Neves, João Marques de Carvalho, Jacques
 Facon, Flávio Bortolozzi, Sérgio Aparecido Ignácio

Session 6: Handwriting 2

Writer Identification for Smart Meeting Room Systems 190
 Marcus Liwicki, Andreas Schlapbach, Horst Bunke, Samy Bengio,
 Johnny Mariéthoz, Jonas Richiardi

Extraction and Analysis of Document Examiner Features from Vector
Skeletons of Grapheme 'th' 201
 Vladimir Pervouchine, Graham Leedham

Segmentation of On-line Handwritten Japanese Text Using SVM for
Improving Text Recognition 213
 Bilan Zhu, Junko Tokuno, Masaki Nakagawa

Application of Bi-gram Driven Chinese Handwritten Character
Segmentation for an Address Reading System 225
 Yan Jiang, Xiaoqing Ding, Qiang Fu, Zheng Ren

Session 7: Language and Script Identification

Language Identification in Degraded and Distorted Document Images . . . 237
 Shijian Lu, Chew Lim Tan, Weihua Huang

Bangla/English Script Identification Based on Analysis of Connected
Component Profiles 249
Lijun Zhou, Yue Lu, Chew Lim Tan

Script Identification from Indian Documents 261
Gopal Datt Joshi, Saurabh Garg, Jayanthi Sivaswamy

Finding the Best-Fit Bounding-Boxes 274
Bo Yuan, Leong Keong Kwoh, Chew Lim Tan

Session 9: Systems and Performance Evaluation

Towards Versatile Document Analysis Systems 286
Henry S. Baird, Matthew R. Casey

Exploratory Analysis System for Semi-Structured Engineering Logs 296
Michael Flaster, Bruce Hillyer, Tin Kam Ho

Ground Truth for Layout Analysis Performance Evaluation 307
A. Antonacopoulos, D. Karatzas, D. Bridson

On Benchmarking of Invoice Analysis Systems 318
Bertin Klein, Stefan Agne, Andreas Dengel

Semi-Automatic Ground Truth Generation for Chart Image Recognition . 330
Li Yang, Weihua Huang, Chew Lim Tan

Session 10: Retrieval and Segmentation

Efficient Word Retrieval by means of SOM Clustering and PCA 342
Simone Marinai, Stefano Faini, Emanuele Marino, Giovanni Soda

The Effects of OCR Error on the Extraction of Private Information 354
Kazem Taghva, Russell Beckley, Jeffrey Coombs

Combining Multiple Classifiers for Faster Optical Character Recognition . 365
Kumar Chellapilla, Michael Shilman, Patrice Simard

Performance Comparison of Six Algorithms for Page Segmentation 375
Faisal Shafait, Daniel Keysers, Thomas M. Breuel

Posters

HVS inspired System for Script Identification in Indian Multi-script
Documents 387
Peeta Basa Pati, A. G. Ramakrishnan

A Shared Fragments Analysis System for Large Collections of Web Pages   397
Junchang Ma, Zhimin Gu

Offline Handwritten Arabic Character Segmentation with Probabilistic
Model 409
Pingping Xiu, Liangrui Peng, Xiaoqing Ding, Hua Wang

Automatic Keyword Extraction from Historical Document Images 421
K. Terasawa, T. Nagasaki, T. Kawashima

Digitizing A Million Books: Challenges for Document Analysis 433
Pramod Sankar K., Vamshi Ambati, Lakshmi Pratha, C. V. Jawahar

Toward File Consolidation by Document Categorization 445
Abdel Belaïd, André Alusse

Finding Hidden Semantics of Text Tables 457
Saleh Alrashed

Reconstruction of Orthogonal Polygonal Lines 470
Alexander Gribov, Eugene Bodansky

A Multiclass Classification Framework for Document Categorization 482
Qi Qiang, Qinming He

The Restoration of Camera Documents through Image Segmentation 493
Shijian Lu, Chew Lim Tan

Cut Digits Classification with k-NN Multi-specialist 505
Fernando Boto, Andoni Cortés, Clemente Rodríguez

The Impact of OCR Accuracy and Feature Transformation on
Automatic Text Classification 516
*Mayo Murata, Lazaro S.P. Busagala, Wataru Ohyama, Tetsushi
Wakabayashi, Fumitaka Kimura*

A Method for Symbol Spotting in Graphical Documents 528
Daniel Zuwala, Salvatore Tabbone

Groove Extraction of Phonographic Records 539
Sylvain Stotzer, Ottar Johnsen, Frédéric Bapst, Rolf Ingold

Use of Affine Invariants in Locally Likely Arrangement Hashing for
Camera-Based Document Image Retrieval 551
Tomohiro Nakai, Koichi Kise, Masakazu Iwamura

Robust Chinese Character Recognition by Selection of Binary-based
and Grayscale-based Classifier 563
Yoshinobu Hotta, Jun Sun, Yutaka Katsuyama, Satoshi Naoi

Segmentation-driven Recognition Applied to Numerical Field
Extraction from Handwritten Incoming Mail Documents 575
Clément Chatelain, Laurent Heutte, Thierry Paquet

Performance Evaluation of Text Detection and Tracking in Video 587
Vasant Manohar, Padmanabhan Soundararajan, Matthew Boonstra,
Harish Raju, Dmitry Goldgof, Rangachar Kasturi, John Garofolo

Document Analysis System for Automating Workflows 599
Steven J. Simske, Jordi Arnabat

Automatic Assembling of Cadastral maps Based on Generalized Hough
Transformation 605
Fei Liu, Wataru Ohyama, Tetsushi Wakabayashi, Fumitaka Kimura

A Few Steps Towards On-the-Fly Symbol Recognition with Relevance
Feedback 617
Jan Rendek, Bart Lamiroy, Karl Tombre

The Fuzzy-Spatial Descriptor for the Online Graphic Recognition:
Overlapping Matrix Algorithm 629
Noorazrin Zakaria, Jean-Marc Ogier, Josep Llados

Author Index 641

Retrieval from Document Image Collections

A. Balasubramanian, Million Meshesha, and C.V. Jawahar

Centre for Visual Information Technology,
International Institute of Information Technology,
Hyderabad - 500 032, India
jawahar@iiit.ac.in

Abstract. This paper presents a system for retrieval of relevant documents from large document image collections. We achieve effective search and retrieval from a large collection of printed document images by matching image features at word-level. For representations of the words, profile-based and shape-based features are employed. A novel DTW-based partial matching scheme is employed to take care of morphologically variant words. This is useful for grouping together similar words during the indexing process. The system supports cross-lingual search using OM-Trans transliteration and a dictionary-based approach. System-level issues for retrieval (eg. scalability, effective delivery etc.) are addressed in this paper.

1 Introduction

Large digital libraries, such as Digital Library of India (DLI) [1] are emerging for archiving large collection of printed and handwritten documents. The DLI aims at digitizing all literary, artistic, and scientific works of mankind so as to create better access to traditional materials, easier preservation, and make documents freely accessible to the global society. More than 25 scanning centers all over India are working on digitization of books and manuscripts. The mega scanning center we have, has around fifty scanners, each one of them capable lof scanning approximately 5000 pages in 8 hours. As on September 2005, close to 100 thousand books with 25 million pages were digitized and made available online by DLI (*http://dli.iiit.ac.in*) as document images.

Building an effective access to these document images requires designing a mechanism for effective search and retrieval of textual data from document image collections. Document image indexing and retrieval were studied with limited scope in literature [2]. Success of these procedures mainly depends on the performance of the OCRs, which convert the document images into text. Much of the data in DLI are in Indian languages. Searching in these document image collections based on content, is not presently possible. This is because OCRs are not yet able to successfully recognize printed texts in Indian languages. We need an alternate approach to access the content of these documents [3]. A promising alternate direction is to search for relevant documents in image space without any explicit recognition. We have been motivated by the successful attempts on

H. Bunke and A.L. Spitz (Eds.): DAS 2006, LNCS 3872, pp. 1–12, 2006.

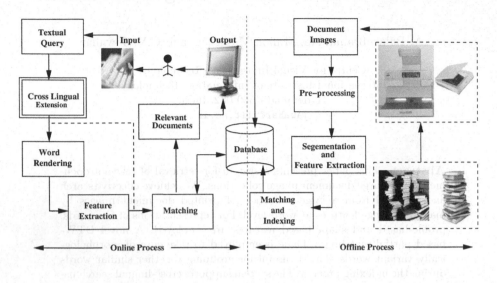

Fig. 1. Conceptual Diagram of the Searching Procedure from Multilingual Document Image Database. A Web Demo for the Above Procedure is Available Online at http://cvit.iiit.ac.in/wordsearch.html.

locating a specific word in handwritten English documents by matching image features for historical documents [4, 5].

We have already addressed algorithmic challenges for effective search in document images [6] . This paper describes the issues associated with the implementation of a scalable system for Indian language document images. A conceptual block diagram of our prototype system is shown in Figure 1. Our system accepts textual query from users. The textual query is first converted to an image by rendering, features are extracted from these images and then search is carried out for retrieval of relevant documents. Results of the search are pages from document image collections containing queried word sorted based on their relevance to the query.

2 Challenges in Design and Implementation of the System

Search and retrieval from large collection of document images is a challenging task, specially when there is no textual representation available. To design and implement a successful search engine in image domain, we need to address the following issues.

Search in images: Search in image space requires appropriate representational schemes and similarity measures. Success of content-based image retrieval(CBIR) schemes were limited by the diversity of the image collections. Digital libraries primarily archive text images, but of varying quality, script, style, size and font.

We need to come up with appropriate features and matching schemes, which can represent the content (text), while invariant to the popular variations.

Degradations of documents: Documents in digital libraries are extremely poor in quality. Popular artifacts in printed document images include (a) Excessive dusty noise, (b) Large ink-blobs joining disjoint characters or components, (c) Vertical cuts due to folding of the paper, (d) Cuts of arbitrary direction due to paper quality or foreign material, (e) Degradation of printed text due to the poor quality of paper and ink, (f) Floating ink from facing pages etc. We need to design an appropriate representational scheme and matching algorithm to accommodate the effect of degradation.

Need for cross-lingual retrieval: Document images in digital libraries are from diverse languages. Relevant documents that users need may be available in different languages. Most educated Indians can read more than one language. Hence, we need to design a mechanism that allows users to retrieve all documents related to their queries in any of the Indian languages.

Computational speed: Searching from large collection of document images pass through many steps: image processing, feature extraction, matching and retrieval of relevant documents. Each of these steps could be computationally expensive. In a typical book, there could be around 90,000 words and processing all of them online is practically impossible. We do all computationally expensive operations during the offline indexing (Section 4) and do minimal operations during online retrieval (Section 5).

Indian languages: Indian languages pose many additional challenges [7]. Some of these are: (i) lack of standard representation for the fonts and encoding, (ii) lack of support from operating system, browsers and keyboard, and (iii) lack of language processing routines. These issues add to the complexity of the design and implementation of a document image retrieval system.

3 Representation and Matching of Word Images

Word images extracted from documents in digital libraries are of varying quality, script, font, size and style. An effective representation of the word images will have to take care of these artifacts for successful searching and retrieval. We combined two categories of features to address these effects: word profiles and structural features. Explicit definitions of these features may be seen in [6].

Word Profiles: Profiles of the word provide a coarse way of representing a word image for matching. Profiles like upper word, lower word, projection and transition profiles are used here for word representation. Upper and lower word profiles capture part of the outlining shape of a word, while projection and transition profiles capture the distribution of ink along one of the two dimensions in a word image.

Structural Features: Structural features of the words are used to match two words based on some image similarities. Statistical moments (such as mean and standard deviation) and region-based moments (such as the zeroth- and first-order moments) are employed for describing the structure of the word image. For artifacts like salt and pepper noise, structural features are found to be reasonably robust.

Some of these features provide the sequence information, while others capture the structural characteristics. Given a document image, it is preprocessed offline to threshold, skew-correct, remove noise and thereafter to segment into words. Then features are extracted for each of the segmented word. They are also normalized such that the word representations become insensitive to variations in font, style, size and various degradations popularly present in document images.

Spotting a word from handwritten images is attempted by pairwise matching of all the words [5]. However for proper search and retrieval, one needs to identify the similar words and group them based on their similarity, and evaluate the relative importance of each of these words and word clusters. Matching is used to compute dissimilarity between word images. We use a simple squared Euclidean distance while computing the dissimilarity.

For matching word images we use Dynamic Time Warping (DTW) that computes a sequence alignment score for finding the similarity of words [6]. The use of the total cost of DTW as a distance measure is helpful to cluster together word images that are related to their root word, which is discussed in Section 4.

DTW is a dynamic programming based procedure [5] to align two sequences of signals and compute a similarity measure. Let the word images (say their profiles) are represented as a sequence of vectors $\mathcal{F} = \mathbf{F_1}, \mathbf{F_2}, \ldots \mathbf{F_M}$ and $\mathcal{G} = \mathbf{G_1}, \mathbf{G_2}, \ldots, \mathbf{G_N}$. The DTW-cost between these two sequences is $D(M, N)$, which is calculated using dynamic programming is given by:

$$D(i,j) = \min \begin{cases} D(i-1, j-1) \\ D(i, j-1) \\ D(i-1, j) \end{cases} + d(i,j)$$

where $d(i,j) = \sum_{k=1}^{N} (F(i,k) - G(j,k))^2$ (the cost in aligning the ith element of $\mathbf{F}$ with jth element of $\mathbf{G}$). Using the given three values $D(i, j-1), D(i-1, j)$ and $D(i-1, j-1)$ in the calculation of $D(i,j)$ realizes a local continuity constraint, which ensures no samples are left out in time warping. Score for matching the two sequences $\mathcal{F}$ and $\mathcal{G}$ is considered as $D(M, N)$, where M and N are the lengths of the two sequences. Structural features can also be incorporated into the framework by computing them for the vertical strips. Detailed discussion of the algorithms is available in [6].

4   Offline Indexing

The simple matching procedure described in Section 3 may be efficient for spotting or locating a selected word-image. However the indexing process for a good

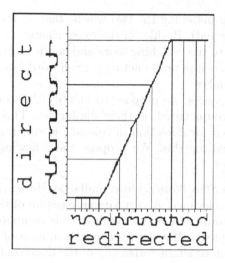

Fig. 2. Plot Demonstrating Matching of Two Words 'direct' and 'redirected' using Dynamic Time Warping and the Optimal Matching Path. Similar Word Form Variations are Present in Indian Languages.

search engine is more involved than the simple word-level matches. A word usually appears in various forms. Variation of word forms may obey the language rules. Text search engines use this information while indexing. However for text-image indexing process, this information is not directly usable.

We take care of simple, but very popular, word form variations taking place at the beginning and end. For this, once sequences are matched, we backtrack the optimal cost path. During the backtracking phase, if the dissimilarity in words is concentrated at the end, or in the beginning, they are deemphasized. For instance, for a query "direct", the matching scores of the words "directed" and "redirected" are only the matching of the six characters, 'd-i-r-e-c-t', of both words. Once an optimal sub-path is identified, a normalized cost corresponding to this segment is considered as the matching score for the pair of words. With this we find that a large set of words get grouped into one cluster. We expect to extend this for more general variations of words.

The optimal warping path is generated by backtracking the DTW minimal score in the matching space. As shown in Figure 2, extracted features (using upper word profile) of the two words 'direct' and 'redirected' are aligned using DTW algorithm. It is observed that features of these words are matched in such a way that elements of 're' at the beginning as well as 'ed' at the end of the word 'redirected' get matched with characters 'd' and 't' of the word "direct". This additional cost is identified and removed while backtracking.

It can be observed that for word variants the DTW path deviates from the diagonal line in the horizontal or vertical direction from the beginning or end of the path, which results in an increase in the matching cost. In the example Figure 2, the path deviates from the diagonal line at the two extreme ends.

This happened during matching the two words, that is, the root word (direct) and its variant (redirected). Profiles of the extra characters ('re' and 'ed') have minimal contribution to the matching score and hence subtracted from the total matching cost so as to compute the net cost. Such word form variations are very popular in most languages.

For the indexing process, we propose to identify the word set by clustering them into different groups based on their similarities. This requires processing the page to be indexed for detection of relevant words in it. Many interesting measures are proposed for this. We propose the following steps for effective retrieval at image level.

Detection of Common Stop Words: Once similar words are clustered, we analyze the clusters for their relevance. A very simple measure of the uniformity of the presence of similar words across the documents is computed. This acts as an inverse document frequency. If a word is common in most of the documents, this word is less meaningful to characterize any of the document.

Document Relevance Measurement: Given a query, a word image is generated and the cluster corresponding to this word is identified. If a cluster is annotated, matching query word is fast and direct. For other clusters, query word image and prototype of the cluster are compared in the image domain. In each cluster, documents with highest occurrence of similar words are ranked and listed.

Clustering: Large number of words in the document image database are grouped into a much smaller number of clusters. Each of these clusters are equivalent to a variation of the single word in morphology, font, size, style and quality. Similar words are clustered together and characterized using a representative word. We follow a hierarchical clustering procedure [8] to group these words. Clusters are merged until the dissimilarity between two successive clusters become very high. This method also provides scope for incremental clustering and indexing.

Annotation: After the clustering process has been completed offline, we have a set of similar words in each cluster. These clusters are annotated by their root word to ease searching and retrieval. Suppose a cluster contains words such as 'programmer', 'programmers', 'programming', 'programs' and 'program'. Then, we annotate the cluster with the root word "program". Likewise all clusters are manually annotated. If the annotation is not available, we identify an image-representative for the cluster. However, presence of image-prototype can slow down the search process. During searching, cluster prototypes are accessed and checked for their similarity with the query word. This makes sure that search in image domain is as fast as search in text domain.

5   Online Retrieval

A prototype web-based system for searching in document images, is also developed. This is presently available at http://cvit.iiit.ac.in/wordsearch.html. The system has many basic features as discussed below.

Web-based GUI: The web interface allows the user to type in Roman text and simultaneously view the text in one of the Indian languages of his choice. Users can also have the option to search with cross lingual retrieval and can specify the kind of retrieval they want to use. Many retrieval combinations are also provided in the advanced search options such as case insensitivity, boolean searching using !, &, | *and parenthesis*, displaying up to 50 search results per page, and various others. There is on the fly character transliteration available. The user can first choose a particular language (such as Hindi, Telugu, etc.) and then see the text in the corresponding language as he keeps typing the query in Roman (OM-Trans).

Delivery of Images: In order to facilitate users access to the retrieved document images, there is a need to control image size and quality. When a book is typically scanned at a resolution of 600 dpi, the original scanned size of a single page is around 12MB as a PNG file. Viewing such page is too slow and needs network resources. It is wise to make these images available in a compressed form. We compress the above image to a size ranging between 30 to 40 KB in TIFF format, by reducing the size of the image. This makes sure that the delivery of images are faster over the Internet. TIFF image format helps us in general for achieving the trade-off between image size and quality. It keeps the quality of the image during the compression process over JPG and BMP formats.

Speculative Downloading: Our system also supports speculative downloading, where some related pages with the currently retrieved page are prefetched for quick viewing during searching and retrieval as per users query. This mechanism is helpful especially when the user is viewing a collection, page by page, with the assumption that he might view the next page also. Speculative downloading is a background process.

Dynamic Coloring: When a user searches for relevant pages to a given query, our system searches and displays the result with dynamic coloring of all the words in the page that are similar to the queried word. This helps users to easily evaluate relevance of the retrieved page to their need. We adopt false coloring mechanism such that each word in a query carries a unique color in a document image. All this coloring happens at runtime (Figure 3) at image level.

Scalability: DLI is a one million book scanning project. Hence it archives huge collection of document images. Searching in this situation raises the question of scalability. The current prototype system searches in three books, that are a mixture of English and other Indian Languages (Hindi and Telugu). Each book on the average consists of 350 pages, and each page with 300 words. This brings the total number of words to 360,000. This is relatively a small number. The system should aid in searching the huge one million book collection and thus the scalability issues come to forth. Indexing this large collection takes immense time. For us indexing is an offline activity. Searching and retrieval is the only online process. That is why the system manages to run fast in the above sample database. Because it only checks keywords of the index to search for similar words with the query. Even with an increase in the size of document images we do not expect much increase in the number of clusters. Because, words are

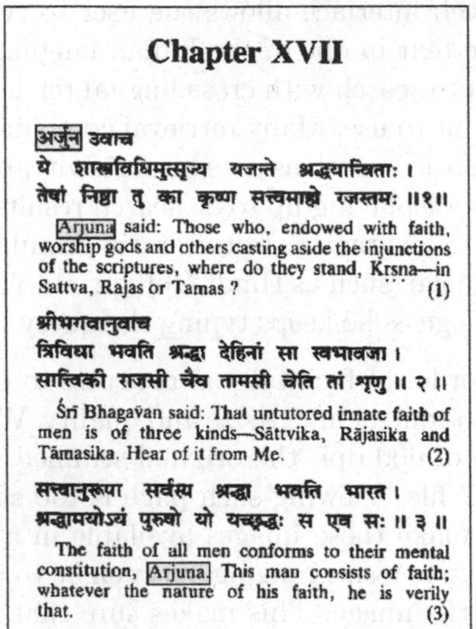

Chapter XVII

अर्जुन उवाच
ये शास्त्रविधिमुत्सृज्य यजन्ते श्रद्धयान्विताः ।
तेषां निष्ठा तु का कृष्ण सत्त्वमाहो रजस्तमः ॥१॥

Arjuna said: Those who, endowed with faith,
worship gods and others casting aside the injunctions
of the scriptures, where do they stand, Krsna—in
Sattva, Rajas or Tamas ?   (1)

श्रीभगवानुवाच
त्रिविधा भवति श्रद्धा देहिनां सा स्वभावजा ।
सात्त्विकी राजसी चैव तामसी चेति तां शृणु ॥ २ ॥

Śrī Bhagavān said: That untutored innate faith of
men is of three kinds—Sāttvika, Rājasika and
Tāmasika. Hear of it from Me.   (2)

सत्त्वानुरूपा सर्वस्य श्रद्धा भवति भारत ।
श्रद्धामयोऽयं पुरुषो यो यच्छ्रद्धः स एव सः ॥ ३ ॥

The faith of all men conforms to their mental
constitution, Arjuna. This man consists of faith;
whatever the nature of his faith, he is verily
that.   (3)

Fig. 3. Search Result with Dynamic Coloring for Query Word 'Arjuna' seen Both in
English and Devanagari

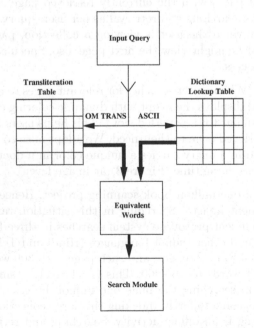

Fig. 4. A Conceptual Diagram that Shows Document Searching in Multiple Languages
using Transliteration and Dictionary Based Approach

Alphabet	a	aa	i	ii	u	uu	....
Hindi	अ	आ	इ	ई	उ	ऊ	....
Telugu	అ	ఆ	ఇ	ఈ	ఉ	ఊ	....
:	:	:	:	:	:	:	
:	:	:	:	:	:	:	
:	:	:	:	:	:	:	

Fig. 5. Sample Entries of the Transliteration Map Built for Cross-lingual Retrieval in English, Devanagari and Telugu

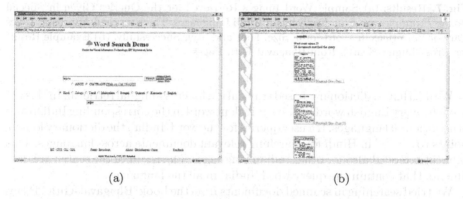

(a)   (b)

Fig. 6. Screenshots of Implementation Results for Cross-lingual Search. (a) An Interface where Users Enter their Query, (b) View of Result of the Search as Thumbnails

limited in every language and they are only the morphological variants of the root word. The system handles addition of new books without re-indexing every time. This saves much time and creating new indexes will be a smooth process. However, we need to deal with delivery of the document images. An increase in the number of pages viewed may slow the transfer process. A good compression technique needs to be applied.

Cross-lingual Search: Our system can also search for cross-lingual documents for a given query. As shown in Figure 4 we achieve this in two ways: transliteration and dictionary-based approaches. Figure 4 is an expanded view of the cross-lingual block diagram presented in Figure 1.

Since Indian scripts share a common alphabet (derived from *Brahmi*), we can transliterate the words across languages. This helps us to search in multiple languages at the same time. We use OM-Transliteration scheme [9]. In OM-Trans scheme, there is a Roman equivalent for all the basic Indian language characters.

Figure 5 shows a sample transliteration map built for this purpose. For Example, "Bhim " can be typed in its Roman equivalent using OM-trans as "Bhima". Then the transliteration table is looked up for searching in Hindi (Devanagari script) and Telugu pages. Their cumulative result is finally displayed back to the user. A screenshot showing implementation result is presented in Figure 6.

program	programs	programming	programmers	Programmers
(a) खरीदा	खरीदी	खरीदे	खरीदना	खरीदने

(b) arjuna	अर्जुन	Arjuna	Arjuna.	अर्जुन
	Arjuna	अर्जुन	तवार्जुन	Arjuna

Fig. 7. Results: (a) Sample Word Images Retrieved for the Queries Given in Special Boxes. Examples are from English and Hindi Languages. The Proposed Approach Takes Care of Variations in Word-form, Size, Font and Style Successfully. (b) Example Result for Cross-lingual Search from Bhagavat Gita Pages.

We also have a dictionary-based translation for cross-lingual retrieval. In this approach, every English word has an equivalent word in the corresponding Indian and other oriental languages. If a user queries for the word 'India', the dictionary lookup points to '   ' in Hindi for searching relevant documents across languages. This table is extended also for other Indian languages. The result of the search are documents that contain the query word 'India' in all the languages.

We tried searching in scanned documents from the book 'Bhagavat-Gita'. Pages from this book contain English and Devanagari text. These pages are of poor quality. We search for the occurrences of the word 'arjuna'. It fetched pages which contain 'Arjuna' in both English and Devanagari. Sample results are shown in Figure 7 (b). In this respect, we need to exploit the available technology at WordNet Project [10] and Universal Language Dictionary Project [11]. WordNet is a lexical database that has been widely adopted in artificial intelligence and computational linguistics for a variety of practical applications such as information retrieval, information extraction, summarization, etc. The Universal Language Dictionary is an attempt to create a list of concepts along with words to express those concepts in several "natural" and "artificial" (constructed) languages.

6 Discussion

We have a prototype system for retrieval of document images. This system is integrated with 'Greenstone search engine' for digital libraries [12]. Greenstone is a suite of software for building and distributing digital library collections via the Internet. Given a textual query, we convert it to image by rendering. Features are extracted from these images and then search is carried out for retrieval of relevant documents in image space. We extend the search to cross-lingual retrieval by transliteration among Indian languages and a table-lookup translation for other languages. Results of the search are presented to the user in a ranked manner based on their relevance to the query word.

Table 1. Performance of the Proposed Approach on Two Data Sets in English, and Hindi. Percentages of Precision and Recall are Reported for Some Test Words.

Language	Data Set	Test*	Prec.	Recall
English	2507	15	95.89	97.69
Hindi	3354	14	92.67	93.71

[1]*Number of words used for testing

We evaluated the performance of the system on data sets from languages such as English and Hindi. Pages of Hindi and English are taken from digital library of India collections. The system is extensively tested on all these data sets. Sample words retrieved are shown in Figure 7 (a).

We measure the speed of the system so as to see its practicality. The system takes 0.16 seconds to search and retrieve relevant documents from image databases and 0.34 seconds to transfer that page for viewing by users over the intranet. In comparison, Greenstone text search takes 0.13 seconds to search and retrieve relevant documents from image databases and 0.31 seconds to transfer that page for viewing by users over the intranet. The speed of our system is almost comparable with the Greenstone text search. This shows the effectiveness of the system. The strategy we followed is to perform text processing and indexing offline. The search then takes place on the representative words indexed. Compressing the image (to a size of few KB) also help us a lot during the transfer of the document image for viewing.

Quantitative performance of the matching scheme is computed on sample document image databases of size more than 2500 words. Around 15 query words are used for testing. During selection of query words, priority is given to words with many variants. We computed recall and precision for these query words, as shown in Table 1. Percentage of relevant words which are retrieved from the entire collection is represented as recall, where as, percentage of retrieved words which are relevant is represented as precision. It is found that a high precision and recall (close to 95%) is registered for all the languages. High recall and precision is registered in our experiment. This may be because of the limited dataset we experimented with, that are similar in font, style and size. We are working towards a comprehensive test on real-life large datasets. Our existing partial matching module controls morphological word variants. We plan to make the module more general so that it addresses many more variations of words encountered in real-life documents. We are also working on avoiding the manual annotation and still retaining the same performance.

7   Conclusions

In this paper, we have proposed a search system for retrieval of relevant documents from large collection of document images. This method of search will be important in using large digitized manuscript data sets in Indian languages.

We have focused on computing information retrieval measures from word images without explicitly recognizing these images. The system is capable of searching across languages for retrieving relevant documents from multilingual document image database. Preliminary experiments show that the results are promising. We are currently working on a comprehensive test on large collection of document images.

Acknowledgment. This work was partially supported by the MCIT, Government of India for Digital Libraries Activities.

References

1. Digital Library of India. (at: http://www.dli.gov.in)
2. Doermann, D.: The Indexing and Retrieval of Document Images: A Survey. Computer Vision and Image Understanding (CVIU) **70** (1998) 287–298
3. Chaudhury, S., Sethi, G., Vyas, A., Harit, G.: Devising Interactive Access Techniques for Indian Language Document Images. In: Proc. of the Seventh International Conference on Document Analysis and Recognition (ICDAR). (2003) 885–889
4. Rath, T., Manmatha, R.: Features for Word Spotting in Historical Manuscripts. In: Proc. of the Seventh International Conference on Document Analysis and Recognition (ICDAR). (2003) 218–222
5. Rath, T., Manmatha, R.: Word Image Matching Using Dynamic Time Warping. Proceedings of the Conference on Computer Vision and Pattern Recognition (CVPR) **2** (2003) 521–527
6. C. V. Jawahar, Million Meshesha, A. Balasubramanian: Searching in Document Images. Proc. of the 4th Indian Conference on Computer Vision, Graphics and Image Processing (ICVGIP) (2004) 622–627
7. Department of Information Technology: Technology Development for Indian Languages. (at: http://tdil.mit.gov.in)
8. Duda, R.O., Hart, P.E., Stork, D.G.: Pattern Classification. John Willey & Sons, New York (2001)
9. Indian Language Transliteration. (at: http://www.cs.cmu.edu/~madhavi/Om/)
10. Vossen, P., Fellbaum, C.: The Global WordNet Association. (at: http://www.globalwordnet.org)
11. Universal Language Dictionary Project. at: http://ogden.basic-english.org (2003)
12. Greenstone Digital Library Software. (at: http://www.greenstone.org)

A Semi-automatic Adaptive OCR for Digital Libraries

Sachin Rawat, K.S. Sesh Kumar, Million Meshesha, Indraneel Deb Sikdar,
A. Balasubramanian, and C.V. Jawahar

Centre for Visual Information Technology,
International Institute of Information Technology, Hyderabad - 500032, India
jawahar@iiit.ac.in

Abstract. This paper presents a novel approach for designing a semi-automatic adaptive OCR for large document image collections in digital libraries. We describe an interactive system for continuous improvement of the results of the OCR. In this paper a semi-automatic and adaptive system is implemented. Applicability of our design for the recognition of Indian Languages is demonstrated. Recognition errors are used to train the OCR again so that it adapts and learns for improving its accuracy. Limited human intervention is allowed for evaluating the output of the system and take corrective actions during the recognition process.

1 Introduction

It is becoming increasingly important to have information available in digital format for effective access, reliable storage and long term preservation [1, 2, 3]. This is catalysed by the advancement of Information Technology and the emergence of large digital libraries for archival of paper documents. One of the projects aimed at large scale archival is Digital Library of India (DLI) [4]. The DLI aims at digitizing all literary, artistic, and scientific works of mankind so as to provide better access to traditional materials and make documents freely accessible to the global society.

Efforts are also exerted to make available the content of these digital libraries to users through indexing and retrieval of relevant documents from large collections of document images [5]. Success of document image indexing and retrieval mainly depends on the availability of optical character recognition systems (OCRs). The OCR systems take scanned images of paper documents as input, and automatically convert them into digital format for on-line data processing. The potential of OCRs for data entry application is obvious: it offers a faster, highly automated, and presumably less expensive alternative to the manual data entry process. Thus they improve the accuracy and speed in transcribing data to be stored in a computer system [1]. High accuracy OCR systems are reported for English with excellent performance in presence of printing variations and document degradation. For Indian and many other oriental languages, OCR systems are not yet able to successfully recognise printed document images of varying scripts, quality, size, style and font. Therefore the Indian language documents in digital libraries are not accessible by their content.

In this paper we present a novel approach for designing a semi-automatic and adaptive OCR for large collection of document images, focusing on applications in digital libraries. The design and implementation of the system has been guided by the following facts:

H. Bunke and A.L. Spitz (Eds.): DAS 2006, LNCS 3872, pp. 13–24, 2006.

To work on diverse collections: It has been realised that, we need to design an OCR system that can register an acceptable accuracy rate so as to facilitate effective access to relevant documents from these large collection of document images. Acceptability of the output of the OCR system depends on the given application area. For digital libraries, it is desirable to have an OCR system with around 90% accuracy rate on 90% of the documents rather than having recognition rate of 99% on 1% of the document collections.

Possibility of human intervention: The main flow of operations of the digitization process we follow in the Digital Library of India is presented in Figure 1. In projects like DLI, there is considerable amount of human intervention for acquiring, scanning, processing and web enabling the documents. The expectation of a fully automatic OCR is impractical at the present situation due to the technological limitations. We exploit the limited manual intervention present in the process to refine the recognition system.

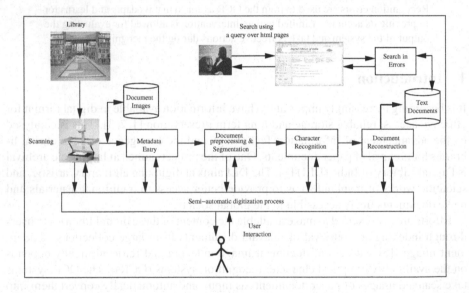

Fig. 1. Block Diagram of the Flow of Operations in Content Generation and Delivery in Digital Libraries

Effectiveness of GUI: There has been considerable amount of research in Indian language OCR [6]. There are many modules in the OCR and most of them are sequential in nature. Failure of even one of the modules can result in making the system unacceptable for real-life applications. Commercial organizations have not taken enough interest to comeup with an Indian language OCR. We argue that, with effective user interfaces to correct possible errors in one or more modules, one can build practical OCR systems for Digital Library of India pages. This can avoid the failure of the entire system due to the failure of selected blocks (say script separation or text-graphics identification).

Availability of limited research: Even with the presence of the first OCR in 1960, English did not have an omni-font recognition system till 1985 [7]. Most of the research in

Table 1. Diversity of Document Collections in DLI. They Vary in Languages, Fonts, Styles and Sizes. Books that are Published since 1850 are Archived which have Different Typesets.

Documents	Diversity of Books
Languages	Hindi, Telugu, Urdu, Kannada, Sanskrit, English, Persian, European, others
Typesets	Letter press, Offset printer, Typewriter, Computer Typeset, Handwritten
Fonts	Ranging from 10 to 20 fonts in each language
Styles	Italics, Bold, Sans serifs, Underline, etc.
Sizes	8 to 45 points
Year of Publication	Printed books from 19, 20 and 21st centuries Ancient manuscripts to 2005

OCR technology has been centered around building fully automatic and high performing intelligent classification systems. Summary of the diverse collections of documents in Digital Library of India is presented in Table 1. Building an omnifont OCR that can convert all these documents into text does not look imminent. At present, it may be better to design semi-automatic but adaptable systems for the recognition problem.

Adaptability requirements: There are many excellent attempts in building robust document analysis systems in industry, academia and research institutions [8, 9]. None of these systems are applied or tested on Indian language real-life documents. Most of the automatic OCR systems were trained offline and used online without any feedback. We argue for a design which aim at training the OCR on-the-fly using knowledge derived from an input sequence of word images and minimal prior information. The resulting system is expected to be specialized to the characteristics of symbol shape, context, and noise that are present in a collection of images in our corpus, and thus should achieve higher accuracy. This scheme enables us to build a generic OCR that has a minimal core, and leave most of the sophisticated tuning to on-line learning. This can be a recurrent process involving frequent feedbacks and refinement. Such a strategy is valuable in situations like ours where there is a huge collection of degraded and diverse documents in different languages [10].

2   Role of Adaptation and Feedback

Recognition of scanned document images using OCR is now generally considered to be a solved problem [11]. Many commercial packages are available for Latin scripts. These packages do an impressive job on high quality originals with accuracy rates in the high nineties. However, several external issues can conspire against attaining this rate consistently across various documents, which is necessary for digital libraries.

Quality: The quality of the original document greatly affects the performance of an OCR system. This is because (i) the original document is old, and has suffered physical degradation, (ii) the original is a low quality document, with variations in toner density, and (iii) many characters are broken which presumably are faint areas on the original not picked up by the scanning process. For example, segmentation errors may occur because the original document contains broken, touching and overlapping characters.

Scanning Issues: Degradations during scanning can be caused by poor paper/print quality of the original document, poor scanning equipment, etc. These artifacts lead to recognition errors in other stages of the conversion process.

Diversity of Languages: Digital libraries archive documents that are written in different languages. Some languages (such as Hindi and Urdu) have complex scripts, while others (like Telugu) have large number of characters. These are additional challenges for the OCRs design.

Any of the above factors can contribute to have insufficient OCR. We need to consider implementation issues and design effective algorithms to address them. Algorithms used at each stage of the recognition for preprocessing, segmentation, feature extraction and classifications affects the accuracy rate. We should allow users to inspect the results of the system at each stage. If user can select the appropriate algorithm or set the most apt parameters, performance of the individual modules and thereby that of the system can be maximised. Designing a system that supports an interactive processing is therefore crucial for better recognition result. We claim that application of a semi-automatic adaptive OCR has a great role in this respect. This will further create dynamism to update existing knowledge of the system, whenever new instances are presented during the recognition process.

2.1 Role of Postprocessor

A post processor is used to resolve any discrepancies seen between recognized text and the original one. It significantly improves the accuracy of the OCR by suggesting, often, a best-fit alternative to replace the mis-spellings. For this, we use a reverse dictionary approach with the help of a trie data structure. In this approach, we create two dictionaries. One is filled with words in the normal manner and the other with the same words reversed. We narrow down the possible set of choices by using both dictionaries. It interacts with the OCR in the following way.

- Get the word and its alternative(s) (if suggested by the OCR).
- Check which of them form valid words and then based on their weights choose the optimal one.
- In case of failure, the postprocessor suggests its own list of alternative words.
- Check with the OCR whether its own suggestion is visually similar with the original one.

In this way, the postprocessor correct recognition errors. Due to the errors in segmentation or classification, the recognition module can have three categories of errors: dele-

Table 2. Performance of the Post Processor on Malayalam Language Datasets. Malayalam is One of the Indian Language with Its Own Scripts.

Error Type	Deletion	Insertion	Substitution
% of errors corrected	78.15	58.39	92.85

tion, insertion and substitution. Table 2 shows percentage of errors corrected by our Malayalam post-processor.

The key issue in document-specific training is that the transcription may be limited or may not be available *a priori*. We need to design an adaptive OCR that learns in presence of data uncertainty and noise. In the case of training, this means that the training transcriptions may be erroneous or incomplete. Thus, one way to produce the required training data is to use words analyzed by the post processor. We design this architecture explicitly, such that the postprocessor accepts words generated by an OCR system and produces error-corrected ones. These words, identified by the postprocessor, are fed back to the OCR such that it builds its knowledge through training for improvement of its performance.

2.2 Role of User Feedback

Designing a mechanism for feedback enables the system to obtain corrective measures on its performance. Users interact with the system and then investigate the output of the system. Based on the accuracy level of the OCR, they will communicate to the system those words in error. This will enable the OCR to gain additional knowledge, based on which retraining is carried out. This mechanism is possible when there is feedback. Thus the feedback will serve as a communication line to obtain more training data that helps to overcome any performance lacuna. This is supported by a GUI which enables to provide feedback to the system concerning a list of words that need corrective action with their full information.

3 Design Novelty of the System

We have a prototype interactive multilingual OCR (IMOCR) system, with a framework for the creation, adaptation and use of structured document analysis applications. IMOCR is a self-learning system that improves its recognition accuracy through knowledge derived in the course of semi-automatic feedback, adaptation and learning. There are various notable goals towards the design and implementation of IMOCR.

- To setup a system that learns through a recurrent process involving frequent feedback and backtracking.
- To manage diverse collection of documents that vary in scripts, fonts, sizes, styles and document quality.
- To have flexible application framework that allows researchers and developers to create independent modules and algorithms rather than to attempt to create an all encompassing monolithic application.
- To allow end users the flexibility to customize the application by providing the opportunity to configure the various modules used, their specific algorithm and parameters.

By doing so the system will be able to interactively learn and adapt for a particular document type. In essence, it provides a framework for an interactive $test \Rightarrow feedback \Rightarrow learn \Rightarrow adapt \Rightarrow automate$ cycle.

3.1 Data Corpus

Our OCR system has been designed under the assumption that vast amount of training samples are not available for every category of document. Rather, it builds a huge collection (or corpus) over time based on the feedback mechanism. The corpus encompass all types of data that are involved in printed documents. The collection contains synthetic data (that varies in scripts, fonts, sizes and styles) and real-life documents (such as books, magazines and newspapers). Having such wealth of data enables the system to learn and accumulate knowledge out of it.

3.2 Design Considerations

From the implementation point of view, the following design considerations have been made:

- The system supports multiple languages in the same framework. Languages currently supported include English, Hindi, Tamil, Telugu and Malayalam.
- Each aspect, right from the GUI to the font-selection are platform independent.
- Dual mode running of the system is enabled by interactive interface as well as batch mode support.
- The application is designed to allow the user to choose the run-time configuration of the system right from the modules, the inner-lying algorithms, the input-output format, the parameters etc. via support for user specified configuration files. The GUI is designed for multi-level access to configuration parameters that scale up for users with various levels of skill.
- A multi-core approach is taken so as to ease development and integration of modules in the future.

3.3 Architecture of the IMOCR

We design the general architecture of an interactive multilingual OCR (IMOCR) system that is open for learning and adaptation. An overview of the architecture of the system is shown in Figure 2. The IMOCR design is based on a multi-core approach. At the heart of the same is an application tier, which acts as the interface between the Graphical User Interface (GUI) and the OCR modules. This application layer identifies the user-made choices, initialises data and document structures and invokes relevant modules with suitable parameters. The GUI layer provides the user with the tools to configure the data-flow, select the plug-ins and supply initialization parameters. The system provides appropriate performance metrics in the form of graphs and tables for better visualization of the results of each step and module during the recognition process.

The last layer is the module/algorithm layer where the actual OCR operations are done. This layer is segmented based on clearly identified functionality. Each module implements a standard interface to be invoked via the application. Each module internally can decide on multiple algorithm implementations of the same functionality that may be interchanged at run-time. This helps in selection and use of an appropriate algorithm or a set of parameters for a book, collection or script. This layer is designed on the principle of plug-ins. The system allows transparent runtime addition and selection

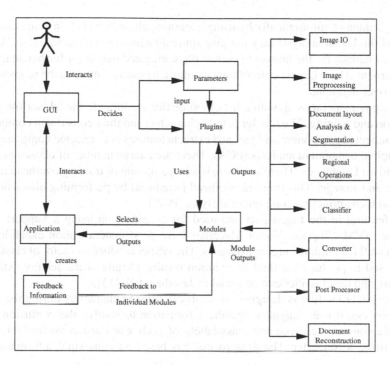

Fig. 2. An Architecture of the Prototype OCR System

of modules (as shared objects/ dynamic libraries) thereby enabling the decoupling of the application and the plug-ins. Feature addition and deployment is as simple as copying the plug-in to the appropriate directory. The other advantages of this approach are lower size of application binary, lower runtime memory footprint and effective memory management (through dynamic loading and unloading, caching etc.).

4 Recognition Module

The recognition module has three main parts: the segmenter, the labeler and the resolver. Scanned images are initially preprocessed to improve the performance of the recognition process [12]. They are binarized and skew corrected. We implement Isodata for binarization and Yin's algorithms [13] for skew detection and correction. The segmentation module is designed to analyze the overall structure of the document and identify sub-regions such as text, tables, images/graphics etc.

Text blocks are further segmented into lines and words. There are several layout analysis algorithms available in literature. The process of segmentation of a page is carried out sequentially in two major steps. The first is separation of text and image regions. Then, the segmentation of text into columns, blocks, text lines and words. The performance of the page layout analysis module depends on the type of document image. Every algorithm has a set of freely tunable parameters, which can be set to give apt results for the document image. However, these parameters are either set by interacting with the human or automatically by using a learning algorithm [14]. In some cases, the output of the layout analysis may not give apt results for any parameter value. We provide a mechanism for the human to correct the segmented output for further analysis of the document. These human corrections can inturn be used to improve the segmentation process over iterations.

The segmenter comes up with a list of words that are input to the labeler for feature extraction and training. The labeler detects characters and their constituent components using connected component analysis and extracts features of connected components using principal component analysis (PCA). There are a large number of classes available in the Indian Languages. Therefore there is a large amount of training overhead in computation and storage. This training overhead is reduced by performing dimensionality reduction using principal component analysis (PCA).

The features in the Eigenspace are used for classification using a Support Vector Machine (SVM). Support Vector Machines have good generalization capability and perform well over Indian language datasets. The labeler produces a vector of class labels that is used to produce the final recognition results. Details of the feature extraction algorithm and the classifier can be found in Jawahar et el. [15].

The resolver module is designed to resolve confusing characters during the recognition process. It uses language specific information to resolve the confusion. Once the confusions are resolved the class labels of each word are converted into UNICODE using a converter. The postprocessor is based on contextual information and

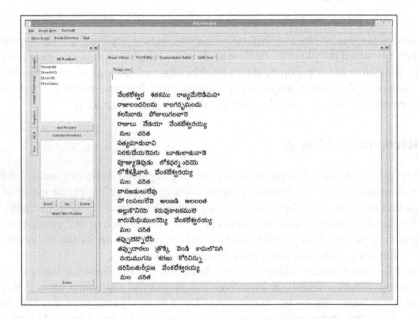

Fig. 3. A Screenshot of Our Prototype Interactive and Adaptive OCR System. The User Interacts for Selection of Algorithms and Parameters, Feedback and Error Correction, Adaptation and Learning.

language-based reverse dictionary approach (as described in Section 2) to correct any mis-recognized words. The post processor can significantly improve the performance of the system. We use a bootstrapping process to retrain the system using the errors corrected by the resolver. The system continously learns through semi-automatic adaptation from feedback; each time gaining knowledge that improves its recognition rate. The feedback is initiated from the result of the resolver.

The output of the postprocessor is a UNICODE string, which can be converted into any language specific font using the converter available. The recognized text is finally reconstructed in various formats including PDF, DOC, RTF, HTML, and Plain text. The output is structurally and visually similar to the input document image as shown in Figure 3.

5 Provision for Learning

In this paper, we have focused on design of a system with capabilities for learning and adaptation. In the previous sections, we described the design criteria to suite these functionalities and the implementation techniques. Improvement in the system, as of now, is limited to the recognition. We also plan to adapt our segmentation work into this framework [14]. Adaptation is primarily done to improve the performance of the system on a specific collection, say a book. After interactively digitizing a few pages, a user can ask the system to retrain and improve the classification performance for the rest of the pages. During retraining, the OCRed words are analysed against the post-processed words to determine the existence of recognition errors. If there is an error, these words are candidates for retraining. To this effect, information related to each word (such as language, font, location indicator coordinates, etc.) are fedback to to the system so that each of its components are added to their respective classes. Finally the system is trained again using the updated datasets to create a new model. This process can repeat multiple times until a saturation (or even over-training) happens on the collections.

An intelligent system should be capable of doing more than adaptation. It needs to identify the appropriate parameters and algorithms without any user interaction and learn to perform better over time. This needs many more functionalities in the system design and implementation. A postprocessor (critique) may run in three modes – student (when a newly seen word is added to the dictionary), mentor (when suggestions are made to the user), and teacher (when the word is replaced in the document). Role of the postprocessor may be set from the user interface or automatically learnt from the confidence level of the recogniser. Similarly, the entire system may want to identify reliable examples for getting trained or learnt from the results. System may use the character (component) images for retraining/refinement depending on the configuration and mode of the system.

The improvement of the performance is presently done by retraining the modules. However, a better alternative will be to refine the performance, provided the algorithms support incremental modes of learning. In our design, the implementation is done such that the retraining or refinement process is transparent to the user. Individual modules can operate in either mode depending on the user setting or algorithmic limitations.

In addition to the adaptation, we have provided provision for long term learning and performance improvement. Adaptation is usually local in nature and is very effective for a specific collection. However, for a new collection, if one can identify a suitable set of model parameters (algorithms), it would further reduce the manual intervention. Such situations are frequent in digital libraries. The settings (parameters) used for one of the books could be an acceptable choice for most books from the same publisher or printed in the same press. We propose to identify the most suited available parameters by modeling the recogniser as a mixture model and selecting the most likely distribution.

6   Performance Analysis of the Prototype System

We have a prototype system that is used for the recognition of document images. The interface is a gate-way to the interactive character recognition. It is an easy to use UI with support for (i) semi automatic operation, (ii) selection of intended regions of image for processing, (iii) display all extracted information (for example, order of segmentation, script, confidence measure, class label, UNICODE etc), (iv) image display at variable resolution, (v) allow for classifier training and display correspondences between image and text.

The system accepts scanned document images in multiple formats such as PGX (PGM, PNM, PPM), TIFF, etc. Scanned images are preprocessed for binarization and skew correction, and then segmented into words. The labeler split words into components and assigned class labels based on which the recognition is performed. Then features are extracted and SVM classifier is used for classification. Algorithms used at each steps for character recognition are already reported in [15, 16]. Recognition results are postprocessed to resolve ambiguity among the candidate words, which is later fedback to the system for creating models that encompasses the new training datasets. The result of the system is reconstructed (see Figure 3) and available in multiple formats such as plain text, HTML, RTF, DOC, PDF etc. The result of the postprocessor is also used for building training data for learning. Our system is semi- automatic for adaptation. Users can have minimal role in due course of the recognition process.

We evaluate the performance of the prototype system on datasets taken from many Indian languages: Hindi, Telugu, Tamil and Malayalam. These datasets are of high quality and used for prototyping and bootstrapping. They are useful for building a pre-

Table 3. Accuracies of DDAG-SVM on Datasets of Various Indian Languages

Name of Language	Number of classes	Accuracy Normal Data	Degraded Data
Hindi	116	98.33	96.54
Telugu	347	97.15	93.14
Tamil	120	99.43	96.24
Malayalam	127	99.72	97.30

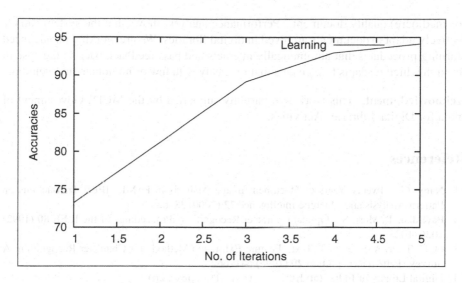

Fig. 4. An Improvement in the Performance of the System Through Learning. It shows Accuracy Vs. Number of Iterations.

liminary version of the training corpus. We add noise using a degradation model as suggested in Kanungo et al. [17]. This degradation simulates the distortions due to imperfection in scanning. The border pixels are eroded using a probabilistic model based on distance from the boundary. We test the system using synthetic data (normal and degraded). The result is shown in Table 3. Such results at the component level are available in many Indian language OCR papers [6]. The errors rates at character level and word level are considerably larger than this. Also the performance degrades highly with the degradation of the input documents.

We now demonstrate how the poor performance on real-life document can be improved using the adaptation strategy discussed in the previous sections. For the first few pages of the book, the accuracy was found to be very low (around 75%) and within few iterations (retrainings) the accuracy improved to close to 95%. This increase is applicable for the specific book, but not generalizable across collections. During adaptation, additional samples of confusing components are added to the training datasets for building improved classifier models. Figure 4 graphically presents the results of the adaptation. It is observed that adapting the system to a maximum of 10 pages is enough for the recognition of an average book with 300 pages. This further indicates how fast the system generalize based on few learnt training data.

7   Conclusions

We have presented a semi-automatic adaptive OCR system. This strategy is important for the recognition of large digitized manuscript datasets of Indian and other oriental languages. The system learns from feedback propagated back through the adaptation process. We claim that interactive OCR lead to better results and is necessary for poor (or mediocre) quality documents. Performance analysis shows that the system can effectively adapt to documents archived in digital libraries. We are working on advanced learning procedures that automatically interacts and pass feedback back to the system through which it adapts to a given situation easily with few or no human intervention.

Acknowledgment. This work was partially supported by the MCIT, Government of India for Digital Libraries Activities.

References

1. Nagy, G.: Twenty Years of Document Image Analysis in PAMI. IEEE Transactions on Pattern Analysis and Machine Intelligence **22** (2000) 38–62
2. Pavlidisi, T., Mori, S.: Optical Character Recognition. Proceedings of the IEEE **80** (1992) 1026–1028
3. O. D. Trier, A. K. Jain, T. Taxt: Feature Extraction Methods for Character Recognition: A Survey. Pattern Recognition **29** (1996) 641–662
4. Digital Library of India. (at: http://www.dli.gov.in)
5. Doermann, D.: The Indexing and Retrieval of Document Images: A Survey. Computer Vision and Image Understanding (CVIU) **70** (1998) 287–298
6. U Pal, B B Chaudhuri: Indian Script Character Recognition: A Survey. Pattern Recognition **37** (2004) 1887–1899
7. Kahan, S., Pavlidis, T., Baird, H.S.: On the Recognition of Printed Characters of Any Font and Size. IEEE Transactions on Pattern Analysis and Machine Intelligence **9** (1987) 274–288
8. Henry S.Baird: Anatomy of a Versatile Page Reader. Proceedings of the IEEE, Special Issue on Optical Character Recognition(OCR), **80** (1992) 1059–1065
9. Bokser, M.: Omnidocument Technoloigies. Proceedings of the IEEE, Special Issue on Optical Character Recognition(OCR), **80** (1992) 1066–1078
10. Ittner, D.J., Baird, H.S.: Language-Free Layout Analysis. In: Proceedings of the 2nd ICDAR. (1993) 336–340
11. Hartley, R.T., Crumpton, K.: Quality of OCR for Degraded Text Images. In: Proceedings of the fourth ACM conference on Digital libraries. (1999) 228–229
12. Gonzalez, R.C., Woods, R.E.: Digital Image Processing. Prentice-Hall (2002)
13. Zhu, X., Yin, X.: A New Textual/Non-textual Classifier for Document Skew Correction. Proc. 16th Int'l. Conf. Pattern Recognition (ICPR'02) **1** (2002) 480–482
14. K S Sesh Kumar, Anoop Namboodiri, C V Jawahar: Learning to Segment Document Images. In: International Conference on Pattern Recognition and Machine Intelligence (to appear). (2005)
15. C. V. Jawahar, M N S S K Pavan Kumar, S S Ravi kiran: A Bilinguagl OCR for Hindi and Telugu Documents and Its Applications. In: International Conference on Document Analysis and Recognition (ICDAR). (2003) 408–412
16. Million Meshesha, C. V. Jawahar: Recognition of Printed Amharic Documents. In: International Conference on Document Analysis and Recognition (ICDAR). (2005) 784–788
17. Tapas Kanungo, Robert M. Haralick, Henry S. Baird, Werner Stuezle, David Madigan: A Statistical, Nonparametric Methodology for Document Degradation Model Validation. IEEE Transaction on Pattern Analysis and Machine Intelligence **22** (2000) 1209–1223

Contribution to the Discrimination of the Medieval Manuscript Texts: Application in the Palaeography

Ikram Moalla[1,2], Frank LeBourgeois[2], Hubert Emptoz[2], and Adel M. Alimi[1]

[1] REsearch Group on Intelligent Machines (REGIM),
University of Sfax, ENIS, DGE,
BP. W-3038 - Sfax – Tunisia
{ikram.moalla, adel.alimi}@ieee.org
[2] Laboratoire d'InfoRmatique en Images et Systèmes d'information (LIRIS),
INSA de Lyon-France
{Flebourg, Hemptoz}@rfv.insa-lyon.fr

Abstract. This work presents our first contribution to the discrimination of the medieval manuscript texts in order to assist the palaeographers to date the ancient manuscripts. Our method is based on the Spatial Grey-Level Dependence (SGLD) which measures the join probability between grey levels values of pixels for each displacement. We use the Haralick features to characterise the 15 medieval text styles. The achieved discrimination results are between 50% and 81%, which is encouraging.

1 Introduction

The Document Image Analysis is a particular research domain which is situated between images analysis, pattern recognition and human sciences especially the science that studies the history of texts. At present time, this research domain is spreading with the succession of the digitization of the ancient manuscripts of the cultural heritage notably in libraries and national archives *etc.* This revolution stimulates new research domains like the automatic extraction of the information for a better accessibility and a correct indexing of digitized documents. Among metadata which can be extracted, the writings styles brings additional information to the contents of the texts. The text layout represents a piece of information introduced in consciously or unconsciously by the writer which can be used to date, authenticate or index a document. The layout of a printed document is characterised by its physical structure and the characters typography (typestyle, size, font *etc.*) while the presentation of an ancient manuscript conceals other levels of interpretation such as the author's personal style of writing, the used calligraphy and the appearance of the document. The philology is a research field which study ancient languages, their grammars, the history and the phonetics of the words in order to educate and understand ancient texts. The philology is mainly based on the content of texts and concerns handwriting texts as well as printed documents. The paleography is a complementary discipline of the philology which collects handwritten texts corpus and knowledge accumulated on these documents. The paleography studies the layout of old manuscripts and their evolutions whereas the classic philology studies the

H. Bunke and A.L. Spitz (Eds.): DAS 2006, LNCS 3872, pp. 25–37, 2006.
© Springer-Verlag Berlin Heidelberg 2006

content of the texts, the languages and their evolutions.   The goals of the palaeographic science are mainly the study of the correct decoding of the old writings and the study of the history of the transmission of the ancient texts. The palaeography is also the study of the writing style, independently from the author personal writing style, which can help to date and/or to transcribe ancient manuscripts. The target of this work consists of making a first methodological and applicable contribution to the automatic analysis of writing styles of old manuscripts for the service of the research in history of texts and for the palaeography science. We are interested more in ancient Latin manuscripts of the Middle Ages which precedes the Renaissance period before the emerging of the printing. The definition of the style is multiple and complicated. We are going to concentrate on a visual and perceptive approach of the style of writings which can be studied with images analysis tools. The recognition of the handwriting style which is connected to the historical period and/or the geographical localization independently of the personal style of the writer   constitutes the main problem of our work.

2   The History of the Latin Writings

We present briefly the various Latin writings and their evolutions in Europe. Since the end of I^{est} century before J.-C, writings were transformed according to the usages. Since the VIIIth until XIIth century, the Caroline was wide spread in the West.

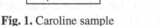
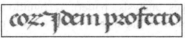

Fig. 1. Caroline sample   **Fig. 2.** Gothic sample

It evolved towards jagged forms to give birth in England to the Gothic writing, which spread in all the Northern Europe.

At the end of the XIVth century, the first humanists resumed the Caroline and created the humanistic. It was that writing which was adopted for printing and which became the basis of our modern writings. For palaeographers, the change from a writing to an other was not made in a radical way but by a slow and progressive evolution, which explains that it is difficult to identify categorically a given writing. For example we observe texts written in Caroline style which contain elements of the Gothic writing. Thus, the palaeographer should be able to quantify exactly the part of mixture of the writings families. For example the class of *Protogothic* writing is an intermediate writing style between the Caroline writing and the Gothic writing (Figs. 1, 2).

Since the XIIth century, the number of observed writing styles in Europe has exceptionally increased. Consequently, the work of palaeographers becomes more difficult especially with the evolution of the *Caroline* into *Gothic* (Fig. 3), and the division of *Gothic* into sub-families such as *Cursive Gothic* scripts, *Textualis Gothic* etc. Like the evolution of the *Caroline* into *Gothic*, the evolution into *Cursive Gothic* script then into *Batarde Gothic* thereafter into *Textualis Gothic* has been gradually made (Fig. 4).

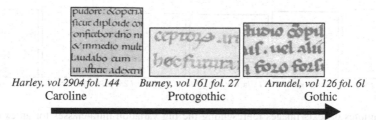

Harley, vol 2904 fol. 144   Burney, vol 161 fol. 27   Arundel, vol 126 fol. 61
      Caroline   Protogothic   Gothic

Fig. 3. Progressive evolution of the Caroline into Protogothic then into Gothic [BL]

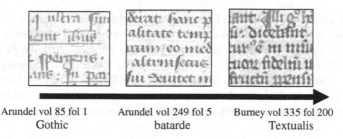

Arundel vol 85 fol 1   Arundel vol 249 fol 5   Burney vol 335 fol 200
     Gothic   batarde   Textualis

Fig. 4. Samples of the evolution from cursive Gothic script into batarde Gothic then into Textualis Gothic [BL]

   ms Thott vol 5554 fol 189v   *ms vol 131 fol 86r*   *ms vol 80 fol 163v*
Cursive Gothic Libraria style   **Cursive Gothic** Formata style   **Cursive Gothic** Currens style

Fig. 5. Samples of text images representing three sub families of cursive script between the 8th and the 16th century [1]

   Yates Thompson   *Arundel Psalms*   *La bible*   *Burney vol 333*
Textualis Gotic Quadrata style   **Textualis Gotic** Semi-Quadrata style   **Textualis Gotic** Prescissa style   **Textualis Gotic** Rotunda style

Fig. 6. Samples of texts images representing the Textualis sub-families of styles between the 8th and the 16th century

The diversification of the writing families in Europe increased until the Renaissance and witnessed the development of writing subfamilies inside every big Gothic family.

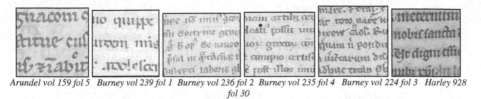

Arundel vol 159 fol 5   Burney vol 239 fol 1   Burney vol 236 fol 2   Burney vol 235 fol 4   Burney vol 224 fol 3   Harley 928 fol 30

Fig. 7. Samples of texts images representing the big variation intra-classes for an example of Textualis Gothic Rotunda style [BL]

So we can distinguish several *Cursive Gothic* subfamilies of (Libraria, Formata and Currens) shown in Fig. 5. Also, the Fig. 6 shows several subfamilies of *Gothic Textualis* such as the *Quadatra*, the *Semi-Quadrata,* the *Prescissa*, the *Rotunda, etc.*

Fig. 7 shows the variability of writings inside the same sub-family as for the *Textualis Gothic Rotunda* class. It illustrates the difficulty in terms of image analysis to define the right features that describes the writing styles in order to find the homogeneity between the various samples of the same writing.

3 State of Art

We can find several work on the characterization of writings for different applications like the checking and the authentification of writer, the pre-classification of writings in terms of legibility for a better recognition in the automatic sorting of the mails and checks. All these studies are related to our problem but these contributions are not all directly re-exploitable for the paleographic study. The distribution of images directions was used to identify the different writings style for their recognition [2]. Fractal analysis measures the degree of autosimilarities in an image; it is a good measure of a writer's style that can serve to classify writings according to their legibility and to detect a modification of a writer for the early diagnostic of Alzheimer's illness [3]. Fractal indication is also susceptible to characterize the different alphabets in the printed texts. [4] characterized different text styles using complexity measures from shapes, legibility and compactness independently of the used alphabet. We can refer other works susceptible to be reused for the recognition of medieval writing such as the recognition of scripts (of words in a particular alphabet) in the multilingual documents. These works use the similarity of graphemes [5], the texture [6], or the analysis of projection profile [7] etc.

The System for Paleographic Inspections (SPI) [8], represents the only tentative for the realization of an automatic assistance system in paleography. [9], it is a local approach that tries to replicate the work of the paleographers. The method consists of isolating manually the representative characters of a writing and to compare them to referential characters from a paleographic database labeled manually. The comparison uses the tangent distance and the rule of the k nearest neighbor *(knn)* that gives k characters the nearest references to the new character. The system SPI only used for testing 37 documents and 4 images per styles and some images are descended from the same documents which is neither representative nor sufficient.

4 Our Proposition

We suggest to recognize the writing styles by using new image analysis methods to assist the historians in the classification and the dating of old Latin manuscript. Indeed, every historical period has been characterized by one or several types of writings. Therefore, the recognition of documents writings allows to know its date and/or its geographical origin.

We are not going to study the page layout of texts, the density of writings, the overlapping of characters, the concentration of diacritics which represent much susceptible information to characterize the style of a document. We limit our work to the classification of the writings into categories defined by paleographers.

Our domain of studies covers the old Latin writings of the VIIIth century until the XVIth. The study of Latin writing preceding the VIIIth century such as the Oncial or the cursive writing doesn't interests the paleographers. By contrast, the assistance to the medieval writing expertise is very useful since the XIIth century. It is for differentiating between main writing families (*Caroline* and *Gothic*) then to finely classify them into subfamilies (*Protogothic, Cursive Gothic, Hybrid Gothic* and *Textualis Gothic*) and then into more precise subgroup (*Rotunda, Quadrata, Semi-Quadrata, Prescissa, Libraria, Currens* and *Formata*) for the *Textualis Gothic* and (*Libraria, Formata* and *Currens*) for the *Gothic cursive* (see Fig. 7).

Our work focuses on the extraction of sufficiently discriminative features in order to be able to differentiate the biggest number of possible Latin writings. This study allows checking the feasibility of an automatic images analysis system that helps paleographers. First we examined the distances between the classes for studying the consistency between results of the images analysis and paleographic expertise.

Second, we refine the discrimination between the main Latin medieval writings then between the writings subfamilies as described in figure 6.

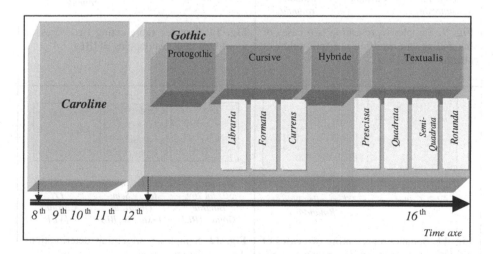

Fig. 8. Different subfamilies distribution of Latin style between the 8th and the 16th century

4.1 The Difficult Conditions

The development of a helping system for the old manuscript expertise is considered a difficult task for many factors:

- The complexity of shapes of writings (Fig. 4, 5, 6), and the variability of writings from the same writing family (Fig. 8).
- The existence of hybrid writings that comes from a mixture of several writings (Fig. 1-3).
- The bad quality for manuscript conservation, for example the fading out of supports and inks (Fig. 9),
- The overlapping of lines and words (Fig. 10), and the presence of writing in the margin and/or between lines (Fig. 11).
- The bad quality of image origins; some colored images quality becomes deteriorated because of the digitization; and others from the digitization of books or microfilms in gray levels. Most images contain deteriorated areas due to a very strong compression (JPEG). Our samples are digitized with different resolutions (Fig. 12).

Therefore, within this difficult context, we analyze the image directly in gray levels without previous filtering, restoration or geometric correction. This choice deprives us from using a big part of the reusable works and in particular all those based on the segmentation.

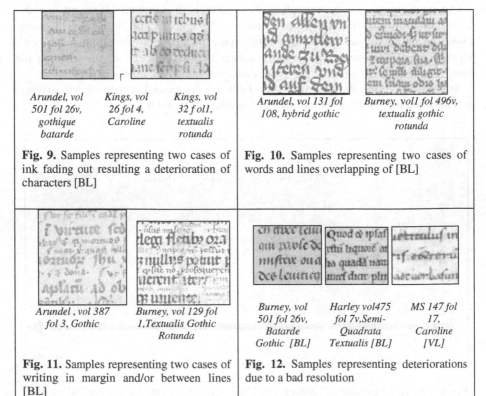

Arundel, vol 501 fol 26v, gothique batarde   *Kings, vol 26 fol 4, Caroline*   *Kings, vol 32 f ol1, textualis rotunda*

Fig. 9. Samples representing two cases of ink fading out resulting a deterioration of characters [BL]

Arundel, vol 131 fol 108, hybrid gothic   *Burney, vol1 fol 496v, textualis gothic rotunda*

Fig. 10. Samples representing two cases of words and lines overlapping of [BL]

Arundel , vol 387 fol 3, Gothic   *Burney, vol 129 fol 1,Textualis Gothic Rotunda*

Fig. 11. Samples representing two cases of writing in margin and/or between lines [BL]

Burney, vol 501 fol 26v, Batarde Gothic [BL]   *Harley vol475 fol 7v,Semi-Quadrata Textualis [BL]*   *MS 147 fol 17, Caroline [VL]*

Fig. 12. Samples representing deteriorations due to a bad resolution

4.2 Our Approach

We distinguish two complementary approaches:

- **Local approach:** we try to replicate the work of paleographers, while attempting to establish some visual similarities between writings relied on very particular features of a letters writing (examples: 'r', 's', 'e', 'a'). Indeed, some particular letters are used by paleographers for the recognition of a writing. These letters must be taken inside words because their graphics change according to the writer when they are situated at the beginning or at the end of words [8] [9].
- **Global approach:** we do not try to replicate the work of paleographers, but to use a more suitable method for the automatic images analysis. The approach consists of analyzing statistically the whole image of a manuscript and to find features which describe writings. The global approach should guarantee the independency of the global measures from the text content, the writer's personal style, the used language, the used letters and of their frequency. If the sample size is meaningful, all the letters are represented and in particular the characteristic letters used by palaeographers.

Moreover, a global analysis allows the inclusion of some ornaments without affecting a statistical analysis because the text occupies a sufficient area.

The global approach advantages are very precious for the analysis of a great variety of documents having different qualities and origins. So we have chosen to work with this approach to overcome the difficult conditions described before.

Because of the lack of previous works in the domain of the global analysis of the medieval manuscripts writings, we have to find image features that verify the following criteria:

- The robustness: image features can be calculated without any image segmentation or any prior processing.
- The writer invariance: the measures should be independent of the writer.
- The invariance to the size: image features must be invariant to the size of the text sample.
- The change of scale: A writing must be invariant to the scale factor, but some images features require to resize the image so as the scale of different writings are comparable.
- The change of ratio: It is the most current geometric transformation to adjust images to an electronic document. The ratio height/width of an image must not influence the final decision. Image features can work differently on images having different ratios. Therfore, we suggest that image maintain all the same ratio.
- The rotation: A writing must remain the same whatever the image orientation can be. In image analysis, describers must be invariant to the same rotation applied to all images.

We suggest to achieve a classification system of writings. If the writing family is found and/or its rate of mixture with other writings is determined, we can give more or less precise date of the document.

4.3 Application of the Cooccurrence on the Medieval Writings

The cooccurrence has been used as a means for characterizing a texture in image analysis. The images of documents present also textures by the repetition of the regular characters, the words and the lines of the text. However we want neither to measure the page layout nor to characterize the management of spaces (density of features, spacing...), we would rather try to characterize writings. We use the cooccurrence just to measure writing variations and not the variations of shapes between themselves. Therefore, we have to do very weak displacements and be assured that we do not compare two adjacent lines or cover a letter horizontally with the neighboring letters. Cooccurrence must be calculated on texts that are normalized in size and displacements must be limited to less than half of the size of the text lines body. We normalize all the images of our experimental database with the overage text body roughly equals 30 pixels to allow the displacements of a distance that exceeds 15 pixels as a maximum.

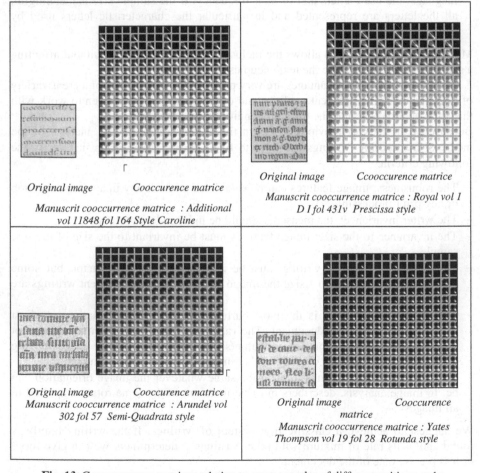

Original image   Cooccurence matrice

Manuscrit cooccurrence matrice : Additional
vol 11848 fol 164 Style Caroline

Original image   Ccooccurence matrice

Manuscrit cooccurrence matrice : Royal vol 1
D I fol 431v Prescissa style

Original image   Cooccurence matrice
Manuscrit cooccurrence matrice : Arundel vol
302 fol 57 Semi-Quadrata style

Original image   Cooccurence
matrice
Manuscrit cooccurrence matrice : Yates
Thompson vol 19 fol 28 Rotunda style

Fig. 13. Cooccurrences matrices relative to some samples of different writings style

For each direction *theta* (θ) and displacement *rau* (ρ), we have a cooccurrence matrix of size NgxNg with Ng is the number of gray levels of the image.

$$Coo(dx = \rho \cos \theta, dy = \rho \sin \theta) = \frac{1}{N} \left[\sum_{x,y} I(x, y) = i \cap I(x + dx, y + dy) = j \right]_{i,j} = \frac{1}{N} \left[M_{i,j} \right]_{(i,j)=0..Ng-1} \tag{1}$$

We use the maximum of information and take a very fine subdivision for the values of ρ and of θ. We have used 16 directions ($\theta \in [0..15]$) and 15 displacements ($\rho \in [1..15]$) that is 16x15 matrices to the maximum. The values of pixels have been decreased from 256 up to 16 values. We do not keep matrices of cooccurrence for $\rho=0$, because they don't correspond to any displacement. The discreet nature of images does not permit to have more than 4 directions for the displacement of 1 pixel, 8 directions for a displacement of 2 pixels etc. It remains 216 non null matrices. Every writing is described by a different signature according to the values of ρ and θ (Fig. 13).

4.4 Verification of Criteria by the Cooccurrence Measures

The cooccurrence matrices relative to samples of different sizes of the same document are approximately similar. Information is considered incomplete for a very small size sample. If the image contains only some words, it does not exist enough information on the intermediate characters.

The cooccurrence is *invariant to text content* because the SGLD are similar on different text areas of the same document. The cooccurrence is *robust* because it does not require any image segmentation nor of text zones, lines, words nor of characters.

The image smoothing modifies greatly the SGLD for the small displacement of *rau* near 1. Because of the specific nature of digitized document, the image smoothing densifies the extreme values of matrices for (i,j)=(0,0),(0,15),(15,0) and (15,15).

The modification of the image ratio is equivalent to the calculation of the cooccurrence with a displacement $\rho(\theta)$ which describe an ellipse and not a circle. The impact on the cooccurrence matrix is equivalent to the change of scale but with a non constant displacement ρ. As we constitute a feature vector from the cooccurrence matrices in the order of ρ and θ, the rotation, the scale and the ratio modify the data position in the feature vector but not the information itself.

The cooccurrence preserves the same information about shapes after the main geometric transformations. But this information is not preserved anymore by the same matrices following ρ and θ. To guarantee that we compare the same information, it is necessary that the images have the same orientation, scale and ratio.

4.5 Images Features

We analyze *n* observations data described by *p* variable with *p* equal to the number of cooccurrence matrices non null multiplied by the number of 12 Haralick describers [10] (With a quantification into 16 values, for ρ and θ, the cooccurrence represents 216 non null matrices of 16x16 values). So we have *n* points in IR^p with p=216x12, *n* is the number of observed images writing.

The features' space are too big in relation with the number of *n* observations for a classifier. There is a limited number of factors among the $p=2592$ variables that participates in the categorization of writings. A manual work of features' selection would be too long and exhausting. Therefore it is necessary to reduce the number of describers by a statistical analysis of the variance.

This analysis allowed us to find the correlated variables and to give a reduced number of factors that are of linear combinations of the origin variable *p*. The data analysis leads to a canonical analysis of the class proximity, then to comparison of the results with those of experts.

5 Analysis of Results

Considering the following references for the 15 classes of the Latin writing:

1 : Caroline	6 : Hybride batard	11 : Textualis Rotunda
2 : Gothic	7 : Textualis	12 : Textualis Formata
3 : Cursive Libraria	8 : Textualis Prescissa	13 : Textualis Libraria
4 : Cursive Formata	9 : Textualis Quadrata	14 : Textualis Currens
5 : Cursive Currens	10 : Textualis Semi-Quadrata	15 : Protogothic

In order to have a general view of the 15 classes, we applied a global discrimination strategy onto the 15 classes.

While applying the PCA (Principle Component Analysis) with only one measure like *f10* that represents the variance of P_{x-y}, we get the factorial map of the Fig.14. This map represents 97% of the variance explained by the first two axes which proves that data is correlated and that we can reduce the number of the characteristics without losing information. This map shows that the different writting form clusters correspond approximately to the classes defined by the palaeographers. This "blind" analysis, without taking into account the classes, shows that the paleographers' classification is coherent and that the writings of the same class are near.

The cooccurrence constitutes a good measure to differentiate between the various writings. However, if these features explain well the variance of observations, they are not necessarily the most discriminative classes. Therefore, we are going to apply the discriminant analysis [11].

Fig. 14. PCA on the 15 classes with f10 characteristic

Contrary to the PCA, the Discriminant Analysis finds linear projections into a subspace that better discriminates a great number of classes if the features are relevant (Fig. 15). Getting a majority of classes separated proves the existence of linear combinations of describers which can solve the problem of medieval writing discrimination. We have obtained a good scattering of classes: 1. Caroline, 3. Cursive Libraria, 4. Cursive Formata, 5. Cursive Currens, 8. Textualis prescissa, 9. Textualis Quadrata, 10. Textualis Semi-Quadrata, 12. Textualis Formata, 13. Textualis Liraria and 14. Textualis Currens. The confusion matrix confirms the good results given by the satisfactory discriminating rates for the writing types relative to these classes (from 48% for the class 12. Textualis Formata up to 100% for the class 5. Cursive Formata). Exceptions concern classes 2. Gothic and 7. Textualis that are not considered as true families as well as the 8. Textualis Prescissa and the 14. Textualis Currens which are not enough statistically represented in our database.

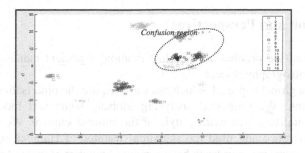

Fig. 15. Result of DA for 15 classes

The writing style 2. *Gothic*, 6. *Hybrid*, 7. *Textualis*, 11. *Textualis Rotunda* and 15. *Protogothic* are the least well separated by the discriminant analysis and show important confusion between them. The four confused classes that are the 2. *Gothic*, the 7. *Textualis*, the 15. *Protogothic* and the 6. *Batarde* do not constitute any real homogeneous writing classes from the image analysis point of view. We think that classes 2. *Gothic* and 7. *Textualis* contain writings non sufficiently described by paleographers and it is therefore normal that these generic classes are confused with their respective subfamilies. We think that *Protogothic* writings are transitory writings between *Caroline* and *Gothic* writings. Dendrogram analysis confirmed that the *Batarde* writing is a *hybrid* writing between the *Cursive Gothic* writings and the *Textualis Gothic* writings.When we omitted the most problematic classes which are the 2. *Gothic*, the 7. *Textualis*, the 15. *Protogothic* and the 6. *Batarde*, we obtained 11 correctly separated classes. Our results show that it exists coherence between image features and the palaeographic classes of medieval writings. We think that *Protogothic* writings do not constitute an independent class which cannot be discriminated from the *Caroline* and the *Gothic* writings. For the *Protogothic* writing, we can provide to palaeographers the rate of mixture between *Caroline* and *Gothic* by taking the distance from the centres of the respective classes. The average rate of discrimination moved from 59% to 81%. It can be improved if we will have a better equilibrated number of samples for classes 8. *Textualis Prescissas* and 14. *Textualis Currens*.

Table 1. Confusion matrix obtained by discriminative analysis onto 11 classes while using the 12 Haralick features

	1	2	3	4	5	6	7	8	9	10	11	%correct
1. Caroline	68	1	0	1	0	0	0	5	0	0	0	91%
2. Cursive Libraria	0	18	1	0	0	0	0	0	0	3	0	82%
3. Cursive Formata	0	1	5	0	0	1	0	0	0	0	0	71%
4. Cursive Currens	0	1	0	8	0	0	0	0	0	0	0	89%
5. Textualis Prescisea	0	0	0	0	2	0	0	2	0	0	0	50%
6. Textualis Quadrata	0	0	0	0	0	49	1	4	2	0	0	88%
7. Textualis Semi-Quadrata	0	0	0	0	0	4	26	9	2	0	0	63%
8. Textualis Rotunda	1	1	0	0	0	5	3	64	1	0	0	85%
9. Textualis Formata	0	1	0	1	0	2	0	1	16	2	0	70%
10. Textualis Libraria	0	2	1	1	0	0	0	0	1	14	1	70%
11. Textualis Currens	0	0	0	0	0	0	0	0	0	2	2	50%
Total	69	25	7	11	2	61	30	85	22	21	3	81%

6 Conclusion and Perspectives

We have exposed the problem of the classification of ancient manuscripts which is useful for the paleography science.

We defined a global approach which does not require the binarisation of images or text segmentation. We suggested analysing globally some text blocks which are enough representative of the writing style of the entire document. We chose to work with the cooccurrence and used the statistical features of Haralick to describe our matrices of cooccurrence in order to have a reduced number of image features.

Our images describers based on the statistical measures of cooccurrence allow to find approximately the classes of writings defined by the palaeographers after the decorrelation by a factorial analysis. The discriminant analysis provides a rate of 59% of global discrimination for the fifteen Latin classes. The discrimination rate increases up to 81 % when we eliminate the four classes causing problems which are not statistically well represented or because of absence of precisions. Indeed the proceeding from one family to another has never been abrupt and some writings can present a mixture of writings features that contributed to its formation. We mention the *Protogothic* and the *Hybrid* as examples. For these writings, we must replace the discriminant analysis by an analysis that measures the rate of mixture with the other definite classes. We also noticed that the *Gothic* and *Textualis* writings are only generic writings that have not been sufficiently described (a hypothesis that remain to be validated by experts in paleography). Contrary to character recognition or scripts separation, classification of medieval writings requires experts in Palaeography to valid our work and confirm the right classification of the images from our database. We found a lot of resources of images on the Web, but we are not sure that the classes given by paleographers are exact. We hope to get the help of paleographers to exploit a bigger number of these resources.

Moreover, we try to increase our collaboration with palaeographers in order to analyse the results from the image analysis point of view and to refine our approach to better fit their needs.

References

1. A. Derolez, "The Palaeography of Gothic Manuscript Books", from the Twelfth to the Early Sixteenth Century", Cambridge Studies in Palaeography and Codicology, Cambridge University Press, 2003. (http://www.moesbooks.com/cgi-bin/moe/39006.html).
2. J. P. Crettez, "A set of handwriting families : style recognition", International conference on Document Analysis and Recognition, Vol 1, page 489, Auguest 1995.
3. V. Bouletreau, "Vers une classification de l'écrit", Thèse de doctorat INSA de Lyon, 1997.
4. V. Eglin, "Contributions à la structuration fonctionnelle des documents imprimés. Exploitation de la dynamique du regard dans le repérage de l'information", Thèse de Doctorat, INSA de Lyon, 13 Novembre 1998.
5. I. Moalla, A.M. Alimi and A. Ben Hamadou, "Extraction of Arabic text from multilingual documents", IEEE International Conference on Systems, Man and Cybernetics, Tunisie, Octobre 2002.
6. T.N. Tan, "Rotation Invariant Texture Features and Their Use in Automatic Script Identification", IEEE Trans. Pattern Analysis and Machine Intelligence, vol. 20, no. 7, 1998, pp. 751-756.
7. S. L Wood, X. Yao, K. Krishnamurthi, L. Dang, "Language Identification for Printed Text Independent of Segmentation", Proc. IEEE ICIP'95, pp. 428-431, 1995.
8. Aiolli, F., M. Simi, D. Sona, A. Sperduti, A. Starita, and G. Zaccagnini. 1999. SPI: a System for Palaeographic Inspections. AIIA Notizie http://www.dsi.unifi.it/AIIA/ vol. 4: 34-38.
9. A. Ciula, "Digital palaeography: using the digital representation of medieval script to support palaeographic analysis", Digital Medievalist 1.1, April 20, 2005
10. R. M. Haralick, "Statistical and structural approaches to texture", Proceedings of IEEE, vol. 67, no. 5, pp. 786{804, 1979.
11. R. O. Duda, P.E. Hart, D.G. Stork, "Pattern classification", second edition
    [VL] http://www.villevalenciennes.fr/bib/fondsvirtuels/microfilms/accueil.asp#item
    [BL] http://prodigi.bl.uk/illcat/searchMSNo.asp

Restoring Ink Bleed-Through Degraded Document Images Using a Recursive Unsupervised Classification Technique

Drira Fadoua, Frank Le Bourgeois, and Hubert Emptoz

LIRIS, INSA de LYON, Bâtiment Jules Verne,
20 Avenue Albert Einstein, 69621 Villeurbanne Cedex, France
{fdrira, Frank.lebourgeois, hubert.emptoz}@liris.cnrs.fr

Abstract. This paper presents a new method to restore a particular type of degradation related to ancient document images. This degradation, referred to as "bleed-through", is due to the paper porosity, the chemical quality of the ink, or the conditions of digitalization. It appears as marks degrading the readability of the document image. Our purpose consists then in removing these marks to improve readability. The proposed method is based on a recursive unsupervised segmentation approach applied on the decorrelated data space by the principal component analysis. It generates a binary tree that only the leaves images satisfying a certain condition on their logarithmic histogram are processed. Some experiments, done on real ancient document images provided by the archives of "Chatillon-Chalaronne" illustrate the effectiveness of the suggested method.

1 Introduction

Historical documents are of great interest to human being. Nowadays, recent techniques help in producing digital copies of these documents to preserve cultural heritage. Nevertheless, the quality of these digital copies depends greatly on the quality of the original documents. These are often affected by several types of degradations limiting their use. In fact, old documents, supported by fragile materials, are easily affected by bad environmental conditions. Manipulations, humidity and unfitted storage for many years affect heritage documents and make them difficult to read. Moreover, the digitizing techniques used in image scanning inevitably further degrade the quality of the document images. A convenient solution to this problem may be the application of restoration methods on these deteriorated document images. Restoration methods can improve the quality of the digital copy of the originally degraded document image, thus improving human readability and allowing further application of image processing techniques such as segmentation and character recognition. A large number of algorithms have been developed by the community. However, each of these methods depends on a certain context of use and is intended to process a precise type of defects.

In this study, we will focus on a particular type of degradation, which is referred to as "bleed-through". This degradation is not only due to ink's seeping through the

H. Bunke and A.L. Spitz (Eds.): DAS 2006, LNCS 3872, pp. 38–49, 2006.

pages of documents after long periods of storage, but also due to the paper porosity, to the chemical quality of the ink, or to the conditions of digitalization. The result is that characters from the reverse side appear as noise on the front side. This can deteriorate the legibility of the document if the interference acts in a significant way. An overview of some restoration techniques tackling this kind of degradation is presented in the first section. In the second section, we propose a new algorithm trying to restore such kind of degraded document images provided by the archives of "Chatillon-Chalaronne". This algorithm performs, recursively, a k-means algorithm on the decorrelated image data with the Principal Component Analysis (PCA) done on the RGB space. It generates a binary tree that only the leaves images satisfying a certain condition on their logarithmic histogram are processed. Our recursive restoration method does not require specific input devices or the digital processing of the backside to be input. It is able to correct unneeded image components and to extract clear textual images from interfering areas through analysis of the front side image alone. The method converges towards the restored version of the degraded document image. The third section shows experimental results that verify the effectiveness of our proposed method.

2   Existing "Bleed-Through" Restoration Methods

Degraded document images, which have been subject to "bleed-through" degradation, contain the content of the original side combined with the content of the reverse side. Examples of such degraded document images provided by "Chatillon-Chalaronne" are shown in the Figure 1. Applying restoration methods on these images could be a solution to extract clear text strings of the front side from this noisy background.

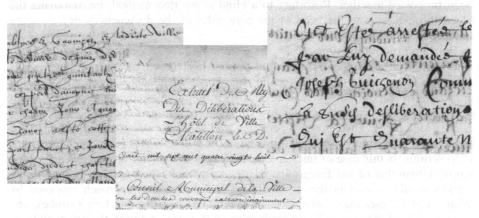

Fig. 1. Examples of "bleed-through" degraded document images

Thresholding techniques are a simple solution for restoring such degradation. Nevertheless, these techniques remain insufficient for too degraded document images. For instance, Leedham and al. [2] compared several thresholding techniques for separating text and background in degraded historical document images. The results prove that neither global nor local thresholding techniques perform satisfactorily.

Indeed, looking for efficient restoration methods becomes an urgent need. Some restoration methods dealing with "bleed-through" removal were proposed. Some of them have successfully resolved this problem but under specific conditions. These methods can be divided into two classes according to the presence of the verso side page document: non-blind ones treating this interference problem using both sides of the document and blind ones treating this problem without the verso side.

The main idea of non-blind approaches is mainly based on the comparison between the front and back page, which requires a registration of the two sides of the document in order to identify the interfering strokes to be eliminated. Examples of as such approaches are reported in [3, 4, and 5]. Sharma's approach [3] simplifies the physical model of these effects to derive a linear mathematical model and then defines an adaptive linear-filtering scheme. Another approach proposed by Dubois and Pathak [4] is mainly based on processing both sides of a gray-level manuscript simultaneously using a six-parameter affine transformation to register the two sides. Once the two sides have been correctly registered, areas consisting primarily of "bleed-through" are identified using a thresholding technique and replaced by the background color or intensity. In [5], a wavelet reconstruction process is applied to iteratively enhance the foreground strokes and smear the interfering strokes. Doing so strengthens the discriminating capability of an improved Canny edge detector against the interfering strokes. All these different non-blind restoration techniques dealt successfully with "bleed-through" removal. Nevertheless, a registration process of both sides of the document is required. Perfect registration, however, is difficult to achieve. This is due to (1) different document skews and (2) different resolutions during image capture of both sides, (3) non-availability of the reverse side and (4) warped pages resulting from the scanning of thick documents. The main drawback of this approach is therefore its dependency on both sides of the documents that must been processed together. Resorting to a blind restoration method, i.e. removing the bleed through without the need of the both sides of the document is often a more interesting solution.

For blind restoration approaches, the restoration process occurs without the verso side. An interesting successfully used approach is based on steered filters. This approach is especially designed for old handwritten document images. A restoration approach [6] proposed by Tan and al. consists in adopting an edge detection algorithm together with an orientation filter to extract the foreground edges and remove the reverse side edges. This approach performs well and improves greatly the appearance of the original document image but it is less or more inefficient when the interference is so serious. In this case of interference, the edges of the interfering strokes are even stronger than that of the foreground edges. As a result, the edges of the interfering strokes would remain in the resultant text image. Another approach proposed by Wang et al. [7] uses directional wavelets to remove images of interfering strokes. The writing style of the document determines the differences between the orientations of the foreground and the interfering strokes. Basically, the foreground and the interfering strokes are slanting along the directions of 45° and 135° respectively. The directional aspect of the transform is capable of distinguishing the foreground and reverse side strokes and effectively removing the appearing interference. This approach produces very interesting results but it remains applicable only to particular cases of character orientation (45° and 135°). All the techniques cited above treat a particular case of degraded document image, where foreground and interfering strokes characters are oriented differently, which is not always the case. Other more flexible techniques exist, among which, we can cite techniques based on Independent Component Analysis [8], adaptive binarization [9], self-organizing maps [10], color analysis [11].

So far, we presented a classification of some methodologies proposed to tackle the "bleed-through" degradation. After this short outline, our choice will directed to a blind restoration method as the verso side is not necessary available.

3 Proposed Method

We propose to proceed with a segmentation approach. In fact, the main idea behind our algorithm is to classify the pixels of the page into three classes: (1) background, (2) original text, or (3) interfering text. This last class must be removed from the original page and replaced by the background color (the average of the detected background pixels for example). "Bleed-through" removal is thus a three-class segmentation problem. Nevertheless, a single clustering step is not sufficient to correctly extract the text of the front side (Fig.2). Thus, we propose to apply a recursive segmentation method on the decorrelated data with Principal Component Analysis. To simplify the analysis and reduce its computational complexity, we will restrict ourselves to the case of a two-class problem: original text or not. The proposed method is built then via recursively dividing the test image into two subsets of classes.

Fig. 2. Results of the 3-means classification algorithm on a degraded image; Top: An extract of a degraded document image; Bottom: Left: Image class n°1, Middle: Image class n°2, Right: Image class n°3

3.1 Justification

The following paragraph will briefly (1) introduce k-means, (2) introduce PCA, (3) explain the importance of applying k-means on PCA, and (4) introduce the logarithmic histogram.

(1) k-means is an algorithm [12] using prototypes to represent clusters by optimizing the squared error function. The prototypes are initially randomly assigned to a cluster. The k-means clustering proceeds by repeated application of a two-step process where the mean vector for all prototypes in each cluster is computed and then prototypes are reassigned to the cluster whose centre is closest to the prototype. The data points are thus decomposed into disjoint groups such that those belonging to same cluster are similar while others belonging to different clusters are dissimilar.

(2) PCA or Principal Component Analysis is an example of eigenvector-based technique which is commonly used for dimensionality reduction and feature extraction of an embedded data. The main justification of dimension reduction is that PCA uses singular value decomposition (SVD) which gives the best low rank approximation to original data. Indeed, PCA can reduce the correlation between the different components where coherent patterns can be detected more clearly.

(3) We propose here to apply k-means (K=2) clustering on the Principal Component Analysis subspace. Pioneering work [13] has shown that PCA dimension reduction is particularly beneficial for K-means clustering. More precisely, we decided to apply the segmentation algorithm on image data decorrelated using a PCA. The PCA is computed on the RGB color space. It improves the quality of classification because of its properties which reduce data space and eliminate associations between data. In representing the document image in a convenient vector space, we will succeed to improve the gathering of elements with approximately similar values in order to make them converging to significant classes.

(4) The logarithmic histogram is a histogram with logarithmic scale. We choose this technique as it is common way to scale histograms for display and then assume that a wide range of luminance values can be clearly represented.

3.2 Description of the Method

A new framework based on a recursive approach is presented here, which relies on two types of analysis: the Principal Component Analysis (PCA) and the k-means algorithm applied recursively on selected generated data image. A scheme of our approach is given in Figure 3. The following steps are performed recursively:

(1) The dimension of an image is reduced and its data is decorrelated using PCA.

(2) The k-means algorithm is applied with parameter k=2, resulting in two classes of image pixels.

(3) The pixels of each class backprojected into the original color space.

(4) The logarithmic histogram of each class image is printed. A comparison between the two class image histograms is established. The one having more dark pixel values is the one associated to the class image that will be used as input to the same algorithm beginning with step1.

The dimension reduction step projects the document image from the original vector space to another reduced subspace generated via PCA. The RGB color space, where each color is represented by a triplet red, green and blue intensity, is used as input.

As shown in Figure 4, the first principal component gives a good approximation of the image compared to the other principal components. For instance, when we project onto the directions with biggest variance, we can not only retain as much information

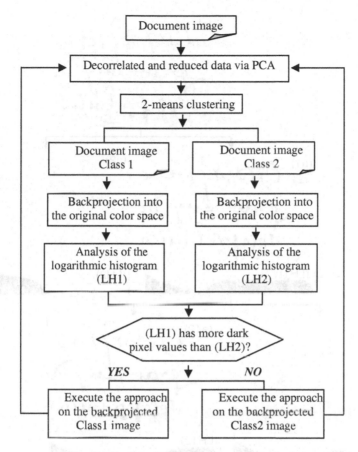

Fig. 3. The flowchart of the proposed method

as possible but also we can deliberately drop out directions with small variance. Indeed, selecting the most significant principal components as input to the k-means clustering algorithm reduces the data enough in order to make the problem manageable while at the same time retaining enough information to perform a successful separation.

Fig. 4. Results of PCA projection; Left: First principal component (99.2% of the total eigenvalues variance); Middle: Second principal component (0.72% of the total eigenvalues variance); Right: Third principal component (0.08% of the total eigenvalues variance)

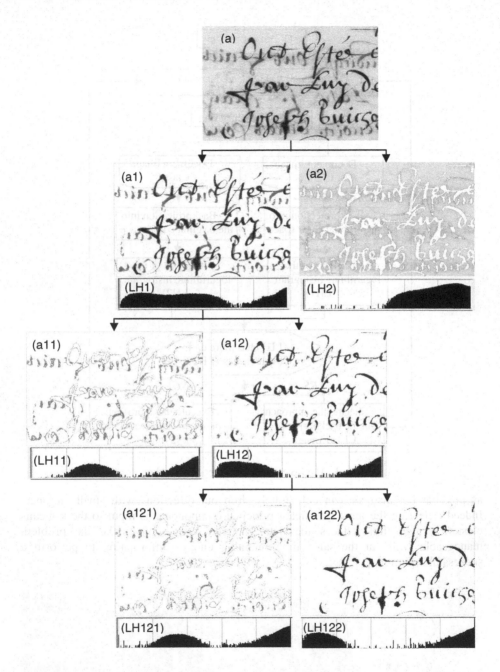

Fig. 5. An extract of the generated tree with our proposed method applied on an extract of a degraded document image (a); (a1), (a2), (a11), (a12), (a121), and (a122) are the different internal nodes of the tree; (LH1), (LH2), (LH11), and (LH12) the logarithmic histogram of (a1), (a2), (a11), and (a12) respectively

The proposed method starts with the whole image set as a single cluster. Then, it is partitioned into disjoint subsets (a1) and (a2), where the inter-cluster distance is maximized. The subsets (a1) and (a2) are then analyzed by studying their logarithmic histogram. The scope here is to allow decomposition only of the leaves images that can lead to the corrected expected image. If we suppose that the text of the original front side is darker than any other interfering text, the analysis of the image logarithmic histogram values could be a solution. This criterion of selection was followed upon the study of the different provided "Chatillon-Chalaronne" document images. By doing so, we can reach automatic final class image detection. Indeed, the subset image corresponding to the logarithmic histogram having the more dark pixel values is further subdivided and so on for the new generated subsets. The process thus leads after a certain number of iterations to two leaves images that one them represents the expected image. This image contains the original text. Figure 5 represents an extract of this tree. As shown in this figure, image (a122) is the expected result. The number of iterations in our method has been determined empirically and set to a fixed number of iterations (=3). The result of the algorithm is a set of classes (the leaves of the tree of recursive function calls), where one class represents the pixels of the original handwriting. We can so notice that the segmentation of the data in a recursive way allows us to refine the final restoration result as soon as we traverse down the binary tree. Our method outperforms other methods that involve a global classification in K classes applied to the entire image (Figure 2). It converges more correctly to the final result.

4 Experimental Results

Experiments were carried out on some samples of degraded image documents to evaluate the performance of our approach (Fig.6, Fig.7). The figure 7 illustrates an example of the restored image resulting from the application of our method on a degraded document image. This figure shows one of the subsets generated after three iterations of the method. This subset represents the front side text and we clearly notice, compared with the test image, that the interfering text has been successfully

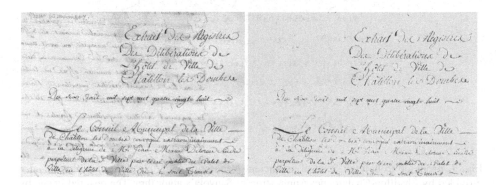

Fig. 6. Left: Scan of an ancient manuscript with "bleed-through" interference provided by Chatillon-Chalaronne. Right: the restored image by the proposed method.

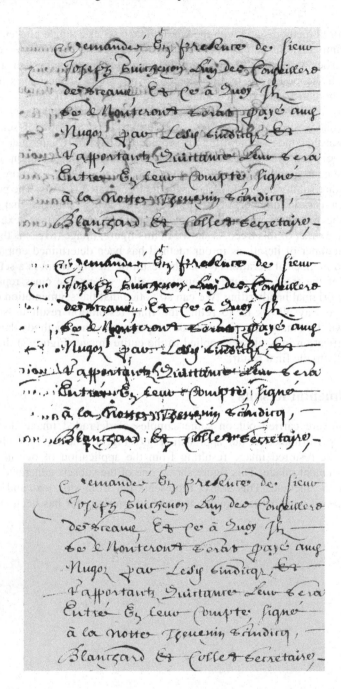

Fig. 7. From top to bottom: Scan of an ancient manuscript with "bleed-through" interference provided by Chatillon-Chalaronne; Application of Sauvola's algorithm; The restored image by the proposed method

removed and replaced by the average of the detected background pixels. This figure illustrates also the fact that classical thresholding techniques such as Sauvola's technique is unable to resolve correctly the problem.

Experimental results illustrate the significant performance of this recursive approach compared to the obtained results of the approach [11] (Fig.8). This approach represents an adaptive segmentation algorithm suited for color document images analysis. It is based on the serialization of the k-means algorithm.

Compared to other existing methods, our method:

(1) does not require specific input devices or the processing of the reverse side of the document to be input. It is able to correct unneeded image components through the analysis of the front side image alone. Our approach can be classified among "blind bleed-through" removal approaches.

(2) does not require any specific learning process such as the case of the self-organizing Maps based approach [10] where a learning process must be performed on each chosen image.

(3) does not require any input parameters as in the case of the serialized k-means based approach. Certainly, this approach gives good results but it is an unsupervised one as the choice of some parameters such as the number of clusters and the color samples for each class are not done automatically.

Fig. 8. From top to bottom: Scan of an ancient manuscript with "bleed-through" interference provided by the archives of "Chatillon-Chalaronne"; the obtained image with our proposed method; the obtained image with the approach [11]

5 Conclusions

We demonstrated in this study the effectiveness of our approach in "bleed-through" removal from degraded document images. This approach consists in combining both Principal Component Analysis (PCA) and K-means. These techniques are applied recursively to separate original text from interfering and overlapping areas of text. The stopping criterion for the proposed recursive approach has been determined empirically and set to a fixed number of iterations. Further research will investigate an automatic determination of this criterion.

The analysis of the image logarithmic histogram values is introduced in order to optimize our recursive approach. Thus, we succeed in automatically detecting the final class image representing the restored version of the degraded document image. Successful experiments were done on real ancient document images provided by the archives of "Chatillon-Chalaronne". Other experiments on other archive document images are in progress.

The application of PCA used as a space reduction and data decorrelation technique has proven to be powerful as a pre-processing step for the k-means classification algorithm, however, the linearity of this transform could limit its application. Indeed, this transform could not detect at all times the different structures in a given image. Resorting to a suitable nonlinear transform could give better results. Moreover, the choice of the k-means and the PCA, widely used techniques in the literature, represents a first step for testing its relevance. Our future research will investigate other techniques and compare the results with those obtained here to evaluate performances.

References

1. H. S. Baird, State of the Art of Document Image Degradation Modelling, invited talk, IAPR 2000 Workshop on Document Analysis Systems, Brazil, December 2000.
2. G. Leedham, S. Varma, A. Patankar, V. Govindaraju, Separating text and background in degraded document images – a comparison of global thresholding techniques for multistage thresholding. In: Proceedings of the 8th international workshop on frontiers in handwriting recognition, pp 244–249, Canada, August 2002,
3. G. SHARMA, Cancellation of show-through in duplex scanning, International Conference on Image Processing (ICIP), vol. 2, pp. 609-612, September 2000 .
4. E. Dubois, A. Pathak, Reduction of bleed-through in scanned manuscripts documents, In: Proceedings of the IS&T conference on image processing, image quality, image capture systems, Montreal, Canada, April 2001, pp 177–180
5. C. L. Tan, R. Cao, P. Shen, Restoration of Archival Documents Using a Wavelet Technique, IEEE Transactions on Pattern Analysis and Machine Intelligence, Vol. 24, 1399–1404, October 2002.
6. C. L. Tan, R. Cao, P Shen, J Chee and J Chang, Text extraction from historical handwritten documents by edge detection, 6th International Conference on Control, Automation, Robotics and Vision, ICARCV2000, Singapore, December 2000.
7. Q. Wang, T. Xia, C. L. Tan, L. Li, «Directional Wavelet Approach to Remove Document Image Interference», ICDAR 2003: p736-740, Edinburgh, Scotland, August 2003.

8. A. Tonazzini, E. Salerno, M. Mochi, L. Bedini, Bleed-through removal from degraded documents using a color decorrelation method, DAS 2004, pp 229-240, 2004.
9. B. Gatos, I. Pratikakis, S. J. Perantonis, An Adaptive Binarization Technique for Low Quality Historical Documents, Document Analysis Systems VI, 6th international workshop, DAS2004, pp.102-113, Florence, ITALY, September 2004.
10. E. Smigiel, A. belaid, H. Hamza, Self-organizing Maps and Ancient Documents, Document Analysis Systems VI, 6th international workshop, pp.125-134, Florence, ITALY, September 2004.
11. Y. Leydier, F. LeBourgeois, H. Emptoz, Serialized k-means for adaptative color image segmentation – application to document images and others, DAS 2004, LNCS 3163, pp. 252-263, Florence, Italy, September 2004.
12. J.A. Hartigan and M.A. Wang. A K-means clustering algorithm. Applied Statistics, 28:100{108, 1979.
13. D. Chris and H. Xiaofeng. K-means Clustering via Principal Component Analysis. Proc. of Int'l Conf. Machine Learning (ICML 2004), Canada. July 2004.

Networked Document Imaging with Normalization and Optimization

Hirobumi Nishida

Document Lab, Software R&D Group, Ricoh Co., Ltd.,
1-1-17 Koishikawa, Bunkyo-ku, Tokyo 112-0002, Japan
hn@src.ricoh.co.jp

Abstract. A system architecture is presented for document imaging in an open, distributed environment over networks, where various kinds of imaging devices can be interconnected remotely. The key components are two sets of image processing operations to transform input images to (1) canonical image representations to absorb different visual appearance due to characteristics of imaging devices or image acquisition conditions (normalization), and (2) optimal image representations according to tasks and preferences of individual users (optimization). Images captured through a diversity of input devices can be delivered to remote sites through networks, and then will be used for a variety of tasks such as printing on paper sheets, browsing on displays, and editing. These diversities can be resolved systematically by placing the normalizations at an upper end (routing servers) and the optimizations at a lower end (clients) of the data flow over networks. In view of this architecture, we describe some instances of the normalizations and optimizations associated with a particular task of highly legible printing of scanned document images. Three essential algorithms are mentioned for optimizing document images: adaptive tone mapping with background cleaning, text super-resolution, and text color clustering. The optimization process is mentioned for highly legible printing, along with some other potential applications and tasks.

1 Introduction

Various kinds of imaging devices can be interconnected remotely in open, distributed environments over networks. Images captured through a diversity of input devices can be delivered to remote sites through networks, and then the stored images will be retrieved for *repurposing* such as printing on paper sheets, browsing on PC, PDA, or cellular phones, and editing, as shown in Fig. 1. This new environment can also be referred to as *asynchronous* in the following sense:

- The sender does not know how, why, or when the delivered image will be used, or the characteristics of output devices at the recipient site (resolution, display area, color gamut, etc.).
- The recipient of delivered images would not know the identity or characteristics (MTF and color) of the input device or the image acquisition conditions at a remote site over the network.

H. Bunke and A.L. Spitz (Eds.): DAS 2006, LNCS 3872, pp. 50–61, 2006.

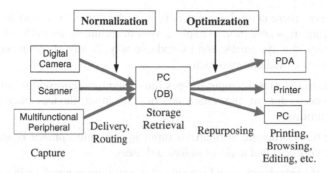

Fig. 1. Document imaging in open, distributed environments

These facts impose new technical challenges on document imaging. Taking an example task of printing out a scanned document image delivered through networks, we often observe the following phenomena and problems in terms of image quality:

- Contrast between text and background is poor.
- Background is colored on the printed image, while it should be white ideally.
- Background needs to be cleaned up to remove "show-through" or noise.
- Moiré phenomena are observed.
- Legibility of small text is poor because of insufficient image resolution.

To resolve these problems, we need to apply some image enhancement suitable for document images. Traditional methods for text image enhancement can be classified into four categories: filtering, contrast enhancement, model-based image restoration, and resolution expansion. Filtering approaches include noise removal using mathematical morphology [6] and second order filters for noise removal without blurring details [11]. Nonlinear tone mapping based on local window statistics [12] is an instance of contrast enhancement. A model-based method of image restoration is proposed based on cluster analysis of causes of OCR errors [5]. Resolution expansion approaches include text bitmap clustering and averaging for generating outlines in arbitrary resolution [2], restoration of optimal high resolution images in terms of an inverse problem based on an objective function composed of bimodality of distribution, smoothness, and intensity [14], and combinations of interpolation and binarization [7]. By combining these techniques, image defects can be resolved and document images can be transformed through various image-processing operations into optimal representations for various tasks (display, print out, OCR, etc.) or preferences of individual users.

There are also new representations and uses of document images in addition to traditional binarized images for OCR and raster images for printing. For instance, the Mixed Raster Content (MRC) Imaging Model, decomposing the document image into foreground (high resolution to be preserved) and background (resolution to be reduced) along with foreground colors (color palettes for text), is now used as a standard (JPM in JPEG2000) for scanned document images [3,4]. The reflowing technique [1] rearranges and reconstructs on Web browsers the document components (text, pictures, etc.) extracted from the image so that the text can be most readable on the specific display.

As can be seen, there could be a diversity of technologies involved in networked document imaging. It is now time to explore system architectures so that we can cope with this diversity in a systematic and extendable way. A key observation is that the diversity can be classified into two factors:

Normalization: transforms the input images into *canonical representations* absorbing specific differences due to the characteristics of input devices and the image acquisition conditions.

Optimization: transforms the normalized input images into *optimal representations* according to *preferences and tasks* of individual users.

The notions of normalization and optimization are quite general. In this paper, as a case study, we focus on the task of highly legible printing of scanned document images. This task of "scan-to-print" is the most common in networked document imaging, because scanned document images are stored in repositories and will be printed by *some* users at a remotely located office many days (or years) later. We describe some instances of the normalization and optimization associated with this particular task.

This paper is organized as follows: In Section 2, we introduce the notions of normalization and optimization in networked document imaging. In Section 3, we outline some algorithms for optimizing scanned document images. In Section 4, the task of highly legible printing of scanned document images is illustrated based on the optimizations. Section 5 is the conclusion.

2 Normalization and Optimization

In this section, we introduce the notions of normalization and optimization in networked document imaging. We also mention image processing techniques for normalization to absorb differences of image appearance due to specific characteristics of individual scanners. Furthermore, some *objective functions* along with image processing algorithms are described for optimizing scanned document images.

Normalization transforms the input images into *canonical representations* absorbing specific differences due to the characteristics of input devices and the image acquisition conditions.

- The canonical representation should be objective and physically determined, because specific differences have been introduced due to artifacts associated with particular input devices.
- Normalized images should enjoy fair quality when output or displayed anywhere, because particular artifacts have been removed through the normalizations.
- No loss of information should be introduced through the normalizations, because only particular artifacts are to be removed.
- The normalizations should be free of parameters specified by end users, because recipients would not know the characteristics of the input device or the image acquisition conditions at a remote site over the network.

- The normalizations should be placed at an upper end (routing servers) of the data flow with batch modes (no user interactions), because the normalizations resolve individual differences of image appearance regardless of tasks or preferences of the recipients.

In contrast to normalization, *optimization* transforms the normalized input images into *optimal representations* according to *preferences and tasks* of individual users

- Preference and tasks are subjective and even psychological.
- Optimal representations also depend on characteristics (resolution, display area, color gamut, etc.) of image output devices.
- The optimizations should be adjustable easily with a few simple parameters specified by end users, because *objective functions* for a particular optimization differ according to tasks, preferences, or characteristics of image output devices.
- The optimizations should be placed at a lower end (clients) of the data flow with interactive modes.

Particular components for image processing and analysis depend on the types of input devices (for instance, flatbed scanners, digital cameras) and tasks in consideration. In this paper, we address the most common task associated with document images: highly legible *printing* of *scanned* document images.

2.1 Normalization

Normalization transforms the input images into *canonical representations* absorbing specific differences due to the characteristics of input devices and the image acquisition conditions. As far as scanners are used as input devices, the following factors possibly introduce specific difference of image appearance:

- Diversities of input devices
  - ➢ Moiré phenomena and graininess of image appearance due to different frequency characteristics (MTF).
  - ➢ Different color characteristics.
- Diversities of image acquisition conditions
  - ➢ Skew
  - ➢ Spherical distortions (bound volumes)
  - ➢ Homographic (perspective) distortions (for camera-type scanners)
  - ➢ Non-uniform illumination

As solutions to image defects due to image acquisition conditions, *rectification* techniques have been investigated extensively in document image analysis. Furthermore, color management has recently been incorporated into many networked imaging devices to maintain color consistency among different devices.

Techniques for suppressing moiré and graininess are often referred to as *inverse halftonning* that restores ideal continuous-tone representations from halftone dot patterns (Fig. 2). Such processing is now included as options in most scanner drivers. However, in network environments, inverse halftoning needs to be applied to image data obtained through an unknown scanner located at a remote site. Therefore, *blind*

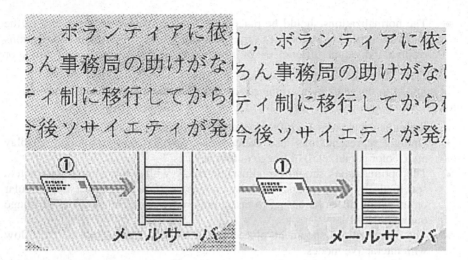

Fig. 2. Original images (left) and result of the inverse halftoning (right)

methods are required without depending on the type or properties of halftoning processes. Practical processing speed must be achieved under software implementation so that images can be processed on routing servers during the image delivery process. A blind, fast algorithm to meet these requirements can be found in Nishida [9].

2.2 Optimization

In general, an optimization problem consists of an objective function and its domain along with constraints. A document image is composed of different types of zones (domains), namely text, pictures, drawings, tables, and rulers, for which different objective functions can be considered in view of image quality and legibility. Typical constraints are the computational resources available. Ideally, computation for optimizations should take only a few seconds with users' interactions on client PCs.

The objective functions also depend the document imaging model. We consider optimization of scanned document images based on the Mixed Raster Content (MRC) imaging model that has attracted much attention with the recent adoption of JPEG2000/Part6 (ISO 15444-6) [4] as a new worldwide standard for encoding color document images.

The MRC (Mixed Raster Content) model is composed of separate background and foreground layers with separate compression methods, and an image mask to blend them together. The scanned document images are first segmented into the picture components and the text components, and the text is divided up again into the binary image and the color. The resulting three layers are compressed separately from each other. Lossless compression is applied to the text layer (a binary image), and therefore, high legibility and OCR accuracy can be achieved. The other two layers (color images) are compressed separately in JPEG2000/Part1 (the image compression within JPEG2000) [3].

Following the MRC model, we find that the following objective functions can be introduced for the three types of image layers:

- Background: The background color (paper color) should be uniform or ideally white. "Show-through" from backside also needs to be cleaned up.
- Binary images for foreground: Legibility of small text should be improved if the image is input in insufficient resolution.
- Color for foreground: Text colors should be clustered into a small number of pallets.

Furthermore, contrast should be enhanced over the entire image to improve text legibility.

As algorithms of image processing and analysis for optimization, the following can be considered on top of layout analysis for page segmentation:

- Adaptive tone mapping with background cleaning for contrast enhancement and background color optimization.
- Text super-resolution for improving legibility of small text.
- Color clustering for text color pallets.

In Section 4, we outline these three algorithms in consideration of computational resources, in particular, to compute image components for optimization within a reasonable time (a few seconds) on PCs.

3 Outline of Algorithms for Optimization

In this section, we outline image processing algorithms for optimizing the above three types of objective functions.

3.1 Adaptive Tone Mapping and Background Cleaning

We address the problems with contrast enhancement between text and background, adaptive control of the tone mapping according to image content, and background cleaning to remove show-through components and noise. A tone mapping is constructed based on statistics of text and background colors, and it is then modified so that black enhancement can be suppressed if the picture portion is large. Furthermore, the background can be cleaned up (or whitened) by mapping background colors to their representative color (or white).

First of all, we need to estimate precisely the text and background colors on the document image. Color document images often contain many photographs and pictures with various colors. Therefore, color or tone histograms obtained from such images are composed of mixture distributions or multi-modal distributions containing many significant valleys and peaks. It is usually difficult to estimate precisely the text and background colors from such mixture distributions, because the histogram also contains spurious peaks and valleys. To avoid analysis of histograms composed of mixture distributions, we note that a color document image is locally composed of two types of regions: foreground and background. Based on this composition, the estimation problem for text and background colors can be reduced to a simple two-class problem:

- Based on some objective function, a subregion containing the true text and background colors is found out.
- The subregion is classified into two classes: foreground and background.
- From the distributions of foreground and background colors, the representative colors and their variations are estimated.

Furthermore, to maintain tone continuity of the midtone areas, black enhancement is suppressed if the picture portion is large. Areas whose colors lie outside the distributions for the text and background correspond to midtone areas, and therefore, the portion of picture areas over the entire image can be estimated based on the intensity distributions of the text and background.

The advantage of the proposed method is that no information on the characteristics of input devices is required; it can estimate parameters specifying the tone mapping based on statistical analysis of image features instead of using knowledge on the characteristics of input devices. This is essential when processing image data input from unknown input devices on remote sites, because *a priori* distributions of text or background colors are not available. Actually, the signal levels for simple white background range widely between 200 and 255 (in 8-bit grayscale) according to tone characteristics and parameter setting (e.g., gamma) of scanners. Examples of the adaptive tone correction and background cleaning/whitening are given in Fig. 5.

3.2 Restoring High-Resolution Binary Images for Text

Following the success of the MRC model, we find that a natural approach to improving legibility of text is to restore high-resolution binary images from the original low-resolution image. It is known theoretically that a gray-scale image in low resolution has the same amount of information as a high-resolution binary image. In practice, we need a method that

- can deal with characters with complex shape structures, such as Kanji,
- can improve OCR accuracy and legibility of text for the human eye (smoothness and linearity of contours and restoration of strokes) at the same time, and
- entails simple computation.

To satisfy the above three requirements, Nishida [10] presents a method for restoring high-resolution binary images from gray-scale images in low resolution. An

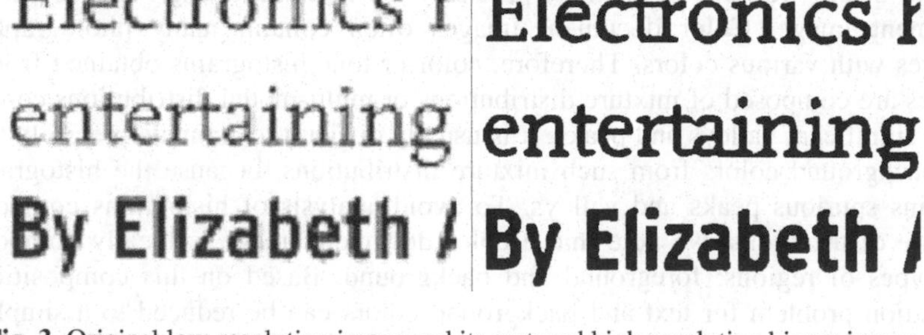

Fig. 3. Original low-resolution image and its restored high-resolution binary image

effective approach to tackling this complex problem is to utilize and integrate various types of information. The new method consists of the following four components:

(1) Generation of the initial high-resolution image by interpolation and local statistics (adaptive binarization)

(2) Complementing missing strokes based on topographic features

Regarding a gray-scale image as a surface, we examine the topographic features ("ridge", "valley", "peak", "pit", "hillside"). They are preserved even on low-resolution images, and therefore, can be used as cues for extracting strokes from text images. Missing strokes are complemented based on the topographic features.

(3) Contour modification: gradient magnitudes and curvatures along the contours

Even if missing strokes can be complemented, the resulting image is still poor in terms of text image quality because of fluctuations along contours. The quality can be improved if it is modified so that curvatures are small and the contour passes through pixels where gradient magnitudes are locally maximized. Contours are modified with the Active Contour Model or Snake.

(4) Contour beautification

Contours are beautified to correct distortions around right angles and fluctuation along horizontal and vertical directions.

Fig. 3 shows an example of the restoration of high-resolution binary images from original low-resolution images [10].

3.3 Text Color Clustering

The specific problem in text color clustering for document images is that text consists mostly of black fonts along with several other colors for emphasizing particular sentences or phrases. Typical profiles of color distributions show that there are a large cluster composed of a majority of colors (corresponding to the dominant color, namely black) and some small clusters, as can be observed from the example of Fig. 4a. We need to pay a particular attention so that small clusters can be picked up to keep them from being merged to the dominant cluster. Furthermore, computational efficiency is also important.

Color clustering has been investigated in the document image analysis area, with emphasis on color-based text extraction from webs or covers of books, magazines, and CDs [13]. There are fewer characters to be considered in these applications than in our problem, and the cluster size is well balanced across the distinct colors.

We take the following approach to the problems of ill-balanced cluster size and computational efficiency:

- Histogram-based clustering is applied separately to each component of a transformed color space, where the components are correlated only weakly.

- The extraction of dominant clusters is followed by the extraction of small clusters corresponding to colors for emphasis or decoration.

We use the YCbCr color space because of its simplicity in the coordinate transformation and independency among the three components. The clustering technique based on Matas and Kittler [8] is applied to each component of YCbCr.

The extraction of dominant clusters proceeds as follows:

(1) The largest clusters (1-D intervals) are extracted from each component of YCbCr.
(2) A 3-D rectangular parallelepiped is generated by taking the Cartesian product of the intervals on Y, Cb, and Cr coordinates. If the number of samples inside this parallelepiped is larger than some specified ratio over the entire samples, a cluster for a dominant color is constructed in the following step (3). Otherwise, the extraction process completes.
(3) A cluster is defined as the parallelepiped, with its representative color being the Cartesian product of the representative values on each.
(4) Histograms on each component of YCbCr are constructed by excluding the colors within the constructed cluster. Repeat from step (1).

For example, the largest cluster is extracted as

$$\{(y, Cb, Cr): y \in [7,14], Cb \in [14,16], Cr \in [14,18]\},$$

including 69.4% of text colors as shown in Fig. 4b. The second largest cluster, occupying 23.2% of text colors as shown in Fig. 4c, is extracted as the three-dimensional parallelepiped [22, 25] x [14, 16] x [14, 18].

Small clusters corresponding to colors for emphasis are extracted in a similar way, but three-dimensional parallelepipeds are constructed for all combinations of extracted clusters on each of Y, Cb, Cr components. Table 1 shows the final results of the whole clustering procedure. There are two dominant clusters (#1 and #2) and four small clusters (#3 to #6).

Table 1. Results of text color clustering

	Cluster Parallelepipeds YCbCr (32levels)	Cluster Centers			Ratio
		YCbCr	RGB (255levels)	Color	
1	[7, 14] x [14, 16] x [14, 18]	(9, 15, 15)	(61, 79, 58)		69.4%
2	[22, 25] x [14, 16] x [14, 18]	(24, 14, 15)	(181, 202, 164)		23.2%
3	[10, 13] x [14, 16] x [17, 18]	(11, 18, 16)	(88, 83, 116)		3.5%
4	[15, 17] x [15, 15] x [15, 16]	(17, 15, 16)	(136, 138, 122)		1.5%
5	[17, 17] x [12, 12] x [16, 16]	(17, 12, 16)	(136, 147, 80)		1.5%
6	[14, 15] x [20, 20] x [9, 10]	(14, 20, 9)	(34, 140, 168)		0.9%

4 Optimization for Highly Legible Printing

We present an example task of highly legible printing of scanned document images. This task of "scan-to-print" is the most common in networked document imaging, because scanned document images are stored in repositories and will be printed by

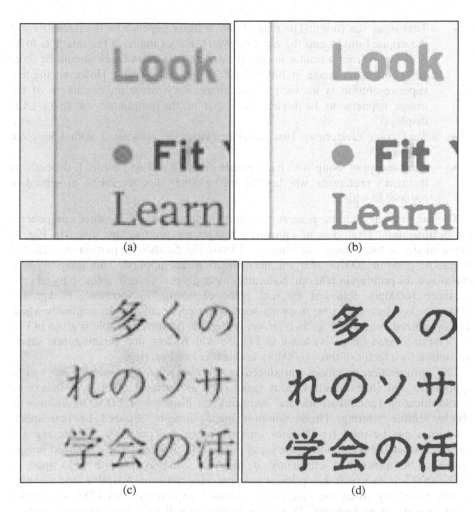

Fig. 5. Examples of optimized images for printing. (a) Normalized original image in 200dpi. (b) Optimized image. (c) Normalized original image. (d) Optimized image.

some users at a remotely located office many days (or years) later. A typical situation is that the document image acquired with a color scanner in low resolution (200 or 300dpi) was stored in a document image database, and is printed out later through a high-resolution printer in 600dpi. This is an asynchronous situation in that the characteristics of the input and output devices are inconsistent and that the person having scanned the document does not know how, why, or when the image will be used in the future.

Regardless of particular tasks or preferences of the user, the normalizations are applied before the image is stored in a canonical representation absorbing specific differences due to the characteristics of input devices and the image acquisition conditions. The optimizations depend on the particular task in hand, the preferences of the user, and also the characteristics of the output device. The user can decide the parameters or options of the optimizations in the following way:

- Text super-resolution: The magnification factor depends on the resolutions of the original image and the output devices. For example, if the image is to be printed out from a printer in 600dpi, the magnification factor should be three and two for the image in 200dpi and 300dpi, respectively. However, the text super-resolution is ineffective and unnecessary when the resolution of the image happens to be higher than that of the output device (e.g., LCD displays).
- Text color clustering: Text super-resolution is associated with text color clustering.
- Tone mapping along with background cleaning and whitening: It depends on the user's preference whether the background color should be preserved or reduced to white.

The output image can be generated from a combination of these three components for optimization. Examples of optimized images for printing are given in Fig. 5. Physical size of these images is 15mm by 15mm. Fig. 5a shows a portion of a scanned magazine page in 200dpi after the normalizations are applied. This image is now optimized for printing in 600 dpi. Naturally, we apply text super-resolution by a factor of three (600dpi), followed by text color clustering. Furthermore, background whitening is selected for tone mapping because the paper color looks originally white. The optimized image for Fig. 5a is shown in Fig. 5b. Another example is given in Fig. 5c. The optimized image is shown in Fig. 5d with background cleaning, text super-resolution by a factor of three (600dpi), and text color clustering.

The optimization processes introduced in this paper are quite simple, but can be applied to and shared with various tasks such as retrieval (OCR and indexing), communication (compression), and browsing on displays or PDA, in addition to highly legible printing. High-resolution binary images obtained by text super-resolution can be used for OCR to improve recall and precision of indexing and retrieval, when the resolution of the input image is insufficient. The optimized images can also be transmitted efficiently if they are compressed with JPM (part of JPEG2000 [4]), to which the optimization processes conform. Adaptive tone mapping is still necessary when the images are browsed on displays and PDA to enhance contrast text and background. Text super-resolution will be a key technology to help senior or visually handicapped people read documents easily on displays, because they can enjoy fine visual quality after text is magnified, as illustrated in Fig. 5.

5 Conclusion

There could be a diversity of technologies involved in networked document imaging. It is now time to explore system architectures so that we can cope with this diversity in a systematic and extendable way. A key observation is that the diversity can be classified mainly into two factors: *Normalization* and *Optimization*. This paper has presented a system architecture for document imaging in an open, distributed environment over networks, composed of the above two sets of image processing operations. In network and Internet environments, digital image data captured through any image acquisition device can be transmitted to remote sites over networks, and the receiver can utilize the image data delivered via networks from unknown input devices. Visual appearance of the document image is quite different according to the characteristics of image acquisition devices and the conditions of image acquisition. Furthermore, different types of image enhancement are required according to users' tasks or preferences. These diversities can be resolved systematically by placing the normalization at an upper end (routing servers) and the optimization at a lower end (clients) of the data flow over networks.

In view of this architecture, we have described some instances of the normalization and optimization associated with a particular task of highly legible printing of scanned document images. In particular, three essential algorithms have been mentioned for optimizing document images: adaptive tone mapping with background cleaning, text super-resolution, and text color clustering. The optimization process has been illustrated for highly legible printing, along with some other potential applications and tasks.

References

[1] T.M. Breuel, W.C. Janssen, K. Popat, H.S. Baird, "Paper to PDA," in *Proc.16th Int. Conf. Pattern Recognition* (Quebec City, Quebec, Canada), vol. 1, 476-479, 2002.

[2] J.D. Hobby and T.K. Ho, "Enhancing degraded document images via bitmap clustering and averaging," in *Proc. 4th Int. Conf. Document Analysis and Recognition*, August 1997.

[3] ISO/IEC 15444-1, Information technology -- JPEG 2000 image coding system -- Part 1: Core coding system, 2000.

[4] ISO/IEC 15444-6, Information technology -- JPEG 2000 image coding system -- Part 6: Compound image file format, 2003.

[5] M.Y. Jaisimha, E.A. Riskin, R. Ladner, and S. Werner, "Model-based restoration of document images for OCR," *Proc. SPIE*, **2660**, 297-308, 1996.

[6] L. Koskinen, H. Huttunen, and J.T. Astola, "Text enhancement method based on soft morphological filters," *Proc. SPIE*, **2181**, 243-253, 1994.

[7] H. Li, O.E. Kia, and D.S. Doermann, "Text enhancement in digital video," *Proc. SPIE*, **3651**, 2-9, 1999.

[8] J. Matas and J. Kittler, "Spatial and feature space clutering: applications in image analysis," in *Proc. Int. Conf. Computer Analysis of Images and Patterns*, 162-173, September 1995.

[9] H. Nishida, "Adaptive inverse halftoning for scanned document images through multiresolution and multiscale analysis," *Pattern Recognition*, **38**(2) 251-260, 2005.

[10] H. Nishida, "Restoring high-resolution binary images for text enhancement," in *Proc. Int. Conf. Image Processing* (Genova, Italy), vol. II, 506-509, September 2005.

[11] G. Ramponi and P. Fontanot, "Enhancing document images with a quadratic filter," *Signal Processing*, **33**, 23-34. 1993.

[12] Y.C. Shin, R. Sridhar, V. Demjanenko, P.W. Palumbo, and J.J. Hull, "Contrast enhancement of mail piece images," *Proc. SPIE*, **1661**, 27-37, 1992.

[13] K. Sobottka, H. Kronenberg, T. Perroud, and H. Bunke, "Text extraction from colored book and journal covers," *Int. J. Document Analysis and Recognition*, **2**, 163-176, 2000.

[14] P.D. Thouin and C.-I. Chang, "A method for restoration of low-resolution document images," *Int. J. Document Analysis and Recognition*, **2**, 200-210, 2000.

Gray-Scale Thinning Algorithm Using Local Min/Max Operations

Kyoung Min Kim[1,2], Buhm Lee[2,*], Nam Sup Choi[2], Gwan Hee Kang[2],
Joong Jo Park[1,3], and Ching Y. Suen[1]

[1] Centre for Pattern Recognition and Machine Intelligence (CENPARMI),
Concordia University, 1455 de Maisonneuve Blvd. West, Montreal, Canada H3G 1M8
{kkm, jjpark, suen}@cenparmi.concordia.ca
[2] Department of Electrical Engineering, Yosu National University, San 96-1,
Dundeok-dong, Yeosu-si, Jeollanam-do, 550-749, Korea
{kkm, buhmlee, nschoi}@yosu.ac.kr
[3] Department of Control and Instrumentation Engineering, Gyeongsang National University,
Gajwa-dong, Jinju-si, Gyeongsangnam-do, 660-701, Korea
jjpark@nongae.gsnu.ac.kr

Abstract. A gray-scale thinning algorithm based on local min/max operations is
newly proposed. Erosion and dilation properties of local min/max operations
create new ridges from the given image. Thus grey scale skeletons can be effectively obtained by accumulating such ridges. The proposed method is quite salient because it can be also applied to an unsegmented image in which objects are
not specified.

1 Introduction

Thinning is one of the most important pre-processing steps for image analysis and
understanding. Many thinning techniques showing quite good results have been developed for binary image [1][2][3]. However, as the generalization of bi-level
thinning, the grey level thinning has been not yet actively studied, even though considerable its own particular applications such as thinning the object of non-uniform
brightness or determining the tinned edge are exist.

As a previous study on grey-level thinning, Peleg proposed the method that uses
the erosion and dilation properties derived from the local min/max operation [4]. This
method has some merits that a pre-processing to divide a given grey image into the
object and background is not required and the extracted edge position usually correspond to the part having large pixel value in the object. However, it shows poor edge
connectivity.

Salari proposed a thinning technique based on ridge tracing in which the skeleton
of an object is obtained by detecting the ridge parts resulted from erosion processing
[5]. Skeleton with single thickness can be obtained and its connectivity is also guaranteed, although it has a restriction that the object in image should be separated in advance. Wang proposed another approach using the connectivity number that thins a

---

* Corresponding author.

H. Bunke and A.L. Spitz (Eds.): DAS 2006, LNCS 3872, pp. 62–70, 2006.

grey image by replacing each pixel value to the minimum value nearby [6]. This method can perform thinning for the object not separated from background. However, in this method some skeletons can be lost and the connectivity is not guaranteed because the connectivity number cannot provide complete information about some feature points like end, node, or crossing points.

In this paper, we proposed a new grayscale thinning method based on local min/max operation. Unlike Salari or Wang's method where the ridges created by eroding only the pixels satisfying some specific conditions are determined as the final skeletons, the proposed method extracts the skeletons by repeatedly carrying out the procedure that detects the ridges newly created by local min operation and then recover the connectivity of disconnected skeleton using connectivity information, after detecting the already existing ridges using the local min/max operation.

The novelty of our approach lies in the fact that the connectivity of skeleton is well reserved, its position corresponds to the part having large pixel value, and separating the object from background is not required.

2 Principles of Greyscale Thinning Algorithm Through Ridge Detection

This chapter will describe the basic principles of the grayscale thinning algorithm being proposed in this research. The ridges detected through grayscale thinning should be as thin as 1 pixel width, have continuous characteristics and should have the highest pixel values within an object. Also, because it is usually difficult to clearly separate objects from the background in grayscale images, a thinning algorithm that can detect ridges even without separation would be appropriate.

One thinning algorithm that can satisfy those conditions is to gradually erode the image until ridges become detectable, and then finally obtaining a skeleton. Fig.1 demonstrates this process in one-dimensional diagram.

First Fig.1(a) shows side-cut of original image, and target skeletons in this image would be located in ①, ② and ③. Performing ridge detection on this image will only find ① as a ridge because ① is already shaped like a ridge but ② and ③ are mostly flat. Fig.1(b) is eroded image of 1(a) with the previously extracted ridge restored on top. Performing ridge detection on this image will find ① and ③ since ① is already a ridge, ③ just became a ridge through the erosion process, and ② still remains flat. Fig. 1(c) is further eroded image of 1(b) with ridges detected in 1(b) restored. In this case ② now becomes a ridge and thus another ridge detection process applied will find all of ①, ② and ③ as ridges. Fig.1(d) shows above erosion detection process repeated several times with the ridges restored. This image will not change any more with further processing. Performing ridge detection on this final image and taking the detected ridge values obtains Fig.1(e). This is the final result of grayscale thinning algorithm and corresponds to the skeleton of the original image.

If the background's grayscale is needed to be kept in order to obtain some other information, Fig.1(d) would be a suitable result. The processing mechanism needed in these grayscale thinning are erosion computation and ridge detection methods. This paper proposes a grayscale thinning algorithm that finds skeletons through performing local min/max operations.

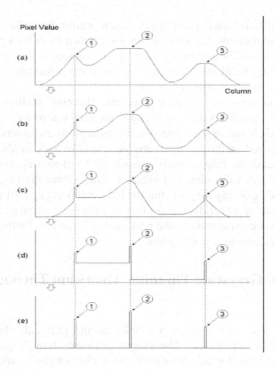

Fig. 1. Process of gray level thinning by proposed algorithm   (a) Original image,   (b), (c), (d) Process of image erosion and ridge detection,   (e) Thinned image

3   The Proposed Gray-Level Thinning Algorithm

Basically, the proposed method needs the erosion operation and ridge detection techniques [7][8]. We employ local min/max operation to implement these techniques. As a parallel neighborhood operation, the local min operation used for image erosion and local max for dilation replace each pixel value of a given image with the maximum and minimum value among itself and its neighbors, respectively. Let $\Pi_\phi = \{\mu_\phi^{ij}; i = 1,2,...,I, \ j = 1,2,...,J\}$ be the $I \times J$, grey-level image array. Then the erosion operation for a pixel at (I, J) is mathematically written as

$$EROSION\{\mu_\phi^{ij}\} = \min_R\{\mu_\phi^{ij}\} \tag{1}$$

$$\Pi_{EROSION} \square \ EROSION(\Pi_G) = \min_R(\Pi) \tag{2}$$

where, $\min_R$ is the notation for the local min operator over the region R.

Then, the positions of ridge pixels in the image can be detected by calculating the difference between the original image Π_G and its opened version obtained by the morphological opening operation, i.e., the ridge image Π_{RIDGE} is obtained by

$$\Pi_{RIDGE} = \{\mu_{RIDGE}^{ij}; i = 1,2,...,I, \ j = 1,2,...,J\} \quad 0 \le \mu_{RIDGE}^{ij} \le 1 \tag{3}$$

where
$$\mu_{RIDGE}^{ij} = \begin{cases} \mu_G^{ij} & if \ \mu_G^{ij} - \max_R\{\min_R\{\mu_G^{ij}\}\} > 0, \\ 0 & otherwise \end{cases}$$

In Π_{RIDGE}, even noise-like ridges can be considerably included, since all possible ridges are detected by eq. (3). The clearer ridge, which has relatively large pixel value when compared to its neighborhood, can be detected by slightly modifying this equation as follows:

$$\mu_{RIDGE\_n}^{ij} = \begin{cases} \mu_G^{ij} & if \quad \mu_G^{ij} - \max_R^{(1)}\{\min_R^{(1)}\{\mu_G^{ij}\}\} > 0 \ \& \\ & \mu_G^{ij} - \max_R^{(2)}\{\min_R^{(2)}\{\mu_G^{ij}\}\} > Height \\ 0 & otherwise \end{cases} \tag{4}$$

where the superscripts (1) and (2) on operation $\min_R$ or $\max_R$ denote the number of iterations of these operations applied to the image. The higher the value of threshold, *Height* is assigned, the larger the pixel values of ridges can be obtained. Then the composite image, Π_{COMPn} is obtained by using Π_{RIDGE} and $\Pi_{EROSION}$ as follows:

$$\Pi_{COMP} = \{\mu_{COMP}^{ij}; i = 1,2,...,I, \ j = 1,2,...,J\} \tag{5}$$

where, $\mu_{COMP}^{ij} = \max_p(\mu_{RIDGE}^{ij}, \mu_{EROSION}^{ij})$, $\mu_{RIDGE}^{ij} \in \Pi_{RIDGE}$, and $\mu_{EROSION}^{ij} \in \Pi_{EROSION}$. Plus, $\max_P()$ denotes the local max operator applied to each pixel on two images, Π_{RIDGE} and $\Pi_{EROSION}$.

The above ridge detection and erosion processes are repeated using the obtained Π_{COMP} as input image again. During this process the erosion operation is what makes ridges visible, and ridge detection is what finds the skeleton. According to this method, the ridges found during the process are part of the final skeleton, and thus newly found ridges through eq.(3) are accumulated on existing ridges using eq.(5). Ridge detection is then repeated to build up the final skeleton. This process is iterated until Π_{COMP} image does not change any further. At this stage ridge detection is applied for one last time and ridges found here are determined to be the final skeleton of the image.

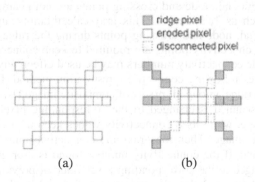

    (a)   (b)

Fig. 2. Connectivity problem: (a) Original image (b) Composite image (Π_{COMP})

However, this method of grayscale thinning will create a connectivity problem between the already obtained ridges and eroded image in terms of pixel values. Fig.2 shows this problem. Fig.2(b) is the Π_{COMP} image after one cycle of above process on Fig.2(a). This connectivity problem in Π_{COMP} image should be resolved.

This disconnection can be restored using grayscale connectivity number information. Grayscale connectivity number is an extension of 8-connectivity number concept for application on grayscale images. The connectivity number $C_8(x_0)$ of central pixel x_0 on 3x3 image area is computed as the number of changes of 8 pixel values f_k, as defined in following equation (6) and (7), from -1 to 1. Pixel scanning is done by one clockwise rotation (i.e. f_8, f_7,..., f_1), ignoring 0 values and taking $x_9=x_1$. Figure 3 shows x_0 and distribution of obtained f_k.

$$f_{2l-1} = \begin{cases} -1, & \text{if } x_{2l-1} < x_0 \text{ and } (x_{2l-1} < x_{2l} \text{ or } x_{2l-1} < x_{2l+1}) \\ 1, & \text{if } x_{2l-1} > x_{2l+1} \text{ and } x_{2l+1} < x_0 \\ 0, & \text{otherwise} \end{cases} \qquad (l=1, 2, 3, 4) \qquad (6)$$

$$f_{2l-1} = \begin{cases} 1 & if \quad x_{2l} > x_{2l+1} \text{ and } x_{2l+1} < x_0 \\ 0 & otherwise \end{cases} \qquad (l=1, 2, 3, 4) \qquad (7)$$

f_4	f_3	f_2
f_5	x_0	f_1
f_6	f_7	f_8

Fig. 3. pixel x_0 and f_k

However the grayscale connectivity number found with this method does not completely provide connectivity status information as contrast to connectivity numbers on binary images. Experiment using grayscale connectivity number found through above method shows that although connected points are correctly detected from the obtained information, detection is not guaranteed on end, node and crossing points. In fact, pixel that was calculated with above method to have value of 2 is guaranteed to be a connectivity point, but end, node and crossing points are not guaranteed to be consistent with values such as 1, 3, and 4. This grayscale thinning algorithm, however, effectively detects end, node and crossing points during the ridge detection process. Therefore only the connectivity points are required to keep connectivity of the skeleton, and the grayscale connectivity numbers may be used effectively.

This algorithm uses following connectivity restoration method: It scans only pixels that are not part of a ridge among all pixels of composite image Π_{COMP} at current stage. The pixel x_0 being scanned is changed to the corresponding pixel value at previous stage composite image, while its 8-connectivity values keep their pixel values of current stage composite image. Then the grayscale connectivity number $C_8(x_0)$ is computed from above data. If the connectivity number found is 2 or greater, the scanned pixel's value is changed to the corresponding pixel value of previous stage composite image. The connectivity of skeleton is then restored, based on the characteristic that pixel values of grayscale image do not change dramatically about its neighboring values. This modified composite image is used again as input image and through iterated ridge detection and erosion process a continuous skeleton can be obtained.

The number of iterations required on this algorithm is automatically determined. However a same final skeleton can be obtained by number of iteration corresponding to 1/2 of maximum ridge width of an object in the image. Therefore if the maximum ridge width of an object in image can be obtained beforehand, number of iteration can be determined before and shorten the required processing time.

4 Experiments and Results

This experiment uses artificial pattern images, character images taken with camera and fingerprint image taken from scanner, all of which are 256-scale grey images. The algorithm's local min/max operations used in erosion and ridge detection uses 4-neighbour as neighboring area. Fig.4 shows experimental results on an artificial 256x190 size pattern image. Since Peleg's method does not recognize connectivity, the upper right and middle pattern shows connectivity problem. Salari's method fails to find proper skeleton on upper right pattern. His method erodes outlines of the object within image relative to the background pixel value, and so erosion can't be performed, and thus the skeleton can't be found, if there is a grayscale distribution shaped as a well within the object that has only little higher pixel values than the background. Wang's method shows problems in connectivity and skeleton shape in upper right pattern and middle pattern. This is because the grayscale connectivity numbers used in this method does not provide sufficient information. In contrast, our proposed method shows much better performance in both connectivity and skeleton shape. One issue is the appearance of unnecessary branches in left pattern, and this happens because proposed method first extract ridges then erodes the new image again to find additional ridges. Peleg and Wang's method also shows similar artifacts in their results. This result obtained final ridges with the value of height set to 30 in eq. (4).

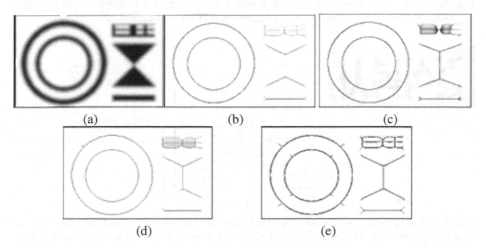

Fig. 4. Thinning results on the pattern image: (a) Original image, (b) Peleg, (c) Salari, (d) Wang, (e) Proposed algorithm

Fig.5 shows experimental results on 256x256 size fingerprint image obtained through thresholding. Peleg's method is result of thresholding with threshold value of 20, and shows problems in both skeleton shapes and connectivity because it does not consider connectivity in the first place. Salari's method fails to find some skeletons by same reasons on Fig.4. Wang's method shows imperfect connectivity due to its

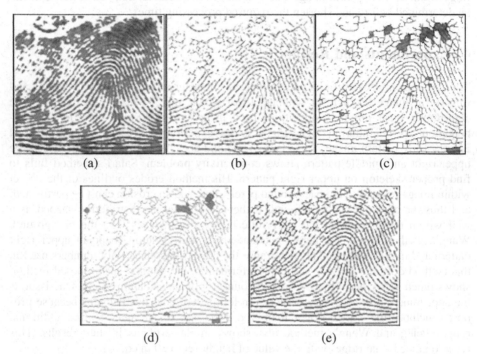

Fig. 5. Thinning results on the segmented finger print image: (a) Original image, (b) Peleg algorithm, (c) Salari algorithm, (d) Wang algorithm, (e) Proposed algorithm

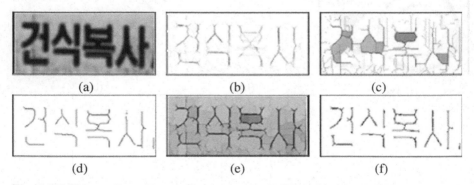

Fig. 6. Thinning results on Korean character image: (a) Original image, (b) Peleg algorithm, (c) Wang algorithm, (d) Wang algorithm(T=220), (e) Proposed algorithm, (f) Proposed algorithm(T=240)

grayscale connectivity numbers. In contrast the proposed method shows much better performance in connectivity and skeleton formation. This result obtained final ridges using height set to 20 in eq. (4).

Fig.6 shows experimental results on image containing characters that are not clearly separated. Salari's method can't be applied in this kind of images. Fig.6(b) is result of Peleg's method, and 6(c) is Wang's method, both performed on original image 6(a). Fig.6(d) is result of thresholding applied on 6(c) with threshold value of 220. Fig. 6(e) is image just before obtaining final ridges using proposed method, and 6(f) is result of thesholding with threshold value of 240. It can be observed that the proposed method provides better results again in terms of skeleton shape and connectivity.

To summarize above experiments: Peleg's method is an early thinning method using local min/max operation that shows connectivity problems. Salari's method can't be applied at all if objects within image aren't completely separated, and fails to perform thinning on circular patterns with different grayscale value than the background. Finally although Wang's method provide better skeleton compared to other methods but still poses connectivity issues. Our proposed method however shows improved characteristics in terms of skeleton shape and connectivity. The skeleton obtained from proposed method has width of around 2 pixels; this may be resolved by applying additional binary image thinning algorithm on final image, but further research seems necessary to obtain 1-pixel wide skeleton.

5 Conclusion

This research proposed a grayscale image thinning method using erosion and dilation functions of local min/max operations. This method extracts skeleton image of grey image using image erosion and ridge detection. The erosion process makes new ridges appear, and then ridge detection is used to extract the skeleton. Although this method uses local min/max operations used in existing Peleg's method it differs in concept of ridge detection and skeleton extraction methods. It is also different than Salari method since ridge is directly extracted and is not dependent on object's outline. This method also uses application of grey connectivity numbers Wang conditionally used to remove pixels to restore connectivity on skeleton.

This method preserves connectivity of obtained skeleton. It is located on the largest pixel value areas in the object, and the method does not require clear separation of objects within image. The major mathematical operations used in this method are simple parallel-processing local min/max operations which reduces processing time required on hardware. Experimental results show much improved performance in skeleton shapes and connectivity when compared with other existing methods.

References

1. L. Lam, S. W. Lee and C. Y. Suen,: Thinning Methodologies - A Comprehensive Survey. *IEEE Trans. Pattern Analysis and Machine Intelligence*, 14 (1992) 869-885
2. V. K. Govindan and A. P. Shivaprasad: A pattern adaptive thinning algorithm, *Pattern Recognition*, 20 (1987) 623-637

3. T. Y. Zhang and C. Y. Suen: A fast parallel algorithm for thinning digital patterns, *Comm. of the ACM*, 27 (1984) 236-239
4. S. Peleg and A. Rosenfeld: A min-max medial axis transformation, *IEEE Trans. Pattern Analysis and Machine Intelligence*, 3 (1981) 208-210
5. E. Salari and P. Sly: The Ridge-Seeking Method for Obtaining the Skeleton of Digital Images, *IEEE Trans. System, Man, and Cybernetics*, 14 (1984) 524-528
6. C. Wang and K. ABE: A Method of Gray-scale Image Thinning : The Case without Region specification for Thinning, *IEEE 11th Int. Conf. on Pattern Recognition*, 3 (1992) 404-407
7. Y. Nakagawa and A. Rosenfeld: A note on the use of local min and max operations in digital picture processing, *IEEE Trans. System, Man, and Cybernetics*, 8 (1978) 632-635
8. K. M. Kim, J. J. Park, M. H. Song I. C. Kim and C. Y. Suen: Detection of ridges and ravines using fuzzy logic operations, *Pattern Recognition Letters*, 25 (2004) 743-751

Automated Scoring of Handwritten Essays Based on Latent Semantic Analysis

Sargur Srihari, Jim Collins, Rohini Srihari,
Pavithra Babu, and Harish Srinivasan

Center of Excellence for Document Analysis and Recognition (CEDAR)
University at Buffalo, State University of New York Amherst, New York 14228, U.S.A
srihari@cedar.buffalo.edu

Abstract. Handwritten essays are widely used in educational assessments, particularly in classroom instruction. This paper concerns the
design of an automated system for performing the task of taking as input scanned images of handwritten student essays in reading comprehension tests and to produce as output scores for the answers which
are analogous to those provided by human scorers. The system is based
on integrating the two technologies of optical handwriting recognition
(OHR) and automated essay scoring (AES). The OHR system performs
several pre-processing steps such as forms removal, rule-line removal and
segmentation of text lines and words. The final recognition step, which
is tuned to the task of reading comprehension evaluation in a primary
education setting, is performed using a lexicon derived from the passage
to be read. The AES system is based on the approach of latent semantic analysis where a set of human-scored answers are used to determine
scoring system parameters using a machine learning approach. System
performance is compared to scoring done by human raters. Testing on
a small set of handwritten answers indicate that system performance is
comparable to that of automatic scoring based on manual transcription.

1 Introduction

Handwritten essays are widely used for student performance evaluation in schools
and colleges. Since this approach to evaluation is efficient and reliable it is likely
to remain a key component of learning. Assessing large numbers of handwritten
essays is a relatively time-consuming and monotonous task. At the same time
there is an intense need to speed up and enhance the process of rating handwritten essays while maintaining cost effectiveness. The assessment can also be
used as a source of timely, relatively inexpensive and responsible feedback about
writing. The paper describes a first attempt at designing a system for reading,
scoring and analyzing handwritten essays from large scale assessments to provide assessment results and feedback. Success in designing such a system will
not only allow instructors to provide timely feedback to students but also can
provide feedback to education researchers and educators.

H. Bunke and A.L. Spitz (Eds.): DAS 2006, LNCS 3872, pp. 71–83, 2006.

Writing done by hand is the primary means of testing students on state assessments. Consider as an example the New York State English Language Assessment (ELA) administered statewide in grades 4 and 8. In the reading part of the test the student is asked to read a passage such as that given in Fig 1 and answer several questions in writing.

Fig. 1. From the New York English Language Arts assessment for Grade 8, 2001 – two of three pages of the story "American First Ladies" are shown

An example of a reading comprehension question based on the passage of Fig. 1 is the following: "How was Martha Washington's role as First Lady different from that of Eleanor Roosevelt? Use information from American First Ladies in your answer." The completed answer sheets of three different students to the question are given in Fig. 2. The answers are scored by human assessors on a seven-point scale of 0-6.

There is significant practical and pedagogical value in computer-assisted evaluation of such tests. The task of scoring and reporting the results of these assessments in a timely manner is difficult and relatively expensive. There is also an intense need to test later in the year for the purpose of capturing the most student growth and at the same time meet the requirement to report student scores before summer break. The biggest challenge is that of reading and scoring the handwritten portions of large-scale assessments.

From the research viewpoint an automated solution will allow studying patterns among handwritten essays that may be otherwise laborious or impossible. For instance metrics can be obtained for identifying difficulties struggling students are having, for measuring repetition of sections from the original passage, for identifying language constructs specific to the population, etc.

The assessment problem is a well-constrained problem in artificial intelligence whose solution will push forward existing technologies of handwriting recognition and automatic essay scoring. Much of artificial intelligence research has

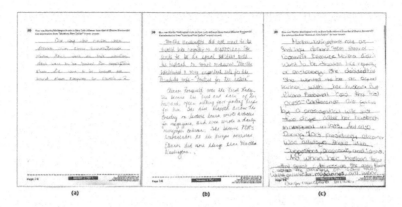

Fig. 2. Sample answer sheets of three students (a-c) based on the reading comprehension passage of Fig. 1. The human assigned scores for these essays, on a scale of 0-6, were 2, 4 and 4 respectively.

progressed in the quest for solutions for specific problems, and this problem promises to be an exciting one both in terms of the task and its use. Solving the problem also promises to reduce costs and raise efficiency of large-scale assessments, which use handwritten essays.

2 Component Technologies and Previous Work

The first step is that of computer reading of handwritten material in the scanned image of an answer booklet page, or optical handwriting recognition (OHR). While computers have become indispensable tools for two of three R's, viz., arithmetic and writing, their use in the third R of reading is still emerging. OHR involves several processing steps such as form (or rule line) removal, line/word segmentation and recognition of individual words. Word recognition relies on a lexicon of words-which could be derived from the passage, question and rubric available in statewide tests. The result of processing the scanned handwritten answer of Fig.2(a) by an OHR system is shown in Fig. 3. The lexicon consisted of words from the passage: 1800s, 1849, 1921, 1933, 1945, 1962, 38000, a, able, about, across, adlai, after, allowed, along, also, always, ambassador, American, etc.

When the lexicon is limited, a majority of the words are correctly recognized although there are errors in some recognized words, and some words are entirely missed. These errors can be reduced by better word segmentation and by using linguistic context in the form of transitional probabilities between words, between parts-of-speech tags, etc. It is possible that certain words, when considered in isolation, are illegible. Local context can resolve such ambiguity. The reading comprehension passage and the rubric provide a rich source of contextual information that can be exploited to get high recognition rates. However, the task itself is one of correct interpretation rather than that of recognizing every illegible word.

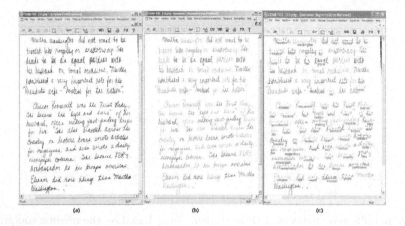

Fig. 3. Results of processing the answer sheet shown in Fig. 2(b) by the OHR system: (a) after forms and rule-line removal, (b) after line and word segmentation (words are shown in different colors), and (c) after word recognition-the word recognizer used a lexicon from the rubric of the question for performing word recognition; only high confidence results are shown

Two basic approaches to automatic essay scoring (AES) are: IR (Information Retrieval)- based and linguistics-based. The IR approach is exemplified by latent semantic analysis (LSA) where keywords and their co-occurrence statistics are used to uncover hidden semantic links between a gold standard and the essay to be evaluated. Linguistic approaches emphasize the use of structures to decode the semantics.

Each of the two areas of OHR and AES has a significant research literature, with virtually no overlap. This research involves integrating concepts and algorithms from each of these areas, which are briefly summarized below.

2.1   Optical Handwriting Recognition (OHR)

OHR is concerned with transforming an image of handwritten text into its textual form. It includes character recognition (OCR), word recognition, part-of-speech tagging, and style recognition. A survey of both on-line (also called dynamic) and off-line (or static or optical) handwriting recognition is [10]. While dynamic handwriting recognition has enjoyed considerable success due to the increasing popularity of tablet PCs and PDAs, OHR has enjoyed success in constrained domains such as postal addresses. To distinguish the two types of handwriting recognition the off-line case is also referred to as optical handwriting recognition (OHR). The higher complexity of OHR stems from the lack of temporal information and the complexity of document analysis.

Prior to OHR there are several pre-processing steps to be performed on document images, e.g., detecting and eliminating extraneous information such as logos, ruled lines and margin lines. Within the handwritten text the ordering of the lines has to be determined and within each line the words need to be segmented.

A system for reading unconstrained handwritten pages known as PENMAN was developed by us [13] which has since been developed into the CEDAR-FOX system for the analysis of handwritten documents for forensic analysis [14] and the CEDAR-OHR system. These systems have tools for gray-scale to binary thresholding, rule line removal, and line/word segmentation. There are interactive user interfaces available for the analysis of the documents by researchers.

Character and Word Recognition: Recognition of characters and words is performed in a two step process of feature extraction followed by classification. Features can be either the raw image pixels or shape descriptors. Features can be at the character level (called analytic recognition) or at the word level (holistic recognition). Word recognition can be performed reasonably well for correctly segmented words with small lexicons. The process is error prone for mis-segmented text and large lexicons. Exploiting statistical dependencies between words was first explored in the OCR domain [3] and then extended to on-line handwriting [12]. There has been considerable success in constrained-domain handwriting recognition, e.g., in handwritten address interpretation [7]. Statistical dependencies between word tags corresponding to parts of speech (POS) rather than to words themselves was also explored by our group. In fact the proposed research will expand on this idea but focus on NEs rather than POS.

Handwriting Interpretation: Handwriting Interpretation is a goal-oriented task where the goal is not so much one of recognizing every character and word perfectly but to perform the overall task in an accurate manner. It involves using basic handwriting recognition tools together with contextual information to solve specific tasks even when there is significant uncertainty in the specific components. Such approaches have found success when the domain is limited and contextual information is available. For instance, in the domain of postal addresses a system was developed for determining the destination irrespective of whether the individual components were correctly written [15]. The strategy was to recognize the most easily recognizable parts of the address first, which in this case consists of the ZIP Code and street number. These two "islands" are used to narrow down the lexicon of choices of the street name, which simplifies the task of recognizing the street name. The recognition of the ZIP Code is constrained by the state name and city name. The mutual constraints lead to a correct interpretation irrespective of spelling errors, mistakes and illegibility. Today, over 90% of all handwritten addresses in the United States are interpreted by OHR. This triangulation is useful for recognition of essay words when constraints imposed by certain words can be used to disambiguate illegible words.

2.2   Automatic Essay Scoring (AES)

Automated essay scoring has been a topic of research over four decades. A limitation of all past work is that the essays or examinations have to be in computer readable form. A survey of previous AES methods has been made by Palmer, et. al (2002). Project Essay Grade (PEG) (Page, 1961) uses linguistic features from which a multiple regression equation is developed. In the Production Automated

Essay Grading System a grammar checker, a program to identify words and sentences, software dictionary, a part-of-speech tagger, and a parser are used to gather data. E-rater (Burstein, 2003) uses a combination of statistical and NLP techniques to extract linguistic features. Larkey (1998) implemented an AES approach based on text categorization techniques (TCT).

A promising approach to AES is based on a technique developed in the information retrieval community known as latent semantic indexing. Its application to AES, known as latent semantic analysis (LSA), uncovers lexical semantic links between an essay and a gold standard. Landauer, et. al. (1998) developed the Intelligent Essay Assessor using LSA. A matrix for the essay is built, and then transformed by the algebraic method of singular value decomposition (SVD) to approximately reproduce the matrix using reduced dimensional matrices built for the topic domain. Using SVD new relationships between words and documents are uncovered, and existing relationships are modified to represent their significance. Using LSA the similarity between two essays can be measured despite differences in individual lexical items. Where a gold standard exists, LSA is a robust approach. It correlates as closely with human raters as human raters correlate with each other (Landauer et al. 2003).

Hybrid systems combine LSA word vector similarity metrics with structure-based linguistic features. One such system is the widely-used ETS E-rater (Burstein, 2003) which has been used to grade essays on the GMAT, TOEFL, and GRE exams. E-rater is trained on about 300 hand-graded essays for each question or prompt. A predictive statistical model is developed from the set of scored essays by beginning with a set of 50-70 features and using stepwise linear regression to select features necessary to assign a score from 1-6. E-rater uses part of speech (POS) tagging and shallow parsing to identify subjunctive auxiliary verbs, more complex clause types (e.g. complement, infinitive, and subordinate clauses), and discourse cue words (e.g. because, in summary, for example). Discourse cue words are used both as individual features and as a way to divide essays into labeled discourse segments. The score is a combination of an overall score and the scores for each discourse segment. Additional features include the presence of words like possibly and perhaps, presence of sentence-initial infinitive phrases, and discourse-deictic words like this and these. To evaluate content and word choice, E-rater uses vectors of word frequencies. The training set is collapsed into six categories (one for each scoring value), and each discourse segment is scored by comparing it with the six categories. The mean of the argument scores is adjusted for the number of arguments (to penalize shorter essays).

3   System Architecture

The basic software structure consists of OHR and AES systems. They are integrated into a single automated assessment platform, which can both assign scores and provide analytic feedback. The system is designed to be interactive so that the user– a researcher or educator– will be able to examine the decisions made, and accept or change the decisions.

The OHR system has two phases/components: (i) Rubric Processor: a system that extracts lexicons, entities and concepts from the reading passage, question and rubric– it compiles various indices including lexicons of words that can be used as features by the answer OHR, and (ii) Answer Processor: a system to analyze and score the scanned answer sheet(s) The answer sheets are scanned as gray scale images at a resolution of 300 pixels per inch. The OHR system is written in C with visual interfaces in Visual C++.

The AES system also has two phases. In the training phase the system parameters are learnt from a set of human-scored samples. In the testing phase these parameters are used in performing the evaluation.

3.1   OHR

Recognition of the scanned document begins with a number of document image pre-processing steps such as extracting the foreground from the background, eliminating non-informative material such as rule lines and other printed markings, determining the presence of handwritten words, their reading sequence, etc. Examples of line/word segmentation and recognition, as performed by the CEDAR OHR system, were seen earlier in Fig. 3. The main tasks for the OHR system are as follows:

(1) Word segmentation: The tasks here are the segmentation of lines and words of handwritten text in the presence of ambiguity. To determine whether a gap is a true gap or not features are taken into account from the current document rather than solely rely on a learning set.

(2) Word recognition: When vocabularies provided to the word recognizer are large contextual information needs to be exploited to dynamically limit word choices during the process of recognition. Contextual information is readily available to the recognizer in the form of the passage to be read and the answer rubric.

After the words in the scanned answer documents are recognized by the OHR system the resulting word sequences are written to text files. These text files are then pre-processed for AES which include the following steps.

a. Removing punctuations and special characters
b. Converting upper case to lower case for generalization
c. Stop word removal - removing common words such as *a* and *the* which occur very often and are not of significant importance
d. Stemming - morphological variants of words have similar semantic interpretations and therefore a stemming algorithm is used to reduce the word to its stem or root form. The algorithm [11]] uses a technique called suffix stripping where an explicit suffix list is provided along with a condition on which the suffix should be removed or replaced to form the stem of the word, which would be common among all variations. For example the word *reading* after suffix stripping is reduced to *read*.

3.2 AES

When a large number of student answers are available, which is the case in statewide assessments, a holistic approach will assist in providing computer automated grades close to those that would be assigned by expert human graders. The Latent Semantic Analysis (LSA) approach can take advantage of the availability of a large training corpus. The training corpus consists of human-scored answer documents. The potentiality of LSA to imitate human judgment has been explored and found to have a strong correlation [4].

The underlying semantics of the training corpus are extracted using LSA and without the use of any other external knowledge. The method captures how the variations in term choices and variations in answer document meanings are related. However, it does not take into consideration the order of occurrence of words. This implies that even if two students have used different words to convey the same message, LSA can capture the co-relation between the two documents. This is because LSA depicts the meaning of a word as an average of the connotation of the documents in which it occurs. It can similarly judge the correctness of an answer document as an average of the measure of correctness of all the words it contains.

Mathematically this can be explained as the simultaneous representation of all the answer documents in the training corpus as points in semantic space, with initial dimensionality of the order of the number of terms in the document. This dimensionality is reduced to an optimal value large enough to represent the structure of the answer documents and small enough to facilitate elimination of irrelevant representations. The answer document to be graded is also placed in the reduced dimensionality semantic space and the by and large term-based similarity between this document and each of those in the training corpus can then be determined by measuring the cosine of the angle between the two documents at the origin.

A good approximation of the computer score to a human score heavily depends on the optimal reduced dimensionality. This optimal dimension is related to the features that determine the term meaning from which we can derive the hidden correlations between terms and answer documents. However a general method to determine this optimal dimension is still an open research problem. Currently a brute force approach is adopted. Reducing the dimensions is done by omitting inconsequential relations and retaining only significant ones. A factor analysis method such as Singular Value Decomposition (SVD) helps reduce the dimensionality to a desired approximation.

The first step in LSA is to construct a t x n term-by-document matrix M whose entries are frequencies. SVD or two-mode factor analysis decomposes this rectangular matrix into three matrices [1]. The SVD for a rectangular matrix M can be defined as

$$M = TSD',$$
(1)

where prime $(')$ indicates matrix transposition, M is the rectangular term by document matrix with t rows and n columns, T is the t x m matrix, which

Table 1. An Example 154 x 31 Term by Document Matrix M, where M_{ij} is the frequency of the ith term in the jth answer document

Term/Doc	D1	D2	D3	D4	D5	D6	D7	D8	...	D31
T1	0	0	0	0	0	0	0	0	...	0
T2	2	1	2	1	3	1	2	1	...	2
T3	0	1	0	1	3	1	2	1	...	1
T4	0	1	0	0	0	1	0	0	...	0
T5	0	1	0	0	0	0	1	0	...	0
T6	0	1	1	0	0	1	2	0	...	0
T7	0	0	0	0	1	0	0	0	...	0
T8	0	0	0	0	1	0	1	0	...	0
T9	...	...	...	...	...	...	...	...	...	...
T154	0	0	0	0	0	0	0	0	...	0

describes rows in the matrix M as left singular vectors of derived orthogonal factor values, D is the n x m matrix, which describes columns in the matrix M as right singular vectors of derived orthogonal factor values, S is the m x m diagonal matrix of singular values such that when T, S and D' are matrix multiplied M is reconstructed, and m is the rank of $M = min(t, n)$.

To reduce the dimensionality to a value, say k, from the matrix S we have to delete $m - k$ rows and columns starting from those which contain the smallest singular value to form the matrix S_1. The corresponding columns in T and rows in D' are also deleted to form matrices T_1 and D'_1 respectively. The matrix M_1 is an approximation of matrix M with reduced dimensions as follows

$$M_1 = T_1 S_1 D'_1. \tag{2}$$

Standard algorithms are available to perform SVD. To illustrate, a document-term matrix constructed from 31 essays from the *American First Ladies* example shown in Fig 1 and Fig 2 are given in Table 1. Since the corpus contains 31 documents with 154 unique words, M has dimensions $t = 154$ and $m = 31$.

Training Phase. The following steps are performed in the training phase:

1) Answer documents are preprocessed and tokenized into a list of words or terms– using the document pre-processing steps described in section 3.1.
2) An *Answer Dictionary* is created which assigns a unique file ID to all the answer documents in the corpus.
3) A *Word Dictionary* is created which assigns a unique word ID to all the words in the corpus.
4) An *index* with the word ID and the number of times it occurs (word frequency) in each of the 31 documents is created.
5) A *Term-by-Document Matrix*, M is created from the index, where M_{ij} is the frequency of the ith term in the jth answer document.

Validation Phase. A set of human graded documents, known as the validation set, are used to determine the optimal value of k. Each of them are passed as query vectors and compared with the training corpus documents. The following steps are repeated for each document.

1) A vector Q of term frequencies in the query document is created, similar to the way M was created
2) Q is then added as the 0th column of the Matrix M to give a matrix M_q
3) SVD is performed on the matrix M_q, to give the TSD' matrices
4) Steps 5-10 are repeated for dimension values, $k = 1$ to $min(t, m)$
5) Delete $m - k$ rows and columns from the S matrix, starting from the smallest singular value to form the matrix S_1. The corresponding columns in T and rows in D' are also deleted to form matrices T_1 and D'_1 respectively
6) Construct the matrix M_{q1} by multiplying the matrices $T_1 S_1 D'_1$
7) The similarity between the query document x (the 0th column of the matrix M_{q1}) and each of the other documents y in the training corpus (subsequent columns in the matrix M_{q1}) are determined by the cosine similarity measure defined as

$$CosineSimilarity = \frac{\sum_{i=1}^{n} x_i y_i}{\sqrt{\sum_{i=1}^{n} x_i \sum_{i=1}^{n} y_i}} \tag{3}$$

8) The training documents with the highest similarity score, when compared with the query answer documents are selected and the human scores associated with these documents are assigned to the documents in question respectively
9) The mean difference between the LSA graded scores and that assigned to the query by a human grader is calculated for each dimension over all the queries
10) Return to step 4
11) The dimension with least mean difference is selected as the optimal dimension k which is used in the testing phase.

Testing Phase. The testing set consists of a set of scored essays not used in the training and validation phases. The term-document matrix constructed in the training phase and the value of k determined from the validation phase are used to determine the scores of the test set.

4   Experimental Results

The corpus for experimentation consisted of 71 handwritten answer essays. Of these essays 48 were by students and 23 were by teachers. Each of the 71 answer essays were manually assigned a score by education researchers. The essays were divided into 47 training samples, 12 validation samples and 12 testing samples. The training set had a human-score distribution on the seven-point scale as follows: 1,8,9,10,2,9,8. Both the validation and testing sets had human-score distributions of 0,2,2,3,1,2,2.

Two different sets of 71 transcribed essays were created, the first by manual transcription (MT) and the second by the OHR system. The lexicon for the OHR system consisted of unique words from the passage to be read, which had a size

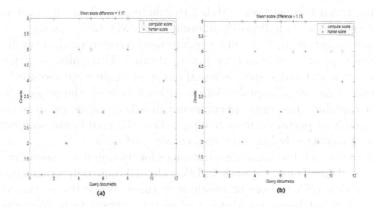

Fig. 4. Comparison of human scores, MT-LSA scores and OHR-LSA scores on 12 student responses to the *American First Ladies* question: (a) MT-LSA scores (open circles) are within 1.17 of human scores (stars), and (b) OHR-LSA scores (open circles) are within 1.75 of human scores (stars)

of 274. Separate training and validation phases were conducted for the MT and OHR essays. For the MT essays, the document-term matrix M had $t = 490$ and $m = 47$ and the optimal value of k was determined to be 5. For the OHR essays, the corresponding values were $t = 154$, $m = 47$ and $k = 8$. The smaller number of terms in the OHR case is explained by the fact that several words were not recognized.

Comparisons of the human-assigned scores (the gold-standard) with (i) automatically assigned scores based on MT is shown in Fig. 4(a) and (ii) automatically assigned scores based on OHR is shown in 4(b). In both plots the human scores are shown as stars (*) and machine-assigned scores as open circles. Using MT the human-machine mean difference was 1.17 (Fig. 4 (a)). This is consistent with a one-point difference between LSA and the gold-standard previously established in large scale testing. Using OHR the the human-machine difference was 1.75 (Fig. 4 (b)). Thus a 0.58 difference is observed between MT and OHR using LSA scoring. Although the testing set is small, these preliminary results demonstrate the potential of the method for holistic scoring and robustness with OHR errors.

5   Summary and Discussion

An approach to automatically evaluating handwritten essays in reading comprehension tests has been described. The design is based on optical handwriting recognition (OHR) and automatic essay scoring (AES). The lexicon for OHR is obtained from the passage to be read by the students. The AES method is based on latent semantic analysis (LSA) which is a holistic method of scoring that has shown much promise. Results on a small testing set show that with manually transcribed (MT) essays, LSA scoring has about a one-point difference from human scoring which is consistent with large scale testing. With the same test set, OHR-LSA scoring has a half-point difference from MT-LSA scoring.

The results point out that despite errors in word recognition the overall scoring performance is good enough to have practical value. This points out that when the evaluation of an OHR system is based not so much on word recognition rates but in terms of the overall application in which it is used, the performance can be quite acceptable. The same phenomenon has been observed in other OHR aplications such as postal address reading where the goal is not so much as to read every word correctly but achieve a correct sortation.

The LSA approach has some disadvantages for its use in a class-room setting since it is based on a holistic approach. Like other IR approaches based on a "bag of words" model, LSA ignores linguistic structures. While the scoring is based on content, it is not based on idea development, organization, cohesion, style, grammar, or usage conventions. Such an approach, known as analytic scoring, will need to take into account linguistic structures. The result of analytic scoring will be more useful to teachers and education researchers. Future work will involve improving the robustness of OHR, particularly in segmenting touching text lines, and the use of information extraction techniques for tighter integration between OHR and AES.

References

1. Baeza-Yates, R. and Ribeiro-Neto, B.: Modern information retrieval. New York: Addison-Wesley (1999).
2. Burstein, J.: The E-rater Scoring Engine: Automated essay scoring with natural language processing. In Automated Essay Scoring (2003).
3. J. J. Hull: "Incorporation of a Markov model of syntax in a text recognition algorithm," in Proceedings of the Symposium on Document Analysis and Information Retrieval, pp. 174-183 (1992).
4. Landauer, T. and D. Laham and P. Foltz.: Automated scoring and annotation of essays with the Intelligent Essay Assessor. In Automated Essay Scoring (2003).
5. Landauer, T.K., P. W. Foltz and D. Laham: An introduction to latent semantic analysis, Discourse Processes, 25, pp. 259-284.
6. Larkey, L.S.: "Automatic essay grading using text categorization techniques, " Proceedings ACM-SIGIR Conference on Research and Development in Information Retrieval, Melbourne, Australia, pp. 90-95.
7. Mahadevan, U., and Srihari, S.N.: "Parsing and recognition of city, state and ZIP Codes in handwritten addresses," in Proceedings of Fifth International Conference on Document Analysis and Recognition (ICDAR), Bangalore, India, pp. 325-328.(1999)
8. Page, E. B.: "Computer grading of student prose using modern concepts and software," Journal of Experimental Education, 62, pp. 127-142.
9. Palmer, J., R. Williams and H. Dreher: "Automated essay grading system applied to a first year university subject - how can we do better?" Informing Science,pp. 1221-1229 June 2002.
10. Plamondon, R., and S. N. Srihari.: "On-line and off-line handwriting recognition: A comprehensive survey," IEEE Transactions on Pattern Analysis and Machine Intelligence, 22(1): 63-84, 2000.

11. Porter, M.F.: "An Algorithm for Suffix Stripping" Program, 14(3),pp. 130-137, 1980.
12. Srihari, R. K., S. Ng, C.M. Baltus and J. Kud: "Use of language models in on-line sentence/phrase recognition," in Proceedings of the International Workshop on Frontiers in Handwriting Recognition, Buffalo, pp. 284-294, 1993.
13. Srihari, S. N., and Kim, G.: "PENMAN: A system for reading unconstrained hand-written page images," in Proceedings of the Symposium on Document Image Understanding Technology (SDIUT 97), Annapolis, MD, pp. 142-153, 1997.
14. Srihari, S. N., B. Zhang, C. Tomai, S. Lee, Z. Shi and Y. C. Shin: "A system for handwriting matching and recognition, " in Proceedings of the Symposium on Document Image Understanding Technology (SDIUT 03), Greenbelt, MD, pp. 67-75, 2003.
15. Srihari, S.N., and E. J. Keubert: "Integration of handwritten address interpretation technology into the United States Postal Service Remote Computer Reader System," Proceedings of the Fourth International Conference on Document Analysis and Recognition (ICDAR 97), Ulm, Germany, pp. 892-896, 1997.

Aligning Transcripts to Automatically Segmented Handwritten Manuscripts

Jamie Rothfeder*, R. Manmatha, and Toni M. Rath*

Department of Computer Science,
University of Massachusetts Amherst, Amherst, MA 01003, USA
{jrothfed, manmatha, trath}@cs.umass.edu

Abstract. Training and evaluation of techniques for handwriting recognition and retrieval is a challenge given that it is difficult to create large ground-truthed datasets. This is especially true for historical handwritten datasets. In many instances the ground truth has to be created by manually transcribing each word, which is a very labor intensive process. Sometimes transcriptions are available for some manuscripts. These transcriptions were created for other purposes and hence correspondence at the word, line, or sentence level may not be available. To be useful for training and evaluation, a word level correspondence must be available between the segmented handwritten word images and the ASCII transcriptions. Creating this correspondence or alignment is challenging because the segmentation is often errorful and the ASCII transcription may also have errors in it. Very little work has been done on the alignment of handwritten data to transcripts. Here, a novel Hidden Markov Model based automatic alignment algorithm is described and tested. The algorithm produces an average alignment accuracy of about 72.8% when aligning whole pages at a time on a set of 70 pages of the George Washington collection. This outperforms a dynamic time warping alignment algorithm by about 12% previously reported in the literature and tested on the same collection.

1 Introduction

Off-line handwriting recognition and retrieval still remains an unsolved problem in the general case for both modern and historical handwriting. In recent years, there has been some work on large vocabulary datasets on both modern [17, 11] and historical documents [6, 13]. Evaluating handwriting recognition and retrieval techniques on large datasets requires annotated (ie. with ground truth) large vocabulary datasets for training and testing. Creating such large annotated datasets is challenging. For large modern datasets (like the IAM database [10]) this has been achieved by having a number of different people copy out in a specified manner articles that they have been provided. Such restrictions include requiring people to use a ruler while writing and to make sure that each

---

* J. Rothfeder and T. M. Rath are now at IBM and Google respectively.

H. Bunke and A.L. Spitz (Eds.): DAS 2006, LNCS 3872, pp. 84–95, 2006.

line corresponds to a line in the original article. Deriving word by word correspondences from the given line by line correspondences is not that difficult especially for clean modern databases like the IAM dataset [10]. The situation is more challenging with historical handwritten documents. In many situations the only text that is available is the handwritten one and the creation of ground truth requires a labor intensive process of manually transcribing each word. This is for example, how the publicly available George Washington dataset of 20 handwritten pages [6] was produced. However, this is a very time consuming process. Given the repetitive boring nature of the task errors are also produced during the transcription process.

For some historical documents an electronic transcription is sometimes available [1]. These may be scholarly transcriptions made for use in historical studies or other related endeavors. For example, electronic transcripts for a portion of George Washington's papers [2] are available from the Library of Congress. The alignment between the scanned images and the transcriptions is not available. That is we do not know the correspondence between the words or lines in the scanned image and the words or lines in the transcript. In many cases the situation is even worse and we do not accurately know which pages line up. This is because each letter that in Washington's papers is transcribed as a unit. On the other hand in Washington's manuscripts, a letter often ends halfway on a page and a second letter begins right after that [3]. An automatic procedure to align the words on the transcript with the words on the handwritten page would be very useful but is very challenging to do. This may be done for example by automatically segmenting the handwritten words and then trying to find an alignment between the segmented boxes and the words in the transcript. If there were no errors in the segmentation or transcription, a simple linear alignment would suffice. That is, by assigning the first transcript word to the first word-image, the second transcript word to the second word-image and so on. This alignment assumes the start and end points are specified. In practice errors in segmentation, or transcription ensure that this approach will not work. The segmentation errors produced make linear alignment impractical. This will happen with any practical segmentor for even a low rate of segmentation errors throws off a linear alignment and would produce useless training/evaluation data. Another source of error comes from words which are broken up at the end of the line and continued on the next page. A segmentor would treat these as two words while in the transcript they only occur as a single word. Besides segmentation errors, there may also be errors in the transcriptions. These errors may occur because of a mistake on the part of the transcriber (historical documents are sometimes hard to decipher) or for example because the transcriber expanded an abbreviation in the original document.

---

[1] Printed transcriptions pose an even greater challenge since optical character recognition errors will also have to be taken into account during alignment.

[2] There are actually multiple writers in this collection for George Washington employed secretaries to help him with his work.

[3] This is probably because these are copies of the actual letters that were sent out.

Here we propose a new algorithm to align the output of an automatic word segmentor on a handwritten page with a transcript. The data we have consists of a set of pages from George Washington's manuscripts. Each page is automatically segmented using the automatic scale space segmentation algorithm reported in [9, 8]. It is shown in [8] that for segmenting historical documents, this algorithm outperforms a gap metrics based algorithm. We also have a transcript corresponding to each page of the manuscript which has been generated by manually labeling the words. Our goal is to assign one or more words from the transcript to each of our automatically segmented word-images. Fig 1 shows an illustration of alignment for two different lines. Each word image is assigned to one or more transcript words. In the case of oversegmentation (or fragmentation), we wish to assign the same transcript word to all fragments of the word image. In the case of undersegmentation (or multiple words in a box), all corresponding transcript words should be assigned to the bounding box.

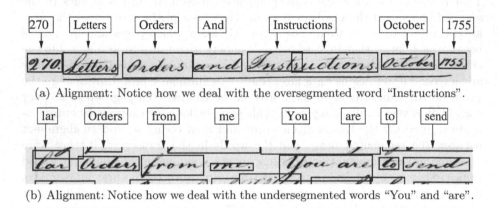

(a) Alignment: Notice how we deal with the oversegmented word "Instructions".

(b) Alignment: Notice how we deal with the undersegmented words "You" and "are".

Fig. 1. Two automatically segmented lines and transcript alignments

We treat the problem as one of aligning two sequences - a sequence of errorful word images and a sequence of words from the transcript. The alignment uses a linear Hidden Markov model and is solved using the Viterbi algorithm to produce the most likely sequence. The HMM models the probability of generating (observing) the word images given the words. The transition model accounts for segmentation errors. The algorithm produces an average alignment accuracy of about 72.8% when aligning whole pages at a time on a set of 70 pages of the George Washington collection. This outperforms a dynamic time warping alignment algorithm (by 12%) previously reported in the literature and tested on the same collection.

Sequence alignment problems have been solved before in a number of language technology areas and bioinformatics. For example, HMM's have been used for sequence alignment in speech recognition [15], the alignment of synthesized speech with speech [7], the alignment of speech recognition output with closed captions in video [12], machine translation [1] and bioinformatics [2] and for aligning parallel corpora in machine translation [4]. For print OCR [3] created groundtruth by using a machine readable description to print the document and then matching character bounding boxes with bounding boxes derived from a scanned image of the document. [18] aligned an imperfect transcript obtained from a scanned image of a printed page with the characters in unsegmented text.

There has, however, been little work in aligning handwritten text to transcripts. Tomai et al. [16] assume that a line by line correspondence of the transcript and handwritten line is provided and that a word by word alignment is required. They use a handwriting recognizer to produce a ranked list of words from a vocabulary for each recognized word image. Different segmentations are then made of each line and the segmentation that has the highest probability, given the line transcript, is selected. Kornfield et al. [5] consider the problem of alignment when line by line correspondences are available and also only when page by page correspondences are provided. They show that the first case is much easier than the second case. They treat word images and transcripts as two time series and then use dynamic time warping to align them.

The rest of the paper is organized as follows: Section 2 introduces the idea of using an HMM to align text with handwritten documents. Then, section 3 describes the the two components of our observation model. Next, we discuss the transition model in section 4. Datasets are discussed in 5. Experiment results are reported in the next section. Finally we conclude the paper.

2   Using a Hidden Markov Model to Align Text

Let H be a handwritten page. Let $S_1, \ldots, S_x$ be a sequence of random variables corresponding to the word-images from H. Let the transcript of H be of length y, this is a sequence of words corresponding to near-perfect segmentation. Given that we have some knowledge about the types of errors that the automatic segmentor produces, our goal is to assign one or more transcript words to each S_i, thus aligning the transcript to the document. To do this we construct the Hidden Markov Model shown in Fig. 2, where the hidden variables are $S_1, \ldots, S_x$, and the observed variables are the feature vectors, $\mathbf{F}_1, \ldots, \mathbf{F}_x$, extracted from each of the word-images (the features are the same as described in [6]). The full joint distribution for our HMM is given by:

$$P(S_1 = s_1, \ldots, S_n = s_n, \mathbf{F}_1 = \mathbf{f}_1, \ldots, \mathbf{F}_n = \mathbf{f}_n) \tag{1}$$

$$= \prod_{i=1}^{n} P(S_i = s_i | S_{i-1} = s_{i-1}) P(\mathbf{F}_i = \mathbf{f}_i | S_i = s_i) \tag{2}$$

After constructing our HMM in this way, we run the Viterbi algorithm to decode the sequence of assignments to each of our S_i, thus assigning one transcript word to each of the word-images. After this, a postprocessing step may be employed to assign more than one transcript word to some of the word-images (this is needed in the case of undersegmentation). This postprocessing step is not discussed in this paper.

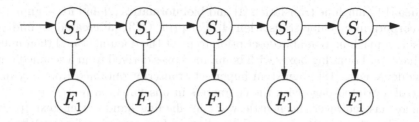

Fig. 2. Graphical model of Hidden Markov Model used for Alignment

The next sections describe the two components of our HMM: the observation model and the transition model.

3   Observation Model - Feature Likelihoods

Let $\mathbf{f}_i$ be the feature vector corresponding to the the the random variable S_i. Our feature vector is 27 dimensional. It is the same set used in Lavrenko et al [6] and consists of scalar features like length of the word or the number of ascenders as well as profile features. Profile features include projection profiles and upper and lower profiles. To obtain a constant length representation, a discrete Fourier Transform is computed over the profiles and only the low order coefficients are used. For more details on the features used see Lavrenko et al [6]. For every vocabulary word w_j in our transcript, we compute the feature-likelihood $P(\mathbf{f}_i|w_j)$, which is a multivariate normal distribution give by:

$$P(\mathbf{f}_i|w_j) = \frac{exp\left\{-\frac{1}{2}(\mathbf{f}_i - \mu_w)^T \Sigma_w^{-1}(\mathbf{f}_i - \mu_w)\right\}}{\sqrt{2^D \pi^D |\Sigma_w|}} \qquad (3)$$

with mean μ_w and covariance matrix Σ_w. $|\Sigma_w|$ is the determinant of the covariance matrix, and D represents the number of features extracted for each of the word images, in our case $D = 27$.

The next step is to estimate μ_w and Σ_w. To do this, we use a training set where the word images boxes are manually corrected (see section 5 for more on experimental datasets). We also need a transcript for each document - the words from which form our vocabulary. The transcripts, along with the manually corrected word-images provide us with a set of pairs in the form {word-image, ASCII-annotation}. If we let the length of our feature vectors be k, then μ_w is a vector of length k containing the mean of all of the feature vectors extracted from word images that have been labeled w_i. In other words, for each word w_i in our vocabulary, we extract a set of feature vectors, $\mathbf{g}_{w,1}, \ldots, \mathbf{g}_{w,k}$ from the training word images that have been labeled with w. Then μ_w is computed as follows:

$$\mu_w[d] = \frac{1}{k}\sum_{i=1}^{k} \mathbf{g}_{w,i}[d], d = 1, \ldots, D \qquad (4)$$

where d is a dimension of the feature vector.

The covariance matrix Σ_w can only be estimated accurately for w_j if there is a sufficient number of word-images in our training set which have been annotated with w_j. Unfortunately, this is never the case and we approximate the covariance matrix using one value, $\Sigma_w \approx \sigma_{avg} * I$, for all words. I is the identity matrix and σ_{avg} is the mean feature variance given by the following:

$$\sigma_{avg} = \frac{1}{D} \sum_{d=1}^{D} \left(\frac{1}{N_{tr} - 1} \sum_{i=1}^{N_{tr}} (\mathbf{g}_{w,i}[d] - \mu[d])^2 \right) \tag{5}$$

where μ is the average of value of all feature vectors in the training set and N_{tr} is the number of all feature vectors, $\mathbf{g}_{w,i}$ in our training set.

Some improvements may be obtained by smoothing the probability estimates especially when the number of training samples is small. A discussion of smoothing for this particular problem requires far more space than is available here and is, therefore, omitted.

4 Transition Model

As mentioned before, errors can be either oversegmentations, undersegmentations, missed word, or extra bounding boxes. If we have an oversegmentation then part of a transcript word will need to be assigned to two or more adjacent

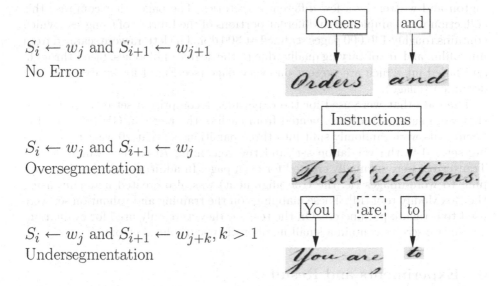

$S_i \leftarrow w_j$ and $S_{i+1} \leftarrow w_{j+1}$
No Error

$S_i \leftarrow w_j$ and $S_{i+1} \leftarrow w_j$
Oversegmentation

$S_i \leftarrow w_j$ and $S_{i+1} \leftarrow w_{j+k}, k > 1$
Undersegmentation

Fig. 3. Different alignment errors and their representations in the transition model. The dangling "are" in the undersegmentation example is not handled by the HMM directly. It could be assigned later using a postprocessing technique not discussed in this paper.

word-images. In the case of undersegmentation, two transcript words will need to be assigned to one bounding box. Extra bounding boxes may be dealt with by assigning a transcript word to more than one word image (as in oversegmentation), and missed-words can be dealt with the same way that undersegmentation is. The following describes a transition model designed to support this behavior.

We can use our transition model to account for segmentation errors by assigning positions in our transcripts in the following way (also see Fig. 3 for an illustration):

1. No error: $S_i \leftarrow w_j$ and $S_{i+1} \leftarrow w_{j+1}$
2. Oversegmentation: $S_i \leftarrow w_j$ and $S_{i+1} \leftarrow w_j$
3. Undersegmentation: $S_i \leftarrow w_j$ and $S_{i+1} \leftarrow w_{j+k}, k > 1$

Where S_i is the random variable corresponding to a word image on the page and w_j is the vocabulary word at position j in the transcript.

The setting of parameters for our model is discussed in section 6.2.

5   Dataset

5.1   Characteristics of the 100 Page George Washington Collection

The 100 Page George Washington Collection (GW100) is a collection of digitized pages, where each page contains one or more letters authored by George Washington and written by a few different secretaries. The pages that comprise this collection were sampled from different portions of the Library of Congress, which contains roughly 140,000 pages scanned at 300 dpi. The letters were scanned from microfilm, and are of varying quality due to the degree of blotches, bleed-through, and faded ink which are present on every page (see Fig. 4 for an example of a document-image).

The data that were used for the experiments comprise a set of word-images that were automatically segmented from each of the pages in GW100. The 100 documents were randomly split into three partitions so that 20 went to a training set, 10 to the validation set, and the remaining 70 to the evaluation set. Transcripts were manually created for each page. In addition, a transcript mapping to word-images (ie. the true alignment) was also created manually using the BoxModify tool [14]. These mappings on the training and validation set were used to estimate parameters. On the test set they were only used for evaluation. These transcripts contain a small number of typographical errors.

6   Experiments and Results

We now discuss the experiments and results. First, we discuss the evaluation procedure. This is followed by a brief discussion of how the parameters are estimated. We then evaluate the alignment algorithm on the test set and discuss the results.

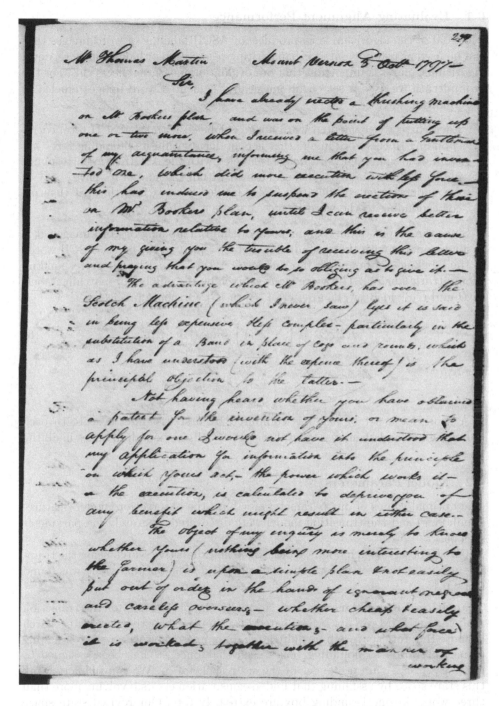

Fig. 4. Image 2360237 from the George Washington Collection. Notice the bleedthrough, faded ink, and blotches.

6.1 Evaluating Alignment Performance

The goal of the algorithm is to produce an ASCII labeling of word images that can be used as training data for handwriting recognition or handwriting retrieval algorithms, and it is important that our evaluation measure reflects this. For the groundtruth we used a set of automatically segmented word images labeled in the following way:

- Each correctly segmented word image is labeled with the ASCII term corresponding to the word image that is contained within its bounding box.
- Each oversegmented word image is labeled with the ASCII term corresponding to the word image that is contained within the sum of its parts.
- An undersegmented bounding box is labeled with each of the ASCII terms corresponding to the word images that are contained within.

Since the output of our alignment algorithm is a labeling of word images, it is easily compared with the groundtruth. Let $B = \{b_1, \ldots, b_r\}$ be the ASCII words in the labeling of a bounding box and let $G = \{g_1, \ldots, g_s\}$ be the corresponding groundtruth labeling. The score for B is given by the number of matching labels in B and G divided by the greater of $|B|$ or $|G|$. Or, more precisely:

$$\sigma(B, G) = \left(\sum_i^r t(i) \right) / max(|B|, |G|) \tag{6}$$

where

$$t(i) = \begin{cases} 1 & \exists j : b_i = g_j \\ 0 & \text{Otherwise} \end{cases} \tag{7}$$

A score for a set of pages is computed by first assigning a score to each bounding box and then averaging this score for all the bounding boxes in all the pages.

6.2 Model Parameters

The optimal values of our parameters for both the observation model (feature-likelihoods) and the transition model were discovered separately via parameter sweeps.

For the observation model, we performed an exhaustive search using the training and validation set to estimate the value of σ. The optimal value was found to be 0.1.

Transition Model Parameters. Normally, the parameters for the transition model in an HMM can not be estimated by a simple exhaustive parameter search because the state space can be quite large. In our case, however, we are assigning transcript words to bounding boxes such that once w_j has been assigned to S_{i-1}, $w_1 \ldots w_{j-1}$ are no longer in the state space of S_i. We can further shrink this state space by assuming that undersegmentation errors involving more than three words in one bounding box are extremely rare. Our revised state space for $S_i = \{w_j, w_{j+1}, w_{j+2}, w_{j+3}\}$. This leaves us with only three parameters to estimate.

The mean percentages of oversegmentation, undersegmentation and missed words in the training set are 0.05, 0.06, and 0.03 respectively. Our initial setting for the transition model was based on these values as follows:

- $P(S_i \leftarrow w_j | S_{i-1} \leftarrow w_j) = 0.05$ - Compensates for oversegmentation.
- $P(S_i \leftarrow w_j | S_{i-1} \leftarrow w_{j-1}) = 0.86$ - Corresponds to correct segmentation.
- $P(S_i \leftarrow w_j | S_{i-1} \leftarrow w_{j-2}) = 0.08$ - Compensates for undersegmentation and missed words.
- $P(S_i \leftarrow w_j | S_{i-1} \leftarrow w_{j-3}) = 0.01$ Compensates for undersegmentation and missed words.

However, a parameter sweep using the training and validation set showed that performance over the validation set was optimized by choosing:

- $P(S_i \leftarrow w_j | S_{i-1} \leftarrow w_j) = 0.001$ - Compensates for oversegmentation.
- $P(S_i \leftarrow w_j | S_{i-1} \leftarrow w_{j-1}) = 0.998$ - Corresponds to correct segmentation.
- $P(S_i \leftarrow w_j | S_{i-1} \leftarrow w_{j-2}) = 0.0008$ - Compensates for undersegmentation and missed words.
- $P(S_i \leftarrow w_j | S_{i-1} \leftarrow w_{j-3}) = 0.0002$ Compensates for undersegmentation and missed words.

It was originally expected that the parameters could be estimated directly from the segmentation errors. This parameter sweep shows this not to be the case. The reason for this is due to very large feature likelihood scores being produced by the observation model. Because the features are normalized before computing the parameters of the observation model, σ_{avg} is a very small value. This produces a very narrow Gaussian. Thus, the likelihood score for any two similar feature vectors may differ by a few orders of magnitude and the transition model must compensate for this.

6.3   Results

When the algorithm was run on the test set, the mean score over the 70 pages was found to be 72.8%. The result was compared with that in Kornfield et al. [5]. The experimental dataset is identical to the one used in our experiments. Alignment is performed by treating the bounding boxes and transcripts like two time series and then using dynamic time warping (DTW) to align them. They evaluated their algorithm by first concatenating the words together that have been assigned to a bounding box, and then computing the Levenshtein distance between the bounding box and the corresponding groundtruth (this measure is close to the measure we use for evaluation). An average score of 60.5% over all bounding boxes was reported when page level alignment was done. Our alignment algorithm, therefore, outperforms their algorithm by about 12%. HMM's incorporate transition probabilities which may explain the better performance.

Kornfield et al. [5] also show that if line break information is available (i.e. line level alignment information is provided) their performance substantially increases to 74.5% (any algorithm will show a substantial improvement in performance when the input is line aligned). Our performance given page alignments is close to their performance using line alignments. The HMM based alignment algorithm presented here would perform even better if line break information were available since the alignment would be much more accurate for shorter sequences. Line break information is rarely available and hence using line break information is not practical for real world problems.

7   Conclusion and Future Work

Aligning transcripts to handwritten data is useful for creating training data. We proposed a new HMM based automatic alignment algorithm for aligning word images and transcripts at page level. This outperformed a previously reported algorithm using dynamic time warping. Future improvements may be obtained by using smoothing for the probability estimates or by using better models. Improvements in segmentation may also improve performance.

Acknowledgments

This work was supported in part by the Center for Intelligent Information Retrieval and in part by the National Science Foundation under grant number IIS-9909073.

References

1. Y. Deng and W. Byrne. Hmm word and phrase alignment for statistical machine translation. In *Proceedings of HLT-EMNLP*, 2005.
2. R. Durbin, S. Eddy, A. Krogh, and G. Mitchison. *Biological Sequence Analysis: Probabilistic Models of Proteins and Nucleic Acids*. Cambridge University Press, 2001.
3. J. D. Hobby. Matching document images with ground truth. *International Journal on Document Analysis and Recognition*, 1(1):52–61, 1997.
4. M. Kay and M. Roscheisen. Text-translation alignment. *Computational Linguistics*, 19(1):121–142, March 1993.
5. E. M. Kornfield, R. Manmatha, and J. Allan. Text alignment with handwritten documents. In *Proceedings of Document Image Analysis for Libraries (DIAL)*, pages 23–24, 2004.
6. V. Lavrenko, T. M. Rath, and R. Manmatha. Holistic word recognition for handwritten historical documents. In *Proceedings of the Workshop on Document Image Analysis for Libraries DIAL'04*, pages 278–287, 2004.
7. F. Malfrre, O. Deroo, and T. Dutoit. Phonetic alignment: Speech synthesis based vs. hybrid hmm/ann. In *Proceedings of the ICSLP*, pages 1571–1574, 1998.
8. R. Manmatha and J. L. Rothfeder. A scale space approach for automatically segmenting words from historical handwritten documents. *IEEE Transactions on PAMI*, 28(8):1212–1225, August 2005.
9. R. Manmatha and N. Srimal. Scale space technique for word segmentation in handwritten manuscripts. In *Proc. of the Second Int'l Conf. on Scale-Space Theories in Computer Vision*, pages 22–33, Corfu, Greece, September 26-27 1999.

10. U. V. Marti and H. Bunke. A full English sentence database for off-line handwriting recognition. In *Proc. of the 5th Int. Conf. on Document Analysis and Recognition, Gangalore, India*, pages 705–708, 1999.
11. U.-V. Marti and H. Bunke. Using a statistical language model to improve the performance of an HMM-based cursive handwriting recognition system. *Int'l Journal of Pattern Recognition and Artifical Intelligence*, 15(1):65–90, 2001.
12. P.J.Jang and A. G. Hauptmann. Learning to recognize speech by watching television. *IEEE Intelligent Systems*, 14(5):51–58, 1999.
13. T. M. Rath, V. Lavrenko, and R. Manmatha. A search engine for historical manuscript images. In *Proceedings of ACM SIGIR'04*, pages 369–376, 2004.
14. T. M. Rath, J. L. Rothfeder, and V. B. Lvin. The BoxModify tool, 2004. (Computer program).
15. D. K. Roy and C. Malamud. Speaker identification based text to audio alignment for an audio retrieval system. In *ICASSP '97*, pages 1099–1102, Munich, Germany, 1997.
16. C. I. Tomai, B. Zhang, and V. Govindaraju. Transcript mapping for historic handwritten document images. In *Proc. of the 8th Int'l Workshop on Frontiers in Handwriting Recognition*, pages 413–418, Niagara-on-the-Lake, ON, August 6-8 2002.
17. A. Vinciarelli, S. Bengio, and H. Bunke. Offline recognition of unconstrained handwritten texts using hmms and statistical language models. *IEEE Trans. Pattern Anal. Mach. Intelligence*, 26(6):709–720, 2004.
18. Y. Xu and G.Nagy. Prototype extraction and adaptive ocr. *IEEE Trans. PAMI*, 21(12):1280–1296, December 1999.

Virtual Example Synthesis Based on PCA for Off-Line Handwritten Character Recognition

Hidetoshi Miyao and Minoru Maruyama

Dept. of Information Engineering, Faculty of Engineering,
Shinshu University 4-17-1 Wakasato, Nagano 380-8553, Japan
{miyao, maruyama}@cs.shinshu-u.ac.jp

Abstract. This paper proposes a method to improve off-line character classifiers learned from examples using virtual examples synthesized from an on-line character database. To obtain good classifiers, a large database which contains a large enough number of variations of handwritten characters is usually required. However, in practice, collecting enough data is time-consuming and costly. In this paper, we propose a method to train SVM for off-line character recognition based on artificially augmented examples using on-line characters.

In our method, virtual examples are synthesized from on-line characters by the following two steps: (1) applying affine transformation to each stroke of "real" characters, and (2) applying affine transformation to each stroke of artificial characters, which are synthesized on the basis of PCA. SVM classifiers are trained by using the training samples containing artificially generated patterns and real characters. We examine the effectiveness of the proposed method with respect to the recognition rates and number of support vectors of SVM through experiments involving the handwritten Japanese Hiragana character classification.

1 Introduction

To recognize handwritten characters, classifiers obtained by techniques of learning from examples are often used[4, 11]. Usually, the performance of the classifiers strongly depends on the quality of the training examples. If a large database which includes almost every possible variation of handwritten patterns is provided, the classifiers learned from the database are likely to perform quite well. However, in practice, collecting a sufficient number of *good* examples is not easy. It is usually costly and time-consuming. Learning algorithms often lack training examples that incorporate enough variations of handwriting. One possible method to overcome this difficulty is to synthesize virtual examples from a small number of real examples [5, 7, 9, 10, 13]. The simplest approach to synthesize training examples appears to be to apply geometrical transformations, such as the affine transform, to character images (i.e., the simple perturbation method[2]). Although this method is effective, an off-line character often lacks information on how it is written. Thus, it is often difficult to generate a set of artificial patterns which contains enough variations of handwriting from the

H. Bunke and A.L. Spitz (Eds.): DAS 2006, LNCS 3872, pp. 96–105, 2006.

character images. If on-line character data is available, the information on strokes can be utilized to synthesize virtual examples for off-line recognition[9, 10, 13].

In our previous paper[13], training examples for SVM classifiers were synthesized by applying the affine transform to each stroke of real training samples, and SVMs were learned on the basis of the generated patterns. Compared to the simple character-wise perturbation, the recognition rate was improved by this method. In this method, artificial patterns are generated on the basis of given specific character samples. When the number of samples is very small, it is likely that augmented patterns cannot efficiently cover the space of every possible character pattern. To overcome this difficulty, we tried to build a model of character patterns and then create virtual character patterns that can be used as "seeds" for pattern synthesis based on the affine transform. To build the character-generation model, DP-based character matching is carried out. Then, from the set of resultant difference vectors, the character generation model is built through the Principle Component Analysis (PCA) technique. To improve the performance of classifiers, SVMs are learned on the basis of the patterns which are generated by the proposed method. We examine the effectiveness of the proposed method through experiments involving the handwritten Japanese Hiragana character classification.

2 Generation of Virtual Examples in the Previous Work

In this chapter, we briefly review our previous method[13].

In our method, we use an on-line character database that contains stroke information to generate artificial character patterns for off-line classification [1, 9, 10]. In the on-line database, we assume that each character is divided into strokes, each of which is a connected component from pen-down to pen-up. We also assume that each stroke is represented as a sequence of 2D coordinates of pen positions. Most Japanese Hiragana characters consist of several strokes.

In our previous work, we simply applied the following affine transformation to each point of a stroke.

$$\mathbf{x}' = \bar{\mathbf{x}} + A(\mathbf{x} - \bar{\mathbf{x}}) + \mathbf{t}, \tag{1}$$

where $\mathbf{t} = (t_x, t_y)^T$ is the translation and $\bar{\mathbf{x}}$ is the center of the bounding box of the stroke. A 2×2 matrix A is given as the product of a shear matrix S and a rotation matrix R

$$A = A(\theta, \varepsilon_x, \varepsilon_y) = R(\theta)S(\varepsilon_x, \varepsilon_y), \tag{2}$$

where $R(\theta)$ and $S(\varepsilon_x, \varepsilon_y)$ are given by

$$S(\varepsilon_x, \varepsilon_y) = \begin{pmatrix} 1 & \varepsilon_x \\ \varepsilon_y & 1 \end{pmatrix}, \quad R(\theta) = \begin{pmatrix} \cos\theta & -\sin\theta \\ \sin\theta & \cos\theta \end{pmatrix}. \tag{3}$$

The transformation in (1) is specified by 5 parameters $(t_x, t_y, \theta, \varepsilon_x, \varepsilon_y)$. They are given uniformly at random for each stroke. After transforming 2D coordinates of strokes, a character image is generated through line thickening.

3   Virtual Example Synthesis Based on PCA

For a character class c, suppose that the number of real on-line samples is $K_c + 1$. One character sample is selected from the real samples as the base sample. The point sequence on the base sample is represented by $\{\mathbf{a}_{c,i} \mid \mathbf{a}_{c,i} = (x^b_{c,i}, y^b_{c,i})^T - \mathbf{P}^b_c, i = 1 \cdots I_c\}$, where $\mathbf{P}^b_c$ is the center position of the bounding box of the base sample. The point sequence on the other K_c real samples is represented by $\{\mathbf{b}^k_{c,j} \mid \mathbf{b}^k_{c,j} = (x^k_{c,j}, y^k_{c,j})^T - \mathbf{P}^k_c, j = 1 \cdots J^k_c, 1 \le k \le K_c\}$, where $\mathbf{P}^k_c$ is the center position of the bounding box of the kth sample. If two point sequences $\{\mathbf{a}_{c,1}, \mathbf{a}_{c,2}, \cdots, \mathbf{a}_{c,i}\}$ and $\{\mathbf{b}^k_{c,1}, \mathbf{b}^k_{c,2}, \cdots, \mathbf{b}^k_{c,j}\}$, are optimally matched, the accumulated distance $g(i, j)$ at DP is calculated by the following expression:

Initial value:

$$\begin{cases} g(i,1) = d(\mathbf{a}_{c,1}, \mathbf{b}^k_{c,1}) + d(\mathbf{a}_{c,2}, \mathbf{b}^k_{c,1}) + \cdots + d(\mathbf{a}_{c,i}, \mathbf{b}^k_{c,1}), & for\ 1 \le i \le I_c \\ g(1,j) = d(\mathbf{a}_{c,1}, \mathbf{b}^k_{c,1}) + d(\mathbf{a}_{c,1}, \mathbf{b}^k_{c,2}) + \cdots + d(\mathbf{a}_{c,1}, \mathbf{b}^k_{c,j}), & for\ 1 \le j \le J^k_c \end{cases} \quad (4)$$

Recurrence formula:

$$g(i,j) = d(\mathbf{a}_{c,i}, \mathbf{b}^k_{c,j}) + min \begin{cases} g(i-1, j-1), \\ g(i-1, j), \\ g(i, j-1), \end{cases} \quad (5)$$

where $d(\mathbf{a}_{c,i}, \mathbf{b}^k_{c,j})$ is the distance between two points, $\mathbf{a}_{c,i}$ and $\mathbf{b}^k_{c,j}$.

Optimal point sequence matching can be attained by calculating the minimum accumulated distance $g(I_c, J^k_c)$ between two patterns and backtracking the path obtained. In this way, we can obtain the corresponding point $\mathbf{b}^k_{c,j(i)}$ for the point $\mathbf{a}_{c,i}$, where $j(1), ..., j(I_c)$ represents the corresponding state between the two patterns. In Figure 1, we show an example of matching results.

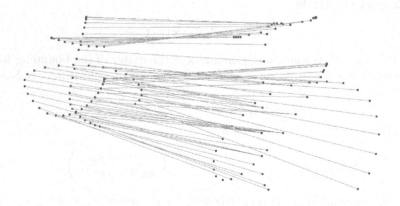

Fig. 1. Example of matching results for a point sequence on two patterns

The average difference vector between the base sample and the kth sample is given by

$$\mathbf{v}_{c,k} = (\; x^k_{c,j(1)} - x^b_{c,1} - \bar{x}_{c,1},\; y^k_{c,j(1)} - y^b_{c,1} - \bar{y}_{c,1}, \cdots,$$
$$x^k_{c,j(i)} - x^b_{c,i} - \bar{x}_{c,i},\; y^k_{c,j(i)} - y^b_{c,i} - \bar{y}_{c,i}, \cdots, \tag{6}$$
$$x^k_{c,j(I_c)} - x^b_{c,I_c} - \bar{x}_{c,I_c},\; y^k_{c,j(I_c)} - y^b_{c,I_c} - \bar{y}_{c,I_c})^T,$$

where

$$\begin{cases} \bar{x}_{c,i} = \dfrac{1}{K_c} \displaystyle\sum_{k=1}^{K_c} (x^k_{c,j(i)} - x^b_{c,i}), \\[2mm] \bar{y}_{c,i} = \dfrac{1}{K_c} \displaystyle\sum_{k=1}^{K_c} (y^k_{c,j(i)} - y^b_{c,i}). \end{cases} \tag{7}$$

We apply PCA to K_c difference vectors $\mathbf{v}_{c,k}$ and obtain eigen vectors $\{\mathbf{u}_{c,1}, \cdots, \mathbf{u}_{c,m}, \cdots, \mathbf{u}_{c,M}\}$ and eigen values $\{\lambda_{c,1}, \cdots, \lambda_{c,m}, \cdots, \lambda_{c,M} \mid \lambda_{c,1} \geq \lambda_{c,2} \geq \cdots \geq \lambda_{c,M} \geq 0\}$. Using the m-largest eigen values and corresponding eigen vectors, the following pattern generation model is obtained:

$$\hat{\mathbf{a}}_{c,m}(\alpha_1, \cdots, \alpha_m) = (\; x^b_{c,1} + \bar{x}_{c,1}, y^b_{c,1} + \bar{y}_{c,1}, \cdots, x^b_{c,I_c} + \bar{x}_{c,I_c}, y^b_{c,I_c} + \bar{y}_{c,I_c})^T$$
$$+ \sum_{n=1}^{m} \alpha_n \mathbf{u}_{c,n} \quad (m \ll M), \tag{8}$$

where α_n represents a normal random variable, $(\alpha_n \sim N(0, \lambda_{c,n}))$. By using this model, we can generate artificial patterns. Examples of generated patterns are shown in Figure 2.

In our method, virtual examples are synthesized by applying the affine transformation described in Chapter 2 to each stroke of the generated patterns.

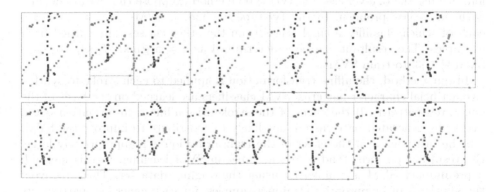

Fig. 2. Examples of patterns generated through the PCA technique (m = 3 in Eq.(8))

4 SVM Learning by Using Virtual Examples

In this chapter, we describe a method to learn SVM by using virtual examples which are generated by the methods described in Chapters 2 and 3. This is based on the method proposed by Miyao et al.[13].

For handwritten Hiragana recognition, we use SVM. SVM is a learning method based on the margin-maximization principle. SVM performs a binary classification by finding the optimal separating hyperplane in the feature space. Suppose that a set of training examples, $\{(\mathbf{x}_i, y_i)\}_{i=1}^N$ $y_i \in \{-1, 1\}$, is given; the SVM classifies the input $\mathbf{x}$ based on the function

$$f(\mathbf{x}) = \sum_{i=1}^{N} \alpha_i y_i K(\mathbf{x}, \mathbf{x}_i) - b \qquad (9)$$

where $K(\mathbf{x}, \mathbf{y})$ is a kernel function which defines the inner product in the feature space. The coefficients α_is are non-zero only for the subset of the input data called support vectors.

The performance of SVM depends on the kernel. We use the RBF (Gaussian) kernel, which outperformed other commonly used kernels in preliminary experiments. The Gaussian kernel is given as

$$K(\mathbf{x}, \mathbf{y}) = \exp(-\|\mathbf{x} - \mathbf{y}\|^2 / 2\sigma^2) \qquad (10)$$

In our work, as an input to the RBF, we used directional feature patterns that have been commonly and successfully used for handwritten character recognition[6]. Each image is normalized to 64×64 pixels. Then, the contour of the normalized image is partitioned into 8×8 blocks. Four patterns emphasizing four directions (vertical, horizontal, left slant and right slant) at every block are detected. As a result, 256 features ($8 \times 8 \times 4$) are extracted. They are treated as components of a 256-dimensional feature vector.

To apply SVM (binary classifier) to a multiclass character recognition problem, we use the one-versus-rest (1vr)-type method. Suppose that we are dealing with an n-class problem. In the 1vr-type method, n SVMs f_i ($i = 1, \cdots, n$), each of which classifies a single class from the other classes, are learned from examples. The resultant class c is determined as $c = \arg\max_i f_i(\mathbf{x})$. We used SVM^{light} [3] to train SVMs.

In our method, the affine transformation is applied to each stroke to synthesize artificial character patterns. SVM classifiers are learned on the basis of the generated patterns. If the effect of the stroke-wise affine transformation is too little, the generated patterns are not likely to contribute to improve the SVM. On the other hand, if the effect of the transformation is inappropriately large, the resultant patterns tend to act as *noise* in SVM learning. In this method, a preliminary SVM is trained by using the original data set. Then, to avoid the synthesis of inappropriate training samples, for each generated pattern, its *effectiveness* is examined by the absolute value of the SVM output. After this data selection process, using the augmented training samples, the final SVM is trained.

5   Experimental Results

To examine the effectiveness of the proposed method, classification experiments were carried out. In the experiments, we used the character database **HANDS-nakayosi_t-98-09**[12]. We selected the 10 Japanese Hiragana characters shown in Figure 3 and trained 1vr-type SVMs. A character data set written by 50 people was used for training. Another data set written by another 50 people was used for testing. For the performance test of the classifiers, 500 patterns for each character class were used.

For each class, the seeds were 50 real handwritten training samples and 50 samples generated according to (8) based on the real samples. Virtual examples were synthesized by applying the affine transformation to the 100 seeds. The parameters of the transformation $(t_x, t_y, \theta, \varepsilon_x, \varepsilon_y)$ used in the experiment were

$$|t_x|, |t_y| < 30, \quad |\theta| < 5(\text{degree}), \quad |\varepsilon_x|, |\varepsilon_y| < 0.3.$$

The training samples for the learning SVMs consist of the seeds and the virtual examples.

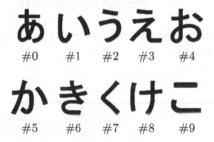

#0   #1   #2   #3   #4

#5   #6   #7   #8   #9

Fig. 3. Target Japanese Hiragana characters

Figure 4 shows a comparison of the recognition rates of SVMs trained using training samples based on a different number of eigen vectors m in (8). In this figure, 'without PCA' represents the results of the SVMs trained by using only real samples and virtual examples synthesized by applying the affine transformation to the real samples (i.e., this is the result for the traditional method[13]). This figure shows that the recognition rates of the proposed method for $m = 5$ are almost the same as those of the SVMs trained with real samples.

Our pattern generation method described in (8) depends on the choice of the base sample. The selection of the base sample may have an effect on the overall performance of the SVMs. To restrict the influence due to the selection of the base sample, we tried to increase the number of base samples. In the experiments, 5 base samples were taken from 50 real training samples, 10 seeds were generated from each base sample through PCA, and a total of 50 seeds were generated. The recognition results using SVMs trained by them are shown in Figure 5. This shows that the recognition rates with $m = 3$ for the proposed method outperformed the traditional method.

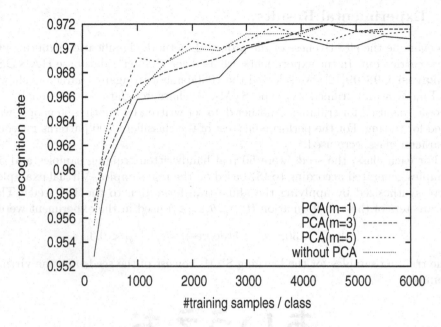

Fig. 4. Comparison of the recognition rates of SVMs trained using training samples based on different m in Eq. (8)

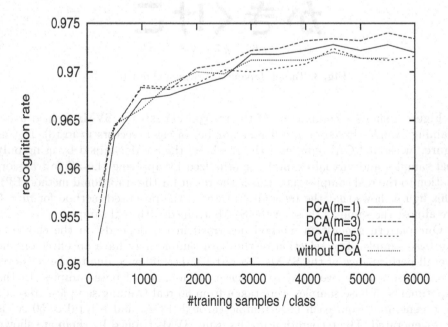

Fig. 5. Recognition rates of SVMs using seeds generated from 5 base samples

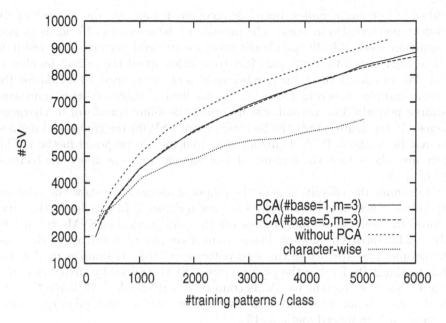

Fig. 6. Relationship between #training samples and #SV

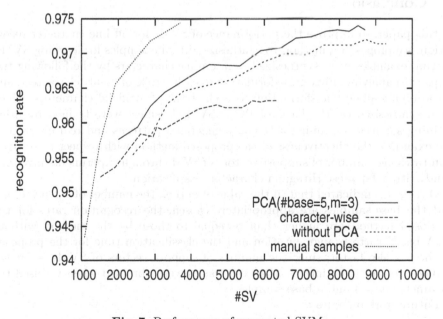

Fig. 7. Performance of generated SVMs

We have shown that the recognition rate of the SVM can be improved by using the artificially generated training samples. Usually, with an increase in the number of training samples, both the recognition rate and the number of SV (support vectors) also increase. The increase of the number of SV leads to slow recognition speed. Ideally we should generate artificial patterns that result in both a high recognition rate and fast recognition speed (i.e., small number of SVs). We examined the total number of SVs of the trained 10 SVMs for the training samples shown in Figure 6. In this figure, 'character-wise' represents a simple perturbation method which applies the affine transform to character images. As the figure shows, the increase rate of #SV for the traditional method denoted by 'without PCA' is higher than that for the proposed method. This figure also shows that the number of base sample does not affect the increase rate of #SV.

To examine the effectiveness of the proposed method, we show the relationship between #SV and the recognition rates in Figure 7. In this figure, the curve denoted by 'manual samples' represents the performance of SVMs trained by only real handwritten samples. These training samples were written by the same (50) people, who also wrote the seed patterns of artificial samples used in the other methods. Preferably, the performance of SVMs trained by virtual examples should come close to that by SVMs trained by real samples. Although the proposed method is not satisfactory, the figure shows that our method outperformes the previously proposed method [13].

6   Conclusion

In this paper, to improve the performance of SVMs for off-line character recognition, we proposed a method to synthesize virtual examples for learning SVMs. Virtual examples were synthesized from on-line characters by the following two steps : (1) applying affine transformation to each stroke of "real" characters, and (2) applying affine transformation to each stroke of artificial characters, which were synthesized on the basis of PCA. SVM classifiers were trained by using training samples containing artificially generated patterns and real characters. We examined the effectiveness of the proposed method with respect to recognition rates and number of support vectors of SVM through experiments involving handwritten Japanese Hiragana character classification.

Our results indicated that, if the value of m (i.e., the number of eigen vectors) and the base samples are appropriately chosen, the recognition rates for the proposed method are higher than or equal to those by the method without PCA-based pattern augmentation and the classification time for the proposed method is also faster, since the number of support vectors of SVMs is further reduced. In our experiments, the best results were obtained when we used the parameter $m = 3$ and 5 base samples.

Future work includes :

- Determining why this method can reduce the number of support vectors more than the method without PCA.
- Designing a method to choose an appropriate number of eigen vectors (i.e. m) and the base samples so that SVM can have higher performance.

References

1. D.Ghosh and A.P.Shibaprasad, "An analytic approach for generation of artificial hand-printed character database from given generative models", Pattern Recognition, Vol.32, pp. 907 – 920 (1999).
2. T.M.Ha and H.Bunke, "Off-line, handwritten numeral recognition by perturbation method", IEEE Trans. PAMI, Vol. 19, No. 5, pp. 535 – 539 (1997).
3. T.Joachims, "Making large-scale SVM learning practical", In *Advances in kernel methods*, Chapter 11, MIT Press (1999).
4. K.Maruyama, M.Maruyama, H.Miyao and Y.Nakano, "A method to make multiple hypotheses with high cumulative recognition rate using SVMs", Pattern Recognition, Vol. 37,No. 2, pp. 241–251 (2004).
5. E.Miller, N.Matsakis and P.Viola, "Learning from one example through shared densities on transformation", Proc. CVPR2000, Vol.1, pp.464–471 (2000).
6. S. Mori, C. Y. Suen and K. Yamamoto, "Historical review of OCR research and development", Proc. IEEE, Vol.80, No.7, pp.1029–1058 (1992).
7. P.Niyogi, F.Girosi, and T.Poggio, "Incorporating prior knowledge in machine learning by creating virtual examples", Proc. IEEE, Vol.86, No.11, pp.2196 – 2207 (1998).
8. V.Vapnik, "Statistical Learning Theory", Wiley, New York (1998).
9. O.Velek, C.-L. Lieu, S.Jaeger and M.Nakagawa, "An improved approach to generating realistic Kanji character images from on-line characters and its benefit to off-line recognition performance" Proc. ICPR 2002, Vol.1, pp. 588 – 591 (2002).
10. O.Velek, S.Jaeger and M.Nakagawa, "A new warping technique for normalizing likelihood of multiple classifiers and its effectiveness in combined on-line/off-line Japanese character recognition", Proc. IWFHR 2002, pp. 177 – 182 (2002).
11. R. Schölkopf and A.J.Smola, "Learning with Kernels", The MIT Press (2002).
12. http://www.tuat.ac.jp/~nakagawa/ipdb/
13. H.Miyao, M.Maruyama, Y.Nakano and T. Hananoi, "Off-Line Handwritten Character Recognition by SVM based on the Virtual Examples Synthesized from On-Line Characters" Proc. ICDAR 2005, Vol.1, pp. 494 – 498 (2005).

Extraction of Handwritten Text from Carbon Copy Medical Form Images

Robert Milewski and Venu Govindaraju

University at Buffalo,
Center of Excellence for Document Analysis and Recognition,
520 Lee Entrance, UB Commons Suite 202,
Amherst NY 14228
{milewski, govind}@cedar.buffalo.edu

Abstract. This paper presents a methodology for separating handwritten foreground pixels, from background pixels, in carbon copied medical forms. Comparisons between prior and proposed techniques are illustrated. This study involves the analysis of the New York State (NYS) Department of Health (DoH) Pre-Hospital Care Report (PCR) [1] which is a standard form used in New York by all Basic and Advanced Life Support pre-hospital healthcare professionals to document patient status in the emergency environment. The forms suffer from extreme carbon mesh noise, varying handwriting pressure sensitivity issues, and smudging which are further complicated by the writing environment. Extraction of handwriting from these medical forms is a vital step in automating emergency medical health surveillance systems.

1 Introduction

This research evaluates several algorithms which extract handwriting from medical form images (see Figure 1) to eventually provide the best handwriting recognition performance. The research copy of the NYS PCR [1] is a yellow-gray carbon mesh where both the handwriting and the mesh around the handwriting have approximately the same intensity. While the density and connectedness of handwriting is heavier then the mesh residue surrounding the handwriting, pressure sensitivity issues can affect the differentiation between the handwriting stroke and the background. The absence of sufficient pen pressure while writing leads to the loss of character information in the carbon copy. This causes character strokes to break after binarization which leads to recognition failures. Prior binarization algorithms have been reported to handle noisy and complicated surfaces [6][10][12]. However, the broken/unnatural handwriting due to ambulance movement and emergency environments, and carbon smearing from unintentional pressure to the form add further complexity to the binarization task. A lexicon driven word recognizer (LDWR) [13] is used for evaluation of the binarization methods. Analysis of the LDWR, as well as a full view of an actual NYS PCR image, can be found in [5].

Section 2 presents an examination of the carbon mesh paper image. Section 3 discusses the results of prior work on the medical forms. Section 4 proposes a new

H. Bunke and A.L. Spitz (Eds.): DAS 2006, LNCS 3872, pp. 106–116, 2006.

strategy for the handwriting foreground extraction. Section 5 compares all algorithms using the LDWR [13]. Section 6 summarizes the findings of this work.

2   Carbon Paper Image

Figure 1 shows an example of the "Objective Assessment" region of the NYS PCR form. It provides an overview of the complex nature of the handwriting on the carbon paper. Figure 2 shows a 400% zoom of one word from Figure 1. It shows the carbon paper mesh integrated with the carbon handwriting stroke. The displayed word *ABD*, in Figure 2, is a common abbreviation for *abdomen*. Since both the background paper and the handwriting are affected by the carbon paper, both the foreground and some parts of the background have identical intensities. This causes many binarization algorithms, which rely on thresholding small areas of the document to fail. The details of these failures are discussed in the following sections. This paper presents an algorithm for binarizing the handwriting on carbon paper while preserving the handwriting stroke connectivity better then the prior algorithms. The inconsistent carbon paper, which shows varying grayscale intensities (see Figures 1 and 2), is referred to as *carbon mesh*.

Pressure sensitivity issues, as a result of light strokes in penmanship, affects the extent to which character connectivity is maintained after binarization. In order for the carbon copy to receive a reasonable representation of the top copy original, the healthcare professional needs to press down firmly with the writing instrument. Since the emergency environment is not conducive to good penmanship, the binarization and cleanup algorithms need to compensate.

Fig. 1. NYS PCR Object Physical Assessment Example

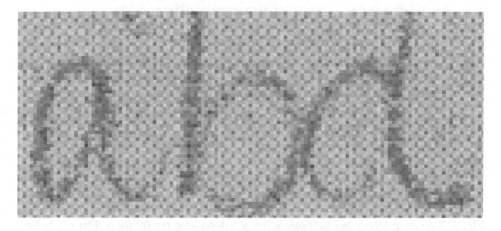

Fig. 2. Grayscale 256 Carbon Mesh Handwriting Example (400% Zoom)

The carbon paper forms also contain guide lines which often interfere with the character strokes. These lines can be detected by those pixels with a grayscale value less then 40; this is consistent across all forms. To reduce stroke fragmentation, it is sufficient to retain the pixels near the line thus keeping most character ascenders and descenders reasonably connected. This form drop out step is performed before binarization.

3 Prior Work

In this section, methods previously described in the literature are compared with the algorithm presented in this paper.

Gaussian, median and mean filtering/smoothing are often used as a base step or an integrated step for noise removal and image enhancement [2][11][18][21]. Mean filter (Figure 3b), shows the least damage to strokes. Median filter (Figure 3c) shows severe character damage. Gaussian Filter (Figure 3d) shows the characters being washed into the background.

Global thresholding algorithms determine a single threshold and apply it to the entire image. In the PCR application, the high pressure sensitive areas are binarized well, whereas medium to low pressure areas run the risk of being classified as background.

Many authors have cited and shown superiority over the Otsu [8][24] algorithm. Since a global threshold is computed, the background paper in many areas of the document merge with the foreground pixels. The Wu/Manmatha [12] method expects at least two histogram intensity peaks. The PCR handwriting strokes have intensities that are the same as the background image with equivalent frequency. This causes large portions of the handwriting to be lost to the background, rendering this technique ineffective.

The Niblack binarization [22] algorithm is an adaptive technique which has been used and compared in many applications such as image and video text detection and

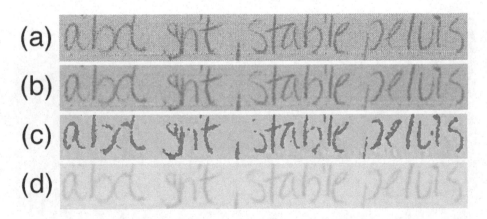

Fig. 3. Smoothing Operations (a) original image + form drop out (b) mean filter (c) median filter (d) Gaussian filter

extraction [7], low quality camera images [9], low quality grayscale utility maps (such as cable and hydro maps with various intensity and noise issues [18]), and low quality historical documents [3]. This algorithm resulted in severe noise, jagged edges and broken character segments. While post-processing improves the algorithm performance substantially, the broken character strokes resulted in lower performance.

Sauvola binarization [14] is a modification of the Niblack algorithm [22] which attempts to suppress noisy areas. Gatos [3] introduced an algorithm which outperformed both Niblack [22] and Sauvola [14]. The Gatos method illustrated that the Sauvola method removed more noise than the Niblack on low quality historical documents. This indicated the potential for the Sauvola method to handle the noise found on the PCR forms. Experimental results in the following sections found the Sauvola method performed better than the Niblack (depending on lexicon size), especially before post-processing.

Logical binarization uses heuristics for evaluating whether a pixel belongs to the foreground or background. It is also common to integrate other adaptive binarization strategies with such heuristics. The Kamel/Zhao algorithm [19] is a logical algorithm which finds stroke locations and then later removes the noise in the non-stroke areas using an interpolation and thresholding step. Various stroke width combinations from 1-10 pixels were tried. However, this algorithm would often classify the stroke as the background thereby making it ineffective.

The Yang/Yan [10] algorithm is a variant of the Kamel/Zhao [19] algorithm. The modifications are to handle low quality images affected by varying intensity, illumination, and artifacts, such as smearing. However, the run analysis step in this algorithm is computed using only black pixels. Neither the foreground or background of the carbon copy medical forms have black pixels; nor are the foreground pixels the same throughout. While both the background and foreground carbon have the same intensities on a specific form, this is not universal. Therefore, the stroke width computation, which is dependent on the run length computation of black or any other specific pixel intensity range, cannot be determined with the carbon paper forms.

In addition to the binarization algorithms, various post-processing strategies are used. The despeckel algorithm is a 3x3 mask which removes a foreground pixel that has no D8 neighbors [11]. The blob removal algorithm is a 9x9 mask which removes small pixel regions that have no neighbors [11]. The Niblack [22] + Yanowitz and Bruckstein method [21] was found to be the best combination strategy here [18]. The Shi and Govindaraju is an image enhancement strategy which has been used on postal mailpieces [17].

4 Proposed Algorithm

4.1 Methodology

Prior algorithms have relied on techniques such as histogram analysis, edge detection, and local measurements. However, these techniques are less effective (see section 5). This motivated the proposed algorithm to use a larger central NxN mask, which determined the intensity of one region, and compare it with the intensities of multiple dynamically moving smaller PxP regions (see Figures 4 and 5).

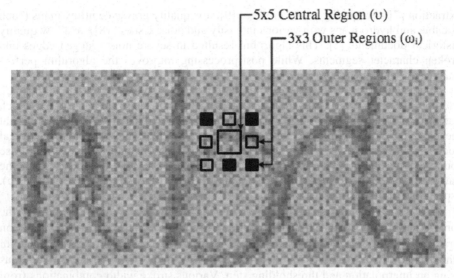

A (ω_i) region which has a lighter mean intensity then (υ)

A (ω_i) region which has a darker mean intensity then (υ)

Fig. 4. Initial Mask Placement Example (N=5 and P=3)

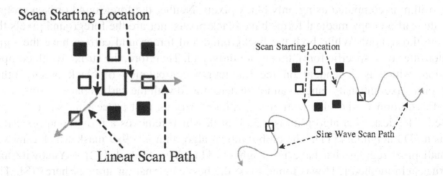

Fig. 5. Scanning Approaches: Linear and Sine Wave

One hypothesis in managing the varying intensities of the carbon mesh and its similarity with the stroke, was to use a wave trajectory for the D8 positioned masks, as opposed to a linear trajectory (see Figure 5). The experiments show that the use of a wave is beneficial for four reasons: (i) the notion of evading a stroke, (ii) finding a background region as close as possible to the central mask (note that the further out from the center mask, the more likely that the carbon mesh of the background can change), (iii) that the best background region to compare to a handwriting stroke may or may not be the edge of the stroke, and (iv) areas surrounding a stroke, in the same trajectory, can be observed. With the inclusion of a stopping condition, our approach does not behave like confined square mask windows, which are relative to a central position, as other global and adaptive approaches pursue. In this context, the wave trajectory for scanning can be thought of as searching for lighter pockets in the intensity fluctuation of the carbon mesh (see Figures 4 and 5).

A sine wave trajectory offers the benefit of beginning at the origin and allowing a continuous trajectory regardless of distance. It allows the control of frequency and amplitude which are necessary to adjust for stroke width. Sinusoidal waves have been used in other contexts for the modeling of human motor function for on-line handwriting recognition feature extraction and segmentation [15], shape normalization of Chinese characters [4], and signal canceling of pathological tremors while writing [16]. Based on these studies, and the knowledge of the English character set, it was possible to scan out from a character stroke, at a certain frequency, allowing a handwriting stroke to be maneuvered, as opposed to traced, in the search for background regions. The sine trajectory can be thought of as a path which continually crosses the handwritten strokes. This allows the background paper on both sides of the stroke, in all directions, and with a dynamic distance, to be evaluated. Intuitively, more space can be searched and both sides of the stroke can be evaluated in the same computational step at variable distances. It is also presumed that in a moving ambulance, carbon smearing is more likely since the writer will press their hand harder to maintain balance in the vehicle. While strokes in the English language contain both curves and straight lines, at the pixel level, they can be considered piecewise linear movements such that a linear scan will trace the stroke and reduce the likelihood of finding the background. Furthermore, holistic features, such as the area in the letter "D", are typically small, and missing the carbon paper inside of such character holes may result in missed background analysis. This motivated the use of a higher sine wave frequency so that the trajectory would pass through the center of holistic features as frequently as possible. Additionally, since the thickness of characters fluctuate, it is difficult to precisely calculate the true stroke width.

4.2 Algorithm

An input grayscale image 0 (black) to 255 (white) is the input and a binarized image is the output. At a given position on the image, there are 9 masks. A single mask is denoted as Ξ. The mean intensity of a single mask is denoted by $M(\Xi)$. The central mask which slides across the image is denoted by (υ) and has a size NxN, such that N ≥ 3 and is odd (e.g. 3x3, 5x5, and 7x7). The size of (υ) is based on the estimated stroke width constant denoted by ϕ. The value of ϕ has been estimated to be 5 pixels, therefore (υ) is of size 5x5. At each (υ) position over the image, 8 masks are initially stationed in each D8 position (Figure 4) and are denoted by ω_i where $1 \leq i \leq 8$. The mask size of (ω_i) is PxP such that $3 \leq P \leq \lceil N/2 \rceil$. Note that $P \leq \lceil N/2 \rceil$ allowing a small mask the opportunity of preserving small holistic features, when moving on the sine curve, while also making sure that the mask will not overlap (υ). Each (ω_i) is initially stationed as close to (υ) as possible so as to avoid the mask overlapping between (ω_i) and (υ). Each (ω_i) moves in its respective D8 direction, either linearly (see Figure 5) or via a sinusoidal wave (see Figure 5). The $M(\omega_i)$ is computed at each position along the trajectory and stops at a position after one cycle and when the current average is less then the previous average on the sine trajectory. A list of mean values, for each position on that trajectory, are denoted by $M(\omega_i)_q$ where q is a coordinate on the sine curve. The minimum mean value for one trajectory is represented by the equation

$M(\omega_i)_{min} = min(M(\omega_i)_{\forall_q})$. Next, a comparison of all the D8 $M(\omega_i)_{min}$ positions are made against $M(\upsilon)$. If there are at least 3-4 (empirically determined) out of 8 of the $M(\omega_i)_{min}$ values which satisfy the equation $|M(\upsilon) - M(\omega_i)_{min}| \geq \kappa$, such that κ is a small constant (we use $\kappa = 10$), then the center pixel of (υ) is classified as a foreground pixel. The value κ defines a tolerance with respect to the intensity fluctuation of the carbon paper and is denoted the *carbon intensity similarity rule*. It is assumed that the new image has been initialized to white background pixels, therefore, it is only necessary to mark the foreground pixels when they are found. A dynamic programming step is used to store each $M(\omega_i)$, corresponding to the appropriate region on the image, to improve the runtime performance.

The sinusoidal path is defined by equation (1).

$$y = 2\phi \sin(\tfrac{1}{2} x) \tag{1}$$

The coordinate (x, y), on a sinusoidal trajectory, is relative to its starting location (origin). A nearest neighbor approach is sufficient for conversion of real coordinates to integer coordinates. Each ω_i is computed on the sine curve trajectory (see Figures 4 and 5). Note that using ϕ amplitude value in equation (1), without the coefficient, will result in a distance of 2ϕ between the highest and lowest y-axis points (ϕ is the stroke width). It is further beneficial to use 2ϕ as the amplitude, yielding a distance of 4ϕ, to account for the possibility of 2 touching strokes (e.g. two touching letters). This places a reasonable guarantee that the curve will efficiently exit a stroke while searching for the background. The constant $\frac{1}{2}$ is used in equation (1) so that the sine frequency does not trace the handwritten stroke.

5   Experimental Results

All tests were performed on 30 PCR's comprising of 1,440 word images and various size lexicons (identified in the LEX column of the tables 1 and 2) using the LDWR handwriting word recognition engine [13]. The linear strategy was outperformed by the Otsu [24] method and a despeckel. However, our technique outperformed all algorithm combinations.

The table columns are abbreviated as follows: (W)u/Manmatha, (K)amel/Zhao, (N)iblack, (S)auvola, (O)tsu, and (SW) for our sine wave approach.

Table 1 Shows the performance of the binarization algorithms without postprocessing. Our algorithm has 9-21% improvement, with various lexicon sizes, over Otsu [24].

Table 1. Binarization Performance (Figure 7)

LEX	W	K	N	S	O	SW
100	3.1%	4.6%	< 1%	19.4%	35.3%	56.5%
1K	< 1%	1.5%	0.0%	10.1%	17.1%	26.9%
4K	0.0%	0.0%	0.0%	4.4%	11.2%	20.3%

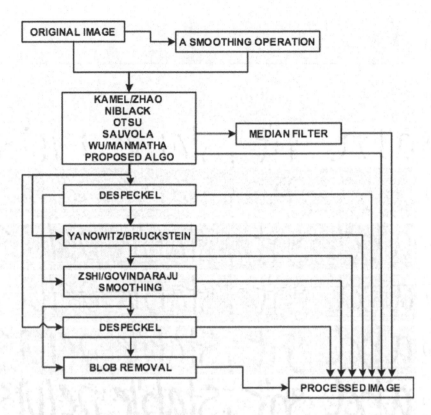

Fig. 6. Image Processing Combinations

Table 2. Combination Performance (Figure 8)

LEX	W	K	N	S	O	SW
100	3.1%	4.6%	46.9%	48.3%	52.6%	59.1%
1K	< 1%	1.5%	26.0%	26.4%	36.1%	40.1%
4K	0.0%	0.0%	17.8%	12.7%	21.2%	25.3%

Figure 7 shows the output of the aforementioned binarization strategies with no post-processing support. The handwriting phrase, from NYS PCR medical form, "abd snt, stable pelvis" means *abdominal soft-not-tender, stable pelvis*. Figure 7e contains heavier noise that is not removed by the LDWR algorithm's pre-processing step, whereas Figures 7f and 7g have noise which is less severe and therefore more easily removed.

Table 2 Shows performance of the binarization algorithms with their best respective post-processing combination from Figure 6. The proposed algorithm + despeckel + blob removal offers 4-7% improvement, with various lexicon sizes, over Otsu [24] + Despeckel.

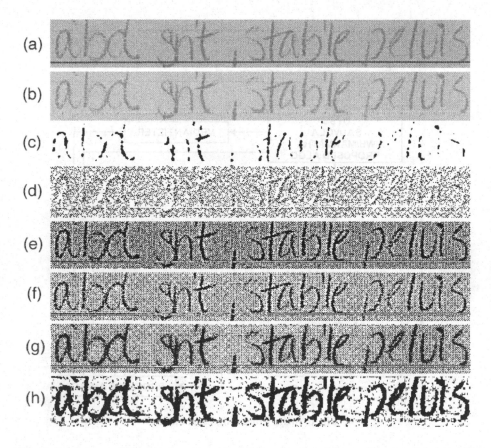

Fig. 7. Comparison of Binarization Algorithms Only: (a) original image (b) original image with form drop out (c) Wu/Manmatha Binarization (d) Kamel/Zhao Binarization (e) Niblack Binarization (f) Sauvola Binarization (g) Otsu Binarization (h) Sine Wave Binarization

Figure 8 shows the output of the aforementioned binarization strategies with each algorithms best post-processing combination.

The percentages in all result tables neglect accept/reject rates due to the complex nature of medical handwriting. The percentages reflect the output of the recognizer, regardless of confidence. Recognizer accept and reject analysis will be included in the handwriting recognition algorithms of future work. Words in the form region were manually segmented by a human. Future research will include the analysis of automated segmentation as well. Stopwords were omitted from both the recognizer lexicon and word images from the form. In addition, the LDWR algorithm uses pre-processing strategies for its own noise removal and smoothing before executing its recognition algorithm [13][20][23]. Therefore, a noisy image submitted to the LDWR algorithm will be internally pre-processed by the handwriting recognizer.

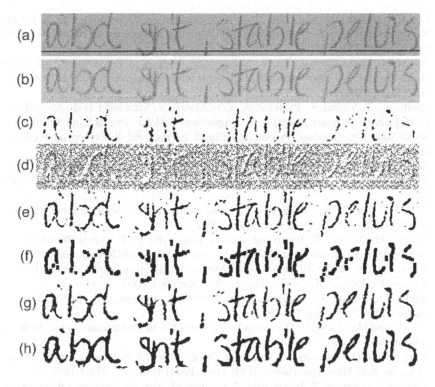

Fig. 8. Comparison of Binarization Algorithms with their Best Post-Processing Strategy: (a) original image (b) original image with form drop out (c) Wu/Manmatha Binarization + unassisted (d) Kamel/Zhao Binarization + unassisted (e) Niblack Binarization + Despeckel (f) Sauvola Binarization + Despeckel + Shi/Govindaraju Region Smoothing (g) Otsu Binarization + Despeckel (h) Sine Wave Binarization + Despeckel + Blob Removal

6 Conclusions

In this paper we describe a binarization algorithm for handling carbon paper medical documents. Improvements of approximately 9-21% (using various lexicon sizes) are obtained over prior binarization algorithms. Approximately 4-7% improvement is obtained using post-processing.

References

1. Western Regional Emergency Medical Services. Bureau of Emergency Medical Services. New York State (NYS) Department of Health (DoH). Prehospital Care Report v4.
2. Hatami, Safar., Hosseini, R., Kamarei, M., Ahmadi, H. Wavelet Based Fingerprint Image Enhancement. IEEE International Symposium on Circuits and Systems (ISCAS). C2005.
3. Gatos, B., Pratikakis, I., Perantonis, S.J. An Adaptive Binarization Technique for Low Quality Historical Documents. 6th International Conference on Document Analysis Systems (DAS). C2004.

4. Liu, C.L., Marukawa, K. Global Shape Normalization for Handwritten Chinese Character Recognition: A New Method. International Workshop on Frontiers of Handwriting Recognition. C2004.

5. Milewski, R and Govindaraju, V. Handwriting Analysis of Pre-Hospital Care Reports. IEEE Proceedings. Seventeenth IEEE Symposium on Computer-Based Medical Systems (CBMS). C2004.

6. Leedham, G., Varma, S., Patankar, A., Govindaraju, V. Separating Text and Background in Degraded Document Images – A Comparison of Global Thresholding Techniques for Multi-Stage Thresholding. Proceedings Eighth International Workshop on Frontiers of Handwriting Recognition. C2002.

7. Wolf, C., Jolion, J.M., Chassaing, F. Text Localization, Enhancement and Binarization in Multimedia Documents. 16th International Conference on Pattern Recognition (ICPR) C2002.

8. Liao, P.S., Chen, T.S., Chung, P.C. A Fast Algorithm for Multilevel Thresholding. Journal of Information Science and Engineering. C2001.

9. Seeger, M., Dance, C. Binarising Camera Images for OCR. Xerox Research Center Europe. 6th International Conference on Document Analysis and Recognition C2001.

10. Yang, Y., Yan, H. An Adaptive Logical Method for Binarization of Degraded Document Images. The Journal of the Pattern Recognition Society. C2000.

11. Sonka, M., Hlavac, V., Boyle, R. Image Processing, Analysis, and Machine Vision; 2nd Edition. PWS Publishing. C1999.

12. Wu, V. and Manmatha, R. Document Image Clean-Up and Binarization. Proc. SPIE Symposium on Electronic Imaging. C1998.

13. Kim, G., and Govindaraju, V.: A Lexicon Driven Approach to Handwritten Word Recognition for Real-Time Applications. IEEE Trans. PAMI 19(4): 366-379. C1997.

14. Sauvola, J. Seppanen, T. Haapakoski, Pietikainen, M. Adaptive Document Binarization. In International Conference on Document Analysis and Recognition, Volume 1. C1997.

15. Beigi, H. Processing, Modeling and Parameter Estimation of the Dynamic On-Line Handwriting Signal. Proceedings World Congress on Automation. C1996.

16. Hsu, D.S., Huang, W.M., Thakor, N.V. StylPen: On-line Adaptive Canceling of Pathological Tremor for Computing Pen Handwriting. IEEE Transactions on Biomedical Engineering. C1998.

17. Shi, Z. and Govindaraju, V. Character Image Enhancement by Selective Region-growing. Pattern Recognition Letters, 17. C1996.

18. Trier, O.D. and Taxt, T. Evaluation of Binarization Methods for Document Images. , IEEE Trans. PAMI, 17 (3). C1995.

19. Kamel, M., Zhao, Extraction of Binary Character/Graphics Images from Grayscale Document Images. CVGIP: Graphics Models Image Processing; 55 (3). C1993.

20. Schurmann, J., et al. Document Analysis-From Pixels to Contents. Processing IEEE Vol. 80 No.7. C1992.

21. Yanowitz, S.D. and Bruckstein, A.M. A New Method for Image Segmentation. Computer Vision Graphics and Image Processing Vol. 46 No.1. C1989.

22. Niblack, W. An Introduction to Digital Image Processing. Englewood Cliffs, N.J. Prentice Hall. C1986.

23. Brown, M.K., Ganapathy, S. Preprocessing Techniques for Cursive Word Recognition. Pattern Recognition, Vol. 16 No. 5. C1983.

24. Otsu, N. A Threshold Selection Method from Gray-Level Histogram. IEEE Transactions on System Man Cybernetics, Vol. SMC-9, No. 1. C1979.

Document Logical Structure Analysis Based on Perceptive Cycles

Yves Rangoni and Abdel Belaïd

Loria Research Center - Read Group, Vandœuvre-lès-Nancy, France
{rangoni, abelaid}@loria.fr
http://www.loria.fr/~rangoni/
http://www.loria.fr/~abelaid/

Abstract. This paper describes a Neural Network (NN) approach for logical document structure extraction. In this NN architecture, called Transparent Neural Network (TNN), the document structure is stretched along the layers, allowing an interpretation decomposition from physical (NN input) to logical (NN output) level. The intermediate layers represent successive interpretation steps. Each neuron is apparent and associated to a logical element. The recognition proceeds by repetitive perceptive cycles propagating the information through the layers. In case of low recognition rate, an enhancement is achieved by error backpropagation leading to correct or pick up a more adapted input feature subset. Several feature subsets are created using a modified filter method. The first experiments performed on scientific documents are encouraging.

1 Introduction

This paper tackles the problem of document logical structure extraction based on physical feature observations within document images. Although this problem has known many solutions, it still remains very challenging for noisy and variable documents.

The literature abounds of structure analysis approaches for different document classes. A survey of the most important approaches can be found in [1]. Most of them are based on formal grammars describing the connection between logical elements. However, these methods have drawbacks because the rules are given by the user and could be not sufficient to handle complex and noisy documents. It is difficult to remove ambiguities and many thresholds must be fixed to process the matching between the physical and the logical structure.

Consequently, a learning-based method seems to be a more adapted solution. Artificial neural network (ANN) approaches allow such a training (rules are learnt) and are known to be more robust to noise and deformation. However, ANN like the classical Multi Layer Perceptron (MLP) is considered as a black box and does not explicit the relationships between the neurons. In the same time, domain-specific knowledge appears essential for document interpretation as mentioned in [2] and it seems useful to keep a part of knowledge in a Document Image Analysis (DIA) system.

H. Bunke and A.L. Spitz (Eds.): DAS 2006, LNCS 3872, pp. 117–128, 2006.

In order to take into account theses two aspects (knowledge and learning), we propose a new ANN approach that use a Transparent Neural Network (TNN) architecture. This method has the same MLP capacities and can act, in the same time, on the reasoning by introducing knowledge. The recognition task is done progressively by propagation of the inputs (local vision) towards the outputs (global vision). Back-propagation movements, during recognition step, are used for an input correction process as the human perception acts. These successive "perceptive cycles" (vision-interpretation) bring a context return which is very helpful for the input improvement.

This paper is organized as follows. In the first section, the TNN architecture is described. The second section details an input feature clustering method to speed up the perceptive cycles. Finally, in the last section experimental results and discussions are reported.

2   The TNN Architecture Description

The proposed TNN architecture is described in Fig. 1. The first layer receives physical features where each element corresponds to a neuron. The following layers represent the logical structure at three different levels, from fine to coarse (see Fig.8 for the whole input and output names).

All the layers are fully connected and all the neurons carry interpretable concepts. This modeling integrates common knowledge on "general" document

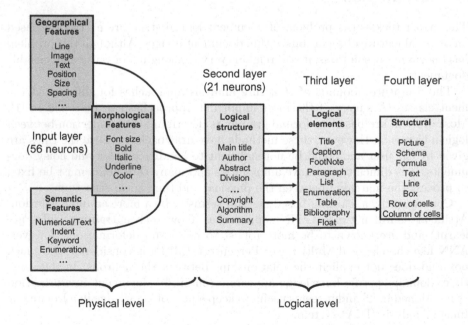

Fig. 1. Neuron semantic for document analysis

structure. It can be more precise if a DTD (Document Type Definition) is given as the DTD organizes the logical element in hierarchy. The real TNN output is the first logical level (the second layer) while the last layers represent the global context (third and fourth layers). They are used to precise the context which is needed for logical structure identification during the perceptive cycles.

This system can be considered as a hybrid method set between a model-driven (DTD integration) and a data-driven approach (training phase). As for a classical MLP, a database is used to train the links between physical and final logical structures. The list of input and output elements is given in Fig. 8.

As the model is transparent and errors can be known for each output layers, the training of the whole network is achieved locally for each consecutive layer pairs. The weight modifications are carried out by an error correction principle. The first stage consists in initializing the weights with random values, then for each couple (Input, Output) of the training database, a predicted value is computed by propagation. The error between the computed output P and the desired output O is then determined. The second stage back-propagates this error in the previous layers. If the activation function is a sigmoid, the value to add to a weight $w_{i,j}$ is $\alpha(O_j - P_i)P_i(1 - P_j)I_i$.

The Fig. 2 shows a small example of a trained TNN that classifies RGB colors in rainbow colors. The green links are used for a positive contribution and the red ones are used for a negative one. The line thickness is proportional to the link weight.

Contrary to a MLP, the recognition process is more complicated. The MLP looks at the maximum output layer component $O_i = argmax\{O\}$ and deduces that the input pattern belongs the ith class. In a TNN system, the outputs are analyzed and two decisions can be chosen (Fig. 3.):

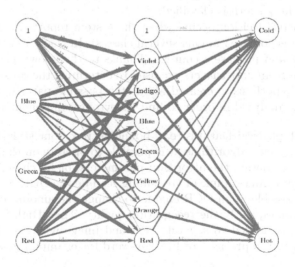

Fig. 2. A TNN classifying RGB pixels in hot and cold colors. It uses rainbow color decomposition in its intermediary layer.

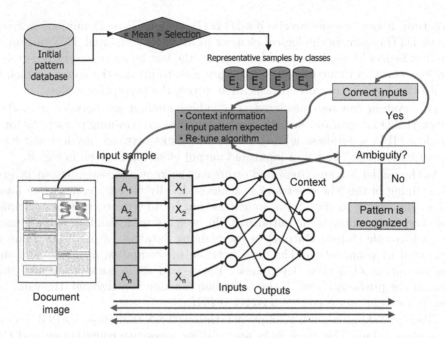

Fig. 3. Perceptive cycles: propagation, analysis, context return, and correction

- the first decision concerns the output when it is close to a unit vector. Thus, the system gives a ruling on a "good" pattern. This means that a class has a sufficient score $\|O\|_\infty \geqslant \varepsilon$ with $0 \ll \varepsilon < 1$ (acceptable class) and this winning class has a score greater than the others $\Gamma(O) = \frac{n((\sum O_i)^2 - \sum O_i^2)}{(n-1)(\sum O_i)^2} \leqslant \eta$ with $0 < \eta \ll 1$ (superior class). If such an output satisfies these rules, the system stops and the pattern is classified.
- the alternative decision occurs when the system reports an ambiguity (i.e. the pattern is confused among several classes). In that case, the latest TNN layers react and propose a context. Thanks to the known neuron semantic, information from upper layers are used to determine the possible or unlikely classes. A hypothesis is created about the possible pattern class and then the input is analyzed in order to find the wrong component values.

As the input physical features (e.g. bounding box, font style, text, etc.) are determined by specific algorithms, it is possible to operate on their precision (or quality) by reconsidering the algorithm parameters, or by changing totally the algorithm method. An example of "re-tuning" can be the OCR settings that give the text. It is possible in an OCR engine to change the amount of computation but changing consequently the recognition quality. The "High Speed" mode is chosen when it is needed to separate text and image whereas "High Quality" mode is preferred if a precise word (a key-word for example) is searched in the text block.

Another example of algorithm "swapping" is the evaluation of word number in a text block. Two solutions can be chosen. The first solution uses RLSA and

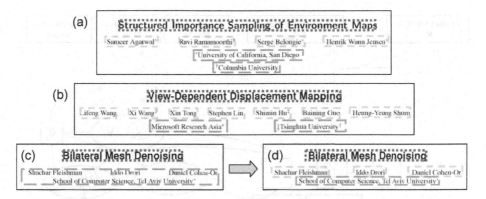

Fig. 4. In (a) and (b), the segmentation and labeling results are correct. Picture (c) shows the result before a context return: the authors are not found. In (d) is the recognition process of (c) after an input correction: title, authors, and locality are found now.

evaluates the number of connected components. The second solution uses an OCR and simply counts the number of words. The first solution is the fastest but gives approximate results whereas the second solution is more time-consuming but more accurate.

With the use of context, new information coming from the training database can be added during the correction. For example, if a segmentation problem occurs, the system finds the "mean" awaited bounding box and corrects the previous bounding box dimensions. This example is not insignificant, because segmentation errors are frequent and penalize the whole physical extraction. The context returns allow often a better segmentation and contribute to better recognition accuracy (see Fig. 4).

3   Input Feature Clustering

In the previous section, the TNN is showed to be able to analyze its outputs and to improve its inputs accordingly. Better results than a MLP can be obtained thanks to the perceptive cycles. However, "high-level" feature extraction is needed for each cycle what remains a time-consuming procedure.

In order to speed-up the global process, the input features are categorized and classified in subsets. The feature subsets are used progressively as TNN inputs. A first feature set is chosen and then if the recognition rate is too low, another set (containing the first and additional features) is selected and so on until reaching the final solution. As the whole features are not necessary needed to classify many patterns the computation is reduced consequently.

Two criteria are used for feature classification: "quality" and "velocity". The "velocity" corresponds to the algorithm execution time given either by experiments or formally by studying the algorithm complexity. For "quality", there is no straightforward measurement method. A specific method based on feature

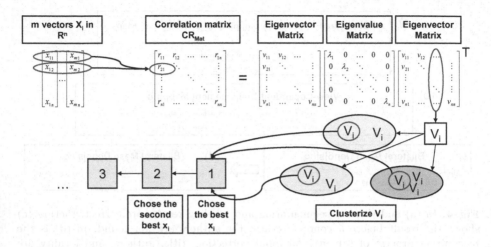

Fig. 5. Data categorization according to predictive capacity

subset selection is proposed. The objective is to determine the best feature combination to feed a pattern classification system. This method is used to create a feature partitioning.

The literature mentions two main feature selection methods: filter and wrapper [3]. The first one selects variables by ranking them with correlation coefficients (it is usually suboptimal for building a predictor, particularly if the variables are redundant). The second one assesses variable subsets according to their usefulness to a given predictor (but the predictor is needed to construct the subsets). As the subsets are needed to construct the TNN architecture, a filter method has been considered. The filter method is also adapted to exclude many redundant variables in the same subset and to keep the most relevant ones.

The Karhunen-Loeve transform is used as a first step in the filter selection method. In [4] we used an extension of the Principal Component Analysis (PCA) in order to build subsets of initial features and not rewrite the features in another base, as the PCA is originally designed.

The eigenvectors V (in absolute value) of the data correlation matrix $CR_{Mat} = (cor(X_i, X_j))$ are computed. The vectors are then clusterized using a Self Organizing Map (SOM) with an Euclidian distance (see Fig. 5.).

The obtained clusters contain similar eigenvectors (i.e. redundant variables). The feature corresponding to the nearest eigenvector from each cluster center is chosen for the creation of a new subset. This subset contains high predictive features which are the least correlated. By fixing the neuron number of the SOM, the number of desired subsets can be chosen.

An important phase of this clustering process is to determine the lower-space dimension q (i.e. the variance to be kept). As no optimal solution exists, some heuristics proposed by the literature have been tested:

- fixed number q: this is a straightforward method where cutting level is imposed by the user.
- fixed percentage: similarly to the previous case, but here the user chooses the first $p\%$ of the eigenvalues.
- cumulated percentage: the number q is determined when the sum of the first variance (eigenvalue) is greater than a given fixed percentage.

These three methods are usual but their choice assumes that the user overcomes its application and can appreciate the dimension to use. These methods are often used in social sciences because it is easier to interpret the data. Two other methods, which are more general and more robust, are based on the shape of the eigenvalue sequence:

- Kaiser method: the average of all the variances is calculated. The space dimension q is determined when the sum of the first variance is greater than this average. Of a wide spread employment, it can be put at fault.
- Cattell method: [5] suggests to find the place where the smooth decrease of eigenvalues appears to level off to the right of the plot (the scree-test). This heuristic is often considered as the most powerful [6]

4   Experimental Results and Discussion

Before introducing results on document image analysis, experiments about "low-level" and highly correlated features are presented.

A first experimentation procedure is employed to illustrate the variable subset creation method. For this purpose, the MNIST database [7] is used. A MultiLayer Perceptron is used to evaluate the group validity. This classifier has the same settings along all the experiments (topology, initial random weights, etc.). Two experiments have been made on this database. The first uses the whole initial pixels of each image (digits are 28×28 pixel images). The second experiment uses resampled images (in a 7×7 format). Thus, we have for the first experiment 784 variables are considered in the first experiment and 49 for the second one.

The MLP is trained with different variable subsets and the recognition rate is chosen as a quality measurement. The subsets are compared to randomly created ones. One thousand of random subsets have been generated and evaluated by the MLP. Then the best one is retained for the comparison. This procedure will be the same for the following experiments about document analysis.

Table 1 shows normalized comparison results between the subset obtained by our method and the best of the random subsets for the initial MNIST database. The Fig. 6 shows the position of the selected pixels in the image. The first picture represents the "mean" digit coming from the whole database ($\frac{1}{n}\sum_{i=1}^{n} I_i$) and in the next three pictures, chosen pixels can be seen. The Table 2 is similar to the Table 1 but here 7×7 pixel images are used for test.

The approach gives good results in spite of the strong influence of each pixel (expecting those on the border) on the classifier. The method keeps the two thirds of the information by keeping less than 4% of features (Table 1: with 25 of the 784 variables, 67.6% of the information is kept).

Table 1. MNIST digit classification accuracy while decreasing the number of features

# features	Method	
	Random	Our selection
784(max)	100%	100%
500	98.4%	99.2%
300	95.9%	98.4%
150	90.5%	96.5%
100	84.2%	94.2%
50	70.9%	87.8%
25	47.1%	67.6%

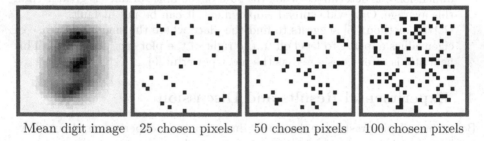

Mean digit image   25 chosen pixels   50 chosen pixels   100 chosen pixels

Fig. 6. Feature subsets created for MNIST database

Experiments concerning the document logical structure analysis are presented below. We have chosen as a main database 74 Siggraph 2003 conference papers [8]. The documents are scientific articles having many and diversified logical structure elements (see Fig. 7 for two examples).

In these 74 documents, 21 logical structures are labeled that represents more than 2000 patterns. The input and output features are presented in Fig. 8. Note that all the physical inputs (geometrical, morphological, and semantic) are numerical values between 0 and 1 after possibly normalization. In general, the number represents a percentage (e.g. the percentage of bold characters in a text block) and for other features that represent a number (e.g. the number k of keywords in a text block) we use the series $\sum_{n=1}^{k} 1/(n+1)$ to have a number between 0 and 1.

As previously, the same protocol for input feature selection is experimented on this document database. We extracted physical information from the document layout. There are 56 features composed of geometrical, typographical, and morphological information (see Fig. 8) and we use once again a MLP as classifier.

Table 3 synthesizes some results of logical structures recognition accuracy according to the eigenvalue choice methods as mentioned at the end of the previous section. The five methods have been tested on different subset sizes.

The choice of the space dimension influences the results quality. Even if the MLP is a classifier able to give good results with few features, choosing too low

Table 2. Resampled MNIST digit classification accuracy while decreasing the number of features

# features	Method	
	Random	Our selection
49(max)	100%	100%
35	94.2%	99.3%
25	81.2%	88.6%
15	56.2%	70.5%
10	43.9%	55.2%

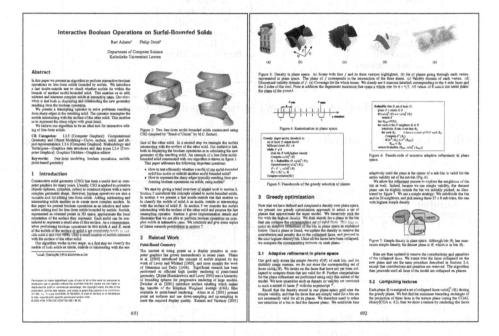

Fig. 7. Two scientific document database samples

or too high eigenvector dimension can be bad for the input feature clustering and consequently for the classifier.

It seems here (and for other tests that have be done on MNIST) that the Cattell method (that set $q = 19$) is most of the time better than Kaiser (with $q = 14$). The two methods, which automatically find the number q, give the same or better results than the classical ones where the user must fix this number. We will retain for the following tests the Cattell method that seems to be the most robust on many experimentations.

As expected and confirmed in Table 4, these "high-level" features lends well to this selection.

In this case, the choice of a small set of features is more difficult. The feature clustering method seems to be appropriate when the number of features is rather

| Logical | Physical | | Semantic |
	Geometrical	Morphological	
Title	Text	Bold	IsNumeric
Author	Image	Italic	KeyWords
Email	Table	Underlined	%KnownWords
Locality	Other	Strikethrough	%Punctuation
Abstract	x position	UpperCase	Bullet
Key words	y position	Small Capitals	Enum
CR Categories	Width	Subscript	Language
Introduction	Height	Superscript	Baseline
Paragraph	NumPage	Font Name	
Section	UpSpace	Font Size	
SubSection	BottomSpace	Scaling	
SubSubSection	LeftSpace	Spacing	
List	RightSpace	Alignment	
Enumeration		LeftIndent	
Float		RightIndent	
Conclusion		FirstIndent	
Bibliography		NumLines	
Algorithms		Boxed	
Copyright		Red/Green/Blue	
Acknowledgments			
Page number			

Fig. 8. Logical outputs and physical inputs for documents

Table 3. Logical structure rate accuracy (in %) according to dimensionality q reducing method

Feature number	Fixed number		Fixed %		% Variance		Kaiser (q=14)	Cattell (q=19)
	Num	Accur.	F%	Accur.	%V	Accur.		
5	2	64.4	2%	61.6	10%	66.5	69.2	68.1
	5	64.3	5%	72.1	20%	67.9		
	10	60.3	10%	64.3	40%	61.4		
	15	59.2	20%	57.8	60%	63.6		
10	2	78.4		79.7		81.1	77.7	82.3
	5	79.8		82.7		73.5		
	10	72.9		77.1		78.4		
	15	70.0		76.6		72.6		
20	2	85.4		82.1		82.3	85.7	86.1
	5	84.9		82.8		86.1		
	10	83.6		83.3		82.3		
	15	82.6		83.3		78.8		
30	2	85.2		82.9		84.2	87.4	88.0
	5	86.8		85.6		85.8		
	10	86.6		86.5		86.7		
	15	86.3		85.4		87.7		

small and can be very powerful in this case (more than 83% of information is kept by dividing the variable number by 5).

Leaving side input features selection, results about complete DIA system are presented. Three input features subsets are created with the previous method.

Table 4. Logical elements classification accuracy while decreasing the number of features

# features	Method	
	Random	Our selection
56(max)	100%	100%
35	86.9%	99.3%
25	65.0%	79.6%
15	51.8%	80.1%
10	35.1%	83.8%
5	17.9%	44.9%

Table 5. Logical classification by MLP and TNN with perceptive cycles

Recognition rates	MLP	TNN			
		C_1	C_2	C_3	C_4
All elements	81.6%	45.2	78,9	90.2	91.7%
Best class	86.9%	66.7	85.3	85.3	99.3%
Worst class	0.0%	0.0	0.0	4.0	28.6%
Recognition time (MLP as reference)	100%	70%	145%	185%	240%

Extraction tools, which can be configured, are used to extract the physical layout. During the recognition phase, the system can choose between the feature subsets and act on extraction tools as mentioned in Section 3. The training stage uses 44 documents and 30 for the test. Test results between a MLP and the TNN at the end of four perceptive cycles are presented in Fig.5.

The perceptive cycles increase the recognition rates. After 4 cycles, the classifier reaches 91.7%. A TNN without perceptive cycles is worse than a MLP (45.2% instead of 81.6%) because TNN does not have many constraints in its intermediate layers. With perceptive cycles, the context returns make it possible to gain in precision while the algorithm complexity increases with a 2.5 factor.

5   Conclusion

We presented in this article a neural network architecture for document logical structure analysis. The method uses a Transparent Neural Network that makes it possible to introduce knowledge in each neuron and to organize in hierarchy the neurons in order to create a "vision" decomposition. The topology can simulate a decomposition hierarchy from fine (the patterns to recognized) to coarse (the global context).

Thanks to this system, we can adapt the computation time according to the pattern granularity and complexity. These "perceptive cycles" as named in cognitive psychology allow simulating in the same system a recognition process that uses automatic and fixed knowledge rules, a hierarchical view, and an interpretation-correction process thanks to hypothesis creation. An input feature clustering was done to speed-up the perceptive cycles.

The TNN gives encouraging results. Although some improvements are in hand, tests are already better than a simple MLP, without adding too heavy computation. In our future works, we will propose a genetic-method to choose representative samples in the database during the context return. Another work will be done to improve the feature subset creation and a method to deal with the final cases of rejected patterns will be presented.

References

1. Mao, S., Rosenfelda, A., Kanungo, T.: Document structure analysis algorithms: A literature survey. SPIE Electronic Imaging (2003)
2. Nagy, G.: Twenty years of document image analysis in pami. PAMI (2000)
3. Guyon, I., Elisseeff, A.: An introduction to variable and feature extraction. Journal of Machine Learning Research (2003)
4. Rangoni, Y., Belaïd, A.: Data categorization for a context return applied to logical document structure recognition. ICDAR (2005)
5. Cattell, R.: The scree test for the number of factors. Multivariate Behavioral Research (1966)
6. Zwick, W.R., Velicer, W.F.: Comparison of five rules for determining the number of components to retain. Psychological Bulletin (1986)
7. LeCun, Y.: (http://yann.lecun.com/exdb/mnist/)
8. Siggraph: http://www.siggraph.org/s2003/. (2003)

A System for Converting PDF Documents into Structured XML Format*

Hervé Déjean and Jean-Luc Meunier

Xerox Research Centre Europe
6, chemin de Maupertuis, F-38240 Meylan
Firstname.Lastname@xrce.xerox.com

Abstract. We present in this paper a system for converting PDF legacy documents into structured XML format. This conversion system first extracts the different streams contained in PDF files (text, bitmap and vectorial images) and then applies different components in order to express in XML the logically structured documents. Some of these components are traditional in Document Analysis, other more specific to PDF. We also present a graphical user interface in order to check, correct and validate the analysis of the components. We eventually report on two real user cases where this system was applied on.

1 Introduction

Enterprise Content Management (ECM) software enables organizations to create/capture, manage/secure, store/retain/destroy, publish/distribute, search, personalize, and present/view/print any digital content [1]. The capture module essentially offers functionalities such as scanning, OCR, indexing. Most of the ECM systems integrate now XML, a format which provides, among other advantages, a way to store documents with metadata and structural information. Due to the dissemination of this format and its adoption as standard, new requests from organizations challenge ECM software to provide more sophisticated functionalities such as document conversion to XML which keeps the structural information. This structural information is not explicitly marked up in most electronic documents. This is particularly true for PDF documents [2]. Even if the version 6 of PDF allows a user to create a file containing structural information, most of them do no contain such information. The use of PDF format as input format for a conversion task can be questionable: since PDF files are very often generated from another format (MS Word, Latex), converting files with the original format could be more efficient. But the everyday life (and customers cases provided by Xerox business units) shows that PDF is now a common exchange format between organizations, and often is the only accessible format.

Portable Document Format (PDF) goal is *"to enable users to exchange and view electronic documents easily and reliably, independently of the environment in which they were created"* [2]. A detailed presentation of this format is out of the scope of

---

* This work is supported by VIKEF Integrated Project co-funded under the EU 6th Framework Programme.

H. Bunke and A.L. Spitz (Eds.): DAS 2006, LNCS 3872, pp. 129–140, 2006.

this article, and we will consider here a PDF document as a sequence of pages, each page being composed of any combination of text (referred as *text objects* in [2]), graphics (*path objects*) and images (*external objects*).

1. A text object consists in one or more characters and layout information (position, fonts)
2. A path object contains vectorial instructions (lines or bezier curves).
3. A image external object defines a rectangular image.

Many PDF converters [3;4;5] are available off the shelf, but often they simply provide a format conversion, and almost no structural information is provided in the final format, except at the very low level (words, lines). Information contained in the original PDF file is in a way simply translated in another format. [6] presents a comparison of some of them.

OCR-oriented software [7;8;9] now provides a functionality to convert PDF through scanning and OCR. The drawback is that information clearly present in the PDF file (text zone, external image) is not used, and the image analysis step can introduce noise (some text may not be recognized as text zone; some images may not be correctly recognized). Nevertheless, this strategy is the only one available when the PDF file only contains images (from scanning).

[6] proposes a method combining both approaches: applying traditional layout analysis on TIFF images generated from PDF combined with low-level content extracted from the PDF file. We present here a system that relies solely on the PDF-extracted content, no longer requiring the conversion to TIFF nor the combination of both approaches. The first steps consist in extracting the native PDF pieces of information: text, path objects, and external objects (Sections 2,3). Then the textual organization of each page and its reading order is computed through a XY-cut-based algorithm (Sections 4,5). In order to extract the logical structure at the document level, we first detect the table of contents (Toc) of the document, and structure it according to the hierarchical information present in its Toc (Section 6). Section 5 and 6 are brief since this work has been reported in [14;18]. We also present a graphical user interface which allows the user to correct each step of the conversion (if necessary). We eventually discuss two user cases where this conversion system has been successfully used.

2 Text Extraction

If PDF allows the preservation of the look of documents, it does not contain or guarantee a correct logical representation of the text. An inspection of the text streams extracted form PDF files reveals first that these streams can correspond to various objects: a character, a partial word, a word, a line,…. Secondly the order of these text streams does not always correspond to the reading order. A word reconstruction component and a reading order component are then necessary in order to correctly extract the text from a PDF file. We will describe here the word reconstruction component we have developed. The reading order component is explained Section 5.

Text objects are extracted from the PDF and a word and line segmentation is produced based on heuristics using the distance between characters and their geometrical positions (similarly to the heuristics present in the Xpdf library [10]). In most cases, this set of heuristics correctly segments the text streams into words and lines. Table 1 shows tokenization some errors provided by this method.

Table 1. Texts before and after correction

Original text	Corrected text
TIGHTENING TORQUES	TIGHTENING TORQUES
Throttle pedal position sensor	Throttle pedal position sensor
Fitting rear seal	Fitting rear seal
Oil vapour full recirculation system (Blow - by)	Oil vapour full recirculation system (Blow -by)
En gine coolant temperatu re sensor	Clutch pedal position sensor
Brake pedal position sensor	Brake pedal position sensor
Checking torsion	Checking torsion
E N G I N E E R I N G	E N G I N E E R I N G
Checking bending	Checking bend ing
Checking torsion	Checking torsion
Run u p	Run up

Even if the errors are marginal, texts which are wrongly tokenized often correspond to logical elements which structure documents, such as document/chapter/ section headings. One possible explanation is that special fonts and layout are used for these elements. It is noteworthy that extracting these elements correctly might be very important since they structure the document (as the reader will see Section 6). To correct these errors, we propose the following method:

1. Text is extracted from PDF using geometrical information.
2. A weighted lexicon is built, based on the tokens present in the document
3. For each line, all the possible tokenizations are generated
4. The best tokenization is selected

After the first extraction using geometrical information, a lexicon is built. Since most of the word segmentation is correctly done, the lexicon mainly contains correct words. The hypothesis we do here is that *words which occur in ill-formed elements will occur correctly in other parts of the document.* We will then use correct tokenized words in order to retokenize bad words. External lexicons can be of course used but, since document conversion mainly involves technical documents (with a domain-specific terminology), the general lexicons may have a bad coverage.

Each token (word of the document) is associated a weight. The weighting schema we use is the following one:

$$W= length(token)*log(frequency(token)+1) \tag{1}$$

where *frequency(token)* corresponds to the number of token occurrences in the document, and *length(token)* is the length in character. We consider that the more frequent a word, the more reliable.

A weighted automaton (see [11]) is built, describing the set of all tokens of the document with their respective weight. Let us call it D (for dictionary).

In order to generate all the possible tokenizations, we apply (through a transducer called T) the following actions over an input string (which corresponds to a line built step 1): a space character is deleted or a space character is inserted.

We associate a weight to both operations. Since most of the errors are corrected by deleting a space character, we give a higher weight to the deletion operation. An automaton is generated for a string we want to re-tokenize such that each letter of the string labels a transition. Let us call this automaton S. S, T and D are composed in order to generate all the tokenization for S: S .o. T .o. D* (* being the kleen star). This final transducer will assign to each possible tokenization a weight using the weights associated to the words (automaton D) and to the operation (transducer T). A Viterbi algorithm is applied over the transducer in order to select the path with the highest weight.

Table 1 shows texts extracted from a PDF file and the new tokenization after our correction component. Tests have been made with correctly tokenized text, and the correct tokenization is kept unchanged by the method. This method also provides dealing with hyphenation. By simply adding a third operation: deleting the hyphen symbol, the resulting automaton will de-hyphenate hyphenated words which occur in the document somewhere else (or in an external lexicon).

3   Image/Text Separation

PDF contains also information about images, mainly using two objects: external objects which allow the insertion of external objects (as raster images), and path objects which allow the description of vectorial elements (the clipping objects are not yet taken into account by our system). A single vectorial image can be composed of thousands of paths. One problem is then to regroup all the elements (paths, text, images) which form the complete image. This is a traditional task for Document Analysis systems to recognize and label parts of pages as text zones and image zones. If these methods can be also used here, we prefer to use the information present in the PDF file. An XY-cut-based algorithm (Section 5) is first applied on external and path objects, first ignoring text. The zone of a path object is defined thanks to the coordinates of each element of the path (an approximation is in practice enough for bezier curves). Ignoring textual elements allows avoiding many situations where images and text zones form non-manhattan zones, a well-known problem for an XY-cut approach. The graphical elements (path objects and images) are then grouped, and the final groups can contain both: images and paths. Text segmentation is explained Section 5. Once elements have been regrouped into zones, the labeling (text/image zone) is done by computing the surface of each type (text, image) in the zone. Since overlap between a text and an image zones can happened, both are merged, and the label of this zone corresponds to the label of the text or image zone which covers the highest surface. This simple approach provides a robust solution in most cases, but fails in the following cases:

1. The page contains a background image: The following heuristic can be used in this case: when an image has a size which is similar to the page size, consider it as background image.

2. an image/schema is composed of different elements which are too distant: in this case the image is oversegmented
3. Text is wrongly integrated into an image zone. This error typically occurs when the author wants to insert an image onto a page, although space is clearly missing.

This component is still under research but the current status is enough in order to correctly detect vectorial images, and consequently can be used for developing other components such as a caption detector.

4 Header Footer Detection

The purpose of this component is to detect zones at the top of the document and at the bottom of the document which correspond to headers and footers. Since one goal of this system is to logically structure documents, the deletion of pages induces the deletions of elements which are directly linked to the page segmentation, typically headers and footers. In order to characterize this zone, we use the following observation: in a header or footer zone, the textual variety is much lower than in the body page (see Table 3). A similar observation is used in [12]. The header/footer detection consists of three main steps: text normalization, textual variability computation and header/footer zone detection.

The only normalization applied (step 1) consists in replacing all digits by a unique character (D). This normalization is due to the frequent use of page/chapter/section numbering and dates in headers/footers.

The text extraction component provides us with the vertical or horizontal positions of textual fragments in a page. To each vertical position, we associated the number of text blocks occurring at this position, and the number of different text blocks occurring at this position. A *textual variability score* for each position i is computed as follows:

$$tv\_score(i) = \frac{\#\,different\ text\ blocks}{\#\,total\ text\ blocks} \tag{2}$$

For example, in the Linux System Administrator's Guide, the texts occurring at the position 108 have a textual variability of 7/93 =0.075 (Table 2). As Table 3 shows, and accordingly with our hypothesis, the position 108 has a very low score (header), while the position 156 (page body) has a very high one.

Table 2. Variability for the position 108 in the Linux System Administrator's Guide

Text at the position y = 108	Nb of occurrences
Installing and Configuring DD/DDDBase-T X/DDDD	25
DD/DDDBase-TX Interface Card Statistics	9
Troubleshooting DD/DDDBase-TX/DDDD	33
Configuring Network Connectivity Using SAM'	5
DDDBase-TX Resources	9
Hardware Regulatory Statements	3
Hardware Reference Information	9
total	93

Table 3. Textual variability according to the position in a page: The Linux System Administrator's Guide

position	# text blocks	#different text blocks	Textual variability
96	5	3	0.6
108	93	7	0.075
122	89	32	0.35
143	1	1	1
155	17	11	0.67
156	47	45	0.96

Once the variability score for each position is computed, we try to identify whether the document has header zones and footer zones. For this, we use the following method:

1. Identify potential headers/footers elements: all elements with a score lower than a given threshold θ (0.5 in practice) are identified as potential headers or footers. The top first potential candidate is identified (starting from the top for the header and from the bottom for the footer). For the header detection, this candidate must occur in the upper half-page, for the footer detection, the candidate must occur in the lower half-page.
2. Merge surrounding elements: We extend the current header zone (resp. footer list) with preceding and following elements if and only if its insertion decreases the textual variability score of the new augmented list. Elements are added incrementally starting from the adjacent elements of the list. Potentially no new element is added. The reduction of the score imposes that the new element has some text in common with the current list. If the final zone does not reach the top (for header) or bottom (for footer) of the page, the zone is invalidated.
3. Return the lowest (resp. highest) position of the header (resp. footer) list. A zone for header and/or a zone for footer are then recognized, and elements occurring in them are considered as header or footer.

This method works very well when headers and footers are homogenous over the entire document. It can partially fail when a document is composed of parts which have different kinds of headers or footers (headers in an annex can be different (e.g. lower) to headers in the document body).

5　Reading Order Computation and Segmentation into Paragraphs

The ordering problem consists in ordering the objects of a page in order to reflect the human reading order. Multiple approaches to this problem have been proposed in the literature [13], exploiting geometric or typographic features of the page objects, or going further in exploiting the content of objects, with or without priori knowledge about a particular document class.

The use of off-the-shelf PDF converters leads to the consideration of layout objects of various granularities, because they may contain one line, or one word, or part of a word, or even a single letter. The pages considered here often contain several hundred of textual objects, and we therefore proposed in [14] a method based on the XY-Cut [15], which takes an optimization approach to the problem and leverages dynamic programming to process efficiently any page.

It is also often important to segment the flow of text into paragraphs. The XY-cut approach can also provide this segmentation when the line spacing indicates the paragraph boundaries.

We evaluated the method thanks to the UW III document image database, which includes 1600 English journal pages. We tested at both the word-level and line-level using the ground truth. The parameters were set to their default values (only taking into account the image resolution factor, since the scale was 4 times larger than with our PDF converters). We observed an error of less than 1% of misplaced objects.

The method is a pure geometric ordering method, of general applicability in the sense that no domain knowledge is used. But there exists geometrically ambiguous pages (rare in our experience with technical documents) and for those, additional features must be taken into account. Fortunately, the score function offers convenient room for improvements with the same approach. This method suffers from the XY-Cut L-Shapes weakness but is fast (20 pages/second on a Pentium 4) thanks to the dynamic programming technique. We are now interested in exploring alternative methods based on 2D relationships [16;17].

6 Toc-Based Structuring

This module aims at structuring a document according to its table of contents (hereafter ToC). First the toc of a document is automatically detected, and in the same step, the ToC entries are linked to their entries in the document body. Finally the hierarchical structure of the toc is used to structure the document accordingly. A more detailed presentation of the method is presented in [18].

In view of the large variation in shape and content a ToC may display, we believe that a descriptive approach would be limited to a series of specific collections. Therefore, we instead chose a functional approach that relies on the functional properties that a ToC intrinsically respects. These properties are:

1. Contiguity: a ToC consists of a series of contiguous references to some other parts of the document itself;
2. Textual similarity: the reference itself and the part referred to share some level of textual similarity;
3. Ordering: the references and the referred parts appear in the same order in the document;
4. Optional elements: a ToC entry may include (a few) elements whose role is not to refer to any other part of the document, e.g. decorative text;

Our hypothesis is that those 4 properties are sufficient for the entire characterization of a ToC, independently of the document class and language.

6.1 The Table of Contents Detection

Three steps permit us to identify the area of the document containing the ToC text. Firstly, links are defined between each pair of text blocks in the whole document satisfying a textual similarity criterion. Each link includes a source text block and a target text block. The similarity measure we currently use is the ratio of words shared by the two blocks, considering spaces and punctuation as word separators. Whenever the ratio is above a predefined threshold, the *similarity threshold*, a pair of symmetric links is created. In practice, 0.5 is a good threshold value to tolerate textual variation between the ToC and the document body while avoiding too many noisy links.

Secondly, all possible ToC candidate areas are enumerated. A brute force approach works fine. It consists in testing each text block as a possible ToC start and extending this ToC candidate further in the document until it is no longer possible to comply with the five properties identified above. A ToC candidate is then a set of contiguous text blocks, from which it is possible to select one link per block so as to provide an ascending order for the target text blocks.

Thirdly, we employ a scoring function to rank the candidate tables of contents. The highest ranked candidate is then selected for further processing. Currently, the scoring function is the sum of entry weights, where an entry weight is inversely proportional to the number of outgoing links. This entry weight characterizes the certainty of any of its associated links, under the assumption that the more links initiate from a given source text block, the less likely that any one of those links is a "true" link of a table of contents.

Once the highest ranked table of contents candidate has been selected, we select the best link for each of its entries by finding a global optimum for the table of contents while respecting the five ToC properties. A weight is associated with each link, which is proportional to the similarity level that led to the link creation. A Viterbi shortest-path algorithm is adequate to effectively determine the global optimum.

6.2 Hierarchical Structuring Using the ToC Hierarchy

The next step is then to find the hierarchical organization of the ToC. This is done in a twofold process:

Entry clustering. The ToC entries are clustered according to their visual characteristics (fonts, positions, case). The assumption made here is to consider that elements belonging to the same hierarchical level share the same visual characteristics. This clustering is done using state-of-the-art algorithms. The output is a set of clusters which correspond to each hierarchical level. If the document hierarchy is not reflected by visual clues, then no hierarchy will be found.

Cluster hierarchy determination. The purpose of this second step is to find the hierarchical relation between clusters. Acknowledging the fact that the first element of the ToC is not necessarily an element belonging to the highest level (a document with a complex front matter for example), we use the following heuristics: the elements (namely ToC Entries) of lowest level more frequently have adjacent elements from the same level as elements of higher levels. For instance, for a document with three hierarchical levels (chapter, section, subsection), subsections very often have at least one adjacent element of the same level (if only ToC entries are taken into account). This heuristics allows us to identify the lowest hierarchical level. The procedure is iterated by ignoring the cluster just identified. The detailed procedure is given in [18].

The result of this procedure is the hierarchical structuring of the ToC entries. The ultimate step simply consists in first marking each heading in the document body with its hierarchical level, and then in structuring the document accordingly. The final document is now segmented in hierarchical sections similarly to the information present in the ToC.

7   The Graphical User Interface

We developed a graphical tool to allow the operator to set up the whole conversion chain for a given collection and validate and/or correct the processing output. The conversion chain set up consists in determining which components to apply and with which parameterization, while the correction/validation activity consists in verifying the quality of the conversion and correcting it if needed. Actually, both activities are interleaved since the setting up involves verifying the output while tuning the settings.

Figure 1 shows a screenshot of the graphical user interface of the tool. User-centered design involving cycles of task analysis, mock-ups and user testing allowed us to design a tool taking into account the main needs:

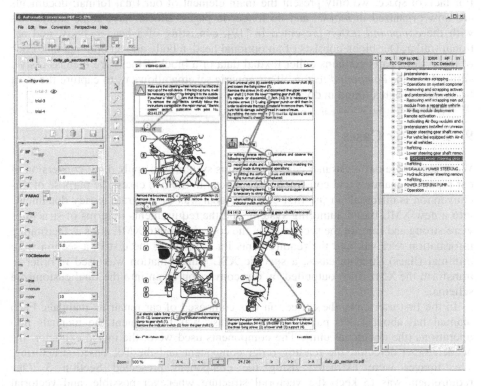

Fig. 1. Left side: the collection, the open documents, the tested configurations. Right side: different perspectives dedicated to each conversion component (here the Toc detector). Center part: decoration for segmentation in blocks and the reading order. In the toolbar appear the different possible main views corresponding to each conversion steps.

- Handling of large collections of documents;
- Fast display of any large document, with instantaneous page browsing and fast document loading (less than 5s for a 1000 page document);
- Capability of customizing both the conversion process and the settings of each conversion step;
- Capability to explore the concurrently possible alternate settings;
- Visual rendering of the conversion output thanks to an intuitive graphical page decoration overlaid;
- An XML display with extensible perspectives offering appropriately customized views, thanks for instance to a series of dedicated XSLT transforms or to dedicated applicative code.
- In-place correction mechanism acting on the overlaid decorations with consistency control;
- A plug-in mechanism to embed future components;

8 Final XML Output

For lack of space, we only present the main element of our final format: documents are now organized in *blocks*, and no longer in pages. Blocks have some similarities with the *compound texton* presented in [19], consisting of a header, body, and optional trailer. Our block consists of an optional head, a body and an optional tail. Each of these three parts contains either textual data or a block. Blocks are then recursive, similarly to the *compound texton*. This generic schema allows us to capture the most frequent structures found in documents.

9 Two User Cases

We present here two customer cases where this system was applied on: conversion of car repairing manuals and construction contracts. In the two cases, the purpose of this conversion is different: in the first case, the goal was to integrate legacy documents into a new XML-based authoring system, and the requirements in terms of structures were strong and fine. In the second case, the conversion into XML aims at facilitating information retrieval, and the requirements for structuring the text in a section were minimal (lines). In both cases, a specific XSL transformation was used in order to transform the XML files outputted by our conversion chain into the final customized schema.

In the first user case, the collection was composed of car repairing manuals. Each manual has about 1,000 pages. The main task was to segment the manuals into operations (the document unit). The components used were: the image extractor, the header/footer detector, the reading order component and the Toc-based structuring. The images were extracted using the component presented Section 3. One requirement was to keep the vectorial structure whenever possible, and vectorial images were converted into SVG. Ad hoc components were developed in order to associate to the image its number where occur below it. The reading order component was very important since most of the pages were two-column pages. A segmentation into paragraphs was achieved by the XY-cut-based module. Some specific structures (warnings, lists) were detected using rules. An estimation done by the customer shows that the use of this automatic system increases by 50% the conversion productivity (done manually before).

In the second user case, the problem was to structure a collection of construction contracts in divisions and sections. Even if the construction documents follow strict guidelines, the documents use various layout standards, depending on the institution. The documents are first scanned, OCR-ed and divided into divisions. Our system was used in order to segment each division into sections. The requirements for the sections were minimal: a simple structuring into lines. The components used for this user case were: the header/footer detector (essentially for the ToC pages), the reading order detector and the toc-based structuring. Each division has a table of contents with 30 to 200 entries (sections). The test set was composed of 25 documents which represent about 12,000 pages for 1600 sections. This represents 10% of a daily conversion (120,000 pages/day). The precision (at the link level) was 92% and the recall 90%. Errors are mainly due to OCR errors and mismatches between the ToC and the document body (e.g. a section in the document does not occur in the ToC).

10   Future Work and Conclusion

We have presented a system able to convert PDF documents into logically structured XML documents. The specificity of our approach relies in the exploitation of the native internal PDF objects rather than using image-based techniques on an image representation of the PDF document. We believe this is advantageous because it is computationally less intensive and potentially more efficient. Indeed exploiting the PDF native objects is helpful also in the sense that some conventional tasks such as image segmentation and labeling become either pointless or can be better done from the native objects.

Our experimentation with some real customer cases allowed us to identify some required improvements, which are now part of our future work list: other specific components such as figure/table caption, footnotes, table, list detectors… Also, the XY-cut segmentation in paragraphs is very sensible to parameters (either a potential under-segmentation or line-segmentation). Other features like fonts, indentation have to take into account. We have also realized the importance of customizing the conversion chain in view of the customer requirements. This customization includes the conformance of the XML output with some precise schema but also requires to both parameterize appropriately each component and to determine the sequence of conversion. While the component parameterization is well supported by the GUI, the customization of the data- and control-flow within the conversion chain deserves some more support. In conclusion, we have found the proposed approach promising and are now working on the identified improvements.

References

1. Wikipedia, www.wikipedia.org
2. PDF Reference, fifth edition, Adobe® Portable Document Format

3. CambridgeDoc : www.cambridgedoc.com.
4. JPedal: www.jpedal.org
5. PDFTron, www.pdftron.com
6. K. Hadjar, M. Rigamonti, D. Lalanne, R. Ingold, *Xed: a new Tool for eXtracting hidden structures from electronic Documents*, DIAL'04, 2004
7. Omnipage 14, Scansoft, www.scansoft.com.
8. ABBYY FineReader, http://www.abbyy.com/
9. Adobe Acrobat Capture
10. Xpdf, http://www.foolabs.com/xpdf/
11. W Kuich, A. Salomaa. *Semirings, Automata, Languages*, in EATCS Monographs, on Theoretical Computer Science, Springer Verlag, 1986
12. Xiaofan Lin, *Header and Footer Extraction by Page-Association*, Hewlett-Packard Technical Report, www.hpl.hp.com/techreports/2002/HPL-2002-129.pdf, 2002
13. R. Cattoni, T. Coianiz, S. Messelodi, C.M. Modena: *Geometric Layout Analysis Techniques for Document Image Understanding: a Review*, ITC-IRST Technical Report #9703-09
14. J.-L. Meunier, *Optimized XY-Cut for Determining a Page Reading Order*, ICDAR, 2005
15. G. Nagy and S. Seth, *Hierarchical representation of optically scanned documents*, International Conference on Pattern Recognition, 1984
16. M. Aiello and A. Smeulders, *Thick 2D Relations for Document Understanding*. 7th Joint Conference on Information Sciences, 2003
17. T. M. Breuel, *High performance document layout analysis*. Symposium on Document Image Understanding, 2003
18. H. Déjean, J.-L. Meunier, *Structuring documents according to their ToC*, DocEng, 2005.
19. D. Dori, D. Doermann, C. Shin, R. Haralick, M. Buchman, D. Ross, I. Phillips, *The representation of Document Structure*. In Hansbooks on optical Character Recognition and Document Analysis, World Scientific Publishing Company, 1996.

XCDF: A Canonical and Structured Document Format

Jean-Luc Bloechle, Maurizio Rigamonti, Karim Hadjar,
Denis Lalanne, and Rolf Ingold

DIVA Group, DIUF
University of Fribourg, Pérolles 2 – Bd de Pérolles 90,
1700 Fribourg, Switzerland
firstname.lastname@unifr.ch

Abstract. Accessing the structured content of PDF document is a difficult task, requiring pre-processing and reverse engineering techniques. In this paper, we first present different methods to accomplish this task, which are based either on document image analysis, or on electronic content extraction. Then, XCDF, a canonical format with well-defined properties is proposed as a suitable solution for representing structured electronic documents and as an entry point for further researches and works. The system and methods used for reverse engineering PDF document into this canonical format are also presented. We finally present current applications of this work into various domains, spacing from data mining to multimedia navigation, and consistently benefiting from our canonical format in order to access PDF document content and structures.

1 Introduction

PDF (Portable Document Format [1]) is nowadays a standard format for exchanging documents through the Internet, thanks to its compactness and robust visualization functionalities. Despite these major capacities, PDF documents are difficult to index for information retrieval tasks because their content is most often disorganized due to optimization reasons, and, therefore, do not respects the reading order. Thus, existing indexing systems always need to preprocess the PDF documents in order to extract and structure the content [17, 4]. In fact, the format presents an important drawback: the documents are created by PDF producers, which 1) privilege layout preservation in spite of physical and logical structures; 2) add a multitude of inconsistencies in the document, e.g. extra blank spaces, over-segmented words, etc. [25]; 3) are unable to generate a PDF document in a unique manner: for instance, a producer might consider a table as a graphic whereas another one could consider the same table as an image.

These lacks imply that PDF efficiency inside the search-engines for information retrieval can be improved, but also that end users would not be able to copy-paste textual parts of a document from PDF viewers maintaining the reading order. Therefore 1) a reconstruction of homogeneous text entities (words, lines, and blocks) extracted from a PDF file and 2) a canonical format organizing the original content in respect of structures and annotations are required before any use of the original content.

H. Bunke and A.L. Spitz (Eds.): DAS 2006, LNCS 3872, pp. 141–152, 2006.
© Springer-Verlag Berlin Heidelberg 2006

This paper is organized as follow: in section 2, we present a taxonomy of the techniques and methods used for extracting information from PDF documents. Section 3 presents the XCDF Canonical Document Format, our proposition for representing electronic document in a unique and structured manner. Section 4 is dedicated to XED, our tool for automatically reverting PDF documents into XCDF. Section 5 describes three different applications using XCDF: an extractor and organizer of TV Schedules, a tool for analyzing logical structures of newspapers and, finally, a multimedia meeting browser based on documents. The last section concludes this paper and announces future works.

2 Taxonomy of PDF Analysis Techniques

Nowadays, different works and researches have been accomplished for recovering hidden physical and logical document structures in PDF files and for deriving specific annotation (for instance the reading order or the table of content). Those methods are summarized in table 1.

Table 1. Taxonomy of techniques for PDF document analysis

Document image analysis	Electronic content analysis		
+ matures techniques	+ accurate results		
+ independent from document	+ access to document hidden information		
	Extending methods	Restructuring methods	
	+ document preserved	+ information easily accessible	
		Conversion	Reverse engineering
			+ content and structures strictly related

The first methodology consists in analyzing the document image to recover the content and the original structures. This method profits of the entire knowledge acquired by researchers in the last decades, applied – in the majority of the cases - to an ideal document, without noise and printed at high resolution [12, 13]. Document image analysis is independent from PDF file inner structure, i.e. documents page can be represented either with PDF primitives (text, graphics and images), or with images. On the opposite, all information contained in electronic documents composed of PDF primitives is ignored.

The second methodology is based on the analysis of documents with electronic content [21]. Parts of these analysis techniques are derived from the classical document image analysis. In general, they make use of the information contained in the electronic version of documents, which is unfortunately rather difficult to access [25]. The main disadvantage of these electronic content-based methods is their complete inefficiency on documents composed only with raster images instead of primitives (text, graphics and images). In [11, 24], we proposed to mix the two methodologies in order to analyze each category of PDF documents.

The second methodology contains two different families of techniques for extracting structures and annotations from documents: extending and restructuring techniques.

In general, extending methods analyze the content of the document in order to reconstitute the original structure and add annotations (e.g. PDF tags on the original raw data without reorganizing document primitives). Specific application and plug-ins often allow an interpretation of those annotations in order to access to structured content and to add new annotations. Extending methods have been applied with interesting results in different works [5, 14, and 18].

Restructuring techniques target to represent the electronic document in a format different from the original PDF such as in XML, which allows accessing easily the information for further uses. The most interesting case of restructuring is the reverse engineering where the document content is analysed in order to be reorganized in respect to the discovered structures. Different researches [3, 7, 8, 9, and 23] and products [29, 15] are based on reverse engineering techniques. Conversion belongs to a special case of restructuring techniques: logical structures are not recovered, PDF files being only transformed into another format, easier to handle. Currently, the amount of PDF converters is very consistent [6, 10, 19, 22, and 30].

In the following sections, we present the XCDF, a canonical format representing analysed PDF; XED, our system for reverse engineering of PDF, is then described; finally, different user-cases and applications are shown.

3 XCDF, an eXhaustive Canonical Document Format

Reverse engineering of PDF files implies the definition of a format able to represent the reorganized document in a structured and unique manner. This task is in general underestimated because most existing works target at recovering structures as a final scope or need only chunks of linearized document information. A canonical format representing electronic documents in a unique and structured manner would greatly help users and researchers to access easily the document content for further works. From our point of view, such a canonical document format must guarantee the full respect of the following principles:

1. All the primitives contained in the original document (texts, graphics and images) must be represented in the new document in an easy, concise and non-ambiguous way;
2. The textual content must be hierarchically structured: homogeneous text blocks containing lines themselves divided into character sequences (called tokens);
3. This format must be user-friendly.

The canonical format is represented in a structured way with a set of well-defined primitives, where the textual content of a page is segmented into blocks, which are themselves divided into lines and, finally, the latter into tokens (syntactical primitives: words, punctuation signs, numbers, special characters and white spaces). Graphical primitives are labeled as threads, frames or general paths. Finally, images are represented with information on their bounding boxes and a reference to their source files. The following partial DTD emphasizes the document hierarchy and describes the main primitives of the canonical format in more details:

```
<!ELEMENT document (fonts?, page+)>
<!ELEMENT fonts (font+)>
<!ELEMENT page (image*, graphic*, frame*, thread*, textblock*,)>
<!ELEMENT graphic (path*)>
<!ELEMENT path (line, cubic, quadratic)*>
<!ELEMENT textblock (textline*)>
<!ELEMENT textline (token*)>
```

This DTD only shows the elements, not their attributes. Each visible element contains attributes for its position, color, style and others specificities. For instance, the "token" element has a special attribute named "content" containing the syntactical text primitives encoded with the UTF-8 standard.

4   XED: The Canonical Format Builder

This section presents XED, a system that reverse engineers original PDF files into a canonical XML form: XCDF. XED proceeds in two main steps: firstly, it converts the PDF document in an internal Java tree, normalizing the primitives of the original document and taking into account all types of embedded resources such as raw images and fonts. Secondly, XED analyzes the internal Java tree document for recovering physical structures and representing them in the canonical format.

The reverse engineering method was developed and tested on a dataset containing documents with complex physical and logical structures such as newspapers. Documents with simpler layout have also been tested successfully so far, without supplemental and specific calibration of the system.

Since the extraction phase has already been exhaustively presented in [11, 24], the following of this section concentrates only on the documents physical structure analysis in order to produce the document canonical representation. The method proceeds in ten key steps:

1. Trim all text primitives in order to remove all superfluous white spaces (being part of text primitives as well as standalone). This is a crucial step because, sometimes, a word could have white spaces between its own letters.
2. Create a layer per angle α existing in the text primitives. The number of layers is then equal to the number of different angles existing in the document.

Following steps are applied for each layer:

3. Apply a linear transformation to rotate the current layer text primitives of an angle $-\alpha$ about the origin of the 2D space (so every text primitive is finally in a horizontal position, its angle being equal to zero).
4. Merge text primitives horizontally to obtain new strings, given a dynamic[1] distance threshold. This results in a basic text segmentation;
5. Tokenize the previous strings using a separators list and obtain isolated pure words, numbers, punctuation signs and special characters. These new-segmented entities are actually textual primitives in the canonical format; henceforth, we will call them "tokens".

---

[1] Thresholds are dynamically generated from the font size and occasionally from other relevant text features.

Fig. 1. Blocks with overlapping bounding boxes are correctly merged

Fig. 2. Result of retroactive merging

6. Merge horizontally the tokens into lines with a dynamic distance threshold, adding required nonexistent white spaces between consecutive token of a line;
7. Merge the lines vertically into blocks given a dynamic distance threshold. This part of the algorithm is similar to connected component detection in image processing (in the paradigm, we can consider lines being pixels and neighbors being adjacent lines). This technique allows to detect overlapped text blocks and to avoid unwanted merging (see fig. 1).
8. Apply retroactive merging. Parse all blocks content in order to recompose over-segmented lines. This over-segmentation is inducted from the dynamic low thresholds generated in step 6: in case of justified lines (fig. 2), the distance between strings increases and, consequently, lines are not always correctly merged. This step corrects all over-segmentation errors in blocks.
9. Apply inverse linear transformation to rotate every text primitive of the current layer back into its original angle.
10. Parse all canonical tokens and label them with a syntactical attribute "word", "number", "white space", "punctuation" or "symbol".

For concision purpose, the ten steps presented above have been simplified and adapted for western newspapers (Latin languages). Arabic and oriental languages are not currently taken into account. Our algorithm is effective with any text angle, since the merging occurs only in a specified layer at a time (text primitives with identical angles). The reading order is perfectly respected; indeed, we sort tokens, lines and blocks before each merging. A relevant feature of our system is its ability to generate the canonical format over any PDF file without specific customization. Indeed, thresholds are not static, they are generated by ratios of dynamic values (font size, interline, etc). Moreover, used ratios (thus thresholds) tend to be minimal, over-segmentation being preferable than under-segmentation.

Fig. 3. Canonical text generation steps

Fig. 3 shows the application of our method on an extract of the International Herald Tribune electronic version. The four images illustrate respectively: the raw segmentation, the canonical tokens, text lines and text blocks. An overview of the XCDF file generated for the current example is presented below (only a subset of element attributes is shown).

```
<textblock x="81" y="374" w="145" h="137">
  <textline x="81" y="374.85" w="145" h="32">
    <token size="32" content="Bush"/>
    <token size="32" content=" "/>
    <token size="32" content="plans"/>
  </textline>
  <textline x="81" y="409" w="140" h="32">
    <token size="32" content="to"/>
    <token size="32" content=" "/>
    <token size="32" content="support"/>
  </textline>
  <textline x="81" y="444" w="116" h="32">
    <token size="32" content="a"/>
    <token size="32" content=" "/>
    <token size="32" content="'"/>
    <token size="32" content="strong"/>
  </textline>
  <textline x="81" y="479" w="105" h="32">
    <token size="32" content="Europe"/>
    <token size="32" content="'"/>
  </textline>
</textblock>
```

An evaluation of the XCDF file generation has been performed on a set of representative Latin newspapers front pages, i.e. *La Liberté*, *Le Monde* and the *International Herald Tribune*. For each newspaper, 10 front pages have been extracted and represented in the canonical format. Table 2 shows the percentage of correct tokens, text lines and text blocks detected, in respect to human judgement.

Table 2. Evaluation of canonical format generation

	La Liberté	*Le Monde*	*International Herald tribune*
% of correct tokens	99.90	99.94	99.94
% of correct text lines	99.24	99.57	99.47
% of correct text blocks	97.00	98.26	98.96

5 Applications Using XCDF and XED

This section presents three applications based on XCDF, the canonical format generated with XED: first, an implementation extracting daily TV schedules is presented; second, a tool for the logical restructuring of newspapers is overviewed; finally, the integration in a multimedia meeting browser is introduced.

TV Schedules

Given our canonical document format, the great deal is now to reconstruct the underlying logical structure of different classes of documents. We first tried to generate the logical information of TV schedules. To reach this purpose, we elaborated a simple DTD corresponding to our requirements (for concision purposes, attributes are omitted):

```
<!ELEMENT tvprogram (tvdate+)>
<!ELEMENT tvdate (tvchannel+)>
<!ELEMENT tvchannel (tvshow+)>
```

We then downloaded various standard PDF files from the Swiss TV website (fig 4). We generated one week of TV schedules for 6 different TV channels, so we got 42 PDF files. After that, we generated the 42 associated XCDF files. Since there, we analysed the canonical files as follows:

1. Removal of superfluous information, in our case: images, graphics, and texts using small fonts;
2. Seeking of the most pertinent information: the TV show times. The simplest way to achieve this was to apply a regular expression over all the remaining text blocks: "\d{2}:\d{2}" in Perl style.
3. Retrieving the text lines corresponding to the TV show times. This was done by analysing relative positions.
4. Label text lines with title and description attributes. This was done simply by querying the font face (bold for title and normal for description).
   We finally got the XML logical structure corresponding to the previous DTD:

```
<tvprogram descripiton="TSR television programs">
 <tvdate year="2005" month="09" day="21">
  <tvchannel channel="TSR2">
   <tvshow p="am" h="06" m="40" t="Zavévu" d="" />
   <tvshow p="am" h="06" m="42" t="TiTeuF" d="Tchernobyl" />
   <tvshow p="am" h="06" m="50" t="Shin Chan" d="Maman a …" />
   <tvshow p="pm" h="20" m="00" t="Banco Jass" d="" />
   <tvshow p="pm" h="20" m="05" t="Le doc nature" d="Jura …" />
  </tvchannel>
 </tvdate>
</tvprogram>
```

The logical file generated from the 42 canonical files was perfect. Of course, the physical layout was not very complex and so was it for the logical layout. This simplicity allowed us to implement a hard coded algorithm. These results prove the relevance of our canonical format and open the field for more complex document logical restructuring.

148   J.-L. Bloechle et al.

Fig. 4. Extract of TV schedule (September 21, 2005)

Dolores

From the canonical document format presented above, Dolores (**Do**cument **Lo**gical **Res**tructuring, a new tool under development) aims at recovering the underlying logical structures of documents (newspaper, scientific papers...). This knowledge could drastically improve search, retrieval and document alignment due to a more precise indexing (profiting of logical information). Currently, Dolores focuses on the newspaper class because it offers a lot of interesting and relevant features: a rich layout with a lot of typographical and topological information as well as deep logical hierarchies.

So, the first step was to define a logical format able to represent, in an adequate way, the logical structure of the newspapers. No pure physical data like position, width, typographical information or even the page on which elements are located are given; instead, a link to the physical representation described by the canonical format is established by means of unique identifiers. The newspaper class logical format is subject-centered, giving a way to group articles belonging to a same theme. It is also designed to ignore topological complications, e.g. an article distributed on different pages. Finally, this format enables to differentiate various types of articles (e.g. news or interviews). Figure 11 shows an example of this logical format applied to an article.

The method we applied to recover the logical structure from newspapers was inspired by the approach introduced by Souafi-Bensafi et al., detailed in [27]. The authors focused on periodic magazines. They labeled the text blocks by means of a naïve bayesian network, justifying this probabilistic approach by the need to recover errors inducted from OCR. As we do not rely on OCR for the physical structure extraction phase but on PDF electronic documents, we opted for artificial neural networks (ANN). So, we kept their bottom-up scheme: first label the basic text blocks (canonial text blocks in our case) with an ANN using mainly topological and typographical information and, later on, reconstruct the logical structure using previously labeled text blocks. More precisely, this reconstruction is based on the one hand on the results of the labeling generated by the ANN, and on the other hand on geometric information. Small deterministic automatons have been implemented in order to describe general article disposition for a given class of newspaper. For example, the typical article shown on fig. 5 begins by a title, followed by the content of the article (which can be composed of text blocks or images). This particular structure is a simple one, but more complex structure can also be described with this mechanism. Rules are then used to reconstruct a logical structure, based on the information detailed above.

Fig. 5. Example of a logical structure

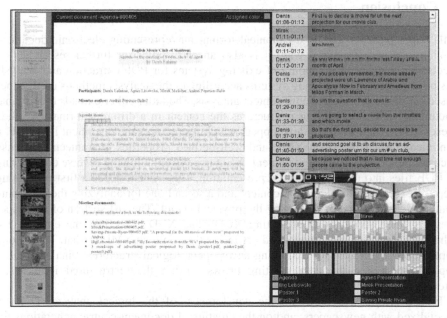

Fig. 6. A screenshot of JFriDoc, a document-centric multimedia meeting browser

Our first experiments gave encouraging results and allowed us to underline some difficulties to overcome. It is relevant to note that these results were first experimentations, but they proved the viability of our approach. More extensive and complete research on logical structure reconstruction will be conducted in the near future.

JFriDoc Multimedia Browser

Building document-centric multimedia meeting browser requires numerous preliminary multimodal analyses. A meeting is an event containing discussed documents, videos of participants and presentations, audio and further. The main tasks required before being able to query or browse meetings, using documents, are multimedia mining and indexing, document structures extraction and finally multimodal document alignment.

XED has been used in different prototypes of multimedia browsers and in particular with an implementation of FriDoc [26], based on JFerret [14, 28].

JFriDoc needs XED for extracting the physical structures from documents, which are then manually annotated with logical information using the Inquisitor tool [26]. Finally, the resulting canonical physical structure is matched with the structured meeting dialogues transcription in order to thematically align them and, thereafter, enrich documents with time indexes [20].

In the next future works, XED will be fully integrated in the multimedia browsers FaericWorld [26], exploring new types of annotation allowing indexing and alignment of documents.

6 Conclusion

This paper presents XCDF, a canonical format for representing electronic document in a unique and structured way; it is also an entry point for further researches on electronic analysis. A taxonomy of existing systems for PDF extraction and analysis has been presented, organizing systems according to the analysis methods used: either based on image or on electronic content analysis. The latter either extends the original document with annotation or restructures the content in a different format. We then presented the algorithm we developped, which restructures the document in XCDF, a canonical format based on XML and well-defined properties guaranteeing an easy access to document structured content. XED is a system allowing reverse engineering of PDF files into their canonical representation. This system needs a first processing step for extracting the electronic content and a second one for analyzing the electronic content, in particular for extracting the physical layout. The last section of this paper presents three applications exploiting XCDF and XED. The first one extracts TV schedules from PDF documents and organizes them into an XML format. The second application is a system for extracting newspapers' logical structures. Finally, the last application is a multimedia meeting browser using the restructured PDF as an interface to access other medias.

Future efforts will focus on the development of the logical analyzer Dolores, specialized with newspapers, and on the creation of document-centric annotations for multimedia browsing, such as classification of document by type (for instance, newspapers, research articles, papers, etc.).

References

1. Adobe PDF reference, http://partners.adobe.com/asn/tech/pdf/specifications.jsp
2. Adobe's Online Converter, http://www.adobe.com/products/acrobat/access_onlinetools. html
3. Anjewierden, A.: AIDAS: Incremental logical structure discovery in PDF document. Sixth International Conference on Document Analysis and Recognition (ICDAR'01), Seattle, USA (2001) 374-377

4. Anjewierden, A., Kabel, S.: Automatic indexing of documents with ontologies. 13th Belgian/Dutch Conference on Artificial Intelligence (BNAIC 2001), Amsterdam, Holland (2001) 23-30
5. Bagley, S. R., Brailsford, D. F., Hardy, M. R. B.: Creating reusable well-structured PDF as a sequence of component object graphic (COG) elements. ACM Symposium on Document Engineering (DocEng'03), Grenoble, France (2003) 58-67
6. BCL, http://www.bcltechnologies.com/document/index.asp
7. Chao, H., Fan, J.: Layout and Content Extraction for PDF Documents. IAPR International Workshop on Document Analysis Systems (DAS'04), Florence Italy (2004) 213-224
8. Chao, H., Xiaofan, L.: Capturing the Layout of electronic Documents for Reuse in Variable Data. Eighth International Conference on Document Analysis and Recognition (ICDAR'05), Seoul, Korea (2005) 940-944
9. Futrelle, R. P., Shap, M., Cieslik, C., Grimes, A. E.: Extraction, layout analysis and classification of diagrams in PDF documents. Seventh International Conference on Document Analysis and Recognition (ICDAR'03), Edinburgh, Scotland (2003) 1007-1012
10. Glance, http://www.pdf-tools.com/en/home.asp
11. Hadjar, K., Rigamonti, M., Lalanne, D., Ingold, R.: Xed: a new tool for eXtracting hidden structures from Electronic Documents. Document Image Analysis for Libraries (DIAL'04), Palo Alto, USA (2004) 212-221
12. Hadjar, K., Hitz, O., Robadey, I., Ingold, R.: Configuration REcognition Model for Complex Reverse Engineering Methods: 2(CREM). 5th International Workshop on Document Analysis Systems (DAS'02), Princeton, New Jersey (2002) 469-479
13. Hadjar, K., Ingold, R.: Arabic Newspaper Page Segmentation. Seventh International Conference on Document Analysis and Recognition (ICDAR'03), Edinburgh, Scotland (2003) 895-899
14. Hardy, M. R. B. , Brailsford, D., Thomas, P.L.: Creating Structured PDF Files Using XML Templates. ACM Symposium on Document Engineering (DocEng'04), Milwaukee, USA (2004) 99-108
15. JFerret, http://mmm.idiap.ch
16. JPEDAL, http://www.jpedal.org
17. Lawrence, S., Bollacker, K., Lee Giles, C.: Indexing and Retrieval of Scientific Literature, Eighth International Conference on Information and Knowledge Management (CIKM'99), Kansas City, USA (1999) 139-146
18. Lovegrove, W. S., Brailsford, D. F.: Document analysis of PDF files: methods, results and implications. Electronic publishing (1995) 207-220
19. MatterCast, http://www.mattercast.com/default.aspx
20. Mekhaldi, D., Lalanne, D., Ingold, R.: From Searching to Browsing through Multimodal Documents Linking. Eighth International Conference on Document Analysis and Recognition (ICDAR'05), Seoul, Korea (2005) 924-928
21. Paknad, M. D., Ayers, R. M.: Method and apparatus for identifying words described in a portable electronic document. U.S. Patent 5,832,530 (1998)
22. PDFTextStream, http://snowtide.com/home/PDFTextStream
23. Rahman, F., Alam, H.: Conversion of PDF documents into HTML: a case study of document image analysis, Conference Record of the Thirty-Seventh Asilomar Conference on Signals, Systems and Computers 2003, USA (2003) 87-91
24. Rigamonti, M., Hadjar, K., Lalanne, D., Ingold, R.: Xed: un outil pour l'extraction et l'analyse de documents PDF. Huitième Colloque International Francophone sur l'Ecrit et le Document (CIFED 2004), La Rochelle, France (2004) 85-90

25. Rigamonti, M., Bloechle, J.-L., Hadjar, K., Lalanne, D., Ingold, R.: Towards a Canonical and Structured Representation of PDF Documents through Reverse Engineering. Eighth International Conference on Document Analysis and Recognition (ICDAR'05), Seoul, Korea (2005) 1050-1054

26. Rigamonti, M., Lalanne, D., Evéquoz, F., Ingold, R.: Browsing multimedia archives through implicit and explicit cross-modal links. 2nd Joint Workshop on Multimodal Interaction and Related Machine Learning Algorithms (MLMI'05), Edinburgh, Scotland (2005) *to be published*

27. Souafi-Bensafi, S., Parizeau, M., Lebourgeois, F., Emptoz, H.: Logical labeling usings Bayesian Networks. Sixth International Conference on Document Analysis and Recognition (ICDAR'01), Seattle, USA (2001) 832-836

28. Wellner, P., Flynn, M., Guillemot, S.: Browsing Recorded Meeting With Ferret. Joint Workshop on Multimodal Interaction and Related Machine Learning Algorithms (MLMI'04), Martigny, Switzerland (2005) 12-21

29. Xed online, http://diuf.unifr.ch/diva/xed

30. xpdf, http://www.foolabs.com/xpdf/home.html

Structural Analysis of Mathematical Formulae with Verification Based on Formula Description Grammar

Seiichi Toyota[1], Seiichi Uchida[2], and Masakazu Suzuki[3]

[1] Graduate School of Mathematics, Kyushu University
ma204035@math.kyushu-u.ac.jp
[2] Faculty of Information Science and Electrical Engineering, Kyushu University
uchida@is.kyushu-u.ac.jp
[3] Faculty of Mathematics, Kyushu University
suzuki@math.kyushu-u.ac.jp

Abstract. In this paper, a reliable and efficient structural analysis method for mathematical formulae is proposed for practical mathematical OCR. The proposed method consists of three steps. In the first step, a fast structural analysis algorithm is performed on each mathematical formula to obtain a tree representation of the formula. This step generally provides a correct tree representation but sometimes provides an erroneous representation. Therefore, the tree representation is verified by the following two steps. In the second step, the result of the analysis step, (i.e., a tree representation) is converted into a one-dimensional representation. The third step is a verification step where the one-dimensional representation is parsed by a formula description grammar, which is a context-free grammar specialized for mathematical formulae. If the one-dimensional representation is not accepted by the grammar, the result of the analysis step is detected as an erroneous result and alarmed to OCR users. This three-step organization achieves reliable and efficient structural analysis without any two-dimensional grammars.

1 Introduction

In this paper, a reliable and efficient structural analysis method for mathematical formulae is proposed for realization of practical mathematical OCR [2]. The purpose of the proposed method is to provide a tree representation for each mathematical formula together with an estimate of its reliability. In case of low reliability, that is, when the tree representation result is suspicious, users can have an alarm from the proposed method.

As shown in **Fig.1**, the proposed method consists of three steps:

1. representation of the two-dimensional structure of each mathematical formula as a tree,
2. conversion of the tree representation to a one-dimensional representation, and

H. Bunke and A.L. Spitz (Eds.): DAS 2006, LNCS 3872, pp. 153–163, 2006.
© Springer-Verlag Berlin Heidelberg 2006

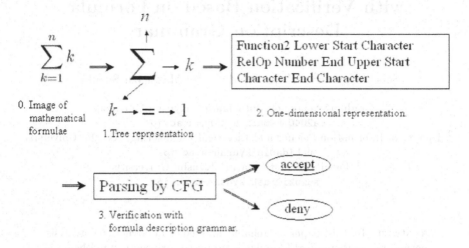

Fig. 1. Flow of the proposed method

3. verification of the one-dimensional representation with a formula description grammar.

In the first step, hereafter called the *analysis step*, a tree representation is constructed for each mathematical formula by considering positional relations between component characters/symbols. This tree construction can be performed very efficiently using the technique proposed in [4, 8]. Furthermore, this analysis step is robust to errors in character/symbol recognition results by a preceding character/symbol recognition engine. For example, the tree representation allows unmatched parentheses. Thus, the following steps should detect two kinds of errors, namely character/symbol-level error (i.e., misrecognitions) and structure-level error.

In the second step, hereafter called the *conversion step*, the tree representation by the analysis step is converted into an equivalent one-dimensional representation. The resulting representation is similar to LATEX representation of mathematical formulae.

In the third step, hereafter called the *verification step*, the one-dimensional representation is parsed by a formula description grammar, which is a context-free grammar (CFG) specialized for mathematical formulae. The prepared grammar is based on a content base interpretation of mathematical formulae (see Section 4). Therefore, the third step corresponds to the final spell check process after recognition in usual OCR. If the one-dimensional representation is not accepted by the grammar, the result of the analysis step is detected as an erroneous result and alarmed to OCR users. Consequently, this step verifies the tree representation provided by the analysis step. Note that the verification step has the potential to detect both of the structure-level errors and the character/symbol-level errors.

Several researchers have considered structural analysis of mathematical formulae. However, most of these methods assume that all the characters/symbols are correctly recognized. Anderson's technique [1] parses using a precedence matrix. Chou [3] devises a two-dimensional stochastic context-free tree grammar, and parses with a generalization of the Cocke–Younger–Kasami algorithm. Applied to two-dimensional grammars, the CYK algorithm is slow on a single processor, though it can be parallelized. Zanibbi [11] has proposed a faster method using two-dimensional grammars, based on tree transformation. Fateman [5] has achieved acceptable speed on a mathematical grammar with left-to-right recursive descent. Okamoto's approach [7] is fast and works solely on the basis of layout, without any grammar whatsoever. A survey of some other methods can be found in [2, 6, 10].

Our technique represents mathematical structure as a tree, using the output of the Eto-Suzuki algorithm [4, 8] applied to individual character recognition results from OCR. This algorithm takes OCR recognition candidates on a page, and arranges them into a tree, optimizing a cost associated to each arrangement. The algorithm can produce several candidate results. The results might include misrecognized characters, or a strange formula structure.

Structural analysis procedures based purely on grammar will fail and provide no structural analysis result when character/symbol-level errors are included. Thus, in the case of failure, OCR users would need to build an *entire* structural analysis result manually. In contrast, the proposed method always can provide some structural analysis result as a tree because it analyzes characters/symbols using only layout information of them. It returns many candidates and their costs after layout analysis. Therefore, if the first candidate is mistaken, it searches for a correct result from other candidates. It rejects candidates that do not conform to a verification grammar that we introduce. This grammar of the verification is based on content rules similar to content mark-up in MathML. By inferring the roles of the symbols, we expect to raise the accuracy of structural analysis.

The remaining part of this paper is organized as follows. Section 2 describes the analysis step for a tree-based structural analysis. Section 3 describes the conversion step for converting the tree representation by the analysis step to a one-dimensional representation. Section 4 describes the verification step using the formula description grammar. Experimental results are provided in Section 5 and in Section 6 a conclusion is drawn.

2   Analysis Step

The analysis step is based on the efficient structural analysis method proposed in [4, 8]. The analysis step provides a tree representation for each mathematical formula. Each component character/symbol of a formula is a leaf of the tree. If two component characters/symbols are "adjacent" (e.g., horizontally adjacent like "2" and "x" of "$2x$", or diagonally adjacent like "x" and "2" of "x^2", or vertically adjacent like "$\sum$" and "x" of "$\sum_x$"), their corresponding leaves are connected by a link. The tree is built as an minimum path algorithm where adjacency, positional relation, and size relation are used as costs. It should be

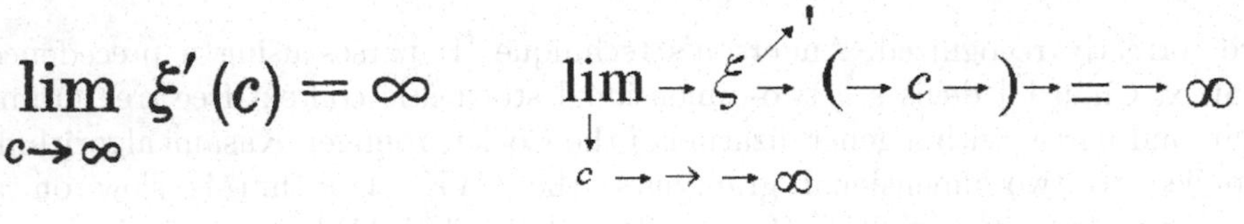

$$\lim_{c \to \infty} \xi'(c) = \infty \qquad \lim_{c \to \to \to \infty} \to \xi \to (\to c \to) \to = \to \infty$$

(a) Original image   (b) Tree representation

Fig. 2. A formula whose structure is perfectly analyzed by the analysis step

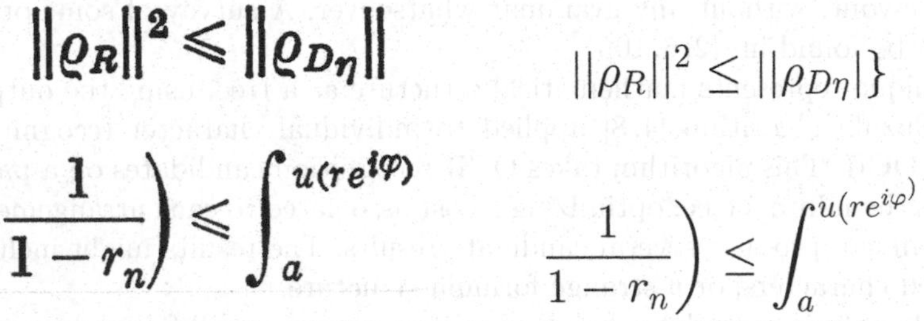

$$\|\varrho_R\|^2 \leqslant \|\varrho_{D\eta}\| \qquad \|\rho_R\|^2 \leq \|\rho_{D\eta}|\}$$

$$\left.\frac{1}{1-r_n}\right) \leqslant \int_a^{u(re^{i\varphi})} \qquad \left.\frac{1}{1-r_n}\right) \leq \int_a^{u(re^{i\varphi})}$$

(a) Original image   (b) Analysis result

Fig. 3. Failures at the analysis step. The upper example includes misrecognition of "|" as "}". The lower example includes a structure-level error where the rightmost parenthesis ")" is treated as a superscript of "e".

noted that this tree can be built with few computations. **Fig. 2** shows several tree representations of formulae provided by the analysis step successfully.

Although the analysis step generally provides correct tree representations, it sometimes fails. This is because the analysis step does not care about the classes of adjacent characters/symbols. For example, the analysis step may allow a strange tree where two "+"s are linked together. In addition, the classes themselves may be erroneous due to the failures by a preceding character/symbol recognition procedure.

Typical failure examples are shown in **Fig.3**. The upper example includes a character/symbol-level error, i.e., a misrecognition of character/symbol. The lower example includes a structure-level error, i.e., error in the structure of the tree, and the position of the right parenthesis is erroneous.

3   Conversion Step

The conversion step of the proposed method connects the preceding analysis step and the succeeding verification step. The result of the analysis step is a tree, i.e., a kind of two-dimensional structure, while the verification step will accept one-dimensional sequences because it is based on a one-dimensional (i.e., usual) CFG. Thus, the role of the conversion step is the transformation of the tree representation into an equivalent one-dimensional representation.

In the conversion, the structure and the component characters/symbols of each mathematical formula are represented by the terminals of **Table 1**. Several

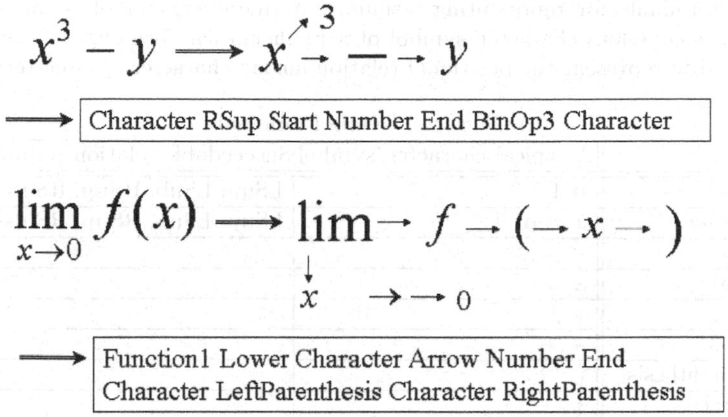

$$x^3 - y \longrightarrow x\overset{3}{\nearrow}\; \text{-}\; \rightarrow y$$

$\longrightarrow$ | Character RSup Start Number End BinOp3 Character

$$\lim_{x \to 0} f(x) \longrightarrow \lim \to f \to (\to x \to)$$
$$\downarrow$$
$$x \quad \to \to 0$$

$\longrightarrow$ | Function1 Lower Character Arrow Number End
Character LeftParenthesis Character RightParenthesis

Fig. 4. Example of a one-dimensional representation of a formula. The tree representation of each formula is also presented.

terms, such as Number, Character, BinOp, etc., represent the category of component character/symbol. Other terms, such as LSup (left superscript), RSub (right subscript), etc., represent the structure of the tree. Roman and Greek letters are classified into the same category(Character). Start and End, are used to specify the range of a super/subscript. The conversion step also prepares the category of each parentheses and punctuation. The choice of category is restricted by existing subarea links.

The conversion rule transforms the tree representation into a one-dimensional representation like the LaTeX description of mathematical formula. The details of the conversion are omitted here. **Fig.4** shows examples of the conversion.

4   Verification Step

The role of the verification step is the detection of structure-level errors and character/symbol-level errors in the result of the analysis step. The verification relies on parsing based on a formula description grammar, which is a context-free grammar specialized for mathematical formulae. Thus, we can implement this verification procedure with any conventional parsing technique for CFG. In the following experiment, we used the well-known chart method for parsing. The terminals used in our CFG are listed in the **Table 1**.

Assume that a mathematical formula "(a)" is wrongly analyzed as "$(a]$". Consider the following grammar:

⟨Start⟩ ::= ⟨Expr⟩

⟨Expr⟩ ::= Character

⟨Expr⟩ ::= LeftParenthesis ⟨Expr⟩ RightParenthesis

⟨Expr⟩ ::= LeftBracket ⟨Expr⟩ RightBracket

Table 1. Terminals for representing formulas. A character/symbol terminal corresponds to a component character/symbol of a mathematical formula. A relation terminal is used to represent the positional relation among character/symbol terminals.

(a) Character/symbol terminals

Terminal	A typical character/symbol	Succeedable relation terminals
Number	$0, 1$	LSup, LSub, RSup, RSub
Character	x, y, α, β	LSup, LSub, RSup, RSub
RelOp	$<, =, >$	
BinOp1	$\div, \times$	
BinOp2	$*, /$	
BinOp3	$+, -$	
LeftParenthesis	$($	
LeftBrace	$\{$	
LeftBracket	$[$	
RightParenthesis	$)$	RSup, RSub
RightBrace	$\}$	RSup, RSub
RightBracket	$]$	RSup, RSub
LeftFloor	$\lfloor$	
LeftCeil	$\lceil$	
LeftAngle	$\langle$	
RightFloor	$\rfloor$	RSup, RSub
RightCeil	$\rceil$	RSup, RSub
RightAngle	$\rangle$	RSup, RSub
OtherParenthesis	$|, \|$	
Point	$", ', ; $	
Function1	$\lim$	Lower
Function2	$\sum, \Pi$	Lower, Upper
Function3	$\sin, \cos$	RSup
Function4	$\int$	RSup, RSub
Arrow	$\leftarrow, \rightarrow$	Upper, Lower

(b) Relation terminals

Terminal	Meaning
Start	Start for range of script
End	End for range of script
RSub	Right subcript
RSup	Right superscript
LSub	Left subscript
LSup	Left superscript
Lower	Lower script
Upper	Upper script

where $\langle \ \rangle$ indicates a non-terminal. This grammar will accept the following sequence representing the formula "(a)":

LeftParenthesis Character RightParenthesis

On the other hand, the above analysis result "(a]" is represented as the following sequence:

LeftParenthesis Character RightBracket

and thus will not be accepted by the grammar. Consequently, a user will have an alarm of an erroneous analysis result according to this verification result.

In practice, we prepare more grammar rules for the verification of various kinds of mathematical formulae; the above tiny example, however, shows the basic approach of the verification step. Note that Anderson's grammar [1] will be helpful to understand the entire rule set.

5   Experimental Results

The verification performance of the proposed method was evaluated by using mathematical formula images extracted from the ground-truthed mathematical document database called INFTY CDB-1 [9]. The ground-truth data for each mathematical formula in INFTY CDB-1 is composed of (i) the correct class of each component character/symbol and (ii) the correct tree structure of the formula.

The experiment focused on the ability of the verification step (i.e., the third step) on detecting the failures at the analysis step (i.e., the first step). The failures at the analysis step are classified into the following two types: misrecognition of component character/symbols (e.g., "/"(slash)→ "l"), and wrong analysis of positional relations (e.g., "x^2A"→ "x2A"). The verification step has the potential to detect both failures.

Figures 5–9 show several results of the proposed method. In each of those figures, formula images (left) and their analysis results by the first step (right) are shown. The analysis results are represented as formulae synthesized by applying the analysis results to the LATEX complier.

Figure 5 shows the results that the verification step could detect the failure of the character/symbol misrecognition at the analysis step. Several characters were misrecognized in the analysis results. For example, in the top example, a mathematical symbol "/"(slash) was misrecognized as "l". In the third example, a character "c" and a symbol "→" touch one another. Thus, they were misrecognized as a single symbol "↦" as shown in the analysis result.

Those results with misrecognitions were successfully detected by the verification step. For example, our CFG does not accept the expression "$\pi l2$" because the CFG requires that digits ("2") should precede letters ("l") if they form a single and horizontally aligned term. The CFG also does not accept the expression "lim, →" because the CFG requires that the first character/symbol of a right subscript should not be an binary operator (e.g., "↦").

Figure 6 shows how that the verification step could detect the failure of the wrong analysis of positional relations at the analysis step. In the first example of this figure, a correspondence of a left parenthesis in the right superscript of the mathematical symbol("$\int$") is wrong. In the second example, the point which a

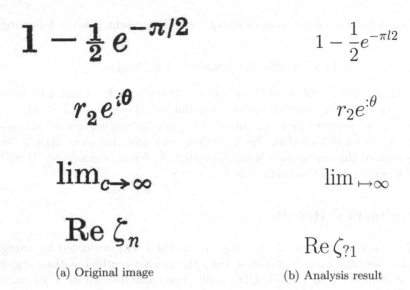

(a) Original image

(b) Analysis result

Fig. 5. Formulae whose character/symbol-level errors were successfully detected by the verification step

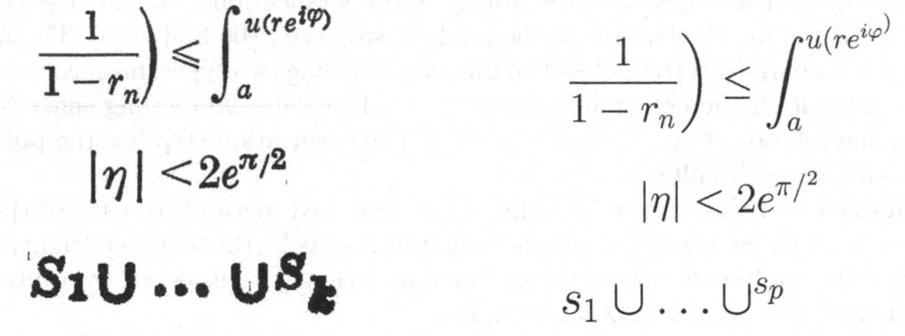

(a) Original image

(b) Analysis result

Fig. 6. Formulae whose structure-level errors were successfully detected by the verification step

mathematical symbol "/"(slash) has a right superscript of "2" is nonsense as a mathematical formula. In the same fashion, the above failure of the positional misrecognition can be detected by this verification.

Figure 7 shows the case that the results of the analysis step include not only misrecognition but also wrong positional analysis. Like the previous examples, this complex failure is also detected by the verification step.

Figure 8 show formulae whose structure-level errors could not be detected by the proposed method. In the first example, the right superscript letter ("$\frac{1}{2}$") of the right square bracket("]") was misrecognized as "g", but this verification is not detected because both of "$\frac{1}{2}$" and "g" are correct as mathematical formulae. In the second example, the position of "A" is wrong. A mathematical symbol

$$||\varrho||^2 \leqslant ||\varrho_{G_i}||$$

$$||\rho||^2 \leq ||\rho_G : ||$$

$$\mu_{S_\bullet}(a'$$

$$\mu_S, (a'$$

(a) Original image   (b) Analysis result

Fig. 7. Formulae whose both character/symbol-level errors and structure-level errors were successfully detected by the verification step

$$D_\Omega[u]^{\frac{1}{2}}$$

$$D_\Omega[u]^g$$

$$||\varrho||_A^2 = \int\int_A \varrho^2 dx\, dy$$

$$||\rho||^2 A = \int\int_A \rho^2 dxdy$$

(a) Original image   (b) Analysis result

Fig. 8. Formulae whose errors could not be detected by the verification step

$$\mu^*$$

$$\mu^*$$

$$\Theta(c) = \int_{l(c)} |*du|$$

$$\Theta(c) = \int_{l(c)} |*du|$$

(a) Original image   (b) Analysis result

Fig. 9. False alarm by the verification step, that is, formulae wrongly detected as erroneous ones

("|") has a possibility of a right subscript like this. Therefore, in this case, there is nothing to detect the failure. The proposed method, however, could not detect this failure because the CFG is insufficient to detect that the character/symbol was misrecognized as a meaningful formula. We can reduce these undetected failures by adding new grammar rules to our CFG.

Figure 9 shows the false alarms by the proposed method. The analysis step could analyze the structure of those formulae successfully. The verification step, however, judged that they are wrong. This is because "*", which is usually a binary operator, appears without a left operand. We will reduce these false alarms by revising our CFG; however, false alarms are less serious than undetected failures. Our method is a verification method and therefore the analysis results detected by the proposed method will be checked by users just as "suspicious" results.

6   Conclusion

We have proposed a reliable and efficient structural analysis method for mathematical formulae, where a verification procedure based on formula description grammar is utilized. First, we assume that the structure of each mathematical formula is analyzed and represented as a tree. Although this analysis can be done efficiently, its result often includes structure-level errors and/or character/symbol-level errors. Thus, the formula description grammar, which is a context-free grammar specialized for mathematical formulae, is used to parse and verify the tree representation. This verification also can be done efficiently, because the tree representation is converted into a one-dimensional representation before parsing. If the one-dimensional representation is not accepted by the grammar, the failing portion will be included in the tree representation but alarmed to users. Experimental results showed that the proposed method can detect some erroneous tree representations successfully.

In the future, we plan to quantitatively evaluate our verification procedure, using data from InftyCDB-1 and *Infty-Reader* [12] which implemented Eto and Suzuki's algorithm. The verification procedure should accept correctly-analyzed formulas and reject incorrectly-analyzed formulas at a high rate. Also, we plan to study how additional semantic information can be used to select structural recognition results from the candidates allowed by our verification grammar.

Acknowledgement

This research is supported by the Kyushu University 21st Century COE Program: "Development of Dynamic Mathematics with High Functionality".

References

1. R.H. Anderson, "Syntax-directed recognition of hand-printed two-dimensional mathematics," Interactive Systems for Experimental Applied Mathematics, M. Klerer and J. Reinfelds, Eds. Academic Press, pp. 436-459, 1968.
2. K. -F. Chan, D. -Y. Yeung, "Mathematical expression recognition: a survey," Int. J. Doc. Anal. Recognit. vol. 3, no. 1, pp. 3-15, 2000.
3. P. A. Chou, "Recognition of equations using a two-dimensional stochastic context-free grammar," Proc. SPIE, vol. 1199, pt. 2, pp. 852-863, 1989.
4. Y. Eto and M. Suzuki, "Mathematical Formula Recognition Using Virtual Link Network," Proc. ICDAR, pp. 430-437, 2001.
5. R.J. Fateman, T. Tokuyasu, B.P. Berman, N. Mitchell, "Optical character recognition and parsing of typeset mathematics," Journal of Visual Communication and Image Representation vol 7 no. 1, pp. 2-15, 1996.

6. U. Garain and B. B. Chaudhuri, "A syntactic approach for processing mathematical expressions in printed documents," Proc. ICPR, vol. 4 of 4, pp.523-526, 2000.
7. M. Okamoto, B. Miao, "Recognition of mathematical expressions by using the layout structure of symbols," Proceedings of First International Conference on Document Analysis and Recognition Saint Malo, pp. 242-250, 1991.
8. M. Suzuki, F. Tamari, R. Fukuda, S. Uchida, and T. Kanahori, "INFTY — An integrated OCR system for mathematical documents," Proc. ACM Symposium on Document Engineering, pp.95-104, 2003.
9. M. Suzuki, S. Uchida, and A. Nomura, "A ground-truthed mathematical character and symbol image database," Proc. ICDAR, vol. 2 of 2, pp. 675-679, 2005.
10. J. -Y. Toumit, and S. Garcia-Salicetti, H. Emptoz, "A hierarchical and recursive model of mathematical expressions for automatic reading of mathematical documents," Proc. ICDAR, pp. 119-122, 1999.
11. R. Zanibbi, D. Blostein, J.R. Cordy, "Recognizing mathematical expressions using tree transformation," IEEE Trans. Pattern Anal. Mach. Intell., vol. 24, no. 11, pp.1455-1467, 2002
12. Infty-Reader, http://www.inftyproject.org/en/download.html.

Notes on Contemporary Table Recognition

David W. Embley[1], Daniel Lopresti[2], and George Nagy[3]

[1] Computer Science Department,
Brigham Young University, Provo, UT 84602
embley@cs.byu.edu
[2] Department of Computer Science and Engineering,
Lehigh University, Bethlehem, PA 18015
lopresti@cse.lehigh.edu
[3] Department of Electrical, Computer, and Systems Engineering,
Rensselaer Polytechnic Institute, Troy, NY 12180
nagy@ecse.rpi.edu

Abstract. The shift of interest to web tables in HTML and PDF files, coupled with the incorporation of table analysis and conversion routines in commercial desktop document processing software, are likely to turn table recognition into more of a systems than an algorithmic issue. We illustrate the transition by some actual examples of web table conversion. We then suggest that the appropriate target format for table analysis, whether performed by conventional customized programs or by off-the-shelf software, is a representation based on the abstract table introduced by X. Wang in 1996. We show that the Wang model is adequate for some useful tasks that prove elusive for less explicit representations, and outline our plans to develop a semi-automated table processing system to demonstrate this approach. Screen-snaphots of a prototype tool to allow table mark-up in the style of Wang are also presented.

1 Introduction

Tables have long been widely used for *presenting* structured information just as printed forms are widely used for *collecting* structured information. Few scientific papers are considered complete without a table or two. There are several government agencies whose main product is tables. Because most of us prefer to "point-and-click" instead of trudging over to the library, tables available on the web are of most use and interest.

We note parenthetically that a successful solution to the table recognition problem will hasten the disappearance of tables, which are in any case an endangered species. Traditional railroad and airplane schedules have already been replaced by on-line Q/A forms. Five-place trigonometric tables were supplanted by ten-digit hand-held calculators. The fat volume of values of the binomial distribution for various n's, k's, and p's is also gone. The British Royal Commission on Mathematical Tables disbanded almost fifty years ago.

Old tables may appear on the web in scanned bitmap form, as in back issues of the *Transactions* in the IEEE Digital Library. Current information, however,

H. Bunke and A.L. Spitz (Eds.): DAS 2006, LNCS 3872, pp. 164–175, 2006.
© Springer-Verlag Berlin Heidelberg 2006

is more likely to be posted as PDF or HTML files, and XML tagging is making headway. Archival material is being gradually converted, most often by manual data entry. Aside from the shift from raw bitmaps to coded forms, an important development is the rapid incorporation of table analysis routines into Microsoft and Adobe software.

Earlier researchers were handicapped by having to build complete low-level table processing software, including OCR, before they could even think about putting table recognition to some use. Most of their hard work yielded only intermediate results. Our purpose here is to initiate discussion on whether we are now in a position to incorporate table recognition in operational applications.

The paper is organized as follows. After describing our view of low-level table processing, we will suggest that this step can now be circumvented by judicious us of common "office" software.[1] The inter-conversion between tables in HTML, PDF, XLM, XLS and DOC files is demonstrated. We then discuss possible table representations for bridging the semantic gap that has so far kept table recognition from being incorporated into routine information retrieval and data extraction applications. The foundations of a *table ontology* for organizing our current understanding of table processing techniques and tools are then sketched. We conclude by briefly outlining our plans to develop a semi-automated table processing system to demonstrate the approach we are proposing, and by describing a prototype tool we have developed for capturing table mark-up in the style of Wang.

2   Low-Level Table Recognition

Low level table recognition implies table representations that allow the formal manipulation of tables without any real understanding of their contents. The "intelligence" comes entirely from the user, who is able to interpret the table in the context of previously acquired knowledge. In Table 1, it is easy to tell that the average "hepth" of "fleck" is approximately 233 "gd," but this does not readily connect with any other piece of generally known information.

Even low-level table recognition requires some analysis. Operations such as computing the average of a row or column of values require, at the minimum, a *geometric model* (i.e., a table frame, grid, array model).

Table 1.

	gonsity (ld/gg)	hepth (gd)
fleck		
burlam	1.2	120
falder	2.3	230
multon	2.5	350

Table 2.

goldam	1.3 ld/gg	320 gd
falder	2.3 ld/gg	230 gd
elmer	2.9 ld/gg	350 gd

---

[1] The functionality we will be illustrating is by no means limited to Microsoft Office, although we use applications from that software suite to illustrate our discussion.

Fig. 1. Array models for Tables 1 and 2

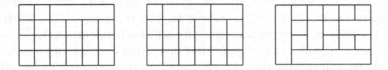

Fig. 2. Array models for more complex tables

For Tables 1 and 2, the model is simple, as shown in Fig. 1. Other tables, with spanning top or side headers, may require merging cells. While all WFT (well-formed table) layouts are topologically equivalent to an array model derived by merging sets of adjacent cells in a regular grid, some models, like the one on the far right in Fig. 2, seem implausible because larger cells are generally above or to the left of smaller cells. We note, however, that a table author may indeed choose to use such a layout to emphasize that a set of columns share a common value in a given row.

Deriving the appropriate array model for a table with multi-line cells without complete rulings has proved difficult. In the last 15 years, over 200 research papers have been published on table recognition [1, 2, 3, 4, 5]. Most published algorithms for cell alignment treat the table as a 2-D array of cells, and attempt to identify the coordinates and contents of each cell. Methods vary depending on whether the table is in scanned bitmap or coded (ASCII, HTML, RTF, PDF) form, ruled, partially ruled or unruled, and on the amount of prior information (including both "external" knowledge base and training data) available. Furthermore, some methods make use only of the layout geometry, while others bring in font, style, lexical and syntactic information extracted from the textual cell contents.

3   Commercial Software

We will demonstrate some of the content-preserving table conversion routines that have been built into Microsoft and Adobe desk-top software. Consider the table appearing in Fig. 3, *Country Data Codes*, rendered by Microsoft Explorer. (FIPS 10-4 codes are intended for general use throughout the US Government. ISO 3166 codes are activities involving exchange of data with international organizations. The Internet country code is the two-letter digraph used by the Internet Assigned Numbers Authority, IANA.) Recent versions of Microsoft Word

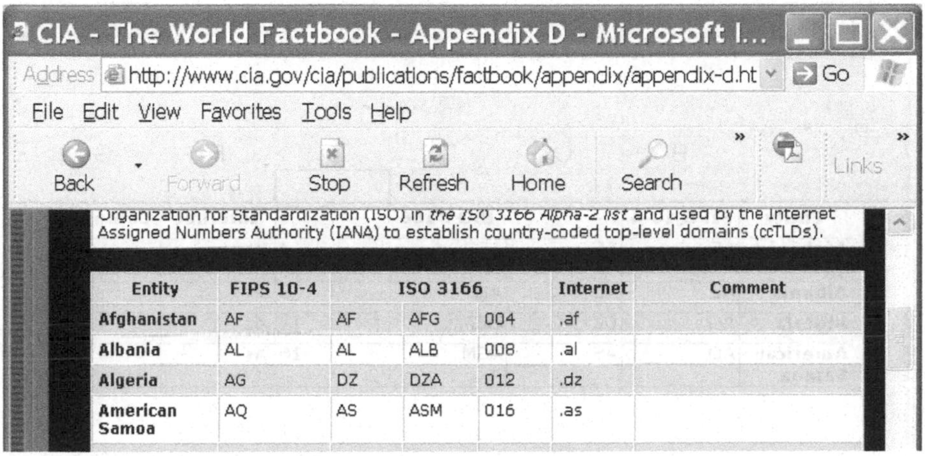

Entity	FIPS 10-4	ISO 3166			Internet	Comment
Afghanistan	AF	AF	AFG	004	.af	
Albania	AL	AL	ALB	008	.al	
Algeria	AG	DZ	DZA	012	.dz	
American Samoa	AQ	AS	ASM	016	.as	

Fig. 3. Table as rendered by Microsoft Internet Explorer 6.0

Entity	FIPS 10- 4	ISO 3166			Internet	Comment
Afghanistan	AF	AF	AFG	004	.af	
Albania	AL	AL	ALB	008	.al	
Algeria	AG	DZ	DZA	012	.dz	
American Samoa	AQ	AS	ASM	016	.as	

Fig. 4. Table copied into Microsoft Word 10.2

are able to copy this table it into a .doc format file without evident loss of information, as seen in Fig. 4. Word is more accurate in this respect than Wordpad, we have found.

From MS-Word, any table can be loaded into MS-Excel, which is a reasonable choice for either automated or interactive cell-level manipulation (cf. Fig. 5). Furthermore, Excel has built-in export routines for transferring the table to a database management system (Microsoft Access).

If the table appeared originally as ASCII text, as it might in an email, it would look like Fig. 6. This tab-separated text file can also be loaded into the spreadsheet program without loss of any layout information.

Another popular file format is Adobe's Portable Document Format, which is essentially enhanced PostScript. Fig. 7 was extracted from a PDF document posted on the website of the Bureau of Labor Statistics. It was then saved using the Adobe Acrobat "table picker" function with the XML tags added. We have not yet been able to automate the recovery of table structure from either PDF or XML, however the prototype tool we shall describe later provides support to facilitate human mark-up of the structure of tables encoded in HTML. Some researchers claim that recovering layout from PDF is done most easily from a rendered pixel map!

	A	B	C	D	E	F	G
1							
2	Entity	FIPS 10-4	ISO 3166			Internet	Comment
3	Afghanist an	AF	AF	AFG	4	.af	
4	Albania	AL	AL	ALB	8	.al	
5	Algeria	AG	DZ	DZA	12	.dz	
6	American Samoa	AQ	AS	ASM	16	.as	
7							
8							

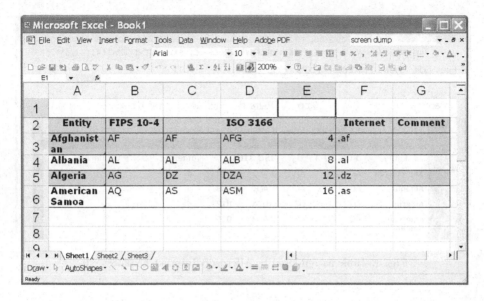

Fig. 5. Table copied from Microsoft Word into Microsoft Excel 10.2

```
Entity           FIPS 10-4   ISO 3166    Internet   Comment
Afghanistan      AF    AF    AFG   004   .af
Albania          AL    AL    ALB   008   .al
Algeria          AG    DZ    DZA   012   .dz
American Samoa   AQ    AS    ASM   016   .as
```

Fig. 6. ASCII version of the table

Table 3. Dissimilarity indexes of labor force projections

Age	BLS projections	Standards of comparison		
		Actual population and—		Census population estimate and—
		BLS participation rate	1988 participation rate	1988 participation rate
Gender, age	1.83	2.02	2.24	2.32
Men, age	1.63	.91	.62	1.37
Women, age	1.91	2.86	2.4	1.32

Fig. 7. Table rendered from a PDF file

4 High-Level Table Recognition

Some of the important applications of high-level table recognition are:

– Recreate an *equivalent* table for human reading by changing the spacing or the font, or by interchanging the rows and columns.

- Enter the attribute-value pairs (e.g., {(*fleck*, *burlam*), (*gonsity*, *1.2*), (*hepth*, 120)}) into a relational database, and re-frame queries in SQL.
- Combine several tables, or extend a selected table by adding information from another table. For example, we could discover that the gonsity of fleck oltan is 2.7 ld/gg, and its hepth is 100 gd, and add this row to Table 1.
- Compare several tables to determine if all or some entries are identical.
- Create conceptual models or ontologies from a large number of tables with interlocking entries. Having seen Table 1, clever software could derive a new average hepth of fleck (300 gd) from Table 2, or an average for all five fleck (274 gd) by combining the two tables. We will discuss below the distant but tantalizing possibility of *machine understanding* of tables.

An issue that keeps recurring in our on-going surveys of table recognition [1, 3, 4] is what should be the output of a table interpretation program. Specific output formats differ widely, but many are equivalent to a spreadsheet where cell contents can be addressed by coordinates. The more advanced methods allow addressing each cell by its row or column header.

The low-level array model is inadequate for answering some queries. The array model is identical for Tables 3 and 4 below. In order to take advantage of the headers in Table 3, it is necessary to first recognize that they are headers and to incorporate them in a higher-level table representation. We therefore attempt to go beyond the current output conventions, along the lines laid out by X. Wang [6] (who was interested in the description and manipulation of tables as *abstract data types*, not in table recognition). In the case of spanning cells, the row and headers form multiple trees. This is captured neatly by the Wang notation. The number of tree-paths necessary to specify a content cell is called the *dimensionality* of the table. (The number of content cells, in contrast, is the *size* of the table.) We stop short of claiming "semantic" interpretation, which is a murky concept in our view.

	Table 3.				Table 4.	

fleck	gonsity (ld/gg)	hepth (gd)		fleck	gonsity (ld/gg)	hepth (gd)
burlam	1.2	120		burlam	1.2	120
falder	2.3	230		falder	2.3	230
multon	2.5	350		multon	2.5	350

Very informally, the Wang Model consists of two components (C, δ), where C is a finite set of labeled domains (or categories), and δ is a mapping from the tree paths labels (or headers) to the possible values. We give the flavor with two examples.

The Wang Model for Table 3 is:

$$C = \begin{cases} (fleck, \{(bulram, \phi), (falder, \phi), (multon, \phi)\}) \\ (characteristic, \{(gonsity, \phi), (hepth, \phi)\}) \end{cases} \tag{1}$$

$$
\delta = \begin{cases}
(\{fleck.burlam, \ characteristic.gonsity\}) \rightarrow 1.2 \\
(\{fleck.falder, \ characteristic.gonsity\}) \rightarrow 2.3 \\
\ldots \\
(\{fleck.multon, \ characteristic.hepth\}) \rightarrow 350
\end{cases} \tag{2}
$$

Note that "characteristic" does not appear in the table at all: we had to invent it in order to provide a root (i.e., a spanning label) for the column-header tree paths to the content cell entries! We call such imputed headers *implicit headers*. The absence of explicit headers is the major difference between high-level and low-level table interpretation. The experienced reader is able to infer them, but it is not easy to devise a robust algorithm that can infer them. The situation is even worse in Table 4, where both implicit headers are missing.

Consider now the more complex table shown in Fig. 7. Here we need a spanning label for "BLS projections" and "Standards of comparison." Let us call this "BLS/STD." Then there are three categories:

$$
C = \begin{cases}
(Age, \ \{(Gender\_age, \phi), \ (Men\_age, \phi), \ (Women\_age, \phi)\}) \\
(BLS \ projections, \phi) \\
(BLS/STD \ (Standards \ of \ comparison \ (Actual \ population \ and- \\
\quad \{(BLS \ participation \ rate, \phi), \ (1988 \ participation \ rate, \phi)\}))) \\
(BLS/STD \ (Standards \ of \ comparison \ (Census \ populations \\
\quad estimate \ and-, \ \{(1988 \ participation \ rate, \phi)\})))
\end{cases}
$$

$$\tag{3}$$

Note that there are two identical column headers called "1988 participation rate." Therefore we need to differentiate the "actual population" and the "1988 participation rates" from the "census population estimates" and the "1988 participation rates." Not an easy table to understand for human or machine! Once the correct label structure is derived, however, the tree-path specifications of the content values are straightforward.

If the logical structure is described completely, i.e., all the headers are present and have been clearly identified, and the geometric structure is specified (say in Excel, with merged cells of the fundamental grid), then it is not difficult to devise an algorithm to obtain a Wang Model of the target table. Such a model fills most of the needs listed at the beginning of this section. It does not, however, imply any true understanding. For instance, even if we know that burlam has only about half the gonsity and hepth of falder, we may not know which is better suited for some purpose, or whether one is likely to be more expensive than the other.

5   External Information

Useful information can often be derived from the text, graphics, or other tables in the same or related documents as the target table. Currently, this is considered outside the domain of table processing, though several research papers have began to explore the topic [7, 8]. Table captions are similar to nearby ancillary information. They do not directly affect the physical or logical structure of the table. Some of the tasks listed above can be readily performed without considering captions.

Footnotes are also often neglected. Wang considers this the greatest shortcoming of her model, because nearly half of the tables she collected had footnotes. From our perspective, however, a footnote is simply cell content that exceeds the physical size of the cell. Footnotes can refer to either header or content cells.

The really important external information is that which does not appear anywhere in the vicinity of the table, but forms part of the users knowledge base. It is possible, however, that such a knowledge base can be assembled from studying a large collection of diverse but related tables. This, in fact, is one of our long term research objectives [9–11].

6   Components of a Table Ontology

Table recognition is a fast-moving target. To keep up with current and future developments, we believe that it is time to assemble the various ideas and tools so that they can be utilized and updated effectively. We believe that the appropriate conceptual and organizational framework for this purpose is an ontology, because an ontology is capable of representing a very broad class of relationships and is essentially open to new constituents and relationships. Some of the components that should be included in any table ontology are listed below.

- Table spotting, location, isolation, demarcation and classification
- Recognition of within-document and external references, including titles, captions, footnotes and citations
- Frame or border detection (box surrounding table)
  - Vertical rules
  - Horizontal rules
  - Line thickness, style, color
- Layout analysis to recover underlying array model
  - Ruled, partially ruled, unruled tables
  - White-space analysis
  - Horizontal text-line segmentation and alignment (single and multiple lines)
  - Vertical text alignment (justification, indentation, centering)
- Font analysis
  - Type size
  - Typeface (at least font family), color
  - Style (bold, italic, sub/superscript)
  - Case (capitalization)
  - Code translation or OCR
- Determination of cell-content similarities and affinities according to
  - Geometry (alignment, size)
  - Typography (type size and face)
  - Lexical category (words, phrases, commensurable decimal/integer values, abbreviations, units)

- • Grammatical construct (part of speech)
  - • Semantics (to the extent possible)
- − Extraction and codification of cell contents
  - • Common and proper nouns (dictionaries and directories)
  - • Phrases
  - • Numeric fields (cardinal, ordinal, interval, integer, decimal)
  - • Common data types (date, time, address, telephone number, email)
  - • Punctuation (ellipsis, parenthesis, hyphen, comma)
  - • Special symbols ($, ditto marks, leaders)
- − Construction of logical table interpretation as a Wang Model or equivalent
  data structure

7   Work in Progress

In this paper we have laid the foundation for work that is still very much in
progress. Our goal — which we shall demonstrate at least in part at the DAS
workshop — is to explore an area of table understanding that has hitherto remained unexamined: the transformation of table data presented in a simple array
model to its full Wang representation. This is perhaps best illustrated in Fig. 8,
where we show the most common formats for encoding tables, transitions between formats that are adequately supported by current commercial software
solutions (solid arrows), transitions that have been the subject of much past research (thin dashed arrows), and the research we are targeting (the thick dashed
arrow in the lower center of the figure).

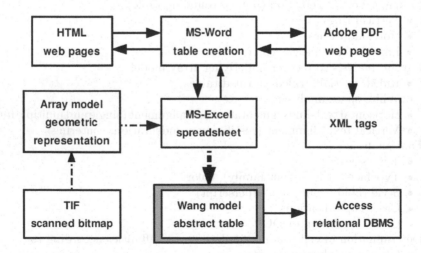

Fig. 8. Existing table conversion software. Solid arrows indicate available commercial
software. Thin dashed arrows show focus of past research systems. Thick dashed arrow
shows planned research.

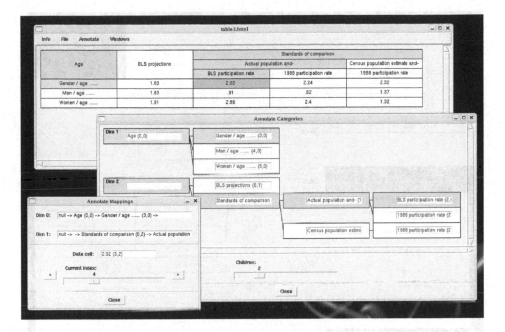

Fig. 9. Screen snapshot of a tool for supporting Wang-style table mark-up

We are currently in the process of implementing a graphical mark-up tool
to semi-automate data capture from web tables, transforming a table in cell
array format into its Wang Model. Our operating hypothesis is that this approach, like past experience with Computer Assisted Visual Interactive Recognition (CAVIAR) [12, 13], will be both more accurate than a fully automated
system while at the same time faster than an unaided human. This work is intended, of course, to be a first step towards the ultimate goal of autonomous
table understanding.

Figures 9 and 10 show screen snapshots of our prototype which is written in
Tcl/Tk, a popular scripting language for developing user interfaces. The table in
Figure 9 should look familiar as it is simply the table from Figure 7 re-rendered
in HTML, the input format used by our tool. The table in Figure 10 is the
canonical example of a 3-D table used by Wang in her thesis [6].

Given an input table, the user first annotates the category structure, which
consists of a set of trees specifying the row and column headers. Each logical
dimension of the table corresponds to a single tree: the table in Figures 9 is
2-D, while Figure 10 shows a 3-D table. Note that every data cell in the table
is uniquely specified (indexed) by a set of paths from the root of a tree to a
leaf: one such path for each tree. After specifying the category trees, the user
then populates the nodes by first clicking on the appropriate cell in the input
table and then on the tree node that represents it. Once the category trees are
completely populated, the mapping from sets of paths to individual data cells
can be stepped through, one by one, with the user selecting at each step the

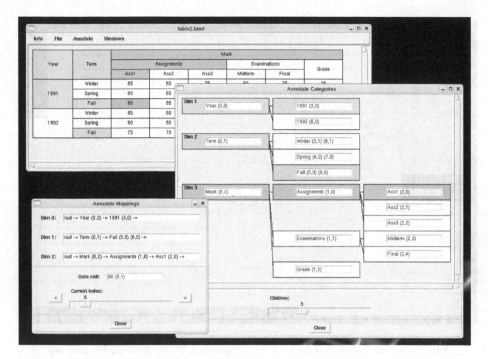

Fig. 10. Another example of Wang-style mark-up created using our prototype tool

appropriate cell in the input table. The tool then outputs the marked-up table in HTML format, with additional tags encoding the Wang structure.

While still just a prototype, this approach appears to be quite effective: the editing time for an expert user to create the annotation shown in Figure 9 was less than 30 seconds, requiring a total of 18 mouse-clicks. The larger, more complicated table in Figure 10, on the other hand, needed two minutes and 40 seconds and 116 mouse-clicks. We continue to work, of course, on refining our tool and plan more extensive user studies in the near future.

We close by citing some other recent developments that appear promising. The work by Pivk, et al. presents an approach for generating F-Logic frames from web tables which can then be used to populate ontologies [14]. They develop not only the methodology, but also an unusually thorough evaluation paradigm. Zanibbi, et al. present a language for representing table recognition strategies which exposes previously hidden assumptions buried within an implementation and offers to shed new light on the decision making process during table processing [15]. Both of these efforts relate to our own.

Acknowledgments

We wish to thank the anonymous reviewers whose comments helped make this a better paper. David W. Embley and George Nagy gratefully acknowledge the support of NSF grants #0414644 and #0414854.

References

1. Embley, D.W., Hurst, M., Lopresti, D., Nagy, G.: Table processing paradigms: A research survey. (2005) In submission.
2. Hurst, M.: The Interpretation of Tables in Texts. PhD thesis, University of Edinburgh (2000)
3. Lopresti, D., Nagy, G.: Automated table processing: An (opinionated) survey. In: Proceedings of the Third IAPR International Workshop on Graphics Recognition, Jaipur, India (1999) 109–134
4. Lopresti, D., Nagy, G.: A tabular survey of automated table processing. In Chhabra, A.K., Dori, D., eds.: Graphics Recognition: Recent Advances. Volume 1941 of Lecture Notes in Computer Science. Springer-Verlag, Berlin, Germany (2000) 93–120
5. Zanibbi, R., Blostein, D., Cordy, J.R.: A survey of table recognition: Models, observations, transformations, and inferences. International Journal on Document Analysis and Recognition **7** (2004) 1–16
6. Wang, X.: Tabular abstraction, editing, and formatting. PhD thesis, University of Waterloo (1996)
7. Douglas, S., Hurst, M., Quinn, D.: Using natural language processing for identifying and interpreting tables in plain text. In: Proceedings of the Symposium on Document Analysis and Information Retrieval (SDAIR'95), Las Vegas, NV (1995) 535–545
8. Hurst, M., Douglas, S.: Layout and language: Preliminary investigations in recognizing the structure of tables. In: Proceedings of the International Conference on Document Analysis and Recognition (ICDAR'97). (1997) 1043–1047
9. Embley, D., Tao, C., Liddle, S.: Automatically extracting ontologically specified data from HTML tables with unknown structure. In: Proceedings of the 21st International Conference on Conceptual Modeling (ER'02), Tampere, Finland (2002) 322–327
10. Embley, D., Tao, C., Liddle, S.: Automating the extraction of data from HTML tables with unknown structure. Data and Knowledge Engineering (2005) (in press).
11. Tijerino, Y.A., Embley, D.W., Lonsdale, D.W., Nagy, G.: Towards ontology generation from tables. World Wide Web Journal **8** (2005) 261–285
12. Zou, J.: Computer Assisted Visual InterActive Recognition. PhD thesis, Rensselaer Polytechnic Institute (2004)
13. Zou, J., Nagy, G.: Evaluation of model-based interactive flower recognition. In: Proceedings of the 17th International Conference on Pattern Recognition. Volume 2. (2004) 311–314
14. Pivk, A., Cimiano, P., Sure, Y.: From tables to frames. In: Proceedings of the Third International Semantic Web Conference (ISWC 2004). Volume 3298 of Lecture Notes in Computer Science. Springer Verlag, Hiroshima, Japan (2004) 166–181
15. Zanibbi, R., Blostein, D., Cordy, J.R.: The recognition strategy language. In: Proceedings of the Eighth International Conference on Document Analysis and Recognition, Seoul, South Korea (2005) 565–569

Handwritten Artefact Identification Method for Table Interpretation with Little Use of Previous Knowledge

Luiz Antônio Pereira Neves[1], João Marques de Carvalho[1], Jacques Facon[2], Flávio Bortolozzi[2], and Sérgio Aparecido Ignácio[2]

[1] UFCG-Universidade Federal de Campina Grande,
Caixa Postal 105, 58.109-970, Campina Grande, Paraíba, Brasil
{neves, carvalho}@dee.ufcg.edu.br
[2] PUCPR-Pontifícia Universidade Católica do Paraná,
Rua Imaculada Conceição 1155,
Prado Velho 80215-901, Curitiba-PR, Brazil
{facon, fborto}@ppgia.pucpr.br,
s.ignacio@pucpr.br

Abstract. An artefact identification method for handwritten filled table-forms is presented. Artefacts in table-forms are smudges and overlaps between handwritten data and line segments which increase the complexity of table-form interpretation. After reviewing some knowledge-based methods, a novel artefact identification method to improve table-form interpretation is presented. The proposed method aims to detect, identify and remove table-form artefacts with little use of previous knowledge. Experiments show the significance of using the proposed artefact identification method to improve table-form interpretation rates.

1 Introduction

Tables, or table-forms, are documents composed by cells, which are determined by intersections of straight line segments, as illustrated in figure 1.

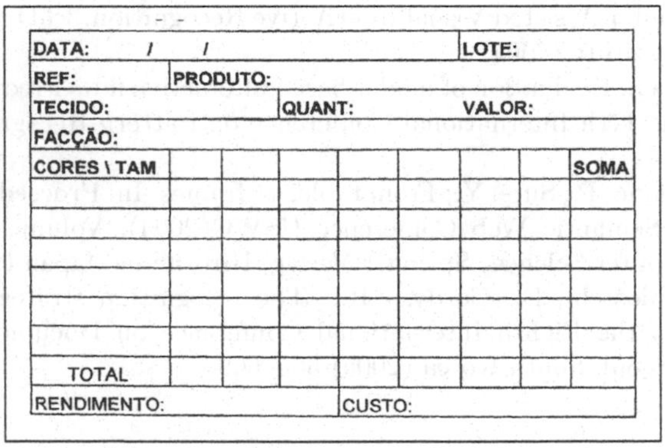

Fig. 1. Example of a table-form document

H. Bunke and A.L. Spitz (Eds.): DAS 2006, LNCS 3872, pp. 176–185, 2006.

Several studies have been presented on table recognition [1], [2], [3], [4], [5], [6], [7], [8], [9]. Some of these researches use tables without imperfections in the horizontal and vertical line segments to reduce the complexity of the problem. In the damaged table case, many researchers use previous knowledge for their interpretations, also aiming to minimize the complexity of the problem.

Since the table-forms considered in this work can be filled in by machines or by hand, overlaps between printed and handwritten information, as shown in figures 2-a and 2-b, might create false intersections. These occurrences are called artefacts. Besides, artefacts can result from faulty table lines, from problems with document acquisition, from binarization problems, or simply from the poor quality of the document, as illustrated by the damaged piece of paper in figure 2-c. Thus, an artefact can be defined as any object, handwritten or not, that produces false table-form intersections. Problems created by artefacts have been partially solved by other researchers. Watanabe [7],[8] presents two procedures, one to be used when no information is previously known and another one when artefacts (noise) characteristics are available in a knowledge base. Couasnon [3] uses previous noise and imperfections knowledge as grammar rules. Arias and Kasturi [1], [2] use the morphological closing operator to eliminate imperfections and to recover the extinguished segment lines for the analysis of the table-form intersections. Liang et al. [10] consider noise and imperfections as previous knowledge. Hori, Doermann [11] and Hirano et al. [12] use table models with noise and imperfections. Shinjo et al. [13] use previous knowledge to detect and correct damages of table corners. Shimotsuji and Asano [14] use table models with imperfections as previous knowledge, to be identified in the interpretation process. Pizano [15] performs image size reduction to eliminate noise and segments, combined with the use of minimum width and distance parameters to eliminate the remaining noise. Tran van Thom [6] performs image size reduction and thresholding for detecting and correcting segments with imperfections.

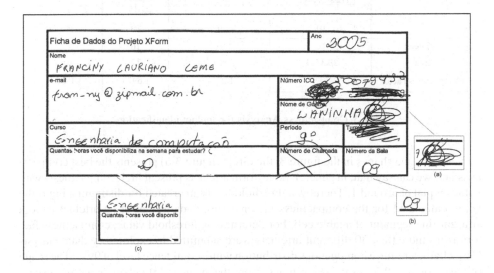

Fig. 2. Examples of artefacts

Analyzing the solutions above, one can conclude that for all methodologies described some form of *a priori* knowledge is needed. The aim of this paper is to propose an artefact analysis method with very little use of *a priori* knowledge, to improve table-form interpretation. This method is described in Section 2. Section 3 presents some experimental results and discussions. Finally, the conclusions are given in Section 4.

2   Artefact Identification

The proposed artefact identification method is based on compactness analysis. Compactness is a property that expresses how large is the area concentrated inside a given perimeter, as shown in figure 3. Compactness is measured by the compactness factor, computed from the perimeter and the area of the analyzed shape. Given a shape of perimeter P and area S, its compactness factor is given by FC, as shown in the equation 1.

$$Fc = \frac{P^2}{4\pi S} \tag{1}$$

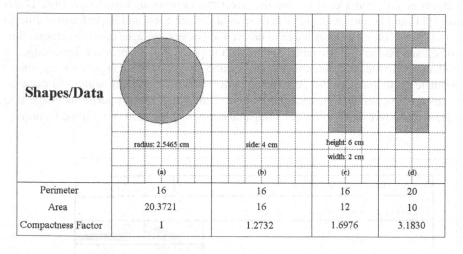

Shapes/Data	radius: 2.5465 cm	side: 4 cm	height: 6 cm width: 2 cm	
	(a)	(b)	(c)	(d)
Perimeter	16	16	16	20
Area	20.3721	16	12	10
Compactness Factor	1	1.2732	1.6976	3.1830

Fig. 3. Compactness Analysis for artefact identification

Verifying the shapes in the figure 3, the circle (figure 3-a) presents the best compactness and we can say that, in general, table-form artefacts present high compactness, with values equal or around 1. Thereby, a threshold has been created for distinguishing if the value calculated for the compactness factor corresponds to that of an artefact or to a straight line segment of a table cell. For determining threshold value, compactness factors from more than 30 different artefacts were submitted to exploratory data analysis [16], characterizing a homogenous distribution with a confidence level of 99%. The range of variation $\mu \pm 2.576 * \sigma$, where μ and σ are the mean and standard deviation respectively, produces inferior and superior limits of 1.21688 and 1.37419, respectvely. The

0.5% of values above the superior limit are not contemplated as artefacts. Therefore, the handwritten data that presents compactness factor below 1.4 is considered an artefact.

Figures 4-a and 4-b show several types of artefacts with the respective compactness factors.

index	artefact	compactness factor
(a)		1.28998
(b)		1.27324
(c)		1.34486
(d)		1.28857
(e)		1.27947
(f)		1.28547

index	artefact	compactness factor
(a)		1.29841
(b)		1.28477
(c)		1.27404
(d)		1.28803
(e)		1.29628
(f)		1.28137

(a)   (b)

Fig. 4. Examples of Artefacts with their compactness factors

index	segment	compactness factor
(a)		1.94365
(b)		4.98904
(c)		1.59781
(d)		5.27407
(e)		3.17814
(f)		1.96736

Fig. 5. Examples of segments that are not artefacts with their compactness factors

Figure 5 shows some table segments with compactness factor values above the established threshold. For figure 5-d, for instance, the compactness factor is 5.27407. This value indicates that the analyzed object is not an artefact, but rather a segment. Therefore, by observing figures 4-a, 4-b and 5, one can conclude that the artefact identification method can make the correct distinction between a handwritten artefact and a table segment.

2.1   Overlap Analysis Step

Overlaps between handwritten data and segments produce misleading values of compactness factors. Analyzing the Pearson variation coefficient [16], [17], using data generated from the horizontal projection profile, it is possible to carry out their elimination. The detection of a peak, which indicates the presence of an undesirable segment among the data, means that an overlap should be deleted, as shown in figure 6-a. By using again the exploratory data analysis [16], one can define the sample variation range which permits elimination of possible undesirable overlaps (table 1). High variability of pixel density values in the horizontal direction (using a confidence level of 90%), characterizes heterogeneous distributions. Then, the range of variation $\mu \pm 1.645 * \sigma$, where μ and σ are the mean and standard deviation respectively, permits to delete the 5% of superior values out of this limit, resulting in overlap elimination, as depicted in figure 6-b. Table 1 shows the data analysis for figure 6-a, where the variation coefficient is high, 74.58%. Therefore, the high standard deviation indicates that the artefact of figure 6-a contains overlaps. Consequently, the overlaps (here the segments) are removed, as illustrated in figure 6-b.

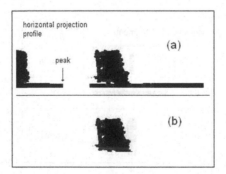

Fig. 6. Example of Artefact with overlapping

Table 1. Analysis of Pearson variation coefficient for figure 6

Analysis	Data	Analysis	Data
Line Numbers	67	Inferior Limit	-15.0473
Mean	66.3284	Superior Limit	147.704
Standard Deviation	49.4685	Variation Coefficient	0.745812

Fig. 7. Examples of analyzed handwritten data, processed without alteration

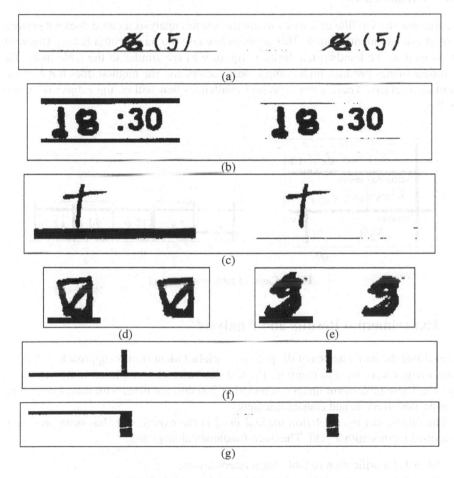

Fig. 8. Examples of artefacts with overlap

Figures 7 and 8 depict some results of artefact analysis and overlap removal. Figures 7-a and 7-b show two successful examples of isolated artefacts without overlap, which represent valid information that must not be removed. Artefact analysis has indicated that the corresponding distributions are homogeneous, since the variation coefficients of figures 7-a and 7-b are 22.96% and 29.32% respectively. So they are not removed.

Figure 8-a shows four overlaps between handwritten data and table lines. These overlaps produce incorrect compactness coefficients. The same occurs in figures 8-b and 8-c. By removing these overlaps, it is possible to correctly identify the true handwritten data. Similarly, overlap analysis makes correct artefact identification easier for figures 8-d and 8-e. Examples of artefacts due to failure in line segments are exhibited in figures 8-f and 8-g, for which overlaps have been correctly eliminated.

2.2 Artefact Cases

Figures 9-a and 9-b illustrate cases where the artefact analysis method does not perform correct artefact identification. This happens because the handwritten letter f (figure 9-a), as well as the handwritten digits 1 (figure 9-b) are similar to the table lines. The resulting shapes produce high compactness factors and the method does not consider them as artefacts. These cases represent challenges that will be the subject of further studies.

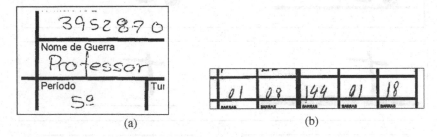

(a)   (b)

Fig. 9. Cases of table with artefact

3 Experimental Results and Analysis

To evaluate the performance of the proposed artefact identification approach, 305 table-form images were used to compose the test database, as exemplified in figures 10, 11 and 12. These table-form images, scanned at 300 dpi, are filled with handwritten data, handwritten overlap, and contain artefacts.

The table-form interpretation method used in the experiments has been previously described by this author [18]. The three fundamental steps are:

Step 1. Identification of table-form intersections;
Step 2. Corner detection and correction;
Step 3. Table interpretation and cell extraction.

The proposed artefact identification approach is inserted between **Steps 2 and 3**. Tests were carried out with and without artefact analysis in order to quantify the improvement produced by the proposed approach. The rate of processed images, shown in table 2, indicates the percentage of images that went through all steps of the methodology. Rejected images are those that did not reach the final processing stage of the methodology. Correctly interpreted images are images that presented no interpretation

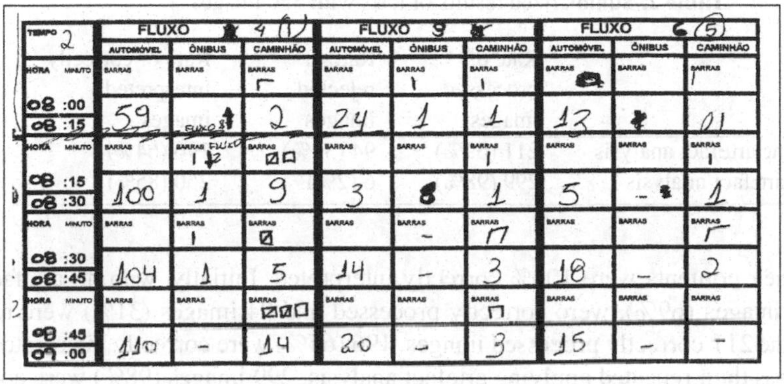

TEMPO 2	FLUXO 4 (1)			FLUXO 9			FLUXO 6 (5)		
	AUTOMÓVEL	ÔNIBUS	CAMINHÃO	AUTOMÓVEL	ÔNIBUS	CAMINHÃO	AUTOMÓVEL	ÔNIBUS	CAMINHÃO
HORA MINUTO	BARRAS	BARRAS	BARRAS	BARRAS	BARRAS	BARRAS	BARRAS	BARRAS	BARRAS
08 :00 08 :15	59		2	24	1	1	12		01
HORA MINUTO	BARRAS	BARRAS	BARRAS	BARRAS	BARRAS	BARRAS	BARRAS	BARRAS	BARRAS
08 :15 08 :30	100	1	9	3		1	5	-	1
HORA MINUTO	BARRAS	BARRAS	BARRAS	BARRAS	BARRAS	BARRAS	BARRAS	BARRAS	BARRAS
08 :30 08 :45	104	1	5	14	-	3	18	-	2
HORA MINUTO	BARRAS	BARRAS	BARRAS	BARRAS	BARRAS	BARRAS	BARRAS	BARRAS	BARRAS
08 :45 09 :00	110	-	14	20	-	3	15	-	-

Fig. 10. Example of table-form in the base of tests

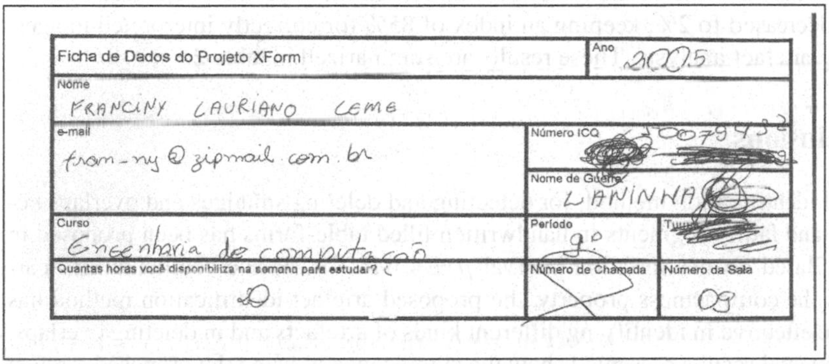

Ficha de Dados do Projeto XForm	Ano 2005
Nome FRANCINY LAURIANO LEME	
e-mail fran-ny@zipmail.com.br	Número ICQ
	Nome de Guerra LANINHA
Curso Engenharia de computação	Período 9º
Quantas horas você disponibiliza na semana para estudar? 20	Número de Chamada / Número da Sala 09

Fig. 11. Example of table-form in the base of tests

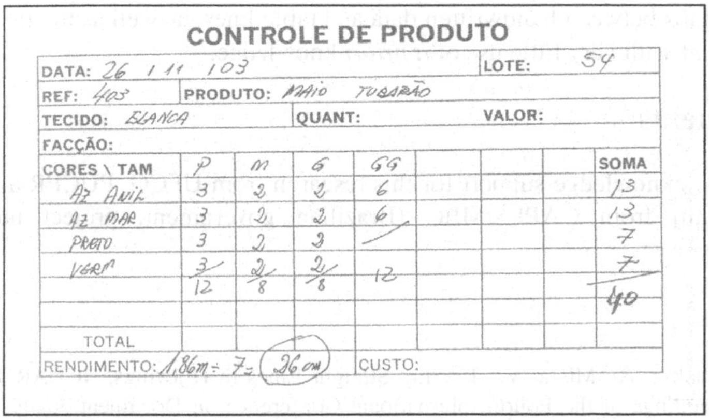

CONTROLE DE PRODUTO

DATA: 26 / 11 / 03						LOTE: 54		
REF: 403	PRODUTO: MAIO TUBARÃO							
TECIDO: BLANCA		QUANT:				VALOR:		
FACÇÃO:								
CORES \ TAM	P	M	G	GG				SOMA
AZ ANIL	3	2	2	6				13
AZ MAR	3	2	2	6				13
PRETO	3	2	2					7
VERM	3	2	2					7
	12	8	8	12				40
TOTAL								
RENDIMENTO: 1,86m ÷ 7 = 26 cm			CUSTO:					

Fig. 12. Example of table-form in the base of tests

Table 2. Summarized results of tests with 350 images

Method	Rate of processed images	Rate of rejected images	Rate of correctly interpreted images
Without using artefact analysis	211 (69%)	94 (31%)	196 (64%)
With using artefact analysis	299 (98%)	6 (2%)	260 (85%)

errors , i.e., their contents were 100% correctly interpreted. Initially, with no artefact analysis, 211 images (69%), were correctly processed and 94 images (31%) were rejected. From the 211 correctly processed images, 196 (64%) were correctly interpreted. The process was then repeated applying artefact analysis. 299 images (98%) were correctly processed and 6 images (2%) were rejected. For the 299 processed images, 260 (85%) were correctly interpreted. A significant result that can be observed is that without artefact analysis 31% of the table-form images in the base were rejected, whereas this index decreased to 2%, keeping an index of 85% for correctly interpreted images, by applying artefact analysis. These results are summarized in table 2.

4   Conclusions

An original identification method, for detecting and deleting smudges and overlaps between data and faulty segments in handwritten filled table-forms has been proposed in this paper. Based on the variation interval $\mu \pm 1.645 * \sigma$, on the coefficient of Pearson and on the compactness property, the proposed artefact identification method has shown to be effective in identifying different kinds of artefacts and in deleting overlaps. The experimental results presented show the significance of using the proposed artefact identification method to improve table-form interpretation rates.

Summarizing the advantages of the method, we mention the possibility of applying it to different types of handwritten filled table-forms for identification of handwritten smudges, of overlaps between handwritten data and table lines, as well as the intersection defects, all that with very little use of *a priori* knowledge.

Acknowledgments

We would like to acknowledge support for this research from UFCG, PUCPR and the PROCAD Program from CAPES/MEC (Brazilian government, project number 153/01-1).

References

1. Arias, J.F., Chhabra, A., Misra, V.: Finding Straight Lines in Drawings. ICDAR 1997 - IEEE In: Proceedings of the Fourth International Conference on Document Analysis and Recognition (1997) 788–791
2. Arias, J.F., Kasturi, R., Chhabra, A.: Efficient Techniques for Telephone Company Line Drawing Interpretation. ICDAR 1995 - IEEE - In: Proceedings of the Third International Conference on Document Analysis and Recognition (1995) 795–798

3. Couasnon, B.: Dmos: A generic document recognition method, application to an automatic generator of musical scores, mathematical formulae and table structures recognition systems. ICDAR 2001 - In: Proceedings of the Sixth International Conference on Document Analysis and Recognition (2001) 215–220

4. Fan, K.C., Lu, J.M., Wang, L.S., Liao, H.Y.: Extraction of characters from form documents by feature point clustering. Pattern Recognition Letters (1995)

5. Hu, J., Kashi, R.S., Lopresti, D., Wilfong, G.T.: Evaluating the performance of table processing algorithms. International Journal on Document Analysis and Recognition **4** (2002) 140–153

6. Thom, R.T.V.: Modélisation de Tableaux pour le traitement Automatique des Formulaires. Laboratoire PSI, Université de Rouen (1997)

7. Watanabe, T., Luo, Q., Sugie, N.: Structure recognition methods for various types of documents. Machine Vision and Applications (1993)

8. Watanabe, T., Luo, Q., Sugie, N.: Layout recognition of multi-kinds of table-form documents. IEEE Transactions on Pattern Analysis and Machine Intelligence (1995)

9. Kieninger, T., Dengel, A.: The t-recs table recognition and analysis system. In: DAS'98 - Proceedings of the Sixth International Conference on Document Analysis Systems (1998) 255–269

10. Liang, J., Ha, J., Haralick, R.M., Phillips, I.T.: Document layout structure extraction using bounding boxes of different entities. WACV 1996 In: Proceedings of the Third IEEE Workshop on Applications of Computer Vision (1996) 278–283

11. Hori, O., Doermann, D.S.: Robust table-form structure analysis based on box-driven reasoning. ICDAR 1995 - In: Proceedings of the Third International Conference on Document Analysis and Recognition (1995) 218–221

12. Hirano, T., Okada, Y., Yoda, F.: Field extraction method from existing forms transmitted by facsimile. ICDAR 2001 - In: Proceedings of the Sixth International Conference on Document Analysis and Recognition (2001) 738–742

13. Shinjo, H., Hadano, E., Marukawa, K., Shima, Y., Saku, H.: A recursive analysis for form cell recognition. ICDAR 2001 In: Proceedings of the Sixth International Conference on Document Analysis and Recognition (2001)

14. Shimotsuji, S., Asano, M.: Form Identification based on Cell Structure. ICPR 1996 - IEEE - In: Proceedings of the 12th IAPR International Conference on Pattern Recognition (1996) 793–797

15. Pizano, A.: Extracting line features from images of business forms and tables. IAPR - In: Proceedings of the 11th International Conference on Pattern Recognition **3** (1992) 399–403

16. Tukey, J.W.: Exploratory Data Analysis. Addison-Wesley (1977)

17. Kazmier, L.J.: Estatística Aplicada a Economia e Administração. Editora McGraw-Hill do Brasil, São Paulo - SP (1982)

18. Neves, L.A.P.: Extração de células de dados manuscritos em tabelas. Master's thesis, Pontifícia Universidade Católica do Paraná - PUCPR (1999)

Writer Identification for Smart Meeting Room Systems

Marcus Liwicki[1], Andreas Schlapbach[1], Horst Bunke[1], Samy Bengio[2],
Johnny Mariéthoz[2], and Jonas Richiardi[3]

[1] Department of Computer Science, University of Bern,
Neubrückstr. 10, CH-3012 Bern, Switzerland
{liwicki, schlpbch, bunke}@iam.unibe.ch
[2] IDIAP, Rue du Simplon 4,
Case Postale 592, CH-1920 Martigny, Switzerland
{bengio, mariethoz}@idiap.ch
[3] Perceptual Artificial Intelligence Laboratory,
Signal Processing Institute, Swiss Federal Institute of Technology,
Lausanne FSTI-ITS-LIAP, Station 11, ELD 243, CH-1015 Lausanne, Switzerland
jonas.richiardi@epfl.ch

Abstract. In this paper we present a text independent on-line writer identification system based on Gaussian Mixture Models (GMMs). This system has been developed in the context of research on Smart Meeting Rooms. The GMMs in our system are trained using two sets of features extracted from a text line. The first feature set is similar to feature sets used in signature verification systems before. It consists of information gathered for each recorded point of the handwriting, while the second feature set contains features extracted from each stroke. While both feature sets perform very favorably, the stroke-based feature set outperforms the point-based feature set in our experiments. We achieve a writer identification rate of 100% for writer sets with up to 100 writers. Increasing the number of writers to 200, the identification rate decreases to 94.75%.

1 Introduction

The aim of a Smart Meeting Room is to automate standard tasks usually performed by humans in a meeting [12, 13, 15, 22]. These tasks include, for instance, note taking and extracting the important issues of a meeting. To accomplish these tasks, a Smart Meeting Room is equipped with synchronized recording interfaces for audio, video and handwritten notes.

The challenges posed in Smart Meeting Room research are manifold. In order to allow indexing and browsing of the recorded data [23], speech [14], handwriting [9] and video recognition systems [4] need to be developed. Another task is the segmentation of the meeting into meeting events. This task can be addressed by using single specialized recognizers for the individual input modalities [15] or by using the primitive features extracted from the data streams [12]. Further tasks deal with the extraction of non-lexical information such as prosody, voice quality variation and laughter. To authenticate the meeting participants and to assign utterances and handwritten notes to their authors, identification and verification systems have to be developed. They are based on speech [11] and video interfaces [5, 18] or on a combination of both [2].

H. Bunke and A.L. Spitz (Eds.): DAS 2006, LNCS 3872, pp. 186–195, 2006.
© Springer-Verlag Berlin Heidelberg 2006

Fig. 1. Picture of the IDIAP Smart Meeting Room with the whiteboard to the left of the presentation screen

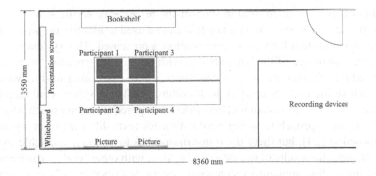

Fig. 2. Schematic overview of the IDIAP Smart Meeting Room (top view)

The writer identification system described in this paper has been developed for the IDIAP Smart Meeting Room [13]. This meeting room is able to record meetings with up to four participants. It is equipped with multiple cameras, microphones, electronic pens for note-taking, a projector, and an electronic whiteboard. Figure 1 shows a picture of this room, and a schematic overview is presented in Fig 2.

The whiteboard shown in Figs. 1 and 2 is equipped with the eBeam[1] system, which acquires the text written on the whiteboard in electronic format. A normal pen in a special casing is used to write on the board. The casing sends infrared signals to a triangular receiver mounted in one of the corners of the whiteboard. The acquisition system outputs a sequence of (x, y)-coordinates representing the location of the pen-tip together with a time stamp for each location. An illustration of the data acquisition process is shown in Fig. 3.

In this paper we describe a system for writer identification using the on-line data acquired by the eBeam interface. Our system uses Gaussian Mixture Models (GMMs)

---

[1] eBeam System by Luidia, Inc. – www.e-Beam.com

Fig. 3. Recording session with the data acquisition device positioned in the upper left corner of the whiteboard

as classifiers which are often used in state-of-the-art speaker verification systems [11]. Our system is text-independent, i.e., any text can be used to identify the writer. In [20] a text-independent system for writer identification is presented. This system uses off-line data, i.e., only an image of the handwriting, with no time information, is available and HMM-based recognizers are used as classifiers. There exist other on-line writer identification and verification systems in the literature [7]. These systems are mainly based on signature, which makes them text dependent compared to our approach which is text independent. An approach to writer verification for texts different from signature has been proposed in [24], but there the transcription has to be made available to the system. To compare the results of our proposed system with other work, we use a modified version of the on-line signature verification system described in [17] as a reference in our experiments. A modification of the system described in [17] has to be made because not all features, i.e., pen pressure, can be extracted from the electronic whiteboard data.

The rest of the paper is structured as follows. In Sect. 2 we present two sets of on-line features for our writer identification system. The Gaussian Mixture Model classifiers are described in Sect. 3. The results of our experiments are presented in Sect. 4. Finally, Sect. 5 concludes the paper and proposes future work.

2   Features

The text written on the whiteboard is encoded as a sequence of time-stamped (x, y)-coordinates. From this sequence, we extract a sequence of feature vectors and use them to train the classifier. Before feature extraction, some simple preprocessing steps are applied to remove spurious points and to fill gaps within strokes [9]. In order to preserve writer specific information, no other normalization operations, such as slant or skew correction, are applied and no resampling of the points is performed. Furthermore, we do not interpolate missing points if the distance between two successive points of a stroke exceeds a predefined threshold [6] as this would remove information about the writing speed of a person.

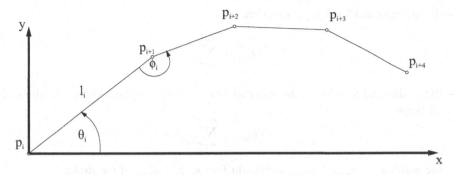

Fig. 4. Point-based features

In this paper we investigate two different approaches for the extraction of the features. In the first approach, we extract features directly from the (x, y)-coordinates of the handwriting (denoted as *point-based* features). In the second approach, we use strokes for the calculation of the features (denoted as *stroke-based* features). A stroke starts with a pen-down movement of the pen and ends with the next pen-up movement. Thus a stroke is a sequence of points during a certain time interval when the pen-tip touches the whiteboard.

The features extracted in the first approach are similar to the ones used in on-line handwriting recognition systems [19] and signature verification systems [7]. For a given stroke s consisting of points p_1 to p_n, we compute the following five features for each consecutive pair of points (p_i, p_{i+1}); for an illustration see Fig. 4:

- the length l_i of the line

$$l_i = d(p_i, p_{i+1})$$

- the writing direction at p_i, i.e., the cosine and sine of θ_i

$$\cos(\theta_i) = \Delta x(p_i, p_{i+1})$$

$$\sin(\theta_i) = \Delta y(p_i, p_{i+1})$$

- the curvature, i.e., the cosine and sine of the angle ϕ_i. These angles can be derived by the following trigonometric formulas:

$$\cos(\phi_i) = \cos(\theta_i) * \cos(\theta_{i+1}) + \sin(\theta_i) * \sin(\theta_{i+1})$$

$$\sin(\phi_i) = \cos(\theta_i) * \sin(\theta_{i+1}) - \sin(\theta_i) * \cos(\theta_{i+1})$$

where $\phi_i = \theta_{i+1} - \theta_i$ (see Fig. 4).

These five features are computed for all the points of each stroke of a text line. We thus get a sequence of five-dimensional feature vectors which can be used for classification. The lengths of the lines l_i implicitly encode the writing speed as the sampling rate of the acquisition hardware is approximately constant.

In the second approach, the extracted feature set is based on strokes. These *stroke-based* features have been designed in the context of this work. For each stroke $s = p_1, \ldots, p_n$ we calculate the following eleven features; for an illustration see Fig. 5:

– the accumulated length l_{acc} of all lines l_i

$$l_{acc} = \sum_{i=1}^{n-1} l_i$$

– the cosine and the sine of the accumulated angle θ_{acc} of the writing directions of all lines

$$\theta_{acc} = \sum_{i=1}^{n-1} \theta_i$$

– the width $w = x_{\max} - x_{\min}$ and height $h = y_{\max} - y_{\min}$ of the stroke
– the duration t of the stroke
– the time difference Δt_{prev} to the previous stroke
– the time difference Δt_{next} to the next stroke
– the total number of points n
– the number of changes n_{changes} in the curvature
– the number of angles n_l of upward writing direction (where $\theta_i > 0$)
– the number of angles n_s of downward writing direction (where $\theta_i < 0$)

The two sets of features presented above provide different information about a person's handwriting. The point-based feature set contains local information about each point of the writing. By contrast, strokes consist of sequences of points and provide rather global information about a handwriting. For example, it is possible to determine whether a person's handwriting is cursive or not from the number of points and changes in the curvature of a stroke. This information is not available from the point-based features.

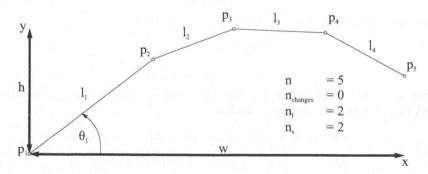

Fig. 5. Stroke-based features

3 Gaussian Mixture Models

In text-independent speaker recognition, Gaussian Mixture Models (GMMs) have become a dominant approach [11, 16]. In this paper we use GMMs to model the handwriting of each person of the underlying population. More specifically, the distribution of feature vectors extracted from a person's on-line handwriting is modeled by a Gaussian mixture density. For a D-dimensional feature vector denoted as $\mathbf{x}$, the mixture density for a given writer is defined as

$$p(\mathbf{x}|\lambda) = \sum_{i=1}^{M} w_i p_i(\mathbf{x}).$$

The density is a weighted linear combination of M uni-modal Gaussian densities, $p_i(\mathbf{x})$, each parameterized by a $D \times 1$ mean vector, μ_i, and $D \times D$ covariance matrix, C_i.

$$p_i(\mathbf{x}) = \frac{1}{(2\pi)^{D/2}|C_i|^{1/2}} \exp\{-\frac{1}{2}(\mathbf{x}-\mu_i)'(C_i)^{-1}(\mathbf{x}-\mu_i)\}.$$

The mixture weights, w_i, furthermore satisfy the constraint $\sum_{i=1}^{m} w_i = 1$. Collectively, the parameters of a writer's density model are denoted as $\lambda = \{w_i, \mu_i, C_i\}$, $i = 1, \ldots, M$. While the general model supports full covariance matrices, only diagonal covariance matrices are used in this paper as they perform better than full matrices in experiments [16].

The following two-step training procedure is used. In the first step, all training data from all writers is used to train a single, writer independent *universal background model (UBM)*. Maximum likelihood writer model parameters are estimated using the iterative Expectation-Maximization (EM) algorithm [3]. The EM algorithm iteratively refines the GMM parameters to monotonically increase the likelihood of the estimated model for the observed feature vectors.

In the second step, for each writer a writer dependent *writer model* is built by updating the trained parameters in the UBM via adaptation using all the training data from this writer. We derive the hypothesized writer model by adapting the parameters of the UBM using the writer's training data and a form of Bayesian adaptation called *Maximum A Posteriori (MAP)* estimation [16]. The basic idea of MAP is to derive the writer's model by updating the well-trained parameters in the UBM via adaptation. The adaptation is a two-step process. The first step is identical to the expectation step of the EM algorithm, where estimates of the sufficient statistics of the writer's training data are computed for each mixture in the UBM. Unlike the second step of the EM algorithm, for adaptation these new statistical estimates are then combined with the old statistics from the UBM mixture parameters using a data-dependent mixture coefficient [16].

The system was implemented using the Torch library [1]. In this implementation, only the means are adapted during MAP adaptation. Variances and weights are unchanged, as experimental results tend to show that there are no effects when they are adapted [16].

4 Experiments and Results

Our experiments are based on the IAM-OnDB database [10], which contains more than 1,700 handwritten texts in on-line format from over 220 writers. During writing on the whiteboard, the data is acquired using the eBeam system which is also used in the

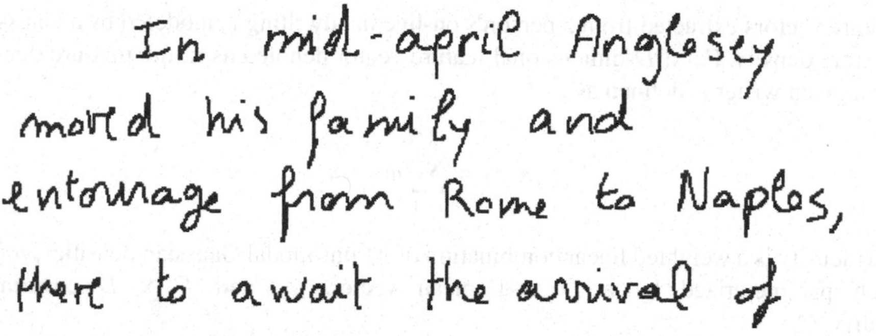

In mid-april Anglesey moved his family and entourage from Rome to Naples, there to await the arrival of

Fig. 6. Example of a paragraph of recorded text

IDIAP Smart Meeting Room [13]. Each writer writes eight paragraphs of text compiled from the Lancaster-Oslo/Bergen corpus (LOB) [8]. The acquired data is stored in XML-format, including the writer's identity, the transcription and the setting of the recording.

One paragraph of text contains 40 words on average. In Figure 6 an example of a paragraph of recorded text is shown. Four paragraphs are used for training, two paragraphs are used to validate the global parameters of the GMMs (see Sect. 3) and the remaining two paragraphs form the independent test set.

The baseline system [17] uses 32 Gaussian mixture components with diagonal covariance matrices. No adaptation is performed and each user model is initialised on its own data set. The nine point-based features used are (x, y) position, writing path tangent angle ϕ, total velocity v, x and y components of velocity v_x, v_y, total acceleration a, and x and y components of velocity a_x, a_y. Note that the pen pressure feature which is used in [17] is not available from the whiteboard data. The data is preprocessed by subtracting the initial point from all samples, so all paragraphs start at $(0, 0)$. Each feature is then normalized in respect to its mean and its variance.

In our system, all training data from each writer is used to train the UBM. The background model is then adapted for each writer using all writer-specific training data. We have increased the numbers of Gaussian from 50 to 400 by steps of 50. In this initial experiment the adaptation factor was set to 0.0, i.e., full adaptation was performed. For the other meta parameters we used standard values [1]. The optimal number of Gaussians was determined on the validation set and this number is then used to compute the identification rate on the test set. The identification rate is determined by dividing the number of correctly assigned text paragraphs by the total number of text paragraphs.

To examine the scalability of the system, we performed the experiments on four sets. First, we randomly choose 50 writers that form the set S_1. Than we added 50 randomly chosen writers to get the second set S_2 ($S_1 \subset S_2$). We continued adding 50 writers to get set S_3 and set S_4, respectively ($S_2 \subset S_3 \subset S_4$).

In Figure 7 the identification rate as a function of the number of Gaussians mixture components on the validation set for the 200 writers experiment with the stroke-based features is shown. On this set, the best identification rate of 96.75% is obtained when using 150 Gaussians. With this number of Gaussians, an identification rate of 93.5% is achieved on the test set.

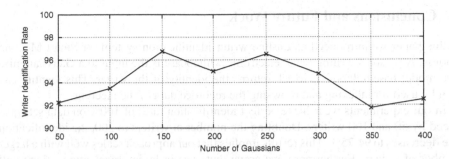

Fig. 7. Identification rate as a function of the number of Gaussians on the validation set

Table 1. Identification rates on the test set (in %)

no. of writers	50	100	150	200
baseline system	94.4	91.4	90.5	85.3
point-based features	98.0	92.5	87.0	85.0
stroke-based features	100.0	100.0	96.7	94.75

Table 2. Identification rates on the test set using different number of paragraphs (in %)

no. of paragraphs	4	3	2	1
stroke-based features	94.75	91.75	86.25	71.25

We repeated the experiments with different number of Gaussians and different adaptation factors and optimized their values on the validation set. The number of Gaussians was varied between 50 and 400 by steps of 50. The MAP factor was increased from 0.0 to 0.5 in steps of 0.1. The other meta parameters were again set to standard values. This optimization further increases the identification rate. Table 1 shows the results on the test set. The performance of the baseline system [17] is comparable to our system when point-based features are used. The stroke-based features perform superior to the point-based features for every number of writers tested. They achieve a perfect identification rate of 100% for 50 and 100 writers. For 200 writers the identification rate is 94.75%.

To investigate how our system performs if fewer data is used for training, we have reduced the number of paragraphs from each of the 200 writers from four paragraphs to one paragraph. The stroked-based features are used in this experiment. The number of Gaussians was varied between 50 to 150 by steps of 50 and the MAP factor was increased from 0.0 to 0.5 in steps of 0.1. Both parameters were optimized on the validation set. The results of our experiments on the test set are given in Table 2. If we use two instead of four paragraphs of text, the writer identification rate of our system using stroke-based features is still better compared to our system using point-based features and the baseline system both trained on all four paragraphs of text (see Table 1).

5   Conclusions and Future Work

In this paper we introduced an on-line writer identification system for Smart Meeting Rooms. A person's writing on an electronic whiteboard is the input to a Gaussian mixture model based classifier, which returns the identity of the writer. This identity can then be used for indexing and browsing the recorded data of the meeting.

In our experiments we achieve perfect identification rates of 100% on data sets produced by 50 and 100 writers. Doubling the number of writers to 200, the identification rate decreases to 94.75%. This results implies that our approach scales well with a larger number of writers. Furthermore, we argue that even in large organizations, there will rarely be more than 200 potential participants to a meeting held in a smart meeting room.

We have introduced two sets of new features extracted from the recorded on-line data. The first set consists of feature vectors from each recorded point, while the second set consists of vectors extracted from strokes. In our experiments the stroke-based features perform consistently better than the point-based features. This indicates that strokes contain more information to characterize a person's handwriting than single points.

In future work we plan to test our writer identification system on a refined scenario. For real world applications it is too time consuming and cumbersome to ask a person to copy large amounts of text before the system can be adapted with the writer's data. Therefore, we intend to further reduce the amount of data which is needed for adapting the GMMs as well as the amount of data needed to test the system. In the current scenario, we use the same data from each writer to train the UBM and the client model. In our future work, we plan to train the UBM with a training set consisting of a disjoint set of persons.

The point-based and the stroke-based feature sets describe different aspects of a person's handwriting. It is reasonable to combine the two sets to get a better performance. Initial experiments show promising results. Another approach to increase the system's performance is to generate multiple classifier systems by varying the system's parameters, e.g., the number of Gaussian components or the adaptation factor.

While our system has been developed for handwriting data acquired by the eBeam whiteboard system, our approach can potentially also be applied to other on-line handwriting data, e.g., data acquired by an electronic pen used on a Tablet PC [21].

Acknowledgments

This work was supported by the Swiss National Science Foundation program "Interactive Multimodal Information Management (IM)2" in the Individual Project "Access and Content Protection", as part of NCCR. The authors would like to thank Dr. Darren Moore for helping us with technical issues of the IDIAP Smart Meeting Room. Furthermore, we thank Christoph Hofer for conducting part of the experiments.

References

1. Collobert, R., Bengio, S., Mariéthoz, J.: Torch: a modular machine learning software library. Technical report, IDIAP (2002)
2. Czyz, J., Bengio, S., Marcel, C., Vandendorpe, L.: Scalability analysis of audio-visual person identity verification. In: Audio- and Video-based Biometric Person Authentication. (2003) 752–760

3. Dempster, A.P., Laird, N.M., Rubin, D.B.: Maximum likelihood from incomplete data via the EM algorithm. Journal of Royal Statistical Society **39** (1977) 1–38
4. Fasel, B., Luettin, J.: Automatic facial expression analysis: A survey. Pattern Recognition **36** (2003) 259–275
5. Grudin, M.A.: On internal representations in face recognition systems. Pattern Recognition **33** (2000) 1161–1177
6. Jaeger, S., Manke, S., Reichert, J., Waibel, A.: Online handwriting recognition: the NPen++ recognizer. Int. Journal on Document Analysis and Recognition **3** (2001) 169–180
7. Jain, A., Griess, F., Connell, S.: On-line signature verification. Pattern Recognition **35** (2002) 2663–2972
8. Johansson, S.: The tagged LOB Corpus: User's Manual. Norwegian Computing Centre for the Humanities, Norway (1986)
9. Liwicki, M., Bunke, H.: Handwriting recognition of whiteboard notes. In: Proc. 12th Conf. of the Int. Graphonomics Society. (2005) 118–122
10. Liwicki, M., Bunke, H.: IAM-OnDB – an on-line English sentence database acquired from handwritten text on a whiteboard. In: 8th Int. Conf. on Document Analysis and Recognition. (2005) Accepted for publication.
11. Mariéthoz, J., Bengio, S.: A comparative study of adaptation methods for speaker verification. In: Int. Conf. on Spoken Language Processing, Denver, CO, USA (2002) 581–584
12. McCowan, L., Gatica-Perez, D., Bengio, S., Lathoud, G., Barnard, M., Zhang, D.: Automatic analysis of multimodal group actions in meetings. IEEE Trans. on Pattern Analysis and Machine Intelligence **27** (2005) 305–317
13. Moore, D.: The IDIAP smart meeting room. Technical report, IDIAP-Com (2002)
14. Morgan, N., Baron, D., Edwards, J., Ellis, D., Gelbart, D., Janin, A., Pfau, T., Shriberg, E., Stolcke, A.: The meeting project at ICSI. In: Proc. Human Language Technologies Conf. (2001) 246–252
15. Reiter, S., Rigoll, G.: Segmentation and classification of meeting events using multiple classifier fusion and dynamic programming. In: Proc. 17th Int. Conf. on Pattern Recognition. (2004) 434–437
16. Reynolds, D.A., Quatieri, T.F., Dunn, R.B.: Speaker verification using adapted Gaussian mixture models. Digital Signal Processing **10** (2000) 19–41
17. Richiardi, J., Drygajlo, A.: Gaussian Mixture Models for on-line signature verification. In: Proc. 2003 ACM SIGMM workshop on Biometrics methods and applications. (2003) 115–122
18. Sanderson, C., Paliwal, K.K.: Fast features for face authentication under illumination direction changes. Pattern Recognition Letters **24** (2003) 2409–2419
19. Schenkel, M., Guyon, I., Henderson, D.: On-line cursive script recognition using time delay neural networks and hidden Markov models. Machine Vision and Applications **8** (1995) 215–223
20. Schlapbach, A., Bunke, H.: Off-line handwriting identification using HMM based recognizers. In: Proc. 17th Int. Conf. on Pattern Recognition. Volume 2. (2004) 654–658
21. Schomaker, L.: From handwriting analysis to pen-computer applications. IEE Electronics & Communication Engineering Journal **10** (1998) 93–102
22. Waibel, A., Schultz, T., Bett, M., Malkin, R., Rogina, I., Stiefelhagen, R., Yang, J.: SMaRT: The Smart Meeting Room Task at ISL. In: Proc. IEEE Int. Conf. on Acoustics, Speech, and Signal Processing. Volume 4. (2003) 752–755
23. Wellner, P., Flynn, M., Guillemot, M.: Browsing recorded meetings with Ferret. In: Machine Learning for Multimodal Interaction. (2004) 12–21
24. Yamazaki, Y., Nagao, T., Komatsu, N.: Text-indicated writer verification using hidden Markov models. In: Proc. 7th Int. Conf. on Document Analysis and Recognition. (2003) 329–332

Extraction and Analysis of Document Examiner Features from Vector Skeletons of Grapheme 'th'

Vladimir Pervouchine and Graham Leedham

Forensics and Security Lab,
Nanyang Technological University, School of Computer Engineering,
N4-2C-77 Nanyang Avenue 639798, Singapore
{pervouchine, asgleedham}@ntu.edu.sg

Abstract. This paper presents a study of 25 structural features extracted from samples of grapheme 'th' that correspond to features commonly used by forensic document examiners. Most of the features are extracted using vector skeletons produced by a specially developed skeletonisation algorithm. The methods of feature extraction are presented along with the results. Analysis of the usefulness of the features was conducted and three categories of features were identified: indispensable, partially relevant and irrelevant for determining the authorship of genuine unconstrained handwriting. The division was performed based on searching the optimal feature sets using the wrapper method. A constructive neural network was used as a classifier and a genetic algorithm was used to search for optimal feature sets. It is shown that structural micro features similar to those used in forensic document analysis do possess discriminative power. The results are also compared to those obtained in our preceding study, and it is shown that use of the vector skeletonisation allows both extraction of more structural features and improvement the feature extraction accuracy from 87% to 94%.

1 Introduction

Handwriting is a personal biometric that has long been considered to be unique to a person. Provided this statement is true, handwriting can be used to identify a person. The methods used by forensic document examiners to determine whether handwriting is genuine, forged, or disguised, are based on a set of established and well documented techniques [1–3]. The techniques have been derived from experience and are generally accepted by the various forensic laboratories. Forensic document analysis of handwriting is the examination of the design, shape, and structures of handwriting. Professional document examiners seek characteristics of handwriting that are consistent in a person's normal writing. These characteristics are called *features* [4, 3, 1].

Whilst the techniques used by forensic document examiners are intuitively reasonable, they still lack a scientific basis. In recent court cases the scientific acceptability of forensic document examination that deals with handwriting analysis has been successfully challenged [5].

H. Bunke and A.L. Spitz (Eds.): DAS 2006, LNCS 3872, pp. 196–207, 2006.

There is a need to determine whether it is possible to establish a sound scientific basis for forensic document analysis. To do this it is necessary to determine to what extent handwriting is unique to an individual and whether the methods of handwriting analysis practised by forensic experts can lead to correct and repeatable results. Since methods of forensic document examiners are based on structural features of handwriting, it is useful to investigate whether those features can be used for writer discrimination. This paper reports the experiments on automatic extraction of some of the document examiner features from images of handwritten grapheme 'th' followed by analysis of discriminating power of the features.

2   Background

2.1   Performance of Forensic Document Examiners

A number of tests have been performed under various conditions to demonstrate that the accuracy of writer identification by forensic document examiners is significantly higher than that of lay people [6, 7, 8, 9]. Establishing these facts means that techniques used by forensic document examiners may indeed allow them to identify authorship with observable accuracy. Hence it is necessary to verify the claim that it is the techniques and not something else (e.g. pure experience from having seen a lot of samples) that mainly contribute to the high writer identification accuracy demonstrated by the experts.

2.2   Establishing Handwriting Individuality

The problem of establishing the individuality of handwriting has received extensive study during recent years [10–12]. The individuality of handwriting is formally defined as "given two well-selected samples of handwriting, we can tell whether they were written by the same person or by two different people with a high degree of confidence." [13, 10]. Further research has been carried out to study the discriminatory power of certain handwriting elements, particularly words [14], characters [15], and digits [16]. It has been shown that certain characters, especially those with ascenders and descenders, as well as capital letters bear more individual information than others which agrees with the statements of forensic document examiners [17, 3]. It has been demonstrated that handwriting can be used to identify a person with high accuracy.

2.3   Document Examiner and Computational Features

The features of handwriting that are commonly used by forensic document examiners to determine the authorship are called document examiner features. Huber and Headrick summarised them in the list of 21 discriminating elements of handwriting [17]. Many document examiner features are defined vaguely and thus do not allow reliable measurement with repeatable results.

Features of handwriting that are defined unambiguously and can be measured from handwriting images are called computational features. It is not necessary that a computational feature corresponds to any document examiner feature. For the study of handwriting individuality any computational features are suitable. However, the open question remains whether the methods used by forensic document examiners allow them to determine the authorship. To answer that question it is necessary to study how useful the document examiner features are for writer discrimination. For this purpose we formalise document examiner features, that is, map them into a set of computational features so that each computational feature represents some structural element of handwriting.

3   Extraction of Features

According to the classification of features of handwriting in relation to the scale of extraction all features can be divided into two categories: macro features and micro features [13]. The macro features are those extracted from the whole document image, from lines, and from words up to the character level. Micro features are those extracted from short consistent character combinations (graphemes), characters, their sub-parts as well as between-character parts (ligatures). Micro features are thought to be more endowed with individual traits and are thought to be harder for the writers to change when attempting to forger or disguise their handwriting. This study is focused on micro features that correspond to document examiner features and which are formalised so that they can be extracted and measured unambiguously and accurately from handwriting images.

3.1   Choice of Features

Grapheme 'th' was chosen for the study because it is the most frequent grapheme in the English language [18]. It accounts for around 4% of all two-character combinations. Also, our previous experiments showed that the discriminative power of the grapheme is higher than that of single characters [19, 20]. The features for study were selected so that they correspond to the structural micro features commonly used by forensic document examiners [17, 3, 1]. Some of the features are shown in Figure 1, and the complete list of features is presented in Table 1.

   The feature set consists of geometrical characteristics of characters, various angular measures, loop characteristics, and stroke features. Definition of height and width as well as the relative position of the top point of 't' T and top point of 'h' H are given in Figure 1. Position of t-bar was a binary feature and was equal to 1 for a t-bar crossing the stem and 0 in the cases of touching, detached, or absent t-bar. It was observed that writers who tend to produce t-bars touching the stem in grapheme 'th' also tend to produce disconnected t-bars in that same grapheme and vice versa. Slant of characters 't' and 'h' was defined as the slant of their stems. Pseudo-pressure was calculated as the gray level of pixels. Retraced strokes were considered as loops hence the total number of loops and retraced strokes was measured. Straightness of strokes (t-bar, t-stem, and h-stem) was defined as the ratio of the total length of the stroke to the distance between its end points. Presence of loops at the top points of 't' and 'h' stems was a binary feature having the value of 1 when a loop was present and the value of 0

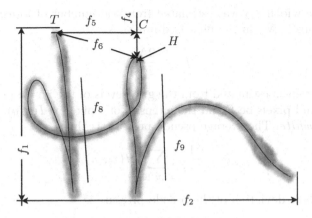

Fig. 1. Some features extracted from grapheme 'th'

Table 1. List of features extracted from grapheme 'th'

Height	f_1	Standard deviation of pseudo-pressure	f_{14}
Width	f_2	Standard deviation of stroke width	f_{15}
Height to width ratio	f_3	Number of strokes	f_{16}
Distance HC	f_4	Number of loops and retraced strokes	f_{17}
Distance TC	f_5	Straightness of t-stem	f_{18}
Distance TH	f_6	Straightness of t-bar	f_{19}
Angle between TH and TC	f_7	Straightness of h-stem	f_{20}
Slant of t	f_8	Presence of loop at top of t-stem	f_{21}
Slant of h	f_9	Presence of loop at top of h-stem	f_{22}
Position of t-bar	f_{10}	Maximum curvature of h-knee	f_{23}
Connected / disconnected t and h	f_{11}	Average curvature of h-knee	f_{24}
Average stroke width	f_{12}	Relative size (diameter) of h-knee	f_{25}
Average pseudo-pressure	f_{13}		

otherwise. Relative size (diameter) of h-knee was defined as the largest horizontal distance between the stem and knee strokes.

3.2   Measurement of Feature Values

The origin of the coordinate system is in the upper-left corner of an image, the abscissa (x) axis is horizontal and directed to the right, the ordinate (y) axis is vertical and directed downwards. Apart from a sample image itself, its binarised version as well as its vector skeleton were used for feature extraction.

Height, width, and height to width ratio were measured from the binarised image by determining the bounding box of the image. The bounding box co-ordinates x_1, y_1, x_2, y_2 correspond to the topmost, leftmost, bottommost, and rightmost black pixels on the image. The feature values were calculated as

$$f_1 = y_2 - y_1 + 1, \; f_2 = x_2 - x_1 + 1, \; f_3 = f_1/f_2 \qquad (1)$$

Average stroke width f_{12} was estimated from the number of foreground pixels N_s and edge pixels N_D in the binarised image as

$$f_{12} \approx \frac{2N_s}{N_D} \tag{2}$$

Pseudo-pressure was estimated from the grey levels of the image pixels. Let the set of foreground pixels be S and the intensity of a pixel be $I(x, y)$, $black = 0 \leq I(x, y) \leq 1 = white$. The average pseudo-pressure is thus

$$f_{13} = \frac{1}{N_S} \sum_{(x_i, y_i) \in S} I(x_i, y_i) \tag{3}$$

And the standard deviation of the pseudo-pressure is

$$f_{14} = \sqrt{\frac{1}{N_S - 1} \sum_{(x_i, y_i) \in S} (I(x_i, y_i) - f_{13})^2} \tag{4}$$

Other features were calculated from grapheme skeletons. The skeletons were produced by a specially developed content-dependent skeletonisation algorithm capable of producing skeletons that are very close to the human perception of the pen tip trajectory [21]. The skeletonisation algorithm also restored some hidden loops. The resultant skeletons were presented as a set of spline-approximated strokes, including retraced strokes and loops.

Slant value was calculated by taking a set of sample points s_i along each spline-approximated stroke that represented the element of interest (ascender, descender, etc.) and calculating the angles of tangents in these points $\alpha_i = \arctan k_i$. The slants f_8 and f_9 were calculated as the weighted average of those angles:

$$\alpha_{slant} = \frac{\sum_i l_i \alpha_i}{L} \tag{5}$$

where l_i is the length of the corresponding curve segment (see Figure 2(a)), $L = \sum_i l_i$ is the total curve length. The slant values were within the range $-\pi/2 \leq \alpha_{slant} < \pi/2$. To extract some features that represent relative position of characters 't' and 'h' in the grapheme, the relative position of top stem points was measured along with the slants of the 'h' and 't' stems. Detection of the top points was made by first detecting all the end points in the upper half of a sample image and then tracing the branches from those end points to determine which of them correspond to the elements of 'th'. All connected components in a sample image were detected. If the top of the stem points belonged to a different connected component, characters 't' and 'h' were disconnected, otherwise they were connected (binary feature f_{11}).

Number of strokes f_{16} and number of loops and retraced strokes f_{17} were available directly from the skeleton as well as the presence of loop at the top of t-stem and h-stem (f_{21} and f_{22}).

Standard deviation of stroke width f_{15} was extracted by taking a set of closely sampled points on the skeleton curves and measuring the cross-section of the strokes on the underlying binarised image as shown in Figure 2(b). The obtained measurements were then used to calculate the feature value.

Straightness of a stroke (t-stem f_{18}, t-bar f_{19}, h-stem f_{20}) was calculated as follows: if the distance between the two end points was d and the length of the stroke was L, the straightness of the stroke was given by

$$straightness = \frac{L}{d} \tag{6}$$

It was close to 1 for a straight stroke, and significantly larger for a curved stroke.

Maximum and average curvature of a stroke (h-knee) f_{23}, f_{24} were calculated by taking closely sampled points along the curve, calculating the curvature at each point, and taking the largest value of the curvature and the average of the curvature.

Relative size of h-knee f_{25} was calculated as the largest distance from h-stem to the h-knee curve as shown in Figure 2(c). It was approximately calculated as the largest horizontal distance between the curves representing the stem and the knee divided by the width of the grapheme f_2.

Algorithms for feature extraction consisted of a main program and subroutines for extraction of particular features. The input to the algorithms was a grapheme image, the output was the feature vector along with additional information which was later used to verify correctness of the feature values. Obviously it was impossible to write algorithms for all possible shapes of the grapheme. However, it was observed that for most samples of each grapheme a wide variety of shapes could be taken into account. Processing of input images was performed in several stages. In each stage some features were extracted and information about the grapheme form, such as position of certain points and correspondence of branches to certain parts of the grapheme, was refined. This information was then used in further stages of the feature extraction.

Sample images of grapheme 'th' for feature extraction were manually segmented from 600 images of the CEDAR letter [10] collected from 200 different writers. The samples were taken only from the beginning of words like 'the'. There were at most 27 samples of the grapheme extracted for each writer.

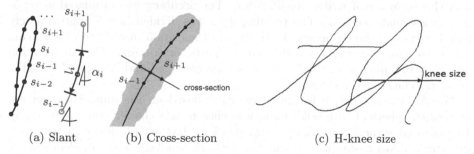

(a) Slant   (b) Cross-section   (c) H-knee size

Fig. 2. Some features of 'th' extracted from a vector skeleton

Automatic feature extraction was carried out on the extracted samples of grapheme 'th' and the results were inspected visually. A sample was considered to be processed incorrectly if either some strokes were detected incorrectly, or the extraction algorithm failed to extract some features. The total extraction error rate was 6%.

In order to make the results of the study comparable to those of the previous study when a raster skeletonisation method was used, samples from the same 165 different writers were chosen for writer accuracy evaluation experiments.

4   Analysis of Feature Usefulness

John et al. [22] analysed several definitions of feature relevance which have been presented in the literature and proposed a definition that includes two degrees of relevance: strong and weak relevance. Strong relevance means that a feature cannot be removed from the feature set without loss of classification accuracy. Weak relevance means that a feature can sometimes contribute to classification accuracy. A feature is irrelevant if it is neither strongly nor weakly relevant, and thus can be excluded from the feature set without loss of classification accuracy.

The definition of weak and strong feature relevance is hard to apply, since it is necessary to know the conditional probabilities $P(\vec{f}_k|j)$ of feature vector $\vec{f}_k$ represents a sample of j-th writer. Another approach can be applied. Suppose there is a set of features and all subsets are found that are equally good for writer classification. "Equally good" means that the classification accuracies achieved when those subsets are used, do not differ significantly — their average values are indistinguishable. There are three classes of features according to their inclusion in the found feature sets: some features are included in all feature sets, some are not included at all, and the rest are included in some of the sets. The first category of features comprises of *indispensable features*, the second category contains *irrelevant features*, and the rest of the features are *partially relevant*.

To find the best feature subsets, the wrapper approach was used. In this approach an induction algorithm is used for evaluation of a feature set. A feature set is assigned a value proportional to its performance — in this study this value was the accuracy of writer classification. The accuracy was evaluated using 5-fold cross-validation [23]. The training data was divided into 5 approximately equal parts and the induction algorithm was then run 5 times each time leaving one subset for test and using the other 4 parts for training. The classification accuracy obtained from the 5 tests was then averaged and associated with the corresponding feature subset.

DistAl, a constructive learning algorithm based on the multi-layer perceptron with spherical threshold units, was chosen as a classification system [24]. Use of a constructive artificial neural network has an advantage of not making any a priori assumption about the network topology. Instead, elements are added to the hidden layer as the learning progresses. The maximum number of elements can be restricted to avoid overfitting. The learning algorithm is fast because it does not use an iterative algorithm to compute perceptron parameters (weights, thresholds). The most time-consuming part is the calculation of inter-pattern distances for each pair of patterns. However, this needs to be performed only once for the whole data. Experiments conducted on both artificial and real data using the DistAl classifier [24] demonstrated classification results comparable to those obtained by other commonly used learning algorithms. Since, in the current study, it is not necessary to obtain the highest classification accuracy possible, but rather the focus is on comparing the classification accuracy of different feature subsets, the DistAl classifier suits the task well.

All feature values were treated as real numbers. Having performed several experiments we chose the normalised Manhattan distance as a distance measure for DistAl because this measure was shown to be suitable for the problem at hand:

$$d\left(\vec{f}_{k_1}, \vec{f}_{k_2}\right) = \frac{1}{M} \sum_{i=1}^{M} \frac{|f_{ik_1} - f_{ik_2}|}{\max f_i - \min f_i} \tag{7}$$

where M was the number of features, and $\min f_i$ and $\max f_i$ were the minimum and maximum values of the i-th feature in the data set respectively.

A genetic algorithm (GA) was used to implement feature subset selection. From the studies of De Jong [25] GAs have been extensively used to solve problems of feature selection in pattern recognition [26–28]. Successful use of a GA together with the DistAl algorithm has also been demonstrated [29]. In this study GA with sharing [30] was used to find the best feature subsets. Original fitness fit_s for feature subset x_s (represented as a binary string) was equal to the average correct classification rate acc_s. Modified fitness was defined as

$$\widetilde{fit}_s = \frac{fit_s}{\sum_j (1 - d(x_s - x_j))} \tag{8}$$

where $d(x_s, x_j)$ is a dissimilarity measure:

$$d(x_s, x_j) = \frac{\sum_m |x_{sm} - x_{jm}|}{M} \tag{9}$$

Here M is the number of features, or the length of binary strings x_s and x_j, representing a feature subset, and x_{sm} is the m-th bit of string x_s. Summation in eq. (8) is performed across the whole population of strings. The following parameters were used for the GA:

- population size of 50;
- uniform crossover [31] with probability of 0.6;
- mutation with probability of 0.03;
- replacement strategy in which best strings from parents and offspring form the next generation;

- linear scaling of fitness function with the factor of 2;
- stop condition was "no new good feature subset during the last 50 generations".

The results of the experiments are presented below.

5   Results and Conclusions

There were a total of 3823 samples of grapheme 'th' taken from 165 different writers, with between 15 and 27 samples per writer. Accuracy of classification was measured by 5-fold cross validation on the DistAl classifier. The best feature sets were searched using a genetic algorithm with sharing.

The optimal feature sets found are presented in Table 2, where a is the average writer classification accuracy achieved when the associated feature set was used, and σ_a is the standard deviation of the accuracy value. The feature values of writer classification accuracy presented in the table are indistinguishable at the 1% confidence level. In a string representing a feature set the value of 1(0) means that the feature is included in (excluded from) the set. The position of a digit in a string in Table 2 corresponds to the index of the feature. Table 1 should be consulted to get the name of the feature.

Based on the optimal feature subsets presented in Table 2, division of the features into three sets of indispensable, partially relevant, and irrelevant can be performed and is shown in Table 3. As seen from the table, there are only two irrelevant features in the set, and 17 out of total of 25 features are indispensable.

Features f_{14} and f_{15}, the standard deviation of pseudo-pressure and standard deviation of stroke width were the two irrelevant features revealed by the experiment. The former feature was aimed at capturing the stability of pen pressure, measured from the gray level of an image. It is likely that evaluation of pen pressure from the image gray level is suitable to capture the overall darkness (pressure), but not suitable for capturing more subtle pressure variations. The latter feature was intended to partially represent a "line quality" feature [17]. It seems that the variation of stroke width does not provide a useful information about individual line quality and rather represents a random noise which

Table 2. Optimal feature subsets of the 'th' feature set, accuracy values, and standard deviations. Bit 1 corresponds to presence of the feature in the subset, bit 0 to absence of it. Features are divided into groups of five for convenience.

feature set $f_1 \ldots f_{25}$	a	σ_a
11111 11111 11000 11101 11111	0.67	0.04
10111 11111 11000 11101 01111	0.67	0.04
11111 11111 11100 11101 01111	0.65	0.05
11011 11111 11100 11111 11111	0.64	0.04
11111 11111 11100 11101 01111	0.64	0.04
11111 11111 11000 11101 00111	0.64	0.04

Table 3. Division of features according to their relevance. Feature indices are presented.

Indispensable features			
Height	f_1	Connected / disconnected t and h	f_{11}
Distance HC	f_4	Average stroke width	f_{12}
Distance TC	f_5	Number of strokes	f_{16}
Distance TH	f_6	Number of loops and retraced strokes	f_{17}
Angle between TH and TC	f_7	Straightness of t-stem	f_{18}
Slant of t	f_8	Straightness of h-stem	f_{20}
Slant of h	f_9	Maximum curvature of h-knee	f_{23}
Position of t-bar	f_{10}	Average curvature of h-knee	f_{24}
		Relative size (diameter) of h-knee	f_{25}
Partially relevant features			
Width	f_2	Straightness of t-bar	f_{19}
Height to width ratio	f_3	Presence of loop at top of t-stem	f_{21}
Average pseudo-pressure	f_{13}	Presence of loop at top of h-stem	f_{22}
Irrelevant features			
Standard deviation of pseudo-pressure	f_{14}	Standard deviation of stroke width	f_{15}

probably depends on writing conditions (pen, paper, writing surface), which were almost identical for all writers in the current study [10].

The errors in feature extraction were mostly due to wide variation of character shapes, some of which were not taken into account by feature extraction algorithms. For practical use of feature extraction algorithms in forensic document analysis tools an interactive extraction algorithms can be implemented on the base of the existing ones, which can improve the feature extraction accuracy further.

From the results obtained we conclude that a number of the features commonly used by forensic document examiners do possess discriminative power. Thus, use of those features for distinguishing writers by samples of their normal unconstrained handwriting is justified. How stable these features are under attempts at forgery or disguise needs to be studied further. Compared to the results obtained in our previous experiments, where the achieved writer classification accuracy on the same data set was 58% [20], use of the new skeletonisation algorithm allowed us to both improve feature extraction accuracy to 94% and extract more structural features, most of which contributed to the set of indispensable features, which in turn resulted in higher accuracy of writer classification of 67%.

References

1. Hilton, O.: Scientific Examination of Questioned Documents. CRC Hall, Florida, USA (1993)
2. Robertson, E.W.: Fundamentals of Document Examination. Nelson-Hall (1991)
3. Harrison, W.R.: Suspect Documents, Their Scientific Examinations. Nelson-Hall, Illinois, USA (1981)

4. Lindblom, B.: Document examination. In Chayko, G.M., Gulliver, E.D., eds.: Forensic Evidence in Canada. 2nd edn. Aurora: Canada Law Book (1999) 505–525
5. *Daubert et al. v. Merrell Dow Pharmaceuticals.* Court case 509 U. S. 579 (1993)
6. Kam, M., Fielding, G., Conn, R.: Writer identification by professional document examiners. Journal of Forensic Sciences **42** (1997) 778–786
7. Found, B., Sita, J., Rogers, D.: The development of a program for characterizing forensic handwriting examiners' expertise: Signature examination pilot study. Journal of Forensic Document Examination **12** (1999) 69–80
8. Kam, M., Gummadidala, K., Fielding, G., Conn, R.: Signature authentication by forensic document examiners. Journal of Forensic Science **46** (2001) 884–888
9. Sita, J., Found, B., Rogers, D.: Forensic handwriting examiners' expertise for signature comparison. Journal of Forensic Sciences **47** (2001) 1117–1124
10. Srihari, S.N., Cha, S.H., Arora, H., Lee, S.: Individuality of handwriting. Journal of Forensic Sciences **47** (2002) 1–17
11. Found, B., Roger, D., Schmittat, R.: A computer program designed to compare the spatial elements of handwriting. Forensic Science International **68** (1994) 195–203
12. Schomaker, L., Bulacu, M., van Erp, M.: Sparse-parametric writer identification using heterogeneous feature groups. In: Proc. 3rd Int'l Conf. Document Analysis and Recognition (ICDAR'95), Montreal, Canada (1995) 545–548
13. Srihari, S.N., Cha, S.H., Lee, S.: Establishing handwriting individuality using pattern recognition techniques. In: Proc. 6th Int'l Conf. Document Analysis and Recognition (ICDAR'2001), Seattle, USA (2001) 1195–1204
14. Tomai, C.I., Zhang, B., Srihari, S.N.: Discriminatory power of handwritten words for writer recognition. In: Proc. 17th Int'l Conf. Pattern Recognition, Cambridge, UK (2004) 638–641
15. Zhang, B., Srihari, S.N., Lee, S.: Individuality of handwritten characters. In: Proc. 7th Int'l Conf. Document Analysis and Recognition (ICDAR'2003), Edinburgh, UK (2003) 1086–1090
16. Srihari, S.N., Tomai, C.I., Zhang, B., Lee, S.: Individuality of numerals. In: Proc. 7th Int'l Conf. Document Analysis and Recognition (ICDAR'2003), Edinburgh, UK (2003) 1096–1100
17. Huber, R.A., Headrick, A.M.: Handwriting Identification: Facts and Fundamentals. CRC Press, LCC (1999)
18. Leedham, C.G., Pervouchine, V., Tan, W.K., Jacob, A.: Automatic quantitative letter-level extraction of features used by document examiners. In Teulings, H.L., Van Gemmert, A.W.A., eds.: Proc. 11th Conf. Int'l. Graphonomics Society (IGS2003), Scottsdale, AZ, USA (2003) 291–294
19. Leedham, C.G., Pervouchine, V., Tan, W.K.: Quantitative letter-level extraction and analysis of features used by document examiners. Journal of Forensic Document Examination (2004) In press.
20. Leedham, C.G., Pervouchine, V.: Validating the use of handwriting as a biometric and its forensic analysis. In Pal, U., Parui, S.K., Chaudhuri, B.B., eds.: Document Analysis: Proc. Int'l. Workshop on Document Analysis (IWDA'05). Allied Publishers Ltd., Chennai (2005) 175–192 Invited lecture.
21. Pervouchine, V., Leedham, C.G., Melikhov, K.: Handwritten character skeletonisation for forensic document analysis. In: Proc. 20th Annual ACM Symposium on Applied Computing, Santa Fe, NM, USA (2005) 754–758
22. John, G.H., Kohavi, R., Pfleger, K.: Irrelevant features and the subset selection problem. In: Proc. 11th Int'l Conf. Machine Learning (ML94), Rutgers University, New Brunswick, NJ (1994) 121–129

23. Weiss, S.M., Kulikowski, C.A.: Computer Systems that Learn: Classification and Prediction Methods from Statistics, Neural Nets, Machine Learning, and Expert Systems. Morgan Kaufmann (1991)
24. Yang, J., Parekh, R., Honavar, V.: Distal: An inter-pattern distance-based constructive learning algorithm. Technical Report ISU-CS-TR 97-06, Department of Computer Science, Iowa State University (1997) Also appeared in Proc. Int'l. Conf. Neural Networks, IEEE, Piscataway, N.J, 1998.
25. Vafaie, H., De Jong, K.: Genetic algorithms as a tool for feature selection in machine learning. In: Proc. 4th Int'l Conf. Tools with Artificial Intelligence (TAI'92), Arlington, VA, IEEE Computer Society Press (1992) 200–203
26. Brill, F.Z., Brown, D.E., Martin, W.N.: Fast genetic selection of features for neural network classifiers. IEEE Trans. Neural Networks 3 (1992) 324–328
27. Bala, J., Huang, J., Vafaie, H., De Jong, K., Wechsler, H.: Hybrid learning using genetic algorithms and decision trees for pattern classification. In: Proc. Int'l Joint Conf. Artificial Intelligence (IJCAI-95), Montreal, Canada (1995)
28. Chen, S., Smith, S., Guerra-Salcedo, C., Whitley, D.: Fast and accurate feature selection using hybrid genetic strategies. In: Proc. Congress on Evolutionary Computation (CEC99), Washington DC, USA (1999)
29. Yang, J., Honavar, V.: Feature subset selection using a genetic algorithm. IEEE Intell. Syst. 13 (1998) 44–49
30. Goldberg, D.E.: Genetic Algorithms in Search, Optimization, and Machine Learning. Addison-Wesley (1989)
31. Syswerda, G.: Uniform crossover in genetic algorithms. In: Proc. 3rd Int'l Conf. Genetic Algorithms, George Mason University, USA, Morgan Kaufmann (1989) 2–9

Segmentation of On-Line Handwritten Japanese Text Using SVM for Improving Text Recognition

Bilan Zhu, Junko Tokuno, and Masaki Nakagawa

Tokyo University of Agriculture and Technology, Naka-cho 2-24-16,
Koganei, Tokyo 184-8588, Japan
{zhubilan, j-tokuno}@hands.ei.tuat.ac.jp,
nakagawa@cc.tuat.ac.jp
http://www.tuat.ac.jp/~nakagawa/

Abstract. This paper describes a method of producing segmentation point candidates for on-line handwritten Japanese text by a support vector machine (SVM) to improve text recognition. This method extracts multi-dimensional features from on-line strokes of handwritten text and applies the SVM to the extracted features to produces segmentation point candidates. We incorporate the method into the segmentation by recognition scheme based on a stochastic model which evaluates the likelihood composed of character pattern structure, character segmentation, character recognition and context to finally determine segmentation points and recognize handwritten Japanese text. This paper also shows the details of generating segmentation point candidates in order to achieve high discrimination rate by finding the combination of the segmentation threshold and the concatenation threshold. We compare the method for segmentation by the SVM with that by a neural network using the database *HANDS-Kondate_t_bf-2001-11* and show the result that the method by the SVM bring about a better segmentation rate and character recognition rate.

1 Introduction

On-line recognition was first employed in real products in 1980s for Japanese input with hard constraints such as character writing boxes. Due to the development of pen-based systems such tablet PC, electronic whiteboard, PDA, Anoto pen, e-pen and so on and the expansion of writing surfaces, handwritten text recognition rather than character recognition is being sought with less constraints since larger writing surfaces allow people write more freely.

The model and system for separating freely written text into text line and estimating the line direction and character orientation was reported in [1]. If the initial segmentation is not good, however, it determines the upper limit of text recognition performance.

Aizawa et al. reported real-time segmentation for on-line handwritten Japanese text by applying features preceding a segmentation point candidate to a neural network in [2]. Okamoto et al. showed that several physical features are effective to segment

H. Bunke and A.L. Spitz (Eds.): DAS 2006, LNCS 3872, pp. 208–219, 2006.

on-line handwritten Japanese text deterministically [3]. We previously proposed a segmentation method for on-line handwritten Japanese text by a neural network [4].

The SVM method [5], [6] for pattern recognition is recently being paid more and more attentions. It is a technique motivated by statistical learning theory and has been developed to construct a function for nonlinear discrimination by the kernel method. SVMs have been successful applied to numerous classification tasks. It is thought that SVMs are the learning models that provides with the best recognition performance in a lot of techniques known now. The key idea of SVMs is to learn the parameters of the hyperplane to classify two classes based on maximum margin from training patterns.

In this paper, we employ a SVM to determine segmentation point candidates for on-line handwritten Japanese text of horizontal writing from left to right. We compare the method for segmentation by the SVM with that by a neural network. We incorporate the method into the segmentation by recognition scheme. We follow the stochastic model proposed in [7] to evaluate the likelihood composed of character pattern structure, character segmentation, character recognition and context and finally determine segmentation points and recognize text.

In this paper, section 2 presents the flow of processing. Section 3 describes text segmentation and a method for generating character segmentation point candidates. Section 4 presents evaluation. Section 5 concludes this paper.

2 Flow of Processing

A stroke denotes a sequence of pen-tip coordinates from pen-down to pen-up while an off-stroke denotes a vector from the pen-up to the next pen-down. Japanese text is composed of several text lines separated by a large off-stroke from a previous line to a new line. Its detection is not difficult. We don't go into this matter in this paper.

We process each text line as follows:

Step1: Generation of segmentation point candidates

Each off-stroke is classified into segmentation point, non-segmentation point and undecided point according to the features such as distance and overlap between adjacent strokes detailed later. A segmentation point should be between two characters while a non-segmentation point is within a character pattern. An undecided point is a point where segmentation or non-segmentation judgment cannot be made. A segmentation unit bounded by two adjacent segmentation points is assumed as a character pattern. An undecided point is treated as two ways of a segmentation point or a non-segmentation point. When it is treated as a segmentation point, it is used to extract a segmentation unit.

Step2: Modification of segmentation point candidates

For text written aslant rather than horizontally or vertically, segmentation point candidates made by the step 1 are modified using the skew space feature defined in [4].

Step3: Segmentation and recognition

A candidate lattice is constructed where each arc denotes segmentation point and each node denotes a character recognition candidate produced by character recognition for each segmentation unit as shown in *Fig. 1*. Scores are associated to each arc or node following the stochastic model evaluating the likelihood composed of character pattern structure, character segmentation, character recognition and context. The Viterbi search is made into the candidate lattice for a handwritten text line and the best segmentation and recognition is determined.

This paper will describe the details of the step 1. For the step 2 and step 3, refer to the literature [4], [7].

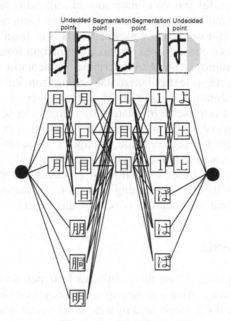

Fig. 1. Candidate lattice

3   Segmentation

First, we extract multi-dimensional features from off-strokes within a text line. Then, each off-stroke is classified into segmentation point, non-segmentation point and undecided point by applying a SVM or a neural network for the extracted features.

3.1   Selection of Off-Stroke Features

First, we define the following terminology:

Bb_{p1}: Bounding box of the immediately preceding stroke
Bb_{s1}: Bounding box of the immediately succeeding stroke
Bb_{p_all}: Bounding box of preceding all the strokes
Bb_{s_all}: Bounding box of succeeding all the strokes
acs: Average character size
D_{Bx}: Distance between *Bb_{p_all}* and *Bb_{s_all}* to x-axis
     D_{Bx} = X coordinate of left position of *Bb_{s_all}* - X coordinate of right position of *Bb_{p_all}*
D_{By}: Distance between *Bb_{p_all}* and *Bb_{s_all}* to y-axis
     D_{By} = Y coordinate of top position of *Bb_{s_all}* - Y coordinate of bottom position of *Bb_{p_all}*
D_{bx}: Distance between *Bb_{p1}* and *Bb_{s1}* to x-axis
     D_{bx} = X coordinate of left position of *Bb_{s1}* - X coordinate of right position of *Bb_{p1}*
D_{by}: Distance between *Bb_{p1}* and *Bb_{s1}* to y-axis
     D_{by} = Y coordinate of top position of *Bb_{s1}* - Y coordinate of bottom position of *Bb_{p1}*

O_b: Overlap area between Bb_{p1} and Bb_{s1}
D_{bsx}: Distance between centers of Bb_{p1} and Bb_{s1} to x-axis
  D_{bsx} = X coordinate of center of Bb_{s1} − X coordinate of center of Bb_{p1}
D_{bsy}: Distance between centers of Bb_{p1} and Bb_{s1} to y-axis
  D_{bsy} = Y coordinate of center of Bb_{s1} − Y coordinate of center of Bb_{p1}
D_{bs}: Absolute distance of centers of Bb_{p1} and Bb_{s1}
Df_b: Difference between Bb_{p_all} and Bb_{s1}
  Df_b = abs(Y coordinate of top position of Bb_{p_all} - Y coordinate of top position of Bb_{s1})

The average character size *acs* is estimated by measuring the length of the longer side of the bounding box for each stroke, sorting the lengths from all the strokes and taking the average of the larger 1/3 of them.

Then, the following 21 features of off-strokes are extracted for segmentation:

f_1: Passing time for the off stroke
f_2: D_{Bx} / acs
f_3: D_{By} / acs
f_4: Overlap area between Bb_{p_all} and Bb_{s_all} / (acs)^2
f_5: D_{bx} / width of Bb_{p1}
f_6: D_{bx} / width of Bb_{s1}
f_7: D_{bx} / acs
f_8: D_{by} / height of Bb_{p1}
f_9: D_{by} / height of Bb_{s1}
f_{10}: D_{by} / acs
f_{11}: O_b / (width x height of Bb_{p1})
f_{12}: O_b / (width x height of Bb_{s1})
f_{13}: O_b / (acs)^2
f_{14}: D_{bsx} / acs
f_{15}: D_{bsy} / acs
f_{16}: D_{bs} / acs
f_{17}: Df_b / acs

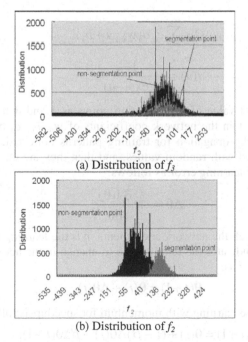

(a) Distribution of f_3

(b) Distribution of f_2

Fig. 2. Distributions of f_2 and f_3 features for training patterns

f_{18}: Length of off-stroke / acs
f_{19}: Sine value of off-stroke
f_{20}: Cosine value of off-stroke
f_{21}: f_2 / the maximum f_2 in text

We examined the distributions of these features using training patterns, and deleted the features such as f_3 shown in *fig. 2(a)* that two classes of segmentation points and non-segmentation points are not clearly divided while retained those such as f_2 shown in *fig. 2(b)* that the two classes are divided to some extent. Moreover, some features have very similar effect. Employment of them at the same time doesn't affect the discrimination rate although it takes processing time. Therefore, we examined the correlation coefficient for each pair of features and selected either one from the pair that has 0.90 or more correlation coefficient. The finally selected features are shown in *table 1*.

Table 1. Selected features

Selected features	Number
f_1, f_2, f_4, f_5, f_6, f_7, f_8, f_9, f_{10}, f_{12}, f_{13}, f_{15}, f_{16}, f_{17}, f_{18}, f_{19}, f_{20} f_{21}	18

3.2   Neural Network

A three-layers neural network can be used for distinguishing two classes of segmentation points and non-segmentation points [8]. We constructed a neural network that has an input layer composed of a feature vector v from an off-stroke plus one additional input, a middle layer of n_{mu} units and the single output. The output O is calculated as follows:

$$O = \sum_{\alpha=1}^{n_{mu}} c_\alpha \, \sigma(\mathbf{w}_\alpha \cdot \mathbf{v} + b_\alpha).$$

$$\sigma(u) = \frac{1}{1 + \exp(-u)}.$$

(1)

We set the target value of segmentation points as 1 and that of non-segmentation points as 0, and obtain the network coefficients of $\mathbf{w}_\alpha$, b_α, c_α by training the neural network using backpropagation for training patterns collected. The network coefficients are initialized with random values, and then they are changed to the direction that will reduce the learning error as follows:

$$\Delta\theta = -\eta \frac{\partial J(\theta)}{\partial \theta}.$$

(2)

where θ represents all the network coefficients, η is the learning rate, $J(\theta)$ is the learning error, and $\Delta\theta$ indicates the relative size of change in the network coefficients. θ is updated at iteration t as:

$$\theta(t+1) = \theta(t) + \Delta\theta(t).$$

(3)

Moreover, we use learning with momentum for speedup as follows:

$$\theta(t+1) = \theta(t) + (1 - \beta)\Delta\theta(t) + \beta\Delta\theta(t-1).$$

(4)

where β is set as 0.9.

For the learning rate η, we initialize it as a large value, and update it at each iteration t as follows:

if(J(t) - J(t -1) >= 0 & & It occurs n_1 times continuous ly) $\eta = \eta - \gamma_1 \eta$.

if(J(t) - J(t -1) < 0 & & It occurs n_2 times continuous ly) $\eta = \eta + \gamma_2 \eta$.

$$(5)$$

where n_1 is set as 3, n_2 is set as 2, γ_1 is set as 0.5, γ_2 is set as 0.1. The learning speed can be remarkably improved by the above method.

For the number of units for the middle layer n_{mu}, we will test several numbers and select the number that makes the smallest learning error.

3.3 Support Vector Machine

The key idea of SVMs is to separate two classes with the hyperplane that has maximum margin. Finding this hyperplane $\omega.x_i + b = 0$ can be translated into the following optimization problem:

$$\begin{cases} \text{minimize} : \dfrac{1}{2}\|\omega\|^2 + C\sum_{i=1}^{l} \xi_i . \\ \text{subject to} : \xi_i \geq 0, y_i(\omega.x_i + b) \geq 1 - \xi_i . \end{cases}$$

$$(6)$$

where $\dfrac{1}{2}\|\omega\|^2$ is for the maximum margin, ξ_i is the learning error of a training pattern i, C is the trade-off between learning error and margin, x_i is the feature vector of a training pattern i, y_i is the target value of a training pattern i, l is the number of training patterns, respectively.

Then, the feature vectors are mapped into an alternative space by choosing kernel $K(x_i, x_j) = \varphi(x_i).\varphi(x_j)$ for nonlinear discrimination. Consequently, it leads to the following quadratic optimization problem:

$$\begin{cases} \text{minimize} : W(\boldsymbol{\alpha}) = \sum_{i=1}^{l} \alpha_i + \dfrac{1}{2}\sum_{i=1}^{l}\sum_{j=1}^{l} y_i y_j \alpha_i \alpha_j \, K(x_i x_j) . \\ \text{subject to} : \sum_{i=1}^{l} y_i \alpha_i = 0, \forall i : 0 \leq \alpha_i \leq C . \end{cases}$$

$$(7)$$

where, $\boldsymbol{\alpha}$ is a vector of l variables and each component α_i corresponds to a training pattern (x_i, y_i). The solution of the optimization problem is the vector $\boldsymbol{\alpha}^*$ for which $W(\boldsymbol{\alpha})$ is minimized and the constraints of the *eq. (7)* are fulfilled. The classification of an unknown pattern z is made based on the sign of the function:

$$G(z) = \sum_{i:SV} \alpha_i y_i \, K(x_i, z) + b .$$

$$(8)$$

We set the target value of segmentation points as 1 and that of non-segmentation points as -1. We obtain the separating hyperplane by solving this optimization problem shown in the *eq. (7)* for training patterns using SVM^{light} [9] that can efficiently handle problems with many thousand support vectors, converges fast with minimal memory requirements.

3.4   Generation of Segmentation Point Candidates

Now, we must consider how to judge segmentation, non-segmentation and undecided points for generating segmentation point candidates.

We could set 0.5 as the threshold *th* because the target value of segmentation points is 1 and that of non-segmentation points is 0, then judge the values of the outputs based on the *eq. (1)* larger than *th* as segmentation points and the others as non-segmentation points for the classification by the neural network. For the classification by the SVM, we could set 0 as the threshold *th* because the target value of segmentation points is 1 and that of non-segmentation points is -1, then judge the values of the outputs based on the *eq. (8)* larger than *th* as segmentation points and the others as non-segmentation points. We could do so if it were only a classification of two classes for segmentation points and non-segmentation points. However, this does not allow the later processing to apply likelihood factors such as character recognition or context to better segment handwritten text.

Fig. 3 shows the distribution of the outputs of the neural network trained for the training patterns. We can set the concatenation threshold th_c and the segmentation threshold th_s for the both sides of *th* and judge values smaller than th_c as concatenation (non-segmentation) points, values larger than th_s as segmentation points, and the others as undecided points to obtain the higher segmentation rate for the step 3 in *Section 2*. The widths $th - th_c$ and $th_s - th$ are not certainly equal, because the distribution of the outputs for two classes of non-segmentation points and segmentation points are unbalanced as shown in *Fig. 3*. Therefore, we take the segmentation measure (the *f* measure according to the *eq. (9)* where r is recall, p is precision) after applying the step 3 for all the combinations of th_c and th_s using the

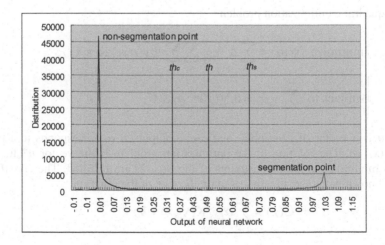

Fig. 3. Distribution of the outputs of the neural network trained for training patterns

training patterns and take the combination of th_c and th_s producing the best segmentation measure f. We employ th_c and th_s determined from the training patterns for the testing patterns, because the distribution of the testing patterns is approximated by that of the training patterns.

$$f = \frac{2}{1/r + 1/p}.$$

$$r = \frac{number\ of\ correctly\ detected\ segmentati\ on\ points}{number\ of\ true\ segmentati\ on\ points}. \tag{9}$$

$$p = \frac{number\ of\ correctly\ detected\ segmentati\ on\ points}{number\ of\ detected\ segmentati\ on\ points\ (including\ false)}.$$

4 Experiments

We extracted text lines of horizontal writing from left to right from the database of character-orientation and line-direction free on-line handwritten Japanese text: *HANDS-Kondate_t_bf-2001-11* collected from 100 people. We took 20 people's patterns as training patterns while 5 people's patterns as test patterns. We used a part of the database since it takes longer time for learning as patterns increase. Their details are shown in *table 2*, where N_{sp}, N_{nsp}, N_{ac} and N_{al} denote the number of true segmentation points, the number of true non-segmentation points, the average number of characters in a text line, the average number of characters written by one people, respectively. We use them to compare the methods for segmentation by the SVM with that by the neural network.

Table 2. Sample patterns

Number Patterns	Text lines	N_{sp}	N_{nsp}	N_{ac}	N_{al}	English letters	Numbers	Karas	Chinese characters	Other characters
Training	2772	27062	79301	11	1193	1231	4647	10715	9949	3292
Testing	695	6887	20196	11	1516	307	1139	2733	2613	790

4.1 Setting Parameters

We tested several neural networks which have the number of units for the middle layer n_{mu} as 2, 4, 6, 8 and 10, and trained the parameters for these neural networks using the training patterns until getting the smallest learning error. We selected the neural network with n_{mu} 4 because it made the smallest learning error.

For the SVM, we used the following radial basis function kernel:

$$K(\mathbf{x}_i, \mathbf{x}_j) = \exp\left(\frac{-\|\mathbf{x}_i - \mathbf{x}_j\|^2}{2\sigma^2}\right). \tag{10}$$

We set σ as 0.4 and C shown in the *eq. (7)* as 100 by testing several values in experiments using the training patterns. Then, we obtained the parameters of the separating hyperplane for the SVM using the training patterns again.

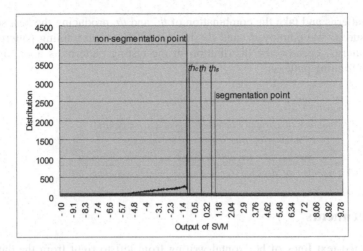

Fig. 4. Distribution of the outputs of the SVM for training patterns

Moreover, we took the distributions of the outputs of the neural network and the SVM for the training patterns. The results are shown in *Fig. 3* and *Fig. 4*. We can see the distribution of the outputs of the SVM is small from −1 to 1, because the training patterns having the outputs from −1 to 1 are regarded as having training errors and the SVM has been trained to have the smallest sum of the training errors.

Then, we measured the f measures according to the *eq. (9)* after applying the step 3 using the training patterns for all the combinations of th_c and th_s within every 0.01 step from 0.0 to 0.5 for th_c and from 0.5 to 1.05 for th_s for the neural network, and within every 0.02 step from −1.1 to 0 for th_c and from 0 to 1.1 for th_s for the SVM, respectively. We took the combination of th_c and th_c producing the best segmentation measure f. According to the result on the training patterns, we set the parameters th_c and th_s as 0.08 and 1.0 for the neural network, -0.98 and 0.98 for the SVM, respectively. The details of the result for the training patterns according to these parameters are shown in *table 3*.

Table 3. The result of segmentation for the training patterns

Off-strokes	Method	Neural Network	SVM
True non-segmentation points	Classified into non-segmentation points	83.24%	91.99%
	Classified into undecided points	16.69%	7.74%
	Classified into segmentation points	0.07%	0.26%
True segmentation points	Classified into non-segmentation points	0.76%	0.58%
	Classified into undecided points	64.18%	6.75%
	Classified into segmentation points	35.05%	92.67%

Table 4. How often off-strokes are classified into thress classes

Off-strokes	Method	Neural Network	SVM
Classified into non-segmentation points		62.25%	68.74%
Classified into undecided points		28.78%	7.49%
Classified into segmentation points		8.97%	23.78%

Table 4 summarises the result from the different viewpoint. It shows how often off-strokes are classified into non-segmentation points, undecided points and segmentation points, because undecided points incur processing time significantly.

4.2 Comparison of Neural Network and SVM

We compare the performance by the SVM and that by the neural network for the training patterns and the testing patterns on a Pentium (R) 4 3.40 GHz CPU with 0.99 GB memory. *Table 5* shows the result, where f, Cr, T_{train}, T_{ac}, T_{ar} denote the f measure after applying the step 3, the character recognition rate after applying the step 3, the time for training the parameters for the neural network or the SVM using the training patterns, the average time for classifying an off-stroke into the three classes, the average time for processing a text line by the three steps mentioned in *Section 2*, respectively.

Table 5. Comparison of the two methods

Performance	Method	Neural Network	SVM
Training patterns	f	0.9600	0.9859
	Cr	72.22%	77.60%
Testing patterns	f	0.9413	0.9578
	Cr	69.76%	72.92%
T_{train}		About 1.5 hours	About 10 hours
T_{ac}		0.009 (ms)	5.845 (ms)
T_{ar}		92.15 (ms)	279.07 (ms)

We also measured the segmentation measure f for classifying only two classes of segmentation points and non-segmentation points by the neural network and the SVM. The result is that the f measure is 0.9045 for the training patterns and 0.8886 for the testing patterns by the neural network, 0.9733 for the training patterns and 0.9268 for the testing patterns by the SVM, respectively.

The *eq. (11)* shows a formula of the average time for processing a text line from components. The terms N_{as}, N_{udp} denote the average number of off-strokes in a text line, the average number of undecided points in a text line, respectively. The terms T_{Se}, T_{Cr}, T_{Lcs}, T_{Las}, are the average time for extracting the features from an off-stroke, the average time of character recognition for a text line, the average time for constructing the candidate lattice for a text line, the average time to search into the candidate lattice for a text line, respectively. The latter three terms depend on how many consecutive undecided points appears, but approximately they have the order of two to the power of N_{udp}.

$$T_{ar} = N_{as}T_{Se} + N_{as}T_{ac} + T_{Cr} + T_{Lac} + T_{Las}$$
$$T_{Cr} = O(2^{N_{udp}})$$
$$T_{Lac} = O(2^{N_{udp}})$$
$$T_{Las} = O(2^{N_{udp}})$$

(11)

From *table 4*, *table 5* and *eq. (11)*, we consider as follows:

(1) The result of the segmentation measure and the character recognition rate by the SVM are better than that by the neural network.
(2) The best neural network has three layers with the middle layer of 4 units. The larger the number of units for the middle layer n_{mu} is, the smaller the learning error should be, but it is practically difficult to find the global minimum for the learning error.
(3) The distribution of the outputs is very small form -1 to 1 for the SVM as shown in *Fig. 4*, which provides reliable margin to discriminate segmentation points and non-segmentation points.
(4) Although the classification time T_{ac} by the SVM is about 649 times longer than that by the neural network because the SVM must count the sum of the support vectors according to the *eq. (8)*, the average time T_{ar} for processing a text line by the SVM is only about 3 times longer than that by the neural network. This is because the segmentation by the neural network has a more number of undecided points, which incurs longer time for character recognition, constructing the candidate lattice and searching into the candidate lattice as shown in *table 4* and the *eq. (11)*. We consider that the average time T_{ar} for processing a text line by the SVM is acceptable because it is not so long.
(5) The training time T_{train} by the neural network is much shorter than that of the SVM.

5 Conclusion

This paper described a segmentation method of on-line handwritten Japanese text. We extracted multi-dimensional features from off-strokes in on-line handwritten text and applied a neural network and a SVM to produce segmentation point candidates. The SVM brought about better segmentation performance and character recognition rate, although its processing time is behind the neural network. By employing the full set of the database, we will report more accurate and reliable evaluation.

Acknowledgement

This research is being supported by Grant-in-Aid for Scientific Research under the contract number (B)17300031.

References

1. M. Nakagawa and M. Onuma, "On-line Handwritten Japanese Text Recognition Free from Constrains on Line Direction and Character Orientation," *Proc. 7th ICDAR*, Edinburgh, 2003, pp.519-523
2. H. Aizawa, T. Wakahara and K. Odaka, "Real-Time Handwritten Character String Segmentation Using Multiple Stroke Features (in Japanese)", *IEICE Transactions in Japan*, Vol.J80-D- II, No.5, 1997, pp.1178-1185

3. M. Okamoto, H. Yamamoto, T. Yosikawa and H. Horii, "Online Character Segmentation Method by Means of Physical Features (in Japanese)", *Technical Report of IEICE in Japan,* PRU, Vol.95, No.43, 1995, pp.93-100
4. Bilan. Zhu and M. Nakagawa, "Segmentation of On-line Handwritten Japanese Text of Arbitrary Line Direction by a Neural Network for Improving Text Recognition," *Proc. 8th ICDAR,* Seoul, Korea, 2005, pp.157-161
5. V.N.Vapnik, *Statistical Learning Theory,* J.Wiley, 1998
6. N.Cristianini and J.Shawe-Talor, *An Introduction to Support Vector Machines,* Cambridge University Press, 2000
7. M. Nakagawa, B. Zhu and M. Onuma, "A Formalization of On-line Handwritten Japanese Text Recognition free from Line Direction Constraint," *Proc. 17th International Conference on Pattern Recognition (ICPR),* Cambridge, England, 2P. Tu-i, 2004
8. R.O. Duda, P.E. Hart, D.G. Stork, *Pattern Classification, Second Edition,* J. Wiley & sons, 2001
9. T. Joachims, "Making large-scale SVM learning practical," in B. Schölkopf, C. J. C. Burges, and A. J. Smola, edits, *Advances in Kernel Methods — Support Vector Learning,* Cambridge, MIT Press, 1999, pp. 169-184

Application of Bi-gram Driven Chinese Handwritten Character Segmentation for an Address Reading System

Yan Jiang[1], Xiaoqing Ding[1], Qiang Fu[1], and Zheng Ren[2]

[1] Department of Electronic Engineering, Tsinghua University, Beijing, China, 100084
{jyan, dxq, fuq}@ocrserv.ee.tsinghua.edu.cn
[2] Siemens AG, D-78467 Konstanz, Germany
zheng.ren@siemens.com

Abstract. In this paper, we describe a bi-gram driven method for automatic reading of Chinese handwritten mails. In destination address block (DAB) location, text lines are first extracted by connected components analysis. Each candidate line is segmented and recognized by our holistic method, which incorporates mail layout features, recognition confidence and context cost. All these are also taken into consideration to identify the DABs from the candidate text lines. Based on them, street address line and organization name line are determined. At last step, edit distance based string matching is performed against given databases. We also discuss the pretreatment to deal with Chinese address databases consisted of a large amount of vocabularies in order to generate keywords for fast indexing during matching. Detailed experiment results on handwritten mail samples are given in the last section.

1 Introduction

OCR (optical character recognition) has been applied in postal automation since 1970s. The first generation of systems is based on postcode recognition, which could only recognize the digits in a specific region on an envelope. Nowadays, it is becoming more and more deficient in satisfying the requirements for faster reading and more detailed treatment of rapidly increasing mails. With the development of pattern recognition, it is now feasible to automatically process all the information on an envelope to boost the recognition performance. There have been various literatures in this area, covering different languages, such as English ([1]), Japanese ([4]) and so on.

Generally speaking, there is no obvious gap between two adjacent characters in a Chinese address line, so a text line should be first segmented into characters for recognition, which has long been an obstacle in Chinese address reading. Although there has been much work considering layout and recognition information in segmentation, it still remains insufficient for some special real world applications like mail reading where high performance in segmentation is needed, since segmentation errors are always incorrigible for post-processing and address

H. Bunke and A.L. Spitz (Eds.): DAS 2006, LNCS 3872, pp. 220–231, 2006.

match. In our proposed method, we incorporate layout cost, recognition cost and contextual cost together based on bi-gram model to achieve a good performance both in segmentation and recognition. Furthermore, we could see that recognition cost and contextual cost are also very important in DAB location, comparing with layout features, they are more discriminating.

Up to now, there are still few efforts considering the work to search and match the Chinese address items in a very large database containing hundreds of thousands of items and our work also focus on this area. We propose a pretreatment method for address database to generate keywords for both searching and matching. The samples which cannot be uniquely identified would be rejected in the keywords searching stage for the consideration of efficiency.

The remainder of this paper is organized as follows: we briefly review bi-gram model based OCR post-processing in Sect. 2; in Sect. 3, we have a short review on Xue's method in extracting text lines from envelopes; in Sect. 4, we introduce our holistic method for address segmentation and apply the evaluated score in DAB location; in Sect. 5, we introduce our basic idea for the pretreatment of the address database and review the definition of edit distance which is used in our string comparison; experiments results are given in Sect. 6.

2 Bi-gram Model

N-gram model has been introduced to natural language processing (NLP) for a long time and it is applied in speech recognition and OCR post-processing. In OCR, a typical character classifier generates several hypotheses for an input image, and the first candidate is not ensured to be correct. Post-processing techniques are studied to select the most likely recognized strings from the candidate characters, the process is formularised as follows:

$$c_{1,k_1^*}, c_{2,k_2^*}, \ldots, c_{T,k_T^*} = \underset{1 \le k_t \le M, 1 \le t \le T}{\arg\max} \ P(c_{1,k_1}, c_{2,k_2}, \ldots, c_{T,k_T} | x_1, x_2, \ldots, x_T) \quad (1)$$

Where $x_1, x_2, \ldots, x_T$ are a series of character images, x_i denotes the i-th character image. The classifier gives M candidate characters for each input character image, which are denoted by $c_{i,k_i} (1 \le k_i \le M)$. The contextual post-processing method select characters from candidate sets to form the most likely string $c_{1,k_1^*}, c_{2,k_2^*}, \ldots, c_{T,k_T^*}$ by maximizing the posterior probability.

By Bayesian formula,

$$P(c_{1,k_1}, c_{2,k_2}, \ldots, c_{T,k_T} | x_1, x_2, \ldots, x_T)$$
$$= \frac{P(x_1, x_2, \ldots, x_T | c_{1,k_1}, c_{2,k_2}, \ldots, c_{T,k_T}) P(c_{1,k_1}, c_{2,k_2}, \ldots, c_{T,k_T})}{P(x_1, x_2, \ldots, x_T)} \quad (2)$$

Bi-gram model only considers the transition probability between two characters, so the probability $P(c_{1,k_1}, c_{2,k_2}, \ldots, c_{T,k_T})$ is simplified as Eq.3.

$$P(c_{1,k_1}, c_{2,k_2}, \ldots, c_{T,k_T}) = P(c_{1,k_1}) \times \prod_{i=1}^{T-1} P(c_{i+1,k_{i+1}} | c_{i,k_i}) \quad (3)$$

Assuming that the current recognition behavior is independent of the previous decisions in the classifier ([3]),

$$P(x_1, x_2, \ldots, x_T | c_{1,k_1}, c_{2,k_2}, \ldots, c_{T,k_T}) = \prod_{i=1}^{T} P(x_i | c_{i,k_i})$$
$$= \prod_{i=1}^{T} P(x_i) \times \prod_{i=1}^{T} \frac{P(c_{i,k_i} | x_i)}{P(c_{i,k_i})} \tag{4}$$

$P(c_{i,k_i})$ is the prior probability determined by the classifier, which could be seen as uniformly distributed ([3]). $P(c_{i,k_i} | x_i)$ could be estimated from recognition distances given by the classifier ([5]).

Combining the above equations, we could simplify the maximization process of posterior probability to the following, in which, Viterbi algorithm is applied ([3]).

$$c_{1,k_1^*}, c_{2,k_2^*}, \ldots, c_{T,k_T^*} = \operatorname*{arg\,max}_{1 \leq k_t \leq M, 1 \leq t \leq T} P(c_{1,k_1}) \prod_{i=2}^{T} P(c_{i,k_i} | c_{i-1,k_{i-1}}) \prod_{i=1}^{T} P(c_{i,k_i} | x_i) \tag{5}$$

We will see the maximum of the right side of Eq.5 is important for both character segmentation and DAB location.

3   Text Line Extraction

The writing style of Chinese envelopes are much different from the western mails. Receiver's information is written in the upper part of the envelope, while sender's information is often written in the lower part. The receiver's name is almost in the center of the image. (Fig. 1) The basic framework of our work is illustrated in

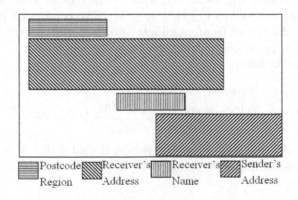

Postcode Region   Receiver's Address   Receiver's Name   Sender's Address

Fig. 1. A typical Chinese envelope layout

Fig.2. In text lines extraction module, connected components are extracted from binary image after preprocessing steps. Each connected component is regarded as a block, which is then categorized into four kinds: noise, text, graphic and image. This classification process is mainly based on the layout features of the connected component, detailed algorithm could be found in [7]. Only text blocks are reserved for the step of text lines extraction. Text lines are generated by

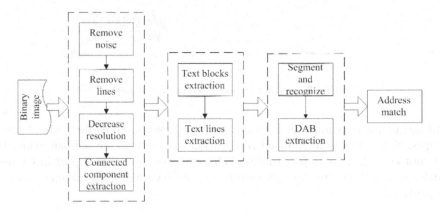

Fig. 2. Framework of our proposed system

merging the text blocks. Layout constraints are taken into account to identify which line a text block belongs to. Then, we merge all the text blocks belonging to the same line together as our extracted candidates, but there maybe more text lines than we expected. We must identify which text line is useful for us from the text line candidates.

For example, six text lines are extracted in Fig.3 (in rectangles). The first text line contains postcode, the fourth text line contains receiver's name and the fifth and six text lines contain sender's information. They are useless for us since we don't intend to process such information. Only the second and the third text line should be identified as DAB. In Xue's work, he presents a bottom-up strategy considering some special characteristics of handwritten Chinese envelopes. But his method may cause some errors simply by considering layout features. In the proposed method, DAB location is not performed directly after text line extraction, instead, all the extracted text lines are sent to the segmentation and recognition module. We will evaluate each line not only by its arrangement features but also by its recognition and contextual cost.

4   Character Segmentation and DAB Location

Chinese characters have very complex structures, and addresses are often written in cursive style. Conventional segmentation methods are based on structural

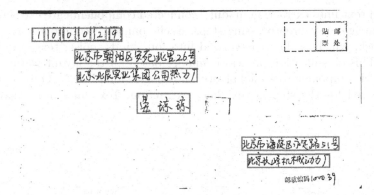

Fig. 3. Extracted text lines by Xue's method

and layout information, but they are not always stable in dealing with Chinese scripts. Some people introduced recognition cost in Chinese segmentation, but it is not enough. Left-right structured characters occupy a large part in Chinese. Both parts of them are valid characters and will own high recognition confidence respectively.

4.1 Over-Segmentation

The general process of character segmentation for Chinese involves an over-segmentation stage at first. Each line image is over-segmented into a series of radicals by structural method. A radical is one part of a character and all radicals are reunited to form character images. An efficient over-segmentation technique could remove overlapping from scripts. We adopt the algorithm proposed by Xue, which cited the work of Tseng and Gao. Only layout information is considered in over-segmentation. Fig.4(b) shows the result of Fig. 4(a) after over-segmentation, each radical is bounded in a rectangle.

4.2 Merge Radicals

For over-segmented radicals, we establish a segmentation graph (Fig.4(c)), the edge from one node to another represents a combination image of some certain radicals and the edge is assigned a cost for the combination. For example, if the over-segmented radicals are denoted by $s_1, s_2, \ldots, s_l$, then the cost of the edge from $Node_i$ to $Node_{i+k}$ is assigned as the cost to combine $s_i, s_{i+1}, \ldots, s_{i+k-1}$.

The widely adopted method to merge radicals is to find the shortest path in the segmentation graph from $Node_1$ to $Node_{l+1}$. Different strategies have been proposed to evaluate the edges' costs, which can be summarized into three main kinds: structural analysis based evaluation, recognition based evaluation and contextual evaluation.

In our method, we first evaluate each edge by Xue's cost function ([7]). Then we apply K-shortest algorithm ([2]) in the segmentation graph according to the layout cost and evaluate each path by our proposed function L. The path with highest score will be selected as our segmentation decision. At the same time, the OCR result of this line image will be given. Our cost function L is formalized as follows, which incorporates layout cost, recognition cost and contextual cost together.

$$L(path) = \frac{1}{n}[\sum_{i=1}^{n} \log P(c_{i,k_i}|x_i) + \log P(c_{1,k_i}) + \sum_{i=2}^{n} \log P(c_{i,k_i}|c_{i-1,k_{i-1}})]$$
$$+ \frac{\lambda}{n}[\log P(x_1, x_2, \ldots, x_n|s_1, s_2, \ldots, s_l)] \tag{6}$$

Where $x_1, x_2, \ldots, x_n$ are the merged images according to *path*, and the third item on the right hand $P(x_1, x_2, \ldots, x_n|s_1, s_2, \ldots, s_l)$ is the confidence to merge $s_1, s_2, \ldots, s_l$ into $x_1, x_2, \ldots, x_n$ according to their layout distribution, the item is estimated from the evaluated layout cost of *path*. λ is a weight factor that is estimated by experiments. The first and the second items are maximized by Viterbi algorithm.

(a) A Chinese address string image

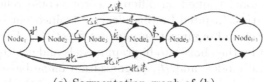

(b) After over-segmentation (each radical is bounded in a rectangle)

(c) Segmentation graph of (b)

Fig. 4. Over-segmentation and merge of radicals

We compare our bi-gram based segmentation result with a previous method proposed by Xue ([7]). Table 1 shows the result containing two content rows which are corresponding to two different methods. The first and the second columns give the number of correctly segmented characters and lines respectively; the third and the fourth columns tell the percentage of the correctly segmented characters and lines. Experiments is carried out on 233 line images containing 3,014 characters which are extracted from Chinese handwritten envelopes.

Table 1. Bi-gram driven segmentation results

	Correct segmentations of characters	Correct segmentations of lines	Ratio of correct segmentations of characters (%)	Ratio of correct segmentations of lines (%)
Xue's method	2,492	55	82.7	23.6
Our method	2,787	144	92.4	61.8

4.3 Recognition and Contextual Information Based Address Line Determination

In Xue's bottom-up method, he uses an empirical evaluation function and identifies the text line with the highest score to be the name line. Then the lines between the first line and the name line are selected as DAB. But this method is not stable in practice, since there maybe some unexpected errors to locate the name line simply by layout analysis. Furthermore, we cannot tell which line contains the geographic location and which line contains organization name by layout feature, since text lines of geographic location and text lines of organization name have no obvious differences.

A more effective method should take both character recognition result and contextual information into account. The proposed method take the context-recognition cost H as the criterion, H is defined as the maximum of the sum of the first item and the second item in Eq.6.

$$H = \max_{1 \leq k_1, k_2, \ldots, k_n \leq M} \frac{1}{n} [\sum_{i=1}^{n} \log P(c_{i,k_i}|x_i) + \log P(c_{1,k_1}) + \sum_{i=2}^{n} \log P(c_{i,k_i}|c_{i-1,k_{i-1}})]$$

(7)

In fact, bi-gram model trained on different corpus could reflect different contextual characteristics. Inspired by this idea, we trained our bi-gram model on geographic addresses and organization names respectively. Each segmented line image is evaluated by the above two bi-gram models and get H_g (geographic address based bi-gram model) and H_O (organization name based bi-gram model) respectively. If a sample is consistent with the domain of the bi-gram model, the value of H will be higher than that is calculated on the corpus which doesn't belong to this domain. Noticing this fact, we could summarize the following rules: (1) if $H_g > H_O$ and $H_g > T$, then we could judge this line image to be a geographic address line; (2) if $H_O > H_g$ and $H_O > T$, then we could judge this line image to be a organization name line. T is a predefined threshold to control the lines to be selected as DAB, since postcode line and name line always have distinctly low H value.

5   Address Matching

Address interpretation is often considered as a string match process. We choose the most suitable address item from a large vocabulary dictionary according to our OCR results. Moreover, we are always required to search and match with acceptable expenditure of time. So the key problem is how to effectively select as small address candidates as possible to include the correct one in a large database.

In our method, keywords are generated for each address item in the pretreatment stage and we establish a lookup table for fast keywords index. For a line image, after the recognition process, we look for the keywords in the recognized string first and select the corresponding address items as candidates (Figure 5).

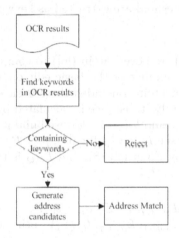

Fig. 5. Flowchart of address searching and matching

5.1 Keyword Generation

For geographic location items, there are twenty items with the same street name averagely, that is, these items are only different in street number. For organization names, it is also a common situation that some organization names are only different in one or two characters. Ambiguous items make it tough for us to identify an item against many similar ones. Furthermore, recognized characters cannot be assured to be entirely correct because some unforeseen errors may be brought by DAB location, character segmentation or recognition. Two principles are essential for keyword generation: (1) the extracted keywords should be easy for searching; (2) OCR result should be rejected if no keywords could be found.

For a Chinese address item, words are piled without gaps between each other. Word segmentation is first applied to split an item into words first. For example, a organization name "北京希盛技术开发有限公司" is segmented into five words: "北京" "希盛" "技术" "开发" "有限公司". "北京" is the city name, "希盛" is the name of the company, "技术" means "technology", "开发" means "development" and "有限公司" means "limited company". It is easy to see that the words "北

京", "技术", "开发" and "有限公司" are helpless to uniquely identify the item. Only the word "希盛" is extracted as the keyword for this name. We give a detailed description for this idea. For an input item, we exam all the segmented words. If a Chinese word contains more than two characters, we exhaust all the two characters combinations, that is, for the word "建国门", we decompose it into "建国" and "国门". For a given string, after word segmentation, we extract a series of two-character words $w_1, w_2, \ldots, w_k$ and their corresponding number of occurrence in address data $N_1, N_2, \ldots, N_k$. The weight for each word is calculated as $\text{Weight}(w_i) = \frac{N_i}{\sum_{j=1}^{j=k} N_j}$ and only the words whose weights are less than a predefined threshold are extracted as keywords for this item.

5.2   Edit Distance

Edit distance is proposed by Levenshtein ([6]) to compare two strings, which is defined as the minimum number of the basic edit operations to transform one string into another. Levenshtein concluded three basic edit operations: deletion, insertion and substitution. Edit distance is calculated by dynamic programming.

For string $a_1 a_2, \ldots, a_P$ and $b_1 b_2, \ldots, b_Q$, we build a $(P+1) \times (Q+1)$ matrix $\{L_{p,q}\}_{0 \le p \le P, 0 \le q \le Q}$, and set $L_{p,0} = p$ for $0 \le p \le P$, $L_{0,q} = q$ for $0 \le q \le Q$. Then $L_{p,q}$ is calculated by Equation (8), and $L_{P,Q}$ is the edit distance between $a_1, a_2, \ldots, a_P$ and $b_1, b_2, \ldots, b_Q$.

$$
L_{p,q} = \begin{cases} L_{p-1,q-1} & \text{if } a_p = b_q \text{ ;} \\ 1 + \min\left(L_{p-1,q-1}, L_{p-1,q}, L_{p,q-1}\right) & \text{otherwise .} \end{cases} \tag{8}
$$

5.3   Geographic Location Items Match

In fact, there are many valid variations for geographic location items. Some parts in a geographic address are not necessary and could be omitted. We try to reflect this feature according to the geographic address model shown below. A common

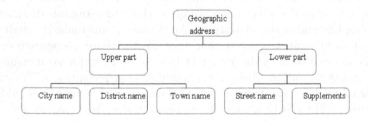

Fig. 6. General structure of Chinese geographic address

Chinese geographic address is composed of five parts and the district name part and town name part are often omitted in general. In addition, there are some suffixes which are written directly behind the address components, such as "市", "县", "区", "镇", "乡" and so on, could be omitted too.

6   Experiments

We collect about 1000 handwritten samples written in different styles. The hand-written character classifier is developed by the department of electronic engineering, Tsinghua University. We collected two address databases: one is full address database, which contains more than 180,000 items in Beijing city (Database I) and the other is street name database which contains more than 7,000 street names in Beijing city (Database II). Each item in Database I is composed of three parts: postcode, geographic location and organization name.

We test DAB location and line discrimination performance. 315 envelopes are taken for this experiment, which contains 630 DAB lines that should be extracted. We will divide this process into two steps: one is text line location and the other is DAB location. The method for the first step is reviewed in Section 3. DAB location step tries to find the text lines of interest. Our contextual-recognition method is compared with Xue's bottom-up strategy.

(a) Fail to extract the text lines containing address information

(b) Some address text lines are missing

(c) Some characters in a text line are missing

Fig. 7. Text line location error classification

Table 2. Text line location errors

Error of Type (a)	Error of Type (b)	Error of Type (c)
16	7	34

In fact, some errors occur at text line location step, we classify those errors into three basic types as shown in Fig.7 and conclude these errors in Table 2.

We abandon the text lines, which cannot be correctly extracted on the envelopes and test our DAB location and line discrimination method on the remaining text lines. There remains 591 text lines that should be identified as either geographic location or organization name from all the extracted text lines. We compare the number of two kinds of errors in DAB location in Table 3. Class A error indicates that a text line which should be identified as DAB is missed; Class B error indicates that a text line which should not be identified as DAB is wrongly accepted. Our proposed line discrimination method is tested in the fourth column of Table 3.

Table 3. DAB location and line discrimination

	Class A errors	Class B errors	Correct rate of discrimination
Xue's method	39	37	—
Proposed method	7	4	97.3%

We have two experiments on Database I and II respectively. In fact, after DAB location, we could tell whether a text line contains geographic information or organization information, so we could compare a recognized string with the corresponding items in Database I. The text line of geographic address and the text line of organization name on the same envelope are matched independently and the results are shown in the first and second column of Table 4. If we combine the matching result of geographic address and organization name on an envelope together, it will reduce the matching errors as shown in the third column of Table 4.

We can find that there are more errors in geographic address match in Database I. Most of these errors are only caused by street number comparison. We may summarize the following problems: (1) many geographic addresses are only different in their street number; (2) there are many confusing characters between Arabic digits, English alphabets and Chinese characters, such as: "13" vs. "B", "3" vs. "ヲ" and so on, it is even difficult for a people to tell whether a character image is a Chinese character, an English character or an Arabic digit without a look at the whole text line; (3) there are no strict contextual constraints to the digits. In another experiment, we compare the extracted geographic address line with the items in Database II. All the items in this database are varied according to the address model and street number comparision is neglected (result is shown in the fourth column of Table 4).

Table 4. Experiments of address match

	Geographic address match (Database I)	Organization name match (Database I)	After fusion (Database I)	Geographic address match (Database II)
Recognition rate	72.8%	84.8%	90.3%	89.8%

7   Conclusions

In this paper, contextual information is taken into consideration for character segmentation by bi-gram model trained on the address corpus which gives better result for cursive handwritten character segmentation. We also see that contextual-recognition cost is also important in DAB location, which makes it possible for precise address line selection and discrimination. We also have discussed two main rules for keywords generation for the purpose of faster search and match.

There still remains some challenging work. First of all, text line location needs to be adapted to diverse writing styles. In matching stage, edit distance with uniform weight for each operation is not suitable for real word application, since the characters in an item are not of same importance. If we could involve address match in character segmentation and recognition stage, it is sure that we could improve our matching of Arabic digits. Additionally, postcode information may help to boost the speed for searching address candidates and improve the matching accuracy to a certain extent. Furthermore, recognition confidence, bi-gram model and string matching could be somewhat combined to find a global optimal solution in the framework of probability theory, which would put our algorithm onto a more stable theoretical foundation.

Acknowledgements. This work has been funded by Siemens AG under contract number 20030829 - 24022SI202.

References

1. El Yacoubi A., Bertille, J.M., Gilloux, M.: Conjoined location and recognition of street names within a postal address delivery line. Proc. 5th International Conference on Document Analysis and Recognition (1995) 1024–1027
2. Jimenez, V.M., Marzal, A.: Computing the K shortest paths: A new algorithm and an experimental comparison. Proc. of the Third International Workshop on Algorithm Engineering, London, July, 1999. LNCS vol. 1668. Springer 15–29
3. Li, Y.X., Ding, X.Q., Tan, C.L., Liu, C.S.: Contextual Post-processing based on the confusion matrix in offline handwritten Chinese script recognition. Pattern Recognition **37**(9) (2004) 1901–1912
4. Liu, C.L., Koga, M., Fujisawa, H.: Lexicon-driven segmentation and recognition of handwritten character strings for Japanese address reading. IEEE Trans. PAMI **24**(11), (2002) 1425–1437
5. Liu, C.L., Masaki, N.: Precise Candidate Selection for large character set recognition by confidence evaluation. IEEE Trans. PAMI **22**(6), (2000) 36–642
6. Levenshtein, V.I.: Binary codes capable of correcting insertions and reversals. Soviet Physics Doklady **10**(8), (1966) 707–710
7. Xue, J.L., Ding, X.Q.: Location and interpretation of destination addresses on handwritten Chinese envelopes. Pattern Recognition Letters **22**(6), (2001) 639–656

Language Identification in Degraded and Distorted Document Images

Shijian Lu, Chew Lim Tan, and Weihua Huang

School of Computing, National University of Singapore, 117543, Singapore
{lusj, tancl, huangwh}@comp.nus.edu.sg
http://www.comp.nus.edu.sg/labs/chime/

Abstract. This paper presents a language identification technique that differentiates Latin-based languages in degraded and distorted document images. Different from the reported methods that transform word images through a character shape coding process, our method directly captures word shapes with the local extremum points and the horizontal intersection numbers, which are both tolerant of noise, character segmentation errors, and slight skew distortions. For each language studied, a word shape template and a word frequency template are firstly constructed based on the proposed word shape coding scheme. Identification is then accomplished based on Bray Curtis or Hamming distance between the word shape code of query images and the constructed word shape and frequency templates. Experiments show the average identification rate upon eight Latin-based languages reaches over 99%. . . .

1 Introduction

With the widespread use of the document capture facilities including document scanner and digital camera, language identification from document images becomes more and more important for applications such as multilingual OCR, multilingual information retrieval, and library digitalization. Traditionally, language identification is frequently addressed in natural language processing areas where languages are differentiated based on the character-coded text [1, 2] or OCR results [3]. N-grams, which represent n adjacent text symbols, are normally utilized for language identification.

Some works have also been reported to identify languages in document images scanned through a document scanner. Unlike various scripts that hold different alphabet structures [4, 5] and texture features [6], Latin-based languages are all printed in the same set of Roman letters and so have similar texture features. As a result, they cannot be differentiated based on alphabets or texture features. Letter sequences, which are generally organized in different fixed patterns (words) for different languages, are therefore widely exploited for Latin-based language identification.

The reported language identification techniques normally begin with a character categorization process, which transforms character images to a number of categories with different codes. Character coding is normally implemented based

H. Bunke and A.L. Spitz (Eds.): DAS 2006, LNCS 3872, pp. 232–242, 2006.
© Springer-Verlag Berlin Heidelberg 2006

on the character shape characteristics including character ascender and descender and character ascent and decent. For example, the works in [5, 7, 8] propose to first group character and other text symbol images into six, ten, and thirteen categories, respectively. With the character categorization results, a set of word shape codes (WSCs) are then created based on the word segmentation results. Finally, languages are differentiated according to the WSC frequency profiles of a single word [5, 7], word pair, and word trigram [8]. Linear discriminate analysis (LDA) [5] and rule based systems [7, 8] are exploited for the final language identification. The reported identification rates reach around 90%.

Though promising identification results have been achieved, some problems still exist. The problems include: 1) Nearly all existing language identification techniques assume that character images are perfectly segmented. They cannot work well with the degraded documents that contain a large number of broken or touching character components. 2) Nearly all existing methods assume that text images are noise free and character ascent and descent can be correctly detected. Unfortunately, noise and character ascent and descent may not be differentiated correctly in lots of cases. 3) Nearly all existing methods require deskew before word shape coding. 4) Nearly all existing methods assume that document images contain a large number of words. Very few works handle language identification in text images that contain just a few word images.

In this paper, we propose a Latin-based language identification technique that is tolerant of noise, segmentation errors, document distortion, and word number problems. For distorted text images, we assume that the skew angle is within 20 degrees, which is quite reasonable for control during the capturing process. For each language studied, a word shape template and a word frequency template are firstly constructed through a WSC training process. Word shape coding is carried out based on the local extremum points [9] and the horizontal intersection numbers, which are both robust to noise, character segmentation errors, and the slight document distortion. Word shape vector and word frequency vector of query images are then constructed based on the same word shape coding scheme. Lastly, languages are identified based on Hamming or Bray Curtis distance between the word shape and frequency vectors of the query images and multiple trained word shape and frequency templates.

2   Word Shape Coding

The proposed language identification technique is presented in this section. In particular, we divide this section into a few subsections, which deal with the image preprocessing, feature extraction, and word shape coding respectively.

2.1   Image Preprocessing

Some preprocessing operations are required before the word shape coding. Firstly, document text must be located and segmented from the background. A number of text detection and segmentation techniques have been reported in the literature. In this paper, we assume that document images are binarized and contain

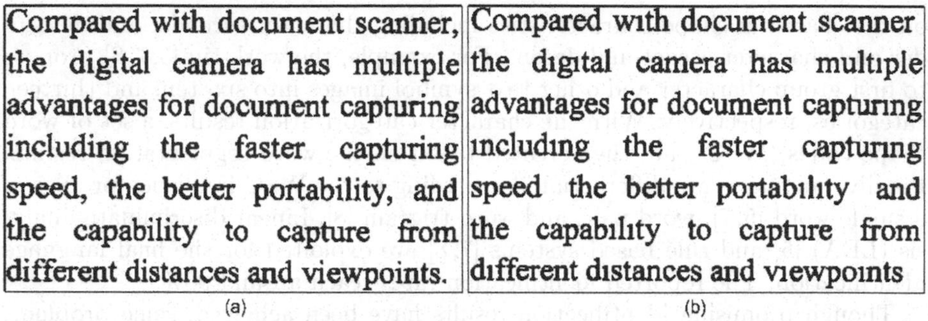

Compared with document scanner, the digital camera has multiple advantages for document capturing including the faster capturing speed, the better portability, and the capability to capture from different distances and viewpoints.	Compared with document scanner the digital camera has multiple advantages for document capturing including the faster capturing speed the better portability and the capability to capture from different distances and viewpoints
(a)	(b)

Fig. 1. (a) Binarized text image; (b) filtered text image

text with noise, segmentation errors, and slight skew distortion with skew angle smaller than 20 degrees.

Preprocessing is thus accomplished through two rounds of size filtering. Noise of small sizes is firstly removed through the first round filtering. We set threshold at 10 because nearly all labeled character components contain much more than 10 pixels. $Size_{mdn}$, the median size of the remaining character components, is then determined through a simple size sorting process. The document components with smaller size including the punctuation, the top part of characters "i", and "j", and character ascent and descent can be further removed through the second round size filtering. The threshold can be determined based on the $Size_{mdn}$:

$$T = k_t \cdot Size_{mdn} \tag{1}$$

where parameter k_t normally lies between 0.2-0.4. We set it at 0.3 in our implemented system. For the binarized text image given in Figure 1(a), Figure 1(b) shows the preprocessing result where small document components have been removed. In later discusses, all character components refer to the ones after these two rounds of size filtering.

Nearly all existing language identification techniques depend heavily on the small document components including the top part of character "i" and "j" and the character ascent and descent such as "$\acute{e}$" and "$\acute{u}$" for character shape coding. Therefore, it is quite difficult to choose a proper threshold for noise removal. As a result, the generated WSCs normally contain lots of errors because these small document components cannot be differentiated from noise of similar size. As our proposed coding scheme does not require these small document components, the preprocessing is able to remove them together with the noise of similar sizes and generate a cleaner text image for ensuing word shape coding.

2.2   Feature Extraction

Two features are exploited for word shape coding. The first refers to the local extremum points that are extracted from upward and downward text boundary. The second is the horizontal intersection number, which counts the intersections between character strokes and the middle line of text lines.

For each labeled character components, the upward and downward character boundary can be determined with a vertical scan line that traverses across the character component from left to right. The first and last character pixels of each scanning round, which correspond to the highest and lowest character pixels, are determined as character upward and downward boundary points. For documents with slight distortion, as we restrict the skew angle within 20 degrees, the boundary of characters ascender and descender such as "*b*" and "*p*" will not cover that of character strokes between x-line and baseline of text lines. Therefore, the extraction of the upward and downward character boundary is tolerant of slight document distortion. For the sample image given in Figure 1, Figure 2(a) shows the extracted text boundary where text is printed in light gray color to highlight the extracted text boundary.

For each labeled character component, its upward or downward boundary actually forms an arbitrary curve that can be characterized by a function f(x). The extrema of the function f(x), which correspond to the local extremum points, can be mathematically defined as below:

Definition : Given an arbitrary curve $f(x)$:
1. We say that $f(x)$ has a relative (or local) maximum at $x = c$ if $f(x) \leq f(c)$ for every x in some open interval around $x = c$.
2. We say that $f(x)$ has a relative (or local) minimum at $x = c$ if $f(x) \geq f(c)$ for every$x$ in some open interval around $x = c$.

For document images scanned through a document scanner, the local extremum points normally take six boundary patterns as illustrated in Figure 3. The downward text boundary also takes six patterns, which are actually 180 degree rotation of the six upward patterns. For the extracted text boundary shown in Figure 2(a), the black dots in Figure 2(b) show the detected extremum points. It should be clarified that some single pixel concave and convex along the text boundary may affect the extremum point detection. These concave and convex with single pixel can be removed using certain logical or morphological operators beforehand.

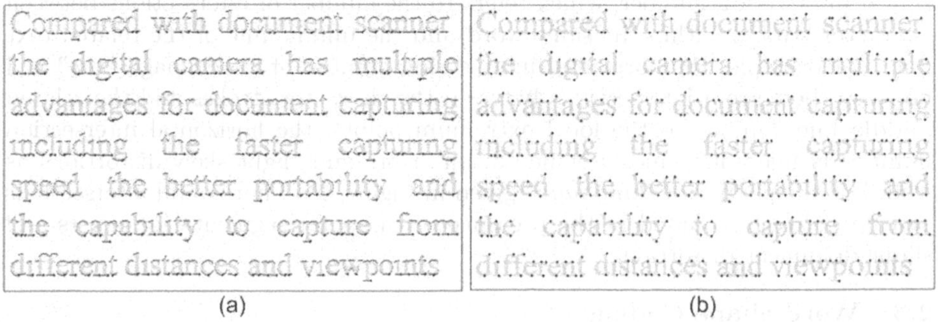
Compared with document scanner
the digital camera has multiple
advantages for document capturing
including the faster capturing
speed the better portability and
the capability to capture from
different distances and viewpoints
(a)
Compared with document scanner
the digital camera has multiple
advantages for document capturing
including the faster capturing
speed the better portability and
the capability to capture from
different distances and viewpoints
(b)

Fig. 2. (a) Upward and downward text boundary; (b) local maximum and minimum boundary points

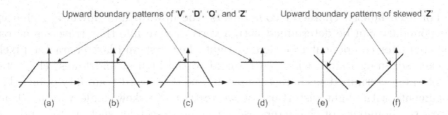

Fig. 3. (a-f): Six upward maximum patterns

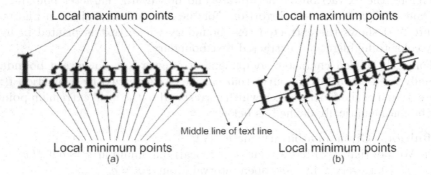

Fig. 4. Local maximum and minimum points and horizontal intersection number in degraded and distorted word image

The local extremum points are tolerant of most segmentation errors and slight document distortions. Figure 4 illustrate these two properties. For word image *"language"* given in Figure 4(a), characters *"g"*, *"u"*, and *"a"* are falsely connected after the binarization process. With traditional character shape coding technique, these three characters will be treated as one and the resulting WSC will be totally different from the actual one. But the local extremum points are able to capture the word shape correctly while characters are connected as shown in Figure 4(a). Similarly, local extremum points can also be detected correctly in presence of slight skew distortion as illustrated in Figure 4(b).

In addition to the local extremum points, another feature we exploit is horizontal intersection number, which refers to the number of intersections between character strokes within the same word and the middle line of the related text line. For example, the horizontal intersection number of word image *"the"* is 4 because there are 4 intersections between the character strokes and the related middle line. Similar to the local extremum points, the horizontal intersection number is tolerant of most segmentation errors and slight skew distortions as well. For sample image *"language"* given in Figure 4, 14 horizontal intersections can be correctly counted in the presence of character segmentation errors and slight document distortion.

2.3   Word Shape Coding

With the local extremum points and horizontal intersection number, each word image can be transformed into a set of electronic WSCs.

Before the word shape coding, it is desired to extract text lines first to facilitate word segmentation and extremum point classification. We extract text lines using the character tracing technique proposed in [10]. With the extracted text lines, word images can be segmented based on the distance between the adjacent extremum points, as the distance between the extremum points adjacent to inter-word blank is much bigger than that between the adjacent extremum points within the same word.

Extremum points can thus be classified based on their positions relative to the x-line and baseline of text lines. In our proposed method, extremum points are classified into three categories with three different codes. The maximum points within the first category lie far above the x-line and they are coded with the number "3". The maximum or minimum points within the second category lie between the x-line and baseline and they are coded with number the "2". The minimum points within the third category lie far below the baseline and they are coded with the number "1". The x-line and baseline can be roughly fitted based on the extremum points extracted from the studied text line.

Combined with the horizontal intersection numbers, word images can thus be transformed to the WSCs and Figure 5 illustrates the WSC format. The first part on the left in Figure 5 refers to the number sequence coded based on the local extremum points. Horizontal intersection number in the middle counts the number of intersections between word strokes and the middle line of text line. These first two parts form the WSC. WSC frequency on the right denotes the occurrence number of the WSC within the studied document image. For example, the word images "*the*" and "*of*" can be coded with the number sequences "33224m", "233n" respectively where parameters m and n refers to the occurrence number of the sample words. Number sequences "3322" and "23" are coded based on the local extremum points and the following numbers "4" and "3" record the horizontal intersection numbers.

The word images within the whole document can thus be coded based on the coding scheme as illustrated in Figure 5. Each word image is translated to a WSC and the whole document is thus transformed into a word shape vector. Each element in the word shape vector records a unique WSC number sequence. For a new WSC translated from a word image, the word shape vector is searched for the element with the same WSC. If such element exists, the occurrence number is increased by one. Otherwise, a new element is created and initialized with the new detected WSC and the occurrence number 1.

The word frequency vector is normalized to facilitate the language identification. For the ith WSC element within the word shape vector, the corresponding frequency element within the frequency vector is defined as:

Coded local maximum and minimum	Horizontal intersection number	WSC occurrence number

Fig. 5. Word shape coding format

$$F_i = \frac{ON_i}{N_w} \tag{2}$$

where parameter N_w denotes the total number of words detected. Parameter ON_i refers to the occurrence number of the i_{th} WSC.

3   Language Identification

We use the proposed word shape codes for language identification. For each language studied, a word shape template and a word frequency template is first constructed through a training process. The language is then determined based on the distance between the word shape and frequency vectors of the query images and multiple trained word shape and frequency templates.

Word shape and frequency templates are constructed through a learning process that accumulates WSCs and the related frequency from multiple training images. For each WSC translated from a word image within a specific training image, the word shape template is searched for the element with the same WSC. If the WSC pattern exists within the WSC template, its occurrence number is increased by one. Otherwise, a new element is created and initialized with the translated WSC. The training process stops automatically while the training images or the WSC patterns within the related template reaches a fixed number. With the constructed word shape template, word frequency template can accordingly be constructed based on the accumulated WSC occurrence numbers using Equation (2).

Language can thus be determined based on the distance between the word shape and frequency vectors of query images and the constructed word shape and frequency templates. For each query image, the word shape and frequency vector can be determined using the word shape coding method described in Section 2. N frequency expectation vectors with dimension same as that of word shape vector can thus be constructed where parameter N refers to the number of languages studied. For each element within the word shape vector of query images, the same WSC pattern is searched throughout each word shape templates. If the same WSC pattern exists with the specific template, the element within the corresponding frequency expectation vector is initialized with the corresponding frequency element within the related word frequency template. Otherwise, the element of frequency expectation vector is set to zero.

As the frequency profile of the WSCs are normally quite similar for documents printed in the same language, Latin-based languages can thus be identified based on the Bray Curtis distance between the word frequency vector of the query image and N constructed frequency expectation vectors. Bray Curtis Distance given below has a nice property that its value always lies between zero and one.

$$D_i = \frac{\sum_{j=1}^{n}(|WEF_j - WF_j|)}{\sum_{j=1}^{n}(WEF_j) + \sum_{j=1}^{n}(WF_j)} \tag{3}$$

where parameter WEF_j represents the jth word expectation frequency within the ith frequency expectation vector. Parameter WF_j corresponds to the jth element of the word frequency vector of query images. The distance D_i is the Bray Curtis Distance calculated for the ith language. As a result, query image is determined to be printed in the language with the smallest D_i.

The identification performance described above may deteriorate while the number of word images becomes too small. For query images with small number of words, the WSC frequency is far different from the word frequency expectation in the related vector. Under such circumstance, the Bray Curtis Distances calculated may be quite close for different languages. We therefore propose to identify languages based on the normalized Hamming distance between word shape vector and the word shape templates while the word number is too small, say, smaller than 50.

The normalized Hamming distance is defined as:

$$HD_i = \frac{1}{N}H(WSV_{query}, WST_i) \qquad (4)$$

where parameter N is equal to the dimension of WSV_{query}, which denotes the number of the unique word shape patterns in the query image. WST_i represents the ith WSC template. Function H count the number of WSCs in WSV_{query} that do not exist in WST_i. Therefore, as WSC in WSV_{query} all appear in WST_i, the normalized Hamming distance of the ith template given in Equation (4) is 0. On the contrary, if no WSC in WSV_{query} appears in WST_i, the normalized Hamming distance is 1.

4   Experimental Results

800 training and testing images are prepared to evaluate the performance of our proposed method. Document texts printed in eight Latin-based languages including English, French, German, Italian, Spanish, Portuguese, Swedish, and Norwegian are tested. Four corpora of text images from different sources including books, articles, and web pages are constructed where the first one is prepared for the word shape and frequency training and the last three are for

Table 1. WSC numbers learned from training images

	English	German	French	Italian	Spanish	Portuguese	Swedish	Norwegian
English	6344	1332	1586	1494	1526	1404	1064	1076
German	1332	8280	1546	1448	1466	1400	1158	1230
French	1586	1546	7472	1620	1646	1552	1232	1210
Italian	1494	1448	1620	6381	1716	1708	1208	1194
Spanish	1526	1466	1646	1716	6811	1808	1278	1188
Portuguese	1404	1400	1552	1708	1808	6144	1124	1102
Swedish	1064	1158	1232	1208	1278	1124	8773	1418
Norwegian	1076	1230	1210	1194	1188	1102	1418	9147

testing. Document images are scanned through a generic document scanner at different resolutions.

The first corpus contains 320 text images scanned at 400 ppi where every 40 are printed in one specific language. The corpus one is prepared for word shape and frequency training as described in Section 3. Table 1 gives the training results where the diagonal items give the numbers of the WSCs learned from the training images and the off-diagonal items give the numbers of WSCs that are shared by two related languages. As Table 1 shows, the average collision rate reaches around 10%. Therefore, the proposed technique can be exploited for language identification. Furthermore, as the trained WSCs contain a large number of short frequently appeared words, the 10% collision rate is actually much higher than the real one. It may be reduced greatly after more sample images are trained and some longer WSCs ones are collected.

The second corpus contains 160 text images with every 20 printed in one specific language. Text images in corpus two are scanned at a lower resolution (200 ppi) and so the binaried images contain more segmentation errors including broken or touching character components. At the same time, different from text images within corpus one where texts are all printed in Time New Roman, texts in corpus two are printed in several different fonts including Arial, Verdana, and Courier. Experimental results show the proposed technique is quite tolerant of text fonts and document degradation. For 160 text images studied, 159 are correctly identified with average identification rate reaching over 99%. Table 2 shows some typical Bray Curtis distances calculated using Equation (3) and four distances are listed for each language studied. As Table 2 shows, the Bray Curtis distances between word frequency vectors and the corresponding frequency expectation vectors are much smaller than those between word frequency vectors and other frequency expectation vectors.

Similar to the corpus two, the third corpus contains 160 text images as well with every 20 printed in one specific language. However, all sample images in corpus three are coupled with slight skew distortion with skew angle controlled under 20 degree. Unlike some methods [7,8] that require document restoration first, word images are transformed to WSCs directly based on our proposed word shape coding scheme. Experiment results show 157 text image are correctly identified with average identification rate reaching over 97%. Therefore, the proposed technique is quite tolerant of slight skew distortion.

Lastly, most reported language identification techniques [5,7,8] cannot identify language in document images that contain just a few words. We therefore construct the fourth corpus to evaluate the performance of our proposed technique with respect to word number. 160 text images are prepared with every 20 printed in one specific language. Test images are directly cut from the 160 testing images in corpus three and each test image contains just one or two text lines with around 20 word images on average. Languages are identified based on the normalized Hamming distance given in Equation (4). Experimental results show that 151 text line images are correctly identified with average identification rate around 94%. The lower identification rate is mainly due to the small number of

Table 2. Bray Curtis distances calculated for text images within corpus two

	English	French	German	Italian	Spanish	Portuguese	Swedish	Norwegian
English1	0.3132	0.6872	0.7292	0.7844	0.7349	0.7819	0.7718	0.7398
English2	0.2438	0.5782	0.7266	0.7534	0.6922	0.8471	0.7491	0.6531
English3	0.3156	0.7275	0.6660	0.8337	0.8244	0.9040	0.6755	0.6988
English4	0.3676	0.7768	0.6720	0.8632	0.8703	0.8930	0.7405	0.7417
French1	0.7000	0.1972	0.5493	0.4485	0.3584	0.5605	0.7193	0.6596
French2	0.6843	0.1850	0.5565	0.4810	0.3626	0.5107	0.7466	0.6350
French3	0.7251	0.2098	0.6101	0.4113	0.4017	0.5594	0.7047	0.6589
French4	0.6944	0.1764	0.4932	0.4553	0.4196	0.4879	0.6553	0.6518
German1	0.6290	0.6959	0.2985	0.7418	0.8002	0.7275	0.6486	0.6763
German2	0.6821	0.7163	0.2541	0.7389	0.8274	0.7748	0.6814	0.6668
German3	0.7069	0.6823	0.2539	0.7353	0.7246	0.7700	0.6742	0.6925
German4	0.6665	0.6849	0.3458	0.7960	0.8050	0.7628	0.6067	0.5949
Italian1	0.7861	0.5149	0.6225	0.2530	0.5542	0.5505	0.7641	0.6149
Italian2	0.7431	0.3933	0.5000	0.1749	0.3943	0.5567	0.6213	0.5824
Italian3	0.6719	0.4873	0.6176	0.2541	0.4956	0.4942	0.7340	0.6464
Italian4	0.7521	0.4038	0.5816	0.2032	0.3984	0.5345	0.6213	0.5458
Spanish1	0.7365	0.3912	0.7740	0.4937	0.2594	0.4283	0.6994	0.6478
Spanish2	0.7167	0.4379	0.7062	0.5213	0.2583	0.5129	0.6658	0.6496
Spanish3	0.7861	0.4276	0.6362	0.5411	0.2282	0.4736	0.7298	0.6437
Spanish4	0.7784	0.4764	0.6873	0.6070	0.2408	0.5930	0.7258	0.7651
Portuguese1	0.7386	0.4841	0.5916	0.6663	0.4638	0.3131	0.7464	0.7562
Portuguese2	0.7693	0.4831	0.6959	0.6922	0.5414	0.1688	0.7951	0.7402
Portuguese3	0.7843	0.6242	0.6811	0.6877	0.6725	0.2458	0.8425	0.8094
Portuguese4	0.7807	0.5610	0.6346	0.7122	0.5952	0.2351	0.7695	0.7224
Swedish1	0.6685	0.6826	0.4480	0.6599	0.6689	0.7307	0.2712	0.4702
Swedish2	0.7032	0.7226	0.5339	0.7978	0.7514	0.7706	0.2617	0.5631
Swedish3	0.6785	0.6995	0.3475	0.6204	0.6389	0.7741	0.2461	0.5389
Swedish4	0.8598	0.8026	0.5334	0.7636	0.6986	0.7803	0.2840	0.5879
Norwegian1	0.7054	0.5514	0.5512	0.5310	0.5460	0.6588	0.4726	0.2134
Norwegian2	0.6220	0.5618	0.4487	0.5574	0.6345	0.6780	0.5000	0.1643
Norwegian3	0.7405	0.6091	0.4851	0.6438	0.6192	0.7750	0.4603	0.1807
Norwegian4	0.5934	0.5706	0.4547	0.5856	0.6129	0.6904	0.4200	0.1581

WSC patterns accumulated within the constructed word shape templates. The identification rates can be improved greatly after more text images are trained and more WSCs and the related frequency information are collected.

Though the proposed technique is able to identify languages from Latin-based text images, some problems still exist. Firstly, the proposed method cannot handle text images with big skew angle. While skew angle is bigger than 20 degrees, upward and downward text boundary and so the local extremum points may not be extracted properly. Under such circumstance, document deskew is normally required before the word shape coding. Secondly, the proposed technique can only handle the Latin-based language identification. For languages typed in different scripts such as Chinese and Arabic, the collision rate is quite high and the coded WSCs are heavily affected by text fonts. We will investigate these two issues in our future work.

5 Conclusion

A Latin-based language identification technique is presented in this paper. The proposed technique is able to identify languages from degraded and distorted text images scanned through a document scanner. Language identification is accomplished through a word shape coding scheme that transforms word images into a set of electronic codes. The local extremum points and the horizontal intersection numbers are exploited for word shape coding and they are both robust to noise, segmentation errors, and slight document distortions. With coded WSCs, languages are identified based on the Hamming or Bray Curtis distance between the word shape and frequency vectors of the query images and the related word shape and frequency templates. Experiments show the proposed technique is able to identify eight Latin-based languages with average identification rate over 99%.

References

1. W. Cavnar, J. Trenkle. N-Gram Based Text Categorization, *3rd Annual Symposium on Document Analysis and Information Retrieval*, Las Vegas, NV, pages 161–175, 1994.
2. T. Dunning. Statistical Identification of Language, Technical report, Computing Research Laboratory, New Mexico State University, 1994.
3. D. S. Lee, C. R. Nohl, and H. S. Baird. Language Identification in Complex, Unoriented, and Degraded Document Images, *International Workshop on Document Analysis Systems*, Malvern, Penn-sylvania, pages 76–98, 1996.
4. J. Hochberg, L. Kerns, P. Kelly and T. Thomas. Automatic Script Identification from Images Using Cluster-based Templates, *IEEE PAMI*, vol. 19, No. 2, pages 176–181, 1997.
5. A. L. Spitz, Determination of the Script and Language Content of Document Images, *IEEE PAMI*, vol. 19, no. 3, pages 235–245, 1997.
6. T. N Tan, Rotation Invariant Texture Features and Their Use in Automatic Script Identifica-tion, *IEEE PAMI*, vol. 20, no. 7, pages 751–756, 1998.
7. N. Nobile, S. Bergler, C. Y. Suen, S. Khoury, Language Identification of On-Line Documents Using Word Shapes, *4th ICDAR*, Ulm, Germany, pages 258–262, 1997.
8. C. Y. Suen, S. Bergler, N. Nobile, B. Waked, C. P. Nadal, and A. Bloch, Categorizing Document Images Into Script and Language Classes, *International Conference on Ad-vances in Pattern Recognition*, Plymouth, England, pages 297–306, November 1998.
9. R. K. Powalka, N. Sherkat, R. J. Whitrow, Word Shape Analysis for a Hybrid Recognition System, *Pattern Recognition*, vol. 30, no. 3, pages 421–445, 1997.
10. S. J. Lu, B. M. Chen, C. C. Ko, Perspective Rectification of Document Images Using Fuzzy Set and Morphological Operations, *Image and Vision Computing*, vol. 23, no. 5, pages 541–553, 2005.

Bangla/English Script Identification Based on Analysis of Connected Component Profiles

Lijun Zhou[1], Yue Lu[1,2], and Chew Lim Tan[3]

[1] Department of Computer Science and Technology,
East China Normal University, Shanghai 200062, China
[2] Shanghai Research Institute of Postal Science,
China State Post Bureau, Shanghai 200062, China
[3] Department of Computer Science, School of Computing,
National University of Singapore, Kent Ridge, Singapore 117543

Abstract. Script identification is required for a multilingual OCR system. In this paper, we present a novel and efficient technique for Bangla/English script identification with applications to the destination address block of Bangladesh envelope images. The proposed approach is based upon the analysis of connected component profiles extracted from the destination address block images, however, it does not place any emphasis on the information provided by individual characters themselves and does not require any character/line segmentation. Experimental results demonstrate that the proposed technique is capable of identifying Bangla/English scripts on the real Bangladesh postal images.

1 Introduction

Language identification acts as an important role in document image processing, especially for multi-lingual OCR systems. Its goal is to automatically classify textual document images, based on analyzing the stroke structure and connections and the fundamentally different writing styles of the different alphabets or character sets. In past years, many algorithms for script identification have been proposed. According to entities analyzed in the process of script identification, the algorithms proposed in the literature could be typically classified to four categories: (a) the schemes based on analysis of connected components [1-2]. (b) the schemes based on analysis of characters, words and text lines[3-7]. (c) the schemes based on analysis of text blocks[8-10]. (d) the schemes based on analysis of hybrid information of connected components, text lines etc.[11-16]. We discuss briefly the principles, merits and weakness of each approach.

1.1 Connected Component Analysis

The approaches based on connected component analysis generally use the intrinsic morphological characteristics of the character sets or strokes of each script. Hochberg et al. [1] presented a system that automatically identifies the

H. Bunke and A.L. Spitz (Eds.): DAS 2006, LNCS 3872, pp. 243–254, 2006.

script form using cluster-based templates. It discovers frequent character or word shapes in each script by means of cluster analysis, then looks for instances of these in new documents and compares a subset of textual symbols from the document to each script's templates. The script with the best match is chosen as the script of the document.

In [2], Spitz presented an approach for automatic determination of the script and language content of document images on the basis of character density or the optical distribution. Based on the spatial relationships of features related to the upward concavities in character structures, the method first classifies the script into two broad classes: Han-based and Latin-based. Language identification within the Han script class (Chinese, Japanese, Korean) is performed by analysis of the distribution of optical density in the text images. They handled 23 Latin-based languages using a technique based on character shape codes.

1.2   Character, Word or Line Analysis

Most methods based on the analysis of character, word or line have been proposed for language identification in multilingual documents. Lee and Kim [3] proposed a scheme for multi-lingual, multi-font, and multi-size large-set character recognition using self-organizing neural network. They determine not the script of the entire document, but the script of individual characters within the document. In [4], Ying et al. carried out language identification by classifying individual character images to determine the language boundaries in multilingual documents.

In [5], John presented Linguini, a vector-space based categorizer used for language identification. Linguini uses dictionaries generated from features extracted from training texts, and compares these against feature vectors generated from test inputs. Features used are N-grams and words, and combinations of both. They also presented an algorithm for detecting and determining the nature of bilingual documents.

In [6], three efficient techniques for identifying Arabic script and English script were presented and evaluated. These techniques address the language identification problem on the word level and on textline level. The characteristics of horizontal projection profiles as well as run-length histograms for text written in both languages are the basic features underlying these techniques.

Tan et al. [7] presented a research in identifying English, Chinese, Malay and Tamil in image documents. The identification process takes place in two main steps. The first step uses bounding boxes of character cells and upward concavities to distinguish between three main classes: Chinese, Latin and Tamil scripts. Then if Latin scripts are detected, they use statistical analysis of word shape tokens of the Latin words in the document to distinguish between English and Malay languages.

1.3   Text Block Analysis

Since visual appearances of different scripts are often distinctive from each other, a text block in each script class may be considered as a unique texture pattern. Thus, texture classification algorithms may be employed to perform script identification. Such texture based approach is presented in [8, 9]. In [8], Peake et al. presented a new scheme based on texture analysis for script identification which did not require character segmentation. Via simple processing, a uniform text block on which texture analysis can be performed is obtained from a document image. Multiple channel (Gabor) filters and grey level co-occurrence matrices are used in order to extract texture features. They used the K-NN classifier to classify the test documents. In [9], Singhal et al. proposed an approach on script-based classification of handwritten text documents in a multilingual environment. They apply denoising, thinning, pruning, m-connectivity and text size normalization in sequence to produce a unique text block. They also use Multi-channel Gabor filtering to extract text features.

Wood et al. [10] proposed a scheme for determining the language classification of printed documents. In that algorithm, the characteristics on the horizontal and vertical projections of the document are used to distinguish European languages, Russian, Arabic, Chinese, and Korean.

1.4 Hybrid Analysis

Most comparatively complex methods are based on hybrid feature analysis. These schemes try to combine the different features extracted from global (text block) and local (text line, word, character and connected components) document entities.

In [12], Pal and Chaudhuri used projection profiles, statistical, topological and stroke based features for identifying English, Urdu, Bangla and Devanagari scripts from a document image. Their work was extended to separation of printed Roman, Chinese, Arabic, Devnagari, and Bangla text lines from a single document[13]. Shape based features, statistical features and some features obtained from the concept of water reservoir, have been used in this technique.

In [15], Chaudhury et al. proposed three trainable classification schemes for identification of Indian scripts. The first scheme is based upon a frequency domain representation of the horizontal profile of the textual blocks. The other two schemes use connected components extracted from the textual region. They have proposed a novel Gabor filter-based feature extraction scheme for the connected components. They also use frequency distribution of the width-to-height ratio of the connected components for script recognition. It is claimed that the Gabor filter-based scheme provides the most reliable performance.

The methods discussed above are summarized in table 1, from which we can notice that very few works have been done in identification of handwritten document images compared to machine generated document images. Most of the script identification techniques available in the literature so far consider printed text only. These techniques, especially those schemes that are based on the overall visual appearance of the text block, are generally incapable of tackling the variations in the writing style, character style and size, spacing between lines/words, etc.

China Post is designing and manufacturing automatic letter sorting machine for Bangladesh Post Office. As a multi-language country, Bangladesh envelopes may be handwritten/printed in Bangla or English. To automatically recognize postcodes or address, Bangla/English script identification in the destination address block (DAB) becomes a crucial step. However, we found that the reported approaches are generally not suitable for our purpose. This is because all these methods apply to a wider range of languages while we specifically would like to maximize the discriminating capability between the Bangla and English scripts for this practical application. In this paper, we propose a novel connected component analysis based approach to identifying Bangla/English scripts on both printed and handwritten envelope images.

Table 1. Summarization of the methods on script identification

Method	Language/Script	Nature
Cluster-Based Templates [1]	Arabic, Armenian, Burmese, Chinese. Cyrillic, Devanagari, Ethiopic, Greek, Hebrew, Japanese,Korean, Roman, Thai	Printed
Analysis of character density or the optical distribution [2]	Han script class(Chinese, Japanese, Korean), 23 Latin-based languages	Printed
Self-organizing neural network [3]	English, Korean and Chinese	Printed
The prototype classification method and support vector machines [4]	Chinese, English and Japanese	Printed
Linguini [5]	Catalan, Danish, Dutch, English, Finnish French, German, Icelandic, Italian Norwegian, Portuguese, Spanish Swedish	Printed
Horizontal projection profiles and run-length histograms analysis [6]	Arabic, English	Printed
Analysis of bounding boxes of character cells and statistical analysis of word shape [7]	English, Chinese, Malay and Tamil	Printed
Texture analysis [8]	Chinese, English, Greek, Korean, Malayalam, Persian and Russian	Printed
Texture classification algorithm [9]	Roman, Devanagari, Bangla and Telugu	Handwritten
Horizontal and vertical projections analysis[10]	European languages, Russian, Arabic, Chinese, and Korean	Printed
Hybrid analysis [12-15]	Indian scripts, Roman, Chinese, Arabic	Printed
Morphological analysis combined with geometrical analysis[16]	Arabic and Latin scripts	Printed and handwritten

2   Proposed Technique for Script Identification

At the first step, the grey scale image is captured from the envelope at the resolution of 200DPI, while a letter is passing by the camera on a letter sorting machine. An adaptive threshold approach is utilized to convert the grey scale image to its binary one, as given in Fig.1(a) and (b). The postal stamp block and other graphic parts are detected and deleted. Such processing is a basic stage, but out of the scope of this paper, and we will not report the corresponding details here. Based on the positional information of the text block, the DAB is extracted for subsequent processing as showed in Fig.1(c) and (d).

For language identification, choosing appropriate features is an important perhaps the most important step. For our purpose, the features used for distinguishing Bangla script and English script are chosen with the following considerations: (a) Easy to detect; (b) Feasible for identification; (c) Independence of font, size and style of the text; (d) Robustness.

The basic alphabets of English and Bangla are shown in Fig.2, from where we can note that English characters are symmetric and regular in the pixel distribution in the vertical direction whereas the difference in the vertical pixel distribution of Bangla characters is prominent. For the English characters, both the location of the lowest and the topmost pixels of each column of the

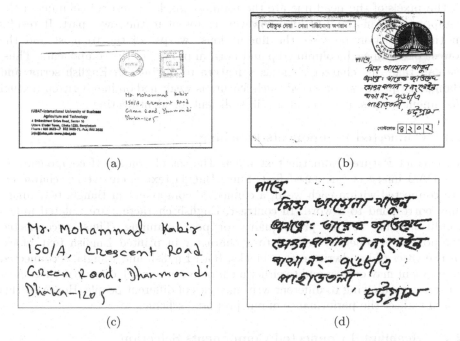

(a) (b)

(c) (d)

Fig. 1. (a) An example of envelop image written in English. (b) An example of envelop image written in Bangla. (c) Detected destination address block of (a). (d) Detected destination address block of (b).

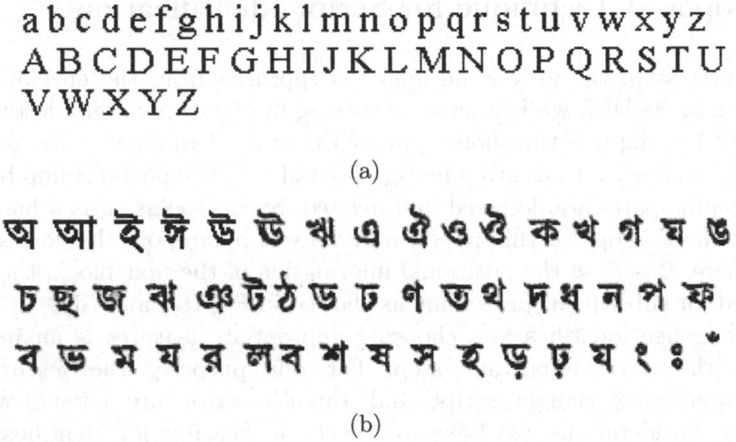

abcdefghijklmnopqrstuvwxyz
ABCDEFGHIJKLMNOPQRSTU
VWXYZ

(a)

অ আ ই ঈ উ ঊ ঋ এ ঐ ও ঔ ক খ গ ঘ ঙ
চ ছ জ ঝ ঞ ট ঠ ড ঢ ণ ত থ দ ধ ন প ফ
ব ভ ম য র ল ব শ ষ স হ ড় ঢ় য় ং ঃ ঁ

(b)

Fig. 2. (a) Basic alphabets of English (b) Basic alphabets of Bangla

components vary regularly. In Bangla, it is noted that many characters of these alphabets have a horizontal line at the upper part which is called the head-line. When two or more characters sit side by side to form a word in this language, the head-line portions touch one another and generate a long head-line. Most of the pixels of the head-line are the topmost pixels of vertical columns of the components. This kind of line, however, is absent in the lower part. It results in the distinction between the fluctuations (warps) of the topmost and the lowest pixels in each column (top and bottom profile) of the components. Thus, we can take this characteristic as a feature to distinguish English script and Bangla script. As we observed, such feature is weakened on handwritten textual document images, however, it is still sufficient for identification.

2.1 Connected Components Labelling

To extract features from the text block, the set of connected components in the DAB image is calculated first. Since Bangla text is cursive i.e. characters are connected within each word, a connected component in Bangla text image may correspond to a word. In contrast, English characters are isolated unless conditions due to low print quality or poor scanning. Thus, a connected component is generally related to a character in printed English text block. In the cases of handwritten text blocks, both English and Bangla, a connected component may correspond to either a character or a word, or several characters within a word owing to different writing styles of different people. However, this doesn't affect the performance of our proposed scheme.

2.2 Meaningful Connected Components Selection

In order to minimize the effect of non-script specific markings and reduce the computational time as well, during the analysis of the connected components profiles (both topmost profile and bottommost profile), absolutely very small elements, relatively very small or large elements are eliminated. This ensures that we consider only meaningful connected components and at the same time we can avoid special noise appearing in the text.

Absolutely very small elements deletion: To select meaningful connected components, we firstly deleted those with small area, currently set at less than 9 pixels. This processing removes noise and assures the veracity of the average area (amount of pixels) of textual components, which is computed as

$$avg = \frac{1}{M} \sum_{i=1}^{M} pix(i) \tag{1}$$

where M is the number of the remaining connected components in the destination address block.

Relatively small elements deletion: Based on the considerations that most relatively small connected components correspond to punctuations or broken parts of characters or strokes which will affect the accuracy of the script identification, the components that are smaller than a predefined threshold should be excluded from further feature analysis. And the corresponding T_s is defined as

$$T_s = \alpha_1 \times avg \tag{2}$$

In our experiment, $\alpha_1 = 0.6$ has been proved to be appropriate.

Relatively large elements deletion: As during the step of destination address block extraction, part of the postal stamp may be included because of the overlapping of them. Also, scratched-out words may be sometimes involved in the DAB. These parts, comparatively large, should be removed too. Here we considered the components which are larger than a threshold T_l as large components. In other words, the component whose area is larger than T_l is eliminated from the profile analysis. T_l is computed as

$$T_l = \alpha_2 \times avg \tag{3}$$

where $\alpha_2 = 5$ has been proved to be a suitable value.

Based on the above processing, the results of connected components filtration of Fig.1(c) and (d) are shown in Fig.3(a) and (b), respectively.

2.3   Connected Component Profiles Analysis

Subsequently, we extract the topmost profile and the bottommost profile of the finally remained connected components respectively, i.e. the topmost pixels and the lowest pixels of vertical columns of the components. To obtain the topmost (bottommost) profile, each vertical column of a particular connected component is scanned from top (bottom) until it reaches a black pixel (p_i). Thus, for a component of width N, we get N such pixels. The topmost profile

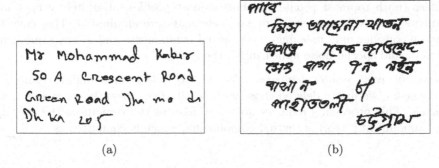

(a)   (b)

Fig. 3. (a) Connected components filtered of Fig.1(c). (b) Connected components filtered of Fig.1(d).

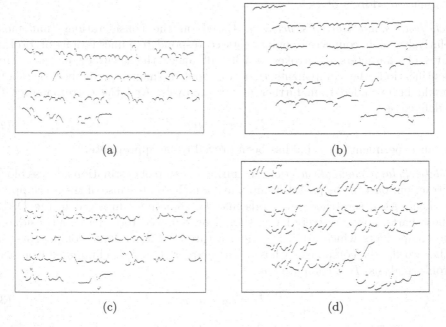

(a)   (b)

(c)   (d)

Fig. 4.   (a) Topmost profile of Fig.3 (a). (b) Topmost profile of Fig.3 (b). (c) Bottommost profile of Fig.3 (a). (d) Bottommost profile of Fig.3 (b).

and bottommost profile of Fig.3.(a) and (b) are showed in Fig.4. To measure the discontinuity of topmost (bottommost) contour line of the component, we traverse from p_i to p_{i+1} , and obtain the difference d_i of two adjacent pixels of the components, and is computed as:

$$d_i = |y_{p_{i+1}} - y_{p_i}|, \qquad 1 \leq i \leq N - 1 \tag{4}$$

where y_{p_i} is the Y-coordinate value of the pixel p_i .

And the total distance of the top border of the component is computed as

$$td(j) = \sum_{i=1}^{N-1} d_i \qquad (5)$$

On the assumption that the text block has M' connected components, its aggregate value of distance of top pixels is produced as

$$ttd = \sum_{j=1}^{M'} td(j) \qquad (6)$$

The aggregate distance of the bottom pixels, then, is obtained in the similar way and is computed as

$$tbd = \sum_{j=1}^{M'} bd(j) \qquad (7)$$

where $bd(j)$ is the accumulative difference of bottom pixels of a connected component which is produced like the $td(j)$ term. Text script is inferred from functions ttd and tbd , on the basis that an English text image will have almost equal value of ttd and tbd whereas the difference in ttd and tbd is obviously large in Bangla text image. A normalized measure of this top/bottom difference D_{tb} is defined as

$$D_{tb} = \frac{ttd - tbd}{\min(ttd, tbd)} \qquad (8)$$

which is generally indicative of an English text block when positive, and a Bangla text block when appeared to be negative. Exception exists in text blocks when the D_{tb} term of English text blocks is negative. However, we also find that the absolute value of D_{tb} in both printed and handwritten English text image is generally small. In contrast, the absolute value of D_{tb} in Bangla text image, either printed text or handwritten text, is comparatively large. To investigate we have done an experiment using 100 images (including English text blocks and Bangla text blocks) which are segmented from the real envelope images provided by Bangladesh Post. Through the experiment, two threshold-value are adopted which have been proved to be suitable, the one is thresh1=0.3, another is thresh2=0.1. We identify the script according to the following rules:

Rule 1: if D_{tb} is larger than thresh1, the script of the text block is identified as Bangla.

Rule 2: if D_{tb} is smaller than thresh2, the script of the text block is identified as English.

Rule 3: otherwise, the image is rejected from script identification.

The confidence level of the identification increases with increasing difference between D_{tb} and the threshold-value.

3   Experimental Results

1200 images have been used for test in our experiments. These samples were captured from real Bangladesh postal images. A small amount of page skew was inevitably introduced in practical environment and the character sizes and writing styles were vastly different. Some samples are showed in Fig.5.

The experimental results are shown in Table 2 and Table 3. It is observed that the accuracy of script identification is very high for printed text, and for handwritten text, the proposed approach can also achieve a satisfactory accuracy of about 95%.

From the experiments, we noticed that the main reason of mis-recognition and rejection are poor quality of envelope images. And the erroneous identifications of English script were found to be mostly due to the lower part connection of

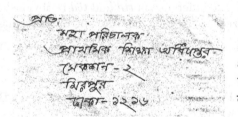

Fig. 5. Examples of destination address block used in the experiment

Table 2. Performance for identifying printed envelope images

	Recognized as		
Script	English	Bangla	Rejected
English	98.00	0.66	1.33
Bangla	0	100.00	0

Table 3. Performance for identifying handwritten envelope images

	Recognized as		
Script	English	Bangla	Rejected
English	94.67	1.33	4.00
Bangla	0	95.33	4.67

the characters or words. As the lower part of the components is connected and the upper part of the components is unconnected, the distance of the topmost pixels increases whereas the distance of the bottom pixels decrease. However, this seldom occurs.

4   Conclusions

In this paper, we present a simple but novel technique for script identification with applications to the destination address block of Bangladesh envelope images. The approach is based upon the analysis of connected component profiles, however, it does not place any emphasis on the information provided by individual characters themselves and does not require any character/line segmentation. During the extraction of features characterizing the visual appearance of the destination address block, special connected components that are either too small or too large are deleted prior to feature analysis. Thus, the approach is robust with respect to noise. It is clear that this approach is insensitive to character size, font, writing style and case variation in the destination address block. Also, the approach is immune from text height, inter-line, inter-word spacings and skew. Experimental results have showed that relatively simple technique can reach a high accuracy level for discriminating among English script and Bangla script.

Acknowledgements

This work is jointly supported by the National Natural Science Foundation of China under grant no. 60475006, and the Contract Project of Bangladesh Post No.PARI-2/2-16/2003/2004.

References

1. J. Hochberg, P. Kelly, T. Thomas, L. Kerns, Automatic Script Identification From Document Images Using Cluster-Based Templates, IEEE Transactions on Pattern Analysis and Machine Intelligence, pp. 176-181,1997
2. A. L. Spitz, Determination of the Script and Language Content of Document Images, IEEE Trans. Pattern Analysis and Machine Intelligence, pp. 235-245, 1997
3. S. W. Lee, J. S. Kim, Multi-lingual, multi-font and multi-size large-set character recognition using self-organizing neural network, Proceedings of International Conference on Document Analysis and Recognition, Vol.1, pp. 28-33, 1995
4. Y. H. Liu, C. C. Lin, F. Chang, Language Identification of Character Images Using Machine Learning Techniques, Proceedings of 8th Intl. Conf. Document Analysis and Recognition, pp. 630-634, 2005
5. M. P. John, Linguini: Language Identification for Multilingual Documents, Proceedings of 32nd Hawaii International Conference on System Sciences, vol.2, pp. 2035-2045, 1999

6. A. M. Elgammal, M. A. Ismail, Techniques for Language Identification for Hybrid Arabic-English Document Images, IEEE Proceedings of the Sixth International Conference on Document Analysis and Recognition, pp.1100-1104, 2001
7. C. L. Tan, T Y Leong and S He, Language identification in multilingual documents, Proceedings of International Symposium on Intelligent Multimedia and Distance Education (ISIMADE'99), pp.59-64, 1999
8. G. S. Peake, T.N. Tan, Script and Language Identification from Document Images, Proceedings of the Workshop on Document Image Analysis, pp.10-17, 1997
9. V. Singhal, N. Navin, D. Ghosh, Script-based classification of Hand-written Text Document in a Multilingual Environment, Research Issues in Data Engineering, pp.47-54, 2003
10. S. L. Wood, Xiaozhong Yao, K. Krishnamurthi, L. Dang, Language identification for printed text independent of segmentation, Proceedings of the International Conference on Image Processing, vol.3, pp.3428-3431, 1995
11. J. Ding, L. Lam, Ching Y. Suen, Classification of Oriental and European Scripts by Using Characteristic Features, Proceedings of fourth International Conference Document Analysis and Recognition, pp.1023-1027, 1997
12. U. Pal, B. B. Chaudhuri, Script Line Separation from Indian Multi-Script Documents, Proceedings of fifth Intl. Conf. Document Analysis and Recognition, pp.406-409, 1999
13. U. Pal, B. B. Chaudhuri, Automatic Identification of English, Chinese, Arabic, Devnagari and Bangla Script Line, Intl. Conf. Document Analysis and Recognition, pp.0790-0794, 2001
14. U. Pal, S. Sinha, B. B. Chaudhuri, Multi-Script Line identification from Indian Documents, Proceedings of the Seventh International Conference on Document Analysis and Recognition, vol.2, pp.880-884, 2003
15. S. Chaudhury, R. Sheth, Trainable Script Identification Strategies for Indian Languages, Proceedings of 5th International Conference on Document Analysis and Recognation, pp.657-660, 1999
16. S. Kanoun, A. Ennaji, Y. LeCourtier, A. M. Alimi, Script and Nature Differentiation for Arabic and Latin Text Images, Proceedings of the 8th International Workshop on Frontiers in Handwriting Recognition, pp. 309-313, 2002

Script Identification from Indian Documents

Gopal Datt Joshi, Saurabh Garg, and Jayanthi Sivaswamy

Centre for Visual Information Technology,
IIIT Hyderabad, India
gopal@research.iiit.ac.in, jsivaswamy@iiit.ac.in

Abstract. Automatic identification of a script in a given document image facilitates many important applications such as automatic archiving of multilingual documents, searching online archives of document images and for the selection of script specific OCR in a multilingual environment. In this paper, we present a scheme to identify different Indian scripts from a document image. This scheme employs hierarchical classification which uses features consistent with human perception. Such features are extracted from the responses of a multi-channel log-Gabor filter bank, designed at an optimal scale and multiple orientations. In the first stage, the classifier groups the scripts into five major classes using global features. At the next stage, a sub-classification is performed based on script-specific features. All features are extracted globally from a given text block which does not require any complex and reliable segmentation of the document image into lines and characters. Thus the proposed scheme is efficient and can be used for many practical applications which require processing large volumes of data. The scheme has been tested on 10 Indian scripts and found to be robust to skew generated in the process of scanning and relatively insensitive to change in font size. This proposed system achieves an overall classification accuracy of 97.11% on a large testing data set. These results serve to establish the utility of global approach to classification of scripts.

1   Introduction

The amount of multimedia data captured and stored is increasing rapidly with the advances in computer technology. Such data include multi-lingual documents. For example, museums store images of all old fragile documents having scientific or historical or artistic value and written in different scripts which are stored in typically large databases. Document analysis systems that help process these stored images is of interest for both efficient archival and to provide access to various researchers. Script identification is a key step that arises in document image analysis especially when the environment is multi-script and multi-lingual. An automatic script identification scheme is useful to (i) sort document images, (ii) help in selecting appropriate script-specific OCRs and (iii) search online archives of document image for those containing a particular script.

Existing script classification approaches can be classified into two broad categories, namely, local and global approaches. The local approaches analyse a list

H. Bunke and A.L. Spitz (Eds.): DAS 2006, LNCS 3872, pp. 255–267, 2006.
© Springer-Verlag Berlin Heidelberg 2006

of connected components (like line, word and character) in the document images to identify the script (or class of script) in the document image. However, these components are available only after line, word and character (LWC) segmentation of the underlying document image. In contrast, global approaches employ analysis of regions comprising at least two lines and hence do not require fine segmentation. Consequently, the script classification task is simplified and performed faster with the global rather than the local approach. This is attractive feature for a fast script-based retrieval systems.

In the category of local approaches, Spitz [1] proposed a method for discriminating Han based (Asian) and Latin based (includes both European and non-European) scripts. This method uses the vertical distribution of upward concavity in the characters of both the scripts. Furthermore, method uses optical density distribution in character and characteristic word's shape for further discrimination among Han and Latin scripts, respectively. Hochberg [2] proposed a script classification scheme which exploits frequently occurring character shapes (textual symbols) in each script. All textual symbols are rescaled to a fixed size (30 × 30) following which representative templates for each script are created by clustering textual symbols from a training data. Textual symbols from a new document are compared to the representative templates of all available scripts to find the best matched script. In India, a multi-lingual multi-script country, languages have scripts of their own, though some scripts like Devanagari, Bengali may be shared by two or more languages. Some classification methods have been proposed for Indian language scripts as well[6, 5]. These use Gabor features extracted from connected components [6] or statistical and topological features [5]. In [6], a connected component is processed only if its height is greater than three-fourth or less than the one-fourth of the average height of characters in document image. The training data is formed by representing each connected component with a feature vector (12 Gabor feature values) and a script label. This scheme has been shown to classify 4 major Indian language scripts (Devanagari, Roman (English), Telugu and Malayalam). A tree based classification scheme for twelve Indian language scripts in [5] uses horizontal profiles, statistical, topological and stroke based features. These features are chosen at a non-terminal node to get optimum tree classifier. These features, however, are very fragile in presence of noise.

In all the above approaches, the success of classification is dependent on the accuracy of character segmentation or connected component analysis. The problem of character segmentation presents a paradox similar to that presented by OCR, namely that character segmentation is best performed when the script of the document is known [4]. Some scripts, such as Chinese, have characters laid out in a regular array which greatly helps in character segmentation. Arabic scripts in contrast, are more difficult to segment due to the overlapping and conjoining of cursive characters during the typesetting process. On the other hand, Indian languages have a mixture of attributes in their scripts which help to segment at word level easily but not at the character level. As a result, one segmentation method does not work well for all the scripts. Due to this limitation, local approaches are slower, computationally expensive and have to be developed with attention to a specific class of scripts.

Global approaches, in contrast, are designed to identify the script by analysing blocks of text extracted from the document image. Wood [3] proposes methods using Hough transforms and analysis of density profile resulting from projection along text lines. However, it is not clear how the projection profile can be analysed automatically to determine the script. A texture based classification scheme in [4] uses the rotationally invariant features from Gabor filter responses. Since the texture images formed by different scripts patterns are found to be consistent, the text blocks are normalized to have equal height and width with uniform spaces between the lines and the words. Many steps are used to make the script texture consistent, as a result of which the scheme is computationally expensive. Chan et al [8, 7] take a biologically inspired approach to text script classification and derive a set of descriptors from oriented local energy and demonstrate their utility in script classification. Testing on a standard or large size data set however, has not been reported.

Global approaches have practical importance in script based retrieval systems because they are relatively fast and reduce the cost of document handling. However, the shortcomings of existing global methods are poorer classification accuracy compared to the local approaches and inability to handle large classes of scripts. We propose a Gabor energy based classification scheme which uses a global approach and demonstrate its ability to classify 10 Indian language scripts. In section (2), we describe the proposed scheme in detail. Results of the scheme tested over a large data set are presented in section (3).

2   The Proposed Scheme

The proposed scheme is inspired from the observation that humans are capable of distinguishing between unfamiliar scripts just based on a simple visual inspection. Examination of the type of processing carried out at the pre-attentive (image data driven processing) level of the human visual system reveals the presence of cells which extract oriented line features. These cells have been shown to be modelled by Gabor functions [10]. With this as a starting point, we consider script identification as a process of texture analysis and classification similar to [4]. However, our analysis treats the line textures as deterministic features.

In general, a texture is a complex visual pattern composed of sub patterns or Textons. The subpatterns give rise to the perceived lightness, uniformity, density, roughness, regularity, linearity, frequency, phase, directionality, coarseness, randomness, fineness, smoothness, granulation etc; as the texture as a whole. Although subpatterns can lack a good mathematical model, it is well established that a texture can be analysed completely if and only if its subpatterns are well defined. For example, consider the images in Fig.1(in first row) showing the cross section of a basket, a pile of seeds and a synthetic image formed by several 'T's. Each of these texture images has its own subpattern such as different size rectangles in the basket texture, different size

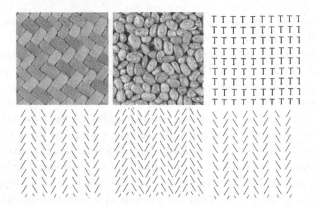

Fig. 1. Sample natural and synthetic textures

ovals in the seed texture and 'T' shape patterns in synthetic texture. In addition to the nature of the subpatterns, the manner in which they are organised can also affect the *look* of the textures. This is seen from the images in the second row of Fig.1. All the synthetic images in this row have the same subpattern. However, from a quick glance, it is seen that the one in the middle looks different from the other two, due to the compactness in the placing of subpatterns. But a more carefully look reveals that the first and third image are actually different. Despite the two images having the same compactness, their perceptions are different due to a rearrangement in the subpatterns. The perception after a quick glance is the result of a global(or coarse) analysis of the three images while the second perception after a more careful observation is a result of a local(or finer) analysis of the images. Script patterns can be considered to be textures formed by oriented linear subpatterns as the curved components are also decomposable into several oriented linear subpatterns. We argue that any script (not a language) can be characterised by the distribution of linear subpatterns across different orientations, the information about which can be obtained by a global analysis of the script image. For example, Chinese scripts are very compact and contain predominantly linear features. In contrast, many Indian scripts are composed of mostly curved features while Roman (English) scripts contain a good mixture of linear and curved features. These scripts can be easily classified using global analysis whereas, local analysis can be reserved for tasks such as distinguishing between (i) two different languages, such as English and French, written in one script or (ii) two similar scripts such as Urdu and Arabic. It is useful to study the extent of classification possible and the accuracy that is attainable using only global features. We use Indian language scripts as a test bed to perform this study.

2.1   Indian Language Scripts

India has 18 official languages which includes Assamese, Bangla, English, Gujarati, Hindi, Konkanai, Kannada, Kashmiri, Malayalam, Marathi, Nepali, Oriya,

Fig. 2. Indian language scripts

Punjabi, Rajasthani, Sanakrit, Tamil, Telugu and Urdu. All the Indian languages do not have the unique scripts. Some of them use the same script. For example, languages such as Hindi, Marathi, Rajasthani, Sanskrit and Nepali are written using the Devanagari script; Assamese and Bangla languages are written using the Bangla script; Urdu and Kashmiri are written using the same script and Telugu and Kannada use the same script. In all, ten different scripts are used to write these 18 languages. These scripts are named as Bangla, Devanagari, Roman(English), Gurumukhi, Gujarati, Malayalam, Oriya, Tamil, Kannada and Urdu. The image blocks of these images are shown in Fig. 2.

Some Indian scripts, like Devanagari, Bangla, Gurumukhi and Assamese have some common properties. Most of the characters have a horizontal lines at the upper part called *headline* and primarily the characters of words in these scripts are connected by a these headlines (shown in Fig. 4). Due to these properties they can be differentiable from the Roman (English), Telegu, Oriya, Urdu and other scripts. Furthermore, some characters have a part extended above the headline in these scripts. Presence of this portion is also useful for script classification. It would be advantageous to capture these distinguishing features using global level processing, if possible, as they can be used in script classification. We next propose a method to extract features through a global analysis of a given text document image and use them to classify the underlying script.

2.2 Preprocessing

Our scheme first segments the text area from the document image by removing the upper, lower, left and right blank regions. After this stage, we have an image which has textual and non-textual regions. This is then binarised after removing the graphics and pictures (at present the removal of non-textual information is performed manually, though page segmentation algorithms such as [12] could be readily been employed to perform this automatically). Text blocks of predefined size (100 × 200 pixels) are next extracted. It should be noted that the text block may contain lines with different font sizes and variable spaces between lines, words and characters. Numerals may appear in the text. We do not perform any processing to homogenise these parameters. It is necessary only to ensure that at least 40% of the text block region contains text.

2.3 Feature Extraction

Log-Gabor Filtering. A traditional choice for texture analysis is to use Gabor filters at multiple scales. Based on our observations of the HVS performance, we have selected oriented local energy features for script classification, with the local energy defined to be the sum of squared responses of a pair of conjugate symmetric filters. One of the major advantage with these features is that it is not necessary to perform analysis at multiple scales which reduces the computational cost of the scheme. Hence, features can be obtained from the image by using a single, empirically determined optimal scale. The optimal scale is one in which filters respond maximally to the given input. This response can be further enhanced by increasing filter bandwidth at the same optimal scale. The maximum bandwidth obtainable from a Gabor filter is only about 1 octave which is a disadvantage as it limits the feature size that can be captured. A log-Gabor filter on the other hand, allows large bandwidths from 1 to 3 octaves which makes the features more effective, reliable and informative [15]. In our scheme, features are extracted using a log-Gabor filter bank designed at a single optimal scale but at different orientations.

Due to the singularity in the log-Gabor function at the origin, one cannot construct an analytic expression for the shape of log-Gabor function in the spatial domain. Hence, one has to design the filter in the frequency domain. On a linear scale, the transfer function of a log-Gabor filter is expressed as

$$\Phi_{(r_o, \theta_o)} = \exp\left\{ -\frac{(\log\left(\frac{r}{r_o}\right))^2}{2(\log\left(\frac{\sigma_r}{r_o}\right))^2} \right\} \exp\left\{ -\frac{(\theta - \theta_o)^2}{2\sigma_\theta^2} \right\} \tag{1}$$

where r_o is the central radial frequency, θ_o is the orientation of the filter, σ_θ and σ_r represent the angular and radial bandwidths, respectively.

The oriented local energy $E_{\theta_o}^{r_o}(x, y)$ at every point in the image defines an energy map. This is obtained as:

$$E_{\theta_o}^{r_o}(x, y) = \sqrt{(O_{\theta_o}^{r_o, even}(x, y))^2 + (O_{\theta_o}^{r_o, odd}(x, y))^2} \tag{2}$$

where $O_{\theta_o}^{r_o, even}(x, y)$, $O_{\theta_o}^{r_o, odd}(x, y)$ are the responses of the even and odd symmetric log-Gabor filters, respectively. The real-valued function given in (1) can be multiplied by the frequency representation of the image and, transform the result back to the spatial domain, the responses of the oriented energy filter pair are extracted as simply the real component for the even-symmetric filter and the imaginary component for the odd-symmetric filter. Let $Z_{(r_o, \theta_o)}$ be the transformed filtered output. The responses of even and odd symmetric log-gabor filters are expressed as:

$$O_{\theta_o}^{r_o, even} = Re(Z_{(r_o, \theta_o)}); \qquad O_{\theta_o}^{r_o, odd} = Im(Z_{(r_o, \theta_o)}) \tag{3}$$

The total energy over the entire image can be computed as as follows:

$$\widetilde{E}(\theta_o) = \sum_{x=1}^{m}\sum_{y=1}^{n}(E_{\theta_o}^{r_o}(x,y)) \tag{4}$$

where $m \times n$ pixels is the size of the text block. This is nothing but the histogram function for the energy map. This energy histogram is a global feature which expresses the oriented energy distribution in a given text block. We will use it to classify the underlying script in the text block.

Features Used for Classification. The oriented energy distribution characterises a script texture as it indicates the dominance of individual subpatterns (lines of different orientation). For instance, the Hindi script is characterised by the dominance of horizontal lines, whereas this is not true for Malayalam (see Fig. 2). Hence, we extract such features that are relevant to the problem in hand.

Oriented local energy responses: The oriented local energy is computed as given in equation (4). A dominance of lines at a specific orientation θ is signalled by a peak in $\widetilde{E}(\theta)$. This is computed for text blocks (extracted as discussed in Sec. 2.2) using log-Gabor filters designed at 8 equi-spaced orientations ($0°, 22.5°, 45°$, $77.5°, 90°, 112.5°, 135.5°$ and $180°$) and at an empirically determined optimal scale. The energy values are normalised for a reliable classification and can be derived as

$$E(\theta_i) = \left\{ \frac{\widetilde{E}(\theta_i)}{max\left\{\widetilde{E}(\theta_j)|j=1,\cdots,8\right\}} \middle| i = 1,\cdots,8 \right\} \tag{5}$$

Here, index i denotes the corresponding orientation ($0°, 22.5°, \cdots, 180°$). We have dropped r_o for convenience, as we computed energy in only one scale. Several used features are extracted from this normalised energy. We describe these features and their method of computation next. The features are presented in the order of their saliency in the final classifier.

1. **Statistical features:** The energy profile for all the ten Indian scripts can be seen in Fig. 3. The shape of energy profiles differ from each other based on the underlying script. The energy in some scripts, like Devanagari which contain more linear patterns, is concentrated more in fewer channels with less spread into the neighbouring channels. On the other hand, energy is distributed more or less evenly amongst neighbouring channels for scripts which have curved shape,like Oriya. To capture such variation in the energy profile, we can use the relative strength in $E(\theta)$ for adjacent orientation channels. This is derived by finding the first difference in $E(\theta)$ as follows

$$\Delta E_i = \begin{cases} E(\theta_i) - E(\theta_{i+1}) & \text{if } i = 1,\cdots,7 \\ E(\theta_8) - E(\theta_1) & i = 8 \end{cases} \tag{6}$$

These eight feature values provide enough discriminant information to perform a first level classification of scripts. Furthermore, the choice features

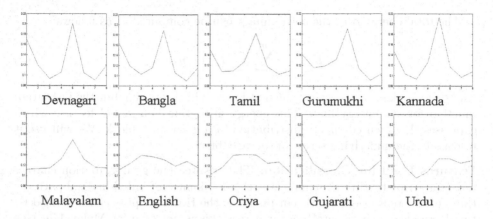

Fig. 3. Energy plots for each Indian language script

also makes our scheme invariant to font size since the $E(\theta_i)$ will proportionally change in each orientation with the change in the font size while the ΔE is less susceptible to change. In order to make the classification robust to skew, it can be observed that skew in the script image results in a shift in the values of ΔE to their neighbouring orientations according to the skew angle but it would not make any change in these average values. Hence, we extract two more features as follows:

$$\overline{\Delta E} = \frac{1}{8} \sum_{i=1}^{8} \Delta E_i; \qquad \overline{E} = \frac{1}{8} \sum_{i=1}^{8} E(\theta_i) \qquad (7)$$

2. **Local features:** The above features capture global differences among scripts. In order to capture the finer differences between similar scripts a set of local features are needed. For instance, Devanagari,Bangla, Tamil and Gurumukhi have similar scripts. A fine analysis is required for their further classification. It is observed that the similar scripts also have similar energy profiles (shape) which is captured in ΔE. However, these energy values $E(\theta_i)$ actually differ drastically in non-adjacent orientation channels. This can be a useful information and hence is captured in the following features. Here, the ratio of energies $E(\theta_i)$ is computed for two non-adjacent orientations θ_i.

3. **Horizontal profile:** Finally, there are some scripts which are distinguishable only by strokes used in the upper part of the words. For instance, Devanagari and Gurumukhi scripts both use a headline but differ in the strokes above the headline. This difference can be captured from the horizontal projection profiles of a whole text block (not of individual text lines as in [6, 5, 4]). The profiles of these scripts' text blocks are shown in Fig. 4. It can be seen that region above *headline* (signalled by three high peak in each profile) differ in both scripts. The average value of peaks in that region is higher for Gurumukhi script.

Fig. 4. Devanagari and Gurumukhi scripts with their corresponding horizontal profile

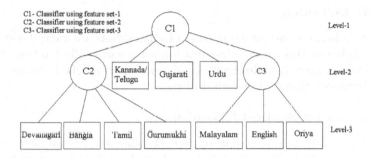

Fig. 5. Classification scheme for Indian language scripts

2.4   Script Classification Scheme

We now propose a hierarchical script classifier for the Indian scripts using the *globally* extracted features listed in the previous section. These features capture discriminating information among the scripts and get more script specific in the successive levels of the classifier. In the highest level, gross information is used for a broad categorisation, whereas in the lower levels categorisation is performed using finer analysis of the underlying script.

The proposed hierarchical classifier uses a two-level, tree based scheme (shown in Fig. 5) in which different sets of principle features are used at the non-leaf

Table 1. Features used in classifier at different levels

Feature set	Features used	Classifier
1	8 ΔE_i values $\overline{\Delta E}$ $\overline{E}$	C1
2	$ratio(E_3, E_7)$ $ratio(E_3, E_1)$ $ratio(E_7, E_1)$	C2
3	$ratio(E_5, E_1)$ $ratio(E_8, E_1)$ Horizontal profile	C3

nodes. The root node classifies scripts into five major classes using feature set-1. In the second level of the scheme, there are five major classes in which three are single member classes. Rest of the two classes have four and three members, respectively. On the respective non-leaf nodes, different feature sets are used, based on their effectiveness in discriminating between members of that sub-class. In the third level, all the leaf nodes belong to a single member class. Table. 1 gives a complete list of feature sets used by each classifier.

3   Experiments and Results

3.1   Data Collection

At present, in India, standard databases of Indian scripts are unavailable. Hence, data for training and testing the classification scheme was collected from different sources. These sources include the regional newspapers available online [14] and scanned document images in a digital library [9].

3.2   Selection for the Best Classifier

In order to identify the most appropriate classifier for the problem at hand, we experimented with different classifiers. Matlab pattern recognition toolbox [11] was used to conduct these experiments. Well known classifiers based on different approaches were chosen for the experiments [13]. These were: k-nearest neighbor, Parzen density, quadratic Bayes, feed-forward neural net and support vector machine based classifiers.

Table. 2 compares the performance of the classification scheme when different classifiers are used at every node of the proposed classifier. It can be seen that the nonparametric classifiers (K-NN and Parzen window) perform the best among all classifiers. The best classification rate obtained is 97.11% with 10 different Indian scripts after testing on a large script test data set (2978 text blocks). This

Table 2. Error rate for different classifiers

Classifier	Remarks	Error rate
Quadratic Bayes normal classifier	Gaussian with full variance	37.34%
Neural network based classifier	Three hidden layers	4.84%
K-Nearest Neighbor Classifier	k is optimized using leave-one-out error estimation	2.89%
Support vector classifier	Polynomial kernel	34.96%
	Redial basis kernel	36.57%
	Exponential kernel	6.98%
Parzen density based classifier	Kernel width is optimized using leave-one-out error estimation	3.16 %

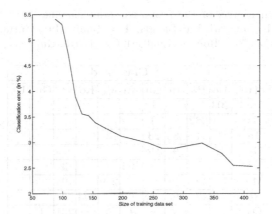

Fig. 6. Dependency of classification error on the training data set size

indicates the effectiveness of the proposed features. Since all these features were globally extracted, the good performance demonstrates the strength and effectiveness of global analysis based classification which is also computationally efficient. This is in contrast to the previous approaches to Indian script Identification which use local analysis (of connected components) and achieve the same level of performance as the proposed approach. Due to the lack of standard (benchmark) Indian scripts data, it is not possible to directly compare the performance of the proposed scheme with previously reported script classification schemes.

3.3 Optimal Size of Training Data Set and Feature Set

In order to determine the optimal size of the training data set required for the best performance of the classifier we tested with varying number of training data set (see Fig. 6). We found that with the size of 264 data set block, our classifier attains best performance with a classification error of 2.89%. This size of data set can easily be collected. A possible reason for the size being small is that the extracted features best represent the discriminant information among scripts. Ten features are used at the root node of the classifier (as explained in section (2.3)). These features are the local energy computed at the output of 8 oriented filters with an orientation resolution of 22.5 °. We examined the influence of the resolution on the classifier performance and our finding was that with a resolution reduction of 50% the performance degrades to 95% (from 97% with 8 oriented filters).

3.4 Performance Analysis

As mentioned earlier, based on testing the proposed scheme on 2978 individual text blocks, the classification accuracy obtained is 97.11%. It was found that a skew of upto 4 degree has no effect on the classifier performance. To improve this robustness further, more rotationally invariant features derived from the oriented energy reponses can be added [4]. A Confusion matrix for the proposed classification scheme is given in Table. 3. The major diagonal term indicates the number

Table 3. Confusion Matrix of the proposed script classifier for 10 different Indian scripts. (Here De=Devanagari, Ba=Bangla, Ta= Tamil, Gu= Gurumukhi, Ka= Kannada, Ma=Malayalam, Ro= Roman (English), Or= Oriya, Guj= Gujarati, Ur= Urdu.)

	Classified									
Actual	De	Ba	Ta	Gu	Ka	Ma	Ro	Or	Guj	Ur
De	203			1						
Ba		282		3						
Ta		1	283	23		3				
Gu	1		9	248						
Ka					596	3		3		
Ma						279		9		
Ro		7	6				264	2		
Or					1	5	8	231	1	
Guj									263	
Ur										243

of correctly classified testing samples while the off-diagonal term indicates the number of misclassified samples. From the matrix, it can be observed that the worst performance is only in the case of Tamil and Gurumukhi. It is interesting to see that both the scripts have similar energy profile (given in Fig. 3) even though they are perceptually different(can be viewed from Fig. 2). Thus it appears that the extracted global features are insufficient to discriminate such cases at present.

4   Conclusion and Future Work

Based on our observation human ability to classify unfamiliar scripts we have examined the possibility of using only global analysis of scripts for identifying them. We have presented a set of local energy based features for accomplishing classification in a hierarchical fashion extracted from oriented log-Gabor filters. These features have been used to develop a script classification scheme for Indian language scripts. The scheme is very simple and practical for a script based retrieval system. It requires a very simple preprocessing followed by a feature extraction process. Test results of the proposed classification scheme has revealed that good performance accuracy (97%) is obtainable using global analysis thereby illustrating its strength and utility. The scheme can be extended to multiple scales to handle scripts printed at a different resolution. The proposed scheme can be used for other language scripts as well with minimal modification.

References

1. A. Spitz., Determination of the script and language content of document images. IEEE Trans. Pattern Anal. Mach. Intell.**19(3)** (1997) 235–245.
2. J. Hochberg, L. Kerns, P. Kelly, and T. Thomas., Automatic script identification from images using cluster-based templates. IEEE Trans. Pattern Anal. Mach. Intell. **19(2)** (1997) 176–181.

3. S. L. Wood, X. Yao, K. Krishnamurthi, and L. Dang., Language identification for printed text independent of segmentation. Proceedings of International Conference on Image Processing **3** (1995) 428–431.
4. T. N. Tan., Rotation invariant texture features and their use in automatic script identification. IEEE Trans. Pattern Anal. Mach. Intell. **20(7)** (1998) 751–756.
5. U. Pal, S. Sinha, and B. B. Chaudhuri., Multi-script line identification from indian document.Seventh International Conference on Document Analysis and Recognition **2** (2003) 880–884.
6. S. Chaudhury and R. Sheth., Trainable script identification strategies for indian languages. Fifth International Conference on Document Analysis and Recognition (1999) 657–660.
7. W. Chan and J. Sivaswamy., Local energy analysis for text script classification. Proceedings of Image and Vision Computing New Zealand (1999) .
8. W. Chan and G. G. Coghill., Text analysis using local energy. Pattern Recognition **34(12)** (2001) 2523–2532.
9. Digital Library of India. http://dli.iiit.ac.in/.
10. M. C. Morrone, D. C. Burr, Feature detection in human vision: A phase-dependent energy model. Proceedings of the Royal Society, London Series B **235** (1988) 221–245.
11. PRTools: A Matlab Toolbox for Pattern Recognition. http://www.prtools.org/
12. A. K. Jain and Y. Zhong., Page segmentation using texture analysis. Pattern Recognition **29** (1996) 743–770.
13. R. Duda, P. Hart, and D. Stork., Pattern Classification. second edition, New York: John Wiley and Sons (2001).
14. http://www.samachar.com/.
15. X. Zhitao, G. Chengming, Y. Ming, and L. Qiang, Research on log Gabor wavelet and its application in image edge detection. Sixth International Conference on Signal Processing, (2002).

Finding the Best-Fit Bounding-Boxes

Bo Yuan[1], Leong Keong Kwoh[1], and Chew Lim Tan[2]

[1] Centre for Remote Imaging, Sensing and Processing,
National University of Singapore, Singapore 119260
{yuanbo, lkkwoh}@nus.edu.sg
[2] Department of Computer Science, School of Computing,
National University of Singapore, Singapore 117543
tancl@comp.nus.edu.sg

Abstract. The bounding-box of a geometric shape in 2D is the rectangle with the smallest area in a given orientation (usually upright) that complete contains the shape. The best-fit bounding-box is the smallest bounding-box among all the possible orientations for the same shape. In the context of document image analysis, the shapes can be characters (individual components) or paragraphs (component groups). This paper presents a search algorithm for the best-fit bounding-boxes of the textual component groups, whose shape are customarily rectangular in almost all languages. One of the applications of the best-fit bounding-boxes is the skew estimation from the text blocks in document images. This approach is capable of multi-skew estimation and location, as well as being able to process documents with sparse text regions. The University of Washington English Document Image Database (UW-I) is used to verify the skew estimation method directly and the proposed best-fit bounding-boxes algorithm indirectly.

1 Introduction

Text blocks in the printed documents are customarily rectangular. In document image analysis, this rectangular contour provides important information about the geometry of the text blocks, such as orientations and dimensions. Normally, text blocks are marked with upright (not best-fit) bounding-boxes as the results of page segmentation processes. However, it is desirable to find the best-fit bounding-boxes of the text blocks so that the intended shape of the blocks can be presented. Finding the best-fit bounding-box of a text block is a minimization problem that searches for the bounding-box with the smallest area among all the possible orientations.

This paper presents an algorithm of finding the best-fit bounding-box of a given text block (textual component group). It can be used to solve certain problems in the field of document image analysis (DIA). Therefore, given a textual document image, the components are first grouped by this grouping function, and then the best-fit bounding-boxes of the individual component groups are detected with the proposed best-fit bounding-box algorithm in this paper.

One of the applications of the proposed best-fit bounding-box algorithm is the skew estimation for textual document images. The skew of a textual document image

H. Bunke and A.L. Spitz (Eds.): DAS 2006, LNCS 3872, pp. 268–279, 2005.
© Springer-Verlag Berlin Heidelberg 2005

is the amount of misalignment of its text lines relative to the edges of the image. Skews are introduced during the digitization process due to the imprecision or difficulty in the placement of the original documents. Skew estimation is one of the important processing steps in document image understanding. There are some in-depth reviews [1]-[3] available for the large array of techniques that have been developed in the research literature [4]-[12]. These skew estimation methods have different detection accuracy, time and space efficiencies, abilities to detect the existence of multiple skews in the same image, and robustness in noisy environments and scan-introduced distortions. The skew estimation method proposed in this paper is capable of detecting and locating multi-skews in a document image, which many of the existing skew detectors are not capable. The full set of the 979 real document images in the University of Washington English Document Image Database (UW-I) is used to evaluate the performances of this skew estimation method. Since there are no publicly available databases with ground truth for directly evaluating of the proposed best-fit bounding-box algorithm, the use of UW-I on skew estimation is an indirect evaluation of the effectiveness of the proposed best-fit bounding-box algorithm.

2   Finding the Best-Fit Bounding-Boxes

The input to the proposed best-fit bounding-box algorithm is a segmented page where the components are properly grouped by *any* page segmentation algorithms. Then, the best-fit bounding-boxes of the individual component groups are detected.

2.1   Components Grouping

We use a simple and efficient component-grouping function that is based on the spatial distances and size similarities among the components [13]. Given two components of areas s_1 and s_2, if the value of the grouping function $f(s_1, s_2)$ in Eq. (1) is larger than the Euclidian distance between the two, they are considered *directly linked*. A component group is a collection of components among which there always exists at least one path of direct links for any two components. This component-grouping process takes the form of acyclic multi-trees called the *component-linking trees*. The coefficient k in Eq. (1) is given a constant value, but can be adjusted by the batch of samples in use.

$$f(s_1, s_2) = \sqrt{\frac{ks_1 s_2}{s_1 + s_2}} \tag{1}$$

The grouping function in Eq. (1) has several desirable properties: (a) it is a distance measure; (b) it is symmetric for any two components; (c) it is rotation invariant; (d) it is resolution invariant, if the aliasing effect is discounted; (e) when the size difference between two components becomes large, the function tends to be determined mainly by the smaller component. Thus, the grouping process biases strongly toward close components with similar sizes, resulting in higher tolerance to the interferences from graphical elements and other source of noises for the textual components.

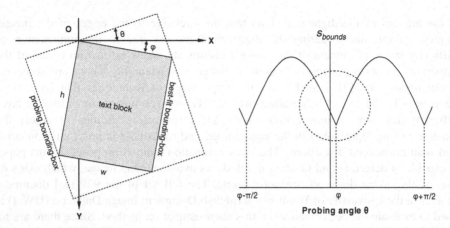

Fig. 1. The configuration for probing the best-fit bounding-box of an ideal text block (left) and the region-of-interest in the area-angle plot (right)

Note that the quality of the component grouping or page segmentation algorithms in use has direct impact on the quality of the best-fit bounding-boxes. The best-fit bounding-boxes are found for whatever blocks that are provided.

It should be pointed out that even though a special component grouping using Eq. (1) is used in this paper, any page segmentation algorithms can be used for the proposed searching algorithm for best-fit bounding-boxes.

2.2   Best-Fit Bounding-Boxes Probing

Given a group of components, its bet-fit bounding-box can be found by minimizing the area of its bounding-box. As shown in Fig. 1 (left), the area of a bounding-box S_{bounds} is:

$$S_{bounds} = \left| w \cos (\theta - \varphi) + h \sin (\theta - \varphi) \right| \left| w \sin (\theta - \varphi) + h \cos (\theta - \varphi) \right|$$

$$= w\,h + (w^2 + h^2) \left| \sin 2\,(\theta - \varphi) \right| / 2 \tag{2}$$

Fig. 1 (right) shows the curve of Eq. (2) which has a period of $\pi/2$. In the context of document image analysis, the circled region is the region-of-interest. Generally, the range of page skews is within than $\pm 3°$ for human scan operators. This practical limit can be used to set the bracket for the minimization process.

For an ideal text block, when the probing angle θ is close to the skew angle φ of the block, the curve of Eq. (2) approximates a triangle. In real documents, this region may not be a symmetric triangle due to the indent of the first line and/or the shorter last line, which can be observed in Fig. 2.

The minimization process uses the bi-section (successive bracketing) method [14]. Given an initial bracket, such as [-9°, 9°] in Fig. 2, its central value is used to recursively divide the left and the right halves. For any bracket, if the central point is smaller than that of the two end-points, this bracket must contain the minimum, and the other branches of bracketing are abandoned. This process continues until the

This article reports on research performed at the Air Force Institute of Technology's School of Systems and Logistics, Wright-Patterson Air Force Base, to study the feasibility of the 4 day workweek in ALCs.[1] But, before we review the research we should briefly review the 4 day workweek concept.

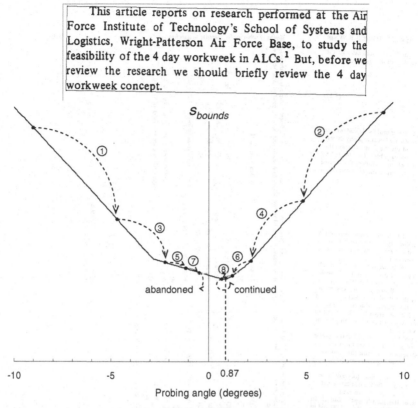

Fig. 2. Bi-section search for the probing bounding-box with the minimum area of a real text block. The curve (bottom) near the minimum is distorted from a symmetric triangular shape due to the indent of the first line and the shorter last line of the text block (top).

width of the current smallest bracket is smaller than, say 0.01°. The middle of this bracket is taken as the orientation of the best-fit bounding-box. The searching range is assumed unimodal.

Even though the proposed best-fit bounding-box algorithm is practically fast enough in its baseline form, there is still room for speedup. One speedup technique is to use the vertices of the convex hulls of the components in the group rather than using the constituting points of the components directly. This alone can achieve an order-of-magnitude reduction in computation time.

To evaluate the efficiency of the proposed best-fit bounding-box algorithm, the full set of the 979 real document images (2592×3300 pixels each) from UW-I are used. Experimental results show that the total time spent on the preprocessing stage (which includes the image input, the connected component analysis, the component filtering and the component grouping) is 1 912 820 milliseconds (or 1.95 seconds per sample), and the total time spent on the proposed best-fit bounding-box algorithm is 40 559 milliseconds (or 0.04 second per sample). Therefore, the computational cost is a non-issue even on legacy computers.

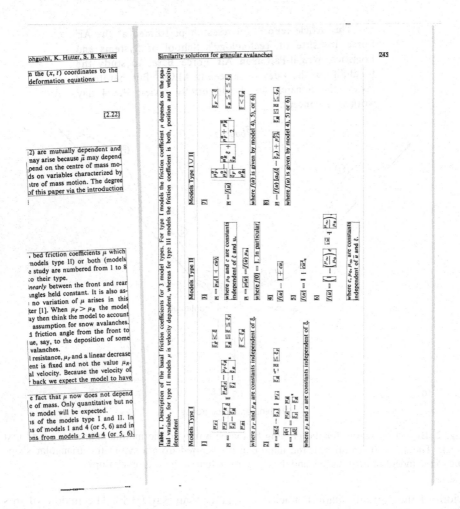

Fig. 3. The best-fit bounding-boxes of the image A002 in UW-I detected by the proposed algorithm in this paper. There are two parts on this image with different skew angles. The components in gray are the filtered-outs from the original image.

Fig. 3 shows the best-fit bounding-boxes of the sample image A002 in UW-I using the component-grouping algorithm in Ref. [13] and the proposed best-fit bounding-box algorithm in this paper. This image is scanned in the 2-up style, which contains an incomplete left page and a complete right page with sparse text. This sample image demonstrates the effectiveness of the proposed best-fit bounding-box algorithm in processing text blocks with distinct orientations, shapes and populations.

Fig. 4 shows the result on another sample image A03I in UW-I. This sample image shows how the component-grouping results affect the results of the best-fit bounding-box algorithm. On the incomplete right page, some of the noises in the dark spine area are wrongly grouped into text blocks by the used grouping function [13]. Therefore, some of the best-fit bounding-boxes are not the best for those text blocks. For this situation, the proposed best-fit bounding-box algorithm is not at fault.

It is also interesting to see how the proposed best-fit bounding-box algorithm works on the individual characters. Compared to the text blocks whose rectangular borders are well defined, the single characters are small and their contours are not intended to reflect the rectangular shape of their glyphs. This means that there may bemore than one local minimum in the areas of the probing bounding-boxes, and the maximum to minimum ratio is not large enough to guarantee meaningful best fit. The image in Fig. 5 shows that in the normal style, the majority of the best-fit bounding-boxes are coincide with the page orientations, even in italic style.

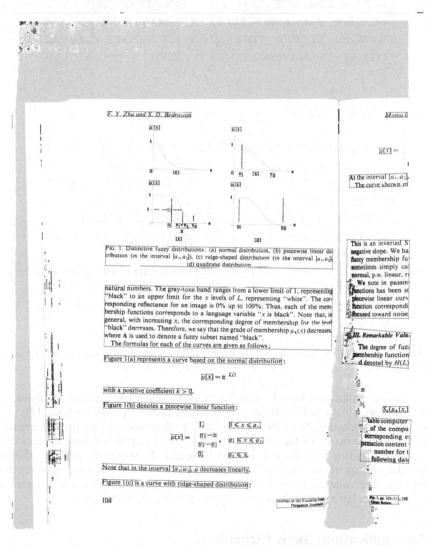

Fig. 4. The best-fit bounding-boxes of the image A03I in UW-I. This image shows that the grouping results have direct impact on the best-fit bounding-boxes. Some blocks in right half contain unfiltered noises that distorted the correct detection of the best-fit bounding-boxes.

Fig. 5. A clip of an article with the best-fit bounding-boxes of its individual characters in italic and normal styles

In many component-based algorithms for document image analysis, the components are abstracted to single points, called fiducial points by Spitz [7], which are sometimes chosen to be the bottom centers or other points along the borders of the upright bounding-boxes of the components [5]. The downside of these choices of the fiducial points is that they are not rotation-invariant. To solve this problem, the best-fit bounding-boxes of the components should be used so that the fiducial points at the borders become rotation-invariant. It is even more applicable for the Chinese and other East Asian languages whose font glyphs are visually rectangular.

3 An Application: Skew Estimation

One of the direct applications of the best-fit bounding-boxes is the multi-skew estimation of a page. A page usually contains several text blocks. The best-fit bounding-boxes of the text blocks may provide important hints for estimating the orientations and locations of the individual blocks as well as the skew of the page as a whole.

There are many established skew estimation methods in literature [4]-[12], but this best-fit bounding-boxes based skew estimation method has the advantage of detecting and locating multiple skews in the same image. Furthermore, this method can be used to detect non-text blocks such as the rectangular graphical inserts or the tables with rectangular borders.

3.1 Weighted Skew of Page

A document image may have more than one part, such as when two facing pages are scanned in the same image. In such a case, each part has text blocks whose best-fit bounding-boxes differ slightly. The images in Fig. 3 and Fig. 4 raise the question of how the skew of a page can be estimated from the individual blocks in the same image.

We take a convolution-based approach [12] to locate the peak values from the resultant orientation histogram of the text blocks. Given a document image, the detected orientation of the best-fit bounding-boxes are accumulated in an accumulator array that has N_{bin} = 9000 bins. This represents an angle range of [-90°, 90°], with an angle resolution of 0.02° per bin.

Given the best-fit bounding-box of a text block with skew angle θ and size n (number of components), the bin index of the text block in the accumulator array is $4500 + \theta / 0.02$, and the increment in this bin is the square-root of the size n. This choice on one hand gives larger weights to the larger text blocks in a hope that the shapes of these larger blocks are closer to rectangles and their true orientation can be more reliably approximated by their best-fit bounding-boxes. On the other hand, the influences of excessively long detected edges can be limited to some extent.

As shown in Fig. 6 (left), the skew histogram of the blocks in the sample image A03I in Fig. 4 has a cluster of discrete values around the largest peak. For the images that contain two pages, such as the sample image A002 in Fig. 3, there will be more than one cluster in the histogram. In order to distinguish the individual clusters that represent different multiple skews and at the same time weight the distribution within the clusters, the histogram is convolved by Eq. (4) with a finite, symmetric kernel generated from an un-normalized Gaussian distribution as in Eq. (3), where σ_{bin} is the variance and μ is a positive integer that represents the half-size of the kernel.

$$k[j] = \exp\left[-\frac{(j-\mu)^2}{\sigma_{bin}^2}\right] \tag{3}$$

$$h_{convol}[i] = \sum_{j=-\mu}^{\mu} h[(i-j-\mu+N_{bin}) \bmod N_{bin}] k[j+\mu] \tag{4}$$

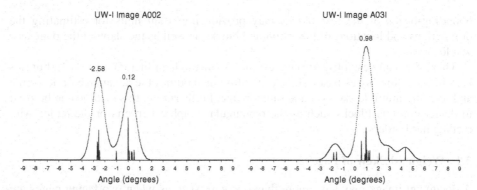

Fig. 6. The orientation histograms of the best-fit bounding-boxes of the images A002 (in Fig. 3) and A03I (in Fig. 4) in UW-I. An un-normalized Gaussian kernel ($\sigma = 0.5°$) as in Eq. (3) is used to smooth the histograms.

In Eqs. (3) and (4), the half-size μ of the Gaussian kernel is set to $3\sigma_{bin}$. The value of σ_{bin} is set to 25 bins, which corresponds to 0.5°. The value of μ is 75 bins. The size of the kernel is 151 bins. The modulo operator in Eq. (4) indicates the wrapping of values at the two endpoints of the histogram.

The convolved histogram in Eq. (4) is used to search for the prominent peaks that correspond to the dominant skew angles in an image. For the raw histogram in Fig. 6 (left), the convolved histogram is show in Fig. 6 (right). This convolved histogram also shows the desired property of the chosen kernel in Eq. (3), which combines the smoothing and area subtraction in one.

3.2 Suite Test Using UW-I

To evaluate the effectiveness and robustness of the proposed best-fit bounding-box based skew estimation method, the real document images from the University of Washington English Document Image Database I (UW-I) are used. In this database, total 979 images are scanned from real printed journals. Many images contain large area of disjoint, non-textual components that are the results of binarization on photographic objects, or the artifacts of the scanning process. Using a widely used document database makes it possible for different groups of researchers to evaluate and compare their algorithms with a common benchmark.

Fig. 7 (top) gives the regression analysis of this suite test, where the linear correlation coefficient is 88.4%. Fig. 7 (bottom) shows the accumulated percentage of samples versus the absolute detection error. It can be seen from these test results that this best-fit bounding-box based skew estimation method performs very well for real world document images.

The execution speed of the proposed skew estimation method is very fast based on the experimental results. It takes less than 2 seconds in average to process a sample image on the Java 5 platform in a 3GHz Pentium 4 computer.

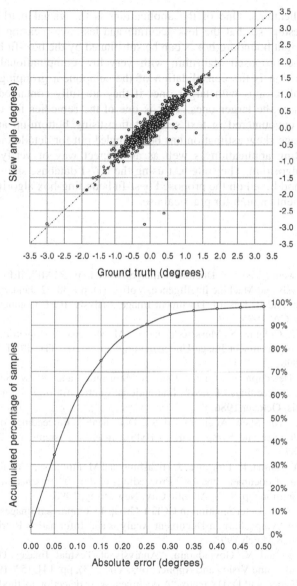

Fig. 7. The regression analysis (top) and the accumulated percentage of samples (bottom) of the 979 real document images in UW-I

4 Conclusions

This paper presents an algorithm for finding the best-fit bounding-boxes of text blocks in scanned document images. This algorithm is based on the principle that the best-bit bounding-box of text block has the minimum area compared to the bounding-boxes with other orientations. This algorithm is reliable, efficient and applicable in a number of applications. One of the applications is the visual marking of the text segmentation results so that the less accurate and less eye-pleasing but simple and widely used upright bounding-boxes can be substituted by the best-fit bounding-boxes produced by the proposed algorithm with very low computational cost. Another potential application is the consolidation of the component grouping results, which merges the small groups with larger ones if they are fully contained in the best-fit bounding-boxes of the larger ones. This is one of the remedies for under-grouping, which is often encountered in text segmentation using bottom-up approaches. The application in page skew estimation has been singled out for detailed investigation, as it is an interesting application as well as an indirect way of verifying the best-fit bounding-box algorithm. The suite test using the UW-I database shows that the skew estimation method based on the proposed best-fit bounding-box algorithm is accurate, robust and efficient enough for practical use.

References

1. G. Nagy, "Twenty Years of Document Image Analysis in PAMI", IEEE Transactions on Pattern Analysis and Machine Intelligence, Vol. 22 (1), pp. 38-62, January 2000.
2. L. O'Gorman, and R. Kasturi. Document Image Analysis. IEEE Computer Society Press, Los Alamitos CA, 1995.
3. R. Cattoni, T. Coianiz, S. Messelodi, and C. M. Modena, "Geometric Layout Analysis Techniques for Document Image Understanding: a Review", ITC-IRST Technical Report #9703-09, 1998
4. W. Postl, "Detection of Linear Oblique Structures and Skew Scan in Digitized Documents", Proceedings of the 8th International Conference on Pattern Recognition, pp. 687-689, Paris, October 1986.
5. H. S. Baird, "The Skew Angle of Printed Documents", Proceedings of the SPSE 40th Annual Conference and Symposium on Hybrid Imaging Systems, pp. 21-24, Rochester, NY, May 1987.
6. Y. Nakano, Y. Shima, H. Fujisawa, J. Higashino and M. Fujinawa, "An algorithm for skew normalization of document images," Proceedings of the 10th International Conference on Pattern Recognition, pp. 8-13, Atlantic City, New Jersey, 1990.
7. A. L. Spitz, "Skew Determination in CCITT Group 4 Compressed Images", Proceedings of the 1st Annual Symposium on Document Analysis and Information Retrieval, Las Vegas, pp. 11-25, 16-18 March 1992.
8. S. N. Srihari, and V. Govindaraju, "Analysis of Textual Images Using the Hough Transform", Machine Vision and Applications, Vol. 2 (3), pp. 141-153, 1989.
9. S. Hinds, J. Fisher, and D. D'Amato, "A document skew detection method using run-length encoding and the Hough transform", Proceedings of the 10th International Conference on Pattern Recognition, pp. 464-468, Atlantic City NJ, 17-21 June 1990.
10. S. Chen, and R. M. Haralick, "An Automatic Algorithm for Text Skew Estimation in Document Images Using Recursive Morphological Transforms", Proceedings of IEEE International Conference on Image Processing, pp. 139-143, Austin TX, 13-16 November 1994.
11. H. K. Aghajan, and T. Kailath, "SLIDE: Subspace-Based Line Detection", IEEE Transactions on Pattern Analysis and Machine Intelligence, Vol. 16 (11), pp. 1057-1073, November 1994.

12. B. Yuan, and C. L. Tan, "Fiducial line based skew estimation", Pattern Recognition, Vol. 38 (12), pp. 2333 – 2350, December 2005.
13. B. Yuan, and C. L. Tan, "A Multi-Level Component Grouping Algorithm and Its Applications", Proceedings of the 8th International Conference on Document Analysis and Recognition, pp. 1178-1181, Seoul Korea, 29 August - 1 September 2005.
14. W. H. Press, B. P. Flannery, S. A. Teukolsky, and W. T. Vetterling, "Numerical Recipes in C : The Art of Scientific Computing", Second Edition, Cambridge University Press, 1992.

Towards Versatile Document Analysis Systems

Henry S. Baird and Matthew R. Casey

Computer Science & Engineering Dept, Lehigh University,
19 Memorial Dr West, Bethlehem, PA 18017, USA
baird@cse.lehigh.edu, mrc8@lehigh.edu

Abstract. The research goal of highly versatile document analysis systems, capable of performing useful functions on the great majority of document images, seems to be receding, even in the face of decades of research. One family of nearly universally applicable capabilities includes document image content extraction tools able to locate regions containing handwriting, machine-print text, graphics, line-art, logos, photographs, noise, etc. To solve this problem in its full generality requires coping with a vast diversity of document and image types. The severity of the methodological problems is suggested by the lack of agreement within the R&D community on even what is meant by a representative set of samples in this context. Even when this is agreed, it is often not clear how sufficiently large sets for training and testing can be collected and ground truthed. Perhaps this can be alleviated by discovering a principled way to amplify sample sets using synthetic variations. We will then need classification methodologies capable of learning automatically from these huge sample sets in spite of their poorly parameterized—or unparameterizable—distributions. Perhaps fast expected-time approximate k-nearest neighbors classifiers are a good solution, even if they tend to require enormous data structures: hashed k-d trees seem promising. We discuss these issues and report recent progress towards their resolution.

Keywords: versatile document analysis systems, DAS methodology, document image content extraction, classification, k Nearest Neighbors, k-d trees, CART, spatial data structures, computational geometry, hashing.

1 Introduction

Computer vision systems, and document analysis systems in particular, are notoriously either overspecialized and fragile, or ruinously expensive (*e.g.* national postal code readers)[1]. The research goal of highly versatile document analysis systems, capable of performing useful functions across the great majority of document images, seems to have receded, even in the face of decades of research [2][3]. Certainly users—*e.g.* in the digital libraries, web search, and intelligence communities—avidly desire such a technology. But this goal too ambitious: a mirage, so ill-defined or open-ended that it is illusory? Or, can some fresh research agenda accelerate our approach to it? This paper takes seriously the potential of such an agenda.

Thus we aim at a *versatility first* research strategy: that is, we attempt to invent document image analysis capabilities that will work reliably across the broadest possible range of cases. This diversity embraces documents and images that: are carefully prepared as well as hastily sketched; are written in many languages, typefaces, typesizes,

H. Bunke and A.L. Spitz (Eds.): DAS 2006, LNCS 3872, pp. 280–290, 2006.

and writing styles; obey a myriad of geometric and logical layout conventions; possess a wide range of printing and imaging qualities; are expressed as full color, grey-level, and black-and-white; may be acquired by geometrically accurate flat-bed scanners, or snapped with hand-held cameras under accidental lighting conditions; are of any size or resolution (digitizing spatial sampling rate); and are presented in many image file formats (TIFF, JPEG, PNG, etc), both lossless and lossy.

Now not every useful functionality is called for on all or even most documents: *e.g.* word-spotting in Amharic is surely a niche application which will be perfected (if it ever is) by special-purpose engineering. So for the purposes of this paper we will restrict our attention to a set of basic capabilities that are, arguably, most broadly useful in that they have been applied very early in the document-processing pipeline. These are the *document image content extraction* tools, able to locate and characterize regions containing handwriting, machine-print text, graphics, line-art, logos, photographs, noise, and other "content types." By "locate" we mean describe the regions in the image where each content type dominates. By "characterize' we mean report estimates of a few basic properties of the regions: *e.g.* for machine-print, report skew angle, number of lines of text, number of words, and perhaps type size and type family. Although high accuracy is always appreciated, for broadly applicable tools such as these are, a lower threshold of competency may be sufficient: in pariticulat, trlie confidence of a decision or ot the value of a property may be as important as accuracy to downstream processing.

Even for this narrowly characterized set of tasks, the severity of our methodological problems is suggested by the lack of agreement within the R&D community on what is meant by a representative set of samples. The gold standard for this in our field is a manually collected set of samples with a published rationale for selection and a detailed protocol for assigning ground truth (*e.g.* UWash CD-ROM DBs[4]). Certainly these methodologies are essential: they have assured long and useful lives for their resulting data bases, and have strongly benefited DAS research. But their costs are dauntingly high—approximately $2M to compile the 3-CDROM UWash DBs—and they are as well known for their omissions as their coverage—*e.g.* the UWash DBs contain only English and Japanese documents. If a document image is seen, later, what does it mean to claim that the training set was representative of it? If we can't make this claim, how great an indictment is it if a classifier, trained on that set, fails on this new sample? What do we say if the user claims that he or she expected our tool to succeed on this sample, because "it was like the training data"? How can sample sets with far broader coverage be affordably collected and ground-truthed?

In Section 8 we propose that this obstacle can be alleviated, if not overcome, by developing a principled way to amplify sample sets using synthetic variations. A particular form of this, which we call *model-based interpolation* may combine the authenticity of "real" samples with the broad and systematic coverage of synthetic samples.

The data sets we need to provide coverage will certainly be vast: far larger than our current databases. To make good use of them, we will need classification methodologies capable of learning automatically from such huge sample sets in spite of their poorly parameterized—or unparameterizable—distributions. In Section 4 we propose that it may be possible, due to recent advances in memory, disk storage, and data structures technology, to design fast expected-time approximate k-nearest neighbors classifiers.

The key insight here is that fast *expected time* performance is a good match for document image analysis problems, since among pages images within a document, and even more strongly among pixels within a single image, we can expect to see the effects of style consistency[5][6]—what Prateek Sarkar called *isogeny*—so that we can hope that the enormous data structures that high-dimensional search trees (*e.g.* non-adaptive k-d trees) tend to require may be manageable using modern paging techniques.

2   A Research Agenda for Versatile Document Analysis

We are investigating strongly versatile algorithms for the **document image content extraction** problem:

Given an image of a document,
find regions containing handwriting, machine-print text, graphics, line-art, logos, photographs, noise, etc.

To solve this problem in full generality—given the great diversity of document and image types—we have decided to emphasize, in our research strategy:

1. *versatility first*: concentrate first on designing methods that work across the broadest possible variety of cases (document and image types);
2. *voracious classifiers*: trainable on billions of samples in reasonable time;
3. *extremely high speed classification*: ideally, nearly at I/O rates (as fast as the images can be read);
4. *amplification*: use real ground-truthed training samples as 'seeds' for massive synthetic generation of pseudorandomly perturbed samples for use in supplementary training;
5. *confidence before accuracy*: good estimates of the confidence of decisions is important; high accuracies are desirable but even modest accuracy can be useful;
6. *near-infinite space*: *i.e.* design for best performance in a near-term future when main memory will be orders of magnitude larger and faster than today; and
7. *data-driven design*: we won't invest much effort in making what are, ultimately, arbitrary engineering decisions such as choice of preprocessors and features; instead, we'll try to allow the training data to determine these automatically as far as we can;

3   Document Image Content

Types of document images we wish to process include color, grey-level, and black-and-white; also, any size or resolution (digitizing spatial sampling rate); and in any of a wide range of file formats (TIFF, JPEG, PNG, etc). We choose to convert all image file formats in a three-channel color PNG file in the HSL (Hue, Saturation, and Luminance) color space; this has the advantage that black-and-white and greylevel images convert into HSL images with fixed values for Hue and Saturation permitting easier comparison with color images using simple metrics.

We are gathering sample page images containing the following types of content: handwriting, machine print, line art, photos, math notation, maps, engineering drawings, chemical drawings, "junk" (e.g. margin and gutter noise),and blank. Sources for these include: the Univ. Washington CD-ROM Data Bases, the UNLV Data Sets, various Library of Congress digital library sites such as the American Memory Project, the ISI Kolkata mathematics notation collection, and Lehigh University digital library sites[1] We can exploit any pre-existing ground-truth metadata with rectangular zones; for other images we have developed an interactive ground-truthing tool. We have begun a systematic statistical sample and analysis of the presence of these content types within these data bases.

4   Statistical Framework for Content Classification

To avoid overspecialization, we choose to classify individual pixels, not extended regions of arbitrarily chosen size and shape. Thus each training and test sample is a pixel in a document image, and each pixel owns d features which are scalar properties extracted by image processing in the vicinity of that pixel.

Our statistical sample space (the "universe") $U = \mathbf{R}^d$, the multidimensional reals. If all we are told about a classification problem is a training set—if we lack, for example, analytic models for the processes that generated the samples—then no reliable and rapidly computable way is known, grounded in pattern recognition theory, for automatically choosing a small number of sufficiently discriminative features that will support highly accurate classification. Thus in practice we will be forced to explore, in a trial and error way, a large space of promising features suggested by insight, experiment, and the literature. Given a set of features, methods are known to select a good subset of them: but it is far easier to propose new features than to select the best ones. For these reasons we expect that the number of features will be large, say $d \approx 100$. A member of the sample space is called $\mathbf{x}, \mathbf{y}, \mathbf{z}$, etc. All samples belong to one of m classes $\mathbf{C} = \{c_j\}_{j=1,\ldots,m}$. The number of content type classes m will, we expect, be ≈ 10. Within the $\mathbf{R}^d$ space we choose to use the Infinity norm (or $\mathbf{L}_\infty$ norm) $\|\mathbf{x} - \mathbf{y}\|_\infty \equiv max_{i=1}^d\{|x_i - y_i|\}$ to capture the notion of feature similarity. Many pattern recognition researchers believe that the choice of metric has less influence on the accuracy of a classifier than the size and representativeness of the training data[8]. Training data consists of a set of samples $\mathbf{T} \subset \mathbf{R}^d$ labeled with their classes. We expect the number of training samples $n \equiv |\mathbf{T}| \approx 1$ billion. We first discuss the problem of classifying a single test sample $\mathbf{x}$ but eventually we expect to batch-classify large sets $\mathbf{X}$ of test samples. Note that in our context $c \ll d \ll n$: this will seriously constrain our engineering options, as we will see.

5   A Nearly Ideal Classifier in This Context

Classification problem

Given $\mathbf{T}$, and a previously unseen sample $\mathbf{x}$,
find   the most probable class c for $\mathbf{x}$.

---

[1] Details are reported in [7].

Adopting a Bayesian approach, we choose $c_{max} = argmax_{c_j \in \mathbf{C}}\{P(c_j|\mathbf{x}, \mathbf{T})\}$ where $P(c_j|\mathbf{x}, \mathbf{T})$ denotes the posterior probability of class c_j given the new observation $\mathbf{x}$ and the prior knowledge expressed in training data TThe *k-nearest neighbors*(kNN) algorithm is of course:

K Nearest Neighbors algorithm

INPUT: $\mathbf{T}, k \in \mathbf{N}^+$, and $\mathbf{x}$
OUTPUT: $c \in \mathbf{C}$
Step 1. within $\mathbf{T}$, find k nearest neighbors of $\mathbf{x}$
    that is, find a set $Y \subset \mathbf{T}, |Y| = k$, s.t.
$$\forall \mathbf{y} \in Y \; \forall \mathbf{z} \in T - Y \; \|\mathbf{x} - \mathbf{y}\| \leq \|\mathbf{x} - \mathbf{z}\|$$
Step 2. within Y, use the ground-truth classes assigned to samples in $\mathbf{T}$ find
the most frequently occurring class, breaking ties at random.

For any particular set of features, assuming that the training data is representative, the kNN algorithm enjoys a valuable theoretical property: as the size of the training set increases, its error rate approaches to no worse than twice the Bayes error[9], which is the minimum achievable by any classifier given the same information. This remarkable performance is due, fundamentally, to its not committing to a specific parametric model for the per-class distributions. This algorithm also generalizes directly to more than two classes (unlike several competing methods such as neural nets and classification trees). Finally, it has has often been competitive in accuracy (if rarely in speed) with more recently developed classifiers including support-vector machines. For these reasons, we consider kNN would be a nearly ideal classifier for this problem, were it were not for the high cost in both time and space of naive implementations and the difficulty of crafting algorithms that approximate its performance in high dimensions.

We have implemented this (for $k = 5$) and, in early small scale experiments, have seen it yield pixel classification rates on the content extraction problem greater than 98% correct. Interestingly, even when per-pixel classification error is as high as 23%, the principal regions and their dominant content types are evident to the eye and (we expect) can be extracted robustly by simple image post-processing[7].

6   Approximations to kNN

Radius Search problem

Given $\mathbf{T}, r \in \mathbf{R}$, and $\mathbf{x}$,
find   all points of $\mathbf{T}$ within radius r of $\mathbf{x}$: that is, the set $Y_r \equiv \{ \mathbf{y} \in \mathbf{T} \; s.t. \|\mathbf{x} - \mathbf{y}\| \leq r \}$

If $r \ll s$, we can expect that finding Y_r will be easier than finding Y_s. (Of course, generally $|Y_r| < |Y_s|$ also, in which case reporting the result of the search will take *longer*. But we choose to neglect runtimes that depend on the size of the output, for reasons that will become clear later.) If $|Y_r| = k$, then radius search is equivalent to kNN. If $|Y_r| \approx k$, then we will say that radius search *approximates* kNN. (Of course, this notion of approximation does not address the key issue, which is how much less accurate radius search classification is than kNN classification.)

It might be cheaper to compute approximations to radius search.

Nested Radius Search problem

Given T, $\{r_i\}_{i=1,\ldots,s} \in \mathbf{R}$, $r_1 < r_2 < \ldots < r_s$, and $\mathbf{x}$,
find sets $\subset \mathbf{T}$ within radii r_i of $\mathbf{x}$: that is,
$$Y_{r_i} \equiv \{\, \mathbf{y} \in \mathbf{T} \ s.t. \ \|\mathbf{x} - \mathbf{y}\| \le r_i \,\}$$

Note that $Y_{r_1} \subseteq Y_{r_2} \subseteq \ldots \subseteq Y_{r_s}$. If $r_k < r_l$, then it may be possible, through judicious choice of data structures and algorithms, to compute Y_{r_l} faster than Y_{r_k}.

Approximate Radius Search problem

Given $\mathbf{T}$, $r \in \mathbf{R}$, $\epsilon \in \mathbf{R}$ and $\mathbf{x}$,
find sets Y^L and $Y^U \subset \mathbf{T}$ such that
$$Y_{r-\epsilon} \subseteq Y^L \subseteq Y_r \subseteq Y^U \subseteq Y_{r+\epsilon}$$

That is, Y^L and Y^U approximate Y_r within ϵ. As $\epsilon \to 0$, $Y^L \to Y_r$ (from below) and $Y^U \to Y_r$ (from above), and so Approximate Radius Search converges to Radius Search. When ϵ is large, it should be easier to solve Approximate Radius Search than to solve Radius Search.

How can Approximate Radius Search be used for classification? Well, if it happens that $|Y^L| = |Y^U|$, then $Y^L = Y^U = Y_r$ and, exactly as in kNN, we can choose the most frequently occurring class in that set. Lets call the frequency of occurrence of each class c_j in Y^L "f_j^L" and similarly, in Y^U, "f_j^U". Let the most frequently occurring classes in these sets be $maxc^L$ and $maxc^U$; if these happen to be the same class, we will of course choose that class. But if they differ, then we have several policy choices:

- we can compute average frequencies for each c_j, e.g. $f_j^{aver} \equiv (f_j^L + f_j^U)/2$, and then choose the class with the highest average frequency;
- we can use the value k from kNN to assist in the decision, for example, if $|Y^L|$ is closer to k than Y^U, we choose the most frequently occurring class in Y^L (and vice versa).

Thus Approximate Radius Search can be used as a basis for classification and offers a range of engineering tradeoffs between accuracy and speed.

7 Approximate Radius Search Under the Infinity Norm

With the Infinity Norm as our metric, then Radius Search becomes a multidimensional range search (or "region query") in which the search regions are hypercubes of radius r centered on the query sample $\mathbf{x}$. Multidimensional range searching is an intensively explored topic[10][11] by researchers in the computational geometry, machine learning, pattern recognition, and graphics research communities. However, special requirements of pattern classification may lead us in fresh directions. For example, in the literature, range searching is commonly discussed as a generalization of *point searching*, which in turn is characterized as a generalization of dictionaries to multidimensional data. Dictionaries are classically designed to support three basic operations: *insert* a single data item, *find* an item (returning its associated metadata, or returning 'not found'), and *delete* an item. Data structures and algorithms for dictionaries are thus *dynamic*: designed to process an arbitrary sequence of these three operations efficiently.

By contrast, in classification, insertions are performed all at once in an offline batch operation (the "training stage") in which all the data (training samples) are simultaneously available. Deletion never occurs (although we may choose to prune ("edit) them or summarize sets of data points statistically rather than storing all of them explicitly). Thus the data structure is *static*. Finding is the only operation which is online and must run fast; and it may also be possible to batch a large set of find operations and so exploit the similarity of sequences of queries for points that are isogenous. Thus much of the literature on dynamic multidimensional search is not directly relevant to classification, and may benefit from a fresh perspective.

Let us review techniques for multidimensional search that may assist us in choosing, adapting, or crafting new data structures and algorithms suitable for classification.

7.1 Adaptive *k*-d Trees

One multidimensional search technique with broad applicability is Bentley's *k*-d trees [12]. The variant of k-d trees most relevant to classification seems to be the *adaptive k*-d tree[13]. Briefly, these partition the set of points recursively in stages: at each stage one of the partitions is divided into two subpartitions; we will assume that it is possible to choose cuts that achieve *balance*, that is, to divide into subpartitions containing roughly the same number of points. Division is by cutting along one of the dimensions $i \in \{1, \ldots, d\}$, *i.e.* by choosing a threshold value and assigning each of the partition's points $\mathbf{x}$ to subpartition (a) or (b) according to whether its $\mathbf{x}_i$ component value is (a) less than, or (b) greater than or equal to the threshold. (In some implementations, the threshold corresponds to a component value for one of the points, which is then stored in the interior node of the search tree; but will we assume here that all points are stored in leaf nodes). Generally, at each stage a different dimension is cut: one simple strategy is to cycle (and if necessary recyle) through the dimensions in a fixed order; another strategy is to cut the currently most populous partition. Cutting proceeds until all partitions contain few enough points to invite a final fast sequential search. The final partitions are generally hyperrectangles (not always hypercubes) with orthogonal sides (parallel to the coordinate axes of $\mathbf{R}^d$).

Balancing each cut ensures that find operations execute in $\Theta(\log n)$ time in the worst case. Consistent with a guarantee of such logarithmic-time finds, Bentley's k-d tree construction achieves an asymptotically minimum number of cuts and thus a minimum number of partitions (close to n/p, where p is the number of points in the final partitions; note that, in our context where $p = 10$ this is still huge, $\approx 10^8$). The threshold value chosen for each cut depends on the distribution of points within the partition to be cut, so the thresholds are not *independently predictable*: that is, none (after the first) can be computed without knowledge of the cut thresholds in some earlier stages. Further, given a previously unseen $\mathbf{x}$ it is not possible to compute the d upper and lower bounds of its k-d hyperrectangle (within which it lies) without traversing the k-d tree. Thus locating $\mathbf{x}$'s k-d hyperrectangle *requires* $\Theta(\log n)$ time.

The pruning power of k-d trees speeds up range searches. Given a query point $\mathbf{x}$ and a radius r, defining a search hypercube, it is straightforward to generalize the find algorithm to explore all k-d tree nodes whose subtrees overlap the search hypercube. The asymptotic runtime of such variants has been studied: [14] reports that the worst-case number of tree nodes explored is $\Theta(d\, n^{1-1/d})$. In our context, this may (or may not) promise much improvement over brute-force search, since (neglecting the multiplicative constant) $d\, n^{1-1/d} \approx 100(10^9)^{0.99} = 100(10^{8.91}) = 10^{10.91} \gg 10^8 \approx n$. Of course this may be a pessimistic bound for several reasons. Whether or not k-d tree range searches are efficient for classification may ultimately be decidable only by experiment.

7.2 Multidimensional Tries

An alternative data structure that assists multidimensional search is a recursive partitioning of the space using *fixed cuts*. Suppose that for each dimension $i \in \{1, \ldots, d\}$, lower and upper bounds L_i and U_i on the values of the components $\mathbf{x}_i$ are known. Then one may choose to place cuts at midpoints of these ranges, *i.e.* at $(L_i + U_i)/2$, and later, when cutting those partitions, recursively cut at the midpoint of the (now smaller) ranges. A search trie can be constructed in a manner exactly analogous to k-d trees with the exception that the distribution of the data is ignored in choosing cut thresholds. It will no longer be possible to guarantee balanced cuts and thus most of the time and space optimality properties of k-d trees are lost. However, there are gains: for example, the values of the cut thresholds can be predicted (they all are of course predetermined by $\{L_i, U_i\}_{i=1,\ldots,d}$). As a consequence, if the total number of cuts r is known, the hyperrectangle within which any query (test) sample $\mathbf{x}$ lies can be computed in $\Omega(r)$ time, and in some realistic models of computation in $\Omega(1)$ time—in either case, extremely fast, faster than computing a single point-to-point distance using the metric. We will call these recursive midpoint-cut trie hyperrectangles *partitions* (they are often called 'bins' or 'cells' in the kNN literature).

Bit-Interleaving. Partitions resulting from tries as above can be addressed using *bit-interleaving*. Let $< d_k, m_k >_{k=1,\ldots,r}$ be a sequence of cuts, where, at cut k, d_k is the dimension chosen to be cut and m_k is the midpoint of the partition chosen for that cut. Among the partitions of feature space that result, a test sample x will fall in a partition that can be described by a sequence of decisions $b_k = (x_{d_k} > m_k)$ taking on the value False ('0') or True ('1') as x lies below or above the cut respectively. Equivalently, any bit-sequence $< b_k >_k = 1, \ldots, r$ of length r determines the boundaries of some partition, and so can be thought of as an address for it. To summarize: given a test sample x and a sequence of r cuts, we can compute in $\Theta(r)$ time the bit-interleaved address of the partition within which x lies.

Now in this context—as in most if not all naturally occurring image pattern recognition problems—we expect that training and test data have a skewed (nonuniform) distribution in feature space, and specifically when r is large that only a small fraction of the resulting small partitions will be occupied by *any* training data. If this assumption holds true in practice, only a few distinct bit-interleaved addresses will occur in even a very large training set, and so it may be possible to use a dictionary data structure to manage them. The feasibility of this approach depends crucially of course on how many distinct values of bit-interleaved addresses occur in practice.

Experiments on our document images where $d = 15$, using $n = 10,000,000$ training samples, varying the number of bits $r < 75$ suggest that the number of occupied partitions, as a function of the length of their bit-interleaved address, is asymptotically roughly cubic. For $r = 50$ the absolute number observed was about 2,100,000, which is of course easily manageable by single-stage hashing where the hash table is contained within main memory.

Also, we have systematically tested the accuracy and speedups of hashed kD trees, where $d = 15$ (again), $n = 1,565,695$ training samples and $254,181$ test samples. When a brute-force 5-NN program is run, it achieves a per-pixel correct classification rate of 78% (and the results look very good to the eye); of course, it runs slowly, requiring about 400 billion distance calculations. By using bit-interleaved address of length 40 bits, hashing speeds up the calculation by a factor of 99.7 for a slight drop in per-pixel accuracy, to 68%. The range of tradeoffs between speed-up and accuracy is shown in Figure 1.

Accuracy remains high (above 60%) until somewhere between 40 bits (5 bytes) and 48 bits; thereafter it falls rapidly. The speed-up factor improves exponentially across the range.

In the above data, errors are of two types. In the first type, we hash into a cell which contains some training samples, but 5NN does not do as well as expected: this means of course that not all of the five nearest neighbors lie within this hash cell. Errors of the second type occur when the cell contains *no data*: that is, no training points hashed into that cell. Errors of the second type are in the minority as long as the bit-interleaved address is less than about 50 bits; but above that, they rise rapidly and dominate the error count. Clearly these errors will be reduced by the addition of more training data.

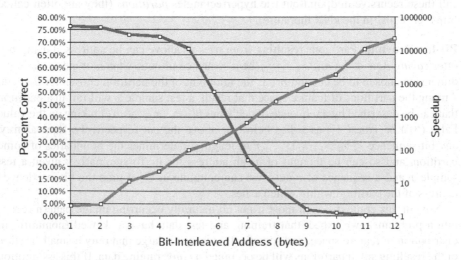

Fig. 1. Tradeoffs between accuracy (percent of pixels correctly classified, labeled on the left scale) and speed-up (factor of decrease in the number of distances computed, compared to brute-force; labeled on the right scale, using a log-scale), as a function of the length of the bit-interleaved address (shown in units of 8-bit bytes)

It is interesting to note that, if we do not count the second type of errors, then accuracy remains high (above 60%) until more than 64 bits are used, for a speed-up of 3401.

The rise and rapid dominance of errors of both types are to be expected when the volume of a hash cell falls below a certain threshold. We can roughly estimate this threshold as follows. We have observed that the distance from a probe point to the farthest of its five nearest neighbors is less than 15 for about 95% of the points. When we use at least 45 bits of bit-interleaved address, we have in effect guaranteed that each of the 15 dimensions have been cut three times, which gives hash cells that are $256/2^3 = 32$ on a side. This is at the boundary of the unpleasant case when the farthest of the five nearest neighbors is likely to fall outside the cell. This rough analysis seems to explain the rapid fall-off of accuracy above 48 bits.

One obvious next step is to dramatically increase the size of the training set and observe how fast the errors of the second type decrease, and the effect also on speed-up.

8 Amplifying Sample Sets

Just a brief note on some ideas for amplifying sets of "real" samples using synthetically generated samples that may answer the objection that synthetic samples are inappropriate for training and testing. The complex processes by which document images are generated—governed by choices of subject, meaning, language, text, illustrations, page layout styles, typefaces, type sizes, printing parameters, image digitization resolution, etc etc—are in many details subject to parameterization by more or less continuously varying numerical values: certainly type size and digitizing gutter widths, line spacing, digitizing resolution, and image degradation parameters; also, less obviously, parameters that characterize typeface families such as stroke width and serif length[15]. Given two "real" images collected and added to a sample set, it is often possible to estimate the values of these parameters. When there is a gap between the two values— e.g. digitizing resolutions of 200 and 400 dpi—we will argue that they span a range of values—including, say 300 dpi—that *could occur* in other sets of real samples. Thus any variation of either image that is generated synthetically by chosing values between the two, within the range that they span, should be admissible as a training or test sample. Given than one such parameter, convex combinations of their values should also be admissable. Synthetic images generated in the way we call *synthetically interpolated*. We have begun the investigation of interpolation tools for this purpose.

9 Discussion and Future Work

However, we may soon face other theoretical and practical obstacles to following this approach in building a fast approximate kNN algorithm. How can we ensure that a partition addressed by a bit-interleaved address contains **all** of the training samples that may fall within the kNN set, or an approximate-radius NN set? It is easy to see that, in the worst case, this extra offline preprocessing (and space requirements) may be exponential in d; even worse, this would require exponential space to store the redundant copies of the test samples. Again this point must be tested empirically.

In a personal communication, Jon Bentley has suggested to us that a hybrid of classification trees (CARTs[16]) and k-d trees may provide a circumvention of these potential problems. Specifically, the first few levels of a CART are compressed using a hashing scheme similar to the bit-interleaving trick.; but it is not yet clear how to make this work.

References

1. Pavlidis, T.: Thirty years at the pattern recognition front. In: King-Sun Fu Prize Lecture, 11th ICPR. (2000), address = Barcelona, Spain)
2. Nagy, G., Seth, S.: Modern optical character recognition (1996)
3. Nagy, G.: Twenty years of Document Image Analysis in PAMI. (IEEE Transactions on Pattern Analysis and Machine Intelligence)
4. I. T. Phillips, S.C., Haralick, R.M.: Cd-rom document database standard. (In: Proc., 2nd IAPR ICDAR), pages = 478–483, year = 1993)
5. Sarkar, P., Nagy, G.: Style consistent classification of isogenous patterns. IEEE Trans. on PAMI **27** (2005)
6. Veeramachaneni, S., Nagy, G.: Style context with second order statistics. IEEE Trans. on PAMI **27** (2005)
7. H. S. Baird, M. A. Moll. J. Nonnemaker, M.R.C., Delorenzo, D.L.: Versatile document image content extraction. In: Proc., SPIE/IS&T Document Recognition & Retrieval XII Conf., San Jose, CA (2006)
8. Ho, T.K., Baird, H.S.: Large-scale simulation studies in image pattern recognition. IEEE Transactions on Pattern Analysis and Machine Intelligence **19** (1997) 1067–1079
9. Duda, R.O., Hart, P.E., Stork, D.G.: Pattern Classification, 2nd Edition. Wiley, New York (2001)
10. Samet, H.: The Design and Analysis of Spatial Data Structures. Addison-Wesley, Reading, Massachusetts (1990)
11. Bentley, J.L.: Multidimensional binary search trees used for associative searching. Communications of the ACM **18** (1975) 509–517
12. Bentley, J.L.: Multidimensional binary search trees used for associative searching. Commun. ACM **18** (1975) 509–517
13. Freidman, J.H., Bentley, J.L., Finkel, R.A.: An algorithm for finding best matches in logarithmic expected time. ACM Trans. Math. Softw. **3** (1977) 209–226
14. Lee, D.T., Wong, C.K.: Worst-case analysis for region and partial region searches in multidimensional binary search trees and balanced quad trees. Acta Inf. **9** (1977) 23–29
15. Knuth, D.E.: Computer Modern Typefaces. Addison Wesley, Reading, Massachusetts (1986)
16. Breiman, L., Friedman, J.H., Olshen, R.A., Stone, C.J.: Classification and Regression Trees. Wadsworth& Brooks/Cole, Pacific Grove, CA (1984)

Exploratory Analysis System
for Semi-structured Engineering Logs

Michael Flaster, Bruce Hillyer, and Tin Kam Ho

Bell Laboratories, Lucent Technologies,
700 Mountain Ave., Murray Hill, NJ 07974, USA
{mflaster, hillyer, tkh}@lucent.com

Abstract. Engineering diagnosis often involves analyzing complex records of
system states printed to large, textual log files. Typically the logs are designed to
accommodate the widest debugging needs without rigorous plans on formatting.
As a result, critical quantities and flags are mixed with less important messages
in a loose structure. Once the system is sealed, the log format is not changeable,
causing great difficulties to the technicians who need to understand the event correlations. We describe a modular system for analyzing such logs where document
analysis, report generation, and data exploration tools are factored into generic,
reusable components and domain-dependent, isolated plug-ins. The system supports incremental, focused analysis of complicated symptoms with minimal programming effort and software installation. We discuss important concerns in the
analysis of logs that sets it apart from understanding natural language text or
rigorously structured computer programs. We highlight the research challenges
that would guide the development of a deep analysis system for many kinds of
semi-structured documents.

1 Introduction

Performance analysis for complex engineering systems often involves sifting through
many large textual log files for a few rare target symptoms. Designed to serve as many
diagnostic needs as possible, such logs typically include mixed printings of time stamps,
numerical quantities, flags, and informal messages, in an order determined by the evolution of the system state. The logs can also be records of interrogations by an external
observer, with variable sequences of queries representing particular monitoring needs.

For fear of regret on losing information, the design of such logs tends to be inclusive,
which creates a cluttered background when one's interest is to detect a specific event.
Moreover, the circumstances under which the logs are designed and studied are often
less than ideal – there could be incomplete functionalities, chatter among different components, and non-deterministic occurrences of problems in a yet-to-be perfect product.
All these contribute to the log documents having a loose structure despite that there is
some intended, and still discernible, regularity.

Engineering logs are rarely customer-facing, and hence are unlikely to be rigorously
designed and cleaned even after the system delivery. In many cases, the system is delivered as a sealed box and it is not possible to change the commands that generate and

H. Bunke and A.L. Spitz (Eds.): DAS 2006, LNCS 3872, pp. 291–301, 2006.

format such logs. Once the system is deployed, logs of specific events are not always easy to regenerate because it may not be possible to reconstruct a particular system state.

Having to deal with such documents is an annoying aspect of many technicians' everyday life. While in principle one can always write specialized programs to search for the interesting phenomena within the logs, the engineers are often domain experts with little interest nor time for sophisticated search programming. Few can afford the luxury of having a dedicated debugging programmer in service. When the important symptoms involve joint occurrences of multiple flags and quantities that are scattered through the logs, or with specific sequential orders, the conditions could be very difficult to express even with complicated search programs. Worse, in highly complex systems with hundreds of critical parameters, events of interests sometimes cannot be articulated for tailored searching before they are recognized as a pattern. Discovery of correlations and causal relationships occurs more likely at the end instead of at the beginning of the debugging process. Thus an exploration tool that can operate with loosely structured documents is an essential aid to a diagnostic process.

Responding to this need, we propose a modular "log analysis" system that is designed to support complex event discovery within semi-structured documents. To address the problem in wide generality, we argue that the system should consist of separated lexical analysis, syntax-directed parsing, semantic translation and report generation, and exploratory analysis components. Wherever possible, generic tools should be used in each component, and the domain-dependent features should be minimized and contained within a set of plug-ins. In this paper we share our experiences in designing one such system that was motivated by real diagnostic scenarios in the telecommunication industry. Our goal is to call for attention to this ubiquitous challenge, and outline open questions for further research to improve such systems.

2   Rigidity of Textual Structures and Levels in Document Understanding

Semi-structured textual logs are predictable to an extent between those of natural language text (such as news stories) and artificial language text (such as computer programs). The technology of formal languages and program compilation is a well researched and mature field of study. Natural language understanding, while still difficult, has received much attention because of intense interests in internet searching. For the in-between continuum of structured or semi-structured text, however, research has been spotty.

Document understanding systems arising as a generalization of Optical Character Recognition systems [17] have had successes on documents with well-defined structure, such as mail addresses, forms, and tables [5][15][16].

These systems enjoy the advantage of having clear expectations of the document format, so that parsers can look for specific blocks, lines, or fields, though the expectations are not necessarily represented as a formal grammar. For these systems, emphasis is often put on the transcription and subsequent clean-up of the imaged text. Occasionally, statistical parsing, by way of computing the joint likelihood of each possible interpretation, is used to select among several syntactic alternatives [5]. For documents without well defined syntax, attention tends to focus on the early stages of image processing, 2D layout analysis, and symbol (character/field/sentence) recognition. They often stop at obtaining logically ordered, tagged and transcribed text blocks.

Our concern is on methods to understand documents with contents that are very structured but there is no full grammar. Typically there are some expectations on the amount, type, and contents of the messages. But the underlying grammar is not available, or the text may not be produced by a single grammar. An example is a debugging trace generated by a program with several concurrent and interacting modules. Another example is a record of interrogation to several entities that produced indefinitely delayed replies. Few tools are known to handle such documents. Typically, their analysis means eyeballing, with aids of text editors (like `emacs`) or simple pattern search utilities such as the unix "grep". If more complex relationships are to be validated, special script programs (like those in `awk`, `perl`, or `python`) are constructed to search for the desired message.

The focus of this paper is to discuss technologies that can assist understanding of such semi-structured text. But just what do we mean by understanding what is in a document? One way of understanding is to focus on the morphology, and to classify which type of document the input is, i.e., a news story, a letter, a table, a form, a dialog, a computer program listing, a message log, etc. Each of these types of documents has a specific texture in terms of regularity in symbol density, line and field spacing, alignment, and repetition [13].

Going deeper, one may want to obtain the messages contained in the document. When the input is a page image, this involves symbol/token segmentation, symbol recognition, or OCR (Optical Character Recognition). This may also include removal of decorative graphics and markup tags, or determining the orientation of the text lines and the logical ordering of the text blocks [3][24]. Additionally, language identification may be needed for mixed language input [22], and context and language models may be called for in symbol recognition. At times, one may defer document classification to or integrate it with this stage if the document type must be disambiguated with symbol recognition. At this stage one gets ready for, but has not begun, extraction of information that connects to the application context.

In this work we analyze the information extraction steps after such early processing. Thus we assume the input to be ASCII text or transcriptions of text images with well delimited text lines in a logical order, and that the input has been accepted as an instance of a document of a known type. We do not consider graphics or decorative text printed in nonlinear layouts. Nor do we assume that the text strictly adheres to a pre-designed format or that we have a way to influence the behavior of the document generator. We explore the space beyond reach by existing specialized tools and commercial products that are designed for the analysis of data or event logs following a particular protocol, such as operating systems logs (e.g. `syslog`), web logs [8], or files generated by data logging software libraries coupled to the observed system. For such specialized tools we refer readers to [14].

We argue that, like steps in program compilation and natural language parsing, there can be cleanly separable stages in a system for extracting information from semi-structured documents. Generic and reusable components can comprise substantial parts

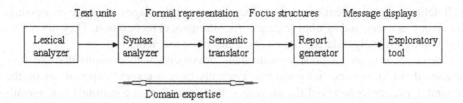

Fig. 1. A modular analysis pipeline for semi-structured text. Like computer program compilers and natural language understanding systems, it has distinct stages with well defined output. Up to the interfaces, the implementation in each stage is independent of those in others. We emphasize that domain-specific designs can be contained within the middle layers, leaving the front-end and back-end utilities generic and reusable.

```
mod1152 2005-05-24 21:46:06
... masterReadX() completed with 300 values of X read
... master initialized
line 557 reached
mod1205 2005-05-24 21:48:32
... !!!alarm thresholdCrossing T23
default value restored
mod567 2005-05-24 22:01:05
... slaveMakeY() paused at counter=46 y=577.03
...
```

Fig. 2. An example log file that records events in several software components. The more important flags and alarms in an intended regular format are mixed with transient, informal debugging messages.

of the system, and domain-dependent drivers can be contained within a middle layer. We describe one such system that has been developed and used to parse and explore complicated engineering logs arising in network diagnosis (Figures 1, 2). Compared to single-shot, *ad hoc* pattern searchers, an important advantage of a modular architecture is that it supports incremental understanding and exploration. In the following sections, we discuss the details of the system, and highlight the problematic areas where practical difficulties have precluded a clean automation.

3   Lexical Analysis, Syntax Guided Morphology Analysis and Shallow Parsing

In this stage, to understand is to parse the document according to the expected syntax. The input to this stage is a sequential chain of text blocks that have all tokens delimited. This could also be a transcription of imaged or audio documents. The output is a formal representation of the document as an internal data structure, which can be optionally serialized in XML or other forms of tagging [7].

The parser can be further decomposed into generic and domain-dependent modules. A generic module can be used for lexical analysis, where the purpose is to break

```
<logfile>
<logline>
<idstr> mod1152 </idstr>
<datestr> 2005-05-24 </datestr>
<timestr> 21:46:06 </timestr>
</logline>
<logline> ... masterReadX() completed with 300 values of X read </logline>
<logline> ... master initialized </logline>
<unknown> line 557 reached </unknown>
...
</logfile>
```

Fig. 3. Output of simple lexical analysis, where fields with recognizable format are marked

down the incoming text into units suitable for comparison to the expected format. In this stage the system tokenizes the input stream, determines field types and looks for identifiers that are markers or delimiters of the expected messages. The identifiers can be symbols, symbol patterns, keywords, or stop words. Examples include the symbol ":" if a dialog is expected, the symbol "=" for key-value pairs, or fields in the form of "YY:MM:DD" for dates (Figure 3). Relevant tools include regular expression matchers, or search utilities taking a simple target symbol/string as an argument. Up to a simple parameterization, such search utilities can be generic, and many tools for this have been produced in early research in computer science. Simple data cleaning, such as repairing an inappropriate line breaks or converting time stamps to standard formats, may belong to this stage.

Based on the expected message format, a subsequent syntax analyzer takes in text segments extracted from this stage and organizes them into the largest legitimate syntactic units (Figure 4). The syntax analyzer has to involve tailored code. If implemented in objected-oriented languages, the code would populate attributes of the objects that represent the target structure. If the structure of the input document follows the known object hierarchy, this can use classical techniques like recursive descent parsing. In less clean scenarios the parser must be tailored to provide more flexibility. For example, when there is indeterministic interleaving of multiple, spontaneous message streams, the parser has to be able to cope with concurrent, dangling structural references.

In practice, there is no guarantee that the object hierarchy is strictly observed in the input. While in program compilation it is perfectly reasonable to reject the input whenever the grammar is violated, pragmatic systems for log analysis must be error tolerant. The emphasis is on the search for useful fragments, and there is less concern in the validity of the format. Structure of the expected input provides guidance to the parser, but it must not be overly controlling or limiting. Moreover, in many log analysis scenarios, the grammar is not available at the outstart. Instead, the expectation is developed

```
<sysXlog>
<modmsg>
<msgheader>
<id> mod1152 </id>
<date> <year> 2005 </year> <month> 5 </month> <day> 24 </day> </date>
<time> <hour> 21 </hour> <min> 46 </min> <sec> 06 </sec> </time>
</msgheader>
<msgbody>
<msg> ... masterReadX() completed with 300 values of X read </msg>
<msg> ... master initialized </msg>
</msgbody>
</modmsg>
...
</sysXlog>
```

Fig. 4. Output of a syntax analyzer that groups the input lines into largest recognizable units

incrementally by inspection and validation. Typically, a sequence of trial-and-error is applied to get rid of exceptions.

An interesting research question is to what extent pattern recognition techniques can be useful in this stage. Syntactic pattern recognition [4] immediately comes into the picture, and techniques such as automatic learning of regular expressions and pattern languages [1][2][19] and, more generally, grammatical inference [12][20][23] may provide help. Grammatical inference is known to be hard, though in recent years there have been moderate successes with re-stimulated interest. In time-pressured analysis scenarios, the difficulty of application of such techniques often denies them of their deserved opportunity. The offer of an easily applicable library of such elements should be welcomed [18].

We believe that, more likely in near-term, assistance would come from a collection of statistical tools for analyzing the text morphology, such as automated search of repeated units, computation of autocorrelation functions on simple quantities like line lengths, and other techniques commonly used in texture analysis, text compression, and cryptoanalysis. These hints can aid the construction of the structural expectation.

A key point we emphasize here is the notion of incremental transformation. Syntax driven tools at this stage do not have to assume all the load of extracting the desired message from the document. Moderate goals, such as translating the document to a machine understandable structure, are sufficient and are often most easily accomplishable with tools designed for this level of processing. For example, while an awk script can easily extract a consecutive block of lines and translate them to a semantically related group of statements, it is not the ideal tool to implement the decision logic needed to look for low level components scattered within deeply nested structures. Semantic understanding can be deferred to the next stage, where target driven tools can be brought in to obtain the message of concern.

4   Deep Parsing, Focus Structure Selection and Target Generation

Documents converted to a formal representation are ready for event discovery and semantic translation. This is the stage where domain-specific knowledge is most intensively applied. Custom code is needed to express the goal of the analysis. Translation tools that are based on common representations of formal documents provide much convenience. For example, for documents parsed into an XML representation, multiple XSLT scripts can be designed to apply tests to and extract contents from different components of the object hierarchy. Whenever necessarily, new data structures can be constructed to facilitate event discovery [21].

Again, rarely is it true that a full understanding can be achieved in a single shot. Conclusions need not be drawn at this stage. Flexibility can be sought from incremental constructions of the translation code, with the goal moderately set at producing new structures to represent grouping of potentially related sets of variables and messages, or at particular focus scales (Figure 5). For example, a translator for a time-stamped log may produce separate tables containing messages produced at the day, hour, or minute scales respectively Analysis of the messages and impacts can be deferred to the next stage.

When repeated analysis is needed on massive dumps, the target of this translation can be tables added to a full-strength relational database. For transient analysis, such

Events			
mod id	date	time	msg
mod1152	2005-05-24	21:46:06	masterReadX() completed with 300 values of X read
mod1152	2005-05-24	21:46:06	master initialized
mod1205	2005-05-24	21:48:32	alarm thresholdCrossing T23
mod567	2005-05-24	22:01:05	slaveMakeY() paused at counter=46 y=577.03
			...

Alarms				
mod id	date	time	alarm type	port id
mod1205	2005-05-24	21:48:32	thresholdCrossing	T23
			...	

Fig. 5. Tables with different emphases created from the same log file

tables can simply be stored as CSV (comma separated values) formatted files ready to be loaded into a display and reporting tool, such as an Excel spreadsheet. In either case, the notion of a record, i.e., a row in a table, represents an entity of analysis. Standard considerations in database design, such as attributes to contain in each record and keys to be chosen, are essential in designing such tables.

A research challenge for this stage is to find the most suitable data structures to support discovery of each type of events. Here events can be simple propositions and their boolean combinations, like "if flag A appears," "if flag A appears but flag B is not seen," or predicates like "if quantity x is less than 0.01." An event may also involve more complex expressions like "flag A occurs 3 times and flag B never occurs more than 2 times before quantity x reaches 100.0." While many questions about the data can be formulated as queries to a relational database, there are limits in the expressive power of such queries. Even if the event definition is well articulated, and stays within coverage of the query language, the decomposition of an engineering question into such queries is not always obvious. It could be a difficult maneuver to ask of the technician who, with intimate knowledge about the observed system, intuitively knows what should happen, but may not be able to tell before the event is first seen. Proper structures of the data and messages to support recognition of such events are much desired. This points back to a fundamental concern in pattern recognition, namely, the quest for the most suitable features and feature representations to support identification of a certain regularity.

5   Exploratory Analysis in Collections of Focus Structures

Once the document is converted to a collection of standard data structures such as tables or object trees, domain independent display and exploratory tools can again be introduced. It is well known that exploratory data analysis can benefit much from visual tools. Therefore we describe, as an example module in this stage, an interactive visual tool we developed for correlation of text strings organized in tables. The tool exploits the power of hypertext links and browsers to support relational querying without the need for a back-end database server.

Given a set of CSV formatted tables, the Java program htmlgen would infer simple connections between the tables. A connection can be as simple as that two tables share a common column name. In that case, the program constructs a set of table-specific web pages, another set of column-specific web pages, plus an index page containing links to both sets of pages. When a user clicks a link to a table-specific page, the next web page he sees contains the corresponding table. If instead he clicks into a column-specific page, he sees all the tables containing that column.

In either case, once presented with one or more tables, he can further click on a column name to sort the table by that column. More importantly, each cell in each table is a hyperlink. On a click at a particular cell, the script program embedded in the web page filters the currently seen tables by the value of this entry at this column. The next display is constructed which shows the filtered table or tables. The user may continue the filtering recursively, or back track and attempt a different filter.

The purpose of this design is to allow the user to see the text surrounded by different contexts. For example, if a column contains an alarm message, consecutive alarms may be seen in one table, and long range dependence among the alarms may be summarized in another table. Tables containing different sets of attributes and sharing several keys would allow projection of complicated message relationships onto different subspaces.

The design of the web pages and the embedded scripts follows the REST (Representational State Transfer) style [6]. The hyperlinks at the cells are constructed on-the-fly as a root site address concatenated with a sequence of operators and operands. The intent is to provide support for completely hassle-free querying by simple clicking. This removes unnecessary obstacles to the thought of the analyst who can now concentrate on the diagnostic tasks rather than struggle with forming proper symbolic queries in correct syntax. Thus the tool is another practice of the design philosophy in Mirage, another graphical tool of ours for numerical exploratory analysis [9][10][11].

A further advantage of the REST style address is that it records the sequence of steps the user has traced to arrive at a particular state of the tables. For example, the address for a page derived from filtering all tables created from the log of May 24, 2005 that contain the key field "modid" with values "modid=mod1152" and "hour=21" would be

```
http://ihost.xyz.com/Xlog/20050524/unique_modid.html?
modid=%20mod1152&hour=%2021
```

which can be bookmarked and revisited at a later time, after the analyst has a chance to pause and digest the information for what happened in the observed system that led to this state. Sometimes insights may come only after he sees the same thing happening under different but similar scenarios. In this way, the tool can support discovery of certain events that can be articulated only after it is seen over and over again.

Our utility for automatically inferring such hyperlinks uses no other knowledge of the table contents. This guarantees that the pages can be rebuilt easily when the table changes. The need arises when the user decides to change the semantic translators to generate tables with different selected components. It also means that tables can be accumulated, recombined, and cross linked in an arbitrary way. This is especially suited for historical archives and for comparisons of system states from different environments and perspectives. The query processor is extremely light-weight: no database installation is involved, and after one application of htmlgen to build the basic sets of web pages, nothing more is needed from the server. The collection of web pages can be taken off-line for querying and browsing. This provides a critical functionality of relational databases – querying in the form of "select ... from ... where ..."– without the need for the expensive, and often intimidating process of installing and populating a full-scale database. Moreover, there is no need for continuous connection to a database server, which provides additional convenience for in-field analysis.

Despite its simplicity, the tool demonstrates powerful consequences when proper considerations are given on extracting and isolating common functionalities in a document analysis process. For further research, one may consider generalization towards more sophisticated schema matching rather than relying on column names, approximate or partial matches rather than exact matches, and facilities for multimedia content retrieval when the table cells feature combinations of text, graphics, images, and others. Meanings of the clicks can be changed with options in the page header. With every cell clickable, use of the display estate can be maximized. Development of sophisticated tools to do these would benefit from many current research activities in pattern recognition.

6 Conclusions

We have witnessed the power of modern internet search engines that rely on primitive keyword matching. Though efficient implementations of such simple searches are highly nontrivial, we have reasons to believe that the technology has only scratched the surface of complex pattern recognition and knowledge discovery from analysis of documents.

In this paper we analyzed the information extraction stages of a document understanding process. We argued the advantages of a modular system architecture, and outlined the relevant pattern recognition challenges at each stage. Starting with a particular demand for engineering diagnosis, we investigated the issues, built a system for practical use, and generalized it to suit many other scenarios where there is a need for progressive annotation, multi-scale and dynamic context display, and exploratory analysis with text. We summarized our observations from this experience as well as from our knowledge of similar systems.

Beyond the engineering diagnosis setting, there are many documents that have some minimal structural regularity that can be subjected to a similar "syntax, semantics, and event discovery" analysis pipeline. Examples are journals, blogs, interviews, plays, court transcripts, news stories, and all kinds of transaction and event records in science and humanities. The analyses of these documents share a common characteristic that the process is explicitly driven by a search for events and patterns. There is a large, unfilled space between trivial keyword matching and the extremely difficult domain of natural language understanding. The popular "bag of words" analysis of documents using techniques like latent semantic indexing does not facilitate complex event searching and thus still leaves many unserved needs.

For text exploration, we developed a tool for automatic hypertext generation that embeds a light-weight query processor into a table display, such that relational projections can be applied without requiring the user to install special software or database servers. We believe that its generality and extreme ease of use can encourage incremental attempts on semantic translation, which allow for continuous accumulation and evolution of discoveries from a document.

Acknowledgements

We thank Phil Bohannon for organizing a text analysis seminar where many ideas presented here were discussed, Narasimhan Raghavan and Suresh Goyal for bringing to us the practical challenge, and Cliff Martin, Steve Fortune, and David James for useful exchanges.

References

1. D. Angluin, Finding Patterns Common to A Set of Strings, *Proc. of the 11th Annual ACM Symposium on Theory of Computing*, Atlanta, 1979, 130 - 141.
2. D. Angluin, Learning Regular Sets From Queries and Counterexamples, *Information and Computation*, Vol. 75, 1987, 87-106.
3. H.S. Baird. Anatomy of a versatile page reader. *Proceedings of the IEEE*, Vol. 80, No. 7, Jul 1992, 1059–1065.
4. H Bunke, A Sanfeliu, *Syntactic And Structural Pattern Recognition: Theory And Applications*, World Scientific, 1990.
5. P. Cullen, T.K. Ho, J.J. Hull, M. Prussak, S.N. Srihari, Contextual Analysis of Machine Printed Addresses, *Proc. of the 4th USPS Advanced Technology Conference*, Washington, D.C., Nov 1990, 779-793.
6. R.T. Fielding, *Architectural Styles and the Design of Network-based Software Architectures*, PhD Dissertation, Information and Computer Science, University of California, Irvine, 2000.
7. K. Franke, I. Guyon, L. Schomaker, L. Vuurpijl, The WANDAML Markup Language for Digital Document Annotation, *Proc. of the 9th International Workshop on Frontiers in Handwriting Recognition*, 563-568.
8. N.S. Glance, M. Hurst, T. Tomokiyo, BlogPulse: Automated Trend Discovery for Weblogs, *Proc. of WWW 2004*, New York, May 17-22, http://www.blogpulse.com/research.html.
9. T.K. Ho, Exploratory Analysis of Point Proximity in Subspaces, *Proc. of the 16th ICPR*, Quebec City, Canada, Aug 11-15, 2002.
10. T.K. Ho, Interactive Tools for Pattern Discovery, *Proc. of the 17th ICPR*, Cambridge, U.K. Aug 22-26, 2004, Vol. 2, 509-512.
11. T.K. Ho, Mirage project site: http://www.cs.bell-labs.com/who/tkh/mirage.
12. V. Honavar, G. Slutzki (eds.), *Proc. of the 4th International Colloquium on Grammatical Inference*, ICGI-98, Iowa, July 12-14, 1998. Lecture Notes in Artificial Intelligence, Vol. 1433, Springer.
13. J. Hu, R. Kashi, G. Wilfong, Document Image Layout Comparison and Classification, *Proc. of the 5th ICDAR*, Bangalore, 1999, 285.
14. Loganalysis.org, http://www.loganalysis.org.
15. D. Lopresti, G. Nagy, Automated Table Processing: An (Opinionated) Survey, *Proc. IAPR Workshop on Graphics Recognition (GREC99)*, Jaipur, Sep 1999, 109-134.
16. S. Madhvanath, V. Govindaraju, V. Ramanaprasad, D.S. Lee, S.N. Srihari, Reading Handwritten US Census Forms, *Proc. of the 3rd ICDAR*, Vol. 1, 1995, 82.
17. G. Nagy, Twenty Years of Document Image Analysis in PAMI, IEEE Trans. PAMI-22, 1, Jan 2000, 38-62.
18. V. Raman, J.M. Hellerstein, Potter's Wheel: An Interactive Data Cleaning System, *Proc. of the 27th VLDB Conference*, Roma, Italy, 2001.
19. P. Rossmanith, T. Zeugmann, Stochastic Finite Learning of the Pattern Languages, *Machine Learning*, Vol. 44, 2001, 67–91.

20. Y. Sakakibara, Grammatical Inference in Bioinformatics, *IEEE Trans. on Pattern Analysis and Machine Intelligence*, Vol. 27, 2005, 1051–1062.
21. J. Shanmugasundaram, K. Tufte, G. He, C. Zhang, D. DeWitt, J. Naughton, Relational Databases for Querying XML Documents: Limitations and Opportunities, *Proc. of the 25th VLDB Conference*, Edinburgh, Scotland, 1999.
22. A.L. Spitz, Determination of the Script And Language Content of Document Images, *IEEE Trans. Pattern Analysis and Machine Intelligence*, Vol. 19, No. 3, 1997, 235–245.
23. M. van Zaanen, The Grammatical Induction Website, http://eurise.univ-st-etienne.fr/gi.
24. T. Watanabe, T. Sobue, Layout Analysis of Complex Documents *Proc. of the 15th ICPR*, Barcelona, Vol. 4, 4447.

Ground Truth for Layout Analysis Performance Evaluation[*]

A. Antonacopoulos[1], D. Karatzas[2], and D. Bridson[1]

[1] Pattern Recognition and Image Analysis (PRImA) Research Lab,
School of Computing, Science and Engineering,
University of Salford, Manchester, M5 4WT, United Kingdom
http://www.primaresearch.org
[2] School of Electronics and Computer Science,
University of Southampton, Southampton, SO16 1BJ, United Kingdom
http://www.ecs.soton.ac.uk/~dk3

Abstract. Over the past two decades a significant number of layout analysis (page segmentation and region classification) approaches have been proposed in the literature. Each approach has been devised for and/or evaluated using (usually small) application-specific datasets. While the need for objective performance evaluation of layout analysis algorithms is evident, there does not exist a suitable dataset with ground truth that reflects the realities of everyday documents (widely varying layouts, complex entities, colour, noise etc.). The most significant impediment is the creation of accurate and flexible (in representation) ground truth, a task that is costly and must be carefully designed. This paper discusses the issues related to the design, representation and creation of ground truth in the context of a realistic dataset developed by the authors. The effectiveness of the ground truth discussed in this paper has been successfully shown in its use for two international page segmentation competitions (ICDAR2003 and ICDAR2005).

1 Introduction

Layout analysis is a very important step in document analysis. Errors made at this stage will propagate in the subsequent OCR and document understanding stages and can adversely impact on the success of the application as a whole.

Over the past two decades a significant number of layout analysis (mostly page segmentation and region classification) approaches have been proposed in the literature. Each approach has been devised for and/or evaluated using relatively narrow-focused application-specific datasets, which more often than not do not reflect the real-world occurrence of documents. As a result, it is difficult to evaluate the practical value of each method and to make a direct comparison between the different approaches.

Whilst the need for objective performance evaluation of layout analysis algorithms is evident, there does not exist a suitable dataset with ground truth that reflects the

---

[*] This work was supported by GCHQ (UK Government Communications Headquarters) and the EPSRC (UK Engineering and Physical Sciences Research Council).

H. Bunke and A.L. Spitz (Eds.): DAS 2006, LNCS 3872, pp. 302–311, 2006.

realities of everyday documents (widely varying layouts, complex entities, colour, noise etc.). A number of layout analysis approaches in the literature have reported evaluation results based on the University of Washington dataset [1] which mostly contains (relatively stylised) technical article images, a large number of which are synthetic (created by the dataset authors using LaTeX and output as images). It is the view of the authors that such a database can be useful but does not reflect the complexities of the majority of widely available documents.

This lack of a representative and practical (in terms of use) dataset can be attributed mostly to the need to subtly balance wide-ranging issues involved in its design as well as to the effort required in its realisation.

While the design of the dataset architecture is of central importance in terms of its usefulness and usability, the crucial (and most influential) element is the design of the *ground truth*. It should be mentioned, for completeness, that ground truth is defined as a representation of the agreed correct result of the ideal layout analysis method (i.e. the result of the method that, if existed, would put an end to the research problem). The ground truth forms the basis for all comparisons with the output of any layout analysis method to be evaluated.

A significant clarification must be made at this point between *performance evaluation* and *benchmarking*. The former involves in-depth analysis of results and is aimed at providing feedback to developers, the latter usually outputs a single value that is used to compare between approaches. Clearly, for in-depth performance evaluation, a more thorough specification and design is required for the dataset in general and for the ground truth in particular.

This paper presents and discusses the issues related to the design, representation and creation of ground truth in the context of the layout analysis performance evaluation dataset developed by the authors. In contrast to previous approaches (the most prominent of which is [1]), the proposed dataset is not only realistic in the selection of documents but it has significant flexibility in the description and use of ground truth. A more accurate region representation scheme is used in favour of using rectangles (unable to describe complex-shaped regions) but without sacrificing ease of use or performance. The additional information describing the physical and logical characteristics of regions ensures the applicability of the ground-truth to a wide range of evaluation scenarios and anticipated future needs (as evidenced by current developments).

The remainder of the paper starts with a brief description of the context within which the ground truth needs to be designed, created and used. In this respect, Section 2 describes the performance evaluation framework while Section 3 presents aspects of the dataset. The main considerations for the design of successful ground truth are discussed in Section 4. The specification of the ground truth and its XML representation are introduced in Section 4.1. An overview of a software tool designed by the authors to support the ground truth creation is given next (Section 4.3). Section 5 concludes the paper.

2 Performance Evaluation Framework

One of the important issues to address and one of the advantages of the ground truth representation described in this paper is the flexibility of its use within different performance evaluation contexts. These can range from simple listings of regions missed/detected etc. to sophisticated evaluation of scenarios (e.g. the detection of headlines and separators) with configurable penalties etc.

A brief description of this wider perspective, in the form of the framework being developed by the authors, is given here to highlight the needs that ground truth has to fulfil within a wider, more-demanding application. The most important objective of the framework is to provide the (layout analysis) algorithm developer with an in-depth analysis of the performance of the method being evaluated. Detailed statistical information is given on the ability of a method in terms of correctly detected, merged, split, partially or wholly missed regions (along with combinations of these conditions as well as the incorrect detection of noise as valid regions) [2]. *Goal-oriented* performance evaluation is enabled through the creation of scenarios (application of sets of weights on the detected errors). An example of this can be when an OCR developer is interested in not missing any text regions and in not merging text regions across columns etc. (to preserve the reading order), while they may not assign high value to the accurate detection of graphic regions.

At a higher semantic level, a scenario may involve the evaluation of logical as well as physical layout characteristics. For instance, in an indexing application the developer may be interested in correctly locating figure captions (for indexing photographs), or article titles and dates (for indexing newspaper articles).

Moreover, the framework is able to summarise the performance of a method by providing scores (based on scenarios) at different levels as required. For instance, a developer who needs to assess the resulting improvement of a newly introduced modification may customise the framework to provide them with both an overall scenario evaluation score but with detailed scores for the tasks that are most affected by the given modification.

It is therefore important that the ground truth must hold information that supports these evaluation tasks.

3 Dataset

In its most crude form, a performance evaluation dataset comprises a set of images and associated ground truth (for each image). The dataset on which layout analysis methods are evaluated has an obvious bearing on the relevance of the evaluation results. This section briefly presents the dataset developed by the authors with two key objectives in mind. First, to give the reader a broader understanding of the contextual issues for ground-truth design in terms of the choice of documents (page images) it needs to describe. Second, to provide an understanding of the overall architecture of which ground truth is part (and within which it is used).

The choice of documents to include in a dataset has to fulfil two major requirements. First, the types (categories) of documents have to be representative of everyday occurrences. Second, the proportion of documents (population in the dataset) between categories should reflect realistic usage and at the same time the documents in each category must be sufficiently varied and numerous to enable meaningful evaluation for specific applications.

To that effect, the authors have established a detailed taxonomy of existing documents (text carriers), based on physical and logical layout characteristics (about 21 document types and 80 subtypes). Document types range from official documents (e.g., certificates) to various drawings and maps, to forms, books, tickets and text in natural scenes, to name but a few. However, certain types of document are more widely distributed and are more targeted by application developers. These are documents that contain information that a wide variety of users need to extract. Examples are office documents, magazine pages, advertisements and technical articles. The dataset created by the authors reflects this situation by containing more instances of these types of document.

It should be noted that the layouts of these types of document vary considerably. Office documents and technical articles have more structured layouts that usually follow simple formatting rules. On the other hand, magazine pages have more complex layouts and advertisements even more so. As it will be seen in the next section, the complexity of layout regions is one of the deciding factors in ground truth design.

The dataset is organised in two broad layers of functionality. The outer layer is a database holding certain physical and administration attributes for each document page in the dataset. Physical attributes include dimensions, the presence (or absence) of colour, whether or not the document is single or multi-columned, the (main)

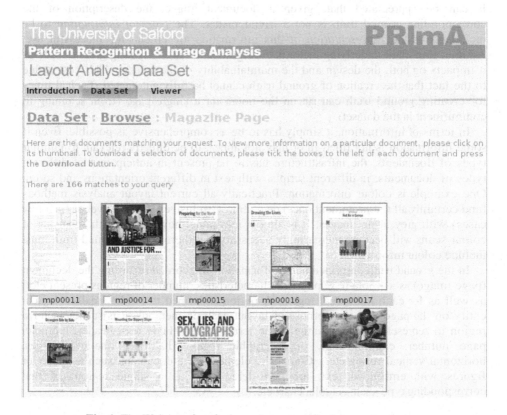

Fig. 1. The Web interface for browsing a specific document category

language of the text, the reading direction, the resolution of the image as well as a characterisation of the complexity of the layout. All these attributes are deemed to be interesting for searching and selecting sets of documents for evaluation (they represent major factors that influence layout analysis methods). Administration attributes are mostly used by the dataset keepers and include authorship and source information, copyright information etc. A web front-end enables both searching of the dataset based on the above attributes as well as browsing of the dataset according to document types (as defined in the established taxonomy). A screenshot of the web interface (browsing magazine pages) can be seen in Fig. 1.

The inner layer of functionality comprises the image-ground truth pair. An image file (or two, as in the case of colour/greyscale documents both the original and a bilevel copy are kept) and its corresponding ground truth description file are linked to each record in the database. The design issues and characteristics of the ground truth description are discussed in the next section.

The current dataset (to be made freely available to researchers) can be found in:
http://www.prima.cse.salford.ac.uk/dataset/.

4 Ground Truth

It can be appreciated that, given a document image, the description of the corresponding ground truth is not a trivial matter. The *types of information* to be included and the *representation* of this information are crucial for successful use. Another important underlying factor is the significant cost of creating ground truth, as it impacts on both the design and the maintainability of the dataset. This cost is due to the fact that the creation of ground truth cannot be fully automated. Typical times for creating ground truth can run in the hours for a single page (from scanning to commitment in the dataset).

In terms of information, it simply has to be as comprehensive as possible. Even if some information is not filled-in or may not appear to be directly relevant to familiar types of documents, the infrastructure has to be present in anticipation of different types of documents, in different scripts, with text in different orientations and so on. One example is colour information. Practically all current layout analysis methods (and certainly all the prominent ones) deal almost exclusively with bilevel or (in a few cases) with grey scale images. It is almost inevitable, however, that the analysis of colour scans will become increasingly necessary and therefore the ground truth must include colour information.

In the ground truth described here, information is recorded regarding the document (page image) as a whole (e.g. physical characteristics, number of regions present etc.) as well as for each individual region. A region is defined to be the smallest logical entity on the page. For the purpose of layout analysis methods, it is sufficient for a region to represent a single paragraph in terms of text (body text, header, footnote, page number, caption etc.), or a graphic region (halftone, line-art, images, horizontal/vertical ruling etc.). Composite elements of a document, such as tables or figures with embedded text, are considered each as a single region (of that corresponding type such as table, chart etc.).

The region-representation scheme plays a critical role in the efficiency and accuracy of the performance analysis strategy. For the comparison between regions (a ground truth region against a region resulting from a method to be evaluated), bounding rectangles are the most efficient representation. However, complex-shaped regions cannot be accurately represented by bounding rectangles. The proposed scheme describes regions using isothetic (having only horizontal and vertical edges) polygons [3]. This representation of regions is very accurate and flexible since each region can have any size, shape and orientation. Furthermore, a region, whose contour is an isothetic polygon, can be represented by a number of rectangular horizontal intervals whose height is determined by the corners of its contour polygon (effectively achieving decomposition into rectangles). This interval structure makes checking for inclusion and overlaps, and calculation of area, possible with very few operations, thus approximating the efficiency of rectangles [4].

In general, ground truth must fulfil the following objectives:

- *Accuracy*, both in terms of absence of human errors and in the inherent ability to represent complex information.
- *Richness of information*, to enable various evaluation scenarios.
- *Efficiency of comparison*, to enable evaluation using large datasets.
- *Ease of understanding*, in terms of representation organisation to facilitate maintenance and use.
- *Ease of creation*, in terms of the ability to achieve the above objectives with the use of a specially designed ground-truthing tool (see below).
- *Anticipation of future requirements*, in terms of extensibility to avoid obsolescence.

4.1 Ground Truth Representation

The ground truth information is represented in XML (addressing, thus, the representation-related goals listed in the previous section). Figure 2 shows a ground truth example of a document containing a single text region (simplified for illustration purposes). The main element is a *Document*, which is the only type of element that can be found in an XML file after the header lines. Inside the Document (between the <document> and </document> tags) two types of element are allowed: the *Document Summary* and a number of *Pages*. The document summary section specifies how many pages there are in the document.

Each page is represented as a separate element, and information about each page is given between the <page> and </page> tags. The image filename attribute is used to indicate the name of the image file on which the ground truth is based. Each page can be decomposed into a number of regions. In the current ground truth version, there are ten distinct types of regions defined: *Text, Image, Line Drawing, Graphic, Table, Chart, Separator, Maths, Noise* and *Frame*. The "page summary" contains the number of occurrences of each type of region in the page, while the page size attributes define the width and height (in pixels) of the page.

Each region must contain a unique ID number to identify it within the document. A number of attributes (their occurrence depending on the type of the region) is

```
<?xml version="1.0" encoding="UTF-8"?>
<!DOCTYPE document SYSTEM
"http://www.prima.cse.salford.ac.uk/dataset/documentlayout.dtd">

<document>
    <document_summary no_pages="1"/>
    <page page_id="1" image_filename="mp00088bw.tif">
        <page_summary no_text_regions="22"
            no_image_regions="0" no_line_drawing_regions="0"
            no_graphic_regions="0" no_table_regions="0"
            no_chart_regions="0" no_separator_regions="0"
            no_maths_regions="0" no_frame_regions="0"
            no_noise_regions="0"/>
        <page_pixel_size width="2340" height="3135"/>
        <text_region id="1" txt_orientation="0"
            txt_reading_direction="Left_To_Right"
            txt_leading="" txt_kerning=""
            txt_font_size="12" txt_type="Paragraph"
            txt_colour="Black" txt_reverse_video="No"
            txt_indented="No" txt_primary_lang="English"
            txt_secondary_lang="None"
            txt_primary_script="Latin"
            txt_secondary_script="None" txt_bgcolour="White"
            txt_reading_orientation="0">
            <coords no_coords="4">
                <point x="10" y="10"/>
                <point x="20" y="10"/>
                <point x="20" y="20"/>
                <point x="10" y="20"/>
            </coords>
        </text_region>
    </page>
</document>
```

Fig. 2. Example of ground truth representation

optional. These attributes describe as many characteristics of the region as possible. Various attributes relevant to text regions are shown in the example of Fig. 2. It is mandatory that each region contains coordinate sets that define its outline (isothetic polygon).

The full Document Type Definition (DTD) file which defines the XML representation of ground-truth information can be found at:

http://www.prima.cse.salford.ac.uk/dataset/documentlayout.dtd.

4.2 Ground Truth Creation

To enable the creation of detailed and flexible ground truth, a semi-automated tool has been designed by the authors. When designing this tool the decision was made to provide full flexibility and the focus was placed on the *creation* of ground truth, rather than the *correction* of the results of a first-pass segmentation process. This is a pragmatic approach to the problem, stemming from previous experience of the authors with ground-truthing [5]. The crucial observation was that the time spent in correcting the errors of segmentation is more often than not significantly longer than following a bottom-up approach to build ground truth information and fewer errors are made (users tend to miss errors made by the first-pass segmentation process).

It is worth mentioning at this point that there are other approaches to "ground truth" creation in the literature (e.g., [6]). In these cases though, the tools are meant to be used in the final stages of an automated process to ensure the validity of the outcome of the conversion process of a paper document into electronic form, while the "ground truth" information sought is also application specific and lacks the depth and breadth needed for performance evaluation.

The ground-truthing tool "*Aletheia*" (from the Greek word for "truth") operates on the bilevel version of the document images and comprises functionality to perform connected component analysis and, subsequently, combine the resulting components into regions (as required by the ground truth specification). In addition, it provides the necessary interface to label the regions identified and specify an appropriate set of attributes for each, customized according to its type. Finally, the software can export the ground truth as an XML file, which fully conforms to the ground truth specification.

Before any editing operations become available, the software performs a connected component analysis of the document image. A fast one-pass algorithm is employed for that purpose. The connected components identified in the image are the base units for the construction of regions. Each target region will comprise a list of components, and will be described by a boundary which will enclose only the specified components, and possibly some white space.

There are four supported methods to group together connected components into a region that affect the way the boundary of the region is derived offering different levels of flexibility. At the lower level the user can select the components of a region one by one. The boundary of the region is then defined as the minimum bounding rectangle which encloses the selected components. A higher-level approach is to use a drag-and-resize operation to specify a rectangle and select all the components inside it. The system then allows the user to either adopt the specified rectangle as the boundary of the region, or shrink the specified rectangle in order to produce the minimum rectangle in the same manner as before. Finally, in order to address cases where complicated region shapes are necessary, the software offers the option to use a freehand drawing method to select components. In this case the user defines a polygon by successively selecting its corner points. The isothetic rectangle boundary in this case is calculated based on the initial polygon, which is reduced in such a way so that most of the white space is removed.

Aletheia also offers more advanced region-editing functions, for instance to combine regions, or to combine existing regions with individual components, while regions can always be dissolved into their constituent components. Following the bottom up approach described above, a higher (region) level segmentation of a document can be obtained in a few minutes.

Subsequent to geometrically defining the regions of the document page the user has to label the resulted regions and define the associated attributes. According to the ground truth specification, *Aletheia* allows each region to be of any of the ten region types defined. By right-clicking a region, the user is presented with a dialog box, which lists the type and associated attributes of each region. The user can then select the type of the region from a drop down list, and specify the values for all attributes associated with the region type. The only attribute the user cannot control is the region ID number, which is assigned and managed automatically by the software. Figure 3 shows the attributes dialog for a text region, and a line drawing region.

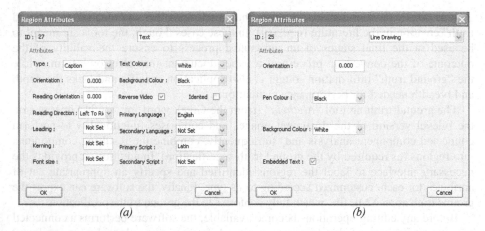

Fig. 3. The attribute dialogs for (a) a Text region and (b) a Line Drawing region

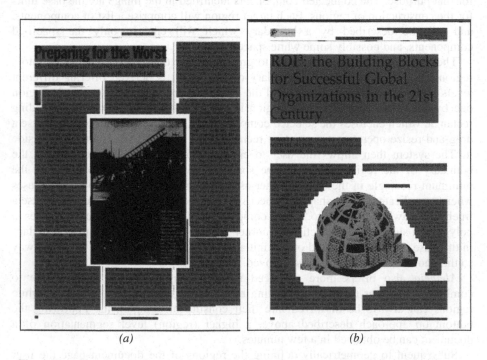

Fig. 4. Examples of the final ground-truth for (a) a Magazine page and (b) a Technical Article page

Figure 4 shows two instances of ground-truth regions created with *Aletheia*. The software visualises the ground-truth information by assigning different colours to regions depending on their type. This facilitates the process of labelling the regions, since the user can easily identify any unprocessed regions. Any regions or components that have not been labelled are automatically marked as noise regions.

Finally, *Aletheia* offers two options for storing the final ground truth description. The first is to export it as an XML file (a series of individual regions, along with their boundaries and detailed attributes) which fully conforms to the ground truth specification as described above. The second option is to save the ground truth representation in the software's own format, which has the advantage of preserving the actual components in addition to the higher-level information, thus facilitating more powerful editing at a later time.

5 Concluding Remarks

This paper has introduced and discussed a number of important issues surrounding ground truth for the evaluation of the performance of layout analysis methods. The focus was on the design, representation and creation stages in the context of a new dataset developed by the authors. The resulting ground truth is the product of the authors' effort over the past few years and reflects their experience with performance evaluation. The ground truth created has been successfully used as the basis for two international competitions, held under the auspices of the International Conference on Document Analysis and Recognition in 2003 [7] (in an earlier version) and 2005 [8].

References

1. Philips, I.T., Chen, S., Ha, J., and Haralick, R.M. English Document Database Design and Implementation Methodology. In *Proceeding of the 2nd Annual Symposium on Document Analysis and Retrieval* (UNLV, USA, 1993). 65–104.
2. Antonacopoulos, A. and Brough, B. Methodology for Flexible and Efficient Analysis of the Performance of Page Segmentation Algorithms. In *Proceedings of the 5th International Conference on Document Analysis and Recognition (ICDAR'99)*, (Bangalore, India, 1999). IEEE-CS Press, 451–454.
3. Antonacopoulos, A. Page Segmentation Using the Description of the Background. *Computer Vision and Image Understanding*, Vol. 70, No. 3 (1998), 350–369.
4. Antonacopoulos, A. and Ritchings, R.T. Representation and Classification of Complex-Shaped Printed Regions Using White Tiles. In *Proceedings of the 3rd International Conference on Document Analysis and Recognition (ICDAR'95)* (Montreal, Canada, 1995). IEEE-CS Press, 1132-1135.
5. Antonacopoulos, A., and Meng, H., A Ground-Truthing Tool for Layout Analysis Performance Evaluation, In *Document Analysis Systems V*, D. Lopresti, J. Hu and R. Kashi (Eds.), Springer Lecture Notes in Computer Science, LNCS 2423, 2002, 236-244.
6. Simske, S.J, and Sturgill, M., A Ground-Truthing Engine for Proofsetting, Publishing, Re-Purposing and Quality Assurance, In *Proceedings of the 2003 ACM Symposium on Document Engineering (DocEng'03)* (Grenoble, France, 2003), ACM Press, 150-152.
7. Antonacopoulos, A., Gatos, B., and Karatzas, D. ICDAR2003 Page Segmentation Competition, In *Proceedings of the 7th International Conference on Document Analysis and Recognition (ICDAR2003)* (Edinburgh, UK, August 2003). IEEE-CS Press, 688–692.
8. Antonacopoulos, A., Gatos, B., and Bridson, D. ICDAR2005 Page Segmentation Competition, In *Proceedings of the 8th International Conference on Document Analysis and Recognition (ICDAR2005)* (Seoul, South Korea, August 2005). IEEE-CS Press, pp. 75–79.

On Benchmarking of Invoice Analysis Systems

Bertin Klein, Stefan Agne, and Andreas Dengel

DFKI GmbH, 67663 Kaiserslautern, Germany
{klein, agne, dengel}@dfki.de

Abstract. An approach is presented to guide the benchmarking of invoice analysis systems, a specific, applied subclass of document analysis systems. The state of the art of benchmarking of document analysis systems is presented, based on the processing levels: Document Page Segmentation, Text Recognition, Document Classification, and Information Extraction. The restriction to invoices enables and requires a more purposeful, i.e. detailed, targetting of the benchmarking procedures (acquisition of ground truth data, system runs, comparison of data, condensation into meaningful numbers). Therefore the processing of invoices is dissected. The involved data structures are elicited and presented. These are provided, being the building blocks of the actual benchmarking of invoice analysis systems.

1 Introduction

An interesting and important breed of document analysis systems is the specific class of systems that is devoted to the analysis of invoices: invoice analysis systems, IAS. There is not only a market for IAS, so that they are economically interesting [DNW+03, KD04b]. Also, they are a useful field to better understand details of the nature of document analysis systems under slightly restricted and thus slightly easier conditions. Lastly it is simply a good chance for a scientific field to potentially provide companies with research results and be elegantly able to prove their applicability [KD04b].

With the advent of IAS, there emerges the need for a benchmarking of IAS. In order, either to assure the correctness of results, or to get clues about required corrections of the results and/or the IAS, it is crucial to (be able to) measure the quality of the results of IASes. The respective scientific discipline and the real, practical activity are called benchmarking.

It is without much doubt, that the following four analysis levels are core constituents of any useful analysis of documents in general and of invoices in particular:

- Document Page Segmentation
- Text Recognition
- Document Classification
- Information Extraction

H. Bunke and A.L. Spitz (Eds.): DAS 2006, LNCS 3872, pp. 312–323, 2006.

It is easy to imagine that if one level produces significantly bad results, then the following levels, depending on these bad results as input, will usually not be able deliver good results. Trying to hunt down the origin of some bad results, one would check the results after each of these four major levels. A benchmark of the complete process, thus needs to comprise benchmarking of the levels enumerated above.

Benchmarking, based on these levels, is well researched, i.e. measures have been developed, to calculate and denote representations of respective qualities. An overview is given in section 2. In order to benchmark an IAS, it is not sufficient to know these levels, their measures and their applicability. A deeper understanding of the practical application is required, i.e. what is been done with invoices, which steps constitute the processing of the invoice. An approach to invoice processing steps is made in section 3. The processing steps with an invoice imply the information fields that are needed from the invoice. The invoice processing practice surely judges IAS by their ablility to provide the required fields with high quality —even if there existed other IAS which were better in some other specific analysis task. Thus, these information fields are the hooks on which to benchmark an IAS. Only after having entered into this mechanism, one can substantiate the specification of ground truth requirements for the respective levels and start the collection and preparation of ground truth data. Finally, the concrete measuring activity can access the measures already introduced in section 2.

2 State of the Art

This section provides an introduction and overview of benchmarking of document analysis systems (of which IAS are a subclass), along the four processing levels of: Document Page Segmentation, Text Recognition, Document Classification, and Information Extraction.

2.1 Document Page Segmentation

Two main classes of approaches for the benchmarking of document page segmentation can be distinguished in the literature: bitmap based approaches that operate at pixel level on the document bitmap and text based approaches that benchmark the segmentation at character level.

Bitmap Based Benchmarking: Randriamasy and Vincent are the names behind the origin of bitmap based evaluation [RV94a, RV94b, RVW94, YV95]. Their work has more recently been revisited, e.g. by [PCL+01] and more prominently e.g by [Bre02]. The document image (e.g. in TIFF format) is used and the zoning ground truth in which the regions are described by polygons. Also the result of the automatic zoning is needed in this format. The evaluation performs a geometrical comparison between the segmentation results and the zoning ground truth by testing the affiliation of each black pixel to corresponding regions. The quality of the segmentation is determined by the number of pixels or characters in the wrongly segmented regions of the document. Thulke et al. [TMD98] classify the errors into 19 different types.

Text Based Benchmarking: Text based evaluation operates on the text output of an OCR system. First the OCR system is applied only to the document image. The resulting output contains segmentation errors and OCR errors. Then the OCR system processes the same document image again, additionally provided with the manually generated zoning ground truth. The resulting text output of the second run contains only OCR errors. For both texts the error correction costs are computed by string matching algorithms (e.g. based on the Levenshtein edit distance). The difference then denotes the costs of correcting the segmentation errors [KRN93, KRNN95].

Being solely text based, SEE [ARR00, ADK03] combines the advantages of bitmap based and traditional text based evaluation systems. Contrary to the bitmap based approaches, SEE is able to evaluate the segmentation of OCR systems which do not provide the results of automatic zoning. Furthermore, the segmentation errors can be classified, which was not possible with the text based evaluation methods. The fact that SEE does not need the manually generated zoning ground truth as input leads to a reduction of effort and cost. As a side effect of this SEE can only approximate the number of true occuring segmentation errors.

2.2   Text Recognition

Text Recognition is the most elaborated field within document analysis with respect to benchmarking, mainly attributable to the extensive work at ISRI. The ISRI tools are a very good basis for the benchmarking of standard text recognition systems [RKN93, RKN94, RJN95, RJN96]. The most important measure at benchmarking the text recognition is the *Character Accuracy*. Further character based evaluation measure are: *Confident Interval, Failure, Throughput, Marked Character Efficiency, Confident Metric,* and *Accuracy by Character Class.* For more measures the characters are not treated isolatedly, but text is considered to consist of words separated by whitespace. The most prominent word-based measures are: *Word Accuracy, Stopword Accuracy, Non-Stopword Accuracy, Distinct Non-Stopword Accuracy, Phrase Accuracy,* and *Accuracy by Word Length.* Moreover, the effect of the class of input data has been considered, leading to: *Page Quality Groups, Fax — Non-Fax, Effect of Resolution, Grayscale — Binary Image, Effect of Font Features,* and *Effect of Skew.* Related research was done at the *University of Washington,*which however was more focused on error models and the creation of synthetic data [Bai93, HB93, Bai95, HB95].

2.3   Document Classification

Most measures of document classification benchmarking base on the model of the contingency table, used to simply display the number of correctly and incorrectly classified documents.

Table 1. Binary contingency table after [Lew91, Lew95]

	Ground Truth	
System	K	$\neg K$
K	a	b
$\neg K$	c	d

In the contigency table, a denotes the number of documents, which have been correctly assigned to the class K, b denotes the number of documents, which have been wrongly assigned to class K; wrong, because they are not documents belonging to that class. Most widely used are *Precision* and *Recall* [Lew91, Lew95], and the *F-Measure* [vR79, Lew95], which is calculated on top of both, precision and recall. Further, there are *Reject Rate*, *Fallout*, *Error Rate*, and *Accuracy*. For an accumulated measure over all classes *Macro Averaging* and *Micro Averaging* are used [vR79, Lew91]. There are also approaches, which consider costs of misclassifications, *Cost Measure* [WK91].

2.4 Information Extraction

The basis to benchmark systems at information extraction are usually so-called *Templates*, patterns supposed to be filled by the system. A template consists of several *Slots*, in which information is entered in form of phrases. A template for the official report of a soccer game could have the slots: `hometeam`, `guest`, `playground` and `result`. The contents of a slot, provided as ground truth by a human is called *Key*, the value found by the system is called *Response*. The comparison of both leads to a distinction of six cases [Chi92, CS93]:

Correct: *Response* = *Key*
Partial[1]: *Response* $\cong$ *Key*
Incorrect: *Response* $\neq$ *Key*
Spurious: *Key* empty, *Response* not empty
Missing: *Response* empty, *Key* not empty
Noncommital: *Key* and *Response* are both empty

Basing on the above [Chi92, CS93, LS91], define the following measures: *Error*, *Undergeneration*, *Overgeneration*, *Substitution*, *Recall*, *Precision*, *F-Measure*, and *Error Rate per Word*.

3 Invoice Processing Step Ontology

In oder to benchmark IASs, supposed to support companies or private persons in their handling of invoices, it is required to develop an understanding, what people do on the reception of an invoice, how the triggered process looks like, and what thus is important for companies or private persons to get from an IAS. Let somebody get the invoice in Figure 1 delivered onto his desk, i.e. either an

---

[1] At Muc-6[MUC95] Partial was not used any more, i.e. PAR was set to 0 for all tests.

agent in a medical insurance company[2], or a private person. What is required to do? We elicited the following differentiation into eleven different steps (not all of them mandatory). Note, that these steps represent some serious ontological committment already (which is why this section is entitled alike).

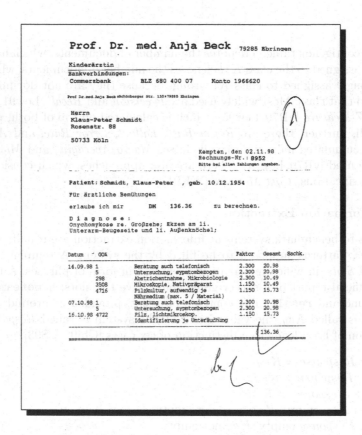

Fig. 1. A typical (in this case medical) invoice

This version elaborates on the version published in [DNW+03]:

1. *Classification.* Determining the class "invoice" triggers the processing steps decribed here. Further subclassing often makes sense.
2. *Retrieval of contract.* The patient needs to be spotted. Consider: addressee, firstname, lastname, birth date. A contract holder, or contract number could be specified, or a relation of patient to contract holder be mentioned ("son").
3. *Retrieval of operation.* Is there a folder with previous documents. Find the treatments and their dates in the invoice, the diagnosis. Conclude possible histories. Compare the (recent or timely related) activities which are logged with the contract (for the patient at hand).

---

[2] Taking a medical invoice as a model does not imply a loss of generality.

4. *Justification of contract plausibility.* Do invoice address and contract address match? Are treatments admitted treatments, and took place while contract existed?

5. *Decide payment target.* Compensate the patient (if he already paid the doctor), the doctor or the doctors invoicing agency. What is: default, general rule in the company, usually better? Does the invoice have a due date, or other time constraints (so that the default rule is modified)?

6. *Collect payment data.* Spot account and bank (name and code of both), a reference number, a payment due date (permitting a delayed payment), comments (perhaps treatments or patient name or dates). Possibly extra comments are required, to explain reductions, etc. ...?

7. *Justification of payment data plausibility.* Is the location of the bank related to the recipient address? Do account name and code match with the data from the contract or possibly a company database of doctors. Does the reference number look genuine (i.e. "2313-AMB-12-1998" could raise doubts, because 1998 looks like a reference to the long ago year 1998)?

8. *Justification of invoice correctness.* Many invoices are not correct! Are all required information fields there, for invoices in general (like adressee, "trading good", tax number of invoicing party etc.), and for medical invoices (25% reduction for hospital treatments, ICD diagnosis code, ...). Are calculations correct? Are balances carried over correctly? Are treatment codes correct and combinations allowed?

9. *Justification of invoice plausibility.* Do treatments coincide and suit the diagnosis? Is the sequence of treatments plausible?

10. *Pay.* Retrieve the amount (claimed amount minus possibly reductions). Fill out bank name and code, account name and code. Provide the invoice-nr and other required reference in the comment field. Provide further comments. Set the due date. Commit.

11. *Archive and log.* Write a line in the contract log. Open or continue an/the operation. Store the invoice. Store the data read. Document the payment. Document and explain any non-standard actions.

It could be problematic, if there occur unusual, special directives on invoices. In practice, it is not problematic. We did not know this from the beginning, but learned it only after a while of practically processing many invoices and large sums [KDF04]. Meanwhile some companies let our system process many invoices without any individual human control. Systems do not need to be perfect for that, it is enough when they commits less —especially less expensive— errors than human agents, which is by the way a reconfirmation that benchmarking, the assessment of errors, should be taken seriously.

This description of an invoice process is a solid ground to start detailing benchmarking of IAS.

4   Information Fields Needed in the Processing Steps

Essentially, what we have provided so far, is sufficient to design a good concept for benchmarking IAS. All the main activities of processing invoices have been presented.[3] It should be clearer now, what is required from an IAS, and how benchmarking could approach IAS. For example it is now clearly imaginable that e.g. sum total is a sensitive information field and any benchmarking would surely closely evaluate the respective system results. Further, benchmarking also wants to distinguish the good from the even better, and a very good system, can outperfrom other good systems, if it was equally good in the area of sensitive data, but also especially good in some speciality e.g. in detecting seemingly minor inconsistencies in the justification tasks.

Although, the different concepts appearing in the processing descriptions might seem a confusing cocktail of very different kinds of concepts. By pinning down what they actually imply for a system, e.g. what values the concepts may take, the confusion starts to appear much easier to master. This is done now. [4]

4.1   Data-Oriented Summary of the Process Steps

With some revisiting and re-ordering, first, the process steps can be clustered together, as they are not so different from each other like they first seem. Second, the quality of the link between input data and output data can be characterized (in the following section). Independent of the algorithm inside some IAS, it is then (and only then) possible to prepare ground truth data for a domain and then benchmark its behavior.

The finally needed information fields are: "payment data", i.e. "payment target", "bank (name and code)", "bank account (name and code)", "reference number". Prior to that, for the justification steps, some more information fields are necessary. Elements, or intermediate results of justification are single notes of "plausibility", e.g. "plausibility of contract data", and their consequences: "acceptance of invoice", "correctness of invoice", "reduction (of claimed amount)", "explanation (of reduction)", "genuine look of a code". One speciality is "urgency", a distance relation on some dates.

All the justification is to a very large degree based on matching patterns, which read as "comparison of data (e.g. addresses)". To a much smaller degree it sometimes bases on a "proximity (or relation) of locations" and also sometimes on the construction of an "interpretable story of dates" (or at least collection and display of dates to the user).

There exist some general processing schemes: "(default) business rule", "law", "general use". Further, note that between the above concepts, which are searched for, and the following concepts, which are those appearing in documents, there

---

[3] Actually, also the software engineers who coded our system [KD04a] started their work with descriptions on such a level. Some people even say, and we partly adhered to that, that a benchmarking concept should be constructed prior to the implementation of a system in order to assure a system meet its requirements well.

[4] Individual mileages may vary. The way we proceed is not unique. It is very usual to encounter differences, when talking about conceptualizations. However, with varying conceptions, as long as they are only consistently used, one can still reach the same result [KBC+05].

are often some bridging concepts. E.g. addressee is part of an address, but can also become a patient or contract holder and a payment target.

4.2   Information Field Concept Classes

The whole set of information fields appearing on invoices can be distinguished into the following set of classes.

1. *Enumerable concepts:* A number of concepts appearing on invoices can be judged as correctly recognized or not, if one only has a database[5] in which all their different possible values are stored, like: "country:= New Zeeland, Italy, Germany, Great Britain, USA,... ". We consider the following concepts to be of that kind: treatment, a patient (respectively a patient identification, usually firstname, lastname, date-of-birth), a diagnosis, location of bank, a doctors address, treatment code, allowed treatment combination.[6]

2. *Record concepts:* There is another kind of database either available in companies anyhow, or possible to construct. They can be used in the first place to map facts to other facts. The database with contracts is the main such database. From there one can retrieve all "contracts" and get their "contract data", i.e. contract number, contract holder, operation, contract duration, contract address, contract coverage (which treatments).

   Other databases could cover "treatment suitabilities for diagnoses", and "possible histories (from treatment to diagnosis to cause)." To extend an invoice system for classes other than invoices, requires a database with the document classes linking to specifications of their required processing.

3. *Visual databases:* Depending on the details of a domain, and given that there is a set of visual matching operations, which are extremely quick, it is in a number of cases found that it is worked with databases of 2 dimensional layout templates (reduced/abstracted representations of real layouts), to map between pages and classes or page snippets and ROI classes (e.g. Figure or Table). (This addresses the implications of the widespread strategy to exploit that many recipients receive many invoices from one sender, who often use fixed basic templates for their invoices, e.g. built-in in their invoicing software [KGKD01].

4. *Labelled concepts:* These are the concepts which are (most often) simply identified, because a keyword indicates what comes next, "From: ....". These concepts can also be treated with a database alike the one for enumerable concepts, but the database has to store the keywords or labels (e.g. "From", "Total", "Sum", "Amount", "Euro", "Diagnosis",...). Concepts of this category are: claimed amount, the patient, the diagnosis.

---

[5] Please read "ontology" instead of "database" from now on, if you know how to store knowledge in ontologies.

[6] In our system, we frequently use this even to actually spot —i.e. not benchmark but spot— occurences of peoples names, including permutations, spelling errors, and OCR errors, which is still very quick with databases of 1 Million names [KDF04].

5. *Syntactic concepts:* This simply bundles all information fields which are convenient to describe with something like a regular expression, or a similar means of abbreviated description. Typical for this category are all kinds of dates: letter date, date of a treatment, payment due date, but also "a calculation (not doing one, but something printed like: "1 + 2 = 3"!). Also addresses are often described syntactically: address, the invoice address, addressee, doctors address. In early applications we described tables of treatments also syntactically (mainly because they often exhibit well- behaved columns with numbers).

   We subsume another group of concepts here, those characterized by their layout. The only occurrences in our example invoice are: subject and reference-field. However, the reference-field can be determined also with a clear reference to its structure. Only the benchmarking of the subject spotting feature needs to be purely based on its look, position, and bold font.

6. *Secondary concepts:* To finish, one more recognition feature to be benchmarked has to be mentioned (c.f. [Sum98]). In general, there exist concepts of elements visible on documents, (called secondary in [Sum98]), which might be identifiable only after other elements have been readily identified. To use the prior, intermediate search results, is a valuable and simple strategy anyhow. If the address was found, no other adress has to be searched, as well as everything belonging to the address, needs not be considered in further searches (for subject, diagnosis, ...). Here, the last concepts come into play, that are simple to find out and represent in the system: "the required information fields for (German) invoices in general", and "required information fields for (German) private medical invoices". Now, for a specific application or class of IAS a benchmarking concept can be constructed based on these building blocks.

5   Conclusion

Good recognition of numbers is obviously very important when dealing with documents about money and its transfer. However, we hope to have contributed to some more understanding of requirements of IAS and dependencies on possibly crucial qualities and features, i.e. on IAS benchmarking.

When we conceived of this paper for the first time a couple of years ago, we wanted to call it something like: "the misunderstanding that there exists something like one ground truth". There is a cornucopia of work pointing out the serious problems, often in conjunction with high costs, when something is too quickly labelled correct or true, and slightly different viewpoints of important stakeholders cause these stakeholders to disagree. However, we have learned from practice that our approach must be more constructive, i.e. we need to try to show ways instead of showing the dead ends. Users or customers dont know what is helpful in the end, and worth their money, but they find it out later, because then the system they chose either makes their life better or not. It is important to assure the users success. Thus, we developed the presented checklist of scenario pieces, which enabled us to (conveniently) assure this in all the scenarios we encountered so far.

We have presented the state of the art of basic benchmarking measures available. Then we have sketched the process, that is initiated when a private person or company receives an invoice. We have derived from this sketch simpler subtasks and the data required for them, which we have grouped into six classes. The sketch of the process should be used for practical projects to assign individual importances to the subtasks and the involved information requirements. These will then inform the choice of state of the art measures to use (E.g. we chose different measures for domains with invoices only below 100 Euro, than for domains with invoices above 100000 Euro, because the importance of the sum total field was specified differently). The classes of data, are the basis to guide the collection of ground truth data (for one customer and his specific "viewpoint") and can also serve to guide their application by the benchmarking system (as the classes tell something about the datatypes).

Future work is devoted to a closer inclusion of tables.

References

[ADK03]   Stefan Agne, Andreas Dengel, and Bertin Klein. Evaluating see — a benchmarking systems for document page segmentation. In *Proceedings of the 7th International Conference on Document Analysis and Recognition ICDAR'03)*, volume I, pages 634 – 638, Edinburgh, Scotland, United Kingdom, August, 3-6 2003.

[ARR00]   Stefan Agne, Markus Rogger, and Jörg Rohrschneider. Benchmarking of document page segmentation. In Daniel P. Lopresti and Jiangying Zhou, editors, *Document and Recognition and Retrieval VII*, volume 3967 of *Proceedings of SPIE*, pages 165 – 171, San Jose, California, USA, 2000.

[Bai93]   Henry S. Baird. Document image defect models and their uses. In *Proceedings of the Second International Conference on Document Analysis and Recognition ICDAR*, pages 62–67, Tsukuba Science City, Japan, October 20–22 1993. IEEE Computer Society Press.

[Bai95]   Henry S. Baird. Document image defect models. In Lawrence O'Gorman and Rangachar Kasturi, editors, *Document Image Analysis*, pages 315–325. IEEE Computer Society Press, 1995.

[Bre02]   T. M. Breuel. Representations and metrics for off-line handwriting segmentation. In *8th International Workshop on Frontiers in Handwriting Recognition*, 2002.

[Chi92]   Nancy Chinchor. MUC-4 evaluation metrics. In *Proceedings of the Fourth Message Understanding Conference (MUC-4)*, pages 22–29, McLean, Virginia, USA, June 16–18 1992. Morgan Kaufmann Publishers, Inc.

[CS93]   Nancy Chinchor and Beth Sundheim. MUC-5 evaluation metrics. In *Proceedings of the Fifth Message Understanding Conference (MUC-5)*, pages 69–78, Baltimore, Maryland, USA, August 25–27 1993. Morgan Kaufmann Publishers, Inc.

[DNW+03]   A. Dengel, P. Nowak, C. Wagner, K. Rehders, B. Klein, D. Schneider, M. Winkler, and Tebel R. Studie automatisierte rechnungseingangsbearbeitung marktpotential, marktübersicht und trends. commercial study, September 2003.

322   B. Klein, S. Agne, and A. Dengel

[HB93]   Tin Kam Ho and Henry S. Baird. Perfect metrics. In *Proceedings of the Second International Conference on Document Analysis and Recognition ICDAR*, pages 593–597, Tsukuba Science City, Japan, October 20–22 1993. IEEE Computer Society Press.

[HB95]   Tin Kam Ho and Henry S. Baird. Evaluation of OCR accuracy using synthetic data. In *Proceedings of the Fourth Annual Symposium on Document Analysis and Information Retrieval SDAIR 95*, pages 413–422, Las Vegas, Nevada, April 24–26 1995.

[KBC⁺05]   A. Kumar, A. Burgun, W. Ceusters, J. Cimino, J. Davis, P. Elkin, I. Kalet, A. Rector, J. Rice, J. Rogers, S. Schulz, K. Spackman, D. Zaccagini, P. Zweigenbaum, and B. Smith. Six questions on the construction of ontologies in biomedicine. In *AMIA*, Washington DC, USA., 2005.

[KD04a]   Bertin Klein and Andreas Dengel. Problem-adaptable document analysis and understanding for high-volume applications. *International Journal on Document Analysis and Recognition*, 2004.

[KD04b]   Bertin Klein and Andreas Dengel. Results of a study on invoice-reading systems in germany. In *IAPR International Workshop on Document Analysis Systems*, 2004.

[KDF04]   Bertin Klein, Andreas Dengel, and Andreas Fordan. *Reading and Learning — Adaptive Content Recognition*, volume 2956 of *LNCS*, chapter *smartFIX*: An Adaptive System for Document Analysis and Understanding, pages 166 – 186. Springer, 2004.

[KGKD01]   B. Klein, S. Gökkus, T. Kieninger, and A. Dengel. Three approaches to industrial table spotting. In *Int. Conf. On Document Analysis and Recognition (ICDAR) '01*, 2001.

[KRN93]   Junichi Kanai, Stephen V. Rice, and Thomas A. Nartker. A preliminary evaluation of automatic zoning. In Kevin O. Grover, editor, *Annual Research Report*, pages 35–45, University of Nevada, Las Vegas, 1993. Information Science Research Institute.

[KRNN95]   Junichi Kanai, Stephen V. Rice, Thomas A. Nartker, and George Nagy. Automated evaluation of OCR zoning. *IEEE Transactions on Pattern Analysis and Machine Intelligence*, 17(1):86–90, January 1995.

[Lew91]   David D. Lewis. Evaluating text categorization. In *Proceedings of the Workshop on Speech and Natural Language*, pages 312–318, Pacific Grove, California, USA, February 19–22 1991.

[Lew95]   David D. Lewis. Evaluating and optimizing autonomous text classification systems. In Edward A. Fox, Peter Ingwersen, and Raya Fidel, editors, *Proceedings of the Eighteenth Annual International ACM SIGIR Conference on Research and Development in Information Retrieval SIGIR '95*, Special Issue of the SIGIR Forum, pages 246–254, Seattle, Washington, USA, July 9–13 1995. ACM Press.

[LS91]   Wendy Lehnert and Beth Sundheim. A performance evaluation of text-analysis technologies. *AI magazine*, 12(3):81–94, Fall 1991.

[MUC95]   *Proceedings of the Sixth Message Understanding Conference (MUC-6)*, Columbia, Maryland, USA, November 6–8 1995. Morgan Kaufmann Publishers, Inc. Inhaltsverzeichnis.

[PCL⁺01]   Liangrui Peng, Ming Chen, Changsong Liu, Xiaoqing Ding, and Jirong Zheng. An automatic performance evaluation method for document page segmentation. In *Proceedings of the Sixth International Conference on Document Analysis and Recognition (ICDAR)*, pages 134 – 137, Seattle, Washington, USA, September 10-13 2001. IEEE Computer Society Press.

[RJN95]   Stephen V. Rice, Frank R. Jenkins, and Thomas A. Nartker. The fourth
            annual test of OCR accuracy. In Andrew D. Bagdanov, editor, *Annual
            Research Report*, pages 11–49, University of Nevada, Las Vegas, 1995.
            Information Science Research Institute.

[RJN96]   Stephen V. Rice, Frank R. Jenkins, and Thomas A. Nartker. The fifth
            annual test of OCR accuracy. Technical Report TR-96-01, Information
            Science Research Institute, University of Nevada, Las Vegas, USA, April
            1996.

[RKN93]   Stephen V. Rice, Junichi Kanai, and Thomas A. Nartker. An evaluation
            of OCR accuracy. In Kevin O. Grover, editor, *Annual Research Report*,
            pages 9–33, University of Nevada, Las Vegas, 1993. Information Science
            Research Institute.

[RKN94]   Stephen V. Rice, Junichi Kanai, and Thomas A. Nartker. The third
            annual test of OCR accuracy. In Kevin O. Grover, editor, *Annual Research
            Report*, pages 11–38, University of Nevada, Las Vegas, 1994. Information
            Science Research Institute.

[RV94a]   S. Randriamasy and L. Vincent. Benchmarking page segmentation algo-
            rithms. In *Proceedings of the 1994 IEEE Computer Society Conference on
            Computer Vision and Pattern Recognition*, pages 411–416, Seattle, Wash-
            ington, USA, June 21–23 1994. IEEE Computer Society Press.

[RV94b]   Sabine Randriamasy and Luc Vincent. A region-based system for the au-
            tomatic evaluation of page segmentation algorithms. In Andreas Dengel
            and A. Lawrence Spitz, editors, *Proceedings of the International Associ-
            ation for Pattern Recognition Workshop on Document Analysis Systems
            DAS94*, pages 29–41, Kaiserslautern, Germany, October 18–20 1994.

[RVW94]   Sabine Randriamasy, Luc Vincent, and Ben Wittner. An automatic
            benchmarking scheme for page segmentation. In *Proceedings of the
            IS&T/SPIE 1994 International Symposium on Electronic Imaging Sci-
            ence and Technology*, volume 2181, pages 217–230, 1994.

[Sum98]   K. Summers. *Automatic Discovery Of Logical Document Structure*. PhD
            thesis, Cornell University, 1998.

[TMD98]   M. Thulke, V. Märgner, and A. Dengel. A general approach to quality
            evaluation of document segmentation results. In S.-W. Lee and Y. Nakano,
            editors, *Proceedings of the International Association for Pattern Recog-
            nition Workshop on Document Analysis Systems DAS98*, pages 79–88,
            Nagano, Japan, November 1998.

[vR79]   C. J. van Rijsbergen. *Information Retrieval*, chapter 7 Evaluation, pages
            144–183. Butterworths, second edition, 1979.

[WK91]   Sholom M. Weiss and Casimir A. Kulikowski. *Computer Systems That
            Learn*, chapter 2 How to Estimate the True Performance of a Learning
            System, pages 17–49. Morgan Kaufmann Publishers, Inc., 1991.

[YV95]   Berrin A. Yanikoglu and Luc Vincent. Ground-truthing and benchmark-
            ing document page segmentation. In *Proceedings of the Third Interna-
            tional Conference on Document Analysis and Recognition*, volume 2, pages
            601–604, Montréal, Canada, August 14–16 1995. IEEE Computer Society
            Press.

Semi-automatic Ground Truth Generation for Chart Image Recognition

Li Yang, Weihua Huang, and Chew Lim Tan

School of Computing, National University of Singapore,
3 Science Drive 2, Singapore 117543
{yangli, huangwh, tancl}@comp.nus.edu.sg

Abstract. While research on scientific chart recognition is being carried out, there is no suitable standard that can be used to evaluate the overall performance of the chart recognition results. In this paper, a system for semi-automatic chart ground truth generation is introduced. Using the system, the user is able to extract multiple levels of ground truth data. The role of the user is to perform verification and correction and to input values where necessary. The system carries out automatic tasks such as text blocks detection and line detection etc. It can effectively reduce the time to generate ground truth data, comparing to full manual processing. We experimented the system using 115 images. The images and ground truth data generated are available to the public.

1 Introduction

In recent years, a number of research works have been done in the area of chart image recognition. Futrelle et al reported their work on diagram understanding [1] back in 1992. Yokokura et al also reported the work on x-y axes detection in chart images [2]. Zhou et al proposed methods chart type determination based on Hough transformation and learning-based approach [3, 4]. We also reported our own model based approach for chart type determination and understanding [5]. While the research activities are continuously carried out and new results are being reported, there does not exist a suitable standard to evaluate the results. In other words, there is no quantitative measurement of the result reported, and there is no public test set and ground truth data available for comparing the results obtained from different systems. Thus, it is desired to develop a system that can generate ground truth data for evaluating the performance of chart image recognition systems from many aspects.

The system proposed here is semi-automatic, which means the system does most of the job automatically while user interactions are required during the ground truth generation process. Since a typical chart image contains both text and graphics, we generate ground truth data for both kinds of information so that they can be used for evaluating both text recognition and graphics recognition. Furthermore, since the ultimate goal of chart image recognition is to understand the logic role of the chart components and to extract the data values carried by

H. Bunke and A.L. Spitz (Eds.): DAS 2006, LNCS 3872, pp. 324–335, 2006.

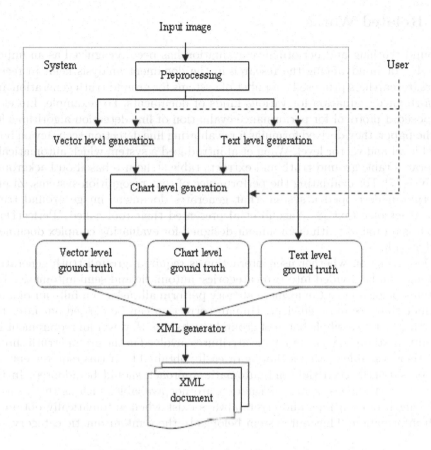

Fig. 1. The proposed ground truth generation system

the chart, we also decided to generate ground truth for chart components and data values.

Figure 1 illustrates the main modules in the proposed system. Pre-processing is performed to the input image first, including text/graphics separation, edge detection, vectorization and text grouping etc. Then ground truth data from text level and vector level are then generated in two different modules. In the next step, data from text level and vector level are combined to generate chart level ground truth. Dashed arrows in the figure indicate that user interactions are required in the modules. In the end, the ground truth data generated for one chart image are stored into an XML document.

The remaining sections of this paper will discuss the details of the proposed system. Section 2 summarizes some related works in ground truth generation. Section 3 introduces the detailed specification of chart ground truth data. Section 4 talks about how the ground truth data are generated. Section 5 presents the results obtained together with some discussion. Section 6 talks about the issue of performance evaluation based on the ground truth data obtained. Section 7 concludes this paper with some future works mentioned.

2   Related Works

Ground truthing and performance evaluation has been recognized as an important factor in advancing the research in the document analysis field. In recent years, researchers proposed a number of systems for ground truth generation and performance evaluation for various kinds of documents. For example, Liu et al proposed a protocol for performance evaluation of line detection algorithms [6]. In the paper, they derived formulas for evaluating line detection accuracy on both pixel level and vector level. Wang et al introduced a system which automatically generates table ground truth and extracts table structure based on background analysis [7]. For evaluating the performance of text recognition systems, Zi and Doermann developed a system that generates document image ground truth from electronic text [8]. Yacoub et al presented their tool called "PerfectDoc" which is a ground truth environment designed for evaluating complex document analysis [9].

Depending on whether user interaction is required, ground truth generation systems can be divided into two categories: automatic and semi-automatic. The systems belonging to the former category perform all tasks in a fully automated manner thus are more efficient. Human correction can be carried out after the system generate a whole batch of ground truth data. However an requirement for the automatic approach is that the attributes involved in the ground truth should be either available at the beginning or easily obtainable. If this requirement can not be satisfied, then the semi-automatic approach should be adopted. In the case of chart images, some information are not available, such as the position and length of each line, and errors always exist when automatically obtaining such information. Thus our system belongs to the semi-automatic category.

3   Ground Truth Data in a Chart Image

As we mentioned previously, the ground truth data generated cover three levels: vector level, text level and chart level. The term "level" is used here to indicate different information granularity of the ground truth data. The order of granularity among various kinds of information in the chart image is:

$$Pixel < vector < text < chart\ component$$

Thus we define four levels of ground truth here. In the following subsections, we will discuss significance, essential attributes and availability of ground truth data at each level.

3.1   Pixel Level Ground Truth

Pixel level ground truth is useful especially for the evaluation of graphics recognition system. It can be used to evaluate the processing capability (Robustness) of image analysis algorithms [6]. The ground truth is basically the original clean image, and the actual image for testing is the degraded image. Since pixel level ground truth comes from clean original image, it may not always be available. For synthetic images, a clean image is available and the pixel values can be used as pixel level ground truth data. However, the images collected from web or scanned in already contain noise and distortions, thus the original pixel values become unknown. As the availability of ground truth for this level is not guaranteed, our system will not include it in the final output, though the image used for ground truth generation is still included.

3.2 Vector Level Ground Truth

Vector level ground truth is the line information in the images, or more precisely the attribute values of the straight line segments and arcs that form the lines. The essential attributes of straight line segments and arcs are the endpoints and the line width. With these attribute values, performance evaluation of vectorization algorithms can be achieved. Details about performance evaluation will be discussed in section 6. For both synthetic and real chart images, vector level ground truth data can be obtained. Although fully automatic extraction of line information is possible using existing vectorization algorithms, human effort is still needed here to manually correct the results to produce the final ground truth. Since higher level symbols (in our case the chart components) are often constructed from lines and arcs, vector level ground truth data not only serve as a standard to evaluate line detection algorithms, but also help to generate higher level ground truth data.

3.3 Text Level Ground Truth

We adopt the traditional representation of text level ground truth data, which consists of text zoning information and the electronic text content. A text zone is indicated by its four boundaries, and it is also an indication of the text location. In our system, each major text group is treated as a whole block and its bounding box is located. There are two reasons for doing so. Firstly, the human effort can be reduced by avoiding specifying the bounding boxes for each individual word. Secondly, it will be easier to assign logical role to a text block. Take the chart title as an example, a typical chart title may contain multiple words and the whole group of words has only one logical role in the chart image. Of course if the text zones are to be used to measure the segmentation capability of OCR systems, then one of the obvious adjustment here is to apply an automatic text segmentation algorithm (such as the x-y cut algorithm) to further locate the bounding box for each word in a text block.

3.4 Chart Level Ground Truth

A chart image has various components and features, but only a subset of them are essential for understanding the chart image. They are summarized in Figure 2. The title of a chart is not always available. If it is available, then it provides contextual information about the chart, together with other textual information in the chart. The axes only exist for some chart types, such as bar chart or line

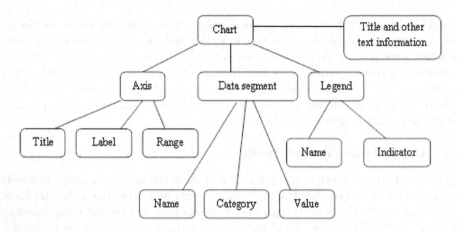

Fig. 2. Essential components in a chart image

chart etc. Besides the position of each axis, axis title, labels along the axis and the axis range are also important for capturing complete axis information. If there are more than one data series presented in the chart, then the legend information is used to distinguish among data series. Legend information includes legend name and legend indicator. Data segments represent data value in different forms for different chart types. For example, there are bars in bar chart, pies in pie chart etc. So in the ground truth data, we not only present the name and value of each data segment, but also specify its form. In case there are more than one data series, the category each data segment belongs to is also recorded.

4   Ground Truth Data Generation

4.1   System Preprocessing

There are several steps in the preprocessing stage:

1. Text/graphics separation. Textual information and graphical information are separated in this step using connected component filtering. A series of thresholds are applied to differentiate text components from graphical components. Most of the text components can be separated from graphics successfully. Characters touching graphics cannot be separated in this case, but the problem can be partially solved later by finding user specified text regions. The text components are binarized and stored in a separate text image, which will be passed as input to text blocks construction step. The graphical components are kept in the original image and will be further analyzed to find the line information.
2. Edge detection. Since all vectorization methods require binary image, edge map is constructed in this step. To effectively identify the edges, the system needs to be given the maximum allowed edge thickness. Edge detection is done by calculating intensity differential among neighboring pixels, followed by gap filling between left edge and right edge.

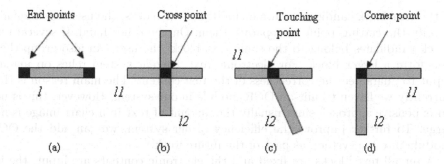

Fig. 3. (a)-(d). Illustration of the set of feature points

3. Text blocks construction. Text block construction is based on the method described in [10] to the text components found previously. The system automatically calculates the text block candidates, after which the user can then refine the result by deciding whether to further split a block or merge some blocks.

4. Vectorization. The purpose of vectorization is to detect line information, or more precisely information of the straight lines and arcs. Here we use the vectorization methods proposed by Liu et al [11, 12] to construct straight lines and arcs respectively. The results are stored in the vector form. The vector of straight line contains starting point, ending point and line width. The content of the vector of arc is similar, except that the arc centre is also stored.

5. Locating Feature points. The feature points include endpoints of straight line segments and arcs, touching points of two lines, cross points and corner points, as illustrated in Figure 3(a) to (d). The point sets are calculated by the system automatically, and will be used as a basis for adjusting the user specified points. If there is more than one feature point near the user selected location, then the nearest feature point will be chosen as the final point.

4.2 Vector Level Ground Truth Generation

As the vectors of straight lines and arcs are already available, the task of the user is to verify the correctness and accuracy of the vectorization result. The vectors are drawn on the original image and the user can manually adjust the endpoints of a vector if it is too long, too short or outside the original line. After the user verify and correct all the vectors, the information stored in the vectors is then saved as the vector level ground truth data. Furthermore, the vector information is also passed on for chart level ground truth generation.

4.3 Text Level Ground Truth Generation

User adjustment can be performed similarly to the text block candidates automatically identified by the system, by refining the boundaries of each candidate.

If the text block candidate contains multiple text blocks, the user can manually specify the cutting point to separate them. On the other hand, if several text block candidates belong to the same text block, the user can also group them and form a larger block. For electronic text, current system relies on manual input to guarantee the correctness of the text content. The main reason is that currently we haven't built an OCR module in our system. However, this is not an expensive approach since usually the amount of text in a chart image is not large. To further improve the efficiency of our system, we can add the OCR module into the system, as part of the future work.

After all text blocks are fixed and the electronic contents are input, the information is saved as text level ground truth. The information will also be used when chart level ground truth is generated.

4.4 Chart Level Ground Truth Generation

As we mentioned, chart level ground truth contains the information of a set of essential chart components. Obtaining such information is not straightforward. The system has to rely on heuristic rules and user interactions to identify the exact position and attributes of the chart components and obtain their values.

To find the graphical chart components, the user just needs to indicate the rough position of the feature points for each component, and then the system will automatically find the precise position by finding the best feature point within a predefined range. If the feature point selected by the system is wrong, the user can still manually adjust the position of the point in four directions.

To find the textual chart components, the user needs to manually specify the correspondence between a text block and its logical role. It is difficult to automate this step, because the text/graphics correspondence is still being studied and no general solution is found yet. data. In this way, the original data values are available for comparison with the extracted data values. For scanned chart

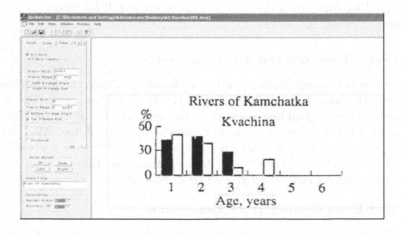

Fig. 4. Snapshot of the system interface

images, the original data values may not be available, thus them need to be calculated based on the information available in the images. There are two cases: if the data values exist in the image in the format of text objects, then the user can help to specify them by input to the system. If the data values are not directly given, then the system will calculate them and the user needs to verify and make correction if there is a large error.

Figure 4 shows a snapshot of the system interface. The input image is placed at the center of the image panel, surrounded by dash boundaries. The tool panels are on the left of the window. The green dots in the input image indicate the feature points used to specify the x-y axis and the bar components. The red dot is the origin of the coordinate system. The snapshot also shows the bounding boxes of all text blocks. The content and logic role of each text block can be specified in the tool panel.

5 Experimental Results and Discussion

5.1 The Data Set

Current data set contains 115 chart images. 75 of them were scanned chart images and the remaining 40 images were downloaded from the internet. The images are either greyscale or color images. The effect of noise results in blurred edge, extra dots and color distortion. More details are shown in Table 1.

5.2 Ground Truth Generated

The proposed system is applied to each image in the data set to generate its ground truth data. Table 2. shows some statistics of the ground truth generated. To generate XML format outputs, a set of tags were defined based on the elements in the ground truth data. The details about XML tag definition can be found in the XML files contained in the ground truth data released on the web, thus they are not discussed here due to limited space in this paper.

5.3 Discussions

Since the original input image is noisy, the lines in the image have distorted edges, which may cause trouble for finding the correct line width. In the vectorization step, the system calculates the width of a line by taking the average width of all

Table 1. The data set

Chart type	Scanned		Downloaded		
	Greyscale	Color	Greyscale	Color	**Total**
Bar chart	61	-	2	12	**75**
Pie chart	-	-	7	18	**25**
Line chart	14	-	-	1	**15**
Total	**75**	**0**	**9**	**31**	**115**

Table 2. Some statistics about the ground truth data generated

Granularity	Elements	Total
Vector level	Straight lines	4377
	Arcs	41
Text level	Text blocks	1587
	Words	2095
Chart level	Chart titles	58
	Axes	180
	Axis labels	1181
	Bars	840
	Pies	116
	Data points (for line chart)	131

small segments in the line. To guarantee the accuracy of the line width detected, the user needs to manually verify it and adjust the line width to a most suitable value if necessary.

There are some special characters in the XML specification that cannot be displayed properly, such as "&" and "<" and ">". Thus to guarantee the completeness of information in the text level ground truth data, we changed these special characters to "and", "less_than" and "greater_than". But then the character set does not match the original set, so we also include a plain text version of the ground truth so that all characters are available, including the special characters.

One of our assumptions is that the lines in the chart components are solid lines. Although in most cases the assumption is valid, there are some exceptions. For example, dash line may be used to connect the data points in a line chart. And sometimes the axes also appear as dash lines. Thus to overcome this weakness, a dash line detection algorithm should be implemented and added to the vectorization process.

On average it took around two to three minutes to process an input image. It may seem a bit slow, comparing to fully automatic processing. But we should consider the necessity of human interaction and correction involved. And the time consumed is definitely much shorter than complete manual processing.

6   Issues on Performance Measure

As the ground truth data become available, we also discuss here how the data can be used to measure the performance of an image recognition system. The system to be evaluated does not need to perform all the tasks and generate all the data to match with the ground truth. It can be a line detection system, a text recognition system or an image understanding system.

At the vector level, we refer to Liu et al's paper about performance evaluation of line detection algorithms [6]. According to Liu, line detection accuracy is indicated by the vector recovery index VRI, which can be obtained by calculating the line detection rate Dv and the false alarm factor Fv:

$$D_v = \frac{\Sigma_{g \in V_g} Q_v(g) \, l(g)}{\Sigma_{k \in V_d} l(g)} \tag{1}$$

where $Q_v(g)$ is total vector detection quality of ground truth vector g and l(g) is the length of the vector, V_g is the set of vectors in the ground truth and V_d is the set of vectors detected.

$$F_v = \frac{\Sigma_{k \in V_d} F_v(k) \, l(k)}{\Sigma_{k \in V_d} l(k)} \tag{2}$$

where $F_v(k)$ is the false alarm factor of the detected line k.

Thus the combined vector recovery index is defined as:

$$VRI = \beta D_v + (1 - \beta)(1 - F_v) \tag{3}$$

where β is the relative importance of detection and 1-β is the relative importance of the false alarm. More details on the term definitions and the formulas can be found in the original paper.

At the chart level, the detection rate of graphical data components can be obtained similarly by calculating the data component recovery index:

$$DRI = \mu D_d + (1 - \mu)(1 - F_d) \tag{4}$$

where μ is the relative importance of detection and 1-μ is the relative importance of the false alarm. And here:

$$D_d = \frac{\Sigma_{k \in C_g} D_d(k) \, S(k)}{\Sigma_{k \in C_g} S(k)} \tag{5}$$

where D_d is the overall detection rate, $D_d(k)$ is the detection rate for ground truth component k and S(k) is the size of ground truth component k, C_g is the set of graphical data components in the ground truth.

$$F_d = \frac{\Sigma_{k \in C_d} F_d(k) \, S(k)}{\Sigma_{k \in C_d} S(k)} \tag{6}$$

where F_d is the overall false alarm rate, $F_d(k)$ is the false alarm rate of the detected component k, C_d is the set of graphical data components detected. $D_d(k)$ and $F_d(k)$ are defined as:

$$D_d(k) = \frac{S(C_d(k) \cap C_g(k))}{S(C_g(k))} \tag{7}$$

$$F_d(k) = 1 - \frac{S(C_d(k) \cap C_g(k))}{S(C_d(k))} \tag{8}$$

where $C_d(k)$ is the detected component and $C_g(k)$ is the ground truth component.

For evaluation of text recognition results, well known IR metrics precision P and recall R are used instead of detection rate and false alarm. Calculation of the precision and recall for character recognition is straightforward:

$$P = \frac{|Ch_g \cap Ch_d|}{|Ch_d|} \tag{9}$$

$$R = \frac{|Ch_g \cap Ch_d|}{|Ch_g|} \tag{10}$$

where Ch_g is the set of characters in the ground truth text and Ch_d is the set of characters recognized. To evaluate the accuracy of text blocks detected, a slight change need to made to equation (9) and (10). Instead of the intersection between two sets, the overlap between two corresponding bounding boxes should be calculated.

The overall performance score S is defined as:

$$S = \Sigma_{i=1}^{n} w_i S_i \tag{11}$$

where Si is the individual score at a single level i, and w_i is the weight assigned to each $S_i(\Sigma w_i = 1)$. Equation (11) is still applicable for systems focusing on only one task, by turn off other performance measures (setting all other weights to zero).

7   Conclusion and Future Work

In this paper, we described our work of ground truth generation from scientific chart images. The system is semi-automatic, which requires user interaction to provide guidance and necessary input to the system and the system automatically does underlying calculation and refinement. The ground truth data can be used to evaluate the performance of document recognition system for various purposes, such as text recognition, graphics recognition and image understanding systems. Currently we have generated ground truth data for 115 images scanned in or downloaded from the internet. The amount will keep increasing as we conduct more and more testing in the future. The generated ground truth data is publicly available, through URL:

http://www.comp.nus.edu.sg/~huangwh/ChartRecognition/GroundTruth/

At the moment, OCR is not integrated into the system, so the content of each text box requires manual input. In the future, an OCR module can be included and then text can be automatically recognized. Then only manual correction is needed, which further minimize the human effort. Another improvement to be made is to include a text segmentation algorithm to automatically divide the text block into small boxes for each individual word.

References

1. R. P. Futrelle, I. A. Kakadiaris, J. Alexander, C. M. Carriero, N. Nikolakis, J. M. Futrelle: Understanding diagrams in technical documents, IEEE Computer, Vol.25, pp75-78, 1992.
2. N. Yokokura and T. Watanabe: Layout-Based Approach for extracting constructive elements of bar-charts, Graphics recognition: algorithms and systems, GREC'97, pp163-174.
3. Y. P. Zhou and C. L. Tan: Hough technique for bar charts detection and recognition in document images, International Conference on Image Processing, ICIP 2000, page 494-497, 2000.
4. Y. P. Zhou and C. L. Tan: Learning-based scientific chart recognition, 4th IAPR International Workshop on Graphics Recognition, GREC2001, page 482-492, 2001.
5. W. H. Huang, C. L. Tan and W. K. Leow: Model based chart image recognition, International Workshop on Graphics Recognition, GREC2003, 30-31 July 2003, Barcelona, Spain.
6. W. Liu, D. Dori: A protocol for performance evaluation of line detection algorithms, Machine Vision and Applications, 1997, vol. 9, pg. 240-250.
7. Y. Wang, R. M. Haralick, I. T. Phillips: Automatic Table Ground Truth Generation and a Background Analysis Based Table Structure Extraction Method ICDAR 2001: 528-532
8. G. Zi, D. Doermann: Document Image Ground Truth Generation from Electronic Text, 17th International Conference on Pattern Recognition, ICPR'04, vol. 2, pp. 663-666.
9. S. Yacoub, V. Saxena and S. Sami: PerfectDoc: A Ground Truthing Environment for Complex Documents, 8th International Conference on Document Analysis and Recognition, ICDAR'05, vol. 1, pg. 452-456.
10. B. Yuan and C. L. Tan: A Multi-level Component Grouping Algorithm and Its Applications, 8th International Conference on Document Analysis and Recognition, ICDAR'05, pg. 1178-1181.
11. W. Liu and D. Dori: Sparse Pixel Vectorization: An Algorithm and Its Performance Evaluation", IEEE Transactions on Pattern Analysis and Machine Intelligence, 1999, vol. 21, pg. 202-215.
12. D. Dori and W. Liu: Incremental Arc Segmentation Algorithm and Its Evaluation, IEEE Transactions on Pattern Analysis and Machine Intelligence, 1998, vol. 20, pg. 424-431.

Efficient Word Retrieval by Means of SOM Clustering and PCA

Simone Marinai, Stefano Faini, Emanuele Marino, and Giovanni Soda

Dipartimento di Sistemi e Informatica - Università di Firenze,
Via S.Marta, 3 - 50139 Firenze - Italy
`marinai@dsi.unifi.it`

Abstract. We propose an approach for efficient word retrieval from printed documents belonging to Digital Libraries. The approach combines word image clustering (based on Self Organizing Maps, SOM) with Principal Component Analysis. The combination of these methods allows us to efficiently retrieve the matching words from large documents collections without the need for a direct comparison of the query word with each indexed word.

1 Introduction

Nowadays, Digital Libraries and archives store large collections of documents in image format. For instance, the *Gallica* Web site maintained by the National Library of France holds more than 70,000 works (mainly books) stored as images, however text-accessible works are limited to a few thousands. For the works stored as images it is frequently possible to access the contents by browsing the table of contents, but it is more complex to perform word searches in the free text. As mentioned in [1] the use of Document Image Retrieval (DIR) techniques is essential to build successful Digital Libraries. Document Image Retrieval aims at finding relevant documents from a corpus of digitized pages relying on image features only. Important sub-tasks include the retrieval of documents on the basis of layout similarity and on the basis of the textual content [2, 3].

In this paper we focus on one specific sub-topic of text-based DIR: word retrieval, that addresses the efficient identification of the occurrences of a given word in the indexed documents. Word retrieval is tightly related to "keyword spotting" where the interest is to locate user defined words from an information flow (e.g. audio streams or sequences of digitized pages) [4–6]. In word indexing the emphasis is not only on the recognition, but also on the efficient indexing and retrieval of words. Several methods have been recently proposed for the effective retrieval of text from both printed and handwritten documents (e.g. [7–9]). Regardless of the word representation and matching strategy adopted all these methods are designed to work with a relatively small collection of documents and the scalability to larger data-sets is an issue. The efficient retrieval of words from large document repositories is the topic of the work described in this paper. Each word is represented by one simple feature vector that is based on word image zoning. The zoning is a particular kind of word representation used for holistic word recognition that consists of overlapping the word image with a fixed-size grid and

H. Bunke and A.L. Spitz (Eds.): DAS 2006, LNCS 3872, pp. 336–347, 2006.

computing some features (e.g. the density of black pixels) in each grid region. Even if more appropriate representations have been proposed, the zoning works reasonably well for printed text with uniform font and allows us to cast the word retrieval as a problem of search in high dimensional vector spaces. As a matter of fact the method described in this paper can work with every word representation that encodes the word into a high dimensional feature vector. Efficient search in high dimensional vector spaces is still the subject of active research. When dealing with low dimensional spaces, then the R-tree [10] (and its variants) can be adopted to reduce the search cost from the linear one. Some methods (e.g. X-Tree [11] or cluster tree [12]) have been proposed to search in high dimensional spaces, however these methods degenerate to the linear complexity when dealing with spaces having more than a few dozens of dimensions.

In this paper we address the word indexing by exploring the effectiveness of a SOM-based word image clustering where the words are grouped considering the image similarity. The idea of using this clustering technique is extended from a previous work that exploited the SOM for character-like object clustering [8]. To reduce the search complexity we project the data in each cluster with Principal Component Analysis (PCA) and then perform an efficient search in the projected space with an appropriate search algorithm (e.g. the X-tree). In the final retrieval step we refine the sorting of the top ranked words by computing the similarity in the original space.

The paper is organized as follows: in Section 2 we describe the use of SOM for word image clustering. In Sections 3 and 4 we analyze the word indexing and retrieval, respectively. Experimental results are reported in Section 5 and some conclusions are drawn in Section 6.

2 Self Organizing Maps of Word Images

The Self Organizing Map (SOM [13]) is a special kind of artificial neural network that is based on competitive learning, where the output neurons of the network compete among themselves. The purpose of SOM training is the computation of an optimal clustering of a collection of patterns in $\Re^n$ (representing words in our case). In the Self Organizing Map the neurons are typically arranged in a two dimensional lattice: the feature map. Each neuron receives inputs from the input layer (vectors in $\Re^n$) and from the other neurons in the map. During the learning the network performs clustering and the neurons are moved in the lattice so as to reflect cluster similarity by means of distances in the map. To each element in the SOM map it is associated one real vector (in $\Re^n$) that can be considered as a prototype of the patterns in the cluster.

One advantage of the use of SOM for word clustering, with respect to other clustering algorithms like k-means, is the spatial organization of the feature map that is achieved after the learning process. Basically, more similar clusters are closer than more different ones. Consequently, the distance among prototypes in the output layer of the SOM can be considered as a measure of similarity between words in the clusters.

In our model the SOM is used to build a word image database where the clusters contain similar words (from a graphical point of view). For the SOM training we modified the SOM_PAK package[1] that implements the standard incremental learning algorithm

---

[1] The package can be found at: http://www.cis.hut.fi/research/som_lvq_pak

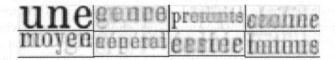

Fig. 1. Eight prototypes obtained from a SOM map trained with the standard training algorithm. Apart from very common words (e.g. "une") the prototypes do not correspond to actual words.

mines facile
raides mètre
huiles heure
lames loutre
toutes bulles
lames fontes

Fig. 2. Some prototypes obtained from one map trained with the modified training algorithm (prototypes correspond to actual words)

([13] page 109). In this algorithm, after each training step the prototype of each neuron is "moved" in the $\Re^n$ space so as to better represent the words belonging to its cluster and to its neighborhoods. This is obtained by replacing the prototype with the arithmetic mean of the patterns belonging to the clusters in the neighborhood.

To evaluate the suitability of the incremental learning algorithm we made some preliminary tests analyzing some maps computed with this algorithm. After sorting the words in each cluster on the basis of their distance from the cluster prototype, we noticed that several occurrences of a given word were spread in the rank. The reason is that different words are put approximately at the same distance with respect to the query, even if their mutual distance is high. This effect is due to the position of the prototypes that usually does not correspond to "actual words" unless the corresponding words are very homogeneous as in the case of stopwords (e.g. see the word 'une' in Figure 1).

To solve the above mentioned problem we modified the incremental learning algorithm. Basically, we update each prototype with the closest training vector among all the patterns in the neighborhood (instead of computing the arithmetic mean). This prototype update is made after each training epoch [2] and also at the end of the training process. From an algorithmic point of view we first scan the training set and associate each input pattern to the closest prototype. Subsequently, we replace the prototype with the closest associated pattern.

This solution provides good results since the final map is uniform and the prototypes usually represent the most frequent words in the dataset. The prototypes shown in Figure 2 are obtained with the modified training algorithm. To suggest the general structure of one trained SOM we show in Figure 3 the contents of two neurons. We can remark that in general the farthest words are loosely related with those closer to the prototype.

---

[2] The epoch is a cycle of presentation of all the patterns to the network.

Fig. 3. Examples of the contents of two neurons. For each neuron we show the words closests to the prototype (on the left) and the farthest words (on the right).

3 Word Indexing

The word indexing is composed by several steps that are sketched in Figure 4 and described in this section.

During the indexing the pages are analyzed by means of one layout analysis tool that identifies the text regions and extracts the words by means of an RLSA-based algorithm. The indexed words are then split into six disjoint index partitions on the basis of their aspect-ratio (the ratio between the word height and width). In doing so the words in each partition have a similar aspect-ratio and the clustering is performed on uniform data.

For each indexed word its aspect-ratio is computed and considered to find the right partition. Next, the word image is linearly scaled to appropriate dimensions, obtaining a vectorial representation whose items contain the average gray level of the pixels belonging to the corresponding grid cell. The main problem of this approach is the high dimensionality of the feature vector (hundreds of dimensions) that is reflected into a long training time for the SOM. However, it should be remarked that this size is a problem only for the training performed during the indexing, but it is not important for the word retrieval.

To reduce the cost of the search in each cluster we also compute, during the indexing, the projection that best represents the data with PCA. The following procedure is repeated for each SOM cluster in order to compute a low dimensional hyperplane by means of Principal Component Analysis (e.g.[14], pag 568). We first compute the mean vector μ and the $n \times n$ covariance matrix Σ of the data in the cluster. The eigenvectors and eigenvalues of Σ are computed and the eigenvectors are sorted according to decreasing eigenvalue. The first h eigenvectors $(e_1, e_2, \ldots, e_h)$ are combined as columns of the $n \times h$ matrix A. It is now possible to project the data in the cluster (for instance one point x) onto the h-th dimensional subspace according to

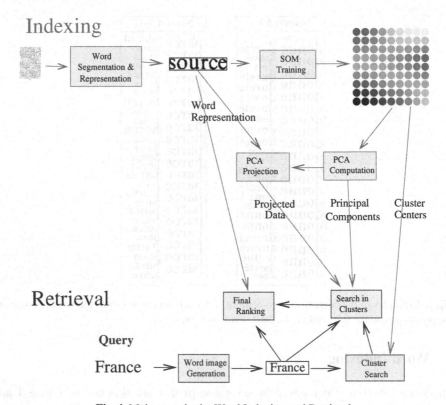

Fig. 4. Main steps in the Word Indexing and Retrieval

$$x' = A^t(x - \mu) \tag{1}$$

Summarizing, the word indexing is composed by the following steps: 1) word segmentation 2) SOM training and PCA computation from a sub-set of the words to be indexed 3) projection of all the indexed words in the lower dimensional space.

4   Word Retrieval

Without taking into account efficiency issues one simple approach for word retrieval would rely on the linear comparison of each indexed word with the query word image. Unfortunately, this approach is not feasible when large word databases are considered. The proposed method takes into account the main features of SOM clustering and PCA to efficiently address the word retrieval problem. Let us describe the four main steps of the word retrieval algorithm.

1. **The Query**
   From the user point of view the queries are made with a simple text-based interface. Starting from the ASCII text one word image is obtained with LATEX by using the *Times* font. This word image is then encoded similarly to the indexed

words: we identify the partitions to be considered, and we scale the image according to the average dimensions of each partition thus obtaining a vectorial word representation.

2. **Cluster Search**

   In the second step we identify the three clusters having prototypes closer to the query in order to restrict the subsequent search. Since we compare the indexed words with one LATEX generated query (and due to the presence of noise in indexed words) it is not usual that all the most similar words are contained in the closest cluster. To tackle this problem we consider the three closest clusters (the number of clusters to retain has been obtained after some preliminary tests). In so doing we reduce on the average the number of patterns to be processed by the subsequent step by a factor 500 (for a map having size of 50 x 30).

   To illustrate the need for the multiple cluster searches we show in Figure 5 the first 31 words in the three clusters closest to the image generated for the query *alcool*. In this case the first cluster contains only a few instances of the word *alcool*, the second cluster does not contain any occurrence of the word, whereas the last one is the most populated.

chimi	chaud	alcool
chimi	chaud	chinoi
chimi	chand	cédent
alcool	chaud	aident
chimi	chaud	cédant
chimi	chaud	cédent
chimi	chaud	alcool
cédent	chaud	alcool
châssi	chand	alcool
aillent	chaud	alcool
cérami	chaud	alcool
chimi	chaud	alcool
alcool	chaud	alcool
alcool	chaud	alcool
nissent	chaud	sistent
cédant	chaud	alcool
chimi	chaud	alcool
alcool	chaud	alcool
chimi	chaud	alcool
alcool	chaud	alcool
chimi	chaud	alcool
chimi	chaud	alcool
alcool	chaud	alcool
cédant	chaud	alcool
alcool	chaud	alcool
chlori	chaud	cédant
nissent	chaud	chloré
abord	chaud	cédent
abord	chaud	alcool
nissent	chaud	alcool
sédant	chaud	alcool

Fig. 5. Left to right: the first words in the three clusters closest to the prototype generated for the query *alcool*

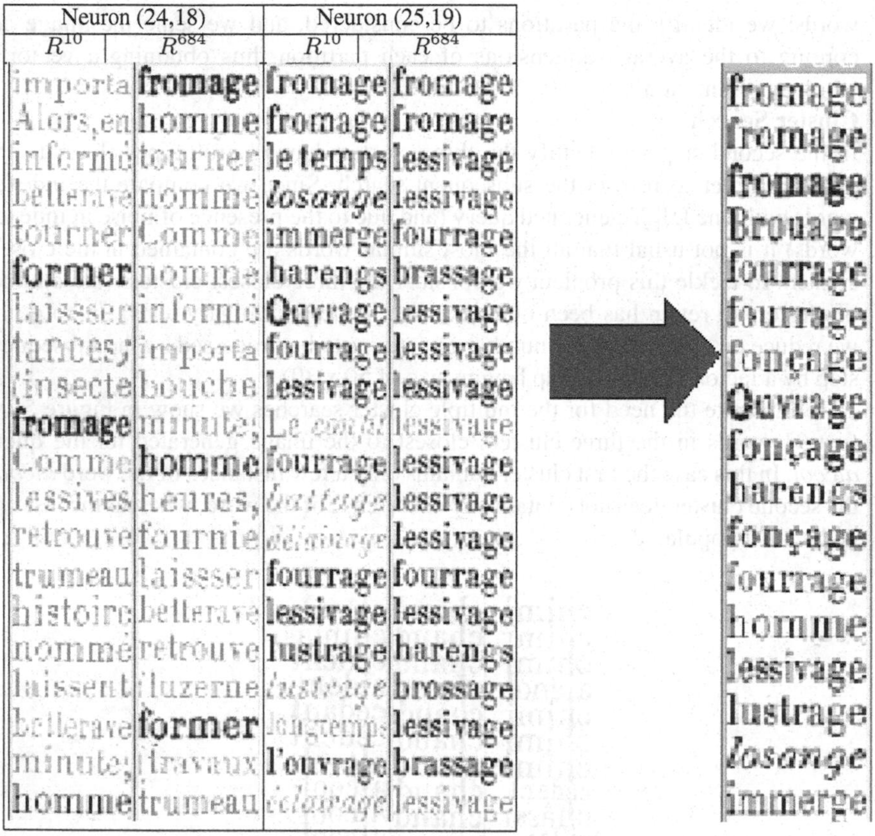

Neuron (24,18)		Neuron (25,19)	
R^{10}	R^{684}	R^{10}	R^{684}
importa	**fromage**	fromage	fromage
Alors, en	homme	fromage	fromage
informé	tourner	le temps	lessivage
betterave	nommé	*losange*	lessivage
tourner	Comme	immerge	fourrage
former	nommé	harengs	brassage
laisser	informé	**Ouvrage**	lessivage
lances,	importa	fourrage	lessivage
(insecte	bouche	lessivage	lessivage
fromage	minute,	Le conf..	lessivage
Comme	**homme**	fourrage	lessivage
lessives	heures,	*battage*	lessivage
retrouve	fournie	*déminage*	lessivage
trumeau	laisser	fourrage	fourrage
histoire	betterave	lessivage	lessivage
nommé	retrouve	lustrage	harengs
laissent	luzerne	*lustrage*	brossage
betterave	**former**	longtemps	lessivage
minute,	travaux	l'ouvrage	brassage
homme	trumeau	éclairage	lessivage

fromage
fromage
fromage
Brouage
fourrage
fourrage
fonçage
Ouvrage
fonçage
harengs
fonçage
fourrage
homme
lessivage
lustrage
losange
immerge

Fig. 6. Ranking of the 20 words closest to the query *fromage*. We show two clusters and the rankings in the original space (R^{684}) and in the projected one (R^{10}). On the right we report the final ranking obtained by merging three lists (one list is not shown on the left).

3. **Search in Clusters** After identifying the three closest clusters we identify the most similar words by means of PCA. During the search in the three clusters we look for the k nearest neighborhoods in the projected spaces. In the left part of Figure 6 we compare the rankings obtained in the projected space and in the original one for the words belonging to two clusters when looking for the word *fromage*. The cluster (24,18) contains one occurrence of the word which is in the first position in the $\Re^{684}$ space, but is in the 10th position in $\Re^{10}$. Two correct words in the other cluster are in the first positions in both spaces. From this example it is clear that the PCA projection approximates the proximity in the n dimensional space thus requiring a refinement in the next step.

4. **Final Ranking**
   The previous step allows us to identify the most similar words in the projected spaces of the three closest clusters. To merge the three lists of top-ranked words and refine the final ranking we compute the distance in the original space between the query word and the words in the three lists. It is worth to remark that the computa-

tion in the original space is performed for a small number of words and therefore it is not problematic from the computational point of view. In the right part of Figure 6 we summarize the final ranking obtained by merging the three lists for the query *fromage* (to simplify the figure only two lists are shown in the left part of the figure).

4.1 Complexity Analysis

To analyze the complexity of the system we compare the computational cost with the costs of two simpler approaches. For each method we consider the search for the words in a given index partition (identified by the query word aspect-ratio) that are more similar to the query word. Both the indexed words and the query one are represented by vectors in $\Re^n$ where n depends on the partition; usually the vector contains hundreds of items (e.g. $n = 684$ for partition number 4). For each method we consider the complexity required for computing the distances, but we do not take into account the computation required to sort the words on the basis of the above mentioned distances (this cost is constant for the three methods).

- **Sequential scan**
  The simplest approach is based on the sequential comparison of each indexed word with the query by considering the original feature vector. Let P be the number of words belonging to the partition, the complexity of retrieval for this approach is therefore:

$$C_r = O(n \cdot P) \tag{2}$$

that is obtained by comparing P vectors with n dimensions.

- **Use of SOM clustering**
  In the second approach we use the method proposed in this paper without the use of the PCA projection. In this case during the indexing it is required to compute the SOM clustering by considering a sub-set of the words to be indexed. Once the optimal SOM is computed we need to identify, for each word to be indexed, the cluster it belongs to. We therefore have an indexing cost:

$$C_i = SOM_t(P') + O(n \cdot P \cdot S), \tag{3}$$

where $SOM_t(P')$ denotes the cost of training the SOM map with the set of words P' (usually $P' \subset P$), and S is the size of the map (in the current experiments the size is 50x30).

Concerning the retrieval cost we should consider two factors: the cost for selecting the appropriate cluster and the cost for computing the distance of the query from all the items in the selected clusters. Let J be the average number of words in each cluster (on the average we have $J = \frac{P}{S}$). The maximum complexity obtained when evaluating three clusters is:

$$C_r = O(S \cdot n + 3 \cdot n \cdot J) \tag{4}$$

- **SOM and PCA**
  The last approach that we consider is the overall method described in this paper including the PCA projection. Let k ($k \ll n$) be the size of the lower dimensional space (in our experiments $k = 10$). In this case the indexing cost is:

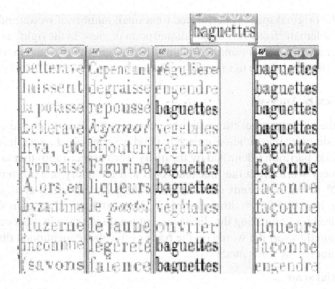

Fig. 7. Screenshot of the word retrieval with the query *baguettes*. On the top we report the LATEX prototype, on the left the rankings in the three selected clusters and the final ranking is shown on the right.

$$C_i = SOM_t(P') + PCA_t(P') + O(k \cdot n \cdot P \cdot S), \tag{5}$$

where $PCA_t(P')$ denotes the cost for computing the PCA eigenvalues and eigenvectors.

The retrieval cost is composed by three parts: the search for the best clusters, the search in the clusters by considering the $\Re^k$ vectors and the final refinement of the rank:

$$C_r = O(S \cdot n + 3 \cdot k \cdot J + 60 \cdot n) \tag{6}$$

Figure 7 reports one additional example of the results achieved with the whole word retrieval approach.

5 Experiments

The experiments described in this paper are made on two books (containing 1280 pages) that are part of an encyclopedia of the XIXth Century [3]. To evaluate the word retrieval we built a pseudo ground-truth by running one commercial OCR engine on the two books. The OCR engine has high recognition performance on this data-set and can be considered as a reasonable approximation of a human validated ground-truth.

The words to be used as queries have been selected from each partition with a particular emphasis on longer words. Basically, we had two types of query words: rare

---

[3] *Les Merveilles De l'Industrie*: downloaded from the web site of the *National Library of France* (http://gallica.bnf.fr).

Table 1. Performance of word retrieval for some frequent (left) and rare (right) words. Frequent words have more than 20 occurrences in the data-set.

Word	Rec	Cor
provient	17	15
femme	19	19
raison	17	9
porter	19	17
terrain	17	17
baguettes	13	11
Bontemps	13	13
Egypte	13	8
chaud	15	1
outil	15	0
vive	11	10
vent	11	1
large	4	4
moulage	18	16
graines	13	8
lignes	11	3
abondance	14	14
demande	11	8
enfants	16	15
incolore	19	15
bambou	10	10
explication	10	10
proportion	17	17
bronze	16	15
Deux	19	15

Word	Rec	Cor	OCR
Savon	10	6	14
intime	11	9	12
drainage	8	8	12
tournesol	1	1	11
grillage	7	7	10
assemblage	7	6	10
horizon	4	3	10
Marie	2	0	10
lande	5	5	8
herbes	4	0	8
Elton	5	4	7
abattre	2	2	6
condiment	2	0	6
japonaise	0	0	6
fromage	3	3	5
mandarin	0	0	5
dosages	4	4	4
barbare, chirurgie	1	1	4
Danemark, kilos	1	1	3
Suger	2	2	2
fumage, vasion	1	1	2
Lorenzo, idiot	1	1	2
Buch	2	0	2
lagunes, Elliot	1	1	1
geoises, argentier	0	0	1

Table 2. Comparison of the performance of the word retrieval with the sequential scan. The meaning of *Rec* and *Top* is the same of Table 1.

Query	Proposed method *Rec/Top*	Sequential scan *Rec/Top*
Canada	>20 / 20	14 / 8
graines	13 / 8	20 / 18
alcool	>20 / 20	>20 / 20
baguettes	13 / 11	9 / 3
Savon	10 / 6	9 / 2
raison	17 / 9	15 / 8

words (a few occurrences among the 1280 pages) and frequent words (occurring hundreds of times in the data-set). Table 1 summarizes the results obtained for some of the test words. For each query we analyzed the list of the 20 top-ranked words and computed two values: *Rec* is the number of correct words found in the list; *Top* denotes the number of subsequent correct words reported at the top of the list. *OCR* denotes the number of words found by the OCR engine. We considered also the following words: *Canada, alcool, peaux, violet, France, Louis, nombre, cylindre, verre, chaque, lorsqu, aniline, volume, soluble, lessive, culture, sulfure, production*. For the latter list of words all the first 20 answers were correct ones.

5.1 Comparison with the Sequential Scan

As discussed in Section 4.1 the proposed approach has a better behaviour with respect to the naive sequential comparison in terms of computational complexity. However, the reduced complexity is useless if we obtain a worst effectiveness. In other terms, the risk is that by using the PCA we loose too much information and some relevant words are not identified by the third step of the retrieval (and therefore cannot be considered in the final ranking). To analyze this aspect we made some preliminary tests comparing the number of correctly retrieved words for the sequential scan and for the proposed approach (see Table 2). We considered six words: in one case (word $alcool$) the two methods provide the same result, whereas in one case (word $graines$) the sequential scan provides better results. However, for the remaining four words the proposed method is not only more efficient, but also more effective, retrieving more correct words.

6   Conclusions

We described a general system for performing word image retrieval by means of a SOM-based word image clustering combined with PCA. The proposed approach addresses the efficiency issues related to the proximity search of large quantities of high dimensional vectors. From the preliminary tests reported in this paper we conclude that the efficiency gain is not obtained at the cost of a reduced retrieval effectiveness.

One restriction of SOM clustering is the need to compute a new set of clusters when dealing with different documents. However, the adaptation to different languages and fonts of the clustering is automatic and does not require additional interaction with the user. Some aspects will require additional investigations, namely the introduction of more appropriate word image distances as well as the use of efficient algorithms to search in the projected spaces (e.g. the X-tree algorithm).

References

1. H. S. Baird, "Digital libraries and document image analysis," in *Proc. 7th ICDAR*, pp. 2–14, 2003.
2. D. Doermann, "The indexing and retrieval of document images: A survey," *Computer Vision and Image Understanding*, vol. 70, pp. 287–298, June 1998.
3. M. Mitra and B. Chaudhuri, "Information retrieval from documents: A survey," *Information Retrieval*, vol. 2, no. 2/3, pp. 141–163, 2000.
4. J. D. Curtis and E. Chen, "Keyword spotting via word shape recognition," in *Proceedings of the SPIE - Document Recognition II*, pp. 270–277, 1995.
5. J. Trenkle and R. Vogt, "Word recognition for information retrieval in the image domain," in *SDAIR*, pp. 105–122, 1993.

6. W. Williams, E. Zalubas, and A. Hero, "Word spotting in bitmapped fax documents," *Information Retrieval*, vol. 2, no. 2/3, pp. 207–226, 2000.
7. K. Kise, M. Tsujino, and K. Matsumoto, "Spotting where to read on pages - retrieval of relevant parts from page images," in *Document Analysis Systems V*, pp. 388–399, Springer Verlag- LNCS 2423, 2002.
8. S. Marinai, E. Marino, and G. Soda, "Indexing and retrieval of words in old docunents," in *Proc. 7th ICDAR*, pp. 223–227, 2003.
9. C. L. Tan, W. Huang, Z. Yu, and Y. Xu, "Imaged document text retrieval without OCR," *IEEE Transactions on PAMI*, vol. 24, pp. 838–844, June 2002.
10. A. Guttman, "R-tree: a dynamic index structure for spatial searching," in *Proc. ACM SIGMOD*, pp. 47–57, 1984.
11. S. Berchtold, D. A. Keim, and H.-P. Kriegel, "The X-tree: an index structure for high-dimensional data," in *Proc. 22nd VLDB*, pp. 28–39, 1996.
12. D. Yu and A. Zhang, "Clustertree: integration of cluster representation and nearest-neighbor search for large data sets with high dimensions," *IEEE Transactions on Knowledge and Data Discovery*, vol. 15, no. 5, pp. 1316–1337, 2003.
13. T. Kohonen, *Self-organizing maps*. Springer Series in Information Sciences, 2001.
14. R. O. Duda, P. Hart, and D. G. Stork, *Pattern Classification*. John Wiley & sons, 2001.

The Effects of OCR Error on the Extraction of Private Information

Kazem Taghva, Russell Beckley, and Jeffrey Coombs

Information Science Research Institute,
University of Nevada, Las Vegas
taghva@isri.unlv.edu

Abstract. OCR error has been shown not to affect the average accuracy of text retrieval or text categorization. Recent studies however have indicated that information extraction is significantly degraded by OCR error. We experimented with information extraction software on two collections, one with OCR-ed documents and another with manually-corrected versions of the former. We discovered a significant reduction in accuracy on the OCR text versus the corrected text. The majority of errors were attributable to zoning problems rather than OCR classification errors.

1 Introduction

Studies have shown that OCR error does not significantly degrade the average effectiveness of information retrieval or text categorization. Recent work suggests that the opposite is the case for information extraction.

In this paper, we offer more evidence for significant degradation in information extraction effectiveness on OCR text. In particular, we examine the performance of two information extractors on corrected and OCR text. We found significant degradation in performance for both extractors on noisy text. Unlike earlier studies, we found that the main source of the degradation was zoning errors in texts containing tabular information rather than classification errors.

In section 2 we describe the problems we attempted to solve using information extraction. Section 3 presents some background concerning experiments on text retrieval and text categorization on OCR text as well as previous experiments applying information extraction to OCR text. We describe our extractors in section 4 and our experiments in section 5. Section 6 reports the effectiveness of using a name-finding module in our extractors. Section 7 presents the results of our experiments. In section 8 we classify and quantify the types of OCR errors affecting the extractors.

2 Problem Description

In order to comply with the Freedom of Information Act (FOIA), documents in a U.S. government online repository must not contain private information such as a person's date of birth or an employee's identification number [1].

H. Bunke and A.L. Spitz (Eds.): DAS 2006, LNCS 3872, pp. 348–357, 2006.

There are two ways to approach the identification and removal of such information. First, one can view this as a *text categorization* task. That is, one attempts to separate documents (or pages) into two categories, those likely to contain private information and those that do not. When the Information Science Research Institute (ISRI) originally began studying this problem, we took the text categorization approach.

One obvious difficulty with this type of solution is what one does with the document or page categorized as containing private information. The document or page as a whole could be removed from the online collection, but then any information therein which is not private is kept from public view. Such a result violates the spirit of the FOIA which strives to make federal agency records publicly accessible insofar as that information is not otherwise protected by law.

Alternately, the private information could be targeted more narrowly and only those items within a document or page that are private would be located and removed. For example, one could automatically *redact* information considered private by replacing likely private strings with the familiar black rectangles. The task of finding such strings of interest is usually called *information extraction*.

Information extraction (IE) is the automatic discovery of information classes in unstructured text. For our tasks, we wish to identify strings in the classes of birth dates and employee identification numbers. This definition of IE is essentially equivalent to the idea that it is the discovery of structured data in unstructured text since the placement of found items into classes such as "birth date" provide the structure [3, 8]. The information discovered likely will be suitable for storage in a relational database, but this is not a necessary feature of IE.

3   Background

Categorization and extraction work at different levels. The categorization task requires in this case a binary decision of labeling a given document as containing privacy or not. On the other hand, the information extraction task consists of identifying all and only the *instances* of privacy information in a given document.

The differences between the two approaches raise an important question for the processing of OCR texts. ISRI has extensively studied the effectiveness of *text retrieval* on OCR versus clean text [15]. Our testing revealed that average precision and recall are not affected by OCR errors. A similar result was found for *text categorization*. Analyzing the application of the BOW [5] text categorizer on OCR text, ISRI determined that the accuracy of text categorization was not significantly affected by the presence of OCR errors, especially if typical dimensionality reduction techniques are applied [17, 16].

In recent studies it has become apparent that the *information extraction* task differs from text retrieval and categorization in that performance is affected for the worse by OCR errors. Miller et al. [7] noted degradation in the accuracy of their Hidden Markov Model (HMM) information extraction system IdentiFinder. They printed copies of Wall Street Journal articles and then ran experiments on progressively degraded images of these with progressively higher word error rates. The system suffered a 0.6 point loss in F1-measure for each percentage point increase in word error. We had similar difficulties applying an address extracting HMM to noisy texts [14].

Jing et al. [4] address the related problem of summarizing documents containing OCR error. They report degradation in performance at every step in the summarizing process. Errors resulted from sentence tokenizers failing to correctly identify sentence boundaries. Syntactic parsers failed to create correct parse trees for the resulting sentence tokens. Sentence reduction operations failed to remove redundant information and correctly combine sentences sharing co-references.

In this paper we offer more support for the conclusion that OCR error degrade the accuracy of IE systems. Specifically we look at two extraction tasks and test the performance of two extraction programs on both OCR and corrected text versions of the data. Both programs show significant degradation when run on OCR text as opposed to corrected text. However, word error caused by classification errors was not the main source of degradation for our systems. Unlike the collection of newspaper articles from a single source tested by Miller et al, our collection of government documents is less homogeneous. Our collection contains documents and forms which display private information in tables. Such data, after passing through zoning algorithms in the OCR system, were sometimes transformed in ways which created difficulties for IE systems like ours which use proximity information to identify items.

4   System Description

ISRI constructed two information extractors for identifying two types of private information. We were looking for (1) birthdates and (2) employee identification numbers appearing in documents collected by the Department of Energy (DOE).

The extractors used in these tasks look for relations among features in the documents. To detect a particular type of private information, it is useful to identify other types of entities which often appear near that particular type. In some cases, to be considered private information, there must be a relationship between data of different types. For example, a date in isolation is not private information. Nor does it become private if it is identified as a birthdate with an identifier such as *date of birth*. A date becomes private information only when it is correctly associated with a person. The statement *John Dough's date of birth is 5/17/55* is private, but the phrase *someone's birthdate is 5/17/55* is not, unless a referent for *someone* is implied contextually.

In some cases, isolated items such as social security numbers are private. However, relational information still proves useful for their identification because the format of a string alone does not guarantee that it is a social security number. Human beings, like machines, cannot identify a social security number in text unless the context provides some evidence. This is fortunate for machines because it ideally requires human authors to provide clues for the identification of items in the context which can in turn be used by a machine.

A set of textual features, such as patterns identifiable be regular expressions, is defined for each extractor. Often a subset of these features serves as an *anchor set*. Occurrences of anchor features are found first, and a context or "window" is defined surrounding them. This context is then searched for other features. All such features provide evidence for the identification (or lack thereof) of the target information type.

The nature of the anchor set differs for the two extraction tasks. The birthdate extractor anchors are keywords and phrases such as *birthdate* and *date of birth*. In the employee identification number extractor, the anchors are patterns for identification numbers.

We describe each extractor in more detail in sections 4.1 and 4.2 respectively.

4.1 Birthdate Extractor

The date of birth extractor functions as follows. First, it tries to find an anchor pattern, which in this case is a key word pattern such as *born, birth date, date of birth*, etc. When an anchor pattern is identified, the program searches a window of pre-defined size for strings that match a set of date patterns. If found, the date is output.

Although a birthdate without a name is not considered to be private information, searching for a name is deemed impractical. For one thing, although we require the person's name to be in the context, we do not actually need to identify that name. Furthermore, experiments (reported elsewhere [11]) have suggested that name-finding algorithms do not improve accuracy for this task. Also, the co-occurrence of birthdate phrases with dates is nearly always associated with a name in the text, i.e. the presence of other features allow us to assume with acceptable accuracy the presence of a name.

4.2 Employee Identification Number Extractor

The employee identification number extractor uses Bayesian probability to combine the evidence provided by multiple textual features. In practice this amounts to a summation of points associated with features found in a context, with each occurrence weighted according to its position.

For each feature f we train two values using positive and negative samples respectively: a) the frequency of f's occurrences in contexts of employee numbers ($frequency(f|eid)$), and b) the frequency of f's occurrences outside any such context ($frequency(f|\overline{eid})$). The value of $frequency$ is defined as

$$frequency = \frac{|occurrences|}{|bytes\ of\ text\ sampled|} \qquad (1)$$

The *anchor set* of features consists of patterns matching employee identification numbers, e.g. "11987". Non-anchor features include the words *employee*, *identification*, and *number* and their many abbreviations. Also included are the names of various employers. Furthermore, when certain features are found consecutively, e.g. *employee identification*, the juxtaposition is regarded as an additional feature, contributing further evidence and more points.

The set of features is next partitioned into subsets, or "groups", such that if x,y are in the group and x contributes evidence, y does not contribute evidence. For example, if *employee* and *emp* occur in a candidate context, only the occurrence with the highest score will count.

The algorithm first seeks an occurrence of an anchor feature, f_a, then establishes a context around f_a. The variable *test_sum* is set as follows:

$$test\_sum = \log\left(\frac{frequency(f_a|eid)}{frequency(f_a|\overline{eid})}\right) \tag{2}$$

Then we search the context for all other defined features. For each occurrence f in the context, we find the textual distance d to f_a. We use a Poisson distribution to estimate the probability of f occurring once within d bytes of f_a. This probability is determined for the in-context frequency ($frequency(f|eid)$) and for the out-of-context frequency ($frequency(f|\overline{eid})$) The score for the occurrence is the logarithm of the quotient of the two probabilities. In a given context, an occurrence counts if and only if it is the highest scoring occurrence among the features of its group in that context:

$$test\_sum = test\_sum + \log\left(\frac{poisson\_prob(d, frequency(f|eid))}{poisson\_prob(d, frequency(f|\overline{eid}))}\right)$$

For a given candidate context, if *test_sum* exceeds an established threshold, the algorithm returns the text matching the anchor pattern.

The Poisson probability p is defined as:

$$p(y) = \frac{\lambda^y e^{-\lambda}}{y!} \quad (y = 1, 2, 3, \ldots) \tag{3}$$

where λ is the mean number of occurrences within a window [6]. In our case, $y = 1$ always.

As with the birthdate extractor, we tested a version of the employee id extractor with a name-finding tool. If a personal name was identified, this fact increased the probability that the anchor match was an employee identification number. Results of these tests are discussed in section 6.

5   Experiments

In order to test the effectiveness of our extraction programs we constructed four document collections. The documents used for these collections consist of Department of Energy documents being considered for inclusion in an online repository. Reports, e-mails, forms and technical documents are included.

For our date of birth finder, we constructed two collections, one with 745 documents and the other with 1076. In the first, 40 contained at least one occurrence of a date of birth and 705 document had no birthdates. In the 1076 document collection, 76 had at least one birthdate and 1000 documents did not. These are denoted as *dob-745* and *dob-1076*.

For testing the employee identification number extractor, we again created two document collections. The first contained 579 documents, 97 of which contained at least one employee id, and 482 without. The second collection contained 617 documents, 95 with occurrences of an employee id and 522 without. These two collections are called *empid-579* and *empid-617*.

For each of the four collections, corrected versions of the documents containing privacy information were manually prepared. Experts then tagged the privacy items using ISRI's MetaMarker tool [13]. This tagging made it possible to evaluate our extractors on an item by item basis more appropriate to the information extraction task.

We evaluate the results using the standard measures of recall, precision, and F1 but in two ways. First, we computed these measures on a per-document basis. At this level, the effectiveness of our programs as document classifiers is determined. That is, we can test how effective the programs are at answering the question, which document contains at least one example of private information of the given type?

Second, we also evaluate our programs as to how well they identify specific instances of a given privacy type. Thus, we can determine how well our programs identify all and only those instances of a given type.

The standard definitions of precision, recall, and F1 appear below. In each case, the formula can be interpreted as referring to *documents* on one hand, and to *specific occurrences of privacy strings* on the other.

$$recall = \frac{\text{number of privacy items located by program}}{\text{total number of privacy items}} \tag{4}$$

$$precision = \frac{\text{number of privacy items located by program}}{\text{total number of items located by program}} \tag{5}$$

$$F1 = \frac{2(Precision \times Recall)}{(Precision + Recall)}. \tag{6}$$

6   Name Finding

The ISRI name-finding algorithm uses a Hidden Markov Model (HMM) whose states consist of various name formats, such as "first-name last-name", "last-name, first-name" (the latter "," is part of the pattern), and so forth [10]. Each input term is identified as having various features. Several knowledge bases are included to determine these features, such as a list common last names, male and female first names, a list of common "non-name" words, and common titles including Mr., Mrs., etc. The name lists were derived from the 1990 census list [2]. Another feature identified is the capitalization pattern of the word. Transition probabilities depend on where connecting marks such as commas appear between words.

We found that including a module for personal name extraction did not help the performance of the birthdate extractor [11]. Our tests on the employee identification number extractor produced somewhat mixed results. Figure 1 compares

Collection	Clean			OCR			Δ_{F1}
	Recall	Precision	F1	Recall	Precision	F1	
Per Document							
with name empid-579	0.970	0.839	0.900	0.938	0.835	0.884	0.016
without name empid-579	0.949	0.968	0.958	0.928	0.968	0.947	0.011
with name empid-617	0.979	0.816	0.890	0.979	0.816	0.890	0.000
without name empid-617	0.979	0.903	0.940	0.979	0.903	0.939	0.001
Per Item							
with name empid-579	0.836	0.656	0.735	0.712	0.309	0.431	0.304
without name empid-579	0.815	0.783	0.799	0.712	0.406	0.517	0.282
with name empid-617	0.768	0.604	0.677	0.678	0.445	0.541	0.136
without name empid-617	0.695	0.683	0.689	0.644	0.556	0.597	0.092

Fig. 1. Effectiveness of Name-finding

the effectiveness of the employee number finder both using a name finding module and not using the module. The results for the two collections, the *empid-579* and the *empid-617*, are shown with per-document and per-item counts.

Although the F1 result is lower when the name-finding module is used, recall for the per-item task can be increased with some loss in precision if name-finding is used. For some tasks, the increased recall may be worth the loss in precision, especially if missing examples of privacy items is considered more costly than identifying false positives.

7 OCR Effectiveness

Figure 2 presents the results of experiments using both the birthdate and employee id extraction programs. The column Δ_{F1} showing the change in F1 reveals that F1 diminished in each case, both on a per-document and per-item basis.

It is interesting to compare the per-document and the per-item mean change in F1. Using a one-sided paired-t test to determine how significant these changes

Task Collection	Clean			OCR			Δ_{F1}
	Recall	Precision	F1	Recall	Precision	F1	
Per-Document							
employee id empid-617	0.979	0.903	0.940	0.979	0.903	0.940	0.000
employee id empid-579	0.949	0.968	0.958	0.928	0.968	0.947	0.041
birthdate dob-745	1.000	0.930	0.964	0.925	0.925	0.925	0.036
birthdate dob-076	0.974	0.961	0.967	0.869	0.957	0.910	0.057
Per-Item							
employee id empid-617	0.695	0.683	0.689	0.644	0.556	0.597	0.092
employee id empid-579	0.815	0.783	0.799	0.712	0.406	0.517	0.282
birthdate dob-745	0.990	0.850	0.915	0.938	0.835	0.884	0.034
birthdate dob-1076	0.678	0.779	0.725	0.464	0.534	0.497	0.228

Fig. 2. Performance on OCR versus clean text

were, it turns out that the per-item degradation in F1 from the clean text test to the OCR test was more significant than the per-document (p-value of 0.036 versus 0.067).

The reason for the difference is that on the per-document level, only one example of private information needs to be identified correctly for the document to be correctly categorized. If there are multiple items in a document, and all but one contain OCR errors, the document will still be correctly marked as containing private information. Individual items not correctly identified on the per-item level are each counted as mistakes. Also, the per-document approach is more like a traditional document categorization task as we noted in section 3. That the per-document approach is less affected by OCR error is consistent with earlier studies showing that text categorization performance is not on average negatively affected by OCR error.

8   Analysis of Results

We discovered two types of OCR error affecting the extractors. The first consists of error traditionally called "classification" errors [18]. A classification error occurs if one or more characters in a string are transformed by the OCR software, or characters are added or deleted. For example, one date was changed from *07/20/1954* to *0?/20/1954*. In several cases, dates and employee ids became completely unrecognizable. In addition, some failures of the extractors could be attributable to OCR-errors in keywords. In one instance, *DATE OF BIRTH* became *DATR OF III RTN*. The counts of these errors are presented in the "Classification" column in figure 3.

A second type of error was caused by zoning. In several of the documents there were tables which listed private information. These were sometimes indicated by column headings. So for example, a list of birthdates would be presented under a single column heading "birthdate". However, the OCR engine occasionally would determine that the heading should be zoned separately from the dates. The heading would then be placed farther from the birthdates than it appears to the eye in the document image. Our experts when creating the corrected text versions of documents sometimes made the text more "readable." This resulted in headings being placed closer to items. These types of errors are enumerated in the "Zoning" column in figure 3. We calculate that 37.5% of the errors were classification errors and 63.5% due to zoning.

Collection	Zoning	Classification	Correctable
dob-745	3	2	1
dob-1076	41	28	15
empid-579	6	5	1
empid-617	10	1	1
Total	**60**	**36**	**18**

Fig. 3. OCR Error Types

9   Conclusion and Future Work

Because OCR text can weaken the usefulness of information extraction programs, steps should be taken to improve the OCR output of such texts. However, it is currently unknown what techniques, if any, can be applied to improve the precision and recall of information extraction programs.

The problems caused by zoning errors will obviously have to be approached differently from classification errors. The classification errors may be correctable to a certain extent using aggressive error correction techniques. For example, spelling correction algorithms enhanced with general and collection-specific lexicons have been shown to improve OCR-accuracy [9, 15]. Such techniques have been incorporated into OCRspell [18] and MANICURE [12].

It should be stressed that the "Correctable" column in figure 3 lists the number of potentially correctable errors. These include keywords, birthdates, or employee id's for which some characters survived the OCR-process. It may be the case that no algorithm will actually correct all the errors. However, only truly impossible cases were excluded, generally those in which no trace of the phrase in question survived. It is a question for further research if indeed ocr-correcting algorithms will be able to correct these errors and if so, which types. In future work we hope to study various ameliorative approaches for dealing with both types of error.

In the case of zoning problems, a minimal strategy would be to expand the size of the context searched around anchor features. Also, more aggressive use of page geometry information from the OCR process to identify columnar information may prove helpful.

Another idea would be to abandon the reliance on "anchor" features. In an extractor dependent on anchor features, extraction fails if the anchor features are note recognized. However, if all features which contribute to the location of an item are given weight in the search, then a desired item may be discoverable even if "anchor" features are corrupted.

References

[1] U.S. Government. The freedom of information act 5 U.S.C. sec. 552 as amended in 2002. Url: http://www.usdoj.gov/oip/foia_updates/Vol_XVII_4/page2.htm. Viewed June 30, 2004.

[2] U.S. Government. Frequently occurring first names and surnames from the 1990 census. http://www.census.gov/genealogy/www/freqnames.html. Viewed August, 2005.

[3] Ralph Grishman. Information extraction: Techniques and challenges. In SCIE1997, pages 10–27, 1997.

[4] Hongyan Jing, Daniel Lopresti, and Chilin Shih. Summarizing noisy documents. In Proceedings of SDIUT'03, pages 111–119, Greenbelt, MD, April 2003.

[5] Andrew McCallum. Bow: A toolkit for statistical language modeling, text retrieval, classification and clustering. http://www.cs.cmu.edu/~mccallum/bow, 1996.

[6] William Mendenhall and Terry Sincich. *Statistics for Engineering and the Sciences*. Prentice Hall, 4th edition, 1995.

[7] David Miller, Sean Boisen, Richard Schwartz, Rebecca Stone, and Ralph Weischedel. Named entity extraction from noisy input: Speech and OCR. In *Proceedings of the Sixth Conference on Applied Natural Languae Processing*, pages 316–324, 2000.

[8] Raymond Mooney and Razvan Bunescu. Mining knowledge from text using information extraction. In *SIGKDD Explorations*, volume 7, pages 3–10, June 2005.

[9] Thomas Nartker, Kazem Taghva, Ron Young, Julie Borsack, and Allen Condit. OCR correction based on document level knowledge. In *Proc. IS&T/SPIE 2003 Intl. Symp. on Electronic Imaging Science and Technology*, volume 5010, pages 103–110, Santa Clara, CA, January 2003.

[10] Lawrence Rabiner and Biing-Hwang Juang. *Fundamentals of Speech Recognition*. Prentice Hall, 1993.

[11] Kazem Taghva, Russell Beckley, Jeffrey Coombs, Julie Borsack, Ray Pereda, and Thomas Nartker. Automatic redaction of private information using relational information extraction. In *Proc. IS&T/SPIE 2006 Intl. Symp. on Electronic Imaging Science and Technology"*. Submitted.

[12] Kazem Taghva, Julie Borsack, and Tom Nartker. A process flow for realizing high accuracy for ocr text. In *SDIUT 2006*. Forthcoming.

[13] Kazem Taghva and Marc Cartright. An efficient tool for XML data preparation. In *Proc. ISNG 2005 Information Systems: New Generations*, Las Vegas, NV, April 2005.

[14] Kazem Taghva, Jeffrey Coombs, and Ray Pereda. Address extraction using hidden markov models. In *Proc. IS&T/SPIE 2005 Intl. Symp. on Electronic Imaging Science and Technology*, San Jose, CA, January 2005.

[15] Kazem Taghva, Thomas Nartker, and Julie Borsack. Information access in the presence of OCR errors In *Proc. of ACM Hardcopy Document Processing Workshop*, pages 1–8, Washington, DC, November 2004.

[16] Kazem Taghva, Thomas A. Nartker, and Julie Borsack. Recognize, categorize, and retrieve. In *Proc. of the Symposium on Document Image Understanding Technology*, pages 227–232, Columbia, MD, April 2001. Laboratory for Language and Media Processing, University of Maryland.

[17] Kazem Taghva, Tom Nartker, Julie Borsack, Steve Lumos, Allen Condit, and Ron Young. Evaluating text categorization in the presence of OCR errors. In *Proc. IS&T/SPIE 2001 Intl. Symp. on Electronic Imaging Science and Technology*, pages 68–74, San Jose, CA, January 2001.

[18] Kazem Taghva and Eric Stofsky. Ocrspell: An interactive spelling correction system for OCR errors in text. *Intl. Journal on Document Analysis and Recognition*, 3(3):125–137, March 2001.

Combining Multiple Classifiers for Faster Optical Character Recognition

Kumar Chellapilla, Michael Shilman, and Patrice Simard

Microsoft Research, One Microsoft Way, Redmond, WA 98052, USA
{kumarc, shilman, patrice}@microsoft.com
http://research.microsoft.com/dpu/

Abstract. Traditional approaches to combining classifiers attempt to improve classification accuracy at the cost of increased processing. They may be viewed as providing an accuracy-speed trade-off: higher accuracy for lower speed. In this paper we present a novel approach to combining multiple classifiers to solve the inverse problem of significantly improving classification speeds at the cost of slightly reduced classification accuracy. We propose a cascade architecture for combining classifiers and cast the process of building such a cascade as a search and optimization problem. We present two algorithms based on steepest-descent and dynamic programming for producing approximate solutions fast. We also present a simulated annealing algorithm and a depth-first-search algorithm for finding optimal solutions. Results on handwritten optical character recognition indicate that a) a speedup of 4-9 times is possible with no increase in error and b) speedups of up to 15 times are possible when twice as many errors can be tolerated.

1 Introduction

Given a classification problem, several approaches exist for building a classifier using machine learning. Different machine learning algorithms produce different classifiers, usually with different classification errors. Several studies have pursued the goal of finding a machine learning algorithm that can solve any classification task with the highest (generalization) accuracy. The quest for such a super classifier and a universal machine learning algorithm for training its architecture still remain elusive. However, its absence has produced several comparable alternatives. This variety has been a boon to approaches that attempt to build better classifiers through combination. Such combination approaches most commonly utilize not only the classification outputs but also the classification confidences returned by each classifier.

Recent investigations [1-6] have concentrated on combining two or more classifiers for improved classification accuracy. The intuition for why such an approach can work lies in the observation that the classification errors produced by radically different classifiers have low correlation [3]. Further, one also observes that the more confident a classifier, the more likely that it is correct and vice versa. When more than two classifiers are available the combination alternatives become much more interesting with a greater potential for producing better qualifiers through combination.

H. Bunke and A.L. Spitz (Eds.): DAS 2006, LNCS 3872, pp. 358–367, 2006.

Today's mobile electronic devices such as cell phones and digital cameras are capable of acquiring images at a sufficiently high resolution (3 MPix) to facilitate OCR of text in these images. There is a simultaneous explosion of software applications targeting these devices that can read and translate words in documents, traffic signs, restaurant menus, travel guides, etc. Given the low processing power of these devices, it is desirable to have high speed OCR systems that can be used on these machines. Though speed is a bottle neck, memory appears to be more freely available as these devices simultaneously target multimedia applications.

In this paper, we investigate the inverse problem wherein classification speed is of interest and we are willing to accept slightly reduced classification accuracy in order to achieve significant speedup. We address the scenario where a set of pre-trained classifiers are available for combination, and we wish to produce various speed-error trade-offs for several different scenarios. For simplicity we assume that retraining during combination is not an option. We present an approach to build and combine classifiers that can significantly improve classification speeds with a pre-specified maximum (usually small) drop in classification accuracy. Section 2 briefly reviews existing classifier combination approaches both for accuracy and speed. The new approach and the underlying optimization problem are presented in Section 3 along with four algorithms for building such cascades. Experimental results are presented in Section 4 and we conclude in Section 5.

2 Background

Combining classifiers for improved optical character recognition (OCR) accuracy is a well studied problem. Simple classifier fusion methods such as minimum, maximum, average, median, and majority voting have recently been studied both theoretically [1] and empirically [3]. Rather than using such simple static rules, a combining classifier can be trained to takes the outputs from two or more classifiers as input and produce a combined output that better models the class posterior probabilities or likelihoods. Such approaches based on learning have greater potential for producing larger improvements in accuracy [2]. Successful applications of classifier combinations include combining fingerprint matches, face and voice recognition and document processing [3-7]. We emphasize that all of these approaches focus on accuracy and invariably result in slower classifiers. The combined classifier is 2-20 times slower with the number of errors dropping by 18%-63% [4-5].

Combining classifiers for speed provides a different approach to improving classifiers. Such sequential combination is commonly addressed to improve not only classification accuracy, but also classification speed. Typically, the quickest classifiers are used first followed by slower (and frequently more accurate) classifiers [8]. Boosting is one such ensemble learning algorithm that sequentially adds weak classifiers to build a strong classifier. Using early stopping during sequential classifier combination can not only produce speed benefits, but also acts as a regularization technique to improve generalization [9].

3 Combining Classifiers for Speed

In this paper we investigate combinations of a class of convolutional neural network classifiers [7]. These networks have two layers of convolutional nodes followed by a hidden layer and an output layer. Such a network achieved the best known error rate of 0.4% [7] for handwritten digit recognition (MNIST). It had 5 nodes in the first convolutional layer, 50 nodes in the second convolutional layer, 100 hidden nodes, and 10 output nodes (one for each digit 0-9). It can process about 250-300 chars/sec on a P4 3GHz machine. The network performs over half a million operations per classification. This network when used for recognizing documents would take over 15 seconds per page and would be too slow.

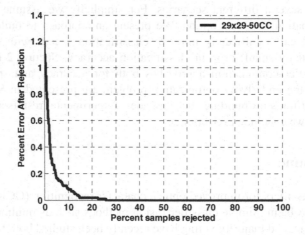

Fig. 1. Rejection curve for a convolutional neural network on MNIST data

The factors contributing to the computation in the classifier are a) the input resolution, b) size of the convolutional layers, c) number of hidden nodes, and d) the number of output classes. The last parameter is defined by the problem and usually cannot be changed. For the remaining settings, smaller values produce faster but less accurate networks [7]. Further, it is well known that one observes a rate of diminishing returns in accuracy as complexity is increased.

The convolutional NN is trained through backpropagation using cross-entropy and learns to predict class probabilities [7]. The output for each class lies in [0,1] and can be used as a confidence measure to reject samples that would be incorrectly classified. Figure 1 presents the rejection curve for a convolutional NN with 50 hidden nodes. The rejection curve is monotonically decreasing indicating that the higher the confidence the less likely that the character will be misclassified. Even though the classifier only achieves an error rate of 1.25% on the MNIST data set, we can improve its error rate to 0.1% or even 0% by rejecting 9% or 26% of the data, respectively. This trade-off is the key intuition behind the proposed cascade architecture.

3.1 Cascade of Classifiers

Figure 2 presents a cascade architecture for combining classifiers using a sequence of thresholds. Characters are processed by the cascade as follows: each input character image is initially presented to the first stage, S_1. If the classification output exceeds the first stage's threshold, t_1, then it is absorbed by the first stage and processing stops. If not, then the sample is rejected (by the first stage) and is passed on to the next stage. This process is repeated till the sample gets absorbed by some stage or we reach the last stage, S_M, in the cascade. The last stage, S_M, has a threshold of $t_M = 0$ and is designed to absorb all characters that reach it. The label assigned to the input character is that assigned by the absorbing stage.

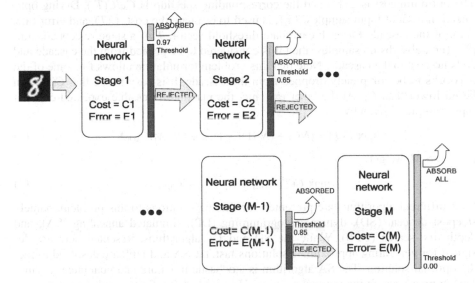

Fig. 2. Cascade of classifiers: Samples rejected at each stage are passed on to subsequent stages. Networks at the front of the cascade are fast and inaccurate while networks towards the end of the cascade are more accurate but slower.

The cascade architecture has several merits for improving processing speed. If faster less accurate nets are placed towards the front of the cascade and slower more accurate nets are placed towards the end of the cascade, one can dramatically reduce the expected processing times for input characters. The speedup and error rate of the cascade is determined by the costs, errors, and thresholds of each stage. Lower cost implies a faster stage.

3.2 Optimization Problem

In this paper, we study such cascades with the stages arranged such that costs monotonically increase from left to right. Mathematically,

$$C_1 \leq C_2 \leq \ldots \leq C_M \tag{1}$$

where M is the number of stages and C_i is the cost of the i-th stage. Given the ordering, the costs are usually normalized such that $C_1 = 1.0$. Unlike the costs the errors are not expected to be monotonically decreasing as we move through the cascade (see Tables 1 and 2). Given this architecture, the goal is to find the fastest cascade with an error rate less than a pre-defined value e_{max}. Though the cascade can be used to improve the error rate of the best classifier, in this paper, e_{max} will be defined to be larger than the error incurred by the best single network in the cascade. The search space of solutions is $S = \{t_1\} \times \{t_2\} \times ... \times \{t_M\}$, where $\{t_i\}$ is the set of all thresholds for stage i. The optimal threshold vector $T_* = [t_{1*}, t_{2*}, ..., t_{M*}]$ is given by

$$T_* = \arg \min \{ C(T) \mid T \in S, e(T) \le e_{max} \} \tag{2}$$

The optimum cost is $C(T_*)$ and the corresponding speedup is $C_M/C(T_*)$. During optimization a set of input samples, $\{x_i\}$, is used to evaluate the cost, $C(T)$, and error rate, $e(T)$, of the cascade for each candidate threshold vector, T. If a stage rejects all samples (i.e., absorbs no samples) then it is considered to be pruned from the cascade and adds no cost to the cascade. Note that this problem formulation allows for some of the networks to be completely dropped from the cascade. It is easy to see that $C(T_*)$ can be no lower than C_1. At the other extreme, the maximum possible expected cost per input sample is given by

$$\max C(T) = (NC_1 + (N-1)C_2 + ... + (N-M)C_M)/N \tag{3}$$

For $N \gg M$, we get

$$\max C(T) = C_1 + C_2 + ... + C_M \tag{4}$$

Four different algorithms are presented for finding solutions to this problem, namely steepest descent (SD), dynamic programming (DP), simulated annealing (SA), and depth-first-search (DFS). While the SD and DP algorithms presented here are designed for generating approximate solutions fast, the SA and DFS are designed to find the optimal solution. The SA algorithm is stochastic in nature and guarantees asymptotic convergence to the optimal solution. However, at any finite number of iterations, the best solution may only be approximate. Brief descriptions of the optimization algorithms are presented below:

Steepest Descent. The algorithm is initialized with $T_0 = [1,1,...,1,0]$, i.e., every stage rejects all samples except for the last stage that absorbs them. Such a solution satisfies the e_{max} constraint and has a cost $C(T_0) = C_M$. During each iteration, the change in cost ΔC_i, $i = 1,2,...,M$ and the change in error Δe_i, $i = 1,2,...,M$ are computed by lowering each threshold t_i to the next possible value while keeping all other thresholds the same. Note that due to the monotonic increase in costs over the cascade $\Delta C_i < 0$, $i = 1,2,...,M$. If the error decreases for any i (i.e., $\Delta e_i < 0$), the best such i with the lowest Δe_i is selected for update. If all $\Delta e_i > 0$, the i with the lowest cost change per unit error change $= -\Delta C_i/\Delta e_i$ is selected for update. The selected threshold is updated to the next lower value and the process is iterated. Search is terminated when the best possible update puts the error above e_{max}. The steepest descent algorithm is sensitive to local optima and is used only as a baseline for comparing algorithms. The algorithm is simple and very fast. Each update takes at most $O(M)$ evaluations and there are at most MN evaluations. Due to the incremental updates to the thresholds during successive evaluations, the cost and error evaluation can be done very efficiently by remembering which samples were absorbed at each of the stages and which ones are affected by the threshold update. The total running time is bounded by $O(M^2N)$.

Dynamic Programming. The dynamic programming algorithm presented here builds a cascade by iteratively adding new stages. It starts with a two stage cascade containing only the first and last stages, S_1, and S_M, respectively. Note that such a two stage cascade has at most N possible threshold vectors. Each threshold vector represents a unique solution with a different second last stage threshold. Let these be represented as N paths of length one, each ending at a unique threshold. Each of these N paths is evaluated. Now consider inserting stage S_2 between S_1, and S_M. Each of the existing N paths can be extended in N possible ways through S_2. All such N^2 extensions are evaluated. For each threshold in S_2, the best path extension (among the N^2 possible extensions) is chosen and retained. This results in N paths of length 2 each passing through a different threshold in S_2 and representing a different cascade with three stages. This process of adding a stage is repeated $M - 2$ times to obtain a set of N paths representing cascades with M stages. The best path among these remaining N paths is picked as the final solution. The algorithm is not guaranteed to find the optimal solution because only N paths are retained during each iteration. The running time is $O(MN^2)$.

Simulated Annealing. A simulated annealing algorithm is presented that simultaneously optimizes all thresholds in the cascade of M stages. As in the case of steepest descent, the initial solution is T_0. At any given temperature, λ, each threshold, t_i, is updated to a neighbor that is $\eta = \text{round}(G(0, \lambda))$ steps away, where $G(0, \lambda)$ is a zero mean Gaussian random variable with standard deviation λ. Note that η can be positive or negative. Any thresholds that fall outside the valid limits (threshold indices: $1-N$ or threshold values $0-1$) are reset to the limit violated. The initial temperature was set to N and the Metropolis algorithm was used to accept better solutions. Further, any solutions that didn't satisfy the e_{max} criterion were also rejected during the updates. The temperature was continuously annealed down to 1.0 with a maximum of one million evaluations ($= E$). The running time is $O(EM)$.

Depth First Search. The above three algorithms do not guarantee finding the optimal solution after a finite amount of computation. A simple depth-first-search was used to search through all possible threshold settings. Every possible cascade with 2 to M stages can be represented as a node in a tree of maximum depth $M - 2$. Nodes at depth d represent cascades of length $d - 2$. The running time is $O(N^{M-1})$, but extensive pruning is possible.

3.3 Experiments

Experiments were conducted with the MNIST and FUGU character datasets. The MNIST dataset consists of 60,000 hand written digits uniformly distributed over 0–9. The FUGU dataset contains a natural distribution of 925,702 Japanese kanji characters with up to 3 strokes (258 classes). For each dataset, 80% of the samples were used for training, 10% were used for validation (to determine when to stop training) and the remaining 10% were used for testing. The validation samples were also used to optimize the thresholds.

A total of 18 MNIST classifiers and 12 FUGU classifiers of varying sizes were trained. The parameters being varied were the input image size (5x5, 7x7, 9x9, 11x11, and 29x29), the number of convolution layers (2 layers or 0 layers), and the number of hidden nodes (50, 100, 200, and 300). Cascades of such trained networks were optimized using the above algorithms. Approximate running times for SD, DP, and SA, on these two problems were 0.25, 45, and 250 seconds, respectively. Due to the computationally intensive nature of DFS, DFS experiments were conducted only on a toy problem consisting of 4 MNIST classifiers and 5000 samples. The quality of the optimal solutions found using DFS are compared with the other algorithms.

4   Results

Training results for MNIST are presented in Table 1. The Train% is the error on the validation set used for stopping training and the Test% is the error on the test set. The best network (stage 18) had a validation error rate of 1.1% and a test error of 1.19%. On the other hand, the fastest network which was 41.6 times faster had an error rate of 26.52%! The validation set was used to optimize the 18-thresholds in the cascade for 11 values of e_{max} ranging from 1.1% (no extra error) to 2.2% (double the error). Figure 3 presents the speedup results obtained using SD, DP, and SA on the MNIST dataset. The speedup rapidly increases with increasing e_{max}. It is quite remarkable that even with no change in error, a 4x speedup is possible using the cascade architecture.

Table 1. MNIST Results: Costs and Errors

SN	Input	Arch.	Cost	Train%	Test%
1	5x5	0,0,50,10	1.00	26.52	27.48
2	5x5	0,0,100,10	1.22	25.06	26.81
3	5x5	0,0,200,10	1.72	25.36	26.76
4	5x5	0,0,300,10	2.24	25.57	27.07
5	7x7	0,0,50,10	1.04	8.82	9.06
6	7x7	0,0,100,10	1.35	8.17	8.38
7	7x7	0,0,200,10	1.99	8.29	8.82
8	7x7	0,0,300,10	2.61	8.04	8.36
9	9x9	0,0,50,10	1.14	4.49	4.65
10	9x9	0,0,100,10	1.53	4.13	4.20
11	9x9	0,0,200,10	2.36	4.03	4.01
12	9x9	0,0,300,10	3.17	3.78	3.89
13	11x11	0,0,50,10	1.26	3.63	3.72
14	11x11	0,0,300,10	3.84	2.35	2.27
15	29x29	0,0,50,10	3.39	3.43	3.36
16	29x29	0,0,300,10	16.3	1.82	1.81
17	29x29	5,50,50,10	23.0	1.20	1.25
18	29x29	5,50,300,10	41.6	1.10	1.19

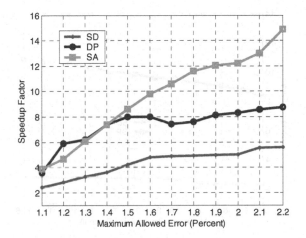

Fig. 3. Speedup factor on MNIST

Table 2. FUGU Results: Costs and Errors

SN	Input	Arch.	Cost	Train%	Test%
1	5x5	0,0,50,258	1.00	52.20	52.02
2	5x5	0,0,300,258	1.06	49.48	49.47
3	7x7	0,0,50,258	1.09	28.56	28.29
4	7x7	0,0,300,258	1.12	20.57	20.53
5	9x9	0,0,50,258	1.96	18.53	18.44
6	9x9	0,0,300,258	2.86	11.91	11.99
7	11x11	0,0,50,258	3.03	14.39	14.27
8	11x11	0,0,300,258	3.25	9.41	9.43
9	29x29	0,0,50,258	3.48	11.88	11.61
10	29x29	0,0,300,258	8.12	7.29	7.23
11	29x29	5,50,50,258	9.37	7.54	7.56
12	29x29	5,50,300,258	17.61	5.79	5.85

The speedup quickly rises above 5x for an e_{max} of 1.2% and reaches 15x for an e_{max} of 2.2%. The curve for DP is wavy with certain lower error settings producing faster solutions. This is because DP only retains the best N paths during each iteration.

Table 2 presents training results for FUGU. The best network (stage 120 has an error rate of 5.79% on the validation set. The error on the test set was 5.85%. On the other hand, the fastest network which is 17.61 times faster had an error rate of 52.20%. The validation set was used to optimize the 12-thresholds in the cascade for 11 values of e_{max} ranging from 5.79% (no extra error) to 11.58% (twice the error). Figure 4 presents the speedup results obtained using SD, DP, and SA on the FUGU dataset. As in the case of MNIST, the speedup rapidly increases with increasing e_{max}. It is interesting to note that using the cascade architecture, an almost 10x speedup is possible with no change in error. The speedup quickly rises to 12x for an emax of 8.95% (55% more errors) and reaches 14x for an emax of 11.58% (twice the number of errors). Over an order of magnitude speedup was possible with little or no change

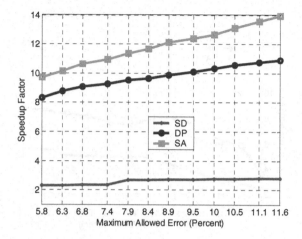

Fig. 4. Speedup factor on FUGU

Table 3. Speedup comparisons against optimal speedup on a toy problem (4 classifiers, 5000 samples)

e_{max}	DFS (optimal)	SA	DP	SA
12.36%	5.1219	1.0250	5.1102	5.0493
15%	7.9754	1.0699	7.9556	7.9193
20%	20.5	1.6314	20.5	20.5

in error rate. We conjecture that the reason for higher speedup factors with FUGU is the natural distribution of characters and an overall larger error rate. Further, the lower slope on the FUGU dataset is due to the lower cost range among constituent networks. At double the error rate, we come close to the maximum possible speedup factor of 17.61.

Table 3 presents results on the toy problem using the four algorithms. DFS finds optimal solutions within a few minutes. On the toy problem, the quality of solutions found using DP and SA closely match those found using DFS. However, further experiments are necessary to determine how well these results generalize to larger problems with more stages and larger validation sets.

5 Conclusion

A cascade architecture for combining classifiers was presented along with four algorithms for optimization. Results on character recognition show that significant speedups can be obtained with little or no change in the error rate. The input to our optimizer is a set of rejection curves computed by potential classifiers (of any type) and the output is a set of thresholds (which potentially eliminate the useless classifiers). The optimizer is called off-line and its output yields a near speed-optimal combination classifier, ready for deployment. Future work will address scaling this approach to much larger data sets, larger cascade sizes, and re-training constituent classifiers in light of the role played by them in the cascade.

References

1. Ludmila IK, "A Theoretical Study on Six Classifier Fusion Strategies," IEEE Trans. On Pattern Analysis and Machine Intelligence, v. 24, No. 2, pp. 281-286, Feb. 2002.
2. RPW. Duin, "The Combining Classifier: To Train or Not to Train?" ICPR (2), pp. 765-770, 2002.
3. J Kittler, M Hatef, RPW Duin, and J Matas, "On Combining Classifiers," IEEE Trans. On Pat. Analysis and Machine Intel., Vol. 20, No. 3, Mar. 1998. Mar. 1998.
4. L Prevost, C Michel-Sendis, A Moises, L Oudot, and M Milgram, "Combining model-based and discriminative classifiers: application to handwritten character recognition," ICDAR'03. 2003.
5. H Hao, CL Liu, and H Sako, "Confidence evaluation for combining diverse classifiers," ICDAR'03, pp. 760-765, 3-6 Aug. 2003.
6. U. Bhattacharya and B. B. Chaudhuri, "A Majority Voting Scheme for Multiresolution Recognition of Handprinted Numerals," ICDAR'03, pp. 16-20, 3-6 Aug. 2003.
7. PY Simard, D Steinkraus, and J Platt, (2003) "Best Practice for Convolutional Neural Networks Applied to Visual Document Analysis," in ICDAR'03, pp. 958-962.
8. S Marinai, M Gori, G Soda, "Artificial Neural Networks for Document Analysis and Recognition," IEEE TPAMI, Vol. 27, No. 1, pp. 23-35.
9. T Zhang and B Yu, "Boosting with early stopping: Convergence and consistency," Annals of Statistics. vol. 33, no. 4, 1538–1579, 2005.

Performance Comparison of Six Algorithms for Page Segmentation

Faisal Shafait, Daniel Keysers, and Thomas M. Breuel

Image Understanding and Pattern Recognition (IUPR) research group,
German Research Center for Artificial Intelligence (DFKI)
and Technical University of Kaiserslautern,
D-67663 Kaiserslautern, Germany
{faisal, keysers, tmb}@iupr.net

Abstract. This paper presents a quantitative comparison of six algorithms for page segmentation: X-Y cut, smearing, whitespace analysis, constrained text-line finding, Docstrum, and Voronoi-diagram-based. The evaluation is performed using a subset of the UW-III collection commonly used for evaluation, with a separate training set for parameter optimization. We compare the results using both default parameters and optimized parameters. In the course of the evaluation, the strengths and weaknesses of each algorithm are analyzed, and it is shown that no single algorithm outperforms all other algorithms. However, we observe that the three best-performing algorithms are those based on constrained text-line finding, Docstrum, and the Voronoi-diagram.

1 Introduction

Document image layout analysis is a crucial step in many applications related to document images, like text extraction using optical character recognition (OCR), reflowing documents, and layout-based document retrieval. Layout analysis is the process of identifying layout structures by analyzing page images. Layout structures can be physical (text, graphics, pictures, ...) or logical (titles, paragraphs, captions, headings, ...). The identification of physical layout structures is called physical or geometric layout analysis, while assigning different logical roles to the detected regions is termed as logical layout analysis [1]. In this paper we are concerned with geometric layout analysis. The task of a geometric layout analysis system is to segment the document image into homogeneous zones, each consisting of only one physical layout structure, and to identify their spatial relationship (e.g. reading order). Therefore, the performance of layout analysis methods depends heavily on the page segmentation algorithm used. Over the last two decades, several page segmentation algorithms have been proposed in the literature (for a literature survey, please refer to [1, 2]).

The problem of automatic evaluation of page segmentation algorithms is increasingly becoming an important issue. Major problems arise due to the lack of a common dataset, a wide diversity of objectives, a lack of meaningful quantitative evaluation, and inconsistencies in the use of document models. This makes

H. Bunke and A.L. Spitz (Eds.): DAS 2006, LNCS 3872, pp. 368–379, 2006.

the comparison of different page segmentation algorithms a difficult task. Meaningful and quantitative evaluation of page segmentation algorithms has received attention in the past. Yanikoglu et al. [3] presented a region-based page segmentation benchmarking environment, named Pink Panther. Liang et al. [4] proposed a performance metric for document structure extraction algorithms by finding the correspondences between detected entities and ground-truth. The quality of page segmentation algorithms was also evaluated by analyzing the errors in the recognized text [5]. However, text-based approaches have found little use since they measure the output of multiple steps and cannot be used to evaluate page segmentation alone. Das et al. [6] suggested an empirical measure of performance of a segmentation algorithm based on a graph-like model of the document.

There has been little effort in the past to compare different algorithms on a quantitative basis. Mao et al. [7] presented an empirical performance evaluation methodology and compared three research algorithms and two commercial products. Their evaluation methodology is based on text-line detection accuracy, so it is particularly useful for evaluating text segmentation approaches. Recent page segmentation competitions [8, 9] address the need of comparative performance evaluation under realistic circumstances. However, a limitation of the competition-based approach is that competing methods only participate if they are implemented and used by a participant. It means several well-known algorithms might not be a part of the comparison at all.

This paper focuses on comparative performance evaluation of six representative algorithms for page segmentation. It is an extension of the work by Mao et al. [7], and adds three more algorithms to the comparison. The algorithms compared in [7] are X-Y cut [10], Docstrum [11], and the Voronoi-diagram based approach [12]. The algorithms added to the comparison in this work are the smearing algorithm [13], whitespace analysis [14], and the constrained text-line finding algorithm [15]. A brief description of the six algorithms used in the comparison will be given in Section 2, followed by the error metric definition in Section 3. Section 4 describes the experiments performed and results obtained, followed by discussion of the results in Section 5 and conclusion in Section 6.

2   Algorithms for Page Segmentation

We selected six representative algorithms for page segmentation. Furthermore, we have introduced a dummy algorithm to determine a bottom line of the possible performance. A brief description of each algorithm and its parameters are described in turn in the following.

2.1   Dummy Algorithm

The dummy segmentation algorithm takes the whole page as one segment. The purpose of this algorithm is to see how well we can perform without doing anything. Then the performance of other algorithms can be seen as gains over that achieved by the dummy algorithm. Using the dummy algorithm also highlights limitations of the evaluation scheme as detailed in Section 3.

2.2   X-Y Cut

The X-Y cut segmentation algorithm [10], also referred to as recursive X-Y cuts (RXYC) algorithm, is a tree-based top-down algorithm.

The root of the tree represents the entire document page. All the leaf nodes together represent the final segmentation. The RXYC algorithm recursively splits the document into two or more smaller rectangular blocks which represent the nodes of the tree. At each step of the recursion, the horizontal and vertical projection profiles of each node are computed. Then, the valleys along the horizontal and vertical directions, V_X and V_Y, are compared to corresponding predefined thresholds T_X and T_Y. If the valley is larger than the threshold, the node is split at the mid-point of the wider of V_X and V_Y into two children nodes. The process continues until no leaf node can be split further. Then, noise regions are removed using noise removal thresholds T_X^n and T_Y^n.

2.3   Smearing

The run-length smearing algorithm (RLSA) [13] works on binary images where white pixels are represented by 0's and black pixels by 1's. The algorithm transforms a binary sequence x into y according to the following rules:

1. 0's in x are changed to 1's in y if the number of adjacent 0's is less than or equal to a predefined threshold C.
2. 1's in x are unchanged in y.

These steps have the effect of linking together neighboring black areas that are separated by less than C pixels. The RLSA is applied row-wise to the document using a threshold C_h, and column-wise using threshold C_v, yielding two distinct bitmaps. These two bitmaps are combined in a logical AND operation. Additional horizontal smearing is done using a smaller threshold, C_s, to obtain the final bitmap. Then, connected component analysis is performed on this bitmap, and using threshold C_{21} and C_{22} on the mean run of black pixel in a connected component and block height, connected components are classified into text and non-text zones.

2.4   Whitespace Analysis

The whitespace analysis algorithm described by Baird [14] analyzes the structure of the white background in document images. The first step is to find a set of maximal white rectangles (called *covers*) whose union completely covers the background. Breuel's algorithm for finding the maximal empty whitespace [15] is used in our implementation for this step. These covers are then sorted with respect to the sort key, $K(c)$:

$$K(c) = \sqrt{\text{area}(c) * W(|log_2\,(\text{height}(c)/\text{width}(c))|)} \tag{1}$$

where c is the cover and $W(.)$ is a dimensionless weighting function. Baird [14] chose a special weighting function using experiments on a particular dataset. We used an approximation of the original weighting function as

$$W(x) = \begin{cases} 0.5 & \text{if } x < 3 \\ 1.5 & \text{if } 3 \leq x < 5 \\ 1 & \text{otherwise} \end{cases} \tag{2}$$

The purpose of the weighting function is to assign higher weight to tall and long rectangles because they are supposed to be meaningful separators of text blocks.

In the second step, the rectangular covers $c_i, i = 1, \ldots, m$, where m is the total number of whitespace covers, are combined one by one to generate a corresponding sequence $s_j, j = 1, \ldots, m$ of segmentations. A segmentation is the uncovered area left by the union of the covers combined so far. Before a cover c_i is unified to the segmentation s_j, a trimming rule is applied to avoid early segmentation of narrow blocks. The unification of covers continues until the stopping rule (3) is satisfied:

$$K(s_j) - W_s * F(s_j) \leq T_s \tag{3}$$

where $K(s_j)$ is the sort key $K(c_j)$ of the last cover unified in making segmentation s_j, $F(s_j) = j/m$, W_s is a weight, and T_s is stopping threshold. At the final segmentation, the uncovered regions represent the union of interiors of all black input rectangles. We take bounding boxes of the uncovered regions as representative of the text segments.

2.5   Constrained Text-Line Detection

The layout analysis approach by Breuel [15] finds text-lines as a two step process:

1. Find tall whitespace rectangles and evaluate them as candidates for gutters, column separators, etc. The algorithm for finding maximal empty whitespace is described in [15]. The whitespace rectangles are returned in order of decreasing quality and are allowed a maximum overlap of O_m.
2. The whitespace rectangles representing the columns are used as obstacles in a robust least square, globally optimal text-line detection algorithm [16]. Then, the bounding box of all the characters making the text-line is computed.

The method was merely intended by its author as a demonstration of the application of two geometric algorithms, and not as a complete layout analysis system; nevertheless, we included it in the comparison because it has already proven useful in some applications. It is also nearly parameter free and resolution independent.

2.6   Docstrum

The Docstrum algorithm by Gorman [11] is a bottom-up approach based on nearest-neighborhood clustering of connected components extracted from the document image. After noise removal, the connected components are separated into two groups, one with dominant characters and another one with characters in titles and section heading, using a character size ratio factor f_d. Then, K nearest neighbors are found for each connected component. Then, text-lines are found by computing the transitive closure on within-line nearest neighbor pairings using a threshold f_t. Finally, text-lines are merged to form text blocks using a parallel distance threshold f_{pa} and a perpendicular distance threshold f_{pe}.

2.7 Voronoi-Diagram Based Algorithm

The Voronoi-diagram based segmentation algorithm by Kise et al. [12] is also a bottom-up algorithm. In the first step, it extracts sample points from the boundaries of the connected components using a sampling rate sr. Then, noise removal is done using a maximum noise zone size threshold nm, in addition to width, height, and aspect ratio thresholds. After that the Voronoi diagram is generated using sample points obtained from the borders of the connected components. Superfluous Voronoi edges are deleted using a criterion involving the area ratio threshold ta, and the inter-line spacing margin control factor fr. Since we evaluate all algorithms on document pages with Manhattan layouts, a modified version of the algorithm [7] is used to generate rectangular zones.

3 Error Metrics

We use text-line detection accuracy [7] as the error metric in our evaluation. The text-lines are represented as bounding boxes enclosing all the characters constituting the text-line. Three types of errors are defined.

1. Ground-truth text-lines that are missed (C), i.e. they are not part of any detected text region.
2. Ground-truth text-lines whose bounding boxes are split (S), i.e. the bounding box of a text-line does not lie completely within one detected segment.
3. Ground-truth text-lines that are horizontally merged (M), i.e. two horizontally overlapping ground-truth lines are part of one detected segment.

These error measures are defined based on set theory and mathematical morphology [7]. Let G be the set of all the ground-truth text-line, and $|G|$ denote the cardinality of the set G, then the overall performance is measured as the percentage of ground-truth text-lines that are not found correctly:

$$\rho = \frac{|C \cup S \cup M|}{|G|} \tag{4}$$

A ground-truth text-line is said to lie completely within one detected text segment if the area overlap between the two is significant. Significance is determined using four tolerance parameters which are identical here to those used in [7].

The main advantages of this approach are that it is independent of OCR recognition error, is independent of zone shape, and requires only text-line level ground-truth. Since a text block can be easily decomposed into text-lines by projecting each block parallel to its baseline and analyzing the resulting one-dimensional profile, the assignment of text-lines to text blocks is not critical. Therefore, the evaluation scheme does not take into account vertical merge errors. However, there is a drawback of this approach. If a segmentation algorithm just takes the whole page as one segment, the split and missed errors vanish

$(C = \emptyset, S = \emptyset)$. Typically for single-column documents, $M = \emptyset$. Hence, without doing anything, the segmentation accuracy can be high if there is a large proportion of single-column document images in the test dataset. This effect was not considered in the original evaluation [7]. In order to check the severity of the problem, we have introduced a dummy segmentation algorithm into the comparison, as discussed in Section 2.1. Furthermore, we report the performance of each algorithm separately for single-column, two-column, and three-column document images. This allows us to assess the strengths and weaknesses of different algorithms.

4   Experiments and Results

The evaluation of the page segmentation algorithms was done on the University of Washington III (UW-III) database [17]. The database consists of 1600 English document images with manually edited ground-truth of entity bounding boxes. These bounding boxes enclose text and non-text zones, text-lines and words. We used the 978 images that correspond to the UW-I dataset pages. Only the text regions are evaluated, and non-text regions are ignored. The dataset is divided into 100 training images and 878 test images. The purpose of the training images is to find suitable parameter values for the segmentation algorithms. The experiments are done using both default parameters as mentioned in the respective papers and tuned/optimized parameters (Table 1). This allows us to assess how much the performance of each algorithm depends on the choice of good parameters for the task. The parameters for the X-Y cut algorithm are highly application dependent, so no default parameters are specified in [10]. The optimized parameter values used for X-Y cut, Docstrum, and Voronoi-diagram based algorithms were the same as in [7]. For the smearing, whitespace, and constrained text-line finding algorithms, we experimented with different parameter values and selected those which gave lowest error rates on the training set.

Table 1. Parameter values used for each algorithm in the evaluation given in Table 2. For dummy, X-Y cut, smearing, and text-line finding algorithms, default and optimized parameters are the same.

Algorithm	Default values	Optimal values
Dummy	None	
X-Y cut	$T_X = 35, T_Y = 54, T_X^n = 78, T_Y^n = 32$	
Smearing	$C_h = 300, C_v = 500, C_s = 30, C_{21} = 3, C_{22} = 3$	
Text-line	$O_m = 0.8$	
Whitespace	$W_s = 42.43, T_s = 34.29$	$W_s = 42.43, T_s = 65$
Docstrum	$K = 5, f_t = 2.578, f_d = 9,$ $f_{pe} = 1.3, f_{pa} = 1.5$	$K = 8, f_t = 2.578, f_d = 9,$ $f_{pe} = 0.6, f_{pa} = 2.345$
Voronoi	$s_r = 6, nm = 11,$ $fr = 0.34, ta = 40$	$s_r = 6, nm = 11,$ $fr = 0.083, ta = 200$

Table 2. The evaluation results for different page segmentation algorithms on 100 train images and 878 test images. The results are reported in terms of percentage of text-lines detection errors (Eq. 4).

Algorithm	Default parameters			Optimized parameters		
	Train	Test		Train	Test	
	Mean	Mean	Stdev	Mean	Mean	Stdev
Dummy	52.2	48.8	39.0	52.2	48.8	39.0
X-Y cut	14.7	17.1	24.4	14.7	17.1	24.4
Smearing	13.4	14.2	23.0	13.4	14.2	23.0
Whitespace	12.7	12.2	20.0	9.1	9.8	18.3
Text-line	8.9	8.5	14.4	8.9	8.5	14.4
Docstrum	8.7	11.2	22.6	4.3	6.0	15.2
Voronoi	6.8	7.5	12.9	4.7	5.5	12.3

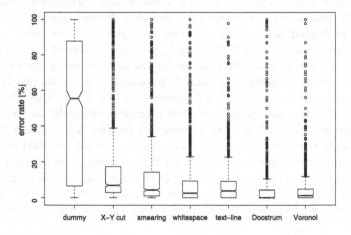

Fig. 1. Box plot for the results obtained with optimized parameters on the test data

We have used the page segmentation evaluation toolkit (PSET) [18] to accelerate the evaluation procedure. The PSET evaluation package implements the training and evaluation scheme by [7], and can be easily extended to evaluate new algorithms and experiment with new metrics and datasets. The average text-line detection error rate for each algorithm is given in Table 2. The high standard deviation in the error rate of each algorithm shows that the algorithms work very well on some images, while failing badly on some other images.

Fig. 1 shows a box plot of the error rates observed for each algorithm. The boxes in the box plot represent the interquartile range, i.e. they contain the middle 50% of the data. The lower and upper edges represent the first and third quartiles, whereas the middle line represents the median of the data. The notches represent the expected range of the median. The 'whiskers' on the two sides show

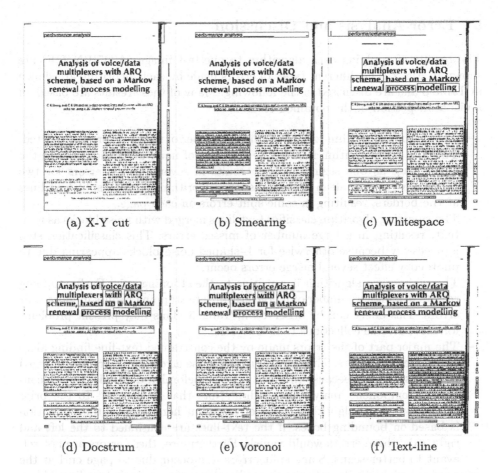

(a) X-Y cut   (b) Smearing   (c) Whitespace

(d) Docstrum   (e) Voronoi   (f) Text-line

Fig. 2. Segmentation results from applying each algorithm to one page image. The page contains a title in large font and a big noise strip along the right border. (a) The X-Y cut algorithm fails in the presence of noise and tends to take the whole page as one segment. (b) The smearing algorithm also classifies the detected regions as text/non-text, and thus misses the lines joined by the noise bar. (c),(d),(e) Due to the large font size and big inter-word spacing, the Voronoi, Docstrum, and whitespace algorithms split the title lines. (f) Due to the noise bar, several characters on the right side of each line in the second column were merged with the noise bar and the text-line finding algorithm did not include these characters.

inliers, i.e. points within 1.5 times the interquartile range. The outliers are represented by small circles outside the whiskers. We can observe the following details: A ranking of the algorithms based on their median error would deviate from the ranking based on the average error. Remarkably, the Docstrum algorithm does not make any errors for more than 50% of the pages in the test set, which is not achieved by any other algorithm. This might be a property that would be preferable in certain applications, while for other applications the average error rate may be more important.

5 Error Analysis and Discussion

The results of applying each algorithm to one test image (A005BIN.TIF) are shown in Fig. 2. The different types of errors made by each algorithm are shown in Table 3 and are discussed in the following. Many of these results are based on a visual inspection of the obtained results.

- The dummy algorithm results in a large number of merge errors as expected.
- The X-Y cut algorithm fails in the presence of noise and tends to take the whole page as one segment. This results in several merge errors for two column pages. For clean documents, the algorithm tends to split text-lines at the borders, resulting in some split errors on each page.
- The smearing algorithm classifies text-lines merged with noise blocks as non-text, resulting in a large number of missed errors. This classification step is necessary because otherwise for L-shaped noise blocks appearing due to photocopy effect several merge errors occur.
- The whitespace algorithm is sensitive to the stopping rule. Early stopping results in a higher number of merge errors, late stopping results in more split errors. This effect can be observed in Table 3. This may present problems for more diverse collections than UW-III.
- The major part of the errors made by the constrained text-line finding algorithm are split errors. The main source of these errors are characters merged with noise blocks, because they are rejected beforehand as noise by the connected component analysis algorithm. Note that in contrast to the prior evaluation of the algorithm, these errors occur here because the evaluation is based on bounding boxes; if the text-lines are continued to the left and right side, these errors would vanish. Furthermore, these errors are not relevant to better scans. Some split errors also occur due to page curl at the border, which results in two separate baselines fit to a single text-line. Merge errors appear when page numbers are in close proximity to journal or article names in footers or headers. Single digit page numbers are missed by the text-line finding algorithm, because it requires at least two connected components to form a line.
- In the Voronoi and Docstrum algorithms, the inter-character and inter-line spacings are estimated from the document image. Hence spacing variations due to different font sizes and styles within one page result in split errors in both algorithms. However, since both algorithms find text regions, and not individual text-lines, huge noise bars along the border do not result in split errors, as the bounding box of the text region includes the characters merged in the noise bar if at least one text line has no merged characters.

Table 4 shows the error rates of the algorithms separated for different document characteristics. First, the documents were separated according to the 'maximum columns number' attribute recorded for each page. There are 362, 449, and 67 one-, two-, and three-column documents in the test set of 878 pages. We can observe that the smearing, whitespace, and text-line algorithms perform

Table 3. Percentage of different types of errors made by each algorithm

Algorithm	Default parameters			Optimized parameters		
	Split	Merge	Missed	Split	Merge	Missed
Dummy	0.0	65.5	0.0	0.0	65.5	0.0
X-Y cut	5.6	7.8	0.4	5.6	7.8	0.4
Smearing	3.8	1.0	5.7	3.8	1.0	5.7
Whitespace	6.6	1.3	0.0	5.0	2.6	0.0
Text-line	5.1	1.3	0.2	5.1	1.3	0.2
Docstrum	4.5	9.0	0.0	2.5	3.6	0.01
Voronoi	4.9	0.8	0.02	2.9	1.3	0.02

Table 4. Text-line detection errors [%] for each of the algorithms separated for one-, two-, and three-column documents, and separated for photocopies or direct scans

Algorithm	No. of columns			Photocopy	
	1	2	3	No	Yes
Dummy	8.3	75.0	88.5	68.7	46.2
X-Y cut	19.9	15.6	11.7	14.7	17.4
Smearing	23.5	7.9	5.8	6.6	15.1
Whitespace	14.5	6.7	5.6	2.9	10.8
Text-line	13.3	5.3	4.4	3.6	9.2
Docstrum	5.8	6.2	5.2	6.2	5.9
Voronoi	6.9	4.6	3.4	2.8	5.8

much worse on one-column documents than on the average. This behavior can be explained by the stronger effect of the noise blocks occurring in photocopied images for these one-column documents, because each line is affected. We further investigated this hypothesis by separating the documents according to their 'degradation type' attribute. There are 776 photocopied and 102 directly scanned documents in the test set and the respective results are shown in Table 4. We can observe that the algorithms performing worse on one-column documents in fact also perform worse on the photocopied images due to the noise blocks. Interestingly, especially the Docstrum algorithm does not gain accuracy for clean documents, while the Voronoi-based algorithm still performs best. The smearing, whitespace and text-line algorithms are most effected by the photocopy effects. This suggests that they would perform better for current layout analysis tasks in which most documents are directly scanned.

The timing of the algorithms cannot be directly compared because of the difference in their output level. Whitespace, Docstrum, Voronoi, and X-Y cut algorithms give text blocks which have still to be separated into text-lines. Whereas the constrained text-line finding algorithm directly gives the text-lines as output. Secondly, the smearing algorithm also includes a block-classification step, which is missing in other algorithms. Furthermore, the Docstrum, whitespace, and constrained text-line finding algorithms depend on the computation of connected components in the image, which were calculated offline and stored in the database. However, an informal ranking of the running times from fastest to slowest is: X-Y cut, Voronoi, Docstrum, whitespace, smearing, and constrained text-line finding. All algorithms completed page processing in an average of less than 7 seconds on a 2GHz AMD PC running Linux.

6   Conclusion

In this paper, we compared the performance of six different page segmentation algorithms on the UW-III dataset using a text-line detection accuracy based performance metric. The evaluation results showed that generally the X-Y cut, smearing, and whitespace algorithms perform poorer than the Docstrum, Voronoi, and constrained text-line finding algorithms. The high variance in the detection error rate prohibits the marking of any algorithm as a clear winner.

We also inspected the results visually and generally observed the following. The constrained text-line finding algorithm is more robust to within page variations in font size, style, inter-character and inter-line spacing than any other algorithm. However, due to page curl and photocopy effect, the characters merged with a noise block are ignored by the text-line finding algorithm resulting in more split errors. Note, though, that the text-line method is not a full-fledged layout analysis method yet. On the other hand, page numbers are more reliably found by Voronoi and Docstrum algorithms. Since each algorithm has different strengths and weaknesses, combining the results of more than one algorithm may yield promising results.

The results also reveal several limitation of the UW-III database. First, all images have the same resolution. This fact favors algorithms with many parameters that can be tuned to the task and contributes significantly to the good results of algorithms based on thresholds on layout distances. Furthermore, the presence of many photocopied pages that are not well binarized is not representative of the majority of scanned documents that are captured today. In summary, although the diversity of layouts found in the UW-III database is good, we consider the variability of physical properties like resolution and image degradation to be too limited for a good evaluation; and we therefore need to test the robustness of algorithms using more heterogeneous document collections. It would be an important step to make available a larger, ground-truthed database with more variability for future research.

Acknowledgments

This work was partially funded by the BMBF (German Federal Ministry of Education and Research), project IPeT (01 IW D03). The authors would also like to acknowledge Joost van Beusekom's work in implementing the run-length smearing algorithm.

References

1. Cattoni, R., Coianiz, T., Messelodi, S., Modena, C.M.: Geometric layout analysis techniques for document image understanding: a review. Technical report, IRST, Trento, Italy (1998)
2. Mao, S., Rosenfeld, A., Kanungo, T.: Document structure analysis algorithms: a literature survey. Proc. SPIE Electronic Imaging **5010** (2003) 197–207
3. Yanikoglu, B.A., Vincent, L.: Ground-truthing and benchmarking document page segmentation. In: Proc. ICDAR, Montreal, Canada (1995) 601–604
4. Liang, J., Phillips, I.T., Haralick, R.M.: Performance evaluation of document structure extraction algorithms. CVIU **84** (2001) 144–159
5. Kanai, J., Nartker, T.A., Rice, S.V., Nagy, G.: Performance metrics for document understanding systems. In: Proc. ICDAR, Tsukuba, Japan (1993) 424–427
6. Das, A.K., Saha, S.K., Chanda, B.: An empirical measure of the performance of a document image segmentation algorithm. IJDAR **4** (2002) 183–190
7. Mao, S., Kanungo, T.: Empirical performance evaluation methodology and its application to page segmentation algorithms. IEEE TPAMI**23** (2001) 242–256
8. Antonacopoulos, A., Gatos, B., Bridson, D.: ICDAR 2005 page segmentation competition. In: Proc. ICDAR, Seoul, Korea (2005) 75–80
9. Antonacopoulos, A., Gatos, B., Karatzas, D.: ICDAR 2003 page segmentation competition. In: Proc. ICDAR, Edinburgh, UK (2003) 688–692
10. Nagy, G., Seth, S., Viswanathan, M.: A prototype document image analysis system for technical journals. Computer **7** (1992) 10–22
11. O Gorman, L.: The document spectrum for page layout analysis. IEEE TPAMI **15** (1993) 1162–1173
12. Kise, K., Sato, A., Iwata, M.: Segmentation of page images using the area Voronoi diagram. CVIU **70** (1998) 370–382
13. Wong, K.Y., Casey, R.G., Wahl, F.M.: Document analysis system. IBM Journal of Research and Development **26** (1982) 647–656
14. Baird, H.S.: Background structure in document images. In: Document Image Analysis, World Scientific, (1994) 17–34
15. Breuel, T.M.: Two geometric algorithms for layout analysis. In: Document Analysis Systems, Princeton, NJ. (2002)
16. Breuel, T.M.: Robust least square baseline finding using a branch and bound algorithm. In: Doc. Recognition & Retrieval, SPIE, San Jose, CA. (2002) 20–27
17. Guyon, I., Haralick, R.M., Hull, J.J., Phillips, I.T.: Data sets for OCR and document image understanding research. In: Handbook of character recognition and document image analysis, World Scientific, (1997) 779–799
18. Mao, S., Kanungo, T.: Software architecture of PSET: a page segmentation evaluation toolkit. IJDAR **4** (2002) 205–217

HVS Inspired System for Script Identification in Indian Multi-script Documents

Peeta Basa Pati* and A.G. Ramakrishnan

Department of Electrical Engineering,
Indian Institute of Science, Bangalore – 560 012, India
pati@ee.iisc.ernet.in

Abstract. Identification of the script of the text, present in multi-script documents, is one of the important first steps in the design of an OCR system. Much work has been reported relating to Roman, Arabic, Chinese, Korean and Japanese scripts. Though some work has already been reported involving Indian scripts, the work is still in its nascent stage. For example, most of the work assumes that the script changes only at the level of the line, which is rarely an acceptable assumption in the Indian scenario. In this work, we report a script identification algorithm, which takes into account the fact that the script changes at the word level in most Indian bilingual or multilingual documents. Initially, we deal with the identification of the script of words, using Gabor filters, in a bi-script scenario. Later, we extend this to tri-script and then, five-script scenarios. The combination of Gabor features with nearest neighbor classifier shows promising results. Words of different font styles and sizes are used. We have shown that our identification scheme, inspired from the Human Visual System (HVS), utilizing the same feature and classifier combination, works consistently well for any of the combination of scripts experimented.

Keywords: Gabor filter, script identification, prototype selection.

1 Introduction

India has 26 official languages represented with 13 unique scripts. Many official documents are multi-script in nature. Besides, there are other Asian countries, where multi-script documents exist. Thus, identification of the script is one of the necessary challenges for the designer of OCR systems dealing with such multi-script documents. Quite a few results have been reported in the literature, identifying the scripts in multi-script documents. However, very few of these works deal with script identification at the word level.

Spitz *et al.* [1] use the spatial relationship between the structural features of characters for distinguishing Han from the Latin script. Asian scripts (Japanese, Korean and Chinese) are differentiated from Roman by an uniform vertical distribution of upward concavities. In the case of the above Asian scripts, the measure

---

* Corresponding author.

H. Bunke and A.L. Spitz (Eds.): DAS 2006, LNCS 3872, pp. 380–389, 2006.
© Springer-Verlag Berlin Heidelberg 2006

of optical density (*i.e.* the number of ON-pixels per unit area) is employed to distinguish one from the other. Hochberg *et al.* [2] use cluster based templates for script identification. They consider thirteen different scripts including Devanagari, an Indian script used to write Hindi, Sanskrit, Marathi and Nepali languages. They cluster the textual symbols (connected components) and create a representative symbol or a template for each cluster. Identification is through comparison of textual symbols of the test documents with those of the templates. However, the requirement of the extraction of connected components makes this feature a local one. Wood *et al.* [3] suggest a method based on Hough transform, morphological filtering, and analysis of projection profile. Their work involves the global characteristics of the text.

Tan [4] has suggested a method for identifying six different scripts using a texture based approach. Textual blocks of 128×128 are taken and filtered with angular spacings of $11.25°$. This method assumes that the script of the text changes at the paragraph level. Roman, Persian, Chinese, Malayalam, Greek and Russian scripts, with multiple font sizes and styles (font invariance within the block), are identified.

Pal and Chaudhuri [5] have proposed a method, based on a decision tree, for recognizing the script of a line of text. They consider Roman, Bengali and Devanagari scripts. They have used the projection profile, besides statistical, topological and stroke-based features. At the initial level, the Roman script is isolated from the other two, by examining the presence of the **headline**[1] (shirorekha). Devanagari is differentiated from Bangla by identifying the principal strokes [5]. In [6], they have extended their work to the identification of the script from a given triplet. Here, they have dealt with almost all the Indian scripts. Besides the headline, they have used some script-dependent structural properties, such as the distribution of ascenders and descenders, the position of the vertical line in a text block, and the number of horizontal runs.

Chaudhuri and Seth [7] have proposed a technique using features such as the horizontal projection profile, Gabor transform and aspect ratio of connected components. They have handled Roman, Devanagari, Telugu and Malayalam scripts.

For most of the above reported works, the textual block taken for the script recognition task is either a mono-script line or a paragraph. However, in the Indian context, in the official documents, technical reports, magazines and application forms, the script could, in principle, vary at the word level. Figure 1 demonstrates this with an example bilingual document containing Devanagari and Roman scripts.

Recognition of the script, using statistical features, at word level has been reported by Dhanya *et al.* [8]. Here the authors tried to differentiate the Tamil and Roman scripts using various feature-classifier combinations. This work has been extended by Pati *et al.* [9]. Here the authors have identified Odiya and Devanagari scripts, besides Tamil, against the Roman script. They use a bank of Gabor

---

[1] Both Devanagari and Bangla scripts have a horizontal line at the top, known as *shirorekha*, which connects the characters in a word.

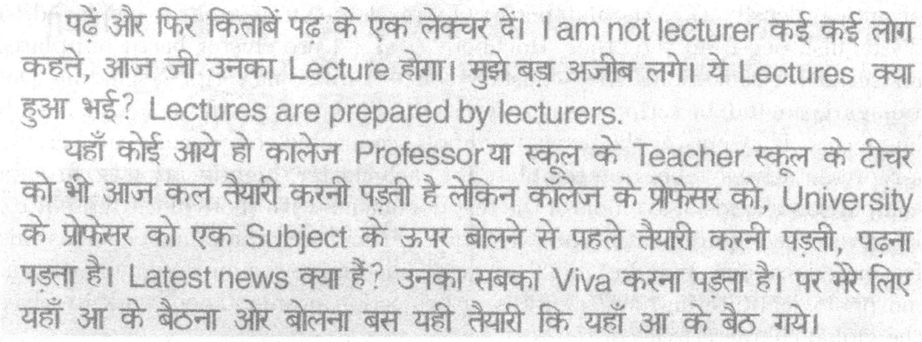

पढ़ें और फिर किताबें पढ़ के एक लेक्चर दें। I am not lecturer कई कई लोग कहते, आज जी उनका Lecture होगा। मुझे बड़ा अजीब लगे। ये Lectures क्या हुआ भई? Lectures are prepared by lecturers.

यहाँ कोई आये हो कालेज Professor या स्कूल के Teacher स्कूल के टीचर को भी आज कल तैयारी करनी पड़ती है लेकिन कॉलेज के प्रोफेसर को, University के प्रोफेसर को एक Subject के ऊपर बोलने से पहले तैयारी करनी पड़ती, पढ़ना पड़ता है। Latest news क्या हैं? उनका सबका Viva करना पड़ता है। पर मेरे लिए यहाँ आ के बैठना ओर बोलना बस यही तैयारी कि यहाँ आ के बैठ गये।

Fig. 1. A sample bi-script document showing interspersed Hindi and English words

filters for feature extraction with linear discriminant classifier for decision making. Besides, redesign of the Gabor functions has allowed to enhance the system efficiency. Pal and Chaudhury [5] have tried to discriminate Roman, Devanagari and Bangla scripts at the word level using a set of structural features and a tree based classifier. They have extended their approach to identify scripts in another triplet, Roman, Devanagari and Telugu scripts [10]. Padma and Nagabhushan [11] have discriminated Roman, Devanagari and Kannada script on similar lines.

In the present work, we significantly extend our earlier work [8, 9] by refining the parameters of the Gabor filters based on our experiments, and also experimenting on a much larger database of words. One of the motivations is to come out with a technique that works for any pairs of scripts, since in the border areas between different states in India, two languages, and hence, two scripts co-exist. Further, since Hindi is the national language, which uses the Devanagari script, we explore the effectiveness of our approach in dealing with documents that use a state language, English and Hindi. Thus, we have evaluated the performance of our technique for recognizing three scripts, namely a local script, Devanagari and Roman. In addition, we also determine how effectively we can determine the script of a word without any a priori knowledge except that it is one of the 5 possible scripts.

2   Data Description

Our database consists of about 1000 scanned documents of different scripts. These documents are scanned from various sources such as (i) laser printed pages, (ii) printed books, (iii) magazines, (iv) newspapers and (v) official documents. We have collected about 4500 words each from Tamil, Kannada, Odiya, Devanagari and Roman scripts [12]. 3000 of these are selected randomly for each script, to form the training set, while the rest 1500 words form the test set. Most of these words have been segmented and collected from actual bilingual documents, with the script varying at the word level. We have assumed that a word contains at least two characters. These words contain a lot of variability in terms of font size and style, as well as the age and nature of the document from which they are collected. We ensure that there are no blank rows or columns at the boundaries of the word image.

3   System Description

Human Visual System (HVS) is best modeled by Gabor functions[2] [15], because the mammalian visual cortex involves a set of parallel filter channels, which are quasi-independent [16] as well as direction dependent [17]. This supports the theory of multi-channel filtering of signals in systems that model biological vision [18]. This scheme has been successful in texture segmentation [19] and researchers have also used it for text page segmentation [20, 21].

There are two approaches taken for script identification in a multi-script scenario. One of them extensively studies the similarities and differences in the structures between the co-occurring scripts while the second method deals with each script as a different texture. In our view, the latter method is more robust as it deals with the script regardless of the size or style of the font. Thus, we use a multi-channel filtering approach, employing Gabor functions, for script identification. This claim of ours is supported by earlier work on page layout analysis [21] and script identification [8, 9].

The Gabor filter bank used has three different radial frequencies (0.125, 0.25 & 0.5) and six different angles of orientation (θ = 0, 30, 60, 90, 120 and 150 degrees). Thus, we have used a radial frequency bandwidth of 1 octave and an angular bandwidth of 30°. The spatial spread of each filter along the $x-$ and $y-$coordinates are determined by the standard deviations of the Gaussians, σ_x and σ_y, respectively. Both of them are functions of the radial frequency and angular bandwidth. The three radial frequencies with six θ's give a combination of 18 odd and 18 even filters. The size of each filter mask is 13 × 13. Each of the word images, without any size normalization, is convolved in the spatial domain with these filters. A 36-dimensional feature vector is formed with the total energy in each of the filtered images forming a feature.

We use linear discriminant (LD) and nearest neighbor (NN) classifiers as the decision makers. Each feature vector acts as a point in a $d-$dimensional space, where d (= 36) is the dimensionality of the feature vector. The NN classifier finds the closest neighbor of the test pattern in this space. It then assigns the class value of this closest pattern to the test pattern. Thus, in a bi-class case, if the test pattern has a closest neighbor from class ω_1, then the test pattern is assumed to be from class ω_1. In LDC, however, we try to find a hyper-plane which best discriminates the classes in this d-dimensional space. In a bi-class case, this hyper-plane divides the feature space into two parts such that the training patterns of the two different classes lie on the opposite sides of this plane. Thus, when a test pattern lies on one side of the hyper-plane, it gets the class value meant for that side of the hyper-plane. A multi-class scenario

---

[2] Gabor [13] introduced these functions, a Gaussian modulated by a complex sinusoid, in 1946 for one-D case which was later extended to 2D case by Daugman [14].

could be considered to be consisting of a number of 2-class scenarios, for LDC evaluation. Thus, by combining the 36-dimensional Gabor features with the LDC or NN classifier, we try to identify the script of a word in bi-script, tri-script and five-script cases.

3000 training patterns is a fairly large set per script. Moreover, quite a lot of samples could be actually very closely placed in the feature space. For deciding the discriminating hyper-plane, only few representing samples which lie on the border of the class are sufficient. Besides, a large training set consumes a lot of computational time while the NN classifier is at work. Thus, it is worth looking at prototype selection mechanisms, where a reduced set called a prototype set takes the place of the training or reference set. This being a small set has the advantage of combined space and computational time efficiency.

Susheela Devi and M N Murthy [22] have proposed an efficient incremental prototype set building algorithm. They have tested their algorithm over a variety of benchmark data sets and reported that it performs consistently. This algorithm has two stages: (i) set growing stage and (ii) set reduction stage. While the set growing stage increases the number of prototypes till all the training samples are recognized, the set reduction technique removes those prototypes which are responsible only for self-classification. We have taken the training sets of all the five scripts and employed a NN classifier for this purpose. We, however, have used only the set growing technique and terminate the process when it achieves 100% recognition accuracy of the training set against the prototype set, for all the five classes.

4   Results

To confirm that our selection of test and training sets are class representative in nature, we tested the accuracy of recognition of the test set against that of the training and vice versa. We use the NN classifier for this purpose. The test set recognition accuracy against the train set is 96.0% while that of the train set against the test set is 94.7%. This shows that the selection of the test and train sets are fairly independent and are class representative in nature.

The prototype selection mechanism was able to reduce the training set to a much smaller set. At the end of the process, we had 291, 290, 258, 570, 485 samples representing the Roman, Devanagari, Kannada, Odiya and Tamil scripts, respectively. Thus, we had a total of only 1894 samples representing 15000 training samples of all the five classes, saving about 87% of memory and computation.

The five scripts we considered for our experiments result in 10 different bi-class problems. We report the accuracies of the bi-class script identification in Table 1. The performance is presented in percentage and give the average recognition accuracies of both the scripts involved. We are presenting the accuracies of the LD and NN classifiers together. In the table, the characters R, D, K, O and T represent the Roman, Devanagari, Kannada, Odiya and Tamil scripts, respectively. It can be observed that both the LD and NN classifiers have performed very well with the Gabor feature vectors, though in most of the cases

Table 1. Recognition rate for pairs of scripts involving various Indian scripts. The figures indicate the average correct recognition of words in both scripts of the test set against the train set and the prototype set using NN or LD classifiers. (R:Roman, D:Devanagari, K:Kannada, O:Odiya and T:Tamil).

			TRAIN SET					PROTOTYPE SET				
			R	D	K	O	T	R	D	K	O	T
		R	–	99.1	99.2	97.8	97.4	–	98.7	98.7	97.6	96.0
		D	99.1	–	99.5	99.1	98.9	98.7	–	99.0	99.1	98.4
	LDC	K	99.2	99.5	–	98.0	99.2	98.7	99.0	–	97.1	99.2
		O	97.8	99.1	98.0	–	98.2	97.6	99.1	97.1	–	97.8
TRAIN		T	97.4	98.9	99.2	98.2	–	96.0	98.4	99.2	97.8	–
SET		R	–	99.4	99.6	98.5	98.8	–	98.9	99.5	97.4	97.6
		D	99.4	–	99.7	99.4	99.2	98.9	–	99.5	98.8	98.0
	NNC	K	99.6	99.7	–	98.2	99.4	99.5	99.5	–	96.2	99.0
		O	98.5	99.4	98.2	–	97.3	97.4	98.8	96.2	–	95.6
		T	98.8	99.2	99.4	97.3	–	97.6	98.0	99.0	95.6	–

the NN classifier performs marginally better. The highest attainable accuracy for the test set against the full training set is 99.7% for the bi-class problem of Devanagari vs. Kannada with a NN classifier while the lowest attainable, with the same classifier, is 97.3% for Odiya and Tamil combination. It could be noted that, the accuracies of the test set against the prototype set is also quite high, though trailing behind the full training set. This could be owing to the following reasons. Since we have tried to attain 100% accuracy for the prototype selection process, there is every likelihood that to attain that accuracy, the spurious patterns have also come into the prototype set. Thus, eliminating such out-lier patterns by the technique proposed by Susheela Devi *et. al.* could be of help. We could also terminate the process a little earlier than attaining 100% accuracy and see how such a prototype set behaves. The good bi-class accuracies obtained indicate that the five classes are well separated in the feature space.

Many official documents in India contain three scripts. They are Roman, Devanagari and the official script of the state, where the document is used. In the second series of experiments therefore, we have attempted discrimination between three scripts, out of which two are Roman and Devanagari. Based on the experiments on pairs of scripts, we expected good separation between scripts in a tri-script scenario using both of the LD and NN classifiers. The results of such experiments are presented in Tables 2 and 3 for LDC and NNC, respectively. The test sets have again been tested for their recognition accuracies against the train and the prototype sets.

The recognition accuracies are generally good. The discrimination between Tamil and combined Devanagari and Roman is relatively low, at 96.4% for the full train set and at 94.4% for prototype set. Here too, the recognition accuracies obtained with the prototype set closely follows the accuracies with the train set. When we compare the results presented in Table 3 (obtained from NNC) with those in Table 2 (obtained from LDC), NN classifier is observed to fare better than the LDC. This is in confirmation with the results for bi-class experiments.

Table 2. Average recognition accuracies for script triplets comprising of Roman (R), Devanagari(D) and Indian local scripts(L). Here L/DR means the average recognition accuracy of the local script against the combined Devanagari and Roman scripts. Values shown are percentages for Gabor feature with LDC as the decision maker.

	TRAIN			PROTOTYPE		
	K	O	T	K	O	T
L/DR	98.7	97.3	96.4	98.4	97.1	94.4
D/RL	98.7	99.0	98.6	97.6	98.7	98.3
R/DL	98.9	97.8	98.2	98.7	96.9	97.7

Table 3. Tri-script recognition rate (in percentage) for the scripts of Kannada (K), Odiya (O) and Tamil (T) with Roman and Devanagari. The Gabor features have been used with NN classifier, against both the training and prototype sets.

	TRAIN			PROTOTYPE		
	K	O	T	K	O	T
Roman	98.9	96.9	97.5	98.8	96.1	96.8
Devanagari	98.7	98.9	98.3	98.1	97.4	97.5
Local	99.3	98.9	97.3	99.3	97.6	96.1
Average	99.0	98.2	97.7	98.7	97.0	96.8

With the NN classifier too, Tamil script has the lowest average accuracy among the three local scripts, for both train and prototype sets.

We have compared our results with the earlier reported results of Pal & Chaudhuri [10] and Padma & Nagabhushan [11][3]. Pal & Chaudhuri have reported an accuracy of 97.2 % for recognition of Devanagari words while Padma & Nagabhushan have reported 97 % for the same script. We achieve a minimum of 97.6 % for the recognition of Devanagari words, against Kannada and Roman. This is the worst case we have when LDC is the decision maker and the test set is compared against the prototype set. The system performs better for combinations involving Kannada and Odiya as local scripts. The discrimination rate of Devanagari words against the other two is 98.7 and 98.3 %, for Odiya and Tamil as the local scripts, respectively, using the prototype set.

Thus a system, using LDC, employed for the discrimination between scripts in a tri-script scenario involving Kannada, Devanagari and Roman scripts would involve the separation of Roman at the first level with an accuracy of 98.9% and the separation between Kannada and Devanagari at the second level, with an accuracy of 99.5%. This makes the overall accuracy of the system to be 98.4% with the train set. A similar arrangement with the prototype set gives 97.7%. The average recognition accuracies for such a tri-script scenario, employing NNC as the decision maker, is 99.0% and 98.7% against the train and prototype sets, respectively. Thus our system, at all its configurations, outperforms the system

---

[3] Since we didn't have access to the databases used by Pal/Chaudhuri and Padma/Nagabhushan, the comparison is just numeric.

Table 4. Recognition rate (in percentage) for a penta-class case involving all the five scripts, using the 36-dimensional Gabor feature with LD and NN classifiers

	TRAIN		PROTOTYPE	
	LDC	NN	LDC	NN
Roman	95.8	96.1	94.4	94.9
Devanagari	97.1	97.5	96.9	95.9
Kannada	89.9	97.2	76.0	95.7
Odiya	93.5	94.5	96.1	91.1
Tamil	91.3	94.5	89.6	91.7
Average	93.5	96.0	90.6	93.9

reported by Padma & Nagabhushan which has a maximum achievable accuracy of 96.7% for the same tri-script scenario.

Since our identification scheme depends on statistical rather than structural features, we have an advantage of taking any number of scripts and identifying them. On the observation that our feature classifier combinations are delivering us very good recognition accuracy, we tried to identify the scripts in a five-script scenario. In this case, any test sample is compared with the reference samples from all the classes by a NN classifier. The LDC classifier finds a discriminant function, which separates the script associated with the function, from rest four scripts. The test pattern is checked with all the discriminant functions for a score which measures its distance from the respective discriminant hyper-planes. The test pattern belongs to the script of the discriminant function yielding the maximum score. Table 4 presents the results of the script identification in this scenario. Consistent with our earlier recorded results, the combination of the NN classifier with the train set yields the best average result. Interestingly, while Kannada fares low with LDC, it is the Tamil and Odiya scripts that fare low with NN classifier.

5   Conclusion and Discussion

By testing with words of different font styles and sizes, we have shown that our identification scheme, utilizing the 36-dimensional feature, works consistently well for any combination of scripts. For example, the average recognition accuracy is 96% and the minimum accuracy for any script is 94.5%, using nearest neighbour classifier employing the full training set (see Table 4). Similarly, the lowest mean identification rate is 97.7% (see Table 3) for the triscript scenario involving Tamil, Devanagari and Roman. The lowest recognition rate in bi-script documents is 97.3% for the case of Tamil against Odiya (see Table 1). However, a preliminary evaluation of the divergence of each of the features, shows that some features have better discriminating property than others. Thus a selected set of features would help in reducing the computation while enhancing the efficacy of the system. Our experiments indicate that such sets need to be uniquely selected for each of the cases separately, on a case by case basis.

The prototype selection mechanism has been successfully able to reduce the train set by about 87%. But the cardinality of the sets for different scripts shows the sets are highly skewed. Kannada gets represented by less than half the number of prototypes needed for the Odiya script. Similarly, Tamil script needs a little less than double the number of prototypes required for Kannada script. This gives us an impression that these two scripts, Odiya and Tamil, are relatively spread out in the feature space while the other three scripts form more compact clusters. When we look at the accuracy results recorded in Tables 1, 2, 3 & 4, we can observe that it is these two scripts which have been consistently faring slightly lower than others, in all cases. Despite all this, the results substantiate our assumption that the HVS inspired system is well suited for script identification in multi-script documents. However, this needs to be tested with other Indian and non-Indian scripts. Further, it will be interesting to compare the results against other features.

Acknowledgment

We would like to express our gratitude to Ms. G. Padmashree, Mr. Keshava and Mr. Ashwin for their help in collection and segmentation of the document images. We also thank the reviewers for improving the presentation of our results and conclusion. This work was supported by the fellowship grant of the Indian Institute of Science, Bangalore, India.

References

1. Spitz, A.L.: Determination of Script and Language Content of Document Images. IEEE transaction on Pattern Analysis and Machine Intelligence **19** (1997) 235–245
2. Hochberg, J., Kelly, P., Thomas, T., Kerns, L.: Automatic script identification from document images using cluster based templates. IEEE transaction on Pattern Analysis and Machine Intelligence **19** (1997) 176–181
3. Wood, S.L., Yao, X., Krishnamurthi, K., Dang, L.: Language identification for printed text independent of segmentation. In: Proc. of Intl. Conf. on Image Processing. (1995) 428–431
4. Tan, T.N.: Rotation invariant texture features and their use in automatic script identification. IEEE transaction on Pattern Analysis and Machine Intelligence **20** (1998) 751–756
5. Chaudhuri, A.R., Mandal, A.K., Chaudhuri, B.B.: Page layout analyser for multilingual indian documents. In: Proceedings of the Language Engineering Conference. (2002) 24–32
6. Pal, U., Chaudhuri, B.B.: Script line separation from Indian muli-script document. In: Proceedings of the International Conference on Document Analysis and Recognition. (1999) 406–409
7. Chaudhuri, S., Seth, R.: Trainable Script Identification Strategies for Indian languages. In: Proceedings of the International Conference on Document Analysis and Recognition. (1999) 657–660
8. Dhanya, D., Ramakrishnan, A.G., Pati, P.B.: Script identification in printed bilingual docuements. Sadhana **27** (2002) 73–82

9. Pati, P.B., Raju, S.S., Pati, N.K., Ramakrishnan, A.G.: Gabor filters for document analysis in indian bilingual documents. In: Proc. of the Int. Conf. on Intelligent Sensing and Information Processing. (2004) 123–126

10. Pal, U., Sinha, S., Chaudhury, B.B.: Word-wise script identification from a document containing english, devanagari and telugu text. In: Proc. of National Conf. on Document Analysis and Recognition. (2003) 213–220

11. Padma, M.C., Nagabhushana, P.: Identification and separation of text words of kannada, hindi and english languages through discriminating features. In: Proc. of National Conf. on Document Analysis and Recognition. (2003) 252–260

12. Pati, P.B.: Indian Script Word Image Dataset, (www.ee.iisc.ernet.in/new/people/students/phd/pati/)

13. Gabor, D.: Theory of communication. J. IEE (London) 93 (1946) 429–457

14. Daugman, J.: Uncertainty relation for resolution in space, spatial frequency and orientation optimized by two-dimensional visual cortical filters. J. Opt. Soc. Am. A 2 (1985) 1160–1169

15. Marcelja, S.: Mathematical description of the response of simple cortical cells. J. Opt. Soc. Am. 70 (1980) 1297–1300

16. Campbell, F.W., Robson, J.G.: Application of Fourier analysis to the visibility of gratings. J. Physiol. 197 (1968) 551–566

17. Morrone, M.C., Burr, D.C.: Feature detection in human vision: a phase dependent energy model. Proc. Roy. Soc. Lon.(B) 235 (1988) 221–245

18. Porat, M., Zeevi, Y.Y.: The generalized gabor scheme of image representation in biological and machine vision. IEEE transaction on Pattern Analysis and Machine Intelligence 10 (1988) 452–467

19. Jain, A.K., Farrokhnia, F.: Unsupervised texture segmentation using Gabor filters. Pattern Recognition 24 (1991) 1167–1186

20. Chan, W., Coghill, G.: Text analysis using local energy. Pattern Recognition 34 (2001) 2523–2532

21. Raju, S.S., Pati, P.B., Ramakrishnan, A.G.: Gabor filter based block energy analysis for text extraction from digital document images. In: Proc. of the First Int. Workshop on Document Image Analysis for Libraries (DIAL'04). (2004)

22. Devi, V.S., Murthy, M.N.: An incremental prototype set building technique. Pattern Recognition 35 (2002) 505–513

A Shared Fragments Analysis System
for Large Collections of Web Pages

Junchang Ma and Zhimin Gu

Department of Computer Science and Engineering,
Beijing Institute of Technology, Beijing 100081, China
swiftma@bit.edu.cn, zmgu@x263.net

Abstract. Dividing web pages into fragments has been shown to provide significant benefits for both content generation and caching. However, the lack of good methods to analyze interesting fragments in large collections of web pages is preventing existing large web sites from using fragment-based techniques. Fragments are considered to be interesting if they are completely or structurally shared among multiple web pages. This paper first gives a formal description of the problem, and then presents our system for shared fragments analysis. We propose a well-designed data structure for representing web pages, and develop an efficient algorithm by utilizing database techniques. Our system is unique in its shared fragments analysis for large collections of web pages. The system has been built and successfully applied to some sets of large web pages, which has shown its effectiveness and usefulness, and may serve as a core building block in many applications.

1 Introduction

The amount of information on the World Wide Web continues to grow at an astonishing speed, and the proportion of dynamic and personalized versus static documents is increasing day-by-day. To efficiently serve and deliver such dynamic and personalized content, several efforts have been made, among which fragment-based publishing and caching of web pages stands out. J. Challenger et al [1] presents a fragment-based publishing system for efficiently creating dynamic web content, which provides a method for web site designers to specify and modify inclusion relationships among web pages and fragments. Fragment-based caching features have already been offered by some products to optimize dynamic content processing on server side, e.g. BEA WebLogic [2], Oracle9iAS [3], Microsoft ASP.NET [4], and IBM WebSphere [5]. Many Java application servers allow programmers to mark a part of a page as cacheable using JSP tags. In ASP.NET such fragment can be explicitly put into a user control, which has its own cache parameters and can be included by pages or other user controls. [6] also uses tags to support fragment caching on a reverse proxy. Proxy+ [7] proposes an approach to enable ASP.NET fragment caching at enhanced web proxies. ESI [8] proposes to cache fragments at CDN stations to reduce network traffic and response time. ESI is a markup language that developers can

H. Bunke and A.L. Spitz (Eds.): DAS 2006, LNCS 3872, pp. 390–401, 2006.

use to identify content fragments for dynamic assembly at network edge servers. Therefore, only those non-cacheable or expired fragments need to be fetched from origin servers, thereby lowering the need to retrieve complete web pages and decreasing the workload of origin servers. These schemes have been shown to accelerate dynamic content generation and reduce network latency.

While performance benefits are important factors to consider, issues such as engineering complexity are of even higher priority. Fragment-based solutions typically rely on the web administrator or the web page designer to manually fragment the pages on the web site. Manual markup of fragments is both labor-intensive and error-prone, and may require considerable reengineering effort. Furthermore, the identification of fragments by hand becomes unrealistic and infeasible as the number of the existing web pages approaches tens of thousands. Thus there is a growing demand for techniques and systems that can automatically detect interesting fragments in web pages, and that are efficient and scalable enough for large collections of web pages.

In this paper, we consider fragments to be interesting if they are completely or structurally shared among multiple web pages, and we present a system that can automatically analyze shared fragments that are cost-effective for fragment-based techniques in large numbers of web pages.

The outline of the paper is as follows: in the next section we present a formal description of the problem. In section 3, we describe the fragments analysis system in detail. In section 4, we evaluate the system. In section 5, we discuss related work. In section 6, we conclude.

2   Problem Definition

Up to now, we have discussed the problem of shared fragments analysis loosely. In this section, we define it precisely. First, we introduce some definitions and notations.

Definition 1. (Nodes Relations) Two nodes in HTML DOM [9] tree are called *similar* iff all the following conditions are satisfied:

- They have the same type and name.
- They both or neither have attributes and children node.
- They have the same set of attribute names (if have).
- Their children nodes lists (if have) have the same length, and all the pairs of children node with the same index in the lists are *similar*.

They are called *equal* iff they satisfy all the following conditions:

- They are *similar*.
- They both or neither have values, if have, their values are same.
- They have the same attribute value for each of the attribute names (if have).
- All the pairs of children nodes (if have) with the same index in their parent's children nodes list are *equal*.

Both definitions are recursive with the base condition being that leaf nodes have no children node and can be compared directly.

Definition 2. (Fragment) For a web page d, let $T(d)$ denotes the HTML DOM tree of d, a *primitive fragment* of d is defined as a node in $T(d)$ of type Element, and two or more adjacent primitive fragments with the same parent are called a *composite fragment*. Both *primitive fragment* and *composite fragment* are called *fragment*. Let $FN(d)$ be the number of fragments in d, associate each fragment in d with a distinct number ranging from 1 to $FN(d)$, which is called its *fragment id*. Let $f(d, x)$ denotes the fragment of *fragment id* x in d, and the set of all the fragments in d is denoted by $F(d)$, $F(d) = \{f(d, x)|x \in [1, FN(d)]\}$.

Definition 3. (Fragments Relations) Two primitive fragments are called *similar/equal* iff their corresponding nodes are *similar/equal*. Two composite fragments are called *similar/equal* iff they have the same number of primitive fragments and all the pairs of them are *similar/equal*. Let $similar(f, f')/equal(f, f')$ denote two fragments f and f' are *similar/equal*. Fragment p is called an *ancestor fragment* of fragment f, or equivalently, f is called a *descendant fragment* of p, iff p directly or transitively contains f. The set of all the ancestor fragments of f is denoted by $PF(f)$, and the set of all the descendant fragments of f is denoted by $DF(f)$.

The *similar* relation defined above captures the characteristics of *structurally* shared fragments, and the *equal* relation captures the characteristics of *completely* shared fragments. Having discussed the necessary definitions and notations, we now present the problem formally.

Problem Statement. Given a set of web pages D, $D_i \in D$, where $i \in [1, |D|]$, and $AF(D)$ denote the set of all the fragments in D, $AF(D) = \bigcup_{i=1}^{|D|} F(D_i)$. Two relations R_{cs} (*Complete Share Relation*) and R_{ss} (*Structural Share Relation*) are defined on $AF(D)$: $R_{cs} = \{(f, f') \in AF(D) \times AF(D)|equal(f, f')\}, R_{ss} = \{(f, f') \in AF(D) \times AF(D)|similar(f, f')\}$. It is easy to see that both of them are equivalence relations. Fix a parameter $M(M > 1)$ called *Minimum Shared Number*, a fragment f in $AF(D)$ is called a *complete shared fragment* iff $\|[f_{R_{cs}}]\| \geq M$, where $f_{R_{cs}}$ is the equivalence class of f on R_{cs}, and f is called a *maximal complete shared fragment* iff it is a *complete shared fragment* and satisfies one of the following conditions:

- $\forall f' \in [f]_{R_{cs}}, \neg \exists p \in PF(f')$ and p is a *complete shared fragment*.
- $\exists H \subseteq [f]_{R_{cs}}, f \in H, |H| \geq M, \forall f' \in H, \neg \exists p \in PF(f')$, and p is a *maximal complete shared fragment*.

The definition is recursive with the first condition as the base condition. *structural shared fragment* and *maximal structural shared fragment* can be defined similarly. Let $CSF(D)$ denotes the set of all the *maximal complete shared fragments* in $AF(D)$, and $SSF(D)$ denotes the set of all the *maximal structural shared fragments* in $AF(D)$. Similarly to R_{cs} and R_{ss}, two equivalence relations R'_{cs} and R'_{ss} are defined: $R'_{cs} = \{(f, f') \in CSF(D) \times CSF(D)|equal(f, f')\}, R'_{ss} = \{(f, f') \in SSF(D) \times SSF(D)|similar(f, f')\}$. The problem is to find the partition of $CSF(D)$ induced by R'_{cs} and the partition of $SSF(D)$ induced by R'_{ss}.

3   Shared Fragments Analysis

In this section, we present the system for the problem defined in section 2. The working process of the system is divided into the following three steps:

1. Parse the given web pages one by one, and store their digest information needed for the analysis into database. We propose a data structure that is suitable for storing in database and efficient for fragment analysis, and provide the steps to transform web pages, which are detailed in section 3.1.
2. Find maximal shared fragments. This step is divided into two sub-steps. First, find the maximal shared *primitive* fragments. Second, merge the *primitive* fragments to find the maximal shared *composite* fragments. It's feasible because any set of maximal shared *composite* fragments can be viewed as multiple sets of maximal shared *primitive* fragments. We provide detailed explanation on the algorithms and implementations in section 3.2 and 3.3.
3. Collect share information. Statistics about fragments and web pages are collected in this step, e.g., size and popularity of fragments, number of shared fragments included by a web page, and the proportion of shared parts contained in a web page. We will not further discuss this step because it is application-specific and relatively easy in terms of implementation.

The system can, although can't simultaneously, analyze both *complete* and *structural* shared fragments. The processes are basically same, and the differences are explained at section 3.1.

3.1   Data Structure

A well-designed data structure for representing web pages is critical to efficient shared fragments analysis in large collections of web pages. The most popular document model is the Document Object Model (DOM) [9]. However, the memory-based DOM tree structure is infeasible for analysis of large collections of web pages, besides, the nodes of DOM tree don't contain sufficient information needed for efficient fragments analysis. These motivate us to store the fragments in DOM tree with augmented information into database, utilizing the mature database techniques in handling large relational data.

The DOM tree of a reasonably sized HTML page may have a few thousand elements. To limit the overhead of storing the elements and exclude very small segments of web pages from being detected as shared fragments, we introduce a parameter MIN_FRAG_SIZE (Minimum Fragment Size), which specifies the minimum size of the *primitive fragment* to be stored. *Composite fragments* are not stored because they can be composed of primitive fragments. Each fragment is stored in the database 'digest' table with *some* fields explained below. For explain convenience, *fragment* normally means the stored fragment in the following paragraphs.

Now we discuss *what* fields about a primitive fragment are stored in database.

First, some basic information about a fragment is stored. Concretely: (1) ID, the primary key of 'digest' table (2) DocID, the identifier of the web page this fragment belongs to (3) FragID, *fragment id* of this fragment. When a DOM tree is being traversed in pre-order, each fragment is numbered an increasing integer starting from 0 (4) StartLineNum, StartColumnNum, EndLineNum and EndColumnNum, the number of the start line, start column, end line and end column of the fragment in the web page respectively.

Second, the relations among fragments are stored. Concretely: (1) Parent-FragID, the FragID of the fragment that directly contains this fragment (2) SiblingFragID, the FragID of the (supposed) next sibling fragment of this fragment (if it hasn't), which has an obvious but important property, namely, *a fragment is a descendant fragment of the current fragment iff they share the same DocID and its FragID is between the FragID, exclusive, and the SiblingFragID, exclusive, of the current fragment.*

Third, information for efficiently comparing fragments and detecting maximal shared fragments are stored. Concretely: (1) HashLow and HashHigh, the lower and higher 8 bytes of the MD5 hash value of the fragment. When finding *complete shared fragments (CSF)*, the hash method is DOMHASH [10], and fragments with the same hash value can be safely called *equal*. While when finding *structural shared fragments (SSF)*, the text data of Text node and attribute value of Attr node are not taken into consideration for hash, and fragments with the same hash value can be safely called *similar* (2) CompleteSize, the size of the data participating in the DOMHASH when finding *CSF*, which represents the actual size of the fragment (3) StructuralSize, the size of the data participating in DOMHASH in spite of *CSF* or *SSF* is currently being detected. *Similar fragments* may have different *CompleteSize* but are certainly have identical *StructuralSize*. *StructuralSize has an important property, namely, if a fragment f is of maximal StructuralSize and is a complete/structural shared fragment, then it is a maximal complete/structural shared fragment.* This property is based on the following observation. For each fragment f' that is equal/similar to fragment f, f' has identical StructuralSize with f, so f' is also of maximal StructuralSize, if there exists a fragment that is an ancestor fragment of f', its StructuralSize must be greater than the maximal StructuralSize, which is impossible.

Having discussed *what* information is stored, we now present the process to *get* the information and store it in database. Given a set of web pages, for each of them, the process is divided into four steps. First, associate each web page with a DocID (Document Identifier). Second, transform the web page to its DOM tree. The DOM parser used by us is based on CyberNeko HTML Parser [11], however, it has been revised so that it can provide the StartLineNum, StartColumnNum, EndLineNum and EndColumnNum fields about a fragment. Third, augment the DOM tree with MD5 hash, CompleteSize and StructuralSize. MD5 hash and StructuralSize are different based on *CSF* or *SSF* is being detected. Finally, assign FragID, ParentFragID and SiblingFragID to fragments whose StructuralSize not less than *MIN_FRAG_SIZE*, and insert them into database.

Since the web pages are converted one by one, the total time needed for this step increases linearly with the number and the total size of the given web pages. Moreover, the maximal memory consumption depends only on the largest web page. Thus, this step is very scalable and can effectively handle large collections of web pages.

3.2 Primitive Fragments Analysis

The process of primitive fragments analysis can be roughly divided into two steps. First, delete non-shared fragments. Second, find maximal shared primitive fragments by repeatedly using the property of StructuralSize.

A fragment is called a *non-shared fragment* iff the number of fragments having share relation with which is less than M (*Minimum Shared Number*). Deleting these fragments can facilitate and speed up the shared fragments analysis. The deletion can be done by grouping all the fragments by hash value and deleting the fragments that are belong to the group whose member count less than M. The pseudo SQL statement of fragments selection is "select ID from digest group by HashLow, HashHigh having count $(*) < M$", and fragments deletion is "delete from digest where id in (list of IDs separated by comma)".

After the first step has been done, all the left fragments are shared fragments. According to the property of StructuralSize, the fragment of maximal StructuralSize is a maximal shared fragment, so are the fragments having the same hash as it, and they constitute an equivalence class of maximal shared fragments. To get all the fragments in the class, the hash value of the fragment of maximal StructuralSize is first obtained by the SQL statement "select HashLow,HashHigh from digest order by StructuralSize limit 1", and then all the fragments having the specified hash value are obtained by the pseudo SQL statement "select ID, DocID, FragID, ParentID, SiblingFragID, CompleteSize, StartLineNum, StartColumnNum, EndLineNum, EndColumnNum from digest where HashLow=specified_hash_low and HashHigh=specified_hash_high". To speed up the queries, indexes for StructuralSize and HashLow are created on 'digest'table.

Once obtaining an equivalence class, it is recorded into database. Two kinds of information are recorded, one is class-level information, and the other is the information of the fragments in the class. Concretely, class-level information is recorded into 'class' table with fields: (1) ClassID, the primary key of 'class' table (2) AvgSize, the average CompleteSize of the fragments in the class (3) ShareNum, the number of fragments in the class (4) LocHash, which will be introduced in the merging process. Information about each fragment in the class is recorded into 'msfrag' table with fields: (1) MSID, the primary key of 'msfrag' table. (2) ClassID, the identifier of the equivalence class this fragment belongs to (3) DocID, FragID, SiblingFragID, CompleteSize, StartLineNum, StartColumnNum, EndLineNum and EndColumnNum.

After recording the equivalence class, the fragments in the class need to be removed from further consideration. In addition, since all the descendants of them cannot be maximal shared fragments, they also need to be removed. All the descendants of a fragment f can be easily found by the pseudo SQL statement "select id from digest where DocID=f.DocID and FragID between f.FragID and f.SiblingFragID". To speed up this query, a multi-column index for DocID, FragID on 'digest' table is created. After removing, an originally shard fragment may not be any more because some of the fragments shared with it are removed for they have ancestors that are maximal shared fragments. So, in the later iteration, the fragments of maximal StructuralSize may not be maximal shared fragments, whereas, their descendant fragments may be. To avoid this complexity, an extra step to delete non-shard fragments can be added in this step, however, which is too expensive simply for this target. We choose to examine whether the detected fragments are real maximal shared fragments, and if not, do not record them, and delete them but remain their children.

To improve database update performance, all the above insertions and deletions are batched, and all the important queries are accelerated by indexes. So, by utilizing the database techniques, this step can handle large numbers of fragments.

3.3   Merging Primitive Fragments

The optimized algorithm to merge maximal shared *primitive* fragments into maximal shared *composite* fragments is still an open issue. However, we have the following observations:

Let $C_1, C_2, \ldots, C_M$ denote the ClassIDs of $M(M > 1)$ equivalence classes of primitive shared fragments, if each of the classes have $N(N > 1)$ fragments, and the list of all their fragments sorted by DocID and FragID is denoted by $LF(C_1, C_2, \ldots, C_M) = (f_{1,1}, \ldots, f_{M,1}, f_{1,j}, \ldots, f_{M,j}, f_{1,N}, \ldots, f_{M,N})$. If $\forall f_{i,j}, i \in [1, M], j \in [1, N], f_{i,j}.ClassID = C_i$ and $\forall f_{i,j}, f_{i+1,j}, i \in [1, M-1], j \in [1, N], f_{i,j}.SiblingFragID = f_{i+1,j}.FragID$. Then $\forall j \in [1, N], f_{1,j}, f_{2,j}, \ldots, f_{M,j}$ can be merged into one fragment. This is illustrated in Fig. 1.

Let $d(f_{i,j})$ denotes the DocID of fragment $f_{i,j}$, $p_{i,j}$ denotes the ParentFragID of $f_{i,j}$, and $DPL(C_i)$ denotes the sorted $d(f_{i,j}),p(f_{i,j})$ list of all the fragments belonging to class C_i, i.e. $DPL(C_i) = (d(f_{i,1}), p(f_{i,1}), \ldots, d(f_{i,N}), p(f_{i,N}))$. In the above conditions, all the adjacent fragments share the same DocID and

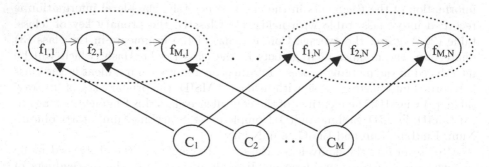

Fig. 1. $C_1, \ldots, C_M$ can be merged into one class, $f_{1,j}, \ldots, f_{M,j}$ can be merged into one fragment

ParentFragID, hence $DPL(C_1) = \ldots = DPL(C_M)$, which can be used as heuristic information when finding equivalence classes for merging. To ease the task of finding such classes, when each class is being recorded in primitive fragments analysis, the 32 bits Rabin [12] hash value of its DPL is stored in the LocHash field. The reason to choose Rabin hash is that it has rare conflict and can be implemented efficiently [12].

The first step of merging primitive fragments is to get the set of LocHash for merging, which can be done by the SQL statement "select LocHash from class group by LocHash having count(*)> 1". Then, for each *LocHash* in the set, get the corresponding list of fragments for merging, this can be done by the SQL statement "select msf.* from class c, msfrag msf where c.ClassID=msf.ClassID and c.LocHash=*LocHash* order by DocID, FragID". To accelerate this query, two indexes are created, one for LocHash on 'class' table and the other for ClassID on 'msfrag' table. Afterwards, try to merge the selected fragments into one class. If succeed, delete old classes and fragments and insert merged class and fragments into database. Otherwise, try to merge part of the fragments. The later case is illustrated in Fig. 2. Due to space limitations, detailed implementations are skipped.

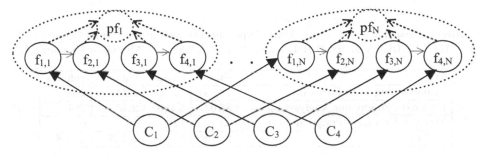

Fig. 2. Classes C_1, C_2, C_3, C_4 have the same LocHash and can't be merged into one, but C_1 can be merged with C_2, and C_3 can be merged with C_4

In this merging process, database queries are accelerated and updates are batched. In the worst case, this step takes much time, which may occur when one web page has a long list of adjacent maximal shared primitive fragments but none of them can be merged, however, it's very rare in practice. So, this step can also handle large numbers of fragments.

4   Evaluation

In this section, we first evaluate the performance of the system, and then present some fragment-level web content characteristics. The evaluations are performed on many large collections of web pages, which were downloaded from known web sites using GNU Wget (http://www.gnu.org/software/wget/wget.html). Due to space limitations, our discussions are restricted to the sina (www.sina.com.cn) and yahoo (www.yahoo. com) web sites. sina and yahoo are the most popular

web site in china and US respectively (reported in http://www.cwrank.com and
http://www.comscore.com/metrix/). The sina data set contains 130,672 files and
1846M bytes, and the yahoo data set contains 7,379 files and 195M bytes. The
parameter M (*Minimum Shared Number*) and *MIN_FRAG_SIZE* are set to 2 and
256 bytes respectively. For each data set, two experiments are performed, namely,
structural shared fragments analysis (denoted by suffix _s) and *complete* shared
fragments analysis (denoted by suffix _c). The four experiments are denoted by
sina_c, sina_s, yahoo_c, and yahoo_s respectively.

4.1 Performance

Table 1 provides a synopsis of the time consumed of the four experiments. The
total time needed for sina_c, sina_s, yahoo_c, yahoo_s is 366, 295, 42, 41 minutes
respectively. Considering that the number and total size of the web pages are very
large, and the task is inherently complex, the time consumed is very reasonable.
Moreover, it can be seen that the total time needed approximately increases
linearly with the number and total size of web pages, which is reasonable and
acceptable. So, the system is expected to be able to effectively handle larger set
of web pages.

Table 1. Breakdown of Analysis Time. Experiments Configuration: Intel Celeron CPU
2.4GHz, 512MB RAM, 40GB IDE DISK, Windows 2000 OS, MySQL 4.1.8 Database.

Steps	sina_c	sina_s	yahoo_c	yahoo_s
Transforming Web Pages (s)	13,254	12,490	2,248	2,198
Primitive Fragments Analysis (s)	8,703	5,189	263	284
Merging Primitive Fragments (s)	32	12	12	6
Total (s)	21,989	17,691	2,523	2,488

The total time is divided into three parts: Transforming Web Pages, Primitive
Fragments Analysis, and Merging Primitive Fragments. The transforming step
takes the most time among the three steps. Fortunately, which is very scalable,
since it simply parses web pages one by one. Time for merging is insignificant,
one reason may be that our merging algorithm isn't optimized and doesn't find
all the worthy fragments. Time for primitive fragments analysis depends on the
concrete characteristics of web pages, and the further analysis is skipped.

4.2 Fragment-Level Web Content Characteristics

Having discussed the performance, we now present some of the web content
characteristics detected by our system, which are illustrated in Fig. 3. It can
be observed that the structural shared fragments analysis has obvious different characteristics from the complete shared fragments analysis except in a).
However, many common behaviors can also be observed.

It can be seen from d) that a large percentage of web pages contain a great
quantity of shared portions, and only a few web pages contain a small percentage

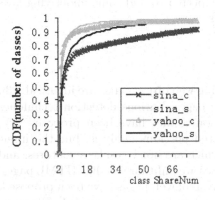

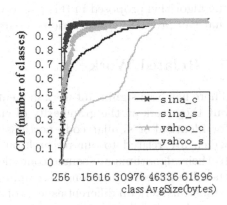

(a) class number distribution versus class ShareNum

(b) class number distribution versus class AvgSize

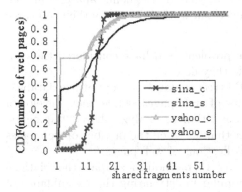

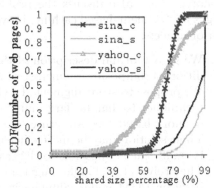

(c) web page number distribution versus shared fragments number

(d) web page number distribution versus shared size percentage

Fig. 3. Various CDF(Cumulative Distribution Function) for different experiments collected from the analysis result. a) CDF of the number of classes versus class ShareNum. b) CDF of the number of classes versus class AvgSize. c) CDF of the number of web pages versus the number of shared fragments contained in web pages. d) CDF of the number of web pages versus the size percentage of shared portions in web pages.

of shared portions. Besides, it can be observed from c) that the number of shared fragments found in a large proportion of web pages is small, and only a fraction of web pages contain large number of fragments. This indicates that our system is appropriate to be used as an automatic fragment tool for fragment-based techniques.

It is clear from a) and b) that a large percentage of classes have relatively small ShareNum and AvgSize, while a few classes have large ShareNum and AvgSize. It should be noted that, since web content characteristics are not the focus of this paper, our findings are very preliminary. However, further studies based on the algorithm proposed in this paper are expected to find some underlying laws that can provide help to various researches.

5   Related Work

There has been significant work in identifying web objects that are identical [13], but they work at the granularity of entire pages. Various detection techniques for identical or similar code portions in source files have been proposed [15], which are related to our research on shared portions analysis, but the input to their algorithms are source code files which are not tree-like structures, and their line-based or function-based approaches are unfit for tree-like HTML pages. Numerous work on different aspects of analysis of web pages have been proposed, exemplified by discovering and extracting objects from web pages [14]. However, none of their work addresses the problem of shared fragments analysis.

The work by Lakshmish Ramaswamy et al [16] is the most related to our research. They also discuss the problem of shared fragments analysis in web pages for fragment-based caching. However, our work differs from theirs on three major aspects:

1. We give a formal description of the problem, and have considered the condition of composite fragments, while they don't.
2. We propose to store augmented DOM trees to database, and utilize database techniques to handle large numbers of web pages, while they develop a memory-based tree structure and algorithm to analyze shared fragments. Their solution may be more efficient than us when the number of web pages is small, but is infeasible for large collections of web pages.
3. They rely on the shingles fingerprinting [13] method to compare the relations between DOM nodes. Shingles is popular in estimating the resemblance of documents, however, which is based on random sampling techniques and improper for small texts that are popular in HTML nodes. While we rely on the semantic information of HTML structure and MD5 Hash to compare their relations, which is more proper.

6   Conclusions and Future Work

This paper makes several contributions:

- We give a formal description of the problem of shared fragments analysis. We have considered both *primitive* and *composite* fragments, and both *complete* and *structural* share relations.
- We propose a well-designed data structure for representing web pages, and provide the steps to transform the web pages. The structure is efficient for fragments analysis, and the transforming steps are scalable.
- We present an efficient algorithm for shared fragments analysis. We divide the algorithm into two steps, and describe the implementation steps and optimization strategies by utilizing database techniques.

– We evaluate the system through a series of experiments, showing its effectiveness in handling large set of web pages and usefulness in fragment-based techniques and studies of web content characteristics.

Our system is unique for its shared fragments analysis and ability to handle large numbers of web pages. However, the merging algorithm has not been optimized, and we will work on this issue in the near future. In addition, based on this system, we also plan to develop refactoring tools for assisting the adoption of fragment-based techniques, and study web characteristics at fragment granularity.

References

1. J. Challenger, etc.: A Publishing System for Efficiently Creating Dynamic Web Content. Proceedings of INFOCOM'00, Mar.2000.
2. BEA WebLogic Server. http://www.bea.com/products/weblogic/server/.
3. Oracle9iAS. http://www.oracle.com/appserver/.
4. Microsoft. Caching Architecture Guide for .NET Framework Applications, 2003.
5. IBM WebSphere. http://www-3.ibm.com/software/webservers/appserv/.
6. Datta A, etc.: Proxy-Based Acceleration of Dynamically Generated Content on the World Wide Web: An approach and Implementation. Proceeding of ACM SIGMOD Intl. Conf. on Management of Data, Jun.2002, pp. 97-108.
7. Chun Yuan, Zhigang Hua, Zheng Zhang.: Proxy+: Simple Proxy Augmentation for Dynamic Content Processing, WCW'03.
8. ESI Consortium. Edge Side Includes. http://www.esi.org.
9. Document Object Model – W3C Recommendation. http://www.w3.org/DOM.
10. Network Working Group. Digest Values for DOM (DOMHASH). RFC2803, Apr.2000.
11. CyberNeko HTML Parser. http://people.apache.org/ andyc/neko/doc/index.html.
12. A.Z. Broder.: Some Applications of Rabin's Fingerprinting Method. In R. Capocelli, A. De Santis, and U. Vaccaro, editors, Sequences II: Methods in Communications, Security, and Computer Science, pages 143-152. Springer-Verlag, 1993.
13. A.Z. Broder. On the Resemblance and Containment of Documents. Proceedings of SEQUENCES-97, 1997.
14. D. Buttler and L. Liu. A Fully Automated Object Extraction System for the World Wide Web. In Proceedings of ICDCS'2001, 2001.
15. T. Kamiya, etc.: CCFinder: A Multilinguistic Token-Based Code Clone Detection System for Large Scale Source Code. IEEE Transactions on Software Engineering. Jul.2002.
16. Lakshmish Ramaswamy, Arun Iyengar,Ling Liu, Fred Douglis.: Automatic Detection of Fragments in Dynamically Generated Web Pages. WWW2004, New York, May.2004.

Offline Handwritten Arabic Character Segmentation with Probabilistic Model*

Pingping Xiu, Liangrui Peng, Xiaoqing Ding, and Hua Wang

Dept. of Electronic Engineering, Tsinghua University,
State Key Laboratory of Intelligent Technology and Systems,
100084 Beijing, China
{xpp, plr, dxq, wangh}@ocrserv.ee.tsinghua.edu.cn

Abstract. The research on offline handwritten Arabic character recognition has received more and more attention in recent years, because of the increasing needs of Arabic document digitization. The variation in Arabic handwriting brings great difficulty in character segmentation and recognition, eg., the sub-parts (diacritics) of the Arabic character may shift away from the main part. In this paper, a new probabilistic segmentation model is proposed. First, a contour-based over-segmentation method is conducted, cutting the word image into graphemes. The graphemes are sorted into 3 queues, which are character main parts, sub-parts (diacritics) above or below main parts respectively. The confidence for each character is calculated by the probabilistic model, taking into account both of the recognizer output and the geometric confidence besides with logical constraint. Then, the global optimization is conducted to find optimal cutting path, taking weighted average of character confidences as objective function. Experiments on handwritten Arabic documents with various writing styles show the proposed method is effective.

1 Introduction

The technique of Optical Character Recognition (OCR) has been the subject of intensive research for decades. In recent years, research on Arabic OCR achieves more and more attentions due to the increasing interaction between western world and Arabic world. As the unique characteristics of Arabic script, it is hard to implement existing frame of segmentation algorithm of other languages. Several most prominent features that are closely relevant to the designing of OCR system are described as follows:

1. There are 28 basic characters in Arabic Script, most of which have four different forms depending on their position in a word.
2. The Arabic characters of a word are connected along a baseline, no matter printed case or handwritten case. This inherent characteristic of connectivity is a crucial challenge to the segmentation algorithm designing. (Fig 1).
3. Many Arabic characters have sub parts (diacritics), which are positioned above or below the main parts of the character. In handwritten script, the relative positions between them vary a lot.

---

* This paper is supported by National Natural Science Foundation of China (project 60472002).

H. Bunke and A.L. Spitz (Eds.): DAS 2006, LNCS 3872, pp. 402–412, 2006.

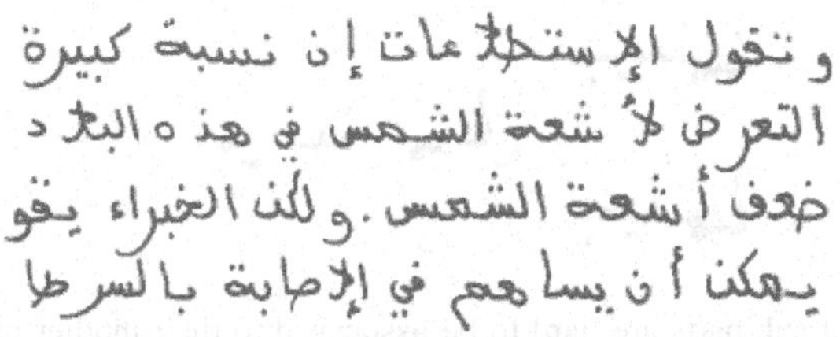

و تخول إلا ستخل عات إن نسبت كبيرة

التعرض لا شعة الشمس في هذ ه البطا د

خدف أ شعة الشمس . و لكن الخبراء يفو

يمكن أ ن يسا هم في الإصابة با لسر طا

Fig. 1. Arabic Script Sample

A typical Arabic recognition system consists of five stages: pre-processing, segmentation, feature extraction, classification and post-processing, among which the specific segmentation module is the most challenging step. For the word segmentation, the analytical approaches that segment the words into individual characters [2-7] are suitable for handling a large vocabulary of words. In this paper, we adopt this kind of approach.

As [11] points out, there are 2 fundamental strategies in analytical segmentation, which are segmentation-then-recognition and segmentation-based strategy. The latter outweighs the former in integrating the extra recognition information, so it is adopted more widely. Within the segmentation-based strategy, there are also 2 different approaches, which are explicit segmentation and implicit segmentation. Usually, the implicit approach is sensitive to the variation of fonts and is characterized by a large computation complexity. Thus, in this paper, we adopt the explicit segmentation.

Explicit segmentation usually consists of two steps, which are over-segmentation and searching. Over-segmentation tries to segment a given word into smaller entities (called graphemes) that are ideally parts of integral characters; based on these graphemes, the searching step finds the best cutting path to obtain the integral characters.

For the over-segmentation step, numerous methods have been proposed in bibliography. The vertical projection histogram is the most direct feature to get the candidate cutting columns [2, 12, 13], however, these systems can not deal with the cases where characters are too close to each other. Also, The morphological stroke extraction [14] and the skeleton analysis [3] are both frequently used, however, none of them shows robust to the handwritten case. Contour analysis [4, 5, 15-18] shows more robust, perhaps because of the simple form of Arabic characters on top contour. In this paper, a contour-based algorithm is presented, which shows robustness through experiments. For the searching step, we propose a model to evaluate candidate solutions with an objective function. The confidence of individual character is integrated with 3 types of information, which are recognition information, segmentation information and logical constraint.

Specific to offline handwritten Arabic application, there remains a problem that has not received enough attention in bibliography, that there are frequently sub parts below or above the main parts, and moreover, the relative position between them often varies a lot in handwriting case (Fig 2), for which we must find the correct association between sub and main parts. Unfortunately, few systems investigated are trying to solve this problem. Most systems simply assume that the correct cutting columns on main parts also cut sub parts correctly [5-7]. In our algorithm, we consider all the possible combination of sub parts and main parts, and propose a 3-queue model to generate the candidate segmentation solutions. This feature shows its advantage when dealing with the cases like Fig 2.

Fig. 2. The cases that sub parts are hard to be associated to their mother main parts. The main parts of characters are too close to each other. As a result, the associating cannot be simply executed through attributing the sub parts to the most near main part.

The rest of the paper is organized as follows: Section 2 introduces our probabilistic segmentation model, and the 3-queue segmentation candidate technique is described in this section. Section 3 illustrates the workflow of the algorithm. Section 4 describes the contour-based over-segmentation step, which generates original segmentation graphemes. Section 5 discusses the experiments and results. The conclusion is in Section 6.

2   The Probabilistic Segmentation Model

In this paper, we propose a new segmentation model for generating segmentation candidates. Fig 3 illustrates that any segmentation candidate can be represented by the corresponding state path in 3-dimentional space. Denote e_i $(0 < i \leq N)$ as the sequence of graphemes segmented from the main parts, e_i^u $(0 < i \leq N^u)$ as the sequence of sub parts above the main part, and e_i^d $(0 < i \leq N^d)$ as that below the main part, all of which follow the left-to-right order. We make the assumption that any valid integral character consists of three sequences of graphemes, each sequence being a consecutive subsequence from e_i $(0 < i \leq N)$, e_i^d $(0 < i \leq N^d)$ and e_i^u $(0 < i \leq N^u)$ respectively. With this assumption, any character sequence $\mathbf{c}_k$ $(0 < i \leq N)$ (sorted from left to right) can be segmented through cutting vector sequences $\mathbf{x}_k = (x_k, x_k^u, x_k^d)$ $(k = 0,1,\dots N)$ (Fig 3),

$$
\begin{cases}
\mathbf{c}_{k+1} = \left\{ e_i \left| x_k < i \leq x_{k+1} \right. \right\} \cup \left\{ e_i^u \left| x_k^u < i \leq x_{k+1}^u \right. \right\} \cup \left\{ e_i^d \left| x_k^d < i \leq x_{k+1}^d \right. \right\} \\
\qquad = c_{k+1} \cup c_{k+1}^u \cup c_{k+1}^d, \quad 0 \leq k < N \\
0 = x_0 \leq x_1 \leq \cdots \leq x_N = N \\
0 = x_0^u \leq x_1^u \leq \cdots \leq x_N^u = N^u \\
0 = x_0^d \leq x_1^d \leq \cdots \leq x_N^d = N^d
\end{cases}
\tag{1}
$$

For $\mathbf{x}_k$ $(k = 0,1,\dots N)$, there is

$$
\mathbf{x}_{k+1} = \mathbf{x}_k + \mathbf{u}_k \quad (\mathbf{x}_k \in X, \mathbf{u}_k \in U, 0 \leq k < N)
\tag{2}
$$

where $X = \left\{ (x, x^u, x^d) \big| 0 \le x \le N, 0 \le x^u \le N^u, 0 \le x^d \le N^d \right\}$, $\mathbf{u}_k$ is restricted

in the space $U = \left\{ (u, u^u, u^d) \big| u \ge 1, u^u \ge 0, u^d \ge 0 \right\} \cup \{(0,0,0)\}$. The cutting

path is represented by $\{\mathbf{x}_k\}$ with the initial and final states constrained to

$\mathbf{x}_0 = (0,0,0)$ and $\mathbf{x}_N = (N, N^u, N^d)$.

The goal of segmentation is to optimize the objective function

$$\text{conf} = \frac{\sum_i n_i \cdot \text{conf}_i}{\sum_i n_i} \tag{3}$$

which is the weighted average of the individual character confidence. n_i is the weight of the corresponding character, which is defined as the number of graphemes in the character.

conf_i, the confidence of i-th character, can be defined as

$$\text{conf}_i = \max_{\text{code}i} \log P(\text{code}_i, \text{img}_i) \tag{4}$$

where code_i is the hypothesis code of i-th character, and img_i is i-th character's image.

$$P(\text{code}, \text{img}) = P(\text{code}|\text{img}) \cdot P(\text{img}) \tag{5}$$

$P(\text{img})$ is related to the probability of the geometric configuration, defined as

$$P(\text{img}) = P(\text{rect}(c)) \cdot P(\text{rect}(c^u)) \cdot P(\text{rect}(c^d)) \cdot P(\text{pos}(c^u, c)) \cdot P(\text{pos}(c^d, c)) \tag{6}$$

$$P(\text{rect}(\varnothing)) = P(\text{pos}(\varnothing, \cdot)) = 1 \tag{7}$$

where c, c^u and c^d are the main, upper part, lower part of img respectively.

$\text{rect}(\cdot)$ represents the pair of $(\textit{width}, \textit{height})$, the parameters of the bounding box of the grapheme, and $\text{pos}(\cdot)$ represents the relative position $(\textit{Xpos}, \textit{Ypos})$ of the two graphemes (taking the centroid of the latter one as reference point). $\text{rect}(c)$, $\text{rect}(c^u)$, $\text{rect}(c^d)$, $\text{pos}(c^u, c)$ and $\text{pos}(c^d, c)$ are all taken as 2 dimensional random variable, which can be assumed as normal distribution. The parameters of the normal distribution can be estimated based on large samples with the EM algorithm.

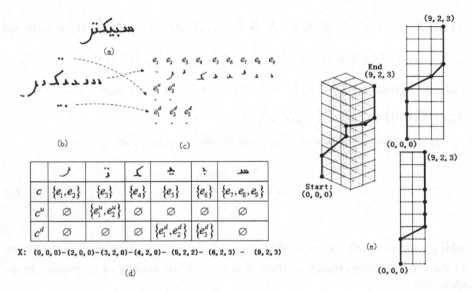

Fig. 3. The cutting mechanism in 3-queue model. (a) is the Arabic word to be cut, (b) is the segmented grapheme sequence of the main part, (c) is the sorted 3- queue grapheme sequences for main part, over-baseline and under-baseline. (d) is the representation of segmented integral characters, each one is combined with 3 components of c, c^u, c^d. (e) the 3-dimensional state space for $\mathbf{x}_k$, the cutting path starts with state (0,0,0) and ends with state (9,2,3).

$P(\text{code}|\text{img})$ is related to the recognition output of the input image i. In our system, we calculate $P(v|i)$ by calculating $P(v_c|c)$, $P(v_u|c^u)$ and $P(v_d|c^d)$ separately, where v_c is the hypothesis code for main part c, and v_u, v_d for c^u and c^d respectively. We define

$$
P(\text{code}|\text{img}) = P(\text{code}, v_c(\text{code}), v_u(\text{code}), v_d(\text{code})|\text{img})
$$
$$
= \max_{v_c, v_u, v_d} P(\text{code}|\text{img}, v_c, v_u, v_d) \cdot P(v_c|c) \cdot P(v_u|c^u) \cdot P(v_d|c^d) \tag{8}
$$

$P(v_c|c)$, $P(v_u|c^u)$ and $P(v_d|c^d)$ are estimated by the statistical recognition module provided in [21]. $P(\text{code}|\text{img}, v_c, v_u, v_d)$ is defined as:

$$
P(\text{code}|\text{img}, v_c, v_u, v_d) = \begin{cases} 1, & v_c, v_u, v_d \text{ can combine to form 'code'} \\ \beta, & v_c, v_u, v_d \text{ cannot combine to form 'code'} \end{cases} \tag{9}
$$

The parameter β determines how strong the logical rule imposed. The logical rule will affect the segmentation more sensitively when β is getting closer to 0.

3 The Workflow of the System

The workflow of our system is presented by Fig 4. The preprocessing phase consists of page decomposition, line cutting, word cutting and normalization. The first 3 steps follow the approach presented in [6], and the normalization step makes the average character height as the unit for all geometric measures. In the segmentation phase, there is a sorting step that executes: 1. splitting the sub parts into two queues: over-baseline and under-baseline; 2. sorting the three queue into left-to-right order. In this step, e_i $(0 < i \leq N)$, e_i^d $(0 < i \leq N^d)$ and e_i^u $(0 < i \leq N^u)$ are obtained. The pre-recognition step recognizes all the possible c, c^u and c^d, storing the recognition information into a database, which will be repeatedly used in searching step. Then, the searching task is facilitated with Dynamic Programming algorithm, which can find global optimal solution, that is, the solution with lowest objective function value $conf^*$, with low computation cost. In this step, the recognition results can be directly obtained at the same time that we get the segmentation solution.

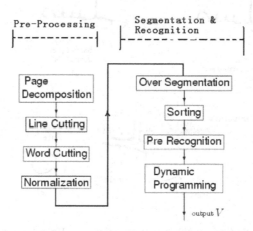

Fig. 4. The overview of the recognition system

4 The Step of Over-Segmentation

Over-segmentation is the step prior to the step of sorting and segmentation (Fig 4), which partitions the connected component of the main part into graphemes. In this step, the contour-based analysis is applied, which can efficiently find the candidate cutting positions with robustness. The rule for choosing candidate cutting positions is listed as following:

- **Rule1** all the local minima of the top contour are treated as candidate cutting points.
- **Rule2** all the points on top contour which have a distance to bottom contour smaller than 4/3 stroke width are treated as candidate cutting points. The stroke width has been calculated through histogram of vertical run-length.

- **Rule3** similar to rule 2, that all the points on bottom contour which have a distance to top contour smaller than 4/3 stroke width are also treated as candidate cutting points.
- **Rule4** the points of top contour, which are on the base line, are treated as candidate cutting points. The base line is extracted with Hough transform [8, 15].
- **Rule5** (the rule for filtering the candidates generated from rule 1,2,3,4) the distance between any two candidate cutting points must be more than 3/2 stroke width, otherwise tick out one point.

These rules are based on the typical characteristic of both printed and handwritten Arabic, that, Arabic characters are usually connected on the baseline. Based on this hypothesis, we take the points located on baseline as the candidate cutting points. Three different contour features can help us to find the candidates, including the local minima (rule 1), the stroke segments with the shape of "bottleneck"(rule 2, 3), and the points lied on the baseline detected by Hough transform (rule 4). Though some extra candidates are introduced, the losing cases are reduced. (Fig 5)

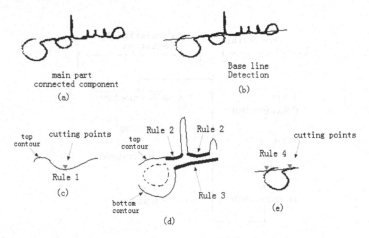

Fig. 5. The rules for finding candidate cutting points. (c) Rule 1 finds local minima on top contour; (d) Rule 2, 3 find segments on contour that are close to the contour on other side. The bold black lines represent the segments that cutting points can be located on. (e) Rule 4 finds candidate cutting point that located on the baseline.

5 Experiments and Results

5.1 Comparative Result

We have a text database of 20000 characters, including various writing styles, with which we segmented and labeled half of the text manually, training the segmentation model and recognition module separately, and chose test samples from another half. We classify them into 5 types (Fig 6). Each type of samples contains about 2000 characters.

Taking $\beta = 0$ (in equation (9)), the results on the 5 test sets are listed in Table 1, from which we can observe that our algorithm performs considerably well on all the 5 sets.

However, with the system that is presented in [6], (using the same training set) we find that the performance deteriorates significantly. (Table 2).

The segmentation rates are all fall behind that of our algorithm, which may be explained as following: this system simply associates the sub parts to the nearest mother main part character. This greatly limits the solution searching, and neglects the logical constraints.

Table 1. Performance of our algorithm

Our method	S1	S2	S3	S4	S5	Average
Total Recognition Rate (%)	69.0	59.4	57.7	54.9	54.9	59.2

Table 2. Performance of the competing method

Competing method	S1	S2	S3	S4	S5	Average
Total Recognition Rate(%)	13.1	11.1	16.5	34.6	38.2	41.3

S1   باكستان تنفي وجود معاتلي القاعدة في كشمير

S2   لسان وزير الدفاع الأمريكي، دونالد رامسفلد ،بأن

S3   غير مسمها دون إحالته إلى القضاء حتى

S4   انتشار وباء الملايا ٤ و نقل الفراشات

S5   المحملّة بالجمرة الخبيثة التي انطلقت

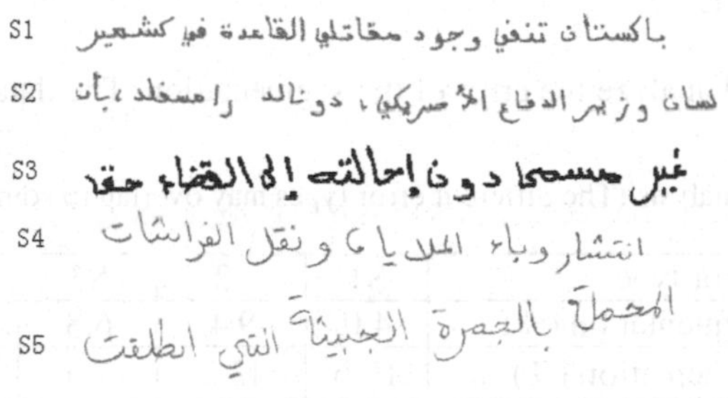

Fig. 6. The test sets for experiments. They are of various writing styles.

5.2 The Significant Role of Logical Rule

The logical rule expressed in $P\left(\text{code}|\text{img},v_c,v_u,v_d\right)$ is crucial to the performance of the algorithm. The parameter of β determines the strength $P\left(\text{code}|\text{img},v_c,v_u,v_d\right)$ imposed on the optimizing process. In basic Arabic characters, the main parts (isolated form) consist of 16 forms including ط, ع, ١, ح, د, ر, س, ى, و, ه, ن, م, ل, ك and ب; the upper sub parts consist of 5 forms including null, • (1-dot), •• (2-dot), •• (3-dot) and ٴ (hazma); and the lower sub parts have 3 forms including null, • and ••. The total combination possible cases would be $16 \cdot 5 \cdot 3 = 240$. However, the valid codes in alphabet include only 28 characters, 10 percent of the 240 possible combinations. It may indicate that the logical constraints can play a considerable role in selecting the correct segmentation.

To infirm this inference by experiments, we design 3 tests: A. let $\beta = 0$; B. let $\beta = 0.2$; C. choose the system presented in [6], (which has been compared with ours above).

Table 3. Comparison of experiments A,B,C

Experiment No.	S1	S2	S3	S4	S5	Average
A (%)	69.0	59.4	57.7	54.9	54.9	58.8
B (%)	49.7	40.9	30.6	47.2	47.1	43.2
C (%)	43.1	44.1	46.5	34.6	38.2	41.3

From the results, we can observe that the results of experiment B fall much behind of that of experiment A, which clearly proves that the logical rule plays a great role in performance. Experiment B's results are close to that of experiment C, which does not use the logical rule and performs directly recognition on combinations of sub and main parts. The results may also indicate that the segmentation-based scheme out-weighs the segmentation-then-recognition scheme, because of the integration of the recognition result.

5.3   Result Analysis

We set $\beta = 0$, and analyze the error of the segmentation. The data is as follows:

Table 4. Error analysis (The different error types may overlap to some specific cases)

Error type	S1	S2	S3	S4	S5
Under-segmentation (%)	4.0	9.4	6.8	12.8	5.8
Over-segmentation (%)	10.6	13.2	7.5	16.4	9.7
Sub-to-main association (%)	2.3	0.8	3.4	4.3	1.6

The errors can be mainly classified into 4 categories:

– Ambiguity in recognition
Since our algorithm use the recognition output as the base for segmenting decision, the right segmentation lies greatly to the correct recognition. Sometimes it is difficult to distinguish the part of character from the integral character, for example, ﺐ, (the tail part of character ﺐ), and the character ا (Alef), share the same shape of a vertical stroke, as a result, they may be difficult to classify by the recognition module. So the tail of ﺐ is quite likely to be cut out as an integral character. In future, we should improve the performance of the recognition module to deal with this kind of problem.

– Failure in over-segmentation
Sometimes the over-segmentation encounters some irregular cases that are still unable to segment. Often it happens where the stroke is too wide, or the characters are too close to each other.

– Ligatures or unique writing conventions

In Arabic, sometimes two or more characters overlap with each other to form a new shape, and these combinations are frequently appeared. In our algorithm, we can treat some of the combinations that appear most frequently as a new character, however, sometimes the frequency of the ligature is low, and the total number of these cases is large. To improve the performance of the system, we have to study these cases more comprehensively.

– Other errors

6 Conclusion

In this paper, a 3-queue model is designed to generate the candidate segmentation solutions. It is mainly aimed to deal with the characteristic of Arabic that the sub parts are isolated from the main parts and their relative positions vary a lot. Specifically, the graphemes are lined in 3 queues, generating a state space that contains all the possible segmentations, in contrast with other "greedy approaches", which takes only the nearest main part as the mother main part of a sub part. Besides, in our model, we integrate the logical and the geometrical constraint together with recognition output in confidence calculating, using probabilistic model. The over-segmentation is designed with contour analysis, which obtains the candidate cutting points through 3 different aspects of contour features.

From our experiments, the robustness of algorithm is verified as the results turn out to be smooth on the 5 selected data sets, which are in different writing style. The comparative experiment is also conducted showing the advantage of our algorithm over traditional ones. However, we have not jet used the lexicon information in this paper, which seems to be much potential in enhancing the performance. In future, we should also try to incorporate the system with the lexicon restriction.

References

1. Al-Yousefi, H. and S.S. Udpa, *Recognition of Arabic characters*. IEEE Transactions on Pattern Analysis and Machine Intelligence, 1992.
2. Amin, A. and J.F. Mari, *Machine recognition and correction of printed Arabic text*. Systems, Man and Cybernetics, IEEE Transactions on, 1989.
3. Amin, A. and H.B. Al-Sadoun. A new segmentation technique of Arabic text. in Pattern Recognition, 1992. Vol.II. Conference B: Pattern Recognition Methodology and Systems, Proceedings., 11th IAPR International Conference on. 1992.
4. Sari, T., L. Souici, and M. Sellami, *Off-line handwritten Arabic character Segmentation algorithm: ACSA*. Frontiers in Handwriting Recognition, 2002. Proceedings. Eighth International Workshop on, 2002: p. 452 - 457.
5. Olivier, C., et al. Segmentation and Coding of Arabic Handwritten Words. in 13th International Conference on Pattern Recognition (ICPR'96). 1996.
6. Jin, J., et al., *Printed Arabic document recognition system*. Vision Geometry XIII. Edited by Latecki, Longin J.; Mount, David M.; Wu, Angela Y. Proceedings of the SPIE, 2004. **5676**: p. 48-55.

7. Cheung, A., M. Bennamoun, and N.W. Bergmann. A recognition-based Arabic optical character recognition system. in Systems, Man, and Cybernetics, 1998. IEEE International Conference on.

8. Pechwitz, M. and V. Maergner. HMM based approach for handwritten Arabic word recognition using the IFN/ENIT - database. in Document Analysis and Recognition, 2003. Proceedings. Seventh International Conference on.

9. Fakir, M., M.M. Hassani, and C. Sodeyama. Recognition of Arabic characters using Karhunen-Loeve transform anddynamic programming. in Systems, Man, and Cybernetics, 1999. IEEE SMC '99 Conference Proceedings. 1999 IEEE International Conference on.

10. Dehghan, M., et al. Holistic handwritten word recognition using discrete HMM and self-organizing feature map. in PROC IEEE INT CONF SYST MAN CYBERN. 2000.

11. Bortolozzi, F., et al. Recent advances in handwriting recognition. in Proceedings of the IWDA'05. 2005.

12. Sarfraz, M., S.N. Nawaz, and A. Al-Khuraidly. Offline Arabic Text Recognition System. in 2003 International Conference on Geometric Modeling and Graphics (GMAG'03). 2003.

13. Najoua, B.A. and E. Noureddine. A robust approach for Arabic printed character segmentation. in Document Analysis and Recognition, 1995., Proceedings of the Third International Conference on. 1995.

14. Motawa, D., A. Amin, and R. Sabourin. Segmentation of Arabic cursive script. in Document Analysis and Recognition, 1997., Proceedings of the Fourth International Conference on. 1997.

15. Bushofa, B.M.F. and M. Spann. Segmentation of Arabic characters using their contour information. in The 1997 13th International Conference on Digital Signal Processing, DSP. Part 2 (of 2).

16. Romeo-Pakker, K., H. Miled, and Y. Lecourtier. A new approach for Latin/Arabic character segmentation. in Document Analysis and Recognition, 1995., Proceedings of the Third International Conference on. 1995.

17. Tolba, M.F. and E. Shaddad, On the automatic reading of printed Arabic characters. Systems, Man and Cybernetics, 1990. Conference Proceedings. IEEE International Conference on, 1990: p. 496-498.

18. Maergner, V. SARAT-a system for the recognition of Arabic printed text. In Pattern Recognition, 1992. Vol.II. Conference B: Pattern Recognition Methodology and Systems, Proceedings., 11th IAPR International Conference on.

19. Elgammal, A.M. and M.A. Ismail. A Graph-Based Segmentation and Feature-Extraction Framework for Arabic Text Recognition. in Sixth InternationalConference on Document Analysis and Recognition (ICDAR'01). 2001.

20. Lethelier, E., M. Leroux, and M.G.L. Poste. An automatic reading system for handwritten numeral amounts on French checks. in Proceedings of the Third International Conference on Document Analysis and Recognition. 1995

21. Wang, H., et al. New statistical method for machine-printed Arabic character recognition. in Proceedings of SPIE -- Volume 5676 Document Recognition and Retrieval XII, Elisa H. Barney Smith, Kazem Taghva, Editors. 2005.

Automatic Keyword Extraction from Historical Document Images

Kengo Terasawa, Takeshi Nagasaki, and Toshio Kawashima

School of Systems Information Science, Future University-Hakodate,
116–2 Kamedanakano-cho, Hakodate-shi, Hokkaido, 041–8655, Japan
{g3103004, nagasaki, kawasima}@fun.ac.jp

Abstract. This paper presents an automatic keyword extraction method from historical document images. The proposed method is language independent because it is purely appearance based, where neither lexical information nor any other statistical language models are required. Moreover, since it does not need word segmentation, it can be applied to Eastern languages where they do not put clear spacing between words. The first half of the paper describes the algorithm to retrieve document image regions which have similar appearance to the given query image. The algorithm was evaluated in recall-precision manner, and showed its performance of over 80–90% average precision. The second half of the paper describes the keyword extraction method which works even if no query word is explicitly specified. Since the computational cost was reduced by the efficient pruning techniques, the system could extract keywords successfully from relatively large documents.

1   Introduction

In this paper an automatic keyword extraction method from historical document images is described. Since the expanding usage of digital archives, we are facing an extreme amount of historical document archives. To make beneficial use of these treasures, it is quite important to make indices of these document images. However, the difficulty of making indices of historical documents leads the fact that only a few documents with great importance are allowed to have their indices that are made by the hand of experts. Therefore, it is now essential to develop systems for making indices of historical document images automatically. Such systems will extend the capability of digital archives.

The difficulty of extracting keywords from historical documents is caused by some reasons. One is that historical documents are mostly handwritten and sometimes are significantly degraded due to the passage of time, therefore traditional OCR (Optical Character Recognition) techniques cannot be easily applied. Moreover, the shortage of lexicons and written character samples make the problems more difficult. Such difficulty about OCR application increases the importance of text retrieval method without recognition.

The idea of text retrieval without recognition is seen in the work of Manmatha et al. [4], which they called "word spotting". Rath and Manmatha proposed a

H. Bunke and A.L. Spitz (Eds.): DAS 2006, LNCS 3872, pp. 413–424, 2006.
© Springer-Verlag Berlin Heidelberg 2006

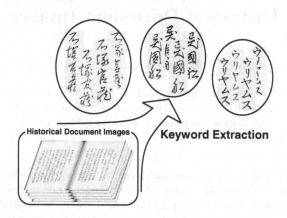

Fig. 1. The purpose of the study

set of features suitable for word image matching [7], and they applied a dynamic time warping method to match the images [8]. Gatos et al. [2] aimed to retrieve texts from historical typewritten Greek documents, where they showed that the use of user's feedback improved the retrieval results. In all of their studies, matching target was a set of segmented words because their works were intended for Western (English or Greek) manuscripts, where word segmentation is possible.

On the other hand, in Eastern languages such as Japanese or Chinese where they do not put clear spacing between words, segmentation into words is practically impossible. A study of word spotting for such a languages was done by Yue Lu and Chew Lim Tan [3], where they developed a method for searching for words in Chinese newspapers. However, it was only applied to machine printed fonts.

The proposed method aims to extract frequently appearing words from historical document images, as displayed in Fig. 1. Although it is mainly intended for handwritten manuscripts of Japanese historical documents, the proposed method is ideally language independent in the sense that it is completely data-driven. It does not need lexical information nor any other statistical language model. Our text retrieval method and keyword extraction method are both based on image matching techniques, i.e. appearance-based. Since we avoid using any lexical or linguistic information, as a natural consequence, the results our method provide will not be a set of true keywords, but a set of frequently appearing words, including not only true keywords but also stopwords or some other meaningless character sequences. However, it is still helpful in making indices of historical documents, because it provides a good list of candidates for keywords.

Our image matching method was inspired by "eigenface" [10, 11] method, which is widely used in the area of face recognition. In this method, face images are compared in reduced dimensional space. We extended the eigenspace method to compare the sequences of images by the use of sliding window technique. The use of sliding window technique in feature extraction from handwritten document images is also seen in literature, e.g. Marinai et al. [5], Fink and Plötz [1], etc.

The proposed method starts with making ranked list sorted by similarity to a query image, as described in our previous study [9]. Section 2 reviews the method for making ranked list, and besides, its performance is evaluated in recall-precision manner. In Sect. 3, we present its extension to keyword extraction, and its experimental results are shown in Sect. 4. Finally, Sect. 5 concludes the paper and discusses the future work.

1.1 Materials

In this paper several experimental results are shown. In such experiments, the materials used were scanned images of "Akoku Raishiki (The diary of Matsumae Kageyu)" (Fig. 2(a)). It is a historiography written by a Japanese government worker in the mid 19th century, which consists of 182 pages, 1553 lines, and 25148 characters. A perfect transcription of the document was available by grace of our civic library.

For use with retrieval evaluation in Sect. 2, we have manually marked every appearing instances in the images for several keywords. In this marking step, the perfect transcription was of course helpful, but final products were surely handmade.

The ground truth of keyword, which is the main objective to be extracted in Sect. 3, was constructed by n-gram statistics and handmade exclusion. First, character strings with at least 10 frequency and at least 3 character length were extracted by n-gram statistics. This constraint was employed for the reason that shorter character strings are tend to be a function word or stopwords. After that, stopwords, meaningless character strings, and duplications were removed by hand. As a result, we have made a set of keywords consist of 23 words (Fig. 2(b)).

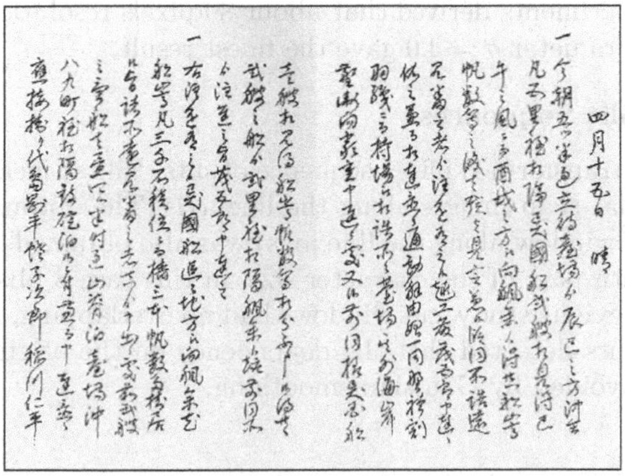

又左衛門 (165)	石塚官蔵 (25)
ウリヤムス (73)	井上富左右 (25)
稲川仁平 (24)	安間純之進 (14)
平山謙次郎 (18)	工藤茂五郎 (11)
蛭子次郎 (13)	藤原主馬 (10)
勘解由 (14)	異人共 (79)
異国船 (30)	応接所 (26)	亀田濱 (14)
本線江引取候 (21)	発砲いたし候 (14)
別紙應接書 (22)	見廻方當番 (23)
二番入津之異船 (10)	沖ノ口役所 (15)
警固之者 (11)	上陸いたし (17)

(a) The first and second pages of scanned images

(b) The ground truth for keyword (frequency)

Fig. 2. Materials used in the experiment: "Akoku Raishiki"

2   Ranked List Making

This section describes the algorithm to make the ranked list sorted by the similarity to a certain given query image. The document image was divided into a sequence of small slit style images, and transformed into a feature space as illustrated in Fig. 3. This method is similar to our previous study [9], but differing in some respects because it includes our recent improvement.

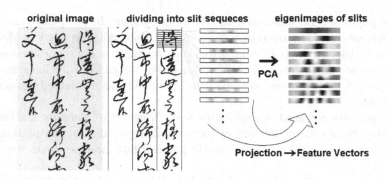

Fig. 3. The original image was transformed into the sequences of features by means of sliding window technique and eigenspace projection

2.1   Preprocessing

Some preprocessing steps needed to be performed before main process. That is, adjustment of image resolution, background removal, line separation, realignment to remove the perturbation of text lines, and Gaussian smoothing. Image resolution and Gaussian smoothing parameter have to be determined with consideration. Our preliminary experiments derived that about 80 pixels resolution per line width and Gaussian parameter $\sigma = 4.0$ gave the finest result.

2.2   Transformation into Slit Sequences

Preprocessed images were then transformed into a sequence of slits. "Slits" mean narrow rectangular windows that scan images along the line axis. The optimal width of the slits (length of the window along the line axis) was also obtained in preliminary experiments as tenth part of the character size: in this case 8 pixel width. Being different to our previous study, cut windows had no overlapping. It is because our recent experiments detected that the dependency on the origins of slit cutting was sufficiently avoided by Gaussian smoothing.

2.3   Eigenspace Projection

Each slit images are transformed into low dimensional descriptors by means of PCA. The covariance matrix of mean-adjusted image vectors was calculated as:

$$C = (\boldsymbol{x}_1 - \boldsymbol{c} \quad \boldsymbol{x}_2 - \boldsymbol{c} \quad \cdots \quad \boldsymbol{x}_m - \boldsymbol{c})(\boldsymbol{x}_1 - \boldsymbol{c} \quad \boldsymbol{x}_2 - \boldsymbol{c} \quad \cdots \quad \boldsymbol{x}_m - \boldsymbol{c})^T, \quad (1)$$

where m represents the number of slit images, x_i represents the image vector of i-th slit, c represents mean image vector. The eigenvectors for the covariance matrix belonging to the d-largest eigenvalues were chosen as $v_1, v_2, \cdots, v_d$. These vectors were called principal vectors, and formed the basis of eigenspace.

Each one of the mean-subtracted images were then projected to these basis vectors, and the generated m d-dimensional vectors became a good descriptor of the original image. These low dimensional vectors allowed us to solve matching problems more easily.

2.4   Matching by Slit Feature Descriptors

After the image document was transformed into vector sequences, the remaining problem was matching the vector sequences.

Let $y(t)$ be the sequence of slit features, where t represents slit ID. Let $A = \{y(t) \mid t_0 \leq t \leq t_0 + \tau\}$ be the feature sequences of the query image, and $B = \{y(t) \mid t_0' \leq t \leq t_0' + \tau\}$ be the arbitrary feature sequences that has the length same to the query. The matching cost between A and B was defined as

$$D(A, B) = \sum_{0 \leq t \leq \tau} d\left(y(t_0 + t),\ y(t_0' + t)\right), \tag{2}$$

where $d\left(y(t_0 + t),\ y(t_0' + t)\right)$ represents the distance between two feature vectors. Computing $D(A, B)$ for all possible Bs, and the feature sequence B which gave the minimum matching cost was selected as the retrieval result. Note that "possible Bs" were much larger in our Japanese case where segmentation into words is impossible, than English case where segmentation into words is possible. We must consider sequences starting from arbitrary slit ID. The number of the times we have to compute D is the same as the number of slits, which is almost ten times larger than the number of characters.

Here, we must mention the definition of the distance between two feature vectors. Although several ways can be used to define this distance, we employed the most common Euclidean distance, i.e.,

$$d\left(y(t_0 + t),\ y(t_0' + t)\right) = \sum_i |y_i(t_0 + t) - y_i(t_0' + t)|^2, \tag{3}$$

where y_i represents the i-th element of vector y. In our preliminary experiments we have found that the Euclidean distance gave the best performance especially when used with DTW described in the subsequent section. When DTW was not used, Manhattan distance and Euclidean distance delivered similar performance.

2.5   Dynamic Time Warping

To make the matching algorithm more robust, we applied dynamic time warping (DTW). DTW is a widely used method in the area of speech recognition. If two time series are given, DTW considers every conceivable time correspondence including non-linear time coordinate transformation, and it outputs the path with minimum matching cost. For our document image retrieval, regarding a slit ID as a time coordinate, sequences of slits can be regarded as a time series.

The time normalized distance between two vector sequences $A = \{y(t) \mid \alpha_1 \le t \le \alpha_n\}$ and $B = \{y(t) \mid \beta_1 \le t \le \beta_m\}$ was defined as follows:

$$D(A, B) = \min \left[\frac{\sum_{\theta=1}^{k} d(y(i_\theta),\ y(j_\theta))}{k} \right], \tag{4}$$

where $(i_1, j_1), \ldots, (i_k, j_k)$ represents the path, satisfying

$$(i_1, j_1) = (\alpha_1, \beta_1) \tag{5}$$

$$(i_k, j_k) = (\alpha_n, \beta_m) \tag{6}$$

$$(i_\theta,\ j_\theta) = \begin{cases} (i_{\theta-1}+1,\ j_{\theta-1}) \\ (i_{\theta-1}+1,\ j_{\theta-1}+1) \\ \text{or } (i_{\theta-1}+1,\ j_{\theta-1}+2), \end{cases} \tag{7}$$

$$1/\alpha\ (i_k - i_1)\ \le\ j_k - j_1\ \le\ \alpha(i_k - i_1). \tag{8}$$

where k represents the length of the path, which takes the same value as n in this definition. Equation (5) and (6) represent boundary condition, (7) represents recurrence, and (8) defines global constraint in order to prevent excessive warps, where α is the stretching allowance ratio. In the following experiment, α was set to 1.2, which showed the best performance in our preliminary experiment.

Equation (8) differs from standard DTW constraint such as parallel band or diamond band because such standard constraints are only used when considering matching problem of separated sequences, i.e. starting points and ending points are strictly specified. On the other hand, our problem considers matching problem of continuous sequences, where arbitrary slit may become a starting point or ending point. This type of problem is also dealt in [6], where CDP (Continuous DP) method was introduced. CDP uses sophisticated recurrence equation and prevent warps with more than twice stretching ratio. Equation (8) is similar to CDP, except that it allows arbitrary limitation of maximum stretching ratio.

2.6   Experimental Evaluation

In order to evaluate the performance of the obtained ranked list, we have adopted a recall-precision evaluation, which is widely used in information retrieval researches. Recall is the ratio of the number of correctly retrieved words to the number of total relevant words. Precision is the ratio of correctly retrieved words to the number of retrieved words. Measuring precisions at various recall levels, the recall-precision curve is produced. Average precision is the mean of the precision values obtained after each relevant word to the query has been retrieved.

In this experiment, we have selected four keywords from the whole document, as shown in Table 1. All selected keywords were human name appearing at least

Table 1. Average-precision for some keywords of "Akoku-Raishiki"

keywords	frequency	average-precision (%)	
		without DTW	with DTW
A. Matazaemon	165	64.12	87.47
B. Uriyamusu	73	71.69	95.23
C. InoueTomizou	25	57.38	92.84
D. IshizukaKanzou	25	58.56	84.20

25 times in the document. For each keyword, each appearing instance was used as a query. The retrieved images were regarded to be correct if the retrieved region and corresponding manually marked region (described in Sect. 1.1) were overlapping sufficiently (in practice, errors less than 20 slits were allowed). The mean of the average precision scores for all queries in each class was calculated for both with-DTW case and without-DTW case, summarized in Table 1.

The result shows that our ranked list was good at its performance, especially when used with DTW.

3   Keyword Extraction

In this section, keyword extraction method is described. Our objective was to extract character strings which appears more than 10 times in the document. To avoid extracting many stopwords, the lower bound of character length in extraction was restricted to 40 slits, which correspond to three or four characters.

First, we introduce a criterion to find out if a certain image region is worthy or not to be selected as a keyword. Then, by applying this criterion to every sub-region in the whole document image, the candidates of keywords were produced. Finally, by clustering the candidates, the set of keywords was constructed.

3.1   Acceptance Check for Each Similarity

In the last section, we have described about the algorithm which gives ranked list sorted by similarity for the given specific image. The next problem is to judge whether this image is keyword or not. This problem has great concern with the judgment of whether the provided similarity is truly coming from correspondence or just only accidental similarity. One idea of making this judgment is to use global thresholding method for matching cost. However, this simple idea ends in failure as illustrated in Fig. 4. In the figure, top 20 ranked matching costs are plotted for three specific images. White circles indicate the valid correspondence, while black circles indicate that similarity was not caused by valid correspondence but by accident. Clearly, the white circles in (b) are higher in position than the black circles in (a) and (c). Therefore, global thresholding method was definitely rejected. Another artifice needed to be employed.

The solution we have found was to normalize distance measure by the energy of image. "Energy of image" means the sum of squared difference of the image

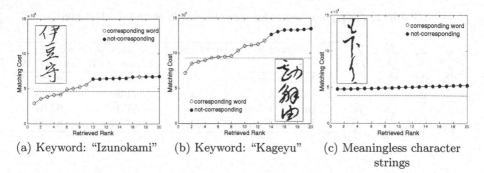

(a) Keyword: "Izunokami"   (b) Keyword: "Kageyu"   (c) Meaningless character strings

Fig. 4. The matching cost of ranked list for different query images

to a plain white image, i.e.

$$\text{Energy of image} = \sum_{\text{all pixels}} |I_{x,y} - 255|^2 \tag{9}$$

$$\approx \sum_{\text{all slits}} d\left(\boldsymbol{y}(t),\ \boldsymbol{w}\right),$$

where $\boldsymbol{w}$ represents the descriptor into which plane white slit image is transformed. Based on this energy, (4) was normalized as

$$\tilde{D}(\boldsymbol{A}, \boldsymbol{B}) = D(\boldsymbol{A}, \boldsymbol{B}) \ / \ \sum d\left(\boldsymbol{y}(t),\ \boldsymbol{w}\right). \tag{10}$$

In Fig. 4, dashed lines represent the energy of images multiplied by 0.20. The figure indicates that a border dividing white circle and black circle is about proportional to energy of query images. Therefore, the normalization described above seems promising.

3.2   Keyword Candidates Extraction from Whole Document

Based on the normalized distance measure, a criterion to extract keyword was defined. That is, an image region was extracted as a candidate of keyword if its average matching cost of top 10 ranked retrieval did not exceed a certain threshold value (Remember that our objective keyword is frequently appearing words at least 10 times). The threshold value we have employed was 0.20, as displayed in Fig. 4. By applying this criterion to every sub-region in the whole document image, we may extract the candidates of keywords.

Theoretically, the above discussion is enough to extract keyword from whole document. However, for all sequences, from whole document, allowing arbitrary length, to conduct the above checking method needs enormous computational cost especially the size of the material was large as in this study. Note again our materials were not segmented into words, therefore we must regard arbitrary slit ID as possibly to be starting point or ending point.

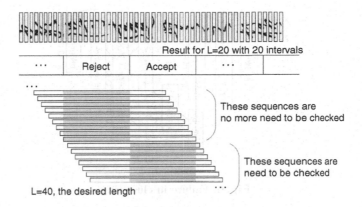

Fig. 5. The pruning method

To reduce the computational cost, pruning was carried out. In pruning, we used the assumption that if a sequence is acceptable as a candidate, the subsequence of it should have been also acceptable. To be exact, this assumption is not perfectly true. However, it is approximately satisfied. Theoretically the average matching cost of subsequence can take a value L/s times larger than the original sequence at extreme case, where L and s are the length of the original sequence and the length of the subsequence, respectively. However, such extreme value rarely appears in practice, which was confirmed in the subsequent experiment.

Under this assumption, now we have to consider only just 40-length slit sequences, because sequences with more than 40 length will be obtained by merger of consecutive 40-length slit sequences.

Therefore let us consider extracting the candidates of keyword with 40-length. The simplest method is to check the average matching cost for all 40-length slit sequences, however it takes too much computational cost. On the other hand, alternative method is to conduct pruning before doing complete search. As a pruning, we checked the average matching cost for 20-length slit sequences at intervals of 20 slit. In this step, about three quarters sequences were rejected although the threshold value was loose than original. After that,40-length slit sequences which includes the accepted 20-length sequences were checked (see Fig. 5). It cost about a quarter of the simplest method, because three quarters sequences were already rejected in the pruning step. We must mention that the computational cost of pruning step was far lower than the subsequent step for two reasons. One is that pruning step scans the document at intervals of 20 slits, therefore the number need to be checked is only 1/20 to original. Another reason is that the computational cost of DTW is quite sensitive to the length of the sequence. Checking with half length is considerably faster than the original length. For these reasons, the computational cost added by the pruning step was far lower than the cost which saved.

Applying above pruning technique recursively, we could reduce computational cost considerably. That is, after 20-length sequences were checked whether or not

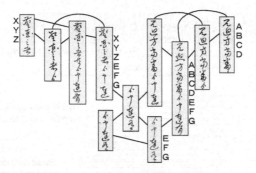

Fig. 6. Failure in clustering

being acceptable, then 30-length sequences were checked, and after that, then 35-length were checked, approaching original 40-length. With the use of this technique, computational cost declined to 6% of thorough search, while 96% of the relevant result were retained.

3.3   Clustering Candidate

The candidates of keywords were extracted in the previous method, however they should be large amount and should have quite many duplications. All that remains to do was transforming it into the set of keywords. For this purpose, a clustering method was applied.

In this process, we used graph theory algorithms. For every candidate of keyword, the starting slit ID was regarded as a vertex of the graph. Two vertices were connected if and only if the matching cost between the images starting from corresponding slit ID were under a certain threshold. After this graph was constructed, every connected parts were output as a keyword cluster. In this definition, connected means that there exists a path (not necessarily an edge) between all pairs of vertices in the cluster. The benefit of this definition is that by merging an image and an image with only slight displacement, redundant output can be avoided.

However, simply applying single connection analysis is prone to invite an unwelcome result. It sometimes connects clusters too much. For example, consider clusters C_1 that includes keyword sequence 'abcd.' If there exists sequences such as 'abcdefg', these sequences are merged into cluster C_1. Furthermore, if there exists sequences such as 'xyzefg', these sequences are also merged into C_1 because their subsequence 'efg' are corresponding. By this way, keyword 'abcd' and 'xyz' are merged into same clusters. It is an unwelcome result.

First attempt to avoid this over-connection was to remove unwanted vertices from graph. Every vertices should have sufficient numbers of adjacent vertices because they were survivors of the keyword candidate extraction. However, there exist some vertices with less numbers of adjacent vertices. Such a less-connected vertices were removed from graph because they were likely to be an error. In practice, we removed vertices which had less than five adjacent vertices.

Another attempt we have made was hierarchical extraction algorithm which could avoid over-connections such as '*abcd*' and '*xyz*' described above. First, longer keywords such as '*abcdefg*' and '*xyzefg*' were clustered. Removing such keywords from graph, then shorter keywords were clustered. By this hierarchical extraction, keyword '*abcd*' and '*xyz*' might not be extracted, however we consider it is also good because keyword '*abcdefg*' was already extracted and '*abcd*' could be found as subsequence in it.

Finally, representative images were chosen from each clusters. The set of representative images were our final output, which is displayed in next section.

4   Experimental Results

The algorithms presented above were applied to the "Akoku Rasishiki," the detail of which is described in Sect. 1.1.

Figure 7(a) shows the extracted candidates of keywords. In the figure, white-back region represents extracted candidates of keywords, while solid box represents the manually marked keywords, the ground truth. In this figure, among sixteen manually marked ground truths, fourteen were extracted as a candidate correctly. Here we must mention that it is not necessary for every keyword to be extracted as a candidate. Since the keyword will appear in the document several times, if the sufficient number of instances are extracted as a candidate, the system is still able to output it as a keyword.

The final result after candidate clustering is displayed in Fig. 7(b), where 46 keyword images were output. As expected, all of these keyword images were frequently appearing images in the document, including stopwords and meaningless character strings. Among of them, 17 valid keywords were contained among 23 ground truth. Recall rate was 74% and precision rate was 37%. Although precision rate was sacrificed because our method did not use lexical information, high recall rate was worthy of remark.

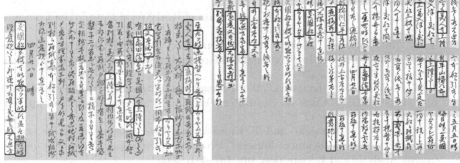

(a) Selected keyword candidate   (b) Final output: Every keyword candidates
     (white back area)   are clustered

Fig. 7. Result of keyword extraction. Solid box represents manually marked keyword.

5   Conclusions and Future Work

In this paper, two main contributions are described. The first half describes the text retrieval method when given a query word. The ranked list sorted by similarity was produced, and it was evaluated in recall-precision manner. The average precision reached over 80–90%. The second half describes the keyword extraction method, which works even if no query is explicitly specified. It is noteworthy that both algorithms works well for Japanese documents, where segmentation into word is practically impossible.

Our future work will focus on considering more sophisticated design for keyword extraction and its clustering. Further experiment, for example applying the method to other languages is also projected, because our method is conceptually independent of languages. Improving the preprocessing for further enhanced performance is also in progress.

References

1. G.A. Fink and T. Plötz "On appearance-based feature extraction methods for writer-independent handwritten text recognition," Proc. of International Conference on Document Analysis and Recognition, pp. 1070–1074, 2005.
2. B. Gatos, T. Konidaris, K. Ntzios, I. Pratikakis, and S. Perantonis, "A segmentation-free approach for keyword search in historical typewritten documents," Proc. of International Conference on Document Analysis and Recognition, pp. 54–58, 2005.
3. Yue Lu and Chew Lim Tan, "Word spotting in Chinese document images without layout analysis," Proc. of IEEE International Conference on Pattern Recognition, pp. 30057–30060, 2002.
4. R. Manmatha, Chengfeng Han and E.M. Riseman, "Word Spotting: A New Approach to Indexing Handwriting," Proc. of IEEE Conf. on Computer Vision and Pattern Recognition, pp. 631–637, 1996.
5. S. Marinai, E. Marino, and G. Soda, "Indexing and retrieval of words in old documents," Proc. of International Conference on Document Analysis and Recognition, pp. 223–227, 2003.
6. R. Oka, "Spotting Method for Classification of Real World Data," The Computer Journal, vol. 41, no. 8, pp. 559–565, 1998.
7. T.M. Rath and R. Manmatha, "Features for Word Spotting in Historical Manuscripts," Proc. of International Conference on Document Analysis and Recognition, pp. 218–222, 2003.
8. T.M. Rath and R. Manmatha, "Word image matching using dynamic time warping," Proc. of IEEE Conf. on Computer Vision and Pattern Recognition, pp. 521–527, 2003.
9. K. Terasawa, T. Nagasaki, and T. Kawashima, "Eigenspace method for text retrieval in historical document images," Proc. of International Conference on Document Analysis and Recognition, pp. 437–441, 2005.
10. M.A. Turk and A.P. Pentland, "Eigenfaces for recognition," Journal of Cognitive Neuroscience, Vol. 3, No. 1, pp. 71–86, 1991.
11. M.A. Turk and A.P. Pentland, "Face recognition using eigenfaces," Proc. of IEEE Conf. on Computer Vision and Pattern Recognition, pp. 586–591, 1991.

Digitizing a Million Books:
Challenges for Document Analysis

K. Pramod Sankar[1], Vamshi Ambati[2], Lakshmi Pratha[1], and C.V. Jawahar[1]

[1] Regional Mega Scanning Centre,
International Institute of Information Technology,
Hyderabad, India
jawahar@iiit.ac.in
[2] Institute for Software Research International,
Carnegie Mellon University, USA

Abstract. This paper describes the challenges for document image analysis community for building large digital libraries with diverse document categories. The challenges are identified from the experience of the on-going activities toward digitizing and archiving one million books. Smooth workflow has been established for archiving large quantity of books, with the help of efficient image processing algorithms. However, much more research is needed to address the challenges arising out of the diversity of the content in digital libraries.

1 Introduction

With the increased availability of economical digital storage media, high speed scanners and high-bandwidth networks, Digital Libraries have received a boost in the last few years. The dream of digitizing the vast knowledge of mankind, and making it available online has now become a realisable goal. As a first step towards this goal, the Digital Library of India (DLI) [1] and the Universal Digital Library(UDL) [2] projects aim at digitizing *one million* books and making them available on the web. One million books is less than one-percent of all the world's published books and represents only a useful fraction of those available.

However the digitization of a million books is in itself a herculean task. If on an average, a book contains 400 pages, then the project will create 400 million digital documents making it the single largest collection available on the web, with as many documents as a tenth of the number of web pages over the entire Internet. If it takes only one second to digitize a single page, it would require about a hundred years of time and 150,000 GB of storage space for the project. Digitizing such massive quantity of data and making it available on the web, for free and non-stop access to anybody-anywhere is clearly a stupendous goal.

The vision of digitizing books was originally conceived at Carnegie Mellon University [3]. A 100 book and a 1000 book pilot projects were successfully completed [4], which paved way for undertaking the goal of 1 million books by 2008, called the Million Book Project (MBP). The project is presently pursued by multiple institutions worldwide in the United States of America, India, China

H. Bunke and A.L. Spitz (Eds.): DAS 2006, LNCS 3872, pp. 425–436, 2006.

and many other countries. The Digital Library of India (DLI) initiative is the Indian part of the UDL and MBP. As of now, the Regional Mega Scanning Center at IIIT-Hyderabad, and associated digitization centres have contributed a major portion of the total content generated within India.

The entire process of digitizing the book consists of various stages such as procuring, scanning, image processing, quality checking and web hosting. Some of the issues involved in creating digital libraries are given in Lesk [5]. The digitization of a million books in a realistic time frame requires the state-of-the-art scanners, and high speed algorithms and software to process the scanned images. An efficient system needs to be built, that pipelines these processes and ensures smooth running of the project, enabling timely delivery of digital content. The system should be robust to various logistical, technical and practical difficulties in handling the work at this large scale. We have succeeded in developing such a system, where a large number of books are digitized each day. The process runs in a highly distributed and layered environment, yet the data flows freely from one stage/centre to another. The statistics from this approach have proved that the envisaged dream could be realized very soon.

The UDL/MBP is the first digitization project aiming at such large quantity of digitization as a million books. Recently, many new projects are being undertaken across the globe, which also aim at digitization of libraries. These include projects like American Memory, Project Gutenberg, Gallicia run by Frances national library, the University of Pennsylvanias Online Books, California Digital library, etc. Project Gutenberg, founded in 1971 by Michael Hart, and built and maintained by hundreds of volunteers, is the longest-running project. As of date it has reached the figure of 16,000 books. Organizations like NSF and DARPA, sponsor a large number of digitization projects in the USA. These initiatives are generally specific to a particular domain. Many projects have recently begun in Europe where the emphasis is on European information resources combining multicultural and multilingual heritage in Europe. Both digitized and born digital material are covered by this initiative. Companies such as Google, Yahoo and Amazon have also undertaken digitization of books on a large scale.

Most of these digitization efforts are either relatively small or too often associated with restricted access. Google Print, for example currently restricts access outside the US even to titles that are in public domain outside the US. Within the US they have a restricted access and some roadblocks to printing and saving images even to public domain titles. Gallica's interface might not be the easiest to use for non-French speakers. The University of Pennsylvania online books project also has to work out on quantitative and quality control issues with respect to its scans, metadata, and interface. The efforts of commercial ventures are associated with a proposed business model to allow for shopping of books based on snippets of content and to reward publishers and authors of copyrighted material.

DLI, however, is a non-commercial project aiming at digitizing non-copyrighted books, mostly of Indian origin. Copyrighted books are digitized and made available online, only with written permission from the author and the publisher. Apart from printed books, a large number of palm leaf manuscripts, which are a part of the Indian heritage, are also being photographed and digitized for the preservation of such delicate storehouses of ancient knowledge.

An insight into the challenges faced by the document image analysis (DIA) community in building digital libraries is discussed in [6] [7]. In this paper, the various challenges realized from the actual implementation of the MBP are discussed and an overview of the procedures employed to work towards the goal is presented. The rest of the paper is organized as follows. Section 2 describes the various issues that affect the digitization process at this large scale. Section 3 gives an overview of the process workflow which is a semi-automatic document analysis system. Section 4 charts the progress and performance of the system at work in the RMSC at IIIT-Hyderabad. Section 5 observes the challenges that we realized while working with the project and we conclude in section 6.

2   System-Level Issues

When the Million Book Project was initiated, it was the first of its kind ever conceived. The challenges faced by the project were many, and as the project progressed, newer challenges arose. The major aspect of the project is its magnitude. Digitization of a million books, firstly, requires being able to procure the given number of books. The type of books could vary in a variety of ways such as the size of the book, quality of paper, clarity of print, font face used, type of binding etc. Old books which are delicate and have deteriorated over time need extra care in handling apart from requiring special routines to process them.

Transferring the procured books to a digitization center calls for heavy logistical inputs. To reduce this, the digitization centres are generally setup in close proximity to the libraries. Such centres should be co-ordinated and managed by Regional Mega Scanning Centres (RMSCs), where the digital content generated by each center is hosted on servers for public access. The storage and transfer of the data generated by each center is a major task. Each center generates tens of GBs of data every day. Since network transfer of such large quantities of data is neither feasible nor economical, it has to be physically moved in HDDs or DVDs. Pipelining the data within the various phases of the digitization process is also a serious tactical issue.

Due to the fact that different libraries have a copy of each of many books, duplicate digitization occurs, which results in wastage of effort and thus valuable resources. To avoid this, there has to be proper synchronization between the various digitization centres and RMSCs. Moreover, the representation of Indian languages content is not standardized. Different organizations use different formats, such as ISCII, ITRANS, OmTrans, Unicode, etc. to code the Indian language documents. This lack of a standard complicates duplicate checking and elimination.

Digital Libraries are also a means of preservation of content for the use of future generations. Hence maintaining good quality in the digitization process is of utmost importance. Also to ensure that all centres adhere to a common set of guidelines, enabling and maintaining a standard [8] for the entire project is essential. Baird [9] gives some guidelines regarding many of the quality control aspects for digital libraries.

Maintaining large amount of digital data on the web, for any time access from anywhere, is a huge challenge. Accurate search and quick retrieval of the digital content against user queries is a major research problem.

Considering these issues, a process workflow was designed and is explained in the next section. Apart from handling the above problems, the system was also robust to many practical situations which threw up further challenges.

3   Semi-automatic Digitization Process

Owing to the magnitude of the project, the digitization process is distributed into different logical steps and over different *wings* within a given digitization center. Since, a distributed environment is apt for the project, we have identified different phases of work that can be distributed over different locations. We designed a process flow that was aimed at achieving a highly automated set up and to create the notion of a distributed environment, which is flexible, yet cohesive. The different stages of the process pipeline are depicted in Figure 1. Each of the component of the workflow is explained below.

The digitization process begins with the procurement of books. A librarian creates the metadata for the books, which is checked for possible duplication against previously digitized books. We have built technology and solution [10] to avoid duplication within our center with minimal network resources.

Scanning: The digitization process starts with the scanning of books. High speed scanners are used to convert books to the corresponding page images. Overhead

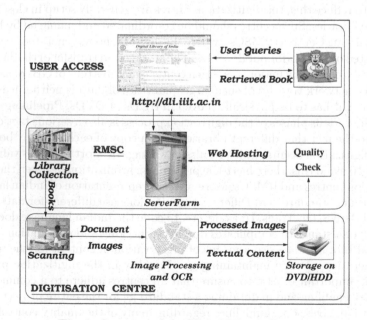

Fig. 1. Overview of the Digital Library Process

scanners scan or photograph the spread of a book from above and can typically scan an A4 sized page at 600dpi in about 2.5 seconds. Theoretically, such a scanner could scan about 10000 pages in a 8 hour shift day. However, due to the fact that an operator needs to turn the pages of the book and give the command for a fresh scan, the obtained throughput is about half this number. In the special case of digitizing palm leaves, high resolution digital colour cameras are used to photograph them.

Image Processing: The raw images generated from the scanning need to be processed for improving the quality. The scanned image needs to be cropped to remove the background. The textual content of a page generally contains a number of artifacts in the form of dots and blotches on the page due to aging of the paper or moth bite, tear or cut in the page, and eroded or incomplete characters. Various image processing operations such as cropping, de-skewing, de-noising, smoothing etc. [11] provided by the ScanFix software, are performed to rid the images of such blemishes. Using this software the operator identifies the most appropriate steps to remove the artifacts as much as possible. He also sets various parameters for the image processing procedures.

The processed images are stored in the TIFF file format using the CCITT 4 Fax compression algorithm. This scheme was found to be very efficient. An image of 4300×2900 resolution, containing only a few words is of 1KB file size, and a document of the same resolution with full text occupies 75KB while the same would need about 150KB in PNG format. A page with images stored in binary format would be of 120KB in TIFF format, compared with about 230KB in PNG format.

We have also experimented with the image processing of palm leaf document images. The software used for books does not support the required functionality for processing palm leaf images. Unlike the white background for book pages, palm leaves have a dark brown background which is non-uniform. Owing to the brittleness of the medium, the documents are prone to tear and damage and the text is found with very heavy noise. No commercially available software is able to handle such extreme conditions and special software is being developed for this purpose. A sample palm leaf and its processed version are shown in Figure 2.

Recognition and Reconstruction: After cropping and cleaning a page image, an OCR is used to extract the text from it. A commercial OCR available with AB-BYY FineReader is used for this purpose. The text output by the OCR is stored in RTF, TXT and HTML formats, in separate folders. The extracted text is used to index the pages and books, to enable search and retrieval for the users.

Quality Checking: To ensure that proper quality is maintained by the digitization center, the digitally converted book is checked for quality at the RMSC [12]. A set of fixed standards were adopted as given in Table 1. The submitted books are checked for quality in each of these aspects and books with more than 80% of the contents containing errors are re-scanned and/or re-processed.

An automatic tool, *QualCheck*, was developed, that searches recursively for books in a given HDD/DVD and automatically checks for all the required con-

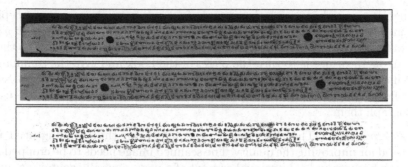

Fig. 2. Palm Leaf images a)unprocessed image b), c) processed images

Table 1. Major quality parameters for processed TIFF images

Parameter	Specification
Dimensions	Same Rows×Columns
dpi	600 or above
Compression	CCITT 4 Facsimile
Margin	300 pixels on all sides
Skew	$< 2°$
Blank Pages	identify and annotate

tents. It then checks for each of the parameters defined for the images, and generates an XML report for each of the errors. A snapshot of the tool is shown in Figure 4 (a). Typically observed errors are missing files from one or more of the folders, non-uniform margins in the processed images and use of a different compression algorithm than specified.

Web-Hosting: The digital book is hosted at the RMSC on Terabyte servers which are clustered as a data farm. An operator performs the post-scanning metadata process, creating structural metadata [10], which is used to easily navigate through the book. A copy of the book is made and stored as a backup in case of any hard disk crash. These books are hosted on the sever and duplicated for the local servers of other RMSCs.

4   Performance of the System

The process flow described in Section 3 was implemented at the RMSC-Hyderabad and the results were very satisfactory. The center was able to achieve a throughput of 140000 pages (about 500 books) each day. Observing the efficiency of the workflow at this center, many other centres have adopted the same pipeline to establish the process at their locations. The following are the performances of each phase of the digitization process.

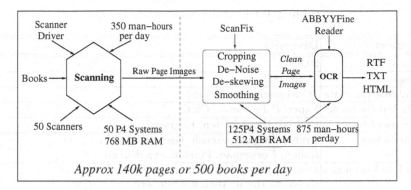

Fig. 3. Scanning Process, Image Processing and OCR schematic diagram with inputs, output and throughput

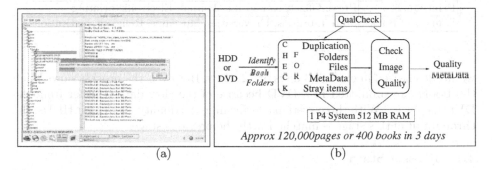

Fig. 4. (a) Snapshot of QualCheck tool (b) quality check performance

Scanning: Figure 3 summarizes the scanning and the image processing stages along with the quantity of inputs and outputs per day. The left side of the dotted line represents the scanning phase. At RMSC-Hyderabad, about 50 scanners are operated in an 8 hour shift per day. The peak throughput obtained was about 140000 pages per day, or 500 books. At this rate, it would take 10 years for a single center to scan a million books. Thus, to increase the overall throughput, the setting up of many such centres, at various locations, is inevitable.

Image processing: The Image processing and OCR stages along with the metrics are depicted on the right side of the dotted line in Figure 3. It was observed that a single desktop PC, can process about 2000 pages per day, performing both image editing and OCR. To match the throughput of the scanning phase, the number of systems allotted for the image processing phase is $2\frac{1}{2}$ times the number of scanners. At RMSC-Hyderabad, the image processing facility has an output of 150000 pages per day, with 125 machines being operated over a 8-hour shift per day.

Quality Check: The Quality check process is depicted in Figure 4 (b). The input to the process is a DVD or HDD containing books submitted. The QualCheck tool needs minimum user input. Once submitted, a HDD containing 400 books

Table 2. Range of digitized content created

Aspect	Diversity
Total Books	90,336
Pages	27,856,099
Publication years	1852-present (for Books)
Medium of books	Paper, Palm leaves, Cloth
Types of books	Printed, Handwritten, Engraved
Languages	Arabic, English, French, German, Greek, Italian, Norwegian, Persian, Spanish, etc.
Indian Languages	Bengali, Hindi, Kannada, Marathi, Sanskrit, Tamil, Telugu, Urdu, etc.
Subjects	Art, Architecture, Autobiography, Astronomy, Commerce, Religious, Economics, Science, Engineering, Geography , Law, Health, History, etc
Print Quality	Press, Offset, Newsprint, Journal, Electronic printing
Sources of Books	State Libraries, Universities, Museums, Religious Institutions

would be checked in close to 3 days or 72 hours. However, the process slows when the books are submitted in a DVD because of the slow data transfer from the DVD hardware. With three systems performing the quality check over HDDs, the throughput of this stage is matched with the previous stages.

4.1   Present Status

Using the procedures stated in this paper, we were able to achieve high quality output and high throughput from the digitization process. In just over an year, RMSC-Hyderabad digitized more than 100,000 books which contain about 25 Million pages. The books are currently online at [1] and are available for free access to anyone, anywhere in the world. These books cover a range of subjects, and languages. The diversity of the digitized content is showcased in Table 2.

More than one third of these books are of Indian language content, spanning 8 Indian languages. Since no commercial OCR is available for Indian language character recognition, the textual content is not available for these books. This severely handicaps searching, which is restricted only to the title and keyword level search. Special techniques need to be developed to search within the books.

Most of the books that are available online from the DLI, date back to before 1920. Many of these books are out of print and could be the last available copies of the same. As part of the initiative to prevent valuable information from being lost, we digitized about 4000 books from the Salar Jung Museum in Hyderabad with more in the process. We are also undertaking further procurement of books from rare collections.

Palm leaves: Digitization of palm leaves is a first-of-its-kind activity undertaken by us. Palm leaves were the storage medium for ancient literature, philosophy and science containing valuable knowledge. The preservation of these manuscripts is one of the more respectable achievements of the project in the context of cultural preservation, apart from other benefits discussed earlier.

5   Challenges Ahead

Thus far, all the books were scanned in binary mode only. This is valid because most of the books being scanned do not have any colour content. Digitizing books in colour would require more sophisticated scanners and better image processing and recognition algorithms and systems.

Trained Manpower: One of the bottlenecks of the project was the lack of trained personnel to operate the scanners and perform the image processing tasks. Since the equipment are costly, much care has to be taken to properly utilize them, and ensure high output without causing any damage. To this end, the operators were put through a thorough training program. The resources required for training could be reduced by using software that is more user friendly.

Duplication: Duplication of work was a major problem that reduced the total output. Since different libraries have a copy of each of the many books, the same books were digitized at different centers. To avoid such duplication of effort and wastage of resources, different meta data files were specified and procedures were laid out [10]. This addresses part of the duplication problem.

Quality of Metadata: Metadata management is an important aspect of the digital library. Frommholz et al.[13] signify this aspect from an information access perspective. A major portion of the sources of books in the project have metadata only in non-digital formats and these have to be entered manually. For the entry of metadata of a book, we largely rely on the librarians for the accuracy and credibility. Sometimes, librarians might not be well advised about the hierarchy and ontology of book classification. We ascertain the fields of metadata by referring to the catalog of OCLC and also by machine aided manual correction of metadata.

Indian Language Content: Most of the established softwares and routines are tuned to handle documents set in the Roman alphabet. The Indian languages, however, are very different, having a large character set and such features as *matras, samyuktakshars, shirorekha* etc. This results in conjunct and compound characters with complex shape variations. In addition, Indian language processing is considerably complex compared to English. These factors complicate optical character recognition, search and indexing. Kompalli et al.[14] give an overview of the challenges in OCR for one of the Indian language script called *Devanagari.* Thus, better software needs to be written to handle Indian languages.

The lack of a standard format for representing Indian language content is another handicap. A standard format needs to be developed and appropriate converters must be made available for converting from one format to the other. Software has to be developed using this standard. The non-standard representation also hampers the web enabling of digital content from scanned books. Web browsers and book viewers should be made "Indian language enabled".

Robust OCR: The OCR software being used gives an accuracy of about 90% - 95%. However, this accuracy is not good enough for a powerful search engine to be built for the digital library. Further improvements in OCR technology are being awaited. In case of noisy images, the performance of the OCR degrades rapidly. Some of the approaches to deal with noisy images are given in [15]. Moreover, OCRs for the Indian languages are still in the research phase, and satisfactory systems need to be built for OCRing Indian language content.

Search in Presence of Errors: Due to the inherent limitations in the OCR design and performance, the accuracy obtained is limited. The commercial OCR being used produces about 5% of errors. If a page contains about 2000 characters, then in a book of 300 pages we could find more than 30000 erroneous characters, which could mean that many erroneous words in a single book. The situation is worse in case of Indian language OCR where the errors are at the component level of each *akshara*. The errors in the component recognition cascade into erroneous letters, and then words. Inspite of these errors, we need to be able to search the content. To achieve this, search in presence of errors needs to be addressed, unlike the exact search that is used so far.

Document Image Compression and Delivery: As was showcased earlier, the storage requirements of the digital content generated from the project is enormous. The storage of such large amounts of data, reliably, is a huge task. With the OCR performance not satisfactory as described above, the preferred delivery of documents will remain to be images for the immediate future. Thus the file size reflects the network bandwidth required for the transfer of page images. One way to reduce the storage requirements is by developing better compression techniques that are tuned for document images. Better bandwidth availability would also improve the utilization of the Digital Libraries by the common man.

Historic Documents: Digitizing palm leaf documents has a large set of challenges associated with it. They need to be handled with enormous care as they are delicate and irreplaceable. As of now, the palm leaves are being photographed one at a time, but better methods have to be invented to improve the rate and quality of digitization. Better scanners have to be designed for this purpose, which can take high definition colour images of the palm leaves while causing no damage to the bundle. The processing of the palm leaf images needs special features and the image processing algorithms must be well tuned to handle heavy noise, tear, cut and background features. Currently, image processing of palm leaf images is pending the appropriate software development.

Human-Computer Interaction: When a user searches for a book or document, he should be able to easily navigate through the book. Better book-readers and intuitive user interfaces need to be developed, so that the user can navigate easily. Personalization of services for easier information access is presented in [13]. Besides, the display technology for Indian language content needs to be developed and standardized, without which it would be difficult to display Indian language text. Web browsers and softwares need to be developed with inherent Indian language support. This would enable the user to search and retrieve books in the native language without having to depend on transliteration.

Non-text Media: Digitization of non-text documents is an imminent challenge ahead. Digitization of paintings and murals is of significance and requires a completely different approach for digitization as well as utilization. Better digitization techniques need to be developed. In case of large documents such as cloth paintings, we would need a mosaicing of many images of high resolution (and small size). Efficient image processing algorithms and special information retrieval mechanisms will need to be built. Digital libraries of sculptures or three dimensional objects will need high performance 3-D scanners and fast methods and software to digitize them. Finally, audio and video libraries would be very popular, but require very robust and efficient search-retrieval expertise.

6   Conclusion

We have made considerable progress with respect to the goal of digitizing a million books. We have established semi-automatic digitization model that works very efficiently and robustly. In this process we have realized further challenges that need to be solved to realize the full potential of the activity. We have discussed in this paper the process workflow which evolved during the execution of the Million Book Project, and the performance statistics of this pipeline. We presented the challenges that were addressed from the effort towards MBP, so far. In light of the recent surge in digital library projects globally and large scale intensification of digitization efforts, we could expect almost all of man's knowledge available in digital form on the web, in the next decade or so. We could expect to see the entire cultural and historical records preserved for future generations and available across the world. Lectures, talks and presentations of teachers and researchers from the best schools in the world would be available to the students in every school, giving education and research activities a significant boost. Appreciation and exchange of art, science, music, movies, culture etc. beyond boundaries will be the real accomplishment of the "Global Village".

Acknowledgments

We would like to acknowledge Prof. Raj Reddy, CMU for his valuable guidance of this project and also for his suggestions towards this paper. We thank Prof. N. Balakrishnan of IISC-Bangalore and Prof. Rajeev Sangal of IIIT Hyderabad for their enormous support and guidance. We acknowledge the financial support received for the project from the Ministry of Communication and Information Technology, Govt. of India and National Science Foundation, USA. Technical and managerial contributions from V. Kiran Kumar and the staff at RMSC, IIIT-Hyderabad is also acknowledged.

References

1. Digital Library of India. (at: http://dli.iiit.ac.in)
2. Universal Library. (at: http://www.ulib.org)
3. Reddy, R.: The universal library: Intelligent agents and information on demand. In: ADL. (1995) 27–34
4. Million Book Project.   at: http://www.archive.org/details/millionbooks (2001)
5. Lesk, M.E.: Understanding Digital Libraries, 2nd ed. Morgan Kaufmann, San Francisco, CA (2004)
6. Baird, H.S., Govindaraju, V., eds.: 1st International Workshop on Document Image Analysis for Libraries (DIAL 2004), 23-24 January 2004, Palo Alto, CA, USA. In Baird, H.S., Govindaraju, V., eds.: DIAL, IEEE Computer Society (2004)
7. Baird, H.S., Govindaraju, V., Lopresti, D.P.: Document analysis systems architectures for digital libraries. In: IAPR Document Analysis Systems Workshop (DAS04), Florence, Italy (2004)
8. Cole, T.W.: Creating a framework of guidance for building good digital collections. First Monday **7** (2002)
9. Baird, H.S.: Digital libraries and document image analysis. In: IAPR 7th Int'l Conf. on Document Analysis and Recognition, Edinburgh, Scotland (2003)
10. Workshop Proceedings, Tools and Resources for Digital Library, IIIT-Hyderabad, 2005.
11. Gonzalez, R.C., Woods, R.E.: Digital Image Processing. Addison-Wesley Longman Publishing Co., Inc., Boston, MA, USA (2001)
12. Vamshi Ambati, K. Pramod Sankar, Lakshmi Pratha, C. V. Jawahar: Quality management in digital libraries. In: International Conference on Universal Digital Library, Hangzhou,P.R.China, Zhejiang University Press (2005)
13. Frommholz, I., Knezevic, P., Mehta, B., Niedere, C., Risse, T., Thiel, U.: Supporting information access in next generation digital library architectures. In Agosti, M., Schek, H.J., Trker, C., eds.: Digital Library Architectures: Peer-to-Peer, Grid, and Service-Orientation. Proceedings of the Sixth Thematic Workshop of the EU Network of Excellence DELOS, Cagliari, Italy (2004) 49–60
14. Kompalli, S., Nayak, S., Setlur, S., Govindaraju, V.: Cahllenges in OCR of devanagari documents. In: IAPR 8th Int'l Conf. on Document Analysis and Recognition, Seoul, Korea (2005)
15. Baird, H.S., Lopresti, D.P., Davidson, B., Pottenger, W.: Robust document image understanding techniques. In: 1st ACM Hardcopy Document Processing Workshop (HDP 2004), Washington, DC (2004) 9–14

Toward File Consolidation by Document Categorization

Abdel Belaïd and André Alusse

LORIA, Campus Scientifique, B.P. 236, Vandoeuvre-Lès-Nancy, France
{abelaid, alusse}@loria.fr

Abstract. An efficient adaptive document classification and categorization approach is proposed for personal file creation corresponding to user's specific needs and profile. This kind of approach is needed because the search engines are often too general to offer a precise answer to the user request. As we cannot act directly on the search engines methodology, we propose to rather act on the documents retrieved by classifying and ranking them properly. A classifier combination approach is considered. These classifiers are chosen very complementary in order to treat all the query aspects and to present to the user at the end a readable and comprehensible result. The application performed corresponds to the law articles stemmed from the European Union data base. The law texts are always entangled with cross-references and accompanied by some updating files (for application dates, for new terms and formulations). Our approach found here a real application offering to the specialist (jurist, lawyer, etc.) a synthetic vision of the law related to the topic requested.

1 Introduction

With the exponential growth of information available on the Web, the information retrieval becomes increasingly difficult. The search engines have more and more difficulty to satisfy the user's requirements. In response to a request, the document retrieval engines turn over sets built more or less well and ordered according to their criteria of relevance. The experiment showed that neither the relevance nor the linearity of presentation are sufficient factors for the user because 1) they do not make it possible to have a global and synthetic vision result, 2) certain documents can escape the criteria of relevance. Moreover, it is not obvious to write a synthesis in order to constitute a file and it is difficult to follow the cross referenced between documents. This implies to develop useful and efficient tools to assist users in searching documents corresponding to his needs in terms of consultation and organization.

The Project PAPLOO positions in this area. It aims is the definition of a generic framework of transformation and document retrieval for personalized use (document synthesis, folder organization according to the topics, document ranking facilitating their search corresponding to the importance and the quality). The main goal of this project is to help the lawyers of the European Community to synthesize or summarize specific subjects treated in various publication of the European Community (decrees, treaties, rules,…).

H. Bunke and A.L. Spitz (Eds.): DAS 2006, LNCS 3872, pp. 437–448, 2006.

A good example being a customs officer intercepting animals transport at the EEC border. He must be able to know the last legislation in use on the animal importation. But the project have other objectives. Avocado, judge, etc. need to build their own consolidated documents, updated automatically, with more or less strong strategy of the appropriation. This implies at least three questions: law classification, crossed consolidation, new text and references.

This paper is organized as follow: in section 2, a brief overview of the whole system is given. Section 3 will be dedicated to file constitution. Experiments and discussions will be done in section 4. Finally, conclusion and future work will be given in section 5.

2   System Overview

The Chain PAPLOO is composed of two distinct parts as shown in Fig. 1. The first part relates to data preparation in terms of OCR (for document images), structure recognition and annotation. The second part concentrates on the constitution of files in terms of reformulation and reformatting. The main language used throughout the chain is XML. Effective research starts after the database constitution enriched by indices (metadata). The user query conditions all the chain. He initialises the total document research (classification, enrichment and reorganization) and allows the constitution of personalized files (documents) by providing the suitable elements of selection. In addition to the personal request, the influence of the user is always present in all the phases of the system through his profile.

The used document are law articles of all kinds belonging to Official Journals (OJ) of the European Union. Documents can be in text format or in PDF which need to be retro-converted. PDF's documents are structured using OCR and retro-conversion processes (Rangoni [1]). In this paper, we will limit our focus on the part related to file constitution.

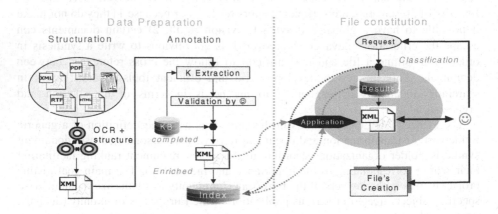

Fig. 1. Chain PAPLOO overview

3   File Constitution

In order to discover sets of similar documents and highlight categories, the categorization, automatic clustering and summarization of documents are possible issues to help the user to solve these problems. A thematic classification allows an organizational vision of the results (Hearst [2]). Moreover, the combination of classification has the potential to provide an accurate, intuitive and comprehensive classified results. Existing work on combining heterogeneous classifiers for information retrieval is widely varied in measures, goals and tasks. Generalization of classifier combination methods were suggested by Lam and Lai [3] and Bennett et. al. [4].

Based on these works, we propose a more dedicated approach for the judicial domain.

3.1   Proposed Solution

The system combines automatic clustering and categorization approaches. Clustering is the process of grouping documents based on similarity of words, or the concepts in the documents as interpreted by an analytical engine. Categorization is the process of associating a document with one or more subject categories.

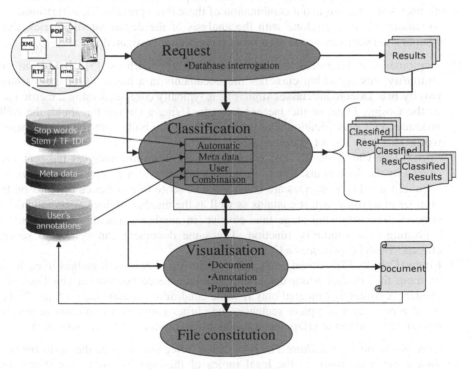

Fig. 2. System overview

In order to discover different point of view on the result set, the system performs several organizations: 1) automatic clustering, 2) metadata categorization, 3) user appreciations. Then, these different classifications are combined: 1) to take into account different points of view, 2) to highlight the main topics (present in the classifiers), 3) to reduce the individual errors, 4) to bring closer the results to the user's concerns.

Fig. 2 shows the system's architecture. First, the user send a request to the database documents Second, he interacts with the different classifications to reorganize the result at glance by acting on the different classifier parameters (removing stop words, performing stemming, pertinence, weight,…). Third, he reads and comments the document by apposing some annotations (finest and personal keywords, more comprehensible by himself…) and at least finalize his file.

Request execution

The documentation base is requested by using a traditional search engine. The query is a set of keywords. The result R is a set of documents where each document d_i is a 4-uplet describing a document result, d_i= (identifier, url, title, summary).

Classification elaboration

Four classifications approaches have been proposed: automatic, using meta-data, using user's annotations and a combination of these three previous classifications.

Automatic clustering: Done with the analysis of the document summaries, three non-supervised statistics-based algorithms have been investigated:

1. Agglomerative Hierarchical Clustering (AHC), Voorhees [5]. Based on the similarity, this algorithm classifies the documents in a hierarchy of classes build two by two. Document/classes similarity is typically computed using a metric such as the Cosine, Dice, or the Jaccard formula. Using a cutting threshold, the AHC produces a C_A classification. The label of classes are build with the most common words shared by the set of documents.
2. Suffix Tree Clustering (STC), Zamir [6]. This algorithm analyses the sentences shared by the documents. Then, it creates a hierarchy. Each sentence constitutes a basic cluster. The sentences are balanced. The score of a sentence depends on the number of words which it contains as well as the number of documents in which it appears. The following stage thus consists in amalgamating these basic clusters according to a similarity function. The same document can belong to several classes. The STC produces a C_S classification.
3. Lingo (Osinski, [7]). Based on the most occurring sentences, it assigns to each one of them the corresponding documents. Each sentence becomes a key label of a cluster. A cluster is validated only if some conditions are satisfied such as: the key word represents a complete sentence, the cluster contains a minimum number of documents, without overlapping, etc. The Lingo produces a C_L classification.

Categorization by metadata: The publication office uses its own thesaurus (or table of index) referring more to the legal topics of this specific base (EuroVoc). The metadata are classified by an expert in the form of a tree of hierarchical indexes. At each leave (i.e. at each path of metadata) will correspond a document classes. As a result of this categorization, a class set C_m is obtained.

User categorization: During document consultation, the user suggests some keywords and scores describing the documents and their interest for his application. For each document d_i, a pair of keywords and associated notes (m_j, n_j) are given. A cross matrix (vector space model, or "bag of word") is established giving for each keyword the associated documents. From this matrix, a similarity or confused matrix (similar to the AHC tree) is computed using Cosine distance on the keywords weighted by the notes. By choosing another cutting parameter, the algorithm produces a C_u classification.

As the user can belong to a group and to a community where the points of view can be completed or generalized, we enlarge the user categorization to the group and to the community. For the group and the community, we put together all the user points of view. This implies to consider all the keywords and to calculate for each one of them the average of the notes given by all the users. The clustering is then similar to the individual grouping. This approach allows the user to share and confront his opinion and the system to have a more global view. This produces two additional classifications: C_G and C_C.

Hence, seven classifications have been obtained by the previous approaches: C_m (metadata), C_A (AHC), C_S (STC), C_L (Lingo), C_U (User), C_G (Group) and C_C (Community).

Classifier combination

These classifications considered individually are not fully satisfying. Each of them is very specialized. To reduce their specific drawbacks, we decided to combine them.

The combination is based on the AHC algorithm with Cosine distance.

Let be C_i a classification, C_i is a set of classes $C_i=\{c_1,c_2,..., c_n\}$ where $c_j=(\omega,\{d_1,...,d_m\})$; ω is the class label and d_i a class document. For the combination, several steps are followed:

All the topics or labels ω are extracted from the all the classifications.

These labels are then used to build the cross matrix M. The label weight depends on its weight classifier and to its occurrence in different classifiers. Weights are assigned to the classifiers according to their accuracy deduced from the experiment. Of course, these values could be refined by the user.

		Documents identifier					
		d1	d2	d3	d4	d5	d6
labels	slaughter	0.0	1.0	1.0	0.0	0.0	1.0
	animal killing	0.0	3.0	0.0	0.0	0.0	1.0
	butchery	0.0	1.0	0.0	0.0	0.0	0.0
	Agricultural activity	1.0	1.0	1.0	0.0	0.0	1.0
	agribusiness	2.0	1.0	2.0	1.0	1.0	3.0
	farm-produce	1.0	1.0	1.0	1.0	1.0	0.0
	aid	3.0	0.0	0.0	0.0	0.0	0.0

Fig. 3. Vector Space Model

Considering this fact, $M_{i,j} = \sum_{k=1}^{n} (d_i \in C_k(\omega_j)) \times p_k$ where p_k is the weight assigned to the classification algorithm and $d_i \in C_k(\omega_j)$ is a binary function (the class ω_j contains or not the document d_i). Fig. 3 shows an example of a cross matrix (vector space model) where the columns represent the 6 document (d_i), while the lines represent the labels (slaughter, animal killing ...). The vector representation for the document d_1 is: $V_{d1} = (0.0, 0.0, 0.0, 1.0, 2.0, 1.0, 3.0)$.

Then, the similarity matrix is computed using the Cosine method (1):

$$D(X,Y) = \frac{\sum_{i=1}^{t} x_i y_i}{\sqrt{\sum_{i=1}^{t} x_i^2 \cdot \sum_{i=1}^{t} y_i^2}}$$

(1)

Finally, we build the hierarchical tree, based on dendogram, a binary tree structure, with the leaves being the individual document points, the internal nodes being (partial) clusters, and the arcs recording the distance between any two (partial) clusters or documents.

Fig. 4 shows the similarity matrix before and after the classification.

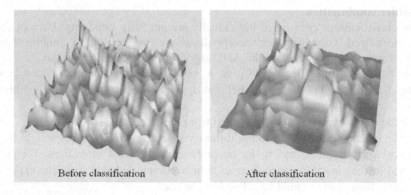

Before classification   After classification

Fig. 4. Similarity matrix

3.2 Classifier Evaluation

In order to help the user to build his file and to adapt the classifier's parameters to solve his needs in a fair way, two objective measurements revealing the cluster qualities were defined. Based on Lamirel [8], concepts of precision and recall used in documentary engineering were adapted to the evaluation of classifications of the documents. The precision measures the percentage of relevant documents among those turn over by the query (N is the number of results, P is the number of relevant documents then Precision = P/N). The recall measures which is the proportion of relevant documents turned over by the system (P is the number of relevant documents retrieved by the system, R is the number of relevant documents in the database, then

Recall = P/R). For our system, the precision measures the classes homogeneity and the recall measures the classes independence.

These table (Fig. 5) shows the classification organisation composed by set of classes. Each class contains documents. Words describe the documents.

Class	Documents	Words					
		t_1	t_2	t_3	...		t_n
C_1	d_1		1				1
	d_2	1	1				1
C_2	d_3			1			
	d_4	1	1	1			
C_n	d_{n-1}	1					1
	d_n			1			

Fig. 5. Repartition of words in documents and in classes

First, the word precision (t_i) in the class C_j is performed as follow (2):

$$P_{C_1}(t_1) = \frac{nbDoc(t_1 \in d)}{nbDoc(C_1)} \qquad (2)$$

(= 1 when all documents of class C contains t).
Then the class precision is determined (3):

$$P_{C_1} = \frac{\sum_1^n P_{C_1}(t_i)}{|C_1|} \qquad (3)$$

(=1 when documents contains the same terms, class is homogeneous, documents are described with same terms).
Finally, the classification precision is determined (4):

$$P = \frac{\sum_1^n P_{C_i}}{|C|} \qquad (4)$$

(=1 means that the division is done in homogeneous classes).
Similarly, the word recall in class is determined (5):

$$R_{C_1}(t_1) = \frac{nbDoc(t_1 \in d, d \in C_1)}{nbDoc(t_1 \in d, d \in \{C_i\})} \qquad (5)$$

(=1 means that the word t_i appearing only on documents of class C_j).

The class recall is performed as follow (6):

$$R_{C_1} = \frac{\sum_1^n R_{C_1}(t_i)}{|C_1|}.$$

(6)

(=1 means that none of the terms constituting C_j belongs to the other classes). Finally, the classification recall is determined (7):

$$R = \frac{\sum_1^n R_{C_i}}{|C|}$$

(7)

(=1 means that the division is done in independent classes).

4 Experiments and Discussion

The method is experimented on a small part of documents of the EC (2000 documents including 453 rules, 368 written questions, 242 treaties, …) which are enough representative to validate the classification approaches.

Fig. 6 shows an example of automatic classification produced by the « lingo » classifier. The request given by the keywords "animals" turn over 120 documents. 17 classes were detected, (the class named "publication of request" contains 14 documents). The sentences which are use to define the name of classes are shared by the documents. Some documents belong to more than one class. In this case, 21 documents are duplicated (141 – 120) . 21 documents are unclassified (others). Fig. 6 shows also an example of AHC classifier and an example of classification combination. The user can discover different organisation of the result sets. The system can help him to explore the documents while proposing different approaches and different topics.

Fig. 6. Example of classifications

Then, in order to enlarge the algorithm comparison, three queries with keywords: "animals", "rice' and "animals transport" are requested. For each classifier, we give the number of documents return by the search engines (Res), the number of classes detected (Cl), the total number of documents classified, one document could be member of several classes (Nb), the number of document unclassified (Un), the assignment coverage Co and the overlap (Ov). Assignment coverage is the fraction of documents assigned to clusters in relation with the total number of inputs (Co=(Res – Un) / Res) and overlap describes the fraction of documents confined to more than one group (Ov=(Nb / Res) –1). Fig. 7 shows these different values for each classifier.

Request	Res.	AHC classification					STC classification				
		Cl.	Nb	Un	Co	Ov	Cl.	Nb	Un	Co	Ov
Rice	55	37	50	5	0.9	-0.09	20	323	0	1	4.87
Animals	119	69	110	9	0.81	-0.08	20	755	5	0.958	5.34
Transport	28	18	28	0	1	0	14	84	14	0.5	2

Request	Res.	LINGO classification					Metadata classification				
		Cl.	Nb	Un	Co	Ov	Cl.	Nb	Un	Co	Ov
Rice	55	6	62	16	0.71	0.12	38	187	1	0.98	2.4
Animals	119	14	131	34	0.71	0.10	79	491	23	0.81	3.13
Transport	28	7	34	10	0.64	0.21	50	138	5	0.82	3.93

Request	Res.	Combination				
		Cl.	Nb	Un	Co	Ov
Rice	55	31	49	6	0.89	-0.11
Animals	119	82	116	3	0.97	-0.03
Transport	28	16	27	1	0.96	-0.04

Fig. 7. Analysis of different queries

We can observe that:

1. In AHC, the number of cluster is huge which implies a problem of legibility and quality of the heading of classes.
2. In STC, the documents are not sufficiently discriminating to deduce interesting regroupings, the overlap (Ov) is important.
3. In Lingo, there are less clusters, but there are more significant.
4. With the metadata, many clusters are detected because the thesaurus is very large.
5. With combination, the covertures of result is improved (almost complete).

Moreover, we observe that combination of these classifiers for the request "animals transport" highlight two important topics: "carcass transport between Europe and ex USSR" and "transport toward Spain" and minimize the title of the set of documents "publication".

The combination gives prominence to the main topics and it reduces the individual errors of each classifier.

To simulate the user's contribution, we have defined 8 users shared in three groups: a customs officer group with two profiles "regulation" and "frontier", a veterinarian group ("sanitary", "disease", "butchery"), a farmer group ("cattleman", "fish breeding", "poultry farming"). For each user we add some keywords according to its concerns, for ex: "foot-and-mouth disease" for the veterinary in the 2nd group in charge of "disease".

We noticed that the cluster deduced from the user contribution is in strongly connection with his concerns (see Fig. 8).

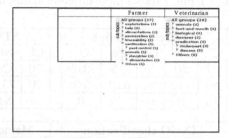

Fig. 8. User's categorization

At least, we obtain a better coverage and dispersion (number of clusters/ number of results) with the contributions of the group and the whole of the users (due to their complementary vision and a best knowledge on the documents). If we analyze the combination of all classifications, we continue to improve the coverage and the dispersion (see Fig. 9). For each user, the first group is the result of the individual annotations and the second is the result of the combination of the classifications.

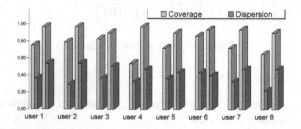

Fig. 9. Measure of coverage and dispersion for individual user's classification and combination of individual, group and all users classification

Fig. 10 shows the precision and recall for some classifications done on the request "animals transport". We can deduce that recall is strong on user's classifications. This implies a good segmentation. Recall and precision are more balanced with the implications of all users due to more view point on the document. A significant lower recall for the combination is observed. The information source is multiple thus implies less independence between classes. We obtain more classes so less independents.

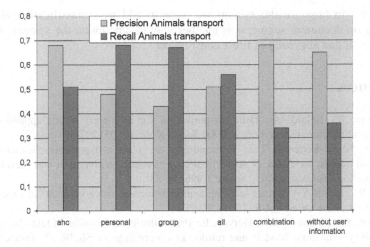

Fig. 10. Precision and recall

Of course, these analysis could be done to observe the influence of different parameters of classifiers. But that shows that they do not have a great impact. In fact, the test is only done with few documents, a hundred only.

However, that makes it possible to analyze the behaviour of each classifier and thus to measure that which is more in connection with the user's concerns.

All these tools and algorithms prepare the constitution of file, the reorganisation of the documents and the historic of them. Studies and measurements done to validate the various techniques allow to identify precise tasks and so to adapt to user's needs. The optimization of parameters and the understanding of each classifier give the highest performance on the system.

5 Conclusion

We have introduced a new system to help the user to build his own file according to his main interests. In order to facilitate the work of the user this system combines several ideas from the information retrieval domain: the sharing of knowledge on documents, the classification technologies and different tools to measure the efficiency of the algorithms. The novelty of the system is the usage of these possibilities drive by the user or recommended by the system.

The first experiments show that the various classification techniques allow a first regrouping of the documents. It is possible to refine this regrouping with the evaluation of the performances and the adaptations of algorithms. It is very useful to understand the possible proximities and relations between the documents. The user finds out more easily the content of the text with the different keywords. This could be a first step to explore the document and to order it in different folders. The second step is the appropriation of the document by the user. He can describe and annotate it. The contributions of different classes of users give more information on the document. Finally, the choice or the combination of these different approaches facilitate the creation of files.

In order to improve the system we have to add new classification algorithms. Working on document segments is another way to ameliorate the system. This work constitutes a first approach of file's constitution.

References

1. Rangoni, Y., Belaïd, A.: Data categorization for a context return applied to logical document structure recognition, ICDAR,Seoul, Korea (2005) 297-301
2. Hearst, M.A., Pedersen J.O.: Reexamining the cluster hypothesis: Scatter/Gather on retrieval results. In Actes of ACM/SIGIR Conference on Research and Development in Information Retrieval, Zurich, Suisse (1996) 76-84
3. Lam, W., Lai, K.Y.: A meta-learning approach for text categorization. In Proceedings of SIGIR-01,, New Orleans, US (2001) 303-309
4. Bennett, P.N., Dumais, S.T., Horvitz, E.: Probabilistic combination of text classifiers using reliability indicators: Models and results. In Proceedings of SIGIR-02, Tampere, Finland (2002) 207-215
5. Voorhees, E.M.: Implementing agglomerative hierarchical clustering algorithms for use in document retrieval, Information Processing and Management, vol. 22, (1986) 465-476,
6. Zamir, O., Etzioni, O.: Web document clustering: a feasibility demonstration, Proceedings of the 19th International ACM SIGIR Conference on Research and Development in Information Retrieval (SIGIR'98) (1998) 46-54
7. Osinski S.: An Algorithm for clustering of Web Search results", Master thesis, Poznan University of technology (2003)
8. Lamirel, J.C., Francois, C., Al Shehadi, S., Hoffman M.: Multi-Topographic new classification quality estimators for analysis of documentary information: Application to patent analysis and web mapping. In Scientometrics international Journal, Vol. 60, No. 3 (2004) 445-462.

Finding Hidden Semantics of Text Tables

Saleh A. Alrashed

Royal Saudi Air Force, Riyadh, Saudi Arabia
Dralrashed@Gmail.com

Abstract. Combining data from different sources for further automatic processing is often hindered by differences in the underlying semantics and representation. Therefore when linking information presented in documents in tabular form with data held in databases, it is important to determine as much information about the table and its content. Important information about the table data is often given in the text surrounding the table in that document. The table's creators cannot clarify all the semantics in the table itself therefore they use the table context or the text around it to give further information. These semantics are very useful when integrating and using this data, but are often difficult to detect automatically. We propose a solution to part of this problem based on a domain ontology. The input to our system is a document that contains tabular data and the system aims to find semantics in the document that are related to the tabular data. The output of our system is a set of detected semantics linked to the corresponding table. The system uses elements of semantic detection, semantic representation, and data integration. In this paper, we discuss the experiment used to evaluate the prototype system. We also discuss the different types of test, the experiment will perform. After using the system with the test data and gathering the results of these tests, we show the significant results in our experiment.

1 Introduction

Documents are one of the most important ways of sharing knowledge between humans. They are constructed using some common assumptions about their structure. Authors intend to convey information in ways allowing readers accurate and effective interpretation of the contents. This is why understanding documents is a relatively easy task for an intelligent human reader. One of the ways that authors use to present information in documents is tables.

The number of tables used per page in scientific papers has increased quite steadily over time. It has grown from 9% of the pages in 1984 up to 32% in 1997 [5]. Document tables have been created by humans to aid understanding of the information, therefore any attempts to reuse their content automatically needs effort to recognise and determine the table's structure and semantics.

Because of the large number of documents that have been published electronically, there is a real need to reuse the contents of these types of documents in investigations. This implies a need for automatic analysis of documents to

H. Bunke and A.L. Spitz (Eds.): DAS 2006, LNCS 3872, pp. 449–461, 2006.

aid human users. As an important part of a document, tables have received attention from researchers trying to locate, analyse, identify and transform them into reusable formats for further analysis by software systems [3, 6, 7]. Most researchers have concentrated on the table itself, identifying its physical and logical structure, without considering the relation between a table and the surrounding text in the document [4].

The problem with isolating tabular data that appears in textual documents from the rest of the text, is that although the table data can be extracted and reused, it is not possible to fully understand its contents and reuse it effectively in other integration processes unless this data has been combined with parts of the text in the same document that are related to that table. This text describes the semantics of the information in the table.

This problem arises for two main reasons. Firstly, the author of the document tends to explain parts of the table in the text around it, and the information in the table does not make sense if the table is completely isolated (semantically) from its document. Even if there are no explanations about the table in the text, the table can not be completely isolated from its domain, especially if it is going to be integrated with other tables without losing some of its usefulness. Secondly, locating all data with related description of the semantics in the table structure makes the table difficult to understand as it extends the size of the table and affects the clarity of presentation. Therefore authors tend to leave parts of the meaning of data to be explained in the surrounding text.

2   Semantics and Representational Conflicts

When trying to integrate data from different sources drawn from the same domain, semantic conflicts and representational conflicts can occur. Semantic conflicts are related to differences in the metadata of the table (attributes, names etc). Such a conflict occurs when different data names represent the same data (synonyms), the same name represents a different data domain (homonyms), or a hidden semantic relationship exists between two or more terminologies. For example the relationship between cost and price or between profit and net-profit, and the similarity between car, vehicle and truck cannot be understood unless we use a domain knowledge base to relate these terms. To overcome conflicts we use semantic metadata, which provides information about the meaning of the available data and any semantic relationships [1]. The sources of semantic information can include ontologies. Madnick [2] defines an ontology as an agreement about a shared conceptualization of a given application domain.

Representational conflicts occur due to the way data is represented and in particular the measurement unit being used. These conflicts are concerned with the values of an attribute. If we have two attributes, which are semantically the same, they are not in conflict when their values are represented in the same way, i.e. in the same units. This is important, if we are bringing attributes together. For example, the values of a price can be represented in pounds or in dollars. If the units are different, there is a representational conflict unless they can be converted to the same representation before they are used together. Thus re presentational metadata provides information about the meaning of the values of an attribute, its representational relationships and its units of representation.

3   Semantic and Representation Detection Framework

SRD (Semantic and Representation Detection framework) is to be a prototype system for discovering and interpreting the context information about tables present in the text of a document containing tabular data, and prepare them for interoperation with other data. Figure. 1 shows the proposed system architecture of the SRD system, which will extract and structure the context data about a table held within a textual document.

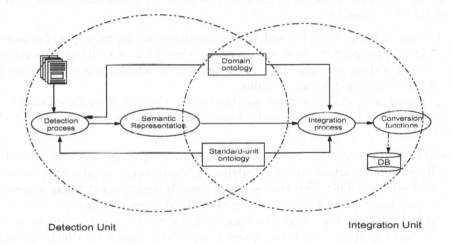

Fig. 1. Semantic and representation detection framework architecture

It consists of two main units and each unit has a number of processes and sub-units. The first is the **Detection Unit**. The main purpose of this unit is identifying, extracting and representing the information about the context of a table's elements given within the text. This information will be used to enhance the table's metadata and thus lead to better use of its contents. It operates on the documents, which are represented in ASCII characters and have tabular data in them.

The second unit is the **Integration Unit**. This is concerned with integrating the detected semantics with other semantics to create a description of a table and its representation. Documents are created by different authors who represent the data using their knowledge of the domain. Therefore the detected semantics might need to be converted into a common representation and terminology before data from this table can be integrated with data from another . In this paper, we discuss the experiment used to evaluate the prototype system. We also discuss the different types of test, the experiment will perform. After using the system with the test data and gathering the results of these tests, we show the significant results in our experiment.[9-11]

4   Experimental Design

In our experiment, we use documents from different sources available on the Internet. The documents were collected randomly, and had to contain tabular data to be valid for the experiment. We have used documents from four primary data sources, as this allows us to detect any differences due to a data source as well. We will investigate the differences between commercial data and non-commercial data sources, and between scientific domains and non-scientific domains with the four types of data source.

In the experiments we have a number of input variables which describe the experiment. These are:

1. The number of domains used. In our experiment we use two types of domain- a scientific (chemistry) and a non-scientific (cars). By using different domains, we will see if there are differences in the number of detected semantics in documents representing different domains.

2. The number of data sources for the domain. For each domain, we used two sources of data. In the cars domain, we used data from the Imotors and Which web sites.

– Which web site: This is a consumer magazine Web site based in the UK. It gives independent, unbiased advice and evaluations on different products and services. This Web site issues a monthly report on different types of car. It reviews many aspects about the cars (e.g. performance, security, and price). Most of the reports contain tables which present the results of an evaluation. With each table, there is text data around it, which explains the table data and important issues about the car. We have extracted 50 pages from this web site. These were selected at random and are different evaluations published on different dates.(See www.Which.co.uk).

– Imotors web site: This is a commercial website. It is one of the fastest, easiest ways to purchase a car online. It has a USA national network of car dealers who provide competitive quotes, and an inventory of thousands of used vehicles. Imotors is now a car-buying service focused on effectively matching consumers with the vehicles they want. Imotors web pages normally consist of a table, which lists the cars that meet the user requirements and a paragraph or two which describe some of the values in the table. We have extracted 100 pages from this web site, which represent different search results.(See www.Imotors.com).

In the scientific domain (chemistry), we used two web sites - the Thermoset web site and the Eastman web site.

– Thermoset is part of The Lord Corporation and traces its roots to 1919. Lord's ideas produced inventions, and led to chemical formulations, bonding processes, elastomers, adhesives, coatings, bonded elastomer assemblies and many more discoveries. They provide on their web site, descriptions and specifications of their products. We have extracted 100 pages from this web site. This website is a commercial website. (See www.thermoset.com).

– Eastman Chemical Company (NYSE:EMN) is a global company which is one of the world's largest suppliers of polyester plastics for packaging. Headquartered in Kingsport, Tennessee, USA, Eastman manufactures and markets more than 1,200 chemicals, fibres and plastic products. On their web site, they evaluate a number of their chemical products so that customers can determine whether a product meets their requirements. We have extracted 50 pages from this web site(See www.Eastman.com).

It is probable desirably to use other data sources to determine whether they show the same behaviour. However there was insufficient project time to identify another source domain with enough documents meeting our needs for a specific domain. Thus, for the two domains chosen we have two different types of sources- a commercial site (Imotors and Thermoset) and an evaluation source (Which and Eastman). Further work is needed to confirm the results hold in other domains.

3. The number of documents from each data source for the commercial data sources is 100 documents and 50 for the evaluation data sources, which makes a total of 300 documents. We have tried to increase the number of documents but consistent sources of these types of documents (documents containing tabular data) are hard to find. The number of documents within each source type is sufficient for the experiment, because as Admantios mentions in [8], 30 items can show the true behaviour of an item with respect to its characteristics being evaluated.

4.1   Experiment Objectives

For our experiments, we have a number of objectives we wish to evaluate. These are:

1. To show that there are hidden semantics - in documents - that are related to a table in that document and they are significant to its interpretation.
2. To show the usefulness of a domain ontology in detecting and using these semantics.
3. To determine the difference between alternative approaches that can be used to detect such semantics and to identify the best approach.
4. To determine whether there is a relationship between the number of semantics in a paragraph and the distance between the paragraph which contains the semantics and the table itself.
5. To identify whether there is a significant difference in the number of detected semantics in different domains.
6. To evaluate the system.

To achieve these objectives, our experiments will analyse the documents and calculate a number of values. These analyses and calculations will be performed twice. The first time, we will perform them manually (fully human, no use of any other system). The second time we will use our system SRD without any human interference. Doing the analysis twice will allow us to compare the two methods and discover if there is a significant difference between a manual approach and the SRD approach. We then do comparisons with the SRD system to determine the effect of using an ontology in the determination of semantics and to identify where the semantics occur in the text in relationship to the table.

The values that are going to be calculated in this comparison are:

1. The number of semantics detected using the table header augmented by the appropriate terms from the domain ontology as the search key (enhanced keywords).
2. The number of semantics detected using the table information (data, meta-data, footer).
3. The number of semantics detected in the paragraphs before the table.
4. The number of semantics detected in the paragraphs after the table.

We use the experimental data to perform the the coming tests.

For Each Data Source

1. Compare the number of semantics detected using the domain ontology to enhance the search keys with the number detected using only keys from the table information.
2. Compare the number of semantics detected in the paragraphs before the table with the number detected in the paragraphs after the table.
3. Compare the total number of semantics detected using our system (SRD) with the total number of semantics detected manually.

For Each Domain. Compare the number of semantics found for the two types of data sources in the domain.

1. Number of semantics in Imotors web pages with number in Which web pages, detected using the table keys enhanced by terms from the domain ontology.
2. Number of semantics in Imotors web pages with number in Which web pages, detected using table information only.
3. Number of semantics in Imotors web pages with number in Which web pages, detected using the paragraphs before the table.
4. Number of semantics in Imotors web pages with number in Which web pages, detected using the paragraphs after the table.
5. Total number of semantics in Imotors web pages with total number in Which web pages.

These tests will also be performed using the chemistry domain web sites when Thermoset web pages will be compared with the Eastman web pages. These tests will also be performed to compare the two sets of commercial web pages, and the two sets of scientific web pages, i.e. a comparison of the Imotors web pages with Thermoset web pages and the Which website with the Eastman website.

5   Experimental Results

We have divided the significant results that we found into two parts, namely tests related to the logical content of the documents, and tests related to the physical structure of the documents.

5.1   Tests Related to Logical Content of Documents

We found that there is a significant number of useful semantics, hidden in a document, which are related to the tabular data in that document. After analysing 300 documents from different data sources, we found that there is hidden data related to the tabular data in the document which can be detected, extracted and represented as beneficial semantics related to that table. These semantics can be used for integrating these tables with data from other data sources.

Our experiment has shown that the number of detected semantics is normally distributed among all the 300 documents with a mean of 9.9 semantics per document. This means that the average number of semantics detected in a document is 9.9. The experiment sample documents can be categorised by the name of the domain that the sample is related to. Also, within each domain there are two types of data sources, commercial and evaluative.

We have used two domain types, scientific (chemistry) and non-scientific (cars). We found that the chemistry domain had fewer semantics than the cars domain, with the chemistry mean equal to 8.3 and the cars domain mean equal to 11.5. Thus, the cars domain has a higher number of semantics per document, and we think that the reasons for this are as follows:

1. The chemistry domain has well-defined concepts, therefore the users or the writers of the documents do not have many alternative terms to identify and describe the concepts. In other words the domain name concepts don't have many synonyms or relationships and are well known to the community.
2. As a result of the first reason, the writers of a document don't have many things to explain in the text.
3. The cars domain has different terminologies between different countries and even between groups of people; therefore the writers of a document in this domain need to explain most of the attributes in their tables, as they are targeting a set of readers with a less coherent background.

We have shown that detecting the hidden semantics will result in a better understanding of a table, and in its enrichment with extra semantics.

Significance Between Different Domains. 80.7 % of the detected semantics have been detected using a domain ontology approach. In our experiments, we used two approaches to detect the hidden semantics. One of these approaches used a domain ontology. This approach gives us most of the semantics that were detected manually in the text, as shown on Table 1. This table, shows the percentage of semantics detected by the domain ontology approach in each data source of the total number of semantics that were detected manually. Thus, most

Table 1. Percentage of semantics detected in documents using domain ontology

Data source name	Domain name	Percentage
Imotors	Cars-Commercial	74.8
Thermoset	Chemistry-Commercial	87.9
Which	Cars-Evaluation	71
Eastman	Chemistry-Evaluation	89.2

of the semantics are detected using a domain ontology approach. Therefore, any event that affects the domain ontology will affect the total number of semantics detected, and any changes in the domain ontology will also affect the detection process. For instance, if the domain ontology becomes richer in concepts, then the total number of semantics that are detected will increase, and vice versa. This led us to conclude that a domain ontology plays an important role in detecting hidden semantics in documents, and any limitations in the domain ontology will also limit the number of semantics detected.

We also found that the number of semantics detected using a domain ontology approach in a non-scientific domain (cars) is higher than in the scientific domain (see table 2). But with respect to the percentage of the total number of semantics detected manually, the scientific domain has a higher percentage, as shown in Table 1.

Table 2. Number of semantics detected in each data source using domain ontology

Data source name	Domain name	number semantics
Imotors	Cars-Commercial	7.18
Thermoset	Chemistry-Commercial	5.53
Which	Cars-Evaluation	4.10
Eastman	Chemistry-Evaluation	2.82

Significance of the Differences Between Data Sources. There seems to be a significant difference between the number of semantics in the commercial and evaluation data sources in both our domains. Comparing the number of semantics detected in commercial data sources in the cars and chemistry domains has shown that they are always higher in the commercial data sources than in the evaluation data sources, see Table 3. However, this needs further investigation to determine if it holds in other domains.

We believe that the large difference between these types of data sources is due to a number of reasons:

1. Commercial data sources try to give the reader as much information as they can to attract him or her to buy their merchandise, whereas in evaluation data source documents they evaluate a product without looking to the need to attract the reader to purchase. This is in part, because they are showing facts which the supplier and the reader might not like.

Table 3. Number semantics for each data source

Data source name	Domain name	Data source type	number semantics
Imotors	Cars	Commercial	9.59
Thermoset	Chemistry	Commercial	6.29
Which	Cars	Evaluation	5.76
Eastman	Chemistry	Evaluation	3.16

2. Commercial data sources have to attract the consumers to buy their products using a small space. Therefore, they put all the information they have into a very short text which makes it a quicker to read and also easier to detect by other systems, whereas in evaluation data sources, the time constraint is not a crucial element as their readers want as full a comparison as possible.
3. The length of a document has an effect on the number of semantics. The evaluation data sources are longer documents than commercial data sources, yet have less table semantics. This needs more investigation, but may indicate they are giving a fuller evaluation in the text of the points being made.
4. Also, most of the documents in the evaluation data sources describe new products and technologies which have not yet been included in the domain ontology. This may be a cause of the smaller number of semantics detected in them, but this needs further investigation.

Significance in the Prototype System. Our system SRD has detected 70 % of the total number of semantics detected manually in the sample documents. By comparing the total number of semantics detected by SRD with the total number of semantics detected manually, we found that for all data sources SRD detected a reasonable percentage of the total semantics, (see Table 4). This Table shows a significant difference between the number of semantics detected by SRD and manually, and we believe that the reason for this is not the method we are using, but two other reasons:

1. There is a weakness in the programming and thus the keyword searching in our system is not as sophisticated as it might be. If we had used a better searching mechanism, we might have achieved better results. For example, when searching for engine size the system is able to detect " engine size " but not able to detect "engines-size" in the text.
2. The domain ontology used is limited. For example, in one of the documents there was a semantic value in the text mentioning that 'the car has 260 HPs' but 'HP' was not a term in the domain ontology, and therefore the SRD system did not detect this semantic.

The high percentage of undetected semantics by the SRD when compared with the manually detected semantics has occurred because of the weakness of the domain ontology used in our system. We found that most of the missing semantics could be related by an ontology if the ontology was expanded. However, without a well defined ontology the missing semantics will remain undetected.

Table 4. Number of semantics detected by SRD and Manually

Data source	Domain name	SRD	Manually	Percentage
Imotors	Cars	9.59	12.38	77.5
Thermoset	Chemistry	6.29	9.09	70
Which	Cars	5.76	9.76	59.1
Eastman	Chemistry	3.16	6.8	46.5

We believe that this point needs more investigation using a richer ontology. However, it shows that an automatic detection system using an ontology is unlikely to achieve 100% due to the difficulty of getting a comprehensive ontology.

5.2 Experimental Significance Related to the Physical Structure of Documents

Adjacent Paragraphs. We found that 75.05 % of the total detected semantics come from the adjacent paragraphs to the table. In Table 5, the commercial data sources from both domains have a very high percentage of their semantics coming from the adjacent paragraphs, while in the evaluation data sources the percentages are not so high.

Table 5. Percentage of semantics in the adjacent paragraphs

Data source name	Domain name	Percentage
Imotors	Cars-Commercial	88.3
Thermoset	Chemistry-Commercial	86.1
Which	Cars-Evaluation	64.8
Eastman	Chemistry-Evaluation	61

We believe there are three reasons for this:

1. The commercial data sources are reasonably short compared to the evaluation documents, and this will affect the spread of the semantics in the paragraphs. In commercial data sources, documents have 2 to 7 paragraphs, whereas in evaluation data sources they can go up to 13 paragraphs.
2. Evaluation data sources tend to talk about one concept or part of the table in each paragraph and start on a new topic in a new paragraph. This leads to the semantics being spread over the document.
3. Commercial data sources try to concentrate the information into one or two paragraphs to hold the reader's attention.

Paragraphs Under the Table. We found that 70 % of the detected semantics appear to be from the paragraphs after the table. It is common that the writer of the document will describe the table after showing it to the reader. In our sample, the table in commercial data sources usually comes in the middle of the

Table 6. The mean of the number of semantics before and after a table

Data source name	Number of Semantics before Table	Number of Semantics after Table
Imotors	3.09	6.50
Thermoset	1.68	4.61
Which	1.98	3.78
Eastman	.76	2.40

document, whereas in evaluation data sources it is normally near the beginning of the documents.

In Figure 7, we can see that the mean of the number of semantics after a table is always higher than the mean of the number of semantics before the table for all data sources. In Imotors, the paragraphs after the table have produced 65% of the total semantics detected in the documents, also in Which they have produced 66%, Thermoset 74%, and in Eastman they have produced 76%. In total the paragraphs after the table give us 68% of the total number of semantics. This tells us that detecting semantics in the paragraphs after the table is more productive than using the paragraphs before the table.

We believe that by concentrating on the adjacent paragraphs and paragraphs under the table, a system will get most of the semantics, if not all of them presented in a document. In some cases, the tables are put at the end of the document, or in a certain place in the text, or refer to it by its number. We treat this type of document as if the table is in the first indicator position in the document text.

Semantics and Indicators. By tracing the types of indicators used in the text, we find that there are a number of types that the writers tend to use to point to the table from the text. The first one, and the most commonly used is indicating a table by its number, for example 'Table 2.1', and this appears when there is more than one table in the document. It is also used when the table is far away from the indicator in the document. The other types of indicators are 'the above table', 'the next table', 'the last table', 'the previous table', 'in the table below' and the use of 'Figure' instead of 'Table' in these phrases. These types of indicator always need to be close to the table. In some cases there is no indicator in the documents, and this is because the document is short and there was only one table.

In Table 7 P is Paragraph, S is Semantics, and I is Indicators. The column heading P with I and S means paragraphs with an indicator and semantics. This analysis shows that paragraphs containing indicators nearly always have semantics in them (Column 3) and that the semantics are always next to the indicator. Comparing between paragraphs, the paragraphs that have indicators have most of the detected semantics in them (Column 4). Therefore, in large documents, it is useful to search for the indicators first and concentrate on the paragraphs that contain them when looking for hidden semantics.

Paragraphs and Indicators. Among those paragraphs that have indicators, the first paragraph has the highest number of semantics in it. We believe that this

Table 7. Percentage of semantics in paragraphs that contain indicators

Data source	P with I	P with I and S	S in P containing I.	S in the 1st P
Imotors	80	100	89.5	51.7
Thermoset	83.3	100	92	38.2
Which	90.9	95	94.7	10
Eastman	88	90	98.2	13.6

result needs more investigation, because the type of documents we used might affect this result. The documents we used are slightly short and might not show the real situation. However, in the evaluation data sources, the writers spread the semantics throughout the documents and sometimes they use different indictors, for example 'in the first column' and 'in the last row' appear in these documents showing a fuller analysis is being undertaken.

6   Conclusion

As an experiment, we applied our system SRD to 300 documents related to two domains, cars and chemistry. For each domain, we used documents from two different data sources, a commercial and an evaluation. The experiment has shown that documents from commercial data sources in doth domains have more semantics than those from evaluation sources. Also, documents from the scientific domain, chemistry, have fewer semantics than documents from the non-scientific domain, cars.

We found from the experiments that it is common that the writer of the document will describe the table after showing it to the reader. We found that 75.05 % of the total detected semantics comes from the paragraphs adjacent to the table. Also, we found that 71.8 % of the detected semantics appear to be from the paragraphs after the table. We believe that by concentrating on the adjacent paragraphs and paragraphs after the table it is possible to get most of the semantics, if not all of them, that are present in the text.

We also found that paragraphs that have indicators always have semantics in them, which are always next to the indicator. Thus, when comparing between paragraphs, the paragraphs with indicators have most of the detected semantics. Therefore, in large documents, it may be useful to search for the indicators first and concentrate on the paragraphs that contain them in the full detection process. By tracing the types of indicators, we found that there are a number of ways that the writers tend to use to indicate to a table in the text. The first one and the most commonly used is indicating to the table by its number for example 'Table 2.1'. The other types of indicators are 'the above table', 'the next table', 'the last table', 'the previous table', 'in the table below' and with 'figure' instead of table. This can be useful in directing the searching mechanism to concentrate on paragraphs that contain these types of indicators. Also, in large paragraphs, the hidden semantic is sometimes close to that indicator.

References

1. Christof Bornhovd (1999): "Semantic Metadata for the integration of Web-based for Electronic Commerce" International Workshop on Advanced Issues of E-Commerce and Web-based Information Systems (WECWIS'99) Santa Clara, California, 1999
2. Madnick , S.E. (1995): From VLDB to VMLDB (Very Many Large Database: Dealing with Large-Scale Semantic Heterogeneity, Proc. 21st VLBD Conf. 1995.
3. O. Hori and D. S. Doermann, Robust table-form structure analysis based on box-driven reasoning, Proceedings of the Third International Conference on Document Analysis and Recognition (Volume 1), 1995,218,IEEE Computer Society
4. Debashish Niyogi, A Knowledge-Based Approach to Deriving Logical Structure from Document Images, Department of Computer Science, SUNY Buffalo, 94-35, 1994,
5. Matthew Hurst,The Interpretation of Tables in Text,University of Edinburgh, 2000
6. Pallavi Pyreddy and W. Bruce Croft, TINTIN: A System for Retrieval in Text Tables,2nd ACM International Conference on Digital Libraries, 1997,
7. M. Yoshida and K. Torisawa and J. Tsujii, A method to integrate tables of the World Wide Web, Proceedings of the First International Workshop on Web Document Analysis ,2001, 31-34, Seattle, Washington, ICDAR'01
8. Adamantis Diamantopoulos and Bodo Schlegelmilch , Taking the Fear Out of Data Analysis,1997,The Dryden Press, London
9. Saleh Alrashed, W. A. Gray,(2002) "Detection Approaches for Table Semantics in Text", Proceedings of the 5th International Workshop,DAS2002, Princeton.
10. Saleh Alrashed and W. A. Gray, Semantic Detection for Tabular Data in Text, In 7th World Multiconference on Systemics, Cybernetics and Informatics,2003, Orlando, Florida , USA, IEEE, Computer Society ,
11. Saleh Alrashed and W. A. Gray, Utilising Semantic Conversion Functions to Link Tabular Data, In The 9th. International Conference on Information Systems Analysis and Synthesis: ISAS '03,2003,IEEE, Computer Society

Reconstruction of Orthogonal Polygonal Lines

Alexander Gribov and Eugene Bodansky

Environmental System Research Institute (ESRI),
380 New York St., Redlands, CA 92373-8100, USA
{agribov, ebodansky}@esri.com

Abstract. An orthogonal polygonal line is a line consisting of adjacent straight segments having only two directions orthogonal to each other. Because of noise and vectorization errors, the result of vectorization of such a line may differ from an orthogonal polygonal line.

This paper contains the description of an optimal method for the restoration of orthogonal polygonal lines. It is based on the method of restoration of arbitrary ground truth lines from the paper [1]. Specificity of the algorithm suggested in the paper consists of filtering vectorization errors using a priori information about orthogonality of the ground truth contour.

The suggested algorithm guarantees that obtained polygonal lines will be orthogonal and have minimal deviations from the ground truth line. The algorithm has a low computational complexity and can be used for restoration of orthogonal polygonal lines with many vertices. It was developed for a raster-to-vector conversion system ArcScan for ArcGIS and can be used for interactive vectorization of orthogonal polygonal lines.

Keywords: Polygonal line, orthogonality, line drawings, maps, vectorization, error filtering.

1 Introduction

The term *orthogonal polygonal lines* will be used to refer to polygonal lines consisting of orthogonal straight segments. There are only two permissible directions for these segments. These are called cardinal directions. Any two segments of an orthogonal polygonal line are either parallel or perpendicular to each other. Any two successive segments are perpendicular to each other. A rectangle is an example of an orthogonal polygonal line.

Orthogonal polygonal lines can be seen at different line drawings, for example, in architectural plans, engineering drawings, and electrical schematics. Fig. 1 shows a fragment of a city map. Most of the building outlines are orthogonal lines.

The results of vectorization of lines from monochrome images usually are corrupted. Because of scanning noise, discretization, binarization, and vectorization errors, even straight lines are converted to polygonal lines after raw vectorization. Fig. 2 shows a monochrome image obtained by scanning a straight line and the result of raw vectorization. The number of segments in a resulting polygonal line and the deviations of these segments from the ground truth straight lines are sometimes used to evaluate vectorization error [2].

H. Bunke and A.L. Spitz (Eds.): DAS 2006, LNCS 3872, pp. 462–473, 2006.

Fig. 1. A fragment of a city map with buildings. Many of the building borders are orthogonal lines.

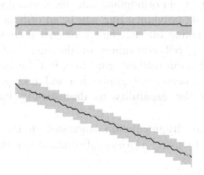

Fig. 2. The monochrome image of straight lines and polygonal lines as a result of raw vectorization

Post-processing usually follows raw vectorization. One of the tasks of post-processing is defragmentation. The goals of defragmentation are data compression and increasing precision. In the past, data compression was more important. The most widely used compression methods solve the problem of data compression by removing some source polygonal line vertices (see, for example, the Douglas-Peucker method in [3]).

The main criterion for removing a vertex is the distance from the vertex of the source polygonal lines to the polygonal line that is a result of compression. Because the location errors of the remaining vertices are not corrected, the precision of vectorization may not be enhanced. In spite of this the Douglas-Peucker compression method is used till now for defragmentation and simplification of polygonal lines.

Recently, because of considerable reduction in price and increasing capacity of computer memory, the problem of data compression has become less important, while the problem of enhancing the precision of vectorization has become more critical.

One approach to the problem of increasing vectorization precision of polylines consisting of geometric primitives follows. A source polygonal line obtained by raw vectorization is divided into nonoverlapping fragments such that each could be approximated with good precision using some geometric primitive (for example, a straight segment, or a circle arc). By finding the optimal approximations of the primitives and the intersections of adjacent primitives, it is possible to build a sequence of primitives that is the restoration of ground truth line. The source polygonal line must be divided in such a way that some functional that is a measure of approximation error will be minimized. The vital importance of such an approach has a definition of the functional.

In [1], such an approach is used with one restriction (after dividing the source line into fragments, they are approximated only with straight segments). The functional value depends not only on the precision of the approximation of fragments of source lines but also on the number of fragments or the number of straight segments of the resulting polygonal line. This method uses only one parameter – the penalty for each segment of the resulting polygonal line.

If the ground truth line is an orthogonal line, the method suggested in [1] does not guarantee that the resulting polygonal line will be an orthogonal line. It is possible to resolve the problem by taking into account geometrical constraints (in this case it is an orthogonality) after a polygonization of the result of raw vectorization (for example, with a beautification method from [4]). But the suggested method resolves the problem with simultaneous polygonization and taking into account geometric constraints. It provides the capability to dramatically increase the accuracy of resulting polylines.

A new method of line fragmentation suggested in this paper differs from the method described in [1] by using *a priori* information that the ground truth line is an orthogonal line.

2 Statement of the Problem

Let p_i, where $i = 0,...,n$, be vertices of polygonal line P_n. Let q_j-th vertices p_{q_j} divide P_n into a set of nonoverlapping polygonal fragments, and $Q_n = \{q_0 = 0, q_1,..., q_m = n\}$ be a set of indexes of the decomposition points of a source polygonal line, where m is a number of segments.

Suppose that cardinal directions of the sought orthogonal polygonal line are horizontal (H) and vertical (V) directions. Let X be one of the cardinal directions and $\perp X$ be a direction perpendicular to X.

Let L_j^X and $L_j^{\perp X}$ be lines having cardinal directions X and $\perp X$ and minimal integral standard deviations $\varepsilon^X_{q_{j-1}, q_j}$ and $\varepsilon^{\perp X}_{q_{j-1}, q_j}$ from the corresponding fragment $(p_{q_{j-1}}, p_{q_j})$ limited with q_{j-1}-th and q_j-th vertices, where $j = 1, ..., m$ of the source polygonal line (see Fig. 3). In Appendix 1, there is an algorithm for building such lines.

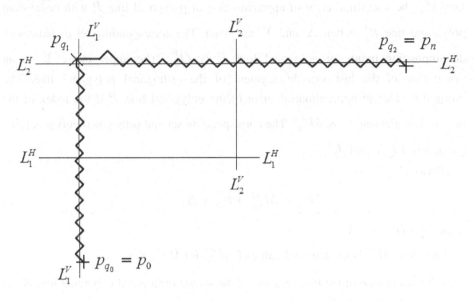

Fig. 3. Polygonal line P_n and horizontal and vertical lines (L_i^H and L_i^V, $i = 1, 2$) are approximations of fragments (p_{q_0}, p_{q_1}) and (p_{q_1}, p_{q_2}), where $q_0 = 0$, $q_2 = n$

The measure of the error of the orthogonal polygonal line approximation is

$$F(Q_n, X, Y, \Delta, m) = m \cdot \Delta + (\varepsilon_{q_0, q_1}^X + \varepsilon_{q_1, q_2}^{\perp X} + ... + \varepsilon_{q_{m-1}, q_m}^Y), \qquad (1)$$

where Δ is a penalty for each straight segment of the resulting orthogonal polygonal line, the second item is the sum of the integral standard deviations, X is the direction of the first segment, and Y is the direction of the last segment of the orthogonal polygonal line.

Lines L_j^X and $L_j^{\perp X}$ are used for building orthogonal polygonal lines. The vertices of the orthogonal polygonal lines are the intersections of adjacent perpendicular lines L_j^X and $L_{j+1}^{\perp X}$. The beginning and the end of the orthogonal polygonal lines are projections of points p_0 and p_n on lines L_1^X and L_m^Y.

The task is to find such set $\hat{Q}_n = \{\hat{q}_0, \hat{q}_1, ..., \hat{q}_{\hat{m}}\}$ and values $\hat{X}$ and $\hat{Y}$ that do the value of the functional (1) minimal. This set $\hat{Q}_n$, directions $\hat{X}$ and $\hat{Y}$, and corresponding orthogonal polygonal line $\hat{R}_n$ are optimal ones.

3 Iterative Algorithm of Decomposition of a Polygonal Line into Fragments

Let M_k^Y be a minimal error of approximation of polygonal line P_k with orthogonal polygonal line R_k^Y when Δ and Y are fixed. The corresponding set of indices of decomposition points of polygonal line P_k is Q_k^Y. The upper index Y is an orientation of the last straight segment of the orthogonal polygonal line. The minimum value of approximation error of the polygonal line P_k if the index of the next to last element i, is $M_{i,k}^Y$. The corresponding set and orthogonal polygonal line are denoted $Q_{i,k}^Y$ and $R_{i,k}^Y$.

Obviously

$$M_{i,k}^Y = M_i^{\perp Y} + \varepsilon_{i,k}^Y + \Delta, \tag{2}$$

where $i = 0,...,k-1$.

Therefore M_k^Y is the minimal value of $M_{i,k}^Y$ for $0 \le i < k$.

If the orientation of the first segment of the sought orthogonal polygonal line $\hat{R}_n$ is unknown and so can be horizontal or vertical, then

$$M_0^H = 0, \; M_0^V = 0. \tag{3}$$

Suppose that all minimal errors of approximation M_i^H and M_i^V of polygonal line P_{k+1} and corresponding sets Q_i^H and Q_i^V, where $i = 1,...,k$ are known. If minimum errors M_{k+1}^H and M_{k+1}^V of P_{k+1} and corresponding set Q_{k+1}^H and Q_{k+1}^V could be found, an iterative algorithm can be build to evaluate an optimal set $\hat{Q}_n$ and optimal orthogonal polygonal line $\hat{R}_n$.

Using the method of least squares, a horizontal or vertical line can be built through the fragment of the source polygonal line between vertices p_i and p_{k+1} and the standard deviation $\varepsilon_{i,k+1}^Y$ and the minimal value of approximation error $M_{i,k+1}^Y$ can be calculated.

By analyzing $M_{i,k+1}^H$, where $i = 0,...,k$, the minimum value of $M_{i,k+1}^H$ and corresponding value $i = i^H$ can be found. Similarly it can be found $i = i^V$.

Sets Q_{k+1}^H and Q_{k+1}^V can be found by adding $k+1$ to sets $Q_{i^H}^V$ and $Q_{i^V}^H$ respectively (attention must be paid to the sequence of superscripts). Thus the problem is resolved.

Repeating this procedure n times sets Q_n^H and Q_n^V will be obtained that provide the minimum values of functional (1) for given values of Δ and Y.

If the last segment of the resulting orthogonal line must be horizontal or vertical then the optimal sets are Q_n^H or Q_n^V respectively. If there is no such requirement for the last segment of the resulting orthogonal line, then the optimal set is

$$\hat{Q}_n = \begin{cases} Q_n^H, M_n^H < M_n^V; \\ Q_n^V, \text{otherwise.} \end{cases} \tag{4}$$

Fig. 4 shows the source polygonal line and orthogonal line obtained using this method.

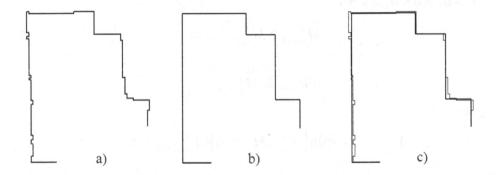

a)   b)   c)

Fig. 4. Orthogonal polygonal line obtained using the described method for $\Delta = 30$ (*a - the source polygonal line, b - orthogonal polygonal line, c - the source and the result line together*)

4   Optimization of the Iterative Algorithm

The algorithm described above has the square calculating complexity. It can be used when the source polygonal line does not have many vertices, for example, an outline of buildings in maps of middle scale. In the case in which the source line has many vertices, the suggested algorithm can cause an essential delay. It is especially inadmissible for interactive modes.

A technique to reduce the calculating complexity of the described algorithm is suggested. There are inequalities that can be used for defining if a given part of the polygonal line P_k can contain the next to last point of decomposition that minimizes $M_{i,k}^Y$. This makes it unnecessary to analyze every vertex p_i, where $i = 0, ..., k-1$ of the polygonal line, while finding a new optimal point i^Y.

This technique is based on two obvious inequalities.

The first arises from the fact that an error of the optimal approximation of a polygonal line with two straight segments is not greater than the error of the optimal approximation of the same polygonal line with one straight segment.

$$\varepsilon^X_{q_1,q_2} + \varepsilon^X_{q_2,q_3} \le \varepsilon^X_{q_1,q_3}, \text{ where } 0 \le q_1 \le q_2 \le q_3 \le n. \tag{5}$$

The second inequality arises from the fact that the minimum error of the approximation of some part of the polygonal line is not greater than the minimum error of the approximation of the whole polygonal line.

$$\min\{M^Y_{q_1}, M^{\perp Y}_{q_1} + \Delta\} \le M^Y_{q_2}, \tag{6}$$

where $0 \le q_1 \le q_2 \le n$, and $\perp Y$ is a direction orthogonal to the direction Y.

From inequalities (5) and (6) it follows (see an Appendix 2) that for $0 \le q_1 \le q < q_2 \le k+1$:

$$M^Y_{q,k+1} \ge \tilde{M}^Y_{q_1,q_2,k+1}, \tag{7}$$

$$M^Y_{q,k+1} \ge \tilde{\tilde{M}}^Y_{q_2,k+1}, \tag{8}$$

where

$$\tilde{M}^Y_{q_1,q_2,k+1} = \min\{M^{\perp Y}_{q_1}, M^Y_{q_1} + \Delta\} + \varepsilon^Y_{q_2-1,k+1} + \Delta, \tag{9}$$

$$\tilde{\tilde{M}}^Y_{q_2,k+1} = \min\{M^Y_{q_2-1}, M^{\perp Y}_{q_2-1} + \Delta\} + \varepsilon^Y_{q_2-1,k+1}. \tag{10}$$

Denote

$$\hat{M}^Y_{q_1,q_2,k+1} = \max\{\tilde{M}^Y_{q_1,q_2,k+1}, \tilde{\tilde{M}}^Y_{q_2,k+1}\}. \tag{11}$$

Suppose the value of the functional of some decomposition of the polygonal line P_{k+1}, where the next to last point of the decomposition does not belong to the half-interval $[q_1, q_2)$ was calculated. Denote this functional F^Y. The next to last point q of decomposition for which $M^Y_{q,k+1}$ becomes minimal can be located inside half-interval $[q_1, q_2)$ only if

$$\hat{M}^Y_{q_1,q_2,k+1} \le F^Y. \tag{12}$$

If this condition is not met, the next to last point of decomposition does not belong to $[q_1, q_2)$ and this half-interval can be skipped. Using this, it is possible to accelerate a search at each step of the described iterative algorithm.

5 Building a Close Orthogonal Polygonal Line

The task of analyzing a case when the source polygonal line is closed as in, for example, the borders of buildings or other area objects can be resolved by reducing it to the previous one.

First, it is necessary to open a source polygonal line, in other words, to find the beginning. The first point and the end point of the source line coincide $p_0 = p_n$.

Let the first point be the upper-left vertex of the source line. Because of such choice of the beginning of the polygonal line the error of approximation is not minimal but the additional error is small. Reorder the vertices so that a new source polygonal line passes around the area object in a clockwise direction.

In this case the first segment of the orthogonal polygonal line is horizontal. Therefore the last segment must be vertical because the line is closed.

While the deriving the above algorithm to build an orthogonal polygonal line, it is assumed that the first segment of the orthogonal line can be either horizontal or vertical. Substituting

$$M_0^H = \infty, \ M_0^V = 0 \tag{13}$$

instead of condition (3) the orthogonal polygonal line with horizontal first segment $X = H$ is obtained. Because the last segment must be vertical, the condition $\hat{Q} = Q_n^V$ is used instead of condition (4).

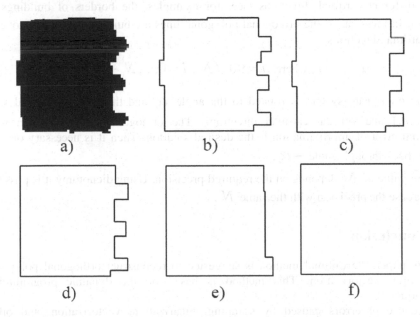

Fig. 5. A building and approximations of its border with orthogonal polygonal lines (*a - raster image of the building with noise and b-f - approximations of building borders obtained with* $\Delta = 30, 100, 300, 1000, 3000$ *accordingly*)

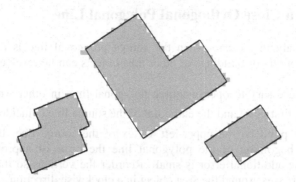

Fig. 6. Image of three buildings and corresponding orthogonal polygonal lines

Fig. 5 shows a monochrome image of a building (with noise) and orthogonal polygonal lines obtained with different values of Δ.

Fig. 6 shows a fragment of a scanned map with three buildings and orthogonal polygonal lines obtained with the suggested method.

6 How to Find Cardinal Directions

Usually cardinal directions are not known in advance. Sometimes different objects have different cardinal directions (see, for examples, the borders of buildings in Fig. 6). In these cases, the orthogonal polygonal lines are built N times with one of the cardinal directions

$$\alpha_i = h \cdot i, \text{ where } h = 90° / N \text{ ; } i = 0, ..., N-1. \tag{14}$$

The coordinate system is rotated to the angle α_i and the task is resolved with horizontal and vertical cardinal directions. The orthogonal polygonal line with minimal error of approximation is the desired solution. Then it is necessary only to turn it back through angle $-\alpha_i$.

The value of N depends on the required precision. Using dichotomy it is possible to increase the precision with the same N.

7 Conclusion

In this paper, the optimal method is suggested to reconstruct orthogonal polygonal lines after vectorization. This method is based on the dynamic programming technique.

Because of errors caused by scanning, binarization, vectorization, and other processes, even straight lines become polygonal lines. One of the goals of post-processing is noise filtering.

In [1], a new method was suggested for filtering errors of vectorization.

A polygonal line obtained as a result of the raw vectorization is divided into no overlapping fragments.[1] The method guarantees the minimum value of the functional that depends on precision of approximation of resulting parts with straight segments and on the number of parts, or the number of segments of the result polygonal line. This method uses one parameter – a penalty for each straight segment of the resulting polygonal line. The error of approximation is calculated as integral standard error. It is possible to modify the method using another measure of the error.

By finding intersections of straight lines obtained as an optimal approximation of fragments a new polygonal line can be built.

Fig. 7. A fragment of the city map from Fig. 1 with borders of orthogonal buildings (the result of processing by ArcScan for ArcGIS)

The method described in this paper is a modification of the method from [1]. Modifying its method with *a priori* information that the sought polygonal line is an orthogonal line provides the method described in this paper. This method guarantees that the resulting polygonal line will be an orthogonal line with almost minimal error compared to the source orthogonal polygonal line.

The method is a combinatorial one and has the quadratic computation complexity. There was a suggested optimization that reduces the number of analyzed solutions, which essentially increases the speed of resolving the task. After optimization, the algorithm can be used for reconstruction of the orthogonal polygonal lines from the source polygonal lines with a large number of vertices, which is common for polygonal lines obtained with vectorization.

The method has been generalized for closed orthogonal polygonal lines, for example, borders of buildings in maps.

---

[1] The polygonal line must have segments roughly equal in size to a pixel; otherwise, it is necessary to perform densification.

The method can also be generalized for the following cases:

- Decomposition of the source polygonal lines into fragments some of which are singular (with zero length)
- Polygonal lines with a fixed angle between adjacent segments differing from 90°
- Polygonal lines with the arbitrary number of permissible directions
- M-dimensional polygonal lines, where $M > 0$

The method has been implemented in ArcScan for ArcGIS. Examples in Fig. 4-7 show the results obtained with the suggested method.

References

1. Gribov A., Bodansky E.: A New Method of Polyline Approximation. Structural, Syntactic, and Statistical Pattern Recognition, Portugal, LNCS 3138, Springer (August 2004) 504-511
2. Phillips I.T., Chhabra A.K.: Empirical Performance Evaluation of Graphics Recognition Systems. IEEE Transactions on Pattern Analysis and Machine Intelligence, Vol. 21, No. 9 (September 1999) 849-870
3. David H. Douglas and Thomas K. Peucker: Algorithms for the Reduction of the Number of Points Required to Represent a Digitized Line or Its Caricature. Canadian Cartographer', Vol. 10, No. 2 (December 1973) 112-122
4. Pavlidis T., VanWyk C.J.: An Automatic Beautifier for Drawings and Illustrations. Computer Graphics, Vol. 19, No. 3, ACM Press (July 1985) 225-234

Appendix 1: Horizontal and Vertical Lines Approximating Some Part of the Polygonal Line

Let t be a parameter equal to the distance from the beginning of the polygonal line till the current point along this line. Let l_{j_1} and l_{j_2} be values of the parameter defining the beginning and the end of the analyzed part of the polygonal line. The horizontal line approximating a given part of the polygonal line can be defined as

$$y = \frac{V_y}{l_{j_2} - l_{j_1}}, \text{ where } V_y = \int_{l_{j_1}}^{l_{j_2}} y(t)dt.$$

The vertical line can be found similarly

$$x = \frac{V_x}{l_{j_2} - l_{j_1}}, \text{ where } V_x = \int_{l_{j_1}}^{l_{j_2}} x(t)dt.$$

Integral standard deviations of these straight lines are defined as

$$\varepsilon_{j_1,j_2}^H = \int_{l_{j_1}}^{l_{j_2}} y^2(t)dt - V_y^2/(l_{j_2} - l_{j_1}),$$

$$\varepsilon_{j_1,j_2}^V = \int_{l_{j_1}}^{l_{j_2}} x^2(t)dt - V_x^2/(l_{j_2} - l_{j_1}).$$

Appendix 2: Derivation of Inequalities (7) and (8)

Let $0 \le q_1 \le q < q_2 \le k+1$.

From inequalities (2) and (6), and obvious inequality $\varepsilon_{q,k+1}^Y \ge \varepsilon_{q_2-1,k+1}^Y$, it is possible to obtain $M_{q,k+1}^Y \ge \min\{M_{q_1}^{\perp Y}, M_{q_1}^Y + \Delta\} + \varepsilon_{q_2-1,k+1}^Y + \Delta$, in other words,

expression (9).

From inequalities (2) and (5) follows $M_{q,k+1}^Y \ge M_q^{\perp Y} + \varepsilon_{q,q_2-1}^Y + \varepsilon_{q_2-1,k+1}^Y + \Delta$.

From an obvious inequality $M_q^{\perp Y} + \varepsilon_{q,q_2-1}^Y + \Delta \ge \min\{M_{q_2-1}^Y, M_{q_2-1}^{\perp Y} + \Delta\}$ it

follows $M_{q,k+1}^Y \ge \min\{M_{q_2-1}^Y, M_{q_2-1}^{\perp Y} + \Delta\} + \varepsilon_{q_2-1,k+1}^Y$, or expression (10).

A Multiclass Classification Framework for Document Categorization

Qi Qiang[1] and Qinming He[1,2]

[1] College of Computer Science, Zhejiang University, Hangzhou 310027, China
qiangqi@yahoo.com
[2] Ningbo Institute of Technology, Zhejiang University, Ningbo 315100, China

Abstract. With a great amount of textual information are available on the Internet and corporate intranets, it has become a necessary to categorize large documents. As we known, text classification problem is representative multiclass problem. This paper describes a framework, which we call Strong-to-Weak-to-Strong (SWS). It transforms a "strong" learning algorithm to a "weak" algorithm by decreasing its iterative numbers of optimization while preserving its other characteristics like geometric properties and then makes use of the kernel trick for "weak" algorithms to work in high dimensional spaces, finally improves the performances of text classification. We analyzed the particular properties of learning with text and identified why this approach is appropriate for this task. Empirical results show that our approach is competitive with the other methods.

1   Introduction

Automated text classification, the supervised learning assignment of labeling free text document to predefined categories based on their content, is a significant component in many data mining and knowledge discovery tasks. Many algorithms for the multiclass problems have been developed recently. One directly considers all data in one optimization formulation. However a more general method is to reduce a multiclass problem to multiple binary problems [1].

In [2] Dietterich and Bakiri described a unifying method for reducing multiclass problems to multiple binary problems based on error correcting output codes. However there might be strong statistical correlations between the resulting classifiers. The design problem of output coding has been introduced [3]. One can regard the design problem as a constrained optimization problem. However this method is extremely time-consuming and has too much variables to solve effectively.

Recently a robust Minimax classifier where the probability of correct classification of future data should be maximized has been provided [4]. No further assumptions are made with respect to the each two class-conditional distributions. The minimax problem can be interpreted geometrically as minimizing the maximum of the Mahalanobis distances to the two classes. "Kernelization" version is also available.

An important feature of the probability machine is that a worst-case bound on the probability of misclassification of future data is always obtained explicitly. We use this probability to build a heuristic algorithm and then solve the design problem of output

H. Bunke and A.L. Spitz (Eds.): DAS 2006, LNCS 3872, pp. 474–483, 2006.

coding more effectively, while overcoming the limitation that the previous methods can be implemented only when given a set of binary classifiers.

Section 2 reviews the standard feature vector representation of text. Section 3 briefly states the output codes framework for multiclass categorization problems. Section 4 reviews the binary minimax machine and introduces resample for robust estimation for mean and covariance matrix. Section 5, the main part of the article, presents new algorithm in detail. In section 6, we report the experimental results. Finally, section 7 presents conclusions and discussion of future directions.

2 Text Categorization

The goal of text categorization is the classification of text into a fixed number of predefined categories. Using machine learning, the objective is to learn classifiers from examples which perform the category assignments automatically. This is a supervised learning problem.

The first step in text categorization is to transform text, which typically are strings of characters, into a representation suitable for the learning algorithm and the classification task. Text Analysis researches suggest that word stems work well as representation units and that their ordering in a text is of minor importance for many tasks. This leads to an attribute-value representation of text. Each distinct word corresponds to a feature, with the number of times word occurs in the text as its value. This representation scheme leads to very high-dimensional feature spaces containing 10000 dimensions and more. Many have noted the need for feature selection to make use of conventional learning methods possible, to improve generalization accuracy, and to avoid overfitting. Following the recommendation of [5], the information gain criterion will be used in this paper to select a subset of features.

3 Design of Output Codes

In this section we briefly review the method for designing of output codes [3]. Let $S = \{(x_1, y_1),...,(x_m, y_m)\}$ be a set of m training examples where each instance x_i belongs to a domain χ. We assume without loss of generality that each label y_i is an integer from the set $\Upsilon = \{1,...,k\}$. A multiclass classifier is a function $H : \chi \rightarrow \Upsilon$ that maps an instance x into an element $y \in \Upsilon$. An output codes M is a matrix of size $k \times l$ over $\mathbb{R}$ where each row of M corresponds to a class $y \in \Upsilon$. Then different binary classifiers $h_1,...,h_l$ can be yielded. We denote the vector of predictions of these classifiers on an instance x as $\overline{h}(x) = (h_1(x),...,h_l(x))$.

We denote the r th row of M by $\overline{M}_r$. Given an example x we predict the label y for which the row $\overline{M}_y$ is the "closest" to $\overline{h}(x)$. Naturally we can perform the calculations in some high dimensional inner-product space Z using a transformation $\overline{\phi} : \mathbb{R}^l \rightarrow Z$ and use a general notion for closeness, then define it through an inner-product function $K : \mathbb{R}^l \times \mathbb{R}^l \rightarrow \mathbb{R}$, which satisfies Mercer conditions [6]. The higher the value of $K(\overline{h}(x), \overline{M}_r)$ is, the more confident we are that r is the correct labels of x according to the classifiers $\overline{h}(x)$. Thus $H(x) = \arg\max_{r \in \Upsilon}\{K(\overline{h}(x), \overline{M}_r)\}$.

Let $[\![\alpha]\!]$ be 1 if the predicate α holds and 0 otherwise, $\delta_{i,j}$ equals 1 if $i = j$, 0 otherwise. Denote by $b_{i,r} = 1 - \delta_{y_i,r}$. We define the 2 norm of a matrix M and introduce slack variables ζ_i. Then the problem of finding a good matrix M can be stated as the following optimization problem:

$$L(M,\zeta,\eta) = \frac{1}{2}\beta\sum_r \left\|\overline{M}_r\right\|_2^2 + \sum_{i=1}^m \zeta_i + \sum_{i,r} \eta_{i,r}\left[K(\overline{h}(x_i),\overline{M}_r) - K(\overline{h}(x_i),\overline{M}_{y_i}) - \zeta_i + b_{i,r}\right] \quad (1)$$

$$subject\ to:\ \forall i,r\ \ \eta_{i,r} \geq 0$$

for some constant $\beta \geq 0$ and $\eta_{i,r} \geq 0$. Let $\overline{1}_i$ be the vector with all components zero, except for the i th component which is equal to one, and let $\overline{1}$ be the vector whose components are all one. We can denote by $\overline{\gamma}_{i,r} = \overline{1}_{y_i} - \eta_{i,r}$.

Finally, the classifier $H(x)$ can be written in terms of the variable γ as:

$$H(x) = \arg\max_r\left\{\sum_i \gamma_{i,r} K(\overline{h}(x), \overline{h}(x_i))\right\} \quad (2)$$

However solving optimization problem (1) is time-consuming. In this paper our algorithm solves this optimization problem heuristically.

4 A Probability Machine

In this section we introduce a minimax probability machine (MPM) [4] proposed by Lanckriet et al., which tries to minimize the probability of misclassification of data.

Let x and y model data from each of two classes in a binary classification problem, with means and covariance matrices given by (x, Σ_x) and (y, Σ_y), respectively. We wish to determine a hyperplane $F(a,b) = \{z \mid a^T z = b\}$, where $a \in \mathbb{R}^n \setminus \{0\}$ and $b \in \mathbb{R}$ which separates the two classes of points with maximal probability with respect to all distributions having these mean and covariance matrices. This is expressed as:

$$\max_{\theta,a\neq 0,b} \theta \ \ s.t \ \ \inf_{x\sim(\overline{x},\Sigma_x)} \Pr\{a^T x \geq b\} \geq \theta$$
$$\inf_{y\sim(\overline{y},\Sigma_y)} \Pr\{a^T y \leq b\} \geq \theta \quad (3)$$

Where the notion (x, Σ_x) refers to the class of distributions that have prescribed mean $\overline{x}$ and Σ_x, but are otherwise arbitrary; likewise for y. In formulation (3) the term θ is the minimal probability of correct classification of future data. Let us denote by $\kappa(\theta) = \sqrt{\dfrac{\theta}{1-\theta}}$. As the result of Marshall and Olkin [7], an optimal hyperplane $F(a_*, b_*)$ exists, and can be determined by solving the convex second order cone optimization problem, with complexity similar to SVM [6]:

$$\kappa_*^{-1} := \min_a \sqrt{a^T \Sigma_x a} + \sqrt{a^T \Sigma_y a} \quad s.t. \quad a^T(\overline{x}-\overline{y})=1, \tag{4}$$

and setting b to the value $b_* = a_*^T \overline{x} - \kappa_* \sqrt{a_*^T \Sigma_x a_*}$, where a_* is an optimal solution of (3). The optimal worst-case misclassification probability is obtained via

$$1-\theta_* = \frac{1}{1+\kappa_*^2} = \frac{\left(\sqrt{a_*^T \Sigma_x a_*} + \sqrt{a_*^T \Sigma_y a_*}\right)^2}{1+\left(\sqrt{a_*^T \Sigma_x a_*} + \sqrt{a_*^T \Sigma_y a_*}\right)^2} \tag{5}$$

Learning large margin classifiers [8] has become an active research topic. SVM [6] aims to find a hyperplane, which can separate two classes of data with the maximal margin. However, this margin is defined in a "local" way, i.e., the margin is exclusively determined by some support vectors, whereas all other points are totally irrelevant to the decision hyperplane. MPM considers data in a global fashion, while SVM actually discards the global information of data including geometric information and the statistical trend of data occurrence. Nonlinear decision boundaries can be obtained by "Kernel" trick that has been used in support vector machine.

5 SWS (Strong-to-Weak-to-Strong) Algorithm

Assume that the binary classifiers are chosen from some hypothesis class H .The following natural learning problems arise,

1. Given a matrix M, find a set binary classifiers $\overline{h}$ which have small empirical loss.
2. Given a set of $\overline{h}$, find a matrix M which has small empirical loss.
3. Find both a matrix M and a set $\overline{h}$ which have small empirical loss.

The previous methods have focused mostly on the first problem. Most of these works have used predefined output codes, independently of the specific application and the learning algorithm. Furthermore, the "decoding" assigns the same weight to each learned binary classifier, regardless of its performances.

The research [3] has mainly concentrated on the code design problem (problem 2). However , solving optimization problem (1) is time-consuming.

We mainly handle the 3rd problem. However it is so hard to solve the designing problem not to mention finding a "good" classifier and a wonderful output codes simultaneously by using general optimization methods. Therefore a heuristic algorithm has been proposed instead of solving directly the optimization problem (1).

In our framework SWS (Strong-to-Weak-to-Strong), we generalize the notion of "weak" algorithm [9]. We can view an algorithm with less iterative step of optimization as a "weak" algorithm and make use of the kernel trick for "weak" algorithm to work in high dimensional spaces, finally improve the performances.

The model of SWS and the heuristic algorithm make it realizable to solve both problems mentioned above with acceptable complexion.

Recently a number of powerful kernel-based learning machines, e.g. SVM [6], Kernel Fisher Discriminant [10] and Kernel Principal Component [11], have been proposed. In KPCA, kernel serves as preprocessing while in SVM kernel has effect on classification in the middle of process.

There could be two stages for kernel to affect the result of our algorithm. The first is in the middle of process as it behaves in SVM. The second is where algorithm transforms several weak classifiers to a strong classifier. For simplicity, from now on, we do not make any distinction between two kernels and transformation $\bar{\phi}$.

5.1 Strong-to-Weak Stage

We use l MPMs as binary classifiers and initially predefine different partitions of the set of the labels, on which l binary weak classifiers are based.

In the Strong-to-Weak stage, we transform "Strong" classifier to "Weak" classifier by equipping less iterative number of optimization while preserving its characteristics like large margin and geometric properties.

On one hand, it significantly decreases total time-consuming in the case of large numbers of classes because each classifier needs less iterative step of optimization.

On the other hand, our algorithm takes the geometric difference of classes into account while other methods ignore the difference because MPM uses Mahalanobis distance that involves geometric information. Therefore SWS preserves the characteristics.

While the algorithm faces the problem with small data sets, estimation errors in the means and covariances of the classes would affect the results. Based on our experiments, we found that adding a regularization term [4] of a classical form has less effect and is sensitive to choices of the parameters. Thus we used some filter methods and found that resample method was well done.

Therefore we are able to use a simple iterative least-squares approach [4] with less iterative step to solve the kernelization version of problem (4) and train the binary classifiers because the algorithm only requires "Weak" learning algorithms.

5.2 Weak-to-Strong Stage

In the Weak-to-Strong stage, we make use of the kernel trick for "Weak" algorithm to work in high dimensional spaces and finally improve the performances. Multiclass classifier obtained in our algorithm becomes a much more "Strong" learning algorithm according to the classification performance.

A few previous heuristics attempting [12] to modify the output codes were suggested. However, they did not yield significant improvements. Unlike those methods, our algorithm implements implicit update in high dimensional spaces by using a transformation $\bar{\phi}: \mathbb{R}^l \to Z$. And the output codes update implicitly occurs in final discrimination from (2):

$$H(x) = \arg\max_{r}\{K(\overline{h}(x), \overline{M}_r^{update})\} = \arg\max_{r}\left\{\sum_i \gamma_{i,r} K(\overline{h}(x), \overline{h}(x_i))\right\} \tag{6}$$

We notice that the saddle point from optimization problem (1) we are seeking is a minimum for the primal variables with respect to ζ_i. We can get

$$\sum_r \eta_{i,r} = 1, \ i.e. \ \overline{\gamma}_i \le \overline{1}_{y_i} \ and \ \overline{\gamma}_i \cdot \overline{1} = 0 \tag{7}$$

And $\overline{1}_{y_i}$ may be viewed as the correct point distribution, $\eta_{i,r}$ could be viewed as the distribution obtained by the algorithm over the labels for each example. Then we can view $\overline{\gamma}_i$ as the difference between the former and the later. It is natural to say that an example x_i affects the solution (6) if and only if $\overline{\eta}_i$ is not a point distribution concentrating on the correct label y_i. Further we can say that only the questionable points contribute to the learning process and regard them as "critical points".

We have realized that it is difficult to solve the optimization problem (1) directly. What have been mentioned above motivate us to develop a heuristic algorithm to solve the problem. We notice that one "critical point" may contribute to more than one class while "support vector"[6] contributes to only one class. Further we believe that it is limitation with SVM. It is typically assumed that the set of labels has no underlying structure, however there exist lots of different relation among category in practice especially in the case of document classification. It means that it is reasonable that one example makes different contributions to some classes or classifiers simultaneously.

We denote the critical degree by element $B_{i,j}^c$ of a $m \times k$ weight matrix B^c. The i th training data contributes to the j th class with degree $B_{i,j}^c$ and row B_i^c of weight matrix is approximation of $\overline{\gamma}_i$. Note that we need a partition of l classifiers into k sets ($l \ne k$). That is to say elements of each set correspond one certain class not one classifier. There are two confidence matrices: $W^c : m \times k$, whose elements are confidences of examples to classes, and $W^m : m \times l$, whose elements are confidences of examples to classifiers. Row W_i^c of confidence matrix is approximation of $\overline{\eta}_i$. We can easily obtain W^c from W^m that can be directly constructed according to margin magnitude $(a^T x - b)$. Therefore we can construct B^c from W^c as shown in Fig. 2. For simplicity, from now on, we do not make any distinction between W^c and W^m. We call them as confidence matrix. Especially $W^c = W^m$ if $l=k$. We then propose a heuristic strategy using vector V^c whose elements are probability outputs of MPMs in Fig. 1 and example margin to build confidence matrix whose elements are feasible solution to the optimization problem (1), further to construct weight matrix.

The algorithm enforces that each row of weight matrix satisfies the constraint (7). It is easy to verify rationality of these approximations for probability and margin indicate contributive degree of an example to a class as $\eta_{i,r}$ behaves.

Get confidence matrix $W^c \leftarrow EvaluateFromClassfier(W^m)$, $W^c : m \times k$ $W^m : m \times l$

Get confidence vector $V^c \leftarrow EvaluateClassfier(V^m)$, $V^c : 1 \times k$ $V^m : 1 \times l$

Repeat $i = 1, ..., m$ $j = 1, ...k$

                if $W^c_{i,:} < 0$ or $W^c_{i,j} > 0$

                    $W^c_{i,j} \leftarrow V^c_j \times W^c_{i,j}$

                else $W^c_{i,j} \leftarrow 0$

end   get fresh confidence matrix

Fig. 1. Algorithm description of constructing confidence matrix. Note: V^c_j has been normalized.

Get fresh confidence matrix $\left[W^c_{i,j}\right]$, $i = 1..,m$ $j = 1,...k$ and sparseRate that controls sparseness

Repeat $j = 1,...k$

        $V_n \leftarrow GetSlackData(W^c_{.,j})$

        $mvalue = \min(V_n)$

        $Removeneg(W^c_{.,j})$ (remove all other negative elements in the j th column)

        $W^c_{.,j} \leftarrow W^c_{.,j} + |mvalue|$

        $mavalue = \max(W^c_{.,j})$ (get maximal value of the j th column)

        $W^c_{.,j} \leftarrow mavalue - W^c_{.,j}$

        $B^c_{.,j} = pickCritical(W^c_{.,j}, sparseness)$

end $B^c_{.,j} = Constrain(B^c_{.,j})$

$m \times k$ matrix B^c whose elements are critical degree of each point to each class

Fig. 2. Algorithm description of constructing weight matrix

One can obtain worst-case bound on the probability of misclassification of future data in MPM. This probability belongs to one binary classifier and each training data x classified by a certain binary classifier has a corresponding margin magnitude in Fig. 1. If this point can be correctly predicted by a classifier h_j, corresponding element of confidence matrix should be $a_j^T x - b^T$ (positive), otherwise this element should be zero that indicates the point rejects the class except for one case, where we should set this element to be $a_j^T x - b^T$ (negative) if no classifiers can correctly predict the corresponding point. Although the value is negative, it actually carries available information that could predict one class, to which this point most possibly belongs. Once all conditions above are available, for each class we pick some maximal negative (their absolute value are small), which indicate that corresponding data reject the class with least degree, from each column of this matrix according to a predefined parameter that controls tolerance level of class to errors if there are some negative in this column. Then algorithm removes all other negative in the same column and adds absolute value of the smallest negative chosen to all the non-zero elements in the same column. We get maximal value in each column and subtract each non-zero element in the same column from this maximal value. Then we choose some elements, whose corresponding data are 'critical points' in descending order according to a parameter that controls sparseness, then construct weight matrix in Fig. 2. We make the matrix elements satisfy the constraint (7). In addition, one can find underlying patterns among classes through relation between data and classes.

After training and constructing weight matrix, one can predicate a label given an instance:

$$H(x) = \arg \max_r \left\{ \sum_i B^c_{i,r} K(\overline{h}(x), \overline{h}(x_i)) \right\}$$ (8)

6 Experiments

In our experiment we set $l = k$, i.e. one-against-rest method that is less competitive as shown in most researches [13,14]. However our experiments report that better performances can be achieved although using one-against-rest method. We use tf×idf and feature selection based on information gained to build training and test data.

The following experiment compares the performance of the new algorithm with five conventional learning methods commonly used for text categorization.

The empirical evaluation is done on the "ModApte" spite of the Reuters-21578 dataset that was compiled by Lewis at AT&T. The ModApte spite, which has 12,902 stories and the average length of 200 words, leads to a corpus of 9603 training stories (75% of the total) and 3299 test stories (25% of the total). Of the 135 potential topic categories only those 90 are used for that reason that there is at least one training and one test example, after preprocessing the training corpus, containing 9962 distinct terms.

We try to replicate the experimental setup in [15, 16], and the best results of all the methods are described in Table 1. Table 2 displays the results of using different iterative steps of optimization for "Weak" algorithm.

Table 1. Precision/recall-breakeven point on the ten largest categories

	Bayes	Rocchio	C4.5	k-NN	SVM	SWS
Earn	95.9	96.1	96.1	97.3	**98.5**	98.0
Acq	91.5	92.1	85.3	92.0	**95.4**	93.5
Money-fx	62.9	67.6	69.4	78.2	76.3	**82.5**
Grain	72.5	79.5	89.1	82.2	**93.1**	92.5
Crude	81.0	81.5	75.5	85.7	89.0	**89.2**
Trade	50.0	77.4	59.2	77.4	78.0	**82.1**
Interest	58.0	72.5	49.1	74.0	76.2	**79.3**
Ship	78.7	83.1	80.9	79.2	87.6	**89.1**
Wheat	60.6	79.4	85.5	76.6	85.9	**86.6**
Corn	47.3	62.2	87.7	77.9	85.7	**90.3**

Table 2. Precision/recall-breakeven point with various iterative numbers of weak algorithm

Iterative numbers	5	10	30	50	100	150
Earn	**98.0**	**98.0**	**98.0**	**98.0**	**98.0**	**98.0**
Acq	92.7	**93.5**	**93.5**	**93.5**	**93.5**	**93.5**
Money-fx	81.2	**82.5**	**82.5**	**82.5**	81.5	81.7
Grain	91.0	**92.5**	**92.5**	**92.5**	**92.5**	90.0
Crude	88.3	**89.2**	**89.2**	**89.2**	**89.2**	87.5
Trade	**82.1**	**82.1**	**82.1**	**82.1**	79.7	78.0
Interest	76.2	**79.3**	**79.3**	**79.3**	78.0	76.5
Ship	89.0	**89.1**	**89.1**	**89.1**	**89.1**	**89.1**
Wheat	86.0	**86.6**	**86.6**	**86.6**	86.1	85.0
Corn	88.7	**90.3**	**90.3**	**90.3**	**90.3**	**90.3**

Best results can be achieved by choosing 2-degree polynomial kernel in SWS.

From Table 1 we observe an interesting phenomenon that our algorithm (SWS) outperforms others in the case that much poor performances could be achieved by all other methods, while in other cases our results are somewhat worse than the best performances.

This phenomenon also inspires us to try to find the reason from the characteristic of MPM that considers data in a geometric fashion, while SVM [6] ignores this kind of information. As known in chapter 4 MPM uses Mahalanobis distance that involves geometric information. It could be the reason that large difference between subspaces of classes leads to poor performance.

It is clear that Table 2 shows the algorithm of SWS can preserve whole performances although decreasing total iterative step of optimization.

7 Conclusion and Future Works

We have introduced a new method for multiclass problems. Results suggest that our algorithm outperforms other algorithms although using one-against-rest strategy.

The subspace of each category of text is quite different from others. This could be the reason why some methods like SVM fail to achieve high performance on some "difficult" datasets where subspaces of different categories are quite different.

Our algorithm takes the geometric difference of classes into account while other methods ignore the difference because MPM uses Mahalanobis distance involving geometric information. Therefore SWS can improve the performance on some "difficult" datasets for taking the different information of subspaces into account.

Generally there are large numbers of categories in text classification problem. Traditional methods are immersed in complex computation.

Our algorithm achieved acceptable complexion through transforming a "strong" learning algorithm to "weak" one. SWS also makes it possible to be insensitive to optimization approach, therefore it can use a simple iterative least-squares approach.

Finally, a nonlinear transformation is utilized to improve the performance.

These characteristics make our method appropriate for text classification.

As we mentioned in section 5, there is a parameter that controls sparseness in the algorithm. How to adaptively tune this parameter is an interesting topic for future work.

Acknowledgements

This research was supported by Ningbo Doctor Science Fund grant 2005A610002.

References

1. Allwein, E., Schapire, R., & Singer, Y.: Reducing multiclass to binary: A unifying approach for margin classifiers. In Machine Learning: Proceedings of the SeventeenthInternational Conference (2000)
2. Dietterich, T. G., & Bakiri, G.: Solving multiclass learning problems via error correcting output codes. Journal of Artificial Intelligence Research, (1995) 2, 263–286
3. Koby Crammer, Yoram Singer: On the Learnability and Design of Output Codes for Multiclass Problems. Proceedings of the Thirteenth Annual Conference on Computational Learning Theory (2000) 35–46
4. Lanckriet, R. G., Ghaoui, L.E., Bhattacharyya, C., and Jordan, M. I.: A robust minimax approach to classification. Journal of Machine Learning Research (2002) 3:555–582
5. Y. Yang and J. Pedersen: A comparative study on feature selection in text categorization. In International Conference on Machine Learning (ICML) (1997)
6. V. Vapnik: The Nature of Statistical Learning Theory. Spinger Verlag, New York (1995)
7. Marshall, A. W. and Olkin, I.: Multivariate Chebyshev inequalities. Annals of Mathematical Statistics (1960) 31(4): 1001–1014
8. Smola, A. J., Bartlett, P. L., Scholkopf, B., & Schuurmans, D.: Advances in large margin classi-fiers. MIT Press (2000)
9. Yoav Freund: Boosting a weak learning algorithm by majority. Information and Computation (1995) 121(2): 256–285
10. S. Mika, G. Rätsch, J. Weston, B. Schölkopf, and K. -R. Müller: Fisher discriminant analysis with kernels. Neural Networks for Signal Processing IX (1999) 41–48
11. B. Schölkopf, A.J. Smola, K. -R. Müller: Nonlinear component analysis as a kernel eigenvalue problem. Neural Computation (1998) 10:1299–1319
12. Aha, D. W., & Bankert, R. L.: Cloud classification using error-correcting output codes. In Artificial Intelligence Applications: Natural Science, Agriculture, and Environmental Science (1997) 11:13–28
13. Hsu, C., & Lin, C. A.: comparison of methods for multiclass support vector machines. Technical report, Department of Computer Science and Information Engineering, National Taiwan University, Taipei, Taiwan (2001) 19
14. J. C. Platt, N. Cristianini, and J. Shawe-Taylor: Large margin DAGs for multiclass classifycation. In Advances in Neural Information Processing Systems, MIT Press (2000) 12:547–553
15. Joachims, T.: Text cateforization with support vector machines: Learning with many relevant features. In Proceedings 10th European Conference on Machine Learning (ECML), Springer Verlag (1998)
16. Taku Kudo and Yuji Matsumoto: Fast methods for kernel-based text analysis. In Proceedings of the 41est Annual Meeting of the Association for Computational Linguistics (2003) 24-31

The Restoration of Camera Documents Through Image Segmentation

Shijian Lu and Chew Lim Tan

School of Computing, National University of Singapore, 117543, Singapore
{lusj, tancl}@comp.nus.edu.sg
http://www.comp.nus.edu.sg/labs/chime/

Abstract. This paper presents a document restoration technique that is able to flatten curled document images captured through a digital camera. The proposed method corrects camera images of documents through image partition, which divides distorted text lines into multiple small patches based on the identified vertical stroke boundary (VSB) and the fitted x-line and baseline of text lines. Target rectangles are then constructed through the exploitation of the characters enclosed within the partitioned image patches. With the constructed target rectangles and the partitioned image patches, global geometric distortion is finally removed through the local rectification of partitioned image patches one by one. Experimental results show that the proposed technique is fast, accurate, and easy for implementation.

1 Introduction

As camera resolution increases in recent years, high-speed non-contact document capture through a digital camera is opening up a new channel for document capturing and processing. Unfortunately, most documents such as the newspaper held in human hands and the book pages bound in a thick volume lie on a curled instead of planar surface. At the same time, the generic optical character recognition (OCR) systems cannot handle the camera text lying on a non-flat surface. Similar to the compensation of rotation induced skew introduced during the scanning process, geometric distortion resulting from the non-flat document surfaces must be removed before captured documents are fed to the OCR systems.

A number of document restoration techniques have been reported in the literature. The proposed techniques can be classified into two categories, namely, "*hard*" approaches [1, 2, 3] and "*soft*" approaches [4, 5, 6], respectively. The difference between the two approaches is whether auxiliary hardware is required or not. In [1], Pilu proposes to remove the geometric distortion using an applicable surface. This method needs the special laser devices to acquire 3D data before the restoration. Moreover, the correction process is quite slow, as the relaxation requires a large number of iteration to converge. In [2], Brown proposes to restore arbitrarily warped documents using the reconstructed 3D model. This method requires the structured lighting system and the complicated calibration process

H. Bunke and A.L. Spitz (Eds.): DAS 2006, LNCS 3872, pp. 484–495, 2006.

to establish the depth map. In addition, the mapping of points on the non-flat surfaces to the ones on the planar images is still a problem. In [3], Yamashita et al propose to flatten the distorted documents through 3D modeling where a stereo vision system is set up for 3D measurements.

Instead of setting up some auxiliary devices, Agam and Wu [4] proposed a new technique that removes the geometric distortion through 3D mesh manipulation. The 3D mesh is constructed based on stereo disparity, which is built with multiple images captured from different viewpoints. Similarly, Cao et al propose to model the non-flat document using a cylindrical surface in [5]. The restoration equation is constructed through the exploitation of the camera imaging geometry and the cylinder directrix. Apart from the cylindrical modeling restriction, this method requires that generatrix of the cylinder model parallel to the image plane. In another work [6] by Liang, general curved documents can be flattened with just a single image captured through an uncalibrated digital camera. But the process is quite slow because the restoration involves the texture flow computation and the developable surface estimation.

In [7], we propose a rectification technique that restores camera documents with perspective distortion to a fronto-parallel view. The rectification is accomplished through the exploitation of the vertical stroke boundary (VSB), x-line and baseline as labeled with (1) and (2) in Figure 1, which are determined using a few fuzzy sets and morphological operators. In this paper, we extend our earlier work to restore the camera documents where texts lie on a non-flat instead of planar surface. We focus on the documents where texts lie on a smoothly curved surface and text line orientations can be modeled using a cubic polynomial. The proposed restoration technique needs no camera calibration, no auxiliary hardware [1, 2, 3] or 3D reconstruction from multiple images [4]. The only thing required is a single document image captured through a common digital camera. In addition, the method assumes no specific 3D surface model as did in [5]. It is able to handle the camera documents captured from different viewpoints provided that the angle between document normal and camera optical axis lies within a reasonable range.

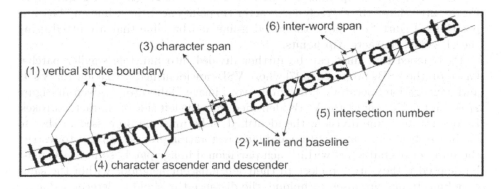

Fig. 1. Text line definition

We propose to restore the camera documents with perspective and geometric distortion through image partition, which divides distorted text lines to multiple small image patches where text can be approximated to lie on a planar surface. The partition is accomplished through the exploitation of the x-line and baseline and the VSBs. For each partitioned image patch, a target rectangle is constructed based on the number and the aspect ratios of enclosed characters. The character aspect ratios are determined based on character span, character ascender and descender, and character intersection numbers as labeled with (3), (4), and (5) in Figure 1. With the constructed quadrilateral correspondences, the global geometric distortion is finally removed through the local rectification of the partitioned image patches one by one.

2   The Proposed Approach

This section presents the proposed document restoration technique. In particular, we divide the description into three subsections, which deal with the camera document partition, the target rectangle construction, and the final camera document restoration respectively.

2.1   Camera Document Partition

The document partition process can be divided into two steps. The first step partitions the distorted document images to multiple text lines based on the x-line and baseline. Combined with the identified VSBs, the second step further divides the partitioned text lines into multiple smaller patches where text can be approximated to lie on a planar surface.

Text lines can be partitioned through the exploitation of the character tip points as proposed in [7]. For text lying over a smoothly curved surface, the orientation of text lines can be modeled well with a cubic polynomial in most cases. We therefore choose a polynomial instead of straight line to fit the extracted character tip points. For distorted word image given in Figure 2(a), Figure 2(b) shows the extracted character tip points near the x-line and baseline positions. Figure 2(c) shows the fitted x-line and baseline that are fitted using the classified character tip points.

Partitioned text lines can be further divided into multiple smaller patches based on the VSBs proposed in [7] where VSBs are identified with a few fuzzy sets and aggregation operators. For sample word image "laboratory" given in Figure 2(a), Figure 2(d) shows the VSBs identified from the left side of character strokes. Before the text line division, the identified VSBs must be processed further to facilitate the document partition and later restoration process. Firstly, to restrict the number of characters within each partitioned image patch, some VSBs must be deleted if they are too close to their left adjacent neighbor within the same text line. In our proposed technique, the distance threshold is determined as:

$$D_{thre} = k_d \cdot VSB_{avg} \tag{1}$$

where parameter VBS_{avg} represents the average length of identified VSBs, which normally reflects the size of the captured characters. Parameter k_d is designed to adjust the width of the partitioned image patches and we set it at 3 so that each image patches enclose as least three characters.

Secondly, for text lines that have no VSBs identified at their left or right end positions, a VSB must be estimated there to enclose all texts that belong to the processed text line. The orientation of the VSB at the text line end position can be determined through the linear interpolation:

$$slp = slp'' + \frac{(x - x'') \cdot (slp' - slp'')}{x' - x''} \tag{2}$$

where x is x coordinates of the leftmost or rightmost text pixel within the studied text line. x', x'' are x coordinates of the centroids of the two VSBs nearest to x. Parameters slp' and slp'' denote the slopes of the straight lines fitted based on that two nearest VSBs. Therefore, the VSBs at the text line end positions can be estimated as the straight line segments that pass through x with orientation determined using Equation (2).

Figure 2(e) shows the processed VSBs where the second VSB in Figure 2(d) is deleted to ensure the width of the partitioned image patches. The rightmost VSB given in Figure 2(e) is constructed to enclose all text within the processed

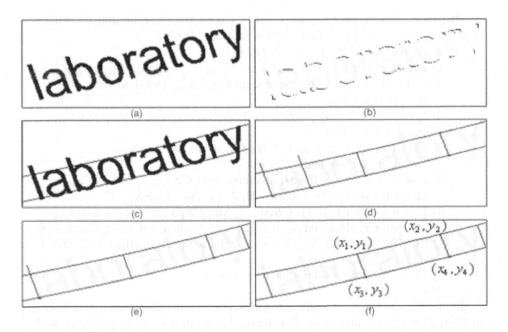

Fig. 2. Document image partition: (a) distorted document text; (b) extracted character tip points; (c) fitted x-line and baseline of text line; (d) identified VSBs; (c) processed VSBs; (d) partition result

text line. Some vertical lines can thus be fitted based on the processed VSBs. Combining the fitted x-line and baseline of the text lines, the distorted word image given in Figure 2(a) can thus be partitioned into three small image patches as shown in Figure 2(f).

2.2   Target Rectangle Construction

For each partitioned image patch, a target rectangle correspondence must be constructed within the target image to rectify that partitioned image patch. We propose to classify characters to six categories with six different aspect ratios. Characters are classified based on the features including character span, character ascender and descender, and character intersection numbers as shown in Figure 1.

Character span is defined as the distance between two parallel straight lines tangent to the left and right sides of character with the orientation same as that of the nearest VSB. Character ascender and descender can be determined based on the distance between the topmost and lowermost character pixels and the x-line and baseline. The last feature, character intersection number, defines the number of intersection between character strokes and the straight line that passes through the character centroid with orientation orthogonal to that of the nearest VSB.

The character classification algorithm can be formalized as follows:

Inputs: Character spans $CSpan$; Character ascender and descender
    $ADInfo$; Intersection numbers $Inter$
Procedure: CC$(CSpan, ADInfo, Inter)$
   1) Initialize i $= 1$
   2) Calculate average character span $CSpan_{avg}$ based on the
       determined $CSpan$.
   3) If $Inter$(i)≥ 3 and $ADInfor=1$(with ascender), character is
       classified as $M, W, @$.
   4) Else if $Inter$(i) ≥ 3 and $ADInfor=0$(no ascender),
       character is classified as m, w.
   5) Else if $ADInfor=1$(with ascender) and $CSpan(i) \geq k_u \cdot CSpan_{avg}$,
       character is classified as $A - H, J - L, N - V, or X - Z$.
   6) Else if $CSpan$(i) $\geq k_l \cdot CSpan_{avg}$ and $CSpan$(i) $\leq k_l \cdot CSpan_{avg}$,
       character is classified as, $a - e, g - h, n - q, u - v, x - z, 2 - 9, \dot{e}, \acute{u} \ldots$
   7) Else if $CSpan$(i) $\leq k_s \cdot CSpan_{avg}$, character is classified as $i, l, I, (,! \ldots,$
       or j.
   8) Else, character is classified as $t, f, or r \ldots .$
   9) i $=$ i $+ 1$

To classify characters into six categories, the average character span $CSpan_{avg}$ in Step 2) is firstly calculated. Parameter k_u, k_l, and k_s in Steps 5), 6), and 7) are three key parameters for character categorization and they are determined as 1.2, 0.7, and 0.3 based on the observation of character aspect ratios in different categories. We have tested 30 camera documents and the categorization rate reaches over 95%. We note that small classification errors will not lead to

Table 1. Restoration and recognition results (IS: image size; CON: number of characters; ET: execution time; RRB: recognition rate before restoration; RRA: recognition rate after restoration)

Classified character categories	Character aspect ratios (R)
M, W, @$\cdots$	1.6 : 1
m, w	1.4 : 1
A-H, J-L, N-V, X-Z $\cdots$	1.2 : 1
a-e, g-h, k, n-q, s, u-v, x-z, 0, 2-9, #, â, ë $\cdots$	0.8 : 1
t, f, r, - $\cdots$	0.5 : 1
i, j, l, I, 1, (,), !, [, —, { $\cdots$	0.2 : 1

the obvious restoration and later recognition errors because the partitioned document patches normally contain no less than three characters as determined by Equation (1).

Based on the proposed character classification technique, all characters are grouped to six categories. Table 1 shows six character categories together with the related aspect ratios.

Similar to character spans, the inter-word blanks as labeled with (6) in Figure 1 must be detected as well to estimate the aspect ratio of target rectangles. The inter-word blanks can be simply located based on the distance between the adjacent characters within, which is normally much less than two VBS_{avg} for adjacent characters within the same word. The contribution of the inter-word blanks to the width of target rectangle can thus be determined based on the relation between the size of inter-word blanks as shown in Figure 1 and the average character span $CSpan_{avg}$.

With VBS_{avg} as the height of target rectangles, the width of target rectangles can thus be determined as:

$$T_w = \sum_{i=1}^{n} R_i \cdot VSB_{avg} \qquad (3)$$

where VBS_{avg} represents the average length of the identified VSBs and parameter n represents the number of characters and inter-word blanks within the partitioned image patch. Parameter R_i refers to the i_{th} aspect ratio of characters and inter-word blanks enclosed.

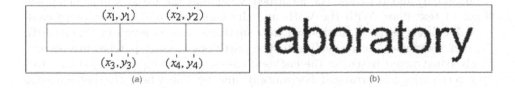

Fig. 3. Document restoration: (a) constructed target rectangles; (b) rectified text

Characters enclosed within the partitioned image patches can be easily located based on the relative position between character centroids and the fitted x-line, baseline, and two straight line segments fitted using the identified VSBs. Target rectangles can thus be restored with the pre-determined height (VBS_{avg}) and the restored width as given in Equation (3). For partitioned image patches given in Figure 2(d), Figure 3(a) shows the corresponding restored target rectangles, which lie on a horizontal line side by side.

2.3   Camera Document Restoration

With the established correspondences between partitioned image patches given in Figure 2(d) and the target rectangles given in Figure 3(a), the distorted camera documents can be restored patch by patch using the rectification homography estimated based on four point mapping algorithm. The rectification homography for a specific pair of quadrilaterals can be estimated as:

$$H = A^{-1} \cdot R \tag{4}$$

where H is the homography matrix and matrixes A, R are constructed using four point correspondences.

$$A = \begin{pmatrix} -x_1 & -y_1 & -1 & 0 & 0 & 0 & x_1'x_1 & x_1'y_1 \\ 0 & 0 & 0 & -x_1 & -y_1 & -1 & y_1'x_1 & y_1'y_1 \\ -x_2 & -y_2 & -1 & 0 & 0 & 0 & x_2'x_2 & x_2'y_2 \\ 0 & 0 & 0 & -x_2 & -y_2 & -1 & y_2'x_2 & y_2'y_2 \\ -x_3 & -y_3 & -1 & 0 & 0 & 0 & x_3'x_3 & x_3'y_3 \\ 0 & 0 & 0 & -x_3 & -y_3 & -1 & y_3'x_3 & y_3'y_3 \\ -x_4 & -y_4 & -1 & 0 & 0 & 0 & x_4'x_4 & x_4'y_4 \\ 0 & 0 & 0 & -x_4 & -y_4 & -1 & y_4'x_4 & y_4'y_4 \end{pmatrix} \quad H = \begin{pmatrix} h_{11} \\ h_{12} \\ h_{13} \\ h_{21} \\ h_{22} \\ h_{23} \\ h_{31} \\ h_{32} \end{pmatrix} \quad R = \begin{pmatrix} x_1' \\ y_1' \\ x_2' \\ y_2' \\ x_3' \\ y_3' \\ x_4' \\ y_4' \end{pmatrix}$$

where the 3 homography matrix is expressed in a vector form and h33 is equal to 1 under homogeneous frame. Four point correspondences (x_i, y_i), (x_i', y_i'), i = 1...4, are taken as the four vertices of the partitioned document patch and the target rectangle as labeled in Figure 2(d) and Figure 3(a). The distorted sample word can thus be restored using the rectification homography and Figure 3(b) shows the restoration result.

Figure 4 illustrates the document restoration process where the distorted camera document given in Figure 4(a) is captured through a digital camera. Figure 4(b) and (c) show the identified VSBs and the fitted x-lines and baselines of text lines. With the VSBs and the x-line and baseline, distorted camera document is then partitioned into small patches as given in Figure 4(d). Target rectangles corresponding to the partitioned image patches are accordingly constructed based on the enclosed characters. As Figure 4(e) shows, target rectangles are arranged horizontally line by line where the bottom edge of all rectangles of the same text line lies on the same horizontal line and the adjacent rectangles share a common vertical edge. With partitioned image patches and the constructed target rectangles, distorted camera document

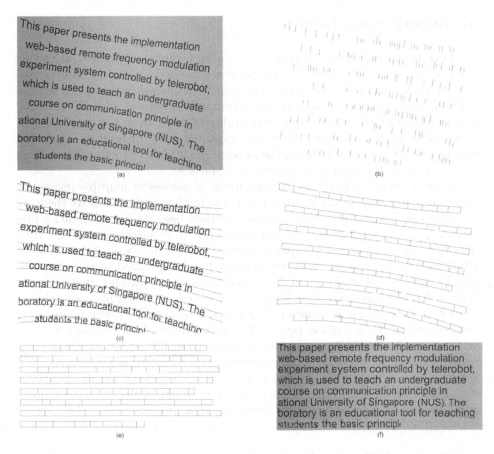

Fig. 4. Perspective and geometric distortion rectification: (a) distorted camera document; (b) identified VSBs; (c) fitted x-lines and baselines; (d) divided image patches; (e) constructed target rectangles; (f) restored document image

given in Figure 4(a) is finally restored patch by patch and Figure 4(f) shows the restored document image.

It should be clarified that character ascender and descender are actually above or below the divided image patches as shown in Figure 4(d). To rectify character ascender and descender correctly, the transformation must be extended above and below a bit beyond the constructed target rectangles as shown in Figure 4(e). The extension range is defined as:

$$E = k_e \cdot VSB_{avg} \tag{5}$$

where VBS_{avg} represents the average length of the identified VSBs. Parameter k_e is designed to adjust the extension range. We determined it as 0.5 in our implemented system so that the transformation is able to cover character ascender and descender and at the same time, it will not reach adjacent text lines.

3   Experimental Results

We have implemented the proposed restoration technique described in Section 2. Experimental results show that the proposed method can restore camera documents with perspective and geometric distortions efficiently. The programs are written in C++ and run on a personal computer equipped with Window XP and Pentium 4 CPU. The system was evaluated with an image database that contains 30 distorted camera documents captured from different distances and viewpoints. At the present stage, the average rectification process takes around 2-3 seconds for document images with size 640×480.

As most researchers rely on 3D measurement devices or multiple images for 3D reconstruction, it is difficult to compare our method with theirs. We therefore evaluate the performance of the proposed method based on the recognition rate of restored document images. In our experiments, 30 sample documents from different sources including newspaper, journal articles, and books are utilized for OCR testing. Documents are firstly captured and digitalized to the electronic images through a digital camera. The camera images are then restored using our proposed restoration technique. Lastly, the restored document images are fed to the OCR software for recognition. We test the recognition performance using Omnipage Pro [8], one of the best OCR software available in the market.

Distorted document images are firstly tested using Omnipage and the average recognition rate is below 10%. This result can be expected, as the generic OCR systems cannot handle the camera documents with perspective and geometric distortions well. Figure 5 shows the recognition results of the 30 restored document images. As the figure shows, the recognition performance of the restored

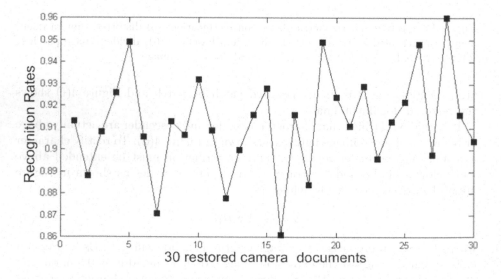

Fig. 5. Recognition rates of the restored document images

image is improved greatly and the average recognition rate reaches over 90%. Even for the worst cases where document may not be partitioned and restored nicely, the recognition rate still reaches over 80%. This is mainly because that the OCR systems are normally tolerant of some minor distortion such as the slight skew and perspective distortions.

The proposed restoration technique is also able to handle the camera documents with only perspective distortion where text lies on a planar instead of curved document surface. Unlike those reported perspective rectification techniques that rely heavily on the document boundary or specific paragraph formatting information [9, 10], our method requires only the VSBs and the x-line and baseline that can be extracted from character strokes directly. Perspective distortion can be removed based on the partitioned image patches and the constructed target rectangles as described in Section 2. For the camera document with perspective distortion given in Figure 6(a), Figure 6(b) shows the restored document image where the bounding box labels the falsely classified characters.

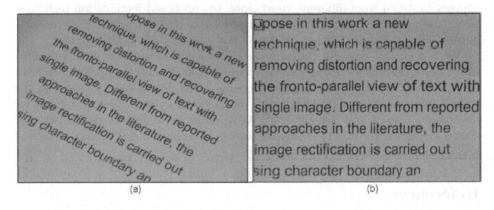

(a)   (b)

Fig. 6. Experiment results: (a) distorted document image; (b) rectified document image

As the proposed technique relies on the VSBs, the x-line and baseline for document restoration, it is able to handle the document text printed in most frequently used fonts. For italic texts, VSBs can still be identified though they do not give the vertical direction. The proposed method may fail when the size of the captured characters is too small. We test some document images with small characters and experiments show that recognition results deteriorate quickly while the average VSBs size becomes smaller than 12 pixels. This can be explained by the fact that VSBs may not be identified properly while characters become too small. Furthermore, the vertical direction cannot be estimated accurately even if the VSBs are correctly identified from characters with small size. This problem can be remedied through the image interpolation, which enlarges the image when the captured characters are too small.

Furthermore, the restoration may fail when the distortion angle between the document normal and camera optical axis is too big. For the 30 document samples we tested, the distortion angle is all within 45 degrees. Experiments show the restoration may fail when the distortion angle becomes bigger. In fact, even human eyes cannot read the text correctly while the distortion angle is bigger than 70 degrees. With the similar reason, the proposed method cannot restore the camera documents with arbitrary geometric distortion such as the image of the creased documents. We will work on the restoration of arbitrarily distorted documents next.

4   Conclusion

In this paper, a computationally efficient technique is proposed to restore the document images with perspective and geometric distortion captured through a digital camera. The restoration is carried out through the image partition, which is implemented based on the identified VSBs and the x-line and baseline of text lines. Different from reported rectification methods that depend heavily on some auxiliary hardware or complicated 3D reconstruction process with multiple images captured from different viewpoints, the proposed rectification technique needs only a single document image captured by a digital camera. Experimental results show that rectification process is fast and easy for implementation.

With a digital camera, the proposed document restoration technique may open a new channel for document capture and understanding. Furthermore, with a little adaptation, it may be applied to some other portable devices such as the digital camera, the mobile phone and the personal digital assistant (PDA) for document capture and management. As a result, these devices embedded with camera sensor need only to store and transmit recognized ASCII text instead of the huge document images.

References

1. M. Pilu, Undoing Paper Curl Distortion Using Applicable Surfaces, International Conference on Computer Vision and Pattern Recognition, Kauai, USA, page 67–72, 2001.
2. M. S. Brown, W. B. Seales, Document restoration using 3D shape: a general deskewing algorithm for arbitrarily warped documents, International Conference on Computer Vision, vol. 2, July 2001, Vancouver, Canada, pp. 367–374.
3. A.Yamashita, A. Kawarago, T. Kaneko, K. T. Miura, Shape Reconstruction and Image Resto-ration for Non-Flat Surfaces of Documents with a Stereo Vision System, International Con-ference on Pattern Recognition, vol. 1, August 2004, Cambridge, UK, page 482–485.
4. G. Agam and C. H. Wu Structural rectification of non-planar document images: application to graphics recognition, Fourth International Workshop on Graphics Recognition Algorithms and Applications, Kingston, Ontario, Canada, pp. 289–298, 2001.
5. H. Cao, X. Ding, C. Liu, A Cylindrical Surface Model to Rectify the Bound Document Image, Ninth IEEE International Conference on Computer Vision, vol. 1, 2003, Nice, France, pp. 228–233.

6. J. Liang, D. DeMenthon, and D. Doermann, Flattening curved documents in images, Interna-tional Conference on Computer Vision and Pattern Recognition, June, 2005, San Diego, USA, pp. 338–345.
7. S. J. Lu, B. M. Chen and C. C. Ko, "Perspective rectification of document images using fuzzy set and morphological operations," Image and Vision Computing, vol. 23, pp. 541–553, 2005.
8. http://www.scansoft.com/omnipage/.
9. C.R. Dance, Perspective estimation for document images, Proceedings of the SPIE Confer-ence on Document Recognition and Retrieval IX, 2002, pp. 244–254.
10. P. Clark, M. Mirmhedi, Rectifying perspective views of text in 3Dscenes using vanishing points, Pattern Recognition, vol. 36, pp. 2673–2686, 2003.

Cut Digits Classification with k-NN Multi-specialist

Fernando Boto, Andoni Cortés, and Clemente Rodríguez

Computer Architecture and Technology Department, Computer Science Faculty, UPV/EHU,
Aptdo. 649, 20080 San Sebastian, Spain
acbbosaf@si.ehu.es

Abstract. A multi-classifier formed by specialised classifiers for noise produced by an image is shown in this work. A study has been carried out in the case of cut images, where tree cases of specialization are considered. Classifiers based on neighbourhood criteria are used, the zoning global feature and the Euclidean distance too. Furthermore, the paper explains a modification of the Euclidean distance for classifying cut digits. The experiments have been carried out with images of typewritten digits, taken from real forms. Trying to obtain a strong database to support the experiments, we have cut images deliberately. The recognition rate improves from 84.6% to 97.70%, but whether the system provides information about the disturbance of the image, it can achieve a 98.45%.

1 Introduction

Human intervention in full scale digitization of documents is tedious because of the large amount of documents to be processed. Nowadays there are some recognition systems in the market for typewritten texts but still they create many problems. The document digitization process is usually made starting with the isolated characters and sometimes this isolation process produces some image disturbances. The noise characters can be obtained through a bad quality of digitization or as a result of a bad segmentation [1] [2] [3].

Many authors use systems based on the combination of classifiers. These systems have different aims [4]: Efficiency [5] [6], improved performance [7] [8] [9], generalisation [10]. Besides, [4] [11] makes a survey of some of the possibilities to combine classifiers and the rules to combine them. In our case, we need a multi-classifier in order to combine classifiers with a different purpose. Each classifier will specialise in a type of problem or distortion and together, by means of a decision rule, will provide a result by common consent.

Another point discussed in this item makes reference to the disturbances produced by digitization or segmentation defects, which will result in noise or blurred numbers, with thickness defects or cuts with loss of structure. Each one of these disturbances has been solved independently, that is with sub-systems which provide a good rate of success with some disturbances but with different results before other types of disturbances.

Many works found in the related bibliography, consider the problem of the cut digits as the problem where the digits must be repaired. These works use algorithms of

H. Bunke and A.L. Spitz (Eds.): DAS 2006, LNCS 3872, pp. 496–505, 2006.

tracking borders techniques, other techniques to obtain the skeleton of an image, dilatation search of rupture points, etc. [1] [2] [12] [13]. We are not going to approach the problem in this way because the needs are different.

The cut digits in the upper or lower part are produce by an improper horizontal segmentation of the code because the cell of the code is badly obtained. Figure 1 shows horizontal improper segmentation, where we can see how the segmentation process produces cut digits. The solution presented in this paper will take place in the recognition phase, specifically in the feature extraction phase.

Fig. 1. Horizontal and vertical segmentation errors

Figure 2 shows the disturbances of our real problem, however in this paper we have only consider the problem of cut digits with lost of structure (type D) and more specifically, with cut digits in upper and lower part, that is, the cell of the digit is cut and the information of the digit is less than the original one. The cut digits in the real problem conform 1% of the total sample, however we have worked with synthetic and homogeneous sample.

We have present in other works, the behaviour of the system for digits with distortions like in the case A and B of the figure 2 [14]. Furthermore we have advances with all the disturbances showed in the figure and nowadays the system is already working in real applications with good results.

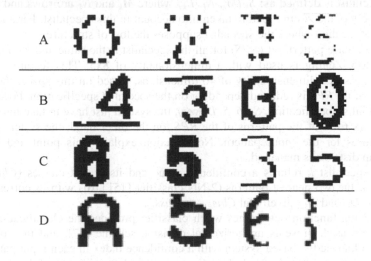

Fig. 2. Real examples of digits with distortions. A: Discontinuous lines (blurred), B: Noise added or annex lines, C: Thickness disturbance and D: Cut digits.

The point of view presented in this work is that, any image with any type of rupture will belong to the sub-space of this type of rupture. A specialised classifier in a sub-space will have a confidence level when sorting out a pattern. A set of classifiers will compete with one another and the classifier with the highest level of confidence will recognise the pattern.

The paper has the following structure. Section 2 describes the Multi-specialist scheme, section 3 shows the solution proposed for cut digits and section 4 an experimental study. Finally the conclusions in section 5.

2 Multiple Specialised Classifiers

The basic aim of the proposed Multiple Specialist Classifier (MSC), is to obtain a multi-classifier formed by specialised simple classifiers for each type of noise produced by an image. Each specialist obtains the features of the input digit, depending on what kind of disturbance is treating, so that the system manage the input patterns in a different way. This is explained in next section.

Specifically, the feature extraction process used is the *zoning* global one [5], which obtains a vector of features which corresponds to the spatial distribution of the black areas of the image. The image is divided in *mxn* cells with the same area for them all, and the percentage of blacks in this area of each cell is calculated.

The decisions adopted by each classifier will be treated jointly in a global discriminating function.

This is a general description of a Multi-classifier (Multi-specialist) [10]: $MSC(ns, \{S_1, ... , S_{ns}\})$, where ns is the number of specialists of the multi-classifier and $\{S_0 .... S_{ns}\}$ the set of specialists for it.

A specialist is defined as: $S_k (M_k, N_k, P_k)$, where M_k and N_k are rows and columns respectively of the zoning feature taken into account in this specialist. Parameter P_k is the part of the digit where the specialist supposes the lost of structure.

The reference pattern set (*RPS*) for all the specialist is the same and the feature extraction too. Zoning is used with a dimensionality of 8x5. This feature extraction generates a space dimensionality of 40 dimensions. Based on this space, the dimensionality of the *RPS* is reduced depending on the specialist specification. For instance, let a specialist specification, $S_k(6, 5, Lower)$, the system just have to take into account the first six rows of the patterns of the *RPS*, on the other hand, the system generate 6x5 features for the input pattern. Next section explains this point and how the Euclidean distance is managed.

Each specialist k returns a confidence value and its output classes ($Class_{k1}$ and $Class_{k2}$) of the two nearest patterns (2-NN classifier [15] [16]) with its corresponding distances, D_{k1} and D_{k2}, given that $Class_{k1} \neq Class_{k2}$.

A decision function determines witch classifier provides the classification result. The system used, presents an horizontal decision scheme [17], and the solution is based in a knowledge based system with a confidence index in each input pattern. So, we have determined to decided class C_{k1} of k specialist, with a confidence value V_k bigger than all the rest specialists. The confidence value for each specialist is $V_k = 1 - D_{k1}/D_{k2}$, this function is the same for all the experiments in this work.

3 Space Dimensionality Variation

This chapter will deal with the solution we have found to palliate the effects of a problem produced by an improper segmentation. This improper segmentation produces digits with a lack of structure or loss of information. The remaining information is not enough to recognise the digit. The lack of structure can be found in the upper part of the image of the digit or in the lower part generally, but sometimes side cuts appear but not so frequently in this environment.

Basically, this is the way to solve this disturbance: The reference patterns or learned set, creates a space of D dimensionality to recognise well formed and standard digits. When we present a cut digit before this dimensional space, it is placed in another point of the space, because, for lack of structure the obtainment of characteristics has created a false pattern. For instance, the more cut is the class 8, in its upper or lower parts, the obtained vector of characteristics will show a point in the space coming nearer to the class 0. However, we can leave aside certain characteristics of the reference pattern set (RPS) and create a dimensional space $D-\Phi$, and try that the Φ features not taken into consideration correspond to the structure missing in the entry pattern.

In short, we generate for the entry pattern $D-\Phi$ characteristics and we apply the distance function with the selected characteristics $D-\Phi$ of the RPS patterns.

Given an RPS pattern of class c $(R_1, R_2, ... R_D)$ within a dimensional space D and an entry pattern or test also class c $(P_1, P_2, ... P_D)$, the Euclidean distance is defined as (1) which will give as a result a value of d_1.

$$\sqrt{\sum_{i=0}^{D}(R_i - P_i)^2} \tag{1}$$

If the entry pattern is cut on the lower part which means that the lower part is missing structure, the calculation of the distance will give a value of d_2 and most probably $d_2 >> d_1$. Therefore, if we have this type of disturbance, the classifier will fail.

If we reduce the space of features $D-\Phi$ for the entry pattern, depending on the loss, the $D-\Phi$ features will appear different to those of the previous $(PC_1, PC_2, ...PC_{D-\Phi})$, but for the RPS the same will be used, even if taking into consideration some of them, that is (2) being d_3 and $d_3 << d_2$.

$$\sqrt{\sum_{i=0}^{D-\Phi}(R_i - PC_i)^2} \tag{2}$$

This is the way to suppose that the digit is cut in its lower part a $\Phi/D*100$ percent. Whether the classifier suppose that the digit is cut in the upper part, the distance is calculated as (3).

$$\sqrt{\sum_{i=0}^{D-\Phi}(R_{\Phi+i} - PC_i)^2} \tag{3}$$

Note that Φ can vary depending on how much cut is supposed the digit to be cut.

The parameter Φ will be always multiple of n, being n the columns of the zoning matrix. In the study explained in next section the parameter Φ will take integer values between n and $3n$.

4   Study of Specialization of Cuts

The experiments have been carried out with images of typewritten digits, taken from real forms and Microsoft sources. 14,750 test digits, out of a total of 100,000, of different real sources, have been considered. We have cut the 14,750 test digits with different percentages in order to have a significant database of cut digits. From this set, 6 different sets of digits have been formed: Digits with a different percentage of cutting on their upper and lower parts (10%, 20% and 30%). Therefore, the total number of digits is 103,250.

The reference set used for all specialists, has been created ad-hoc, with well defined or conformed images of typewritten digits of Microsoft sources.

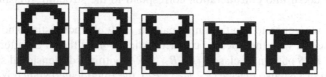

Fig. 3. Example of data base used

The simulator of the multi-classifier used has enabled us to specify the parameters of each specialist as well as their combination parameters.

A finite number of specialists has been used in the diverse experiments which are differentiated in the parameters of extraction of characteristics (M_k and N_k).

The real system used to isolate the digits, provide information about the position of the lack of structure. Therefore, the recognition process has information about the quality of the image, whether is cut or is not cut. The management of this information is important to increase the reliability of the system. We have made an experimental

Table 1. Specification of the specilists used in the study. The Parameters M_k, N_k, are the zoning matrix rows and columns respectively and P_k is the situation of the lack of structure.

S_k	Description (specialisation)	M_k	N_k	P_k
S1	Image without cuts	8	5	$\varnothing$
S2	Little cut upper part	7	5	Upper
S3	Little cut lower part	7	5	Lower
S4	Moderate cut upper part	6	5	Upper
S5	Moderate cut lower part	6	5	Lower
S6	Excessive cut upper part	5	5	Upper
S7	Excessive cut lower part	5	5	Lower

study taking into account that the system has the possibility to know this information and more than this information, in order to make a general study of the system. We have considered three cases: first, the system has all the possible information of the digit (*Case A*), the position of the lack and the amount of the lack. Second, the system has only the information about the position of the lack of structure (*Case B*) and finally the system has not any information about the structure of the digit (*Case C*).

So, the knowledge of the information is used to know what is the best specialist to recognize an input pattern.

4.1 Specialisation of the Classifiers

The experiments have been carried out with the different test sets both separately and jointly. Therefore, primarily we are going to see which are the maximum percentages of success for each separate specialist, which means that each specialist will form an only independent system to observe how it reacts in front of all the disturbances. The following table shows this study.

Table 2. Results for the specialization. The last column shows the average for each specialist separately. The first column shows where the tested digit is cut and the last line shows the average covering the best results (*Case A*).

		No Cut	Little(10%)	Moderate(20%)	Excessive(30%)
Upper	S_1	**99,76**	98,03	76,06	43,57
	S_2	95,8	**99,23**	95,6	84,95
	S_4	73,93	93,76	**98,22**	**97,8**
	S_6	36,68	61,21	89,77	96,8
Lower	S_1	**99,76**	98,97	93,03	67,58
	S_3	94,27	**99,06**	**99,36**	94,46
	S_5	60,73	83,43	98,26	**99,27**
	S_7	37,91	51,75	80,8	96
Case A		*99.76*	*99.15*	*98.79*	*98.54*

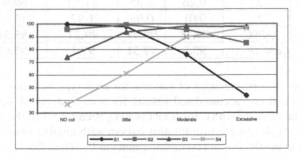

Fig. 4. The axis X: cut level. Axis Y: % recognition for each specialist classifier.

In the table 2 we can see how each system better recognises a class of images (it is a specialist). If we knew beforehand which is the best specialist for each digit, the obtained recognition would be 99.06% (the average of the row *Case A*) against 84.6% (the average of the row S_1) as obtained only with the specialist S_1 (specialised in well conformed images). It is plain to see how S_1 recognises, more or less accurately, uncut digits and not very cut digits (10%), but when the images are badly cut, the recognition rate decreases considerably. The behaviour of the other classifiers is totally different, as shown in the figure 4.

4.2 Adaptability of the System to the Loss of Information

In the following experiment, the system does not know how much cut the image is and which the best specialist for the pattern is. It only knows that the digit is cut on its upper or lower part. Therefore, the specialists for the digits cut on their upper or lower part will compete in a multi-classifier (two multi- specialists with four specialists each one), MSC_1 *(1, {{S_1, S_2, S_4, S_6}})* and MC_2 *(4, {S_1, S_3, S_5,. S_7})*, both multi-classifiers jointly conform a unique system where the images with cuts in the upper part are classified with MSC_1 and the images cut in the lower part are managed with MSC_2. The results for this compound system is the case 2 explained previously and it is calculated like and average of MSC_1 and MSC_2.

Table 3. Results with lose of information. Each cell represent the percentage of patterns well recognized with a specialist and with a kind of images. The MSC_2 and MSC_1 rows are the hit rates for each type of images with MSC_2 and MSC_1 classifers repectively. The last row are the average results for MSC_2 and MSC_1 rows (*Case B*).

		No Cut	Little	Moderate	Excessive
MSC₂	S_1	88,01	34,41	10,93	8,88
	S_2	9,65	59,27	39,39	7,75
	S_4	1,23	4,03	43,60	56,61
	S_6	0,82	1,80	4,92	22,75
	MSC₂	**99,70**	**99,53**	**98,84**	**95,99**
MSC₁	S_1	93,15	49,61	8,58	3,59
	S_3	6,06	47,50	57,20	17,79
	S_5	0,26	2,35	31,52	60,69
	S_7	0,01	0,03	1,97	13,27
	MSC₁	**99,48**	**99,49**	**99,27**	**95,34**
Case B		**99,6**	**99,51**	**99,1**	**95,67**

Table 3 shows the percentages of success for each type of images, the results for each specialists and the accumulated results for both systems. A lower recognition average of the table is shown (*Case B vs Case A*), because when the digit is very cut, specialists S_1, S_2 or S_3 can confuse the test pattern with another class. For example, a digit of class 8 excessively cut resembles a non cut 0. When the digit, which by now is very cut, the specialists S_1, S_2 or S_3, classifies almost all the patterns because the certainty of the specialist for this pattern is the most adequate. If the pattern is very cut, specialists S_4, S_5, S_6, and S_7, become more important, in spite of specialists S_1, S_2, and S_3, are still classifying some patterns. The average recognition for this experiment is 98.45% (average of the row *Case B*) against 84.6% corresponding to all digits against only specialist S_1, even if the recognition rate is lower than in the previous experiment (99.06% in *Case A*).

In the multi-specialist system of the following experiment there is a specialist S_1 specialised in uncut digits and specialised in digits cut in the upper and lower parts, $S_2, S_3, S_4, S_5, S_6, S_7$.

The multi-classifier is defined as **MSC_3** (7, {$S_1, S_2, S_3, S_4, S_5, S_6, S7,$ }).

The Table 4 shows the percentages of success for each specialist, the accumulated addition for each column represents the percentage of success for each type of cut, the right column represents the average of the system.

Table 4. Results for *MSC3*. L: Little, M: Moderate, E: Excesive. Each cell represent the percentage of patterns well recognized with a specialist and with a kind of images. Last row is the percentage recognition for each tipe of images with MSC_3.

Specialist	No cuts	Images cut upper			Images cut lower		
		L	M	E	L	M	E
$S1$	82,62	45,44	7,58	3,27	31,90	7,81	5,59
$S3$	9,29	3,29	1,04	0,35	58,89	38,81	7,33
$S5$	1,15	1,08	0,27	0,08	3,86	43,44	56,21
$S7$	0,74	0,30	0,03	0,02	1,60	4,20	22,29
$S2$	5,53	46,92	56,70	17,27	2,78	3,59	3,07
$S4$	0,24	2,32	31,36	59,59	0,19	0,47	0,55
$S6$	0,01	0,03	1,97	12,84	0,00	0,00	0,00
MSC_3	99,57	99,39	98,95	93,43	99,22	98,33	95,04

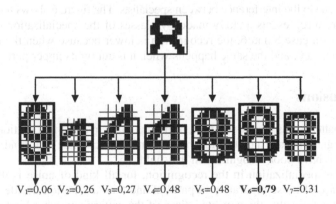

V_1=0,06 V_2=0,26 V_3=0,27 V_4=0,48 V_5=0,48 **V_6=0,79** V_7=0,31

Fig. 5. System behaviour with cut digits. The image shows the reference pattern and the confidence value for each specialist.

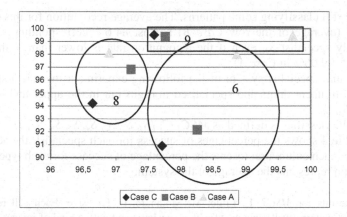

Fig. 6. Axis X is the percentage of success for digits cut in their lower part, and axis Y is the percentage of success of digits cut in their upper part. *Case A* knows where and when the digit is cut, *Case B* only knows where the digit is cut and *Case C* does not know anything, only that the digit can be cut or well conformed.

These results clearly show that each specialist is, generally speaking, a specialist in a class of patterns, even if sometimes recognition is shared with other specialist. 82.62% of the uncut images are well classified by specialist S_1. Images moderately cut in the lower part are mainly correctly recognised by specialists S_3 and S_5. The total average of the recognition rate is 97.70% (*Case C*).

Figure 5 shows how the space dimensionality variation helps to recognize cut digits. The specialist S_6 has the best confidence value because it only uses the first 6 rows of its features to calculate the Euclidean distance and the features of the entry pattern in same dimensionality space are taken into consideration.

The difficulty to recognise some classes increases with the number of specialists in the system. It is due to the interference between specialists. The figure 6 shows this behaviour.

The figure 6 represents a study made by classes of the specialisation of each system. Same as in case 8 and 6, the recognition is lower because when the digit is very cut it looks like a 0, and the same happens when it is cut on its upper part.

5 Conclusions

The noisy patterns has been one of the problems in the pattern recognition. While the human recognition have not too much problems to recognize this kind of patterns, OCR systems have poor recognition in this field.

For us the specialization in the recognition, for all kind of noise is the base. We treat each case of noise separately in parallel and then a criterion decide. So the system provide two results, the expected class of the pattern and what kind of noise has the image, depending on which specialist has responded.

We have study different specializations, the difference of each one is the knowledge of the context. If the type of noise is known the recognition is easier because the system know what is the most efficient specialist. On the other hand when the context information is smaller the specialists have to decide between them in a multi-classifier. This is important in some segmentation systems where the knowledge of the context is possible.

We have obtained a recognition rate of 97.70% with cut digits, even though we can improve the recognition rate to 98.45% using information provided by the segmentation process, the non specialist system obtains for the same data 84.6%.

References

1. Whichello, A. P.,Yan, H.: Linking broken character borders with variable sized masks to improve recognition. Pattern Recognition Vol. 29 (8) (1996) 1429-1435
2. Rodriguez, C., Muguerza, M., Navarro, M., Zárate, A., Martín, J. I.,Pérez, J. M.: A two-stage classifer for broken and blurred digits in forms. ICPR 98 Brisbane, Australia Vol. 2 (1998) 1101-1105
3. Omachi, S., Sun, F.,H., A.: A noise-adaptive discriminant function and its application to blurred machine-printed kanji recognition. IEEE Transactions PAMI Vol. 22 (3) (2000) 314-319
4. Kittler, J., Hated, M., Duin, R. P. W.,Matas, J.: On combining classifiers. IEEE Transactions PAMI Vol. 20 (3) (1998) 226-239
5. Rodriguez, C., Soraluze, I., Muguerza, J., Martín, J. I.,Álvarez, G.: Hierarchical classifiers based on neighbourhood criteria with adaptive computational cost. Pattern Recognition Vol. 35 (12) (2002) 2761-2769
6. Alpaydin, E., Kaynak, C.,Alimoglu, F.: Cascading multiple classifiers and representations for optical and pen-based handwritten digit recognition. 7th IWFHR Amsterdam Vol. (2000) 453-462
7. Ho, T. K., Hull, J. J.,Srihari, S.: Decision combination in multiple classifier systems. IEEE Transactions PAMI Vol. 16 (1) (1994) 66-75
8. Bauer, E.,Kohavi, R.: An empirical comparison of voting classification algorithms: Bagging, boosting, and variants. Machine Learning Vol. 36 (1-2) (1999) 105 - 139
9. Aksela, M., Girdziusas, R., Laaksonen, J., Oja, E.,Kangas, J.: Class-confidence critic combining. 8th IWFHR Ontario, Canada Vol. (2002) 201-206
10. Ha, T. M.,Bunke, H.: Off-line, handwritten numeral recognition by pertubation method. IEEE Transactions PAMI Vol. 19 (5) (1997) 535-539
11. Erp, M. v., Vuurpijil, L.,Shomaker, L.: An overview and comparison of voting methods for pattern recognition. 8th IWFHR Ontario, Canada Vol. (2002) 195-200
12. Yu, D.,Yan, H.: Reconstruction of broken handwritten digits based on structural morphological features. Pattern Recognition Vol. 34 (2001) 235-254
13. Wang, J.,Yan, H.: Mending broken handwriting with a macrostructure analysis method to improve recognition. Pattern Recognition Letters Vol. 20 (1999) 855-864
14. Cortés, A., Boto, F.,Rodriguez, C.: Noisy digit classification with multiple specialist. Pattern Recognition and Data Mining (LNCS 3686) Vol. 1 (2005) 601-608
15. Dasarathy, B. V.: Nearest neighbor (nn) norms: Nn pattern classification techniques. I. C. S. Press (1991)
16. Devroye, L., Györfi, L.,Lugosi, G.: A probabilistic theory of pattern recognition. N. Y. Springer-Verlag (1996)
17. Rahman, A. F. R.,Fairhurst, M. C.: Multiple classifier decision combination strategies for character recognition: A review. International Journal on Document Analysis and Recognition Vol. 5 (4) (2003) 166-194

The Impact of OCR Accuracy and Feature Transformation on Automatic Text Classification

Mayo Murata, Lazaro S.P. Busagala, Wataru Ohyama,
Tetsushi Wakabayashi, and Fumitaka Kimura

Mie University, Faculty of Engineering,
1577 Kurimamachiya-cho, Tsu-shi, Mie 5148507, Japan
{mayo, busagala, ohyama, waka, kimura}@hi.info.mie-u.ac.jp

Abstract. Digitization process of various printed documents involves generating texts by an OCR system for different applications including full-text retrieval and document organizations. However, OCR-generated texts have errors as per present OCR technology. Moreover, previous studies have revealed that as OCR accuracy decreases the classification performance also decreases. The reason for this is the use of absolute word frequency as feature vector. Representing OCR texts using absolute word frequency has limitations such as dependency on text length and word recognition rate consequently lower classification performance due to higher within-class variances. We describe feature transformation techniques which do not have such limitations and present improved experimental results from all used classifiers.

1 Introduction

In recent years, the main means of information exchange has been changing from the traditional printed information to the digital data. This is due to the fact that digital data such as text, image, and audio can be transferred and retrieved faster, more flexibly and more easily. Activities such as digital publishing and the digital library might become the main sources of information in the near future. As the matter of fact digitization projects have been taking place [7], [8]. Since there have been a need to make archives accessible through digital information systems, other traditional libraries might be considering converting printed archives into digital data. Digitized materials might need techniques from automatic text classification (ATC) to be applied to different domain applications such as automatic indexing for Boolean information retrieval systems; document organization; information filtering and hierarchical categorization of web pages.

When working with printed documents there might be two ways to generate digital texts which are keying texts into computer system and using optical character recognition (OCR) systems where by text materials are extracted from digital text images. LDI project team [7] argues that Harvard University Library keying process cost approximately 10-13 times more expensive per page than using uncorrected OCR. They refer to uncorrected OCR due to the fact that OCR-generated texts generally have errors [1], [2]. The authors in [3] showed the impact of OCR accuracy on automatic text classification such that as OCR recognition rates dropped down, the classification

H. Bunke and A.L. Spitz (Eds.): DAS 2006, LNCS 3872, pp. 506–517, 2006.

performance decreased. In this paper, we describe feature transformation techniques for OCR-generated texts and present improved experimental results from all used classifiers.

This paper is organized as follows. The next section presents a brief survey on relevant research works in the literature. Section 3 describes the feature transformation techniques used. In section 4 we present the experimental setup. The results and a short discussion are given in section 5. We conclude and describe future study in section 6.

2 Related Works

This paper describes techniques for transforming features from OCR-generated documents. The literature shows rare research works done previously on OCR in relation to automatic text classification (ATC). This section gives a brief survey from research works that might be relevant.

The work in [9] reports on OCR text representation for learning with a focus on different techniques for automatic construction of relevant features from Germany language documents. Their study considered various features including all words, elimination of stop-words, morphological and composite analysis and use of n-grams. Although some important results are given, the fact that they used different language datasets, their work is remarkably different in various ways. Not only didn't they perform feature transformation techniques but also they didn't use the benchmark collection to text categorization from which we generated image text documents to study the impact of transformed features on OCR-generated documents.

Frasconi et al. [10], [11] performed experiments on text categorization for multi-page documents extracted by an OCR system. They used contrarily untransformed word counts i.e., bag of words to represent the texts. They also used information gain technique for feature selection to reduce the number of features hence dimension reduction. However we employ principal component analysis (PCA) after using term selection techniques for dimension reduction.

The authors in [3] investigated the impact of OCR accuracy on automatic text classification using absolute word frequency as an OCR text representation technique. Since absolute frequency depends on text length we give techniques to solve this problem (see section 3).

Most of the works (*if* not all) mentioned above and that in [12], exhibit notable differences with this paper. The biggest difference is that they reported experimental results from OCR texts represented by untransformed features. Hence we focus on transformed features for representing OCR texts. Experimental results reveal improved classification performance.

3 Feature Transformation Techniques

3.1 Normalization to Relative Word Frequency

The limitation of using absolute word frequency is dependency on text length consequently lower separability of feature space. Fig. 1 shows how the feature vectors length differ for a given sample distribution of absolute word frequency. Relative word frequency y_i in expression (1) does not depend on text length such that the within-class variances are smaller than for absolute word frequency hence feature space can gain more separability.

$$y_i = \frac{x_i}{\sum_{i=1}^{n} x_i}$$ (1)

Whereby, x_i is the absolute word frequency of word i and n is the number of different words. Fig. 1 shows how the feature vectors have smaller variations in lengths after feature transformations.

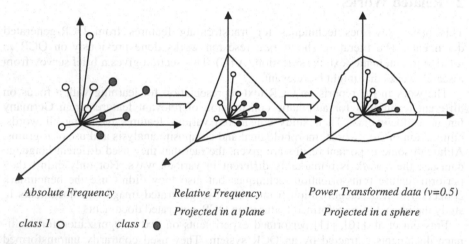

Absolute Frequency   Relative Frequency   Power Transformed data (v=0.5)
                            Projected in a plane   Projected in a sphere
class 1 O   class 1 ●

Fig. 1. Shows how the absolute frequency can be converted to relative frequency then to power transformed features in 3-dimensional space. When the feature is transformed, vector length variation in the category becomes smaller than the absolute frequency. The separability of the feature space increases hence classification rates can be expected to be improved too.

3.2 Power Transformation

Another variable transformation is the power transformation which is expressed as:

$$z_i = x_i^{v} \quad (0 < v < 1)$$ (2)

This was employed to improve the classification accuracy. Power transformation improves the symmetricy of the distribution of the frequency $x_i \geq 0$ which is noticeably asymmetric near the origin. The final effect is to improve performance of parametric classifiers derived on Gaussian assumption.

4 Experimental Setup

4.1 Used Data

In order to study the impact of transformed features for OCR-generated documents in the automatic text classification, a training sample is required. Therefore, we used the Reuters-21578 text benchmark collection for English text classification. The Reuters-21578 is composed of 21578 articles manually classified to 135 categories.

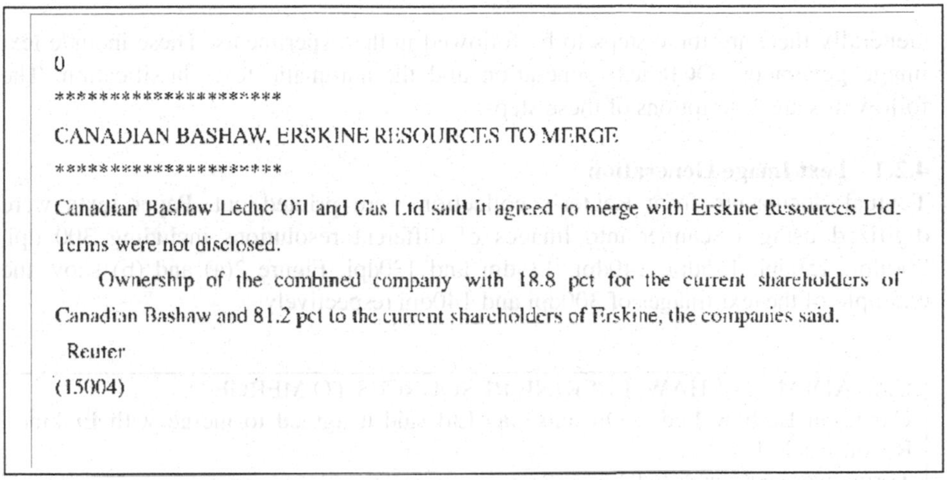

0

****

CANADIAN BASHAW, ERSKINE RESOURCES TO MERGE

****

Canadian Bashaw Leduc Oil and Gas Ltd said it agreed to merge with Erskine Resources Ltd. Terms were not disclosed.

Ownership of the combined company with 18.8 pct for the current shareholders of Canadian Bashaw and 81.2 pct to the current shareholders of Erskine, the companies said.

Reuter

(15004)

(a) 300 dpi

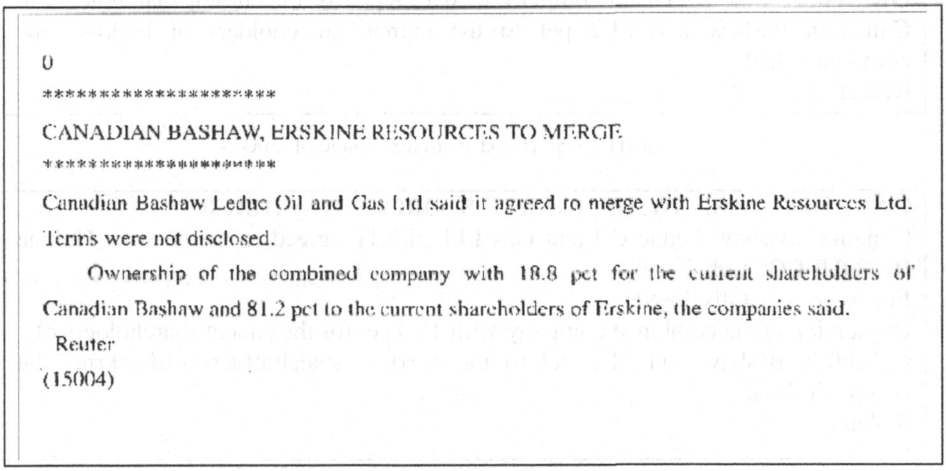

0

****

CANADIAN BASHAW, ERSKINE RESOURCES TO MERGE

****

Canadian Bashaw Leduc Oil and Gas Ltd said it agreed to merge with Erskine Resources Ltd. Terms were not disclosed.

Ownership of the combined company with 18.8 pct for the current shareholders of Canadian Bashaw and 81.2 pct to the current shareholders of Erskine, the companies said.

Reuter

(15004)

(b) 140 dpi

Fig. 2. Examples of the text images

In the experiments, a total of 750 articles i.e., 150 articles per category randomly selected from five categories (acq, crude, earn, grain, trade), were used. Since the sample size is not large enough, the sample was divided into three subsets each of which included 50 articles per category. When a subset was tested, the rest of the two subsets were used as learning sample in order to keep the learning sample size as large as possible while keeping the independency between the samples for learning and testing. Classification tests were repeated for three subsets and the average classification rates were computed.

4.2 Experiments

Generally there are three steps to be followed in the experiments. These include text image generation, OCR text generation and the automatic text classification. The followings are descriptions of these steps.

4.2.1 Text Image Generation

Textual documents from Reuter's collection were printed out. Paper texts were digitized using a scanner into images of different resolutions including 300 dpi, 200dpi, 150dpi, 145dpi, 140dpi, 135dpi and 130dpi. Figure 2(a) and (b) show the example of the text images of 300dpi and 140dpi respectively.

CANADIAN BASHAW, ERSKINE RESOURCES TO MERGE
Canadian Bashaw Leduc Oil and Gas Ltd said it agreed to merge with Erskine Resources Ltd.
Terms were not disclosed.
Ownership of the combined company with 18.8 pet for the current shareholders of Canadian Bashaw and 81.2 pet to the current shareholders of Erskine, the companies said.
Reuter

(a) The ASCII text from text image of 300dpi

CANADIAN yASHAW. HR^KJNh kI';SOlJRCn,S TO V1HRGR
Canadian Bashaw Leduc Oil and Gas I.Id s;ilii IT agreed ro merge wirii Hnkine RL^OUI-CCS Ltd.
Forms were not disclosed.
Ownership of ihe combined company with 1^.8 pet for the cuncnt shareholders of C,m;idi,in B^sbaw and 81.2 pel to ihc eiirrL'nt sbaicholLlcrs cifF.rskrne, die companies said.
Rt-'uter

(b) The ASCII text from text image of 140dpi

Fig. 3. Examples of the ASCII texts converted by OCR software

4.2.2 Text Generation by an OCR System

The text images generated above were converted into ASCII texts by OCR software "OKREADER2000". Examples are given in Figure 3(a) and (b).

The obtained texts were compared with the original texts in the Reuters collection to compute the average character recognition rates and the average word recognition rates for each dpi value. The average character recognition rates can be defined by:

$$c = \frac{(s-t)}{s} \times 100 \qquad (3)$$

Whereby, s and t are the numbers of total characters and the number of miss-recognized characters, respectively. The average word recognition rate can be defined by:

$$v = \frac{(w-u)}{w} \times 100 \tag{4}$$

Whereby, w and u are the numbers of total words and the number of miss-recognized words, respectively.

4.2.3 Automatic Text Classification
Automatic Text Classification was done as described in the following subsections:

I) Feature Vector Generation
First a lexicon consisting of all different words in a learning text set was generated and the alphabetic order of the word list was created. Then the feature vector was composed of the frequencies of the lexicon words found in textual documents. The features extracted can be represented in form of the feature vector X which can be denoted as:

$$X = \left(x_1, x_2, \cdots, x_n\right)^T \tag{5}$$

Whereby, n is dimensionality (size of lexicon), x_i is the frequency value of ith word and T refers to the transpose of a vector.

II) Dimension Reduction
Dimension reduction (DR) in Automatic Text Classification is essential due to the following among other basic two reasons. First in text classification high dimensionality of the term space may be problematic in terms of computational time and storage resources. Second, DR tends to reduce over-fitting. In the experiments we selected word frequencies, $n > 2$, and we used Principal Component Analysis (PCA) technique to extract significant components and to further reduce the dimensionality [3], [5].

III) Learning
Various classifiers were trained accordingly using a learning sample as follows. The Euclidean distance classifier involved computing the mean vector of each class. The linear discriminant function required computation for the weight vector determined by the mean vector of each class and the pooled within covariance matrix of all classes. Training the projection and the modified projection distances needed the computation of the eigenvectors and the eigenvalues of each of the individual category's covariance matrix [4]. Support Vector machines (SVMs) are methods that find the optimal hyperplane during training. In the experiments, C-support vector classification methods (C-SVC) with linear and radial basis (RBF) functions were used. Particularly, we used the SVM library (LIBSVM Version 2.33) developed by Chang and Lin [6].

VI) Classification
The feature vectors of reduced dimensionality were classified to the category with the distance (or the discriminant function) of which was minimum. Referring to the subject field manually given to each article in Reuters-21578, the classification rates, R were calculated by

$$R = \frac{x}{(x+y)} \times 100 \tag{6}$$

Whereby, x and y are the numbers of articles correctly classified and incorrectly classified, respectively [5].

5 Empirical Results

In this section we present experimental results from different features that include absolute word frequency, relative word frequency and their power transformations.

Table 1 shows the classifiers' classification rates versus character recognition rates and the word recognition rates from absolute word frequency at different resolutions. On this table it might be observed that, as the resolution of text images decreased, the character recognition and word recognition rates by an OCR system also decreased. In other words at relative higher resolutions, it was possible to obtain less recognition errors by OCR systems. Similarly, classification rates of OCR texts decreased with increase in OCR errors.

Table 1. OCR Text classification rates (%) for absolute frequency vs. character recognition rates (%) and word recognition rates (%) by an OCR system at different resolutions (dpi)

Resolution (dpi)	130	135	140	145	150	200	300
Word recognition rates	41	53.8	63.7	72.1	84.3	92.9	97.2
Character recognition rates	57.7	71.6	82.8	89.8	96	98.4	99.3
Euclidean distance	44.9	51.9	58.4	62.1	67.2	70.7	74.3
Linear discriminant function	65.7	74.8	80.1	86.0	88.3	89.9	91.1
projection distance	75.2	83.3	87.1	88.4	90.1	90.7	91.2
Modified projection distance	78.1	86.3	89.3	91.6	92.5	92.8	93.1
SVM-Linear	76.1	84.9	87.5	89.9	92.0	92.9	93.3
SVM- RBF	64.5	76.8	82.0	86.3	89.5	91.3	92.1

The summarized best classification rates from all features using different classifiers are given in table 2. It is notable that transformed features improved the performance of all used classifiers. Performing power transformation on relative frequency for example made all classification rates to rise as high as over 91%.

Table 1 and 2 also reveal that modified projection distance (MPD) outperformed all the classifiers used in terms of accuracy and robustness. In other words, this classifier gave out the highest classification rates even when there were more OCR errors. For example when OCR word recognition rate was 41%, MPD was accurate by 78.1% - when absolute frequency was used as feature vector. This was improved to 91.7% [1] by employing power transformation on relative frequency (PTR). And when OCR word recognition rate was 97.2%, the MPD's classification accuracy was improved from 93.1% to 96.1% - when PTR was used as feature vectors.

Table 2. The summary of results showing the best classification rates in % at 300dpi

Classifiers	Absolute Frequency		Relative Frequency	
	without power transformation	with power transformation	without power transformation	with power transformation
Euclidean distance	74.3	89.6	86.0	91.1
Linear discriminant function	91.1	92.8	93.9	94.5
Projection distance	91.2	94.9	93.3	95.7
Modified projection Distance	93.1	95.3	94.7	96.1
SVM-Linear	93.3	95.1	94.3	95.3
SVM- RBF	92.1	93.5	94.4	95.3

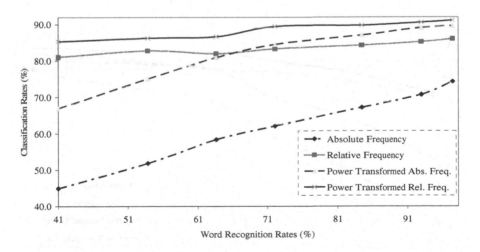

Fig. 4. Word recognition rates vs. classification rates for Euclidean distance classifier with improved results after feature transformation

The relationships between the OCR texts' classification rates of each classifier and word recognition rates are shown in figures 4 to 8. These figures also show the

---

[1] Note that 91.7% is a detail which is not reported in table 1 and 2. It was obtained at resolution 130dpi.

performance of each classifier with all feature types that is absolute word frequency, relative frequency and their power transformations.

By observing figures 4 to 8 it can be learnt that the classification rates were significantly improved by using the relative frequency instead of the absolute word frequency. For instance the accuracy of Euclidean distance classifier was improved by 11.7% at 300dpi and by 36.2% at 130dpi. In addition, power transformation on absolute frequency (PTA) also improved the performance of all used classifiers. However, it is clear that the use of PTA gave out more classification errors when there were more OCR errors in generating texts.

Power transformation on relative frequency (PTR) further improved the classification accuracy of each classifier used. For example the accuracy of Euclidian distance classifier was finally improved cumulatively by 16.8% at 300dpi and by 40.4% at 130dpi. PTR improved classification accuracy such that all classifiers exhibited over 91% classification rates.

Not only did the classifiers performance rose by doing power transformation on relative frequency, but also the robustness of classifiers increased such that even when OCR systems gave a lot of unacceptable amount of errors the performances were considerably higher than using untransformed features in representing OCR texts for classification purposes. For example at highest level of OCR errors, when PTR was used, the worst classifier performed as high as 85.5% accuracy and the best classifier came up with 91.7% accuracy.

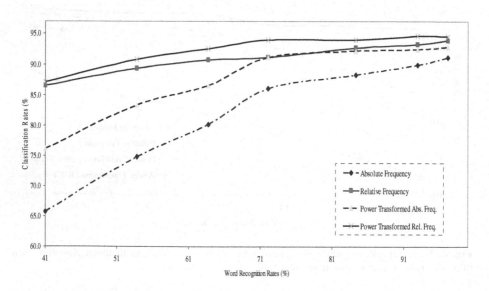

Fig. 5. Word recognition rates vs. text classification rate for linear discriminant function with improved performance after feature transformation

It is also interesting to note that transformed features particularly relative frequency do not heavily depend on word recognition rates by the OCR systems. In such a way that, the differences in accuracy between the absolute frequency and the transformed features, increase as the word recognition rates by OCR systems decrease.

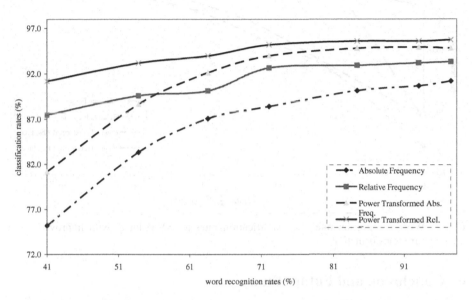

Fig. 6. Word recognition rates vs. text classification rate for projection distance with improved performance after feature transformation

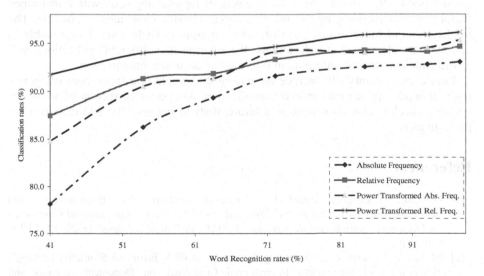

Fig. 7. Word recognition rates vs. classification rates for Modified Projection Distance with improved results after feature transformation

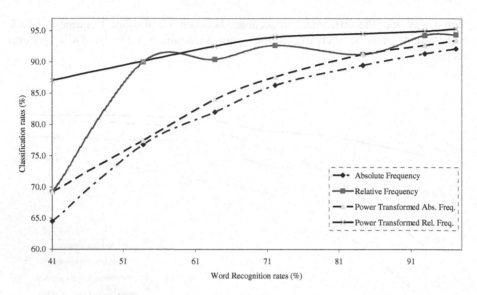

Fig. 8. Word recognition rates vs. classification rates for SVM-linear with improved results after feature transformation

6 Conclusion and Future Study

In this paper we have shown the impact of using transformed features for OCR-generated documents in automatic text classification. The findings show that using transformed features significantly improved the performance of all used classifiers. Even when OCR systems gave a lot of errors by representing texts with transformed features it was encouraging to obtain as higher classification rates as possible. The implications of these results are that, with error-prone OCR texts it is possible to automate the classification tasks and use the automation in different applications such as information retrieval, information filtering and document organization.

Future experiments will include increasing the sample size from more categories for real world applications in text classification. Also error correction of words by spelling check is also remaining as a future study to improve the text classification performance.

References

[1] Ohta,M., Takasu,A., Adachi,J.: "Retrieval Methods for English-Text with Missrecognized OCR Characters", *Proceedings of the Fourth International Conference on Document Analysis and Recognition (ICDAR),* pp.950-956, August 18-20, 1997,Ulm, Germany.

[2] Myka, A., Guntzer. U.: "Measuring the Effects of OCR Errors on Similarity Linking", *Proceedings* of the Fourth International Conference on Document Analysis and Recognition (ICDAR), pp.968-973, August 18-20, 1997, Ulm, Germany.

[3] Zu, G., Murata, M., Ohyama, W, Wakabayashi, T. and Kimura, F.: "The impact of OCR accuracy on Automatic Text Categorization", *Proceedings of Advanced Workshop Content Computing*, pp. 403-409, 2004.

[4] Fukumoto,T., Wakabayashi,T. Kimura,F. and Miyake,Y.: "Accuracy Improvement of Handwritten Character Recognition By GLVQ", *Proceedings of the Seventh International Workshop on Frontiers in Handwriting Recognition Proceedings*(IWFHR VII), 271-280 September 2000.

[5] Guowei Zu, Wataru Ohyama, Tetsushi Wakabayashi, Fumitaka Kimura,: "Accuracy improvement of automatic text classification based on feature transformation" *DocEng'03 (ACM Symposium on Document Engineering 2003)*, pp.118-120, November 20–22, 2003, Grenoble, France

[6] C.C. Chang, and C.J. Lin : "LIBSVM -- A Library for Support Vector Machines (Version 2.33)", *http://www.csie.ntu.edu.tw/~cjlin/libsvm/index.html*, (2002.4)

[7] Library Digital Initiative Project Team, Harvad University Library: "Measuring Search Retrieval Accuracy of uncorrected OCR: Findings from the Harvad-Radcliffe Online Historical Reference Shelf Digitization Project"   A research report available at *http://preserve.harvard.edu/resources/ocr_report.pdf*, (Aug. 2001)

[8] Bicknes, D.A: "Measuring the accuracy of the OCR in the Making of America". A research report available at http://*www.hti.umich.edu/m/moagrp/moaocr.html* (1998)

[9] Junker, M and Hoch, R.: "An experimental evaluation of OCR text representations for learning document classifiers". *International Journal on Document Analysis and Recognition*. Springer-Verlag, pp. 116-122, 1998

[10] Frasconi, P., Soda, G. and Vullo, A: "Text Categorization for Multi-page Documents: A Hybrid Naïve Bayes HMM Approach". *1st ACM-IEEE Joint Conference on Digital Libraries(JCDL'01)* Roanoke Virginia (June, 2001)

[11] Frasconi, P., Soda, G. and Vullo, A: "Hidden Markov Models for Text Categorization in Mult-page Documents". *Journal of Intelligent Information Systems, 18:2/3, 195–217, 2002*(2002).

[12] Taghva, K., Nartker, T., Borsack, J., Lumos, S., Condit, A. and Young, R.: "Evaluating Text Categorization in the Presence of OCR Errors," *Proceedings of the Symposium on Electronic Imaging Science and Technology*, pages 68-74, San Jose, CA, January 2001.

A Method for Symbol Spotting
in Graphical Documents

Daniel Zuwala and Salvatore Tabbone

LORIA-UMR 7503,
Campus Scientifique, B.P. 239,
54506 Villers-les-Nancy Cedex, France
{dzuwala, tabbone}@loria.fr

Abstract. In this paper we propose a new approach to find symbols in graphical documents. The method is based on a representation of the document in chain points extracted from the skeleton. We merge successively these chain points into a dendrogram framework and according to a measure of density. From the dendrogram, we extract potential symbols which can be recognized after.

1 Introduction

Symbol recognition is more than ever a problem that is discussed in scientific community [1]. Several approaches have been proposed and one kind is based on the structural representation of documents [6–10]. These approaches are often very powerful to spot symbols but they suffer of large complexity and they are not robust against the noise. Another kind of approaches is based on features descriptors [2–5] . These descriptors are either considering the contour of the object or either considering the whole object. They are robust against noise and occlusion, but they need the document to be clearly segmented, which is a problem since symbols are often embedded with other graphics layers.

In our previous work [11], we have proposed a method to automatically detect potential symbols without knowledge. However this method was only working on special kind of symbols that had a loop contour. Moreover, it was time-consuming to detect the loop symbols since we were looking for loop in a graph. In this paper, we proposed a new method that do not have the loop structure constraint, but only the constraint that the symbol is defined by a single connected component. We have also overcome the time consuming problem, by developing a new algorithm to detect symbols. The method is based on a structural representation of the document which is decomposed into different chain points. Then, we merge successively these chain points in order to retrieve symbols. Finally we used the photometric information to discard or accept symbols with respect to symbol model. This method is fast, and can be seen as a first processing, in order to have a set of candidate symbols that may be interesting with respect to a symbol query.

H. Bunke and A.L. Spitz (Eds.): DAS 2006, LNCS 3872, pp. 518–528, 2006.

The paper is organized as follows. In section 2 we explain our approach. Examples and experimental results are given in section 3. Limit and future investigations are provided in section 4.

2   The Method

2.1   Low Level Processing

The documents are usually scanned in grey levels, and a binarization is done in order to be able to extract symbols from graphical documents (see Fig 1). Then, the skeleton is defined using the 3-4 distance transform ([12]) (see Fig 2). Finally, we extract from the skeleton image a set of chain points. These chains are composed of connected points that have only two neighbors, and the extremities are either junction points (ie more than two neighbors) or terminal points (ie only one neighbor) as indicated in Fig 3.

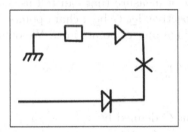

Fig. 1. Binarized document

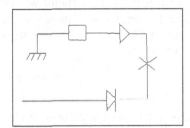

Fig. 2. Extracted skeleton

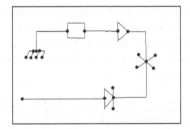

Fig. 3. Document with junctions and terminal points

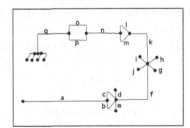

Fig. 4. Defined chain points (denoted a,b,c,...)

At the end of these low level processing, the whole document is decomposed into a set of chain points (Fig 4).

2.2   Main Processing

The idea is to merge these chain points in order to segment the symbols belonging to a document. We assume that the symbols we are looking for are defined by a set of compact connected chains (Fig 5).

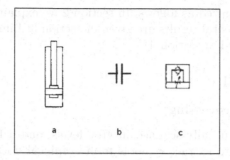

Fig. 5. Examples of symbols that can be recognized or not. Symbol (a), may not be recognized because it is not compact enough. Symbol (b), will not be recognized because it is composed of two disconnected components. Symbol (c), will be recognized.

So in order to find them, we have to define a measure that can tell us, how compact a set of chain points is. In this perspective, let C be a chain points, x_i a point of C, $i \in [1, n_C]$ where n_C is the total number of points in C. We define the density of C as:

$$density(C) = \frac{\sum_{i=1}^{n_C} d(x_i, x_C^G)}{n_C}$$

where, x_C^G is the barycenter of the chain point C defined by $x_C^G = \frac{1}{n_C}\sum_{i=1}^{n_C} x_i$, and $d(x_i, x_C^G)$ a distance (we have taken here, the Euclidean distance).

The idea is to merge successively these chains into a dendrogram structure that can be seen as a graph representation. The nodes of the graph are the chain points, and the edges describe the relation between the chain points. For example, if C_1 and C_2 are directly connected (ie they have common extremities), there is an edge between them. To each edge we assign a value to know how relevant is a merge between two corresponding nodes. The value that we assign to the edge (C_1, C_2) is the following:

$$value(C_1, C_2) = density(C_1)density(C_2)\frac{(n_{C_1} + n_{C_2})density(C_1C_2)}{n_{C_1}density(C_1) + n_{C_2}density(C_2)}$$
$$(1)$$

where n_{C_1}, n_{C_2} are weighted coefficients on the number of merges that already happened in clusters C_1 and C_2. The second part of the expression formula :

$$\frac{(n_{C_1} + n_{C_2})density(C_1C_2)}{n_{C_1}density(C_1) + n_{C_2}density(C_2)}$$

is here to take into account the evolution of the density. Before the merge, we have two nodes of density: $density(C_1)$ and $density(C_2)$. After the merge we will have one density : $density(C_1C_2)$. We look at the ratio between them, in order to measure how the density has evolved before and after the merge. So it means that we are looking for the smallest evolution of the density. But this term alone is not sufficient because if we take a large chain of points, the evolution with a neighbor chain will be very small. To avoid this behavior we add the first term:

$$density(C_1)density(C_2).$$

This term underlines small density chain points. So *value* (formula 1) is a measure that tells that we want a small evolution of the density but also that we want a small density chain point first.

```
for each node in the graph
      calculate the density of the node
end for
for each edge in the graph
      calculate the value of the edge
      insert the edge in a queue Q sorted by increasing value
end for
while Q not empty do
      pop the first edge of Q
      create a new node from this edge
      update the value of edges that have changed because of the new node
end while
```

Fig. 6. Algorithm to construct the dendrogram

We show a sample of a dendrogram in Fig 7 provided from the algorithm defined on Fig 6. At the beginning (level 0), we have small chain points. Then we successively merge them (as indicated by Fig 6). Finally, we obtain a binary tree.

Once we have constructed the dendrogram, we have to find how to extract the best partition (ie the partition that give us the decomposition of symbols). Fig 8 shows the evolution of the measure *value* during the dendrogram construction for the document in Fig 4.

The following figures 9, 10 and 11 show the partition we get when $n = 22, 26, 30$. n is a parameter on the number of merges that have been done since the beginning of the processing, it is related to the level in Fig 7). From these figures, we can remark that for $n = 22$, we find out that there is still some symbols that have not been merged. For $n = 26$ all the symbols are good and for $n = 30$ some symbols have merged with lines.

So it seems difficult to find the right value of n. Of course we don't have to select a single n, but a range. However we get a full partition of the document and we are not able to make a difference between candidate symbols and garbage symbols (like lines network). So many symbols are returned. That's why we have developed another method in order to filter the number of potential symbols returned.

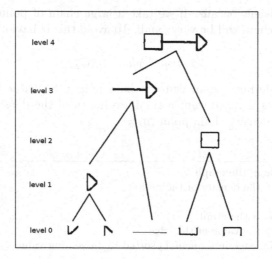

Fig. 7. A dendrogram

Evolution of value during dendrogram construction

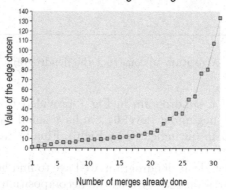

Fig. 8. Evolution of *value* during the dendrogram construction

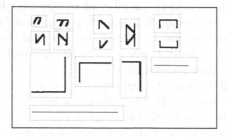

Fig. 9. Partition found with $n = 22$

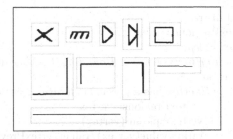

Fig. 10. Partition found with $n = 26$

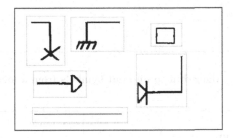

Fig. 11. Partition found with $n = 30$

2.3   Another Method to Extract the Symbols

Instead of having a global view of the dendrogram, let's have a local view of it. A dendrogram is a binary tree, where the leafs are the initial chain points that we have extracted from the skeleton image. If for each leaf, we start looking the evolution of *value* from the leaf to the top of the tree, we will have a local view. The algorithm is described in Fig 12.

We have two parameters to set. The first one, *BoundingBoxMax* is only here to skip chain points that are inconsistent (ie we don't look the symbols that are too big). It represents the maximum size of potential symbols. If we have no clue on the size of the symbols in the documents we can set *BoundingBoxMax = BoundingBox(document)*. The second one, *ratioMax*, is here to limit the evolution of *value*. When *ratio* is above *ratioMax* we suppose that the candidate symbol has merged with another chain points that do not belong to the symbol.

Let's look at the results we have with this method (see Figs 13, 14 and 15). For *ratioMax = 1.2*, we notice that some symbols are incomplete. For *ratioMax = 1.5*, we have all, and only the symbols. For *ratioMax = 1.8*, we have a symbol that have merged with other stuff. So we can observe that we have significantly reduce the number of symbols. However we have added a parameter *ratioMax* that have some influences on the results. As said above, one solution would be to gather all the results return from *ratioMax=1.2* to 1.8, with a step of 0.1. Of course, we increase the number of potential symbols returned but we are rather sure, we do not miss one.

```
for each leaf in tree
        − vertexPrevious = leaf
        − vertex = leaf
    if BoundingBox(vertex) < BoundingBoxMax do
            − ratio = 1
            while ((vertex has a parent)and(ratio < ratioMax)) do
                    − vertexPrevious=vertex
                    − vertex=parent(vertex)
                    − ratio=value(vertex)/value(vertexPrevious)
            end while
            if (ratio < ratioMax) return vertex
            else return vertexPrevious
    end if
end for
```

Fig. 12. Algorithm to find out symbols from a local view

Fig. 13. Results with $ratioMax = 1.2$ **Fig. 14.** Results with $ratioMax = 1.5$

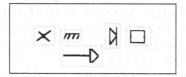

Fig. 15. Results with $ratioMax = 1.8$

2.4   Boosting the Search of Candidate Symbols

As shown before, we can have a same symbol that has been too much merged with other stuff, or that has been not enough merged. In order to detect symbols, a way to not check all the potential symbols is to organize them into a tree, like they were in the dendrogram. Figs 16 and 17 represent the symbols with a tree organization and without. That way, if we find a match with a symbol model, we don't have to look for a match with its children.

2.5   Descriptors

In order to find if the candidate symbols match the model, we are going to use a simple descriptor based on geometric moment[13]. The output of the descriptor

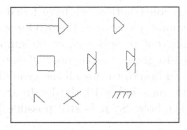

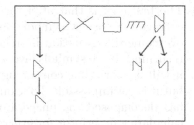

Fig. 16. Without tree organization. We have 9 matches to do.

Fig. 17. With tree organization. Between 5 and 9 matches to do.

is a 4 dimensional vector. We compute the Euclidean distance between the two vectors to know if the symbols match together. That is, if this distance is below a fixed threshold, they match.

This descriptor is very simple, but it is fast. We may have to find better descriptors but it is not the subject of this paper. We will see in the experimentation section that the descriptor is not always discriminant. However, here the main idea is to have a system that can quickly display a set of candidate symbols.

3   Experimentation and Perspectives

Tests have been conducted on five different documents (Fig 19 and 20 are a sample of them). The queries symbols are presented in Fig. 18 and Table 1 shows the results obtained with our approach. We have reported on this table the number of symbols found related to the query compared to the real number belonging to the document. We also add the rank of the symbols retrieved.

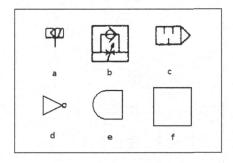

Fig. 18. Symbols to recognize

The results appeared promising. Considering all the experimentations we have made, we have found 35 symbols over 42. For the first image, everything has been recognized, but with variable ranks. We may reasonably hope that with a better descriptor, the ranks returned will be better. We notice that we have miss some symbols. There can be two reasons:

526   D. Zuwala and S. Tabbone

– The first one, is that after the dendrogram construction, we have failed to extract the correct symbols, and so we cannot recognized them. One can overcome this situation by relaxing the different parameters, or by simply returning all the symbols involved in the dendrogram construction. Of course it will be more time consuming to calculate a descriptor for all the symbols, but it is not impossible. For example, for the image in Fig 19, the dendrogram has decomposed the image around 1000 symbols. So it is still possible to calculate a descriptor for every symbols.
– The second reason, is that the method has failed to merge the correct chain points. This could be solved by finding a better definition of the density. Another improvement to overcome this situation should be to not only con-

Table 1. Results obtained with the proposed method. Number of symbols found / Number of symbols in the document. In parenthesis, the different rank of the symbols found.

Symbols	a	b	c	d	e	f
Test 1	4/4 (1;2;3;4)	4/4 (2;4;5;10)	4/4 (3;6;7;10)	0/0	0/0	0/0
Test 2	0/0	0/0	0/0	2/2 (2;4)	2/2 (1;2)	4/6 (1;2;3;5)
Test 3	0/0	0/0	0/0	2/3 (3;5)	4/4 (1;2;3;4)	0/0
Test 4	0/0	0/0	0/0	2/2 (1;2)	0/0	3/7 (3;4;5)
Test 5	0/0	0/0	0/0	4/4 (2;3;101;102)	0/0	0/0

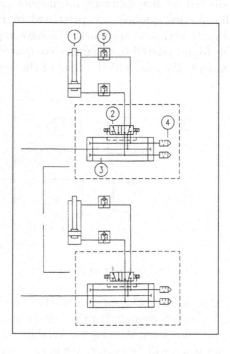

Fig. 19. Document test 1

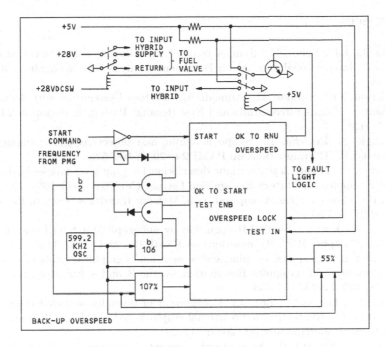

Fig. 20. Document test 2

sider the density of the chain points that are directly connected, but also the chain points that are connected n step later (with n integer greater than 1). Doing so, we will have a more global view of the document instead of the current local view during the construction of the dendrogram.

All the processing (from the skeletization to the output results) take about 5 seconds on Pentium IV (2.8GHz) on a document image of size 1200X2000 pixels.

4   Conclusion

We have proposed a new method to find symbols which do not need to be already segmented or disconnected from graphical documents. This method doesn't made any assumption on the symbols to find, and so can be applied to many different symbols. It assumes only that a symbol is a set of compact chain points, that is often the case. The results that we obtain are encouraging even if we have pointed out several drawbacks. In particular, a better descriptor is needed to improve immediately the performance of the approach. Futures works will be devoted to:

- define a better density measure. In particular the one we have used is more dedicated to concentric distribution. It will be possible to take into account elliptic distribution.
- extent the method to chain points that may be connected n step later (with n integer greater than 1).

References

1. Cordella, L.P., Vento, M.: Symbol recognition in documents: a collection of techniques? International Journal on Document Analysis and Recognition **3** (2000) 73–88
2. Belkasim, S.O., Shridar, M., Ahmadi, M.: Pattern Recognition with Moment Invariants: A Comparative Study and New Results. Pattern Recognition **24** (1991) 1117–1138
3. Belongie, S., Puzicha, J.: Shape matching and object recognition using shape contexts. IEEE Transactions on PAMI **24** (2002) 509–522
4. Ghorbel, F.: A complete invariant description for gray level images by harmonic analysis approach. Pattern Recognition Letters **15** (1994) 1043–1051
5. Lin, B.C., Shen, J.: Fast Computation of Moment Invariants. Pattern Recognition **24** (1991) 807–813
6. Llados, J., Jose, J.: Symbol Recognition by Subgraph Matching Between Region Adjancy Graphs. IEEE Transactions on PAMI **23** (2001) 1137–1143
7. Messmer, B.: Automatic learning and recognition of graphical symbols in engineering drawings. In: Graphics Recognition: methods and applications (GREC'95), LNCS 1072. (1996) 123–134
8. Park, B.G, Lee, K.M., Lee, J.: Recognition of partially occluded objects using probabilistic ARG (attributed relational graph)-based matching. Computer Vision and Image Understanding **90** (2003) 217–241
9. Ramel, J.Y, Emptoz, H.: A structural representation adapted to handwritten symbol recognition. In: Graphics Recognition: methods and applications (GREC'99), Jaipur, India. (1999) 259–266
10. Yan, L., Wenyin, L.: Engineering drawings recognition using a case-based approach. In: International Conference on Document Analysis and Recognition, Edinburgh. Volume **2886** (2003) 190–194
11. Tabbone, S., Wendling L., Zuwala D.: A Hybrid Approach to Detect Graphical Symbols in Documents. In: Document Analysis Systems, Volume **3163** (2004),342–353
12. Sanniti di Baja, G.: Well-shaped, stable, and reversible skeletons from the (3,4)-distance transform, In:Journal of Visual Communication and Image Representation, **5** (1):107-115, March 1994.
13. Hu, M. K.: Visual pattern recognition by moment invariants, In: IEEE Trans. Inform. Theory, **8**, 1962.

Groove Extraction of Phonographic Records

Sylvain Stotzer[1,2], Ottar Johnsen[1], Frédéric Bapst[1], and Rolf Ingold[2]

[1] University of Applied Sciences of Fribourg, CP 32
1705 Fribourg, Switzerland
{sylvain.stotzer, ottar.johnsen, frederic.bapst}@hefr.ch
www.eif.ch/visualaudio
[2] DIVA Group, DIUF, University of Fribourg, Pérolles 2 - Bd de Pérolles 90,
1700 Fribourg, Switzerland
rolf.ingold@unifr.ch

Abstract. Historical sound documents are of high importance for our cultural heritage. The sound of phonographic records is usually extracted by a stylus following the groove, but many old records are in such bad shape that no mechanical contact is possible. The only way to read them is by a contactless reading system. A phonographic document analysis system was developed using an optical technique to retrieve the sound from old records. The process is straightforward: we take a picture of each side of the disc using a dedicated analog camera, we store the film as our working copy, and when needed, we scan the film and process the image in order to extract the sound. In this paper, we analyze the imaging issues and present the algorithm for extracting the groove position and therefore the sound of the records.

1 Introduction

Cutting a disc was the only way to store sounds until the introduction of magnetic tape in the early 50's. Therefore there are huge collections of phonographic records, for example in radio stations and national sound archives. Such archives include pressed discs produced by record companies as well as direct cut discs obtained by the direct recording and available only as single copies with often a great cultural value. These discs are fragile and are deteriorating with time [1]. Worse, many records would be destroyed by the movement of the stylus from even the best turntables. Thus, we risk loosing an important cultural heritage.

On a turntable, a needle follows the groove's radial position. The radial velocity of the stylus is converted into an electrical signal corresponding to the sound. Therefore, the image of the record contains the sound information, as can be seen on Fig. 1. This observation has lead to the VisualAudio system:

1. An analog picture of a disc is taken, in order to preserve the sound information in case the original disc deteriorates.
2. When needed, the film is digitized using a specially designed rotating scanner.
3. The sound is then extracted from the digital image by measuring the radial displacement of the groove.

H. Bunke and A.L. Spitz (Eds.): DAS 2006, LNCS 3872, pp. 529–540, 2006.
© Springer-Verlag Berlin Heidelberg 2006

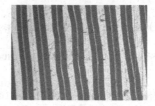

Fig. 1. Top view of a 78 rpm record: the modulations of the groove are visible

Other optical techniques have been proposed to read phonographic records, but without the intermediate photographic step. Poliak et al presented an optical turntable using an optical fiber to follow the groove [2]. Such a technique is not suitable for severely damaged disc, where the groove has big discontinuities. Fadeyev et al. use methods derived from the particle physics instrumentation to recover audio data from musical cylinders and discs. They introduced a 2D imaging technique for 78 rpm monaural discs, and a 3D surface measuring technique using confocal scanning microscopy [3].

The concept of VisualAudio has been introduced in [4], and we described the acquisition process and gave an estimation of the resolution and of the expected extracted signal quality [5], [6]. In this paper we analyze the image and processing issues for record pictures in VisualAudio. Section 2 outlines the image acquisition part of the system. Section 3 describes the groove and record images as well as the main alterations produced by the different steps of the acquisition process, leading to the edge model presented in section 4. Based on this model and on the knowledge of the phonographic record, we present the image processing algorithms used to extract the groove position in Sections 5, 6, 7 and 8. This paper focuses on monophonic 78 rpm (rotations per minute) records, as these are more fragile and more concerned by degradation and preservation issues. Differences between 78 rpm and 33⅓ rpm record will be briefly exposed in Section 9. Finally Section 10 describes the results and system evaluation, followed by a brief conclusion in Section 11.

2   The VisualAudio Image Acquisition

The image acquisition of the VisualAudio system consists of two steps: the photography of the record, and scanning of the negative film. These stages are described in the next two subsections.

2.1 Photography

The groove position must be evaluated very accurately, requiring high image resolution. This can be done with microscope optics. Unfortunately the depth of the groove exceeds the microscope depth of field (DOF). Many discs also have a warping of up to 1 mm. Using the intermediate photography step allows us to work with a larger DOF while imaging the disc, but ensures that the image to be digitized (the film) fits in the reduced DOF required by the microscope's optics.

Most discs are black, and thus their surface has a very low reflectivity factor, as most of the light is absorbed. But since the discs are bright, their reflectivity is mainly specular, meaning that most of the reflected light has a reflective angle equal to the incidence angle. Thus we use a strong lighting that illuminates the disc uniformly from the lens point of view to ensure sufficient contrast between grooves and intergrooves.

Several kinds of cameras and films have been used to determine the equipment that best suits the specific needs of this project. A dedicated camera has been designed in order to satisfy high-resolution needs for record pictures [6].

2.2 Scanning

A dedicated rotating scanner has been built to digitize the record pictures [6]. The film lies on a glass turntable. The light source illuminates the film by transparency. A linear CCD camera is located above on the same axis as the light source and digitizes the film with 2048 sensors. On one rotation of the film, we scan a ring of the disc image (Fig. 2). By radial displacements of the camera, adjacent rings are scanned in order to digitize the whole record. The sampling rate of the camera combined with the turntable speed defines the image sampling frequency, ranging from 65 to 130 k-samples per ring. This frequency combined with the disc speed defines the sampling frequency of the output audio signal, ranging from 84 to 169 kHz for 78 rpm records.

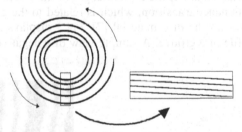

Fig. 2. The rotating scanner acquires one ring of the disc picture in a rectangular image file

As the camera is mounted on a 10x magnification optic and as the sensor size is 10x10 μm, each captured pixel corresponds to a 1x1 μm area. As the glass tray rotates, each CCD-sensor integrates the light on a rotating length of the film, resulting in non-isometric pixels, which size varies from 1x3.5 μm up to 1x15 μm depending on the sampling rate and the radial position on the disc.

2.3 Advantages of the VisualAudio Sound Extraction System

The proposed sound extraction system will not replace standard turntables, but the photographic and image processing methods present numerous advantages over classical stylus playback:

- The optical method is contactless and can be applied on any record.
- Taking a picture of the discs is a quick way to store an analog copy of the sound content in its current state of conservation.

- The document encoding is the same as on the original support: the groove displacement.
- The film is a stable medium, which can be preserved for more than hundred years.
- The ideal storage conditions for films and for discs are similar.
- The extraction process is independent of the recorded speed (16, 33⅓, 78 rpm...) and of the material used to build the record.
- This extraction process is free of the transient noise produced by the mechanical resonance of the turntable arm on a damaged groove.
- The image of a groove shows several edges, which represent the same audio signal. This is very useful for advanced signal correction.

3 Image Description

3.1 Groove Image

As the light reflection on the disc is specular, the groove's shape has an important impact on the disc picture. During the photographic step, flat sections of the disc (intergroove) reflect the light perpendicularly to the camera objective and thus appear as black on the negative film. While the walls of the round monophonic grooves don't reflect light perpendicularly to the camera, the bottoms of the grooves do. The top edges between the intergrooves and the grooves are usually sharp and will result in a clear-cut luminance transition, but the bottom edges of the round shaped grooves will result in a blurred luminance transition, which is related to the groove curvature and the specular reflectance of the disc material [7]. Fig.3 displays an approximation of the 1-D intensity profile of a groove. A sample view of a negative picture of a record is shown on Fig 4.

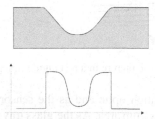

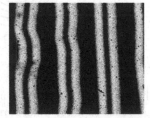

Fig. 3. 78 rpm round shaped groove cut view and its approximate luminance model

Fig. 4. 78 rpm record photography on a negative film

3.2 Image Degradations

Several degradations may occur during the image acquisition process:

Needle damage: If the disc has been played on regular turntables, the groove's wall may have been damaged by the needle at some places. This produces flatter areas in the wall, leading in a darker trace on the photography of the groove (Fig. 5).

Support degradations: Original support degradations (scratches, surface cracking...) or objects on the surface (dust, fungus...) may cause luminance change at the photographic step, causing trace cuts or spots on the acquired image.

Optics: The optical blur is produced by the out of focus blur and the Airy disk. Two separate optical systems are used in the VisualAudio process: the camera and scanner. Their resolutions have been described in details in [6]. The out of focus blur may vary on the whole record surface, due to the warping and the possible surface imperfections. Thus if the edge detection is not accurate enough, the optics blur may lead to a low frequency shift over the edge position. The out of focus blur may also be different at the top and the bottom of the groove.

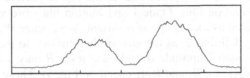

Fig. 5. Grey level intensity profile of a groove, as acquired by the VisualAudio scanner. The left wall has been damaged by the needle, which produced lower intensities in the middle of the white trace.

Motion blur: The motion blur is produced by the displacement of the groove relatively to the camera during the acquisition of a single sample. As the CCD camera is aligned with the center of the rotation glass tray, this motion blur appears only on the radial direction. The displacement due to the spiral and the off-axis are both smaller than 0.01 μm and can be neglected [6]. Thus the motion blur is bounded by the maximum amplitude of the sound that modulates the groove:

$$m_{audio} = \frac{V_{max}}{n \cdot rps} \tag{1}$$

where V_{max} is the maximum recorded velocity, n the number of samples per rotation and rps is the recorded speed in rotation per second. With a sampling frequency of 130 k-samples/rotation, and considering V_{max}=32cm/sec for a 78 rpm disc [8], then m_{audio}=1.89μm. As the motion blur is signal dependent, it is space-variant on the image. Thus if the edge detection is not precise, the motion blur may lead to a shift over the edge position that is proportional to the derivative of the signal.

4 VisualAudio Groove Model

As the sizes of the objects to detect (intergrooves, bottom and walls of the groove) are larger than the blur size, we assume that neighboring objects won't interfere in the edge detection process. Thus we may simplify the groove model and separate it in four distinct step edge models, having the same characteristics but not the same parameter values.

An 1-D edge model of an ideal object boundary could be represented by a step function $Au(x-x_0)+B$ where x_0 is the position of the edge, A is the step amplitude, B the base grey level and the unit step function $u(x)$ defined as [7]:

$$u(x) = \begin{cases} 0 & if \ x \le 0 \\ 1 & otherwise \end{cases} \tag{2}$$

Blur on this edge is usually modeled by the Gaussian blurring kernel [9], [10]:

$$g(x, \sigma) = \frac{1}{\sqrt{2\pi}\sigma} e^{-x^2/2\sigma^2} \tag{3}$$

where σ is an unknown scale constant. Noise can be modeled as uncorrelated, zero-mean, Gaussian distributed additive with a standard deviation γ and could be integrated in the model as an additive parameter $n(x, \gamma)$.

We define σ_t and σ_b as the optical blur at the top respectively the bottom of the groove, and σ_m the motion blur. Optical and motion blurs are space-dependent, but they may be considered as locally space-invariant. We assume that the groove bottom curvature is regular, defining σ_s as the size of the blur due to the round shape of the groove bottom. The step amplitude A and base level B may vary between the two traces, taking values A_1, A_2, B_1 and B_2 (as seen on Fig. 5). These assumptions lead to the following 1-D edge models of a groove having its four edges e_1, e_2, e_3 and e_4 at positions x_1, x_2, x_3 and x_4:

$$e_1(x) = [A_1 u(x - x_1) + B_1] * g(x, \sigma_t) * g(x, \sigma_m) + n(x, \gamma) \tag{4}$$
$$e_2(x) = [A_1 (1 - u(x - x_2)) + B_2] * g(x, \sigma_b) * g(x, \sigma_m) * g(x, \sigma_s) + n(x, \gamma)$$
$$e_3(x) = [A_2 u(x - x_3) + B_2] * g(x, \sigma_b) * g(x, \sigma_m) * g(x, \sigma_s) + n(x, \gamma)$$
$$e_4(x) = [A_2 (1 - u(x - x_4)) + B_1] * g(x, \sigma_t) * g(x, \sigma_m) + n(x, \gamma)$$

If we rescale the step amplitudes to have unique values for A and B, edges are symmetric two by two: the top e_1 and e_4, and the bottom of the groove e_2 and e_3.

5   Image Analysis Algorithm

The image analysis is performed on each dimension separately. Several reasons lead to a 1D edge detection process:

1. As pixels are non-isometric, we have much more accuracy for localization in the radial direction than on the tangential one.
2. The groove is perpendicular to the CCD camera during one sample acquisition. Small displacements of the groove are considered as motion blur (see Sect. 3.2)
3. Uses of the second dimension for the edge detection process would result in a low-pass filtering of the extracted sound signal.

Thus the edge detection process will be applied on each line of acquisition separately, and the process is time independent. The second direction information will be used later to detect and correct the signal in a post-processing step (see Sect. 8).

The image analysis algorithm is applied in three steps: first, the edge detection is performed on each line acquired by the camera. Then the groove reconstruction joins the extracted edges in the time dimension, and finally the detection and correction step is applied to cancel the damages and impulses on the extracted signal.

6 Edge Detection

6.1 VisualAudio Edge Detection Algorithm

To retrieve the location of a single edge with high accuracy, we should detect the position of the middle of the transition between the luminance levels A and B in order to be independent from the space-varying blurs (i.e. optics blur and motion blur) over time. Unfortunately the step amplitude A is difficult to retrieve due to the degradations explained in section 3. Therefore it will be almost impossible to locate the edge at the middle of the transition, thus producing a bias b_i on the extracted signal that is signal dependent. But as the edges are symmetric two by two, the bias b_i due to a space-variant degradation on an edge is compensated by the bias $-b_i$ on the symmetric edge. Thus the average of all edges of the trace produces negligible bias.

The edge detection is performed in two steps for each line captured by the camera: coarse and fine edge detection. These steps are detailed in the subsections 6.2 and 6.3.

6.2 Coarse Edge Detection

The purpose of the coarse edge detection is to detect the traces roughly on a smooth de-noised image. Thus we detect the presence of all the grooves and get an approximate location of the edges. Knowing these locations we can easily have a precise estimation of the local step amplitude A and base value B, even in case of large luminance variation over the image. This is done by taking the maximal, respectively minimal, value between two neighboring detected traces, or a median estimation of these extremes. This coarse edge detection skips also part of the false detections that are induced by dust or damages, as it locates only objects having the desired size (the size of the traces). Coarse edge detection is implemented by a convolution with a double box filter $b(x)$ defined by a $\lambda x1$ kernel $[-1 \ldots -1 \, 0 \, 1 \ldots 1]$. The result of this convolution is a smooth approximation of the derivative of the intensity profile (Fig. 6), which extremum locate the edges. As the 78 rpm groove width and trace width w are constant over the whole record, the scale of the double box filter is $\lambda = \alpha w$ with α being between 0.3 and 0.8.

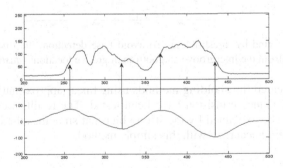

Fig. 6. Intensity profile of a groove (*above*) and the smooth derivative approximation obtained by convolution with the double box filter (*below*). Minima and maxima locate the edges roughly (*arrows*).

Another way to detect approximately the traces over the image would be to initialize the process as described above at the beginning of the image processing, and then to propagate this information over time using the edges detected at the time i to get the location of the edges at time $i+1$. However, due to scratches or other physical damage of the record, trace cuts may occur all over on the image (even during the initialization step) and lead to the loss of some grooves. Such time propagated information has also the disadvantage to propagate errors. Therefore choice has been made to have this coarse scale edge detection at each sampling time.

6.3 Fine Edge Detection

The purpose of the fine edge detection is to locate the edge accurately. One of the constraints given by the model is to detect the position relatively to the local step amplitude A and base value B to keep the edges symmetric two by two. The simplest method to satisfy this constraint is to use an adaptive threshold t defined as follows:

$$t = B + \beta A, \quad \beta \in [0,1] \tag{5}$$

In practice β should be restricted to the [0.2, 0.7] in order to be noise robust. As the white areas (high amplitude on the intensity profile of Fig. 6) are noisier, a low β value produces results that are more robust to noise and degradations. Subpixel accuracy is then achieved by linear interpolation between the two consecutives pixels $p(x)$ and $p(x+1)$ which satisfy $p(x) \geq t$ and $p(x+1) \leq t$ (or the opposite).

The white traces are noisier than the intergroove and may contain some darker areas that could mislead the edge detection. To avoid such false detection, the thresholding process is applied starting from the intergroove or from the bottom of the groove. Edges are then located at the first major discontinuities higher than t (Fig. 7).

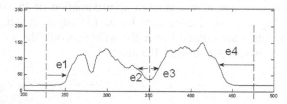

Fig. 7. Edges are found by thresholding. To avoid false detection, the fine edge detection is processed starting from the intergroove and bottom of groove locations (*dashed lines*).

More sophisticated thresholding methods using linear approximation or parametric fitting of the luminance transition have been tested. The results were similar to this method. This can be explained by the strong blur that smoothes the image, producing the same positioning accuracy with this simple method.

7 Groove Reconstruction

Once the 1-D edge detection is performed in the radial direction, detected edge positions must be put in a row to rebuild the recorded signal in the time, corresponding to the 2nd dimension of the image. These vectors will be defined as the extracted sound signals s_1, s_2, s_3 and s_4 retrieved from the four edges of the groove.

As we know the position $s_i(j)$ of an edge i at time j and as we know the maximal displacement of the groove (equation (1)), we may define a margin for the edge at time $j+1$. This margin is defined for each edge at each sampling time and does not overlap with the neighboring traces margins at time i. The edge position $s_i(j+1)$ is then chosen among all the candidates inside the margin to minimize either :

$$| s_i (j) - s_i (j+1)| \quad or \quad |2 s_i (j) - s_i(j-1) - s_i (j+1)| \tag{6}$$

Thus the use of these margins is a first rough denoising process. Most of the time, candidates are unique inside a margin, but these margins are a helpful tool to follow the trace in case of a cut or damaged trace. The margin displacement depends on the signal and the sampling frequency. In case of trace cuts, the margin displacement is driven either by the displacement of:

a) the other edge of the same trace (if existing).
b) the edges of the other trace of the same groove.
c) all the other traces in the image.

The average of all the other traces displacement will result in an approximation of the low frequencies component of the signal, i.e. the spiral of the record and the off-axis due to the bad centering of the film on the scanner.

Finally the relative position of each groove is quantified by the sum its four edges.

8 Edge Correction

Some samples of the extracted signals s_i cannot be defined by the edge detection and groove construction steps. Moreover some samples are corrupted and must be corrected according to the neighboring samples. To solve these issues we use a corrupted samples detection/correction scheme.

In order to be signal independent, the corrupted samples detection is applied on the second derivative $\partial^2 s_i$ of the extracted signal s_i. The detection is performed using a double-threshold method [11]. The high threshold τ_h is used to detect the impulses and the lower threshold τ_l to estimate the impulsion duration and to determine the samples to correct. Both τ_h and τ_l are defined using the standard deviation σ of $\partial^2 s_i$ defined on a local window, typically over 1000 samples:

$$\tau_h = a\sigma \text{ and } \tau_l = b\sigma \qquad \text{with } a > b > 1 \tag{7}$$

The factors values are usually about $a=4$ and $b=2$. The corrupted samples detection process is then applied in two steps:

1. Detect the samples j with $\partial^2 s_i(j) > \tau_h$
2. Starting from j, all the contiguous samples with $\partial^2 s_i(k) > \tau_l$ are marked as corrupted.

The corrupted samples correction is performed either by interpolation or by using the other edges information. As the signal is oversampled and the displacement of the groove over consecutive time samples has relatively small amplitude, short corrections up to 5 samples (which is much smaller than the wavelength of the highest recorded frequency) are performed by interpolation using first or second order polynomials.

In case of physical damages on the record, the sound signal can be extracted using only the information from the undamaged edges and traces. Most of the scratches are not perpendicular to the groove, meaning that the extracted signal from the different edges will be damaged at different sampling time. Thus correct value of the corrupted samples can be estimated by using the other edges. To avoid the effect of the edge detection bias on the signal, we must cancel this bias by using the following combination of s_2, s_3 and s_4 to replace a damaged area on edge s_1:

$$s_1 = s_2 + s_3 - s_4 \tag{8}$$

9   Groove Extraction Comparison Between 78 rpm and 33⅓ rpm

The technology improvement of the 33⅓ rpm microgroove over the 78 rpm leads to several differences in the image of a record. Those affect the signal to noise ratio of the extracted sound from 33⅓ rpm (SNR_{33}) in comparison with the SNR_{78} as follows:

- 33⅓ rpm grooves have a triangular shape. The consequence is that the bottom of the groove is not visible on the acquired image, and that we get only one trace to represent each groove. This limits the quality of the extraction and correction steps. As the extracted signal is averaged using two edges instead of four, the SNR_{33} is then 3 dB lower.
- The 33⅓ rpm microgrooves have less deviation, meaning that we get less dynamic for the displacement measurement. As the 78 rpm groove deviation is three times bigger than on 33⅓ rpm records, SNR_{33} is $20\log_{10}(3) = 9.5$ dB lower.
- With the 33⅓ rpm records, the in-band noise is enhance by a factor 78/33 compared to the 78 rpm, as the speed increase puts more noise out of band. Thus the SNR_{33} is then 3.7 dB lower.

Therefore the sound extraction for 33⅓ rpm results in lower quality than for 78 rpm:

$$SNR_{33} = SNR_{78} - 16.2\text{dB} \tag{9}$$

This is not an issue as 33⅓ rpm are less concerned by preservation. However the reading of stereo microgroove 33⅓ rpm is also possible with the VisualAudio system in order to have a complete system and to be able to read as many records as possible. For example test records are a very useful tool to measure the quality of a sound extraction system, but they are almost only available on 33⅓ rpm.

10   Evaluation and Results

10.1   Edge Detection Quality

The precision of the edge detection scheme can be estimated by measuring the residual noise on the signal extracted from an unmodulated groove. The advantage of this kind of test is that it can be performed on any record as such unmodulated grooves can be found at the beginning and at the end of each track.

To evaluate the accuracy of the edge detection process, differences were measured between consecutive detected edges positions on unmodulated grooves. The standard deviation of these measurements reaches 0.5 pixels (=0.5µm) for 33 rpm records and 0.3 pixels for 78 rpm records. This demonstrates that the groove extraction reaches subpixel accuracy and that the resolution of this system is sufficient to extract good quality sound from the image of phonographic records.

10.2 Quality of the Extracted Signal

33⅓ rpm test records contain sinewave tracks used to evaluate the tracking ability. These tracks can be used in our system to measure a signal to noise ratio (SNR), as well as to detect the presence of harmonics and intermodulations.

Current SNR measurements reach 36dB for the extraction of a 300Hz track on a test record. As this track is amplified by 15dB, the SNR_{33} for a non-amplified record would be 21dB. Therefore we can estimate the SNR_{78} using equation (9):

$$SNR_{78} = SNR_{33} + 16.2dB = 37.2dB \qquad (10)$$

This estimation of SNR_{78} is comparable to the recorded quality of the 78 rpm.

Several harmonics may also be present in the sound extraction of a sinewave. The amplitude of the second harmonic gives information about the edge detection bias. The extraction results presented on Table 1 have been performed on a 300 Hz frequency extracted from a 33⅓ rpm test record. The output level is given in dB for each extracted edge, as well as for the sum of both edges. The sum enhances the signal by 6 dB over each edge, which corresponds to the expected gain for amplification by a factor 2. On the other hand, the sum of both edges reduces the 2nd harmonic by 16 dB. This means that part of the 2nd harmonic is due to a symmetric phenomenon that appears on both edges and which is canceled by summing both signals. Different values for the threshold β lead to similar results and observations.

Table 1. Output level for a 300 Hz track extraction using an adaptive threshold with $\beta = 0.2$

	Edge 1	Edge 2	Edge1+Edge2
Signal (300Hz)	-63 dB	-64 dB	-57 dB
2nd harmonic (600 Hz)	-93 dB	-92 dB	-109 dB

11 Conclusion

Based on the described process, a photography camera, dedicated scanner prototype and extraction software have been developed. This system is fully functional and has demonstrated that we can take photography of a record and extract the sound out of the picture by image processing techniques. The extracted sound quality for 78 rpm records is comparable to the sound of a turntable. It is also possible to extract sound from records damaged by scratches or affected by fungus. The reading of more severely damaged records is still under development, as for example broken records or direct cut disc with shrinkage of the recording layer.

Collaborations with sound archives are currently starting, and the VisualAudio system should begin shortly to preserve the sound from large collections of old phonographic records.

Several recovered sound samples can be found at www.eif.ch/visualaudio.

Acknowledgements

The authors thank C. Milan and T. Fumey for their help in this project.

This project is funded by the Gebert Rüf Foundation (project P024/03) and the Swiss National Science Foundation (project 21-64984.01).

References

1. Bradley, K. et al: Guidelines on the Production and Preservation of Digital Audio Objects. IASA – TC04 (2004) ISBN 87-990309-1-8
2. Poliak, J., Robert, P., Goy, J.: Optical Fibre Turntable for Archive Records, Proceedings of the 92nd Convention AES, Vienna, Austria (1992)
3. Fadeyev, V. , Haber, C.: Reconstruction of Mechanically Recorded Sound by Image Processing, J. Audio Eng. Soc. (2003) 51(12): 1172-1185
4. Cavaglieri, S., Johnsen, O., Bapst, F.: Optical Retrieval and Storage of Analog Sound Recordings. AES 20th International Conference, Budapest (2001)
5. Stotzer, S., Johnsen, O., Bapst, F., Sudan, C., Ingold, R.: Phonographic Sound Extraction Using Image and Signal Processing, IEEE Proceedings 2004 ICASSP (2004) 4:289-292.
6. Stotzer, S., Johnsen, O., Bapst, F., Milan, C., Ingold, R.: Phonographic Sound Extraction using Photography and Signal Processing, Digital Signal Processing, Elsevier, to be published
7. Elder, J.: The Visual Computation of Bounding Contours. PhD Thesis, Mc Gill University, Dept. of Electrical Engineering (1995)
8. Temmer, S.F. (ed.): Disk Recording Volume 1 (Anthology), Audio Engineering Society, New York (1980)
9. Canny, J.: A computational approach to edge detection. IEEE Trans. on Pattern Analysis and Machine Intelligence (1986) 8(6):679-698
10. Pentland, A.P.: A new sense for depth of field. IEEE Tran. PAMI (1987) 9(4):523–531
11. Esquef, P., Biscainho, L.W.P., Diniz, P.S.R., Freeland, F. P.: A double threshold-based approach to impulsive noise detection in audio signal. Proc. X European Signal Processing Conf. (EUSIPCO 2000), Tampere, Finland (2000) 2041-2044

Use of Affine Invariants in Locally Likely Arrangement Hashing for Camera-Based Document Image Retrieval

Tomohiro Nakai, Koichi Kise, and Masakazu Iwamura

Graduate School of Engineering, Osaka Prefecture University,
1-1 Gakuen-cho, Sakai, Osaka, 599-8531 Japan
nakai@m.cs.osakafu-u.ac.jp, kise@cs.osakafu-u.ac.jp,
masa@cs.osakafu-u.ac.jp

Abstract. Camera-based document image retrieval is a task of searching document images from the database based on query images captured using digital cameras. For this task, it is required to solve the problem of "perspective distortion" of images, as well as to establish a way of matching document images efficiently. To solve these problems we have proposed a method called Locally Likely Arrangement Hashing (LLAH) which is characterized by both the use of a perspective invariant to cope with the distortion and the efficiency: LLAH only requires $O(N)$ time where N is the number of feature points that describe the query image. In this paper, we introduce into LLAH an affine invariant instead of the perspective invariant so as to improve its adjustability. Experimental results show that the use of the affine invariant enables us to improve either the accuracy from 96.2% to 97.8%, or the retrieval time from 112 msec./query to 75 msec./query by selecting parameters of processing.

1 Introduction

Document image retrieval is a task of searching document images relevant to a user's query. For meeting diverse needs from users, a wide variety of queries have been employed [1]. With document images as queries, the task of finding similar or equivalent document images has been considered. For scanned documents it is called "document image matching" or "duplicate detection" [2, 3]. This paper concerns a kind of document image matching with camera captured documents as queries. We call this task "camera-based document image retrieval". The technique of camera-based document image retrieval can be used as bases of several applications. For example, we can extract annotations of documents by retrieving original documents based on captured query images with annotations and comparing them.

In order to deal with camera captured images, various kind of problems including perspective distortion, uneven lighting and focusing should be solved [4, 5]. We are concerned here with the problem of perspective distortion. An ordinary way of dealing with the distortion is to normalize the image by estimating parameters of perspective transformation [6]. However, the normalization relies heavily on wide justified text regions that are not necessarily included in or successfully extracted from camera captured images.

H. Bunke and A.L. Spitz (Eds.): DAS 2006, LNCS 3872, pp. 541–552, 2006.
© Springer-Verlag Berlin Heidelberg 2006

Another way is to retrieve images regardless of perspective distortion. Geometric hashing (GH) [7] is a well-known way of indexing and retrieval of images regardless of geometric distortion. GH employs feature points extracted from images to register images in the database as well as to retrieve images using queries. A drawback of GH is that its computational complexity is far beyond linear to the number of feature points: it is $O(N^5)$ where N is the number of feature points in the image under perspective distortion. Thus it is difficult to apply GH for the retrieval of images with a lot of feature points such as document images.

To solve this problem, we have proposed a method of indexing and retrieval for images represented by coplanar points [8]. In this paper we call this method Locally Likely Arrangement Hashing (LLAH). In LLAH, each feature point is registered in the hash table with features defined based on arrangements of neighboring feature points. The method is called "locally likely arrangement" because possible arrangements of neighboring points in a local area are enumerated and registered. Since the computational complexity of LLAH is $O(N)$, efficient retrieval has been realized.

In [8], we have employed a perspective invariant called the cross-ratio for calculation of features from the feature points. Calculation of the cross-ratio requires five feature points, which limit adjustability of balancing computational complexity and accuracy of the method. In this paper, we introduce features calculated from less feature points (four points) to improve the adjustability. It is based on the fact that the transformation of feature points in the local area can be approximated as affine transformation even under perspective transformation. As an invariant, therefore, we utilize an affine invariant. From the experimental results using 10,000 database images and 235 query images, it is shown that, as compared to the cross-ratio, use of the affine invariant enables us to improve either the accuracy from 96.2% to 97.8%, or the retrieval time from 112 msec./query to 75msec./query by selecting parameters of processing.

2   Locally Likely Arrangement Hashing

2.1   Geometric Invariants

In LLAH, we use geometric invariants calculated from f coplanar points. Geometric invariants are the values which keep unchanged under geometric transformation. There are several types of geometric invariants depending on the types of geometric transformation. Different types of geometric invariants require different numbers of f.

1. **Cross-Ratio**
   The cross-ratio is known as an invariant of perspective transformation. It is used in our previous work [8] since query images captured by digital cameras suffer from perspective transformation. The cross-ratio is calculated using coordinates of five coplanar points ($f = 5$) ABCDE as follows:

$$\frac{P(A,B,C)P(A,D,E)}{P(A,B,D)P(A,C,E)} \tag{1}$$

   where P(A,B,C) is the area of a triangle with apexes A, B, and C [9]. Since the cross-ratio is a perspective invariant, its value keeps unchanged even if coordinates of points ABCDE change by perspective distortion.

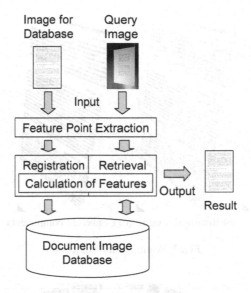

Fig. 1. Overview of processing

2. Affine invariant

We also have invariants for affine transformation. Affine transformation is more restrictive than perspective transformation since it preserves the parallelism of lines. Because perspective transformation of a small limited area can be approximated as affine transformation, it would be possible to apply an affine invariant instead of the cross-ratio.

In this paper we utilize an affine invariant defined using four coplanar points ($f = 4$) ABCD as follows:

$$\frac{P(A, C, D)}{P(A, B, C)} \tag{2}$$

Although the values of invariants are continuous, they must be converted into discrete values in order to be used as indices of the hash table. In LLAH, continuous values are converted into k discrete values by taking into account their frequency: the discretization step is finer for values occurring more frequently. To be precise, discrete values are assigned in proportion to the frequency of values of invariants using a histogram of values of invariants obtained in a preliminary experiment.

2.2 Overview of Processing

Figure 1 shows the overview of processing. At the step of feature point extraction, a document image is transformed into a set of feature points. Then the feature points are inputted into the registration step or the retrieval step. These steps share the step of calculation of features. In the registration step, every feature point in the image is registered into the document image database using its feature. In the retrieval step, the document image database is accessed with features to retrieve images by voting. We explain each step in the following.

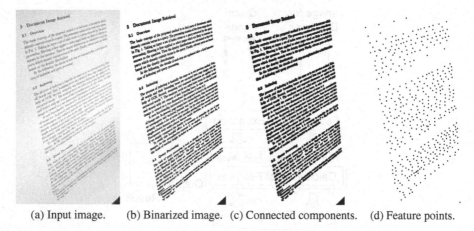

(a) Input image.   (b) Binarized image.   (c) Connected components.   (d) Feature points.

Fig. 2. Feature point extraction

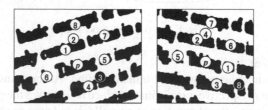

Fig. 3. Change of nearest feature points by perspective distortion

2.3   Feature Point Extraction

An important requirements of feature point extraction is that feature points should be obtained identically even under the perspective distortion, noise, and low resolution. To satisfy this requirement, we employ centroids of word regions as feature points.

The details of processing are as follows. First, the input image (Fig. 2(a)) is adaptively thresholded into the binary image (Fig. 2(b)). Next, the binary image is blurred using the Gaussian filter whose parameters are determined based on an estimated character size (the square root of the mode of areas of connected components). Then, the blurred image is adaptively thresholded again (Fig. 2(c)). Finally, centroids of word regions (Fig. 2(d)) are extracted as feature points.

2.4   Calculation of Features

The feature is a value which represents a feature point of a document image. In order to realize successful retrieval, the feature should satisfy the following two requirements. One is that the same feature should be obtained from the same feature point even under distortion. If different features are obtained from the same feature point at registration and retrieval processes, the corresponding document image cannot be retrieved. We call this requirement "stability of the feature". The other requirement is that different

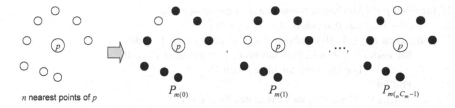

Fig. 4. All possible combinations of $m(=7)$ points from $n(=8)$ nearest points are examined

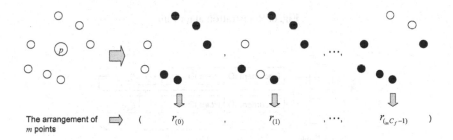

Fig. 5. The arrangement of $m(=7)$ points is described as a sequence of invariants calculated from all possible combinations of $f(=5)$ points

features should be obtained from different feature points. If the same feature is obtained from different feature points, not only the corresponding document image but also other document images are retrieved. We call this requirement "discrimination power of the feature". Both two requirements, the stability and the discrimination power, have to be satisfied for successful retrieval.

Let us explain the stability first. The simplest definition of the feature of a feature point p is to use f nearest feature points from p ($f = 5$ for the cross-ratio, and $f = 4$ for the affine invariant). However, nearest feature points can be changed by the effect of perspective distortion as shown in Fig. 3. Hence the invariant from f nearest points is not stable. In order to solve this problem, we utilize feature points in a broader local area. In Fig. 3, it is shown that 7 points of 8 nearest points are common. In general, we assume that common m points exist in n nearest neighbors under some extent of perspective distortion. Based on this assumption, we use common m points to calculate a stable feature. As shown in Fig. 4, common m points are obtained by examining all possible combinations $P_{m(0)}, P_{m(1)}, \cdots, P_{m(_nC_m-1)}$ of m points from n nearest points. As long as the assumption holds, at least one combination of m points is common. Thus a stable feature can be obtained.

Let us move to the second requirement. The simplest way of calculating the feature from m points is to set $m=f$ and calculate the cross-ratio or the affine invariant from f points. However, such a simple feature lacks the discrimination power because it is often the case that similar arrangements of f points are obtained from different feature points. In order to increase the discrimination power, we utilize feature points of a broader area. It is performed by increasing the number $m(> f)$. As m increases, probability that different feature points have similar arrangement of m points decreases. As shown in

1: **for each** $p \in \{\text{All feature points in a database image}\}$ **do**
2:     $P_n \leftarrow$ The nearest n points of p (clockwise)
3:     **for each** $P_m \in \{$ All combinations of m points from $P_n\}$ **do**
4:         **for each** $P_f \in \{$ All combinations of f points from $P_m\}$ **do**
5:             $r_{(i)} \leftarrow$ The invariant calculated with P_f
6:         **end for**
7:         $H_{\text{index}} \leftarrow$ The hash index calculated by Eq. (3).
8:         Register the item (document ID, point ID, $r_{(0)}, \cdots, r_{(_mC_f-1)}$) using H_{index}
9:     **end for**
10: **end for**

Fig. 6. Registration algorithm

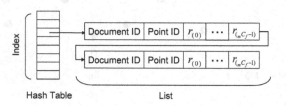

Hash Table   List

Fig. 7. Configuration of the hash table

Fig. 5, an arrangement of m points is described as a sequence of discretized invariants $(r_{(0)}, r_{(1)}, \cdots, r_{(_mC_f-1)})$ calculated from all possible combinations of f feature points taken from m feature points.

The following is the summary of calculation of features. For each feature point, its n nearest points are obtained. Then all possible $_nC_m$ combinations of m points are generated from n points. Features are defined as sequences of invariants by taking $_mC_f$ combinations from m points in a certain fixed order.

2.5 Registration

Let us turn to the registration step. Figure 6 shows the algorithm of registration of document images to the database. In this algorithm, the document ID is the identification number of a document, and the point ID is that of a point.

Next, the index H_{index} of the hash table is calculated by the following hash function:

$$H_{\text{index}} = \left(\sum_{i=0}^{_mC_f-1} r_{(i)} k^i \right) \bmod H_{\text{size}} \tag{3}$$

where $r_{(i)}$ is the discrete value of the invariant, k is the level of quantization of the invariant, and H_{size} is the size of the hash table.

The item (document ID, point ID, $r_{(0)}, \cdots, r_{(_mC_f-1)}$) is registered into the hash table as shown in Fig. 7 where chaining is employed for collision resolution.

1: **for each** $p \in$ {All feature points in a query image} **do**
2:      $P_n \leftarrow$ The nearest n points of p (clockwise)
3:      **for each** $P_m \in$ { All combinations of m points from P_n} **do**
4:          **for each** $P'_m \in$ { Cyclic permutations of P_m} **do**
5:              **for each** $P_f \in$ { All combinations of f points from P'_m} **do**
6:                  $r_{(i)} \leftarrow$ The invariant calculated with P_f
7:              **end for**
8:              $H_{\text{index}} \leftarrow$ The hash index calculated by Eq. (3).
9:              Look up the hash table using H_{index} and obtain the list.
10:             **for each** Item of the list **do**
11:                 **if** Conditions 1 to 3 are satisfied **then**
12:                     Vote for the document ID in the voting table.
13:                 **end if**
14:             **end for**
15:         **end for**
16:     **end for**
17: **end for**
18: Return the document image with the maximum votes.

Fig. 8. Retrieval algorithm

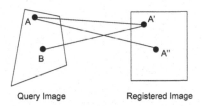

Query Image   Registered Image

Fig. 9. Incorrect correspondence

2.6   Retrieval

The retrieval algorithm is shown in Fig. 8. In LLAH, retrieval results are determined by voting on documents represented as cells in the voting table.

First, the hash index is calculated at the lines 5 to 8 in the same way as in the registration step. At the line 9, the list shown in Fig. 7 is obtained by looking up the hash table. For each item of the list, a cell of the corresponding document ID in the voting table is incremented.

However, the sequence of invariants $r_{(0)} \cdots r_{(_mC_f-1)}$ is not necessarily identical for items with the same value H_{index} of the hash function. In order to remove items with different sequences of invariants, the following condition is employed.

Condition 1: All values of $r_{(0)} \cdots r_{(_mC_f-1)}$ in the item are equal to those calculated at the lines 5 to 7 for P'_m.

If only the condition 1 is employed, we face the following two types of inconsistency shown in Fig. 9: (Type 1) A point (A) in the query image corresponds to more than one point (A' and A") in a registered image. (Type 2) A point (A') in a registered image corresponds to more than one point (A and B) in the query image. In order to avoid such inconsistent correspondences, following conditions are employed.

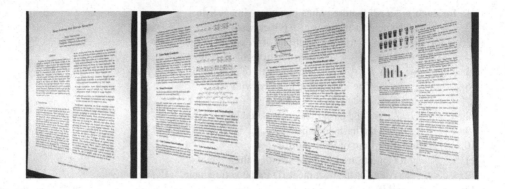

Fig. 10. Examples of query images

Fig. 11. Examples of images in database

Condition 2: It is the first time to vote for the document ID with the point p.
Condition 3: It is the first time to vote for the point ID of the document ID.

The conditions 2 and 3 are aimed at removal of types 1 and 2 inconsistency, respectively.

3   Experimental Results

3.1   Overview

In order to examine effectiveness of the affine invariant, we measured accuracy and processing time. Query images were captured from a skew angle using a digital camera CANON EOS Kiss Digital (also known as EOS-300D; 6.3 million pixels) with a lens EF-S 18-55mm USM. The size of query images is 2,048 × 3,072. The number of query images was 235 (We added 185 images to 50 images in [8]). Figure 10 shows examples of query images. As documents in the database we employed 10,000 page images converted with 200 dpi from PDF files of single- and double-column English papers collected mainly from CD-ROM proceedings. Their size is about 1,700 × 2,200. Figure 11 shows examples of images in the database. Note that the pages

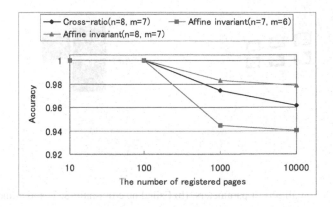

Fig. 12. Accuracy of retrieval

in the database look quite similar because most pages are from scientific papers formatted according to the same style file. Experiments were performed on a workstation with AMD Opteron 1.8GHz CPUs and 4GB memory. We used some sets of parameters n, m, k with which both high accuracy and short processing time were realized in a preliminary experiment. The value of k is set to the best with n and m. A set of parameters is described as cross-ratio(n, m) (cross-ratio with parameters n and m) or affine(n, m) (affine invariant with parameters n and m). As for the cross-ratio, parameters were set to $n = 8, m = 7, k = 18$ (cross-ratio(8, 7)). As for the affine invariant, parameters were set to $n = 7, m = 6, k = 25$ (affine(7, 6)) and $n = 8, m = 7, k = 7$ (affine(8, 7)). H_{size} was set to 1.28×10^8.

3.2 Accuracy of Retrieval

We first analyzed the relationship between the size of the database (the number of registered pages) and the accuracy of retrieval (the rate that the correct page receives the maximum votes).

Figure 12 shows the results. Both the cross-ratio and the affine invariant yielded high accuracy. The highest accuracy was obtained with affine(8, 7). Second was cross-ratio(8, 7) and third was affine(7, 6). This is due to the discrimination power of the feature. Affine(8, 7), cross-ratio(8, 7), and affine(7, 6) have $_7C_4 = 35$, $_7C_5 = 21$, and $_6C_4 = 15$ invariants in their feature, respectively. More invariants in the feature resulted in higher accuracy.

Figure 13(a) shows an examples of query images which caused a failure on retrieval. For this query image, the correct image in the database was not retrieved with cross-ratio(8, 7), affine(8, 7), and affine(7, 6). This is because this query image is covered with many figures and little text regions. Since the current feature point extraction utilizes centroids of word regions, it does not work well to such images. Figure 13(b) shows another example of erroneous cases. For this image, retrieval was failed with cross-ratio(8, 7) and affine(7, 6). However, thanks to the discrimination power of affine(8, 7), the correct image was obtained in spite of the small text regions.

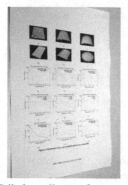

(a) Failed on all sets of parameters. (b) Failed on cross-ratio(8, 7) and affine(7, 6).

Fig. 13. Erroneous cases

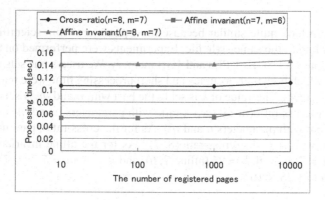

Fig. 14. The relationship among the number of registered pages and processing time

As shown in Fig. 12, the growth of the number of pages decreases the accuracy. This is because a larger database is more likely to have different pages with the same features.

3.3 Processing Time

Figure 14 shows results of experiments about processing time. Contrary to the case of accuracy, affine(7, 6) showed the highest performance. Second was the cross-ratio(8, 7) and third was affine(8, 7). We consider this was caused by the difference of computational complexity for calculating features. This figure also indicates that the increase of the number of registered pages extended processing time. We consider this was due to the increase of collision in the hash table.

3.4 Discussion

From the experimental results, it is shown that the affine invariant can be used as an invariant for the retrieval of perspectively distorted document images. This is because each part of the document images is approximately affine transformed. Therefore it is expected that the cross-ratio or the affine invariant can be used as an invariant for the retrieval of non-perspectively distorted document images if the distortion of each local area is approximated as perspective or affine transformation.

4   Related Work

LLAH can be considered to be a method of planar object recognition if registered document images are viewed as object models. There have been many methods of object recognition which utilize invariants as LLAH does. In this section, we describe similar methods and differences from them.

4.1   Geometric Hashing

In GH, all feature points of models are registered into the hash table using 2 to 4 selected points for defining a local coordinate basis. The number of points b for the basis depends on the kind of invariance: $b = 2$ for similarity, $b = 3$ for affine, and $b = 4$ for perspective transformation. Registration is performed on every possible basis. Retrieval is performed by looking up the hash table using selected bases and voting. GH is similar to the LLAH in the following points.

- invariant indexing of feature points,
- registration of an object by registering all feature points,
- utilization of the hashing and the voting techniques.

However, LLAH is superior to GH in terms of computational complexity. In LLAH, features are calculated from limited neighboring points for each feature point. Hence the computational complexity of the LLAH is $O(N)$ where N is the number of feature points in each model. On the other hand, in GH each feature point is registered using every possible basis. Hence the computational complexity of the registration process is $O(N^{b+1})$. For example, for the case of perspective transformation, the computational complexity of GH is $O(N^5)$ since four points are necessary for the basis. For example, since a document image in the database for the experiments has 630 feature points on average, use of GH requires $630^5 = 10^{14}$ times of point registration to the hash table for each registered image. Thus GH is prohibitive for retrieval with many feature points such as document images.

4.2   Other Methods

Many invariant-based object recognition methods such as [10] and [11] have so far been proposed. However, improvement of the discrimination power of the feature is not employed in these methods. For example, the feature is simply a cross-ratio of five connected line segments in [11]. It is difficult in our case to adopt such a simple indexing, because a huge number of points have similar values of the invariant. In order to avoid this problem, the arrangement of points in the broader area is employed in LLAH; this discriminative feature realizes both high accuracy and computational efficiency.

5 Conclusion

We have proposed a method of camera-based document image retrieval. The method is characterized by the ways of improving both the stability and the discrimination power of the feature defined based on the invariants. High accuracy and efficiency of LLAH were shown by the experimental results. It is also shown that the affine invariant can be used in LLAH. The affine invariant is not invariant under perspective transformation which occurs on camera captured images. However, in methods which focus on local areas such as LLAH, the affine invariant can be used as an approximated invariant. Since the affine invariant requires fewer points than the cross-ratio, its use enables us to make retrieval system adjustable: accuracy oriented or speed oriented. Future work includes experiments with partially captured images of queries and an extension of the method to object retrieval in scene images.

References

1. D. Doermann. The Indexing and Retrieval of Document Images: A Survey. *Computer Vision and Image Understanding*, **70**, 3, pages 287–298, 1998.
2. J. J. Hull. Document image matching and retrieval with multiple distortion-invariant descriptors. *Document Analysis Systems*, pages 379–396, 1995.
3. D. Doermann, H. Li and O. Kia. The detection of duplicates in document image databases. *Proc. ICDAR'97*, pages 314–318, 1997.
4. D. Doermann, J. Liang and H. Li. Progress in camera-based document image analysis. *Proc. ICDAR'03*, pages 606–616, 2003.
5. P. Clark and M. Mirmehdi. Recognising text in real scenes. *IJDAR*, **4**, pages 243–257, 2002.
6. S. Pollard and M. Pilu. Building cameras for capturing documents. *IJDAR*, **7**, pages 123–137, 2005.
7. H. J. Wolfson and I. Rigoutsos. Geometric hashing: an overview. *IEEE Computational Science & Engineering*, Vol. 4, No. 4, pages 10–21, 1997.
8. T. Nakai, K. Kise and M. Iwamura. Hashing with Local Combinations of Feature Points and Its Application to Camera-Based Document Image Retrieval. *Proc. CBDAR'05*, pages 87–94, 2005.
9. T. Suk and J. Flusser. Point-based projective invariants. *Pattern Recognition*, 33, pages 251–261, 2000.
10. B. Huet and E. R. Hancock. Cartographic indexing into a database of remotely sensed images. *WACV96*, pages 8–14, 1996.
11. C. A. Rothwell, A. Zisserman, D. A. Fosyth and J. L. Mundy. Using projective invariants for constant time library indexing in model based vision. *Proc. BMVC*, pages 62–70, 1991.

Robust Chinese Character Recognition by Selection of Binary-Based and Grayscale-Based Classifier

Yoshinobu Hotta[1], Jun Sun[2], Yutaka Katsuyama[1], and Satoshi Naoi[1]

[1] FUJITSU LABORATORIES LTD.,
4-1-1 Kamikodanaka, Nakahara-ku, Kawasaki, 211-8588 Japan
{y.hotta, katsuyama, naoi.satoshi}@jp.fujitsu.com
[2] FUJITSU R&D CENTER Co., Ltd.,
Eagle Plaza B10th floor, Xiaoyun Rd No.26, Chaoyang Dist. Beijing, 10016, P.R. China
sunjun@frdc.fujitsu.com

Abstract. As the spread of digital videos, digital cameras, and camera phones, lots of researches are reported about degraded character recognition. It is found that while the grayscale-based classifier is powerful for degraded character, the performance for clear character is not so good as binary-based classifier. In this paper, a dynamic classifier selection method is proposed to combine the two classifiers based on an estimation of the degradation level and the recognition reliability of the input character images. Experimental results show that the proposed method can achieve better recognition performance than the two individual ones.

1 Introduction

As the spread of digital videos, digital cameras, and camera phones, lot of researches about degraded character recognition are reported [1]-[5]. However, there is a problem that the recognition accuracy of degraded character classifier for characters without degradation is lower than that of conventional classifier that utilize character contour of binary images as a feature vector. Although a general recognition method for characters with degradation or without degradation has been proposed in [1], it is uncertain that the method is effective or not for uncertain fonts because numbers of tested fonts in the paper is limited. In addition, the method is effective only for collapsed characters, not for scratched characters. In general, the contrast of a camera-captured image is lower than that of scanned images and the image is influenced by vibration of a user or so. Therefore collapse or scratch may occur simultaneously when certain binarization methods are applied. Figure 1 shows a camera captured image of "営団日比谷線" and the global binarization result. Not only scratch (" 比 " and "谷"), but also collapse ("線") are caused.

In this paper, a degraded character classifier is used to deal with grayscale images in recognizing low-resolution characters to avoid the above binarization problem. Meanwhile, characters without degradation are recognized by binary-based classifier in

H. Bunke and A.L. Spitz (Eds.): DAS 2006, LNCS 3872, pp. 553–563, 2006.
© Springer-Verlag Berlin Heidelberg 2006

which contour direction of character strokes is used as the character feature (hereafter, "binary-based classifier"). To select one of these two classifiers, "degradation level" of input characters is newly defined, and each classifier is used properly based on the estimated degradation level. Some definitions of degradation are proposed [5][6] so far, but the binary image input is assumed and only single font is considered [5] or only alphabetic characters are considered [6].

Fig. 1. Camera captured string and the binarized images

In Section 2, both binary-based and grayscale-based classifiers are described. In Section 3, "degradation level" for grayscale character images is newly defined, and recognition accuracy of both classifiers according to the degradation level is shown. Selection of classifier is described in Section 4. Section 5 shows the experimental result. Finally, the conclusion is set out in Section 6.

Note that background of the characters is assumed to be uniform and input image is grayscale (0-255). Also each character is assumed to be cut out in advance.

2   Character Classifier

2.1   Grayscale-Based Character Classifier

The grayscale-based classifier for degraded character recognition is based on the degradation model [3][4]. First a binary character image is size-normalized to 32×32 pixel. Let black pixel be 1, and white pixel be 0. Next image decimating and zooming are executed to the image, thus 32×32 grayscale image is generated. Many types of degradation image can be generated by changing decimating size of the character. Algorithm of decimating is Supersampling and that of zooming is Cubic interpolation. Pixel values by raster scanned image with 1,024 dimensions are used as the character feature, x. Next, x is normalized to x' by definite canonicalization [7] in order to decrease the blurring influence. Let n be the dimension of the feature.

$$c = (1/\sqrt{n},...,1/\sqrt{n}) \tag{1}$$

$$x' = x - (c \cdot x)c \tag{2}$$

Then x' is regulated into unit length, x''. That is, $(x'',c) = 0, \| x'' \|^2 = 1$.

Feature selection by Principal Component Analysis (PCA) is first conducted to reduce computational complexity and memory cost and then similarity between the input feature and the reference feature is calculated by the subspace method. Procedures are described as follows.

[Learning phase]

1) Construction of unitary eigenspace : the unitary eigenspace is constructed in a way similar to the traditional eigenspace-based method. The mean vector of every category is used to calculate the covariance matrix of unitary eigenspace. Suppose the character image with size $N*N$ represent a vector, $x = [x_1, x_2, ..., x_{N*N}]^T$, using the raster scanning order. The covariance matrix for the unitary eigenspace is calculated as:

$$COV_{sb} = \frac{1}{P}\sum_{i=1}^{P}(m_i - m)(m_i - m)^T, \quad (3)$$

where P is the number of category. m is the mean vector for all training samples. m_i is the mean vector for the i th category. The first n eigenvectors of matrix COV_{sb} corresponding to the first n biggest eigenvalues are recorded as: $U = [u_1, u_2, ..., u_n]^T$, which spans the unitary eigenspace. Usually, the dimension of the unitary eigenspace is far lower than the dimension of original image for noise removal and data compression.

2) 1st feature extraction using the unitary eigenspace: the feature vector for the i th category is obtained by casting its mean vector to the unitary eigenspace:

$$c_i = U^T(m_i - m). \quad (4)$$

Conventional PCA based methods perform recognition in the above unitary eigenspace.

3) Individual eigenspace construction: the performance of conventional PCA method is not always satisfactory, since for many recognition tasks such as character recognition, the feature distribution for every category is not the same. Thus, an individual eigenspace is built for every category using the 1st feature of all the samples belonging to the same category. The auto-correlation matrix for the 1st feature of the i th category is:

$$W_i = \frac{1}{M_i}\sum_{j=1}^{M_i}(y_i^{(j)} - c_i)(y_i^{(j)} - c_i)^T, \quad i = 1,2,...,P \quad (5)$$

where $y_i^{(j)} = U^T(x_i^{(j)} - m)$ is the 1st feature vector of the j th training sample $x_i^{(j)}$ in the i th category, M_i is the number of training samples for the i th category. The first n_1 eigenvectors of W_i corresponding to the first n_1 eigenvalues are recorded as: $\tilde{U}_i = [u_1^i, u_2^i, ..., u_{n_1}^i]$, $i = 1,2,...,P$, which spans the individual eigenspace for the j th category.

[Recognition phase]

1) 1st feature extraction: for a testing image f, the feature in the unitary eigenspace, y, is extracted using the unitary eigenspace U as $y = U^T(f - m)$.

2) Coarse classification using 1st feature: the coarse classification is performed by comparing the similarity with the 1st feature of the mean vector of every category, c_i, $i = 1, 2, ..., P$ with the 1st feature of testing image. d candidate categories are generated as the result of coarse classification.

3) 1st feature reconstruction: reconstruct the 1st feature of image, f, using the individual eigenspace of the d categories from the coarse classification:

$$\eta_i = \tilde{U}_i^T (y - c_i), \tag{6}$$

$$\hat{y}_i = \tilde{U}_i^T \eta_i + c_i, \tag{7}$$

where η_i is the project coefficient of the 1st feature y on the i th individual eigenspace. $\hat{y}_i$ is the reconstructed feature of y.

4) Final classification using optimal reconstruction: for every of d candidate categories, the reconstruction error of the 1st feature is obtained as:

$$\varepsilon_i = \|y - \hat{y}_i\|. \tag{8}$$

The category of optimal reconstruction, that is, the minimum reconstruction error, ε, is selected as the final recognition result.

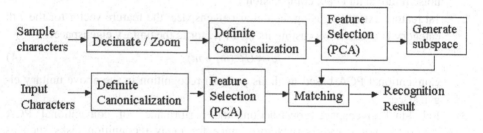

Fig. 2. Whole flow

2.2 Binary-Based Character Classifier

A conventional method is used as a binary-based character classifier. After a binary character image is inputted, size-normalization is conducted first, and contour direction of character stroke is extracted as feature vector. The feature dimension is set to 288 and the city-block distance is used in matching.

3 Degradation Level for Grayscale Image

3.1 Definition of Degradation Level

The degradation level for grayscale character images is defined here. It is difficult to calculate local information such as corner of character stroke when Chinese multifont characters are considered. Therefore, global information is used to evaluate the degradation level. The degradation level is calculated as follows.

1) Inputted grayscale character image is size-normalized to $N \times N$.
2) Definite canonicalization is conducted to the input feature and the feature is regulated into unit length.
3) The density of each pixel value is linearly transformed to 0-255.
4) Count gray pixel value (1-254) among all pixels and define degradation level as follows.

$$\text{Degradation level} = 100 \times (\text{total number of gray pixels}) / (N \times N) \qquad (9)$$

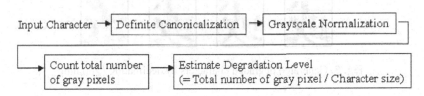

Fig. 3. Calculation flow of degradation level

A character in low quality, " 愛 ", and its density histogram are shown in Figure 4. Vertical axis of the histogram means frequency.

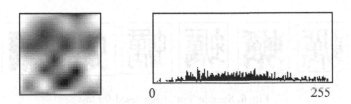

Fig. 4. A degraded character of "愛 " and its density histogram

As the degradation of a character becomes larger, the total number of grayscale pixels also increases. The degradation level here is regarded as a guidepost to evaluate the degradation. When the degradation is small, this value is almost zero regardless of fonts.

3.2 Recognition Accuracy of Each Classifier According to the Degradation Level

Experiments are conducted to investigate the relationship between the degradation level and the recognition accuracy of each classifier. When test data is inputted, recognition result and the degradation level by each classifier is recorded. After many test data are inputted, the recognition accuracy at each degradation level is calculated.

3.2.1 Learning Data
JIS first level kanji, totally 2,965 categories of 19 fonts are used as learning data. Each character image is size-normalized to 32×32 and it is decimated by 7 degrees, 8×8,

12×12 ,..., 32×32, respectively. Next, the decimated image is zoomed back to 32×32. Various fonts such as Mincho, Gothic, Round-gothic, Kaku-gothic etc. are included. The total number of characters used in learning is about 390,000 characters (=2,965×19×7). Figure 5 shows the example of generated degraded characters. The left end shows the image without degradation and the right end shows the image that is decimated to 8×8 and zoomed back to 32×32. On the other hand, the binary-based classifier is trained by clear character images only.

Fig. 5. Generated degraded characters by decimating / zooming

3.2.2 Test Data
JIS first level kanji of 6 fonts, which are different from those of learning data, are used as test data. 7 degrees of degraded images are generated as well. Various fonts such as Gona, Middle-Gothic, etc. are included. The total number of characters is about 120,000 (=2,965×6×7). Figure 6 shows 6 fonts images without degradation.

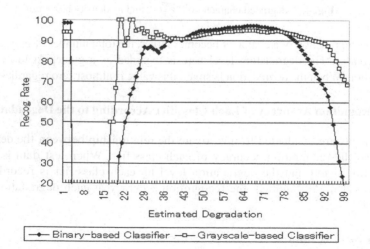

Fig. 6. Sample font images used for test

Fig. 7. Recognition accuracy of each classifier according to the degradation level

3.2.3 Experimental Result

Figure 7 shows the recognition accuracy of each classifier according to the degradation level. Horizontal axis means estimated degradation level and vertical axis means its recognition rate. When degradation level is very low (0-3), the recognition rate of binary-based classifier is higher than that of grayscale-based classifier. As for the level from 4 to 16, there is no character with this degradation. When the level is low (17-36), recognition rate of grayscale classifier is higher, but almost all cases are caused by simple shape characters such as " —", and these are special cases. The total number of characters with middle degradation level (37-78) is a lot, and recognition rate of binary-based classifier is higher at these levels. As the degradation level increases, the recognition rate of the binary-based classifier drops dramatically, whereas that of grayscale-based classifier is relatively stable.

Table 1. Overall recognition rate for the entire test dataset

	Recognition rate (%)
Binary-based classifier	85.1
Grayscale-based classifier	91.2

3.3 Reliability Distribution of Each Classifier According to Degradation Level

3.3.1 Experimental Data

Learning data are the same data as that in 3.2.1. The reliability distribution is examined by using part of the same data as that of 3.2.2, the data without degradation and the data with maximum degradation. The total number of characters for one set of data is 17,790 (=2,965×6). Hereafter, level0 shows the data without degradation and level6 shows the data with maximum degradation. Let the recognition distance of 1st candidate be $d1$, and that of 2nd candidate be $d2$, and reciprocals of them are $r1$, $r2$, respectively. We define recognition reliability, r, as $r = r1/(r1+r2)$.

3.3.2 Reliability Distribution of Binary-Based Classifier

In Figure 8-11, horizontal axis means standardized reliability of r and vertical axis means frequency. Black curve means the frequency of correctly recognized characters and white curve means that of misrecognized characters. In Figure 8, the distribution peaks of two graphs are apart whereas those in Figure 9 almost overlap. From these figures, it can be said that the recognition reliability of the binary-based classifier for degraded characters is unreliable.

3.3.3 Reliability Distribution of Grayscale-Based Classifier

Compared with above figures, the distribution peaks of correctly recognized data and misrecognized data (Figure 11) for level6 data are separated. It can be said that recognition reliability of the grayscale-based classifier for degraded characters is more reliable.

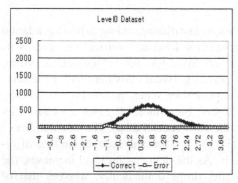

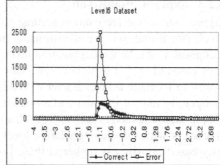

Fig. 8. Reliability distribution of level0 data   **Fig. 9.** Reliability distribution of level6 data

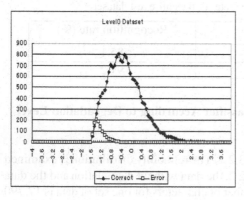

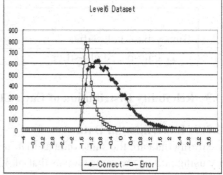

Fig. 10. Reliability distribution of level0 data   **Fig. 11.** Reliability distribution of level6 data

4   Selection of Classifier

Lots of researches about classifier combination are reported, in which recognition results or recognition reliabilities of multiple classifiers are used. But from the point of time complexity, it is desirable that fewer classifiers are used. Also recognition reliabilities are unreliable when degradation is large. Therefore we adopt the classifier selection method based on the degradation level of input characters in combining classifiers (Figure 12). First the degradation level of input character is estimated as described in 3.1. If the degradation level is larger than predetermined threshold (*Th1*), then grayscale-based classifier is used. And binary-based classifier is used for the characters with low/middle level degradation. But binary-based classifier sometimes misrecognizes simple-shaped characters shown in Figure 7, therefore grayscale-based classifier is used when the recognition reliability of binary-based classifier is lower than the predetermined threshold (*Th2*). Threshold of degradation level and recognition reliability is determined by the steepest descent method. *Th1* and *Th2* are set to 82 and -0.7, respectively.

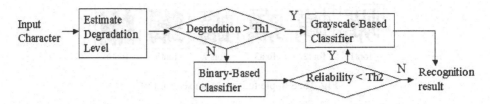

Fig. 12. Selection of binary-based and grayscale-based classifier

5 Experiment

Learning data for each classifier is the same as that used in 3.2.1. Also the data in 3.2.2 are used as learning data for deciding the threshold of degradation level and recognition reliability. 6 fonts data are used as test data that are different from those in 3.2.1 or 3.2.2 (Figure 15). Seven degrees of degradation images are generated in the same way as 3.2.1 or 3.2.2. The total number of characters is about 120,000.

Table 2 shows the comparison of recognition accuracy. Figure 13-14 shows the recognition accuracy according to degradation level. As for learning data, recognition rate of the proposed method is higher than other classifiers at almost all the degradation levels (Figure 13). As for test data, the recognition rate of the proposed method is

Table 2. Comparison of recognition accuracy

	Recog. rate (learning data)	Recog. rate (test data)
Binary-based	85.1%	83.5%
Grayscale-based	91.2%	92.1%
Proposed	93.6%	92.9%

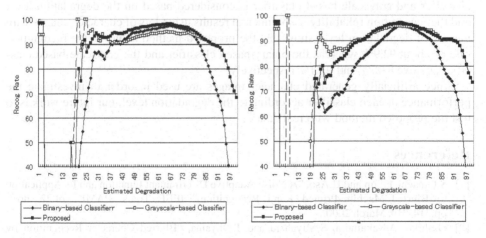

Fig. 13. Recognition accuracy of learning data   **Fig. 14.** Recognition accuracy of test data

font1   font2   font3   font4   font5   font6

Fig. 15. Sample font images used for test

Table 3. Comparison of recognition accuracy for test data at each font

	Font1	Font2	Font3	Font4	Font5	Font6
Binary-based	84.0%	88.9%	90.2%	88.6%	85.6%	63.6%
Grayscale-based	90.0%	95.1%	95.5%	94.3%	92.3%	85.5%
Proposed	92.6%	96.2%	96.2%	95.3%	93.1%	83.4%

higher only when the degradation level is at the middle levels (around 67). Even so, the total number of characters at middle level is too much, thus recognition accuracy of proposed method for entire data is highest. Table 3 shows the comparison of recognition accuracy for test data at each font. The proposed method is effective for many fonts except a very thick font (font6). Even when the degradation is low, the recognition reliability of binary-based classifier seems to be unreliable for a very thick font.

6   Conclusion

In this paper, the degradation level for grayscale character image is newly defined and the binary-based classifier that uses character contour feature and the grayscale-based classifier that uses pixel value of images as a feature are investigated according to the degradation level. It is found that recognition result or reliability of binary-based classifier is not reliable when input character is degraded, thus selection of binary-based classifier and grayscale-based classifier is considered based on the degradation level and the recognition reliability. Experimental results using lots of character images with variety of degradation level show that the proposed method achieves the recognition rate of about 92.9% whereas the binary-based classifier and the grayscale-based classifier achieve 83.5% and 92.1% respectively.

Since artificially generated character images are used in order to investigate the performance of each classifier according to the degradation level, our future work is to test the proposed method with real data.

References

[1] S.Omachi, F.Sun and H.Aso, "A Noise-Adaptive Discriminant Function and Its Application to Blurred Machine-Printed Kanji Recognition," IEEE Trans. PAMI, vol.22, no.3, pp.314-319, March 2000.
[2] O.Shiku, A.Nakamura, S.Miyahara and T.Ohyama, "Blurred Character Recognition by Complementing Features of Blurred Regions," IEICE D-II, Vol.J87-D-II, No.3, pp.808-817, 2004 (in Japanese).

[3] H.Ishida, S.Yanadume, T.Takahashi, I.Ide, Y.Mekada and H.Murase," Recognition of Low-Resolution Characters by a Generative Learning Method," Proc. of the 1st Int'l Workshop on Camera-Based Document Analysis and Recognition (CBDAR2005), pp.45-51, 2005.

[4] J.Sun, Y.Hotta, Y.Katsuyama and S.Naoi, "Low Resolution Character Recognition by Dual Eigenspace and Synthetic Degraded Patterns," Proc. of the 1st ACM Workshop on Hardcopy Document Processing, pp.15-22, 2004.

[5] M.Sawaki, H.Murase and N.Hagita,"Character Recognition in Bookshelf Images by Automatic Template Selection," Proc. of ICPR '98, Vol. 2, pp.1117-1120.

[6] H.S.Yam and E.H.B.Smith, "Estimating Degradation Model Parameters from Character Images," Proc. of Seventh ICDAR, pp.710-714, 2003.

[7] T.Iijima, "Theory of Pattern Recognition," Series of basic information technology 6, *Morikita Publishing Company Ltd*, 1989.

Segmentation-Driven Recognition Applied to Numerical Field Extraction from Handwritten Incoming Mail Documents

Clément Chatelain, Laurent Heutte, and Thierry Paquet

Laboratoire PSI, CNRS FRE 2645, Université de Rouen,
76800 Saint Etienne du Rouvray, France
clement.chatelain@univ-rouen.fr

Abstract. In this paper, we present a method for the automatic extraction of numerical fields (ZIP codes, phone numbers, etc.) from incoming mail documents. The approach is based on a segmentation-driven recognition that aims at locating isolated and touching digits among the textual information. A syntactical analysis is then performed on each line of text in order to filter the sequences that respect a particular syntax (number of digits, presence of separators) known by the system. We evaluate the performance of our system by means of the recall precision trade-off on a real incoming mail document database.

1 Introduction

Today, firms are faced with the problem of processing incoming mail documents: mail reception, envelope opening, document type recognition (form, invoice, letter, ...), mail object identification (address change, complaint, termination, ...), dispatching towards the competent service and finally mail processing. Whereas part of the overall process can be fully automated (envelope opening with specific equipment, mail scanning for easy dispatching, printed form automatic reading), a large amount of handwritten documents cannot be yet automatically processed. Indeed, no system is currently able to read automatically a whole page of cursive handwriting without any *a priori* knowledge. This is due to the extreme complexity of the task when dealing with free layout documents, unconstrained cursive handwriting, and unknown textual content of the document. Nevertheless, it is now possible to consider restricted applications of handwritten text processing which may correspond to a real industrial need. The extraction of numerical data (file number, customer reference, phone number, ZIP code in an address, ...) in a handwritten document whose content is expected (incoming mail document, see figure 1) is one particular example of such a realistic problem.

This paper presents a method for automatically extracting numerical fields from incoming mail documents in order to provide information about the sender: a phone number may be used to identify the customer, the ZIP code his location, the customer code is used to dispatch the document to the competent service,

H. Bunke and A.L. Spitz (Eds.): DAS 2006, LNCS 3872, pp. 564–575, 2006.

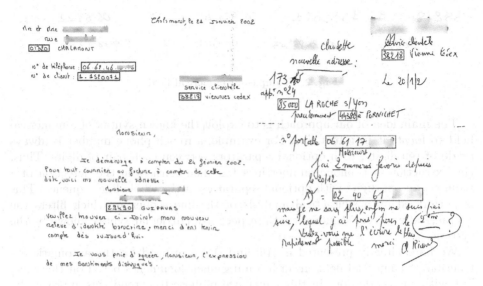

Fig. 1. Incoming mail document examples

etc. Our method is based on a syntactical analysis of the lines of text, to decide whether a numerical field is present or not. For that, a segmentation-driven recognition is performed on each component of the line, in order to locate the isolated and touching digits. The result of this recognition feeds a syntactical analyser that finds the best label sequence of each line of text, using the known syntax of the numerical field we want to detect (number of digits, presence of separator).

This paper is thus organized as follows. In section 2 we present an overview of the proposed system with a brief description of each processing stage. Section 3 presents the segmentation-driven recognition system. We present in section 4 our experimental results on a database of real handwritten incoming mail documents. Conclusion and future works are drawn in section 5.

2   Overview of the Proposed System

We aim at localizing and recognizing numerical sequences such as ZIP codes, customer codes, phone numbers, etc. in unconstrained handwritten documents (see figure 1). It is a very challenging problem since we do not have any *a priori* knowledge about the documents that could help us to locate the fields: the numerical fields may be situated either in the header or in the body of the text. Hence, methods such as those used for example to locate a ZIP code in a handwritten adress [7, 9] do not suit our problem because they are based on strong *a priori* knowledge. Furthermore, numerical fields have no linguistic constraints: any digit can follow an other (see figure 2). Thus, our approach cannot be lexicon-directed as in many classical word recognition systems [8].

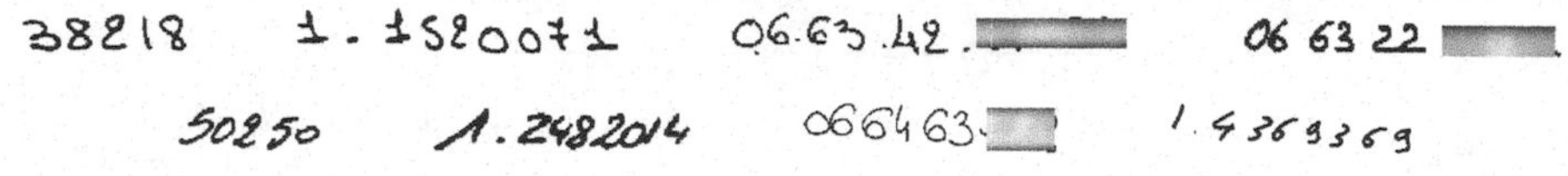

566   C. Chatelain, L. Heutte, and T. Paquet

Fig. 2. Examples of numerical fields

The main idea of our approach is to exploit the known syntax of a numerical field to locate it in a text line. For example, a french phone number is always made of ten digits, with optional separators between each pair of digits. Thus, the extraction of a phone number in a text line consists in the detection of a sequence of ten digits with optional separators in the whole line sequence. This is performed by a syntactical analysis of the line sequence, which filters the syntactically correct sequences with respect to a particular syntax known by the system.

We have already presented in [16] and [15] a method for the automatic extraction of numerical fields from incoming mail documents based on this idea, but without recognition. In this paper, we propose to extend this approach by means of a segmentation-driven recognition, in order to extract and to recognize simultaneously the numerical fields from the documents.

Let us recall the principles of this approach (see figure 3). A line model is defined, which provides the syntactical constraints of a text line that may contain a numerical field. The model is composed of states describing the patterns that can occur in a text line: patterns that belong to a numerical field (digit, separator) or not (reject: word, fragment of word, etc.). Through a classification stage, we align the models on the text lines to filter the syntactically correct sequences. This implies that we need a classification system able to discriminate the components that belong to a numerical field (isolated and touching digits, separators) from the others (Reject).

| Handwritten Document | → | Line segmentation | → | Classification | → | Syntactical analysis | → | location and recognition of numerical fields |

Fig. 3. Overview of the proposed system

The state definition and the classification system are the main differences between our previous approach and the one presented in this paper.

In the previous approach, we made the choice to avoid a segmentation task, and thus to directly classify the connected components with a restricted number of classes: "digit", "double digit", "separator" or "reject", without trying to determine the numerical value of the digit and the double digit components. The numeral classification was performed in a second time, once the fields were extracted. Although this approach had the benefit to be fast, the classification task was difficult, principally due to the heterogeneity of the reject class, and in a lesser degree to the low inter-class variability between the digit and double digit classes. Moreover, the system was unable to detect the fields that contain touching digits composed with more than two digits.

In the present approach, we propose to overcome these problems and to perform simultaneously the localisation and the recognition of the numerical sequences by applying a segmentation-driven recognition on each connected component. We process all the connected components of the document by considering them successively as an isolated, a double, or a triple digit, with a segmentation method and a strictly numeral classifier. Once the numeral recognition is performed, a reject class confidence value is estimated according to the digit classifier outputs to avoid the consideration of a reject class. The separator confidence value is estimated thanks to a small specific classifier. Hence the segmentation-driven recognition outputs a 3-level recognition hypothesis for each component, which are concatened to produce a trellis over all the line.

While performing a segmentation-driven recognition, the syntactical analysis has to find the best path in a 3-level trellis, whereas only one level was considered in the previous approach. The exploration of the trellis is performed by dynamic programming [2]. Figure 4 presents the models for a line which can contain a ZIP code, a customer code or a phone number, where arrows represent authorized transitions between states. Note that while in most cases a text line does not contain any numerical field, the model allows the line to be exclusively composed of reject patterns (i.e. does not include digits).

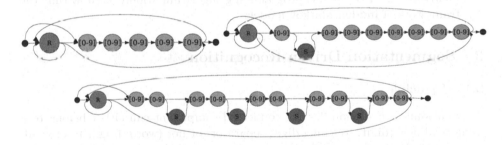

Fig. 4. Models for a line containing a ZIP code, a customer code and a phone number

Hence the three stages of our approach are the following ones (figure 3):

- **Line segmentation:** the connected components are extracted from the document and grouped into lines, according to a classical method [5]. The handwritten document is thus converted into sequences of connected components (see figure 5, and [16] for more details).
- **Segmentation-driven recognition:** during this stage, we search for numeral patterns. Numerical fields are mainly composed of isolated digits and separator components, but may also contain touching digits components (figure 2), which are hard to detect due to their high variability in size and shape. In this paper, we consider a segmentation-based strategy. Each connected component is submitted to a segmentation-driven recognition stage

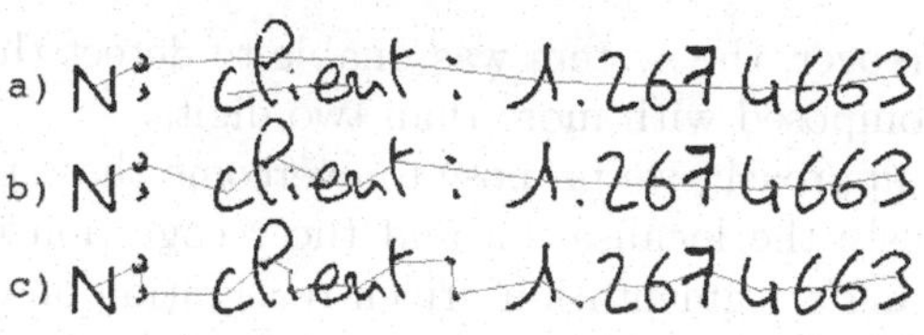

a) N° client : 1.2674663
b) N° client : 1.2674663
c) N° client : 1.2674663

Fig. 5. The three steps for the line segmentation process: a) the big components are grouped together according to a distance criterion, b) alignments which are too close are merged, c) isolated components are grouped with the closest line

which recognize successively the component as an isolated digit, a double or a triple touching digit component. For that, we use a digit classifier with outlier rejection properties, able to output low confidence values when an outlier is encountered. The segmentation-driven recognition module thus outputs a trellis of recognition hypotheses. This stage is detailed in section 3.

– **Syntactical analysis:** this last stage filters the syntactically correct sequences with respect to a particular syntax known by the system, and searches among these sequences the best one according to the confidence values of the recognition hypotheses. Thus, a global decision is taken over the entire line and proposes a set of best paths which can contain or not a numerical field. The best path retrieval is achieved by the famous *forward algorithm* [2], a dynamic programming algorithm widely used within the framework of hidden Markov models.

3   Segmentation Driven Recognition

3.1   Principle

As mentionned in section 2, each connected component can either belong to a numerical field (digit, touching digit, separator) or not (word, fragment of word, noise, etc.). In this latter case, the precise nature of the component is unnecessary, and all these components should be considered as "reject". The classification problem is thus reduced to the discrimination of isolated digits, touching digits and separators from the remaining components (reject). We propose a two-stage recognition method for the component recognition.

First, a segmentation-driven recognition is performed in order to identify the numeral components: isolated or touching digit. Rather than considering a reject class in the classification problem, which is contraindicated due to the extrem heterogeneity of these patterns [12], we propose to design a classifier focused on the numerals. Hence, we avoid the difficult modelisation of a reject class. Thus, thanks to a 10-class digit classifier and a segmentation method, we investigate each connected component successively as being an isolated, a double or a triple digit (see figure 6). Note that touching digit may contain more than three digits, but they are extremely rare, and thus not considered in our work. Thus, the segmentation-driven recognition provides hypotheses of digit classes on 3 levels.

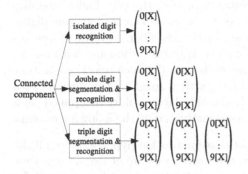

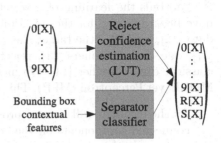

Fig. 6. Recognition of the components: Connected components are recognized as an isolated digit, a double or a triple digit. 'X' denotes a confidence value output by the digit classifier.

Fig. 7. In a second stage, reject and separator confidence values are estimated according respectively to the digit classifier outputs and a specific separator classifier

The second stage of the component recognition system is dedicated to the reject and separator identification among the digit recognition trellis. Indeed, as we do not consider reject and separator classes, the confidence values must be estimated during post processing identification stage. For that, we re-estimate the confidence values of each recognition hypothesis in the trellis by adding a reject and a separator confidence value (see figure 7). The reject confidence value is estimated with respect to the digit classifier confidence values, while the separator confidence value is estimated according to a specific classifier. One can see that we need a digit classifier whose confidence values are exploitable, i.e. these values must be high enough when an isolated digit is submitted, and low otherwise.

We now describe the components of the segmentation-driven recognition: the numeral classifier, the touching digit recognition method using a segmentation method, and the reject and separator confidence estimation procedure.

3.2   Handwritten Numeral Classifier

Usually, a good discrimination between the digit classes is the main criterion to design a handwritten digit classifier. This is due to the fact that the digit classifiers are mostly designed for the recognition of restricted and strictly numerical field (ZIP codes, amount on bankcheck, numerical field extracted from forms, etc.). In our case, the problem is rather different because the digit classifier is requested on each connected component of the whole page of handwriting. Thus, the digit classifier has to perform both:

- A discrimination task: when a digit is encountered, the classifier must be able to output the right digit class with a high confidence value.
- A detection task: as the digits to identify only represent a very small part of the documents, the classifier must have a strong outlier rejection ability in order to reject all the other connected components.

This second task is by far the most difficult: indeed, the very high variability of the outlier patterns (words, fragments of word, noise, stroke, touching digits, etc.) forbids the learning of a reject class for the classifier. Several techniques have been designed for the rejection of outlier: training a classifier with outlier data [12], modeling the target classes and perform a distance rejection strategy [17], one class classifiers [11], reject outliers with respect to the outputs of a classical digit classifier [14]. We have chosen this latter solution, applied on a MultiLayer Perceptron (MLP). This choice is motivated by the following reasons:

- As the classifier will have to process the segmentation hypothesis for all the connected components on the entire document, we cannot use a large time consuming classifier during the decision stage (this constraint prohibits for example multiclass SVM). An MLP well suits this condition because it is one of the fastest classifier during the decision stage.
- If the use of model-based classifiers (RBF, one class classifier, etc.) allows a distance-based rejection strategy, these classifiers provide generally quite poor results in discrimination, whereas MLPs perform very good results, especially in high dimensional spaces [3, 13].

We have thus designed a MLP trained on 130,000 digits, with a structural/ statistical feature set. This feature set developped in our previous work [10], is made of 117 features and has been shown to achieve an efficient and robust discrimination of handwritten characters such as digits, uppercase letters or even graphemes.

In order to evaluate the capacity of our classifier to reject ouliers, we have built a database with both digits and outliers patterns. We consider the Receiver-Operating Characteristic (ROC) curve [6] which is a graphical representation

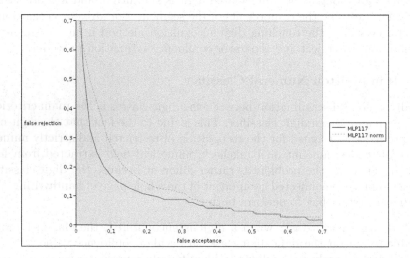

Fig. 8. ROC Curve for the MLP before and after the softmax function that scales MLP outputs into *a posteriori* probabilities

of the trade-off between the false negative (digit rejection) and false positive (outlier acceptation) rates for every possible cut off (confidence value of the first proposition of the MLP). Figure 8 shows the ROC curve for the MLP before and after the softmax function [1] that scales MLP outputs to *a posteriori* probabilities by means of a normalised exponential.

The resulting trade-off is slightly better before the softmax function, thus one can conclude that the analysis of the confidence values must be performed before the softmax function. On a test base of 33,000 digits, the classifier has a recognition rate of 97.78%, 99.20% and 99.60% (without rejection) respectively in TOP 1,2,3.

3.3 Touching Digit Recognition

The aim of this module is to find the best segmentation hypothesis when a double or a triple digit is submitted to the recognizer. For that, a descending segmentation-driven recognition is performed:

First, we make the hypothesis that we have to deal with a double digit connected component. In this case, the component is segmented in two parts according to a set of segmentation paths. These resulting digits are submitted to

Drop fall	ascending left	ascending right	descending left	descending right
cutting path				
digit classifier output	0[98] 8[82]	2[27] 8[35]	0[73] 8[36]	0[92] 8[34]
confidence product	81	09	26	32

Fig. 9. Double digit recognition: several cutting paths are generated and are submitted to a digit classifier. The path who maximizes the confidence product is retained (in this example, the first path).

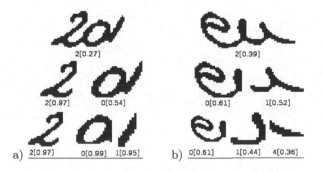

a)   b)

Fig. 10. Each component is recognized with a segmentation-driven recognition strategy as an isolated, double or triple digit. This provides a 3-level recognition trellis. Here, the recognition results are presented on a triple digits(a) and a fragment of word (reject)(b). The confidence values are lower for the reject components.

the digit recognizer, and the path which maximizes the product of confidence values is retained (see figure 9). Among these two digits, the one that has the lowest confidence value is regarded again as a double digit and is segmented in two parts according to the same principles of segmentation. Thus, we obtain for each component a 3-level recognition trellis (figure 10).

The segmentation paths are generated by the "drop fall" segmentation algorithm [4], which simulates the path of an acid drop falling from above the character and sliding along the contour. When the drop falls in a valley, it cuts the character and continues its path. This algorithm provides four possible paths, depending on the drop movement rules (left or right) and orientation (ascending or descending).

3.4   Reject and Separator Confidence Estimation

We need to estimate the probabilities for each pattern in the trellis to be a reject and a separator. The 10 digit classes recognition hypothesis are then converted in twelve classes: 10 numeral + Reject + Separator, each one associated to a confidence value (see figure 6). Once the two confidence values are estimated, the softmax function is applied on the twelve classes to approximate *a posteriori* probabilities [1].

The probabilities of reject and separator classes are estimated as follows:

Reject Confidence Value Estimation: the confidence value for the reject class is estimated with a Look Up Table (LUT) according to the confidence value of the first proposition of the digit recognizer. The LUT has been generated by considering the behaviour of the digit classifier on a database of 2300 digits and 4000 outliers. Statistics on the confidence value of the first proposition provides the LUT shown in figure 11.

Separator Confidence Value Estimation: the confidence value for the separator class is estimated by a small specific 2-class MLP classifier. This classifier

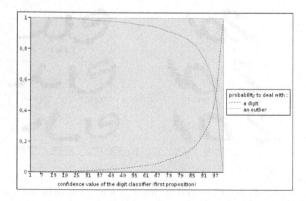

Fig. 11. Look up table for the reject confidence value. This LUT outputs the probability to deal with an outlier for a given digit confidence value.

have been trained on a database composed of separators and outliers (digits, word, fragment of word, noise), with a 9-contextual feature set described in [15]. The recognition rate is 96% (without rejection). As separators are always isolated and are usually small components, we assume that the second and third levels of the trellis cannot be a separator. Therefore, the confidence value of the separator class is directly used for the first level hypothesis of the trellis.

4 Results

The syntactical analysis is performed on each line of the documents, searching in the line trellis (see figure 12) the best path according to the syntactical constraints of the models defined on figure 4.

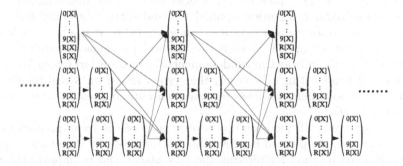

Fig. 12. Line trellis obtained by concatenation of the components trellis

We have evaluated our approach on a database of 293 handwritten incoming mail documents containing ZIP codes, phone numbers and customer codes. The syntactical analysis of the text lines is performed successively according to the three syntax models. A field is considered as "well recognized" if and only if all the components that belong to this field and only these ones have been labelled as the right numeral value of the field.

Let us recall that our method aims at extracting numerical fields for handwritten documents. Therefore, the best mean to analyse the performance of our system is the trade-off between recall and precision rates. The recall and precision rates are defined as:

recall = nb of fields well recognized / nb of fields to extract
precision = nb of fields well recognized / nb of fields proposed by the system

As the forward algorithm provides the n best alignment paths, a field well detected in "TOP n" means that the right recognition hypothesis for a field stands in the n best propositions of the syntactical analyser. It is obvious that the larger n, the more the recall increases, and the more the precision decreases. Table 1 shows the recall-precision trade-off for different values of n.

One can remark that our method is able to locate and recognize nearly 50% of the numerical fields from a document, with a precision of 20%. While increasing n,

Table 1. Recall and precision for the system when considering the n best paths

	TOP1	TOP2	TOP3	TOP4	TOP5
recall	0.49	0.53	0.56	0.59	0.60
precision	0.21	0.12	0.08	0.06	0.05

the system reaches a recall of 60% with a poor precision of 5%. Note that in an industrial application, the system could benefit from a customer database containing the researched fields and then would be able to filter the false alarms.

5   Conclusion and Future Works

In this article, we have presented a syntax directed method coupled with a segmentation-driven recognition applied to handwritten incoming mail documents, in order to locate and recognize numerical fields. It is a very challenging problem because we are faced with the classical problems encountered when dealing with totally unconstrained documents (lack of a priori information, high variability of handwriting). However, the system tested on a real handwritten incoming mail document database has given encouraging results as we obtain a recall of near 50%.

Our future work will focus on the improvement of the recall-precision trade-off. In particular, we plan to improve the precision rate by designing a specific field verification method for filtering the false alarm, and to improve the recall rate by combining our previous approach (without segmentation [15]) with the one presented in this paper.

References

1. BRIDLE, J. S. " Probabilistic interpretation of feedforward classification network outputs, with relationships to statistical pattern recognition ". In Neurocomputing: Algorithms, Architectures and Applications, F. F. Soulie and J. Herault, Eds., NATO ASI. 1990, pp. 227-236.
2. RABINER, L. R. " A tutorial on hidden markov models and selected apllications in speech recognition ". In Readings in Speech Recognition. Kaufmann, 1990, pp. 267-296.
3. BISHOP, C.M., Neural Networks for Pattern Recognition. Oxford University Press, 1995.
4. CONGEDO, G., G. DIMAURO, S. IMPEDOVO and G. PIRLO, " Segmentation of numeric strings ", ICDAR'95, vol. 2, 1995, pp. 1038-1041.
5. LIKFORMAN-SULEM, L. and C. FAURE, "Une méthode de résolution des con its d'alignements pour la segmentation des documents manuscrits ", Traitement du signal, vol. 12, 1995, pp. 541-549.
6. BRADLEY, A.P., " The use of the area under the roc curve in the evaluation of machine learning algorithms ", Pattern Recognition, vol. 30, 1997, pp. 1145-1159.
7. DZUBA, Gregory, Alexander FILATOV and Alexander VOLGUNIN. " Handwritten zip code recognition. " . In ICDAR (1997), pp. 766-770.

8. KIM, G. and V. GOVINDARAJU, " A lexicon driven approach to handwritten word recognition for real-time applications ", IEEE Trans. on PAMI, vol. 19, no. 4, 1997, pp. 366-378.
9. SRIHARI, S.N. and E.J. KEUBERT, " Integration of handwritten address interpretation technology into the united states postal service remote computer reader system ", ICDAR'97, 1997, pp. 892-896.
10. HEUTTE, L., T. PAQUET, J.V. MOREAU, Y. LECOURTIER and C. OLIVIER, " A structural/statistical feature based vector for handwritten character recognition ", Pattern Recognition Letters, vol. 19, 1998, pp. 629-641.
11. TAX, D.M.J. and ROBERT P. W. DUIN. " Combining one-class classifiers". In MCS '01 (London, UK, 2001), Springer-Verlag, pp. 299-308.
12. LIU, C.L., K. NAKASHIMA, H. SAKO and H. FUJISAWA, " Handwritten digit recognition using state-of-the-art techniques", IWFHR, 2002, pp. 320-325.
13. LIU, J. and P. GADER, " Neural networks with enhanced outlier rejection ability for off-line handwritten word recognition pattern recognition", Pattern Recognition, vol. 35, 2002, pp. 2061-2071.
14. PITRELLI, J.F. and M.P. PERRONE, " Confidence-scoring post-processing for off-line handwritten-character recognition verification", ICDAR'03, vol. 1, 2003, pp. 278-282.
15. CHATELAIN, C., L. HEUTTE and T. PAQUET, " A syntax-directed method for numerical field extraction using classifier combination ", 9th International Workshop on Frontiers in Handwriting Recognition, Tokyo, Japan, 2004, pp. 93-98.
16. KOCH, G., L. HEUTTE and T. PAQUET, " Numerical sequence extraction in handwritten incoming mail documents ", ICDAR, vol. 1, 2004, pp. 369-373.
17. MILGRAM, J., R. SABOURIN and M. CHERIET, " An hybrid classification system which combines model-based and discriminative approaches ", 17th Conference on Pattern Recognition (ICPR2004), Cambridge, U.K., 2004, pp. 155-162.

Performance Evaluation of Text Detection and Tracking in Video

Vasant Manohar[1], Padmanabhan Soundararajan[1], Matthew Boonstra[1], Harish Raju[2], Dmitry Goldgof[1], Rangachar Kasturi[1], and John Garofolo[3]

[1] University of South Florida, Tampa, FL
{vmanohar, psoundar, boonstra, goldgof, r1k}@cse.usf.edu
[2] Advanced Interfaces Inc., State College, PA
hraju@advancedinterfaces.com
[3] National Institute of Standards and Technology, Gaithersburg, MD
john.garofolo@nist.gov

Abstract. Text detection and tracking is an important step in a video content analysis system as it brings important semantic clues which is a vital supplemental source of index information. While there has been a significant amount of research done on video text detection and tracking, there are very few works on performance evaluation of such systems. Evaluations of this nature have not been attempted because of the extensive effort required to establish a reliable ground truth even for a moderate video dataset. However, such ventures are gaining importance now.

In this paper, we propose a generic method for evaluation of object detection and tracking systems in video domains where ground truth objects can be bounded by simple geometric shapes (polygons, ellipses). Two comprehensive measures, one each for detection and tracking, are proposed and substantiated to capture different aspects of the task in a single score. We choose text detection and tracking tasks to show the effectiveness of our evaluation framework. Results are presented from evaluations of existing algorithms using real world data and the metrics are shown to be effective in measuring the total accuracy of these detection and tracking algorithms.

1 Introduction

Text embedded in video frames often carries important information such as time, place, name, topics and other relevant information. These semantic cues can be used in video indexing and video content understanding. To extract textual information from video, which is often referred to as *Video Optical Character Recognition*, the first essential step is to detect and track the text region in the video sequence. There have been several published efforts addressing the problem of text area detection in video [1]. Performance metrics assume significance in the presence of such numerous systems with high claims on accuracy and robustness.

Empirical evaluation is highly challenging, due to the fundamental difficulty in establishing a valid "ground truth" or "gold standard". This is the process of establishing the "ideal output" for what *exactly* the algorithm is expected to generate. The secondary challenge with quantitative validation is assessing the relative

H. Bunke and A.L. Spitz (Eds.): DAS 2006, LNCS 3872, pp. 576–587, 2006.
© Springer-Verlag Berlin Heidelberg 2006

importance of different types of errors. In this work, we adopt a comprehensive evaluation framework that carefully examines and finds solutions to each of these factors.

Earlier works on empirical evaluation of object detection and tracking [2–8], either present a single measure that concentrates on a particular aspect of the task or a suite of measures that look at different aspects. While the former approach cannot capture the performance of the system in its entirety, the latter results in a multitude of scores which makes it difficult to make a relative comparison between any two systems.

Similarly, while evaluating tracking systems, earlier approaches either concentrate on the spatial aspect of the task, i.e., assess correctness in terms of number of trackers and locations in frames [5, 7] or the temporal aspect which emphasizes on maintaining a consistent identity over long periods of time [3]. In the very recent works of [4, 8], a spatio-temporal approach towards the evaluation of tracking systems is adopted. However, these approaches do not provide the flexibility to adapt the relative importance of each of these individual aspects. Finally, majority of these undertakings make little effort in actually comparing the performance of existing algorithms on real world applications using their proposed measures.

In this paper, we apply two comprehensive measures that we have used in our evaluations of computer vision algorithms for face detection and tracking in boardroom meetings videos [9]. While the detection measure looks just at the spatial aspect, we approach with a spatio-temporal concept for the tracking measure. By adopting a thresholded approach to evaluation (See Secs 3.1 and 3.2), the relative significance of the individual aspects of the task can be modified. In the end, text detection and tracking is picked as a prototype task for evaluation and select algorithm performances are evaluated on a reasonable corpus.

The remainder of the paper is organized in the following manner. Section 2 briefs the ground truth annotation process which as explained earlier is a vital part of any evaluation. Section 3 briefs the detection and tracking metrics deployed in this evaluation. Section 4 explains the one-to-one mapping which is integral to this evaluation. Section 5.1 details the experimental results describing the behavior of the measures for different types of detection and tracking errors. Section 5.2 discusses and evaluates the results of three text detection algorithms and a tracking algorithm on a data set containing video clips from broadcast news segments. We conclude and summarize the findings in Section 6.

2   Ground Truth Annotations

Having a consistent and reliable ground truth is imperative to carrying out a scientific evaluation. There are many different ways to create a reference annotation for evaluation purposes. Domain characteristics such as spatial resolution of objects, temporal persistence of objects, object movement in the video and scene transitions decide the way annotation is carried out so that the marking is consistent and reliable. Also, in selecting a specific annotation approach, one has to keep in mind that object detection and tracking is essentially a lower level task in a video understanding system, the output of which is passed on to a higher level system which extracts semantic meaning from it. For instance, the result of a text detection and tracking system is often used by an *OCR* system that pulls out textual information producing indexible keywords. Thus, the objective of performance evaluation is to identify a system that best generates an output which can be fed to any reasonable OCR system to obtain satisfying recognition results. To achieve this, the reference annotations should be such an ideal output.

In this paper, the method used for ground truthing is one in which text regions are bounded by a rectangular box with features of the region used as guides for marking the limits of the edges. If the features are occluded, which is often the case, the markings are approximated. Unique IDs are assigned to individual text objects and are consistently maintained over subsequent frames.

There are many free and commercially available tools which can be used for ground truthing videos such as Anvil, VideoAnnex, ViPER [10] and many others. In our case, we used ViPER [1] (Video Performance Evaluation Resource), a ground truth authoring tool developed by the University of Maryland.

Fig 1 shows a sample annotation using ViPER for text in a broadcast news segment.

Fig. 1. Sample annotation of text in broadcast news using rectangular boxes. Textual features such as readability, size and font are used as guides for marking the edges of the box. Internally, a unique Object ID is maintained for each of the text objects shown which helps in measuring the performance of tracking. Courtesy: CNN News.

2.1   Annotation Guidelines

In order to reduce the intra-annotator variability (the same annotator marking the boxes inconsistently at different times) and inter-annotator variability (mismatch between different annotators), a clear and exhaustive set of guidelines

---

[1] http://viper-toolkit.sourceforge.net

is established. These were strictly and diligently adhered to while creating the reference annotations. Further, considerable effort was directed in developing a ground truth that is rich with details. Hence, each text block is associated with a set of attributes which characterizes the region both from an evaluational and informational point of view. This section explains the set of guidelines and additional flags used in this evaluation for the text annotation task.

Every new text area is marked with a box when it appears in the video. Moving and scaling the selection box tracks the text as it moves in succeeding frames. This process is done at the line level (with offsets specified for word boundaries) until the text disappears from the frame.

There are two types of text:

- Graphic text is anything overlaid onto the picture. Example, the "abc" logo in Fig 1.
- Scene text is anything in the background/foreground of what is actually being filmed. Example, all text regions on the newspaper in Fig 1.

Text readability consists of three levels. Completely unreadable text is signified by READABILITY = 0 (green boxes in Fig 1) and is defined as text in which no character is identifiable. Partially readable text is given READABILITY = 1 (blue boxes in Fig 1) and contains characters that are both identifiable and non-identifiable. Clearly readable text is assigned READABILITY = 2 (red boxes in Fig 1) and is used for text in which all letters are identifiable.

The OCCLUSION attribute is set to TRUE when the text is cut off by the bounds of the frame or by another object. The LOGO attribute is set to TRUE when the text region being marked is a company logo imprinted in stylish fonts. Example, the texts "The Washington Post" and "abc" in Fig 1.

Of all the objects of interest in video, text is particularly difficult to be uniformly bound. For this reason, text regions are marked meticulously based on a comprehensive set of rules, namely,

- All text within a selected block must contain the same readability level and type.
- Blocks of text must contain the same size and font. Two allowances are given to this rule. A different font or size may be included in the case of a unique single character and the font color may vary among text in a group.
- The bounding box should be tight to the extent that there is no space between the box and text. The maximum distance from the box to the edge of bounded text may not exceed half the height of the characters when Readability = 2 (clearly readable). When Readability = 0 or 1 the box should be kept tight but does not require separate blocks for partial lines in a paragraph.
- Text boxes may not overlap other text boxes unless the characters themselves are specifically transposed atop one another.

The additional set of attributes described above is used in deciding whether a particular text region should be evaluated. The specific settings for evaluating a text region used in this evaluation are - TEXT-TYPE = Graphic, READABILITY = 2, OCCLUSION = FALSE and LOGO = FALSE.

All other regions are treated as "Don't Care" where the system output is neither penalized for missing nor given credit for detecting. It has to be noted that each of these attributes can be selectively specified to be included in evaluation through the scoring tool that we have developed.

2.2 Annotation Quality

It has been well appreciated in the research community that when manual labeling is involved, it is important to evaluate the consistency of labeling empirically. This becomes extremely critical when the marking involves subjective concepts like object bounds and readability. For this reason, 10% of the entire corpus was doubly annotated and checked for quality using the evaluation measures. Using the thresholded approach described in Secs 3.1 and 3.2, we found that at 60% spatial threshold, the average SFDA and the average ATA scores for the doubly annotated corpus were 0.97 and 0.90 respectively. This process assures that the reference annotations are reliable which is essential for genuine evaluations.

The threshold for a given application is derived from spatial disagreements between the annotators in the 10% double annotated data. The motivation behind this is to eliminate the error in the scores induced due to ground truth inconsistencies in terms of spatial alignment. Also, such an approach of arriving at the spatial threshold reflects the difficulties in how humans perceive the task. It has to be noted that though we get a good performance at 60% spatial threshold on the double annotations, we run the actual evaluations at a threshold of 10%. By adopting this method, systems are less penalized for spatial alignment errors.

3 Performance Measures

The performance measures that were used in the evaluation were proposed and discussed in detail in [9]. The performance measures are based primarily on area calculations of the spatial overlap between the ground truth objects and the system output. To generate the best score for an algorithm's performance, a one-to-one mapping is performed between the ground truth and system output objects such that the metric scores are maximized. All of the measure scores are normalized to a scale from 0, the worst performance, to 1, the best performance.

Secs 3.1 and 3.2 discuss the frame based detection measure and the sequence based tracking measure respectively, while Sec 4 briefs the one-to-one matching strategy.

The following are the notations used in the remainder of the paper,

- G_i denotes the ith ground truth object and $G_i^{(t)}$ denotes the ith ground truth object in t^{th} frame.
- D_i denotes the ith detected object and $D_i^{(t)}$ denotes the ith detected object in t^{th} frame.
- $N_G^{(t)}$ and $N_D^{(t)}$ denote the number of ground truth objects and the number of detected objects in frame t respectively.

- N_G and N_D denote the number of unique ground truth objects and the number of unique detected objects in the given sequence respectively. Uniqueness is defined by object IDs.
- N_{frames} is the number of frames in the sequence.
- N_{frames}^i, depending on the context, is the number of frames the ground truth object (G_i) or the detected object (D_i) existed in the sequence.
- N_{mapped} is the number of mapped ground truth and detected objects in a frame or the whole sequence depending on the context (detection/tracking).

3.1   Detection – Frame Based Evaluation

The Sequence Frame Detection Accuracy **(SFDA)** is a frame-level measure that penalizes for fragmentations in the spatial dimension while accounting for number of objects detected, missed detects, false alarms and spatial alignment of system output and ground truth objects.

The frame-based detection measure **(FDA)** which was used is defined as,

$$FDA(t) = \frac{\text{Overlap\_Ratio}}{\left[\frac{N_G^{(t)} + N_D^{(t)}}{2}\right]} \tag{1}$$

$$\text{where, Overlap\_Ratio} = \sum_{i=1}^{N_{mapped}} \frac{|G_i^{(t)} \cap D_i^{(t)}|}{|G_i^{(t)} \cup D_i^{(t)}|} \tag{2}$$

Here, the N_{mapped} is the number of mapped objects, where the mapping is done between objects which have the best spatial overlap in the given frame t.

To calculate the Sequence Frame Detection Accuracy (SFDA), the FDA scores from each frame are summed together and normalized by the total number of frames which either has a ground truth or a detected object. This normalization accounts for both missed detections and false alarms. This formula can be expressed as,

$$SFDA = \frac{\sum_{t=1}^{t=N_{frames}} FDA(t)}{\sum_{t=1}^{t=N_{frames}} \exists(N_G^{(t)} \ OR \ N_D^{(t)})} \tag{3}$$

Relaxing Spatial Alignment. For many systems, it would be sufficient to just detect the presence of an object in a frame, and not be concerned with the spatial accuracy of detection. To evaluate such systems, we employed a thresholded approach to evaluation of detection. Here, the detected object is given full credit even when it overlaps just a portion of the ground truth. OLP_DET is the spatial overlap threshold.

$$\text{Overlap\_Ratio\_Thresholded} = \sum_{i=1}^{N_{mapped}} \frac{Ovlp\_Thres(G_i^{(t)}, D_i^{(t)})}{|G_i^{(t)} \cup D_i^{(t)}|} \tag{4}$$

where,

$$Ovlp\_Thres(G_i^{(t)}, D_i^{(t)}) = \begin{cases} |G_i^{(t)} \cup D_i^{(t)}|, & \text{if } \frac{|G_i^{(t)} \cap D_i^{(t)}|}{|G_i^{(t)}|} \geq OLP\_DET \\ |G_i^{(t)} \cap D_i^{(t)}|, & otherwise \end{cases}$$

3.2   Tracking – Sequence Based Evaluation

For the tracking evaluation, we use the Average Tracking Accuracy (**ATA**) measure. This measure is a spatio-temporal measure which penalizes fragmentation in both the temporal and spatial dimensions. It also accounts for number of objects detected and tracked, missed objects, and false alarms. A one-to-one mapping between the ground truth objects and the system output is determined by computing the measure over all combinations of system output objects and ground truth objects and using an optimization strategy to maximize the overall score for the sequence.

We first determine the Sequence Track Detection Accuracy (**STDA**) which, is the performance of tracking on all ground truth objects. The $STDA$ is calculated as,

$$STDA = \sum_{i=1}^{N_{mapped}} \frac{\sum_{t=1}^{N_{frames}} \left[\frac{|G_i^{(t)} \cap D_i^{(t)}|}{|G_i^{(t)} \cup D_i^{(t)}|} \right]}{N_{(G_i \cup D_i \neq \emptyset)}} \tag{5}$$

Finally, the Average Tracking Accuracy (**ATA**) is the STDA score normalized by the number of objects in the sequence. It is defined as,

$$ATA = \frac{STDA}{\lceil \frac{N_G + N_D}{2} \rceil} \tag{6}$$

In cases when it is desirable to measure the tracking aspect of the algorithm and not be concerned with the detection accuracy, we can relax the detection penalty by using an area thresholded approach similar to the technique described in Sec 3.1.

4   Matching Strategies

From Eqs 2 and 5, it is clear that both the detection and the tracking measures distinguish between individual objects at the frame and at the sequence level respectively. The maximal scoring is obtained for the *optimal* ground-truth and system output pairs. Potential strategies to solve this assignment problem are the weighted bi-partite graph matching [11] and the Hungarian algorithm [12].

Assume that there are N ground truth objects and M detected objects. A brute force algorithm would have an exponential complexity, a result of having to try out all possible combination of matches (n!). However, this is a standard optimization problem and there are standard techniques to get the optimal match. The matching is generated with the constraint that the sum of the chosen function of the matched pairs is minimized or maximized as the case may be. In

	DT_1	DT_2	...	DT_M
GT_1	x			
GT_2		x		
⋮				
GT_N		x		

usual assignment problems, the number of objects in both cases are equal, i.e, when $N = M$. However, this is not a requirement and unequal number of objects can also be matched.

There are many variations of the basic Hungarian strategy most of which exploit constraints from specific problem domains they deal with. The algorithm has a series of steps which is followed iteratively and has a polynomial time complexity, specifically some implementations have $O(N^3)$. Faster implementations have been known to exist and have the current best bound to be at $O(N^2 log N + NM)$ [13]. In our case, we take advantage of the fact that the matrix is mostly sparse by implementing a hash function for mapping sub-inputs from the whole set of inputs.

5   Results and Analysis

5.1   Analytical Observations

For an object detection and tracking task the errors that can affect the metric scores can be due to a single or a combination of the following errors, namely, spatial inaccuracy, temporal inaccuracy, missed detects and false alarms. In our earlier work, we presented a detailed analysis of the influence of missed detects and false alarms on the metric scores. In a text detection and tracking scenario, most likely the outputs will be used to drive the text recognition module to extract the transcriptions before deriving semantic information. To this extent, we focus on the effects of spatial and temporal inaccuracies as these are as important as the other errors. For the purpose of completeness, we also present the analytical equations that drive the metrics in the case of missed detects and false alarms. We have developed an evaluation tool which reports each of the above components as auxiliary measures. These can be used for debugging purposes by algorithm developers to identify strengths and weaknesses of an approach and also for determining the operating point for their algorithm.

Effect of Spatial Inaccuracy. Assume a ground truth, G_i, and a corresponding detected object, D_i, of the same size ($|G_i|$). Fig 2 shows the effect of percentage overlap of ground truth on the overlap ratio. The main motivation behind taking the ratio of the spatial intersection of the two bounding boxes with their spatial union instead of the ground truth object size is to penalize bigger detected objects with the same spatial overlap with the ground truth.

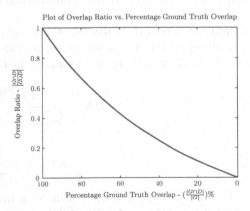

Fig. 2. Plot of overlap ratio vs. percentage ground truth overlap between a ground truth object and a detected object of the same size

For a ground truth, G_i and a detected object, D_i, that overlaps $x_i\%$ of G_i, we can derive "Overlap_Ratio" in Eq 2 for G_i as a function of x_i.

$$\text{Overlap\_Ratio(i)} = \frac{x_i}{1 + \frac{|D_i|}{|G_i|} - x_i} \tag{7}$$

Effect of Temporal Inaccuracy. There are two kinds of temporal inaccuracies that induce errors in the tracking task, namely,

- Incorrect object ID propagation in time. In this case, there can still be perfect detection.
- Missed object frames during tracking. In this case, it is treated as missed detects at the frame level by the detection measure.

Assuming that there are no false alarms and perfect spatial accuracy for the detected objects, we can analytically characterize the SFDA and the ATA measures for temporal inaccuracies as shown in Eqs 8 and 9.

$$\text{SFDA} = \frac{\sum_{i=1}^{N_D} N_{det\_frames}^i}{\frac{\sum_{i=1}^{N_D} N_{det\_frames}^i + \sum_{j=1}^{N_G} N_{frames}^j}{2}} \tag{8}$$

where, $N_{det\_frames}^i$ is the number of frames the output box D_i ideally detected the ground truth G_i irrespective of identification.

$$\text{ATA} = \frac{\sum_{i=1}^{N_{mapped}} \frac{N_{trk\_frames}^i}{N_{frames}^i}}{\left[\frac{N_G + N_D}{2}\right]} \tag{9}$$

where, $N_{trk\_frames}^i$ is the number of frames the output box D_i ideally detected and tracked (identified) the ground truth G_i.

Effect of Missed Detects. Given an ideal detection and tracking for the remaining objects in the sequence, we can characterize the SFDA and the ATA measures for missed detects as shown in Eqs 10 and 11.

$$\text{SFDA} = \frac{\sum_{i=1}^{N_D} N_{frames}^i}{\frac{\sum_{i=1}^{N_D} N_{frames}^i + \sum_{j=1}^{N_G} N_{frames}^j}{2}} \tag{10}$$

$$\text{ATA} = \frac{N_D}{\left[\frac{N_G + N_D}{2}\right]} \tag{11}$$

It can be seen that there will be a uniform degradation of the ATA score while the SFDA score will exhibit a non-uniform behavior. Clearly, the SFDA score is influenced by temporally predominant objects (existing in more frames) in the sequence, while the ATA score is independent of the frame persistence of objects.

Effect of False Alarms. Having looked at the effect of missed detects on the SFDA and the ATA, it is fairly straightforward to imagine the effect of false alarms on the measure scores. Given an ideal detection and tracking for all the objects in the sequence, we can analytically characterize the SFDA and the ATA measures for false alarms as shown in Eqs 12 and 13.

$$\text{SFDA} = \frac{\sum_{j=1}^{N_G} N_{frames}^j}{\frac{\sum_{i=1}^{N_D} N_{frames}^i + \sum_{j=1}^{N_G} N_{frames}^j}{2}} \tag{12}$$

$$\text{ATA} = \frac{N_G}{\lceil \frac{N_G + N_D}{2} \rceil} \tag{13}$$

Just as missing a predominantly occurring object decreases the SFDA score by a higher extent, introducing an object in a large number of frames affects the SFDA score more. However, the ATA score is affected by the number of unique objects (different object IDs) inserted into the sequence.

5.2   Text Detection and Tracking Evaluation

In this section, we describe the framework that we use in our evaluation of text detection and tracking algorithms. We evaluated three text detection algorithms and a text tracking algorithm using the measures discussed. The algorithm outputs were obtained from the original authors and thus can be safely assumed that the reported outputs are for the optimal parameter settings of the algorithm without any implementation errors. For anonymity purposes, these algorithms will be referred to as Algo 1, Algo 2 and Algo 3. The source video was in MPEG-2 standard in NTSC format encoded at 29.97 frames per second at 704x480 resolution (Aspect Ratio – 4:3).

The algorithms were trained on 50 clips, each averaging about 3 minutes (approx. 5400 frames) and tested on 30 clips, whose average length was the same as that of the training data. The ground truth was provided to algorithm developers for the 50 clips to facilitate training of algorithm parameters.

Fig 3 shows the SFDA scores of the three text detection algorithms on the 30 test clips. It also reports the SFDA scores thresholded at 10% spatial overlap, missed detects, and false alarms associated with each sequence. By adopting a thresholded approach, we alleviate the effect of errors caused due to spatial anomalies. Thus, the errors in the thresholded SFDA scores are primarily due to missed detects and false alarms. One can observe a strong correlation between the SFDA scores and the missed detects/false alarms. All three algorithms have reasonably low missed detection and false alarm rates with Algo 1 being the lowest in majority cases. As a result of thresholding, the average increase in scores for Algo 1, Algo 2 and Algo 3 is 29.56%, 63.54% and 24.55% respectively. This shows that Algo 1 and Algo 3 have good localization accuracy which is important if these outputs are to be used by a text recognition system.

Fig 4 shows the ATA scores of a text tracking system on the test set. Additionally, ATA scores thresholded at 10% spatial overlap, missed detects, and false alarms associated with each sequence are reported.

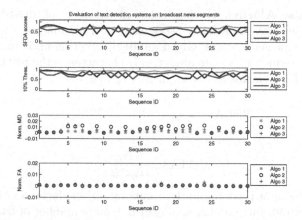

Fig. 3. Evaluation results of three text detection systems. Missed Detects (MD) and False Alarms (FA) are normalized with respect to total number of evaluation frames.

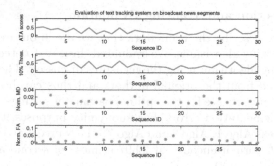

Fig. 4. Evaluation results of a text tracking algorithm. Missed Detects are normalized with respect to total number of unique ground truth objects in the sequence and False Alarms are normalized with respect to total number of unique system output objects in the sequence.

It can be observed from the results that the tracking algorithms are not as accurate as the detection algorithms. This is a direct result of inconsistent ID tracks. Fig 4 also shows that induction of *random* false alarms is detrimental to the performance of the tracking system. Through more analysis using the auxiliary measures discussed in Sec 5.1, we observed that these false alarms generally do not persist for more than a couple of frames. This gives an idea that trackers should perhaps look for evidence in the spatio-temporal space before declaring an object's presence.

6   Conclusions

A comprehensive approach to evaluation of object detection and tracking algorithms is presented for video domains where an object bounding approach to ground truth annotation is followed. An area based metric, that depends on spatial overlap between ground truth objects and system output objects to generate the score, is used in the case of an object bounding annotation. For the detection task, the SFDA metric captures both the detection capabilities (number of objects detected) and the goodness of detection (spatial accuracy). Similarly, for the tracking task, both the tracking capabilities (number of objects detected and tracked) and the goodness of tracking (spatial and temporal accuracy) are taken into account by the ATA metric. Evaluation results of text detection and tracking systems on broadcast news segments show the effectiveness of the metrics in capturing their performance. Results show that the state-of-the-art is fairly mature in the detection of clear, readable text that is overlaid on video. It can also be seen that text tracking systems suffer from irregular identification and insertion of sporadic false alarms.

References

1. Jung, K., Kim, K.I., Jain, A.K.: Text information extraction in images and video: a survey. Pattern Recognition **37** (2004) 977–997
2. Antani, S., Crandall, D., Narasimhamurthy, A., Mariano, V.Y., Kasturi, R.: Evaluation of Methods for Detection and Localization of Text in Video. In: Proceedings in International Workshop on Document Analysis Systems. (2000) 507–514
3. Black, J., Ellis, T.J., Rosin, P.: A Novel Method for Video Tracking Performance Evaluation. In: Proceedings of IEEE PETS Workshop. (2003)
4. Brown, L.M., Senior, A.W., Tian, Y., Connell, J., Hampapur, A., Shu, C., Merkl, H., Lu, M.: Performance Evaluation of Surveillance Systems Under Varying Conditions. In: Proceedings of IEEE PETS Workshop. (2005)
5. Collins, R., Zhou, X., Teh, S.: An Open Source Tracking Testbed and Evaluation Web Site. In: Proceedings of IEEE PETS Workshop. (2005)
6. Hua, X., Wenyin, L., Zhang, H.: Automatic Performance Evaluation for Video Text Detection. In: Proc. International Conference on Document Analysis and Recognition. (2001) 545–550
7. Nascimento, J., Marques, J.: New Performance Evaluation Metrics for Object Detection Algorithms. In: Proceedings of IEEE PETS Workshop. (2004)
8. Smith, K., Gatica-Perez, D., Odobez, J., Ba, S.: Evaluating Multi-Object Tracking. In: Proceedings of IEEE Empirical Evaluation Methods in Computer Vision Workshop. (2005)
9. Manohar, V., Soundararajan, P., Raju, H., Goldgof, D., Kasturi, R., Garofolo, J.: Performance Evaluation of Object Detection and Tracking in Video. In: Proceedings of Asian Conference on Computer Vision. (2006) 151–161
10. Doermann, D., Mihalcik, D.: Tools and Techniques for Video Performance Evaluation. In: ICPR. Volume 4. (2000) 167–170
11. Papadimitriou, C.H., Steiglitz, K.: Combinatorial optimization: algorithms and complexity. Prentice-Hall, Inc., Upper Saddle River, NJ, USA (1982)
12. Munkres, J.R.: Algorithms for the Assignment and Transportation Problems. J. SIAM **5** (1957) 32–38
13. Fredman, M.L., Tarjan, R.E.: Fibonacci Heaps and their uses in Improved Network Optimization Algorithms. Journal of ACM **34** (1987) 596–615

Document Analysis System for Automating Workflows

Steven J. Simske[1] and Jordi Arnabat[2]

[1] Hewlett-Packard Labs, Mailstop 85, 3404 E. Harmony Road,
Fort Collins, CO 90528, USA
Steven.Simske@hp.com
[2] Hewlett-Packard Espanola, Av. Graells, 501
98190 Sant Cugat del Valles, Spain
Jordi.Arnabat@hp.com

Abstract. When a user places a document in a capture device—copier, multi-functional printer [MFP], or scanner—the user expects good output to be produced regardless of the document type. There are a variety of means to achieve improved output, in which the settings on the copying device are tuned to the content characteristics of the document. These settings can be automated across the range of scanned context extremes from photo (blurring, no snapping) to fully-text (sharpening, aggressive snapping) documents. This procedure is "document auto typing", and relies on a fast and accurate assessment of the content of the captured image. We herein describe the development of seven distinct systems for document analysis, and through the comparison of these systems arrive at an efficient and accurate document analysis system for automating the copying settings. We discuss the applicability of this method to other automated workflows in document capture.

1 Problem Statement

We have developed a repertoire of seven different document analysis systems to analyze the content scanned. Each of the algorithms described here can be performed at low (30-100 ppi) resolution. We define them and provide a description of their relative advantages and disadvantages here (see also Table 1):

1. High-Level Document Classification: Photo, Text and Mixed. This is a trinary classification: we determine if the document has text or photo, or else mixed (text AND photo). This algorithm has excellent performance, since it ends its search for text/photo as soon as it verifies the presence of text/photo. This classification scheme implicitly imposes a "region manager" on the classification with the following characteristics: uniform background regions and line drawings are considered "text" regions, since they do not require the same type of specialized image processing (blurring, no snapping) as photos, and are not deleteriously affected when treated as text (sharpening, aggressive snapping). The main disadvantage of this approach appears in multi-page document copying, in which image quality (IQ) variability of the text on different pages of a multi-page document may occur due to page-to-page classification variability.

2. Low-Level Document Classification: Percent Text, Photo. In addition to assigning a document to {text/photo/mixed}, we determine the relative amount

H. Bunke and A.L. Spitz (Eds.): DAS 2006, LNCS 3872, pp. 588–592, 2006.
© Springer-Verlag Berlin Heidelberg 2006

(percentage) of text and photo present. This option can be accommodated with a simple "slider" motif: the minimum/maximum for the slider is 0/100 percent text. However, using this, text will vary in its sharpness considerably with a mixed document set, and the output is more sensitive to classification errors.

3. Neighborhood Analysis—High and Low Frequency Sites. Here, each pixel is classified by the amount of variance in its neighborhood. This is roughly equivalent to edge detection. Only the resulting edges are sharpened. All non-edge pixels are treated as if they are photos. This algorithm is quite fast, and provides uniform appearance across multiple-page documents. However, it can result in artifacts in some regions that lower image quality (this is dependent on print quality, text font, etc.). It will, however, generally result in similar-appearing text regions throughout a multiple-page document.

4. Neighborhood Analysis—Filtered High-Frequency Sites. Simple zoning analysis is performed to prevent sharpening of large, low-edge containing (e.g. photo) regions. This further improves the correlation of sharpening with text and line drawings.

5. Region Analysis and Region-Specific Pipelines. A zoning analysis engine (e.g. [1]) is used to segment and classify specific region types, including but not limited to text, line drawings, tables, photos and graphics. This provides a uniform appearance of like region types across corpora of any size. There is, generally, a decline in performance by roughly an order of magnitude in comparison to the previous methods. Moreover, when there are zoning mistakes, the effects on the output can be quite noticeable—for example, when photos and text are mistaken.

6. By Region with (OCR) Feedback. In this option, region analysis as described in option 5 above is combined with optical character recognition (OCR) to improve the segmentation and classification. That is, OCR results are used to determine the probabilities that zoning was correct in the first pass, and thus improve the zoning output in the second pass. While this greatly improves text classification, it has high memory, performance and other resource costs. However, it does provide searchable text as output, with obvious implications in searching, clustering, summarizing, archiving and topic-tracking.

Table 1. Relative comparison of the 7 options above. All seven of these systems have been built—or incrementally improved—and tested during the past year. These data are for a Windows-based laptop computer with Pentium III processor, 256 MB of RAM, and 1.13 GHz CPU clock.

Option	Time (/page)	Error (pct)	Appearance Flaws
1. High-level	0.3 sec	2-25%	Moderate
2. Pct	0.5 sec	<20%	Moderate
3. Edge-based	0.2 sec	0%	Severe
4. Filtered-edge	0.7 sec	0-2%	Severe
5. Region-based	1.5 sec	2-30%	Moderate
6. Regions+OCR	7.5 sec	0.5-10%	Moderate
7. Template	1.6 sec	0.5-5%	Moderate

7. By Region with Template/Corpus Feedback. When the output closely matches a template, the zoning results are "snapped" to the template, providing increased accuracy without a substantial impact on performance. However, this method generally fails in practice, since most documents to be copied have no template in place.

2 Design and Implementation

We chose Option 1 (with an estimate for Pct, Option 2, which can be used with a slider) for use on a high-speed, walk-up copier. This improves the output image quality for text-only or photo documents over the default "mixed" mode otherwise applied to all documents independent of their content. For this to succeed, most text and photos must be typed correctly, with virtually no mixed documents mistyped. Performance is also an issue (<0.5 sec on the test system). The steps involved are outlined here:

1. Threshold. We used dual-Gaussian fitting (Modified from [2]). The sub-threshold black pixels form a Threshold Map.

2. Find Solids. We then find solid areas of non-uniform hue or intensity, which represent photos. We first scrub any black shadows along the edge of the scanbed, then adaptively determine the amount of run-length smearing to generate sufficient regions to estimate skew correctly but not so many that we sacrifice performance. This estimate is based on the number of black runs rather than using full region formation. After smearing the map, we form regions from the black pixels on the map. Solid (potential photo) regions are, for example, greater than 1 square inch in area and contain 70% or more black pixels, among other possible factors. In general, solid regions have areas with long black runs while "nonsolid" (potential text) regions do not have a high percentage of long black pixel runs. These solid regions are then scrubbed from the Threshold Map, but their boundary information is stored for later analysis.

3. Nonsolid Skew Estimate. The left over pixels are then tested for skew. We use a robust, fast modified Hough transform method.

4. Estimate Text Area. Projection profiles are then formed both horizontally and vertically at the angle of skew to estimate the amount of text on the document. The projection profile statistics are: (1) The number of pixels in the run (length of run in pixels), (2) The number of black pixels in the run (number of "1's" in the thresholded map for the particular run) and (3) The percent of black pixels = (2) / (1). Text can be easily gleaned from projection profiles. EFIGS text, for example, will generally have ascenders and descenders around an x-height, with typically 15-50% black pixels in the x-height area for the length of text in the projection (Asian and other languages will tend to have, like EFIGS languages, other characteristics, such as <= 3X variability in black pixels in all text runs). Because salient text will generally be spaced in repetitive lines, the statistics for text presence go up with more text lines. After this step, if text is present we know the final classification will now be "text" or "mixed". If text is not present, we will need to search for text using projection profiles over solid regions, as discussed in the next section.

5. Estimate Photo and Drawing Areas. The solid regions are next investigated. First an Edge Map is created. The edges overlying every solid region are then smeared to create a New Threshold Map that can be analyzed for text presence, as in (4) above. The amount of potential text over these regions is added to the text area in step (4) and the decision on text is made.

6. Determine Typing. The solid regions are then analyzed—using the histograms of the non-edge pixels –to see if they are uniform backgrounds. If any of the solid regions are not uniform backgrounds, then the final typing is Mixed (text already present) or Photo (no text present).

3 Results

The document auto-typing above is then used to control the copier settings for tone-scale, color table, sharpening and snapping. The software was developed testing on an existing 50-document corpus and then tested on a separate 205-document corpus (generated and maintained by the HP copier image quality team in Boise, ID, USA). For this test set, only 1.6% of documents were made worse than the default (Mixed) setting. Thus, the system provides a precision of 98.4%. Additionally, 87.8% of those scanned documents requiring an altered setting were so identified (this corresponds to recall in machine learning vernacular). Accuracy, which is determined from 2pr/(p+r) where p is precision and r is recall, is thus 92.8%. In everyday usage, the value for accuracy depends on the relative mixture of document types scanned, and will approach 100% for simple text document copying. The remaining 12.2% (those which did not have correct "recall") of the documents tested were typed as default (importantly, there were no extreme Text/Photo or Photo/Text misclassifications—this means that none of the documents was mistyped to be worse than a default setting on the copier).

The algorithm was tested on a Windows-based laptop computer with Pentium III processor, 256 MB of RAM, and 1.13 GHz CPU clock (comparable to resources available on a walk-up copier). The mean processing time for this "test system" was 0.28 sec/document, with a standard deviation of 0.07 sec and a range of 0.17-0.76 sec.

4 Competitive Approaches

Currently shipping copiers allow settings to be made manually on the copier control panel. This includes multifunctional printers and document scanners, which focus on business documents, and usually default to text or near-text mixed modes (i.e. they use sharpening and snapping). All-in-one devices also have multiple modes, but many times default to a more photo-centric processing mode. However, low-end devices such as desktop scanners and all-in-ones have shipped a region-based zoning analysis approach [3] to improving output quality. This analysis, however, is prone to more mistakes since so many (segmentation, classification, bit-depth, etc.) decisions are made on each document page. The per-page failure rate is thus greater than 5%, and the time for analysis is typically an order of magnitude greater than that of the method presented here. Allowing users to correct the analysis, such as is commonplace for a preview-scan workflow motif [4], is not generally acceptable for copier auto-typing. Comparatively, our method is faster (0.3 sec on the "test system") and more accurate, and is suitable for implementation in high throughput devices such as 50 ppm machines without deleteriously affecting performance or processing accuracy.

5   Discussion

Seven methods of improving the automatic image quality of a scanned document are outlined herein. The approach used for a given system will be chosen based on performance requirements, resources available, and the accuracy expected by the users. For example, our choice of Option 1 was natural given it provided high performance (mean processing time of < 0.3 sec), relatively high accuracy (> 90%) and no severe errors (no "text only" documents in the sample corpus were misclassified as "photo only" documents, and vice versa) occurred. Additionally, only two different "quality" settings for text are observed: high quality for "text only" documents and moderate quality for "mixed" documents.

The automatic classification of documents is of interest for a number of other applications, in addition to the need for copier output quality as described here. One such application is the automatic archiving of documents that are scanned and copied. This may be required for auditing, payment, security, etc., reasons. When the documents are assigned to "text", "photo" and "mixed" classes, there can be a considerable savings over a default archiving scheme. For example, "text" pages are typically archived at 400 ppi, 1-bit/pixel before compression, while "photo" pages are typically archived at 200 ppi, 24-bit/pixel before compression. Archiving a "mixed" page requires preserving both the higher resolution and the greater bit depth settings of the "text" and "photo" classes, respectively. Before compression, then, "mixed" pages require 24 times as much memory as "text" pages, and 4 times as much memory as "photo" pages. Compression further exacerbates the difference in archiving. Other applications of the automatic document analysis system used herein include preliminary template matching and preliminary document classification for a document indexing system.

Acknowledgments

The authors thank helpful colleagues—especially Nehal Dantwala, Peter Bauer and Óscar Mártinez—for their comments and suggestions in this work.

References

1. Wahl, F.M., Wong, K.Y. and Casey, R.G.: Block segmentation and text extraction in mixed/image documents. Computer Vision Graphics and Image Processing, Vol. 2, pp.375-390, 1982.
2. Kittler, J. and Illingworth, J.: Minimum error thresholding. Pattern Recognition, Vol 19, no. 1, pp. 41-47, 1986.
3. Lee, J.P., Simske, S.J. and Dawe, J.T.: Segmenting a document into regions associated with a data type, and assigning pipelines to process such regions. U.S. Patent 6,880,122, Apr. 12, 2005.
4. Simske, S.J. and Arnabat, J.: User-directed analysis of scanned images. Proc. DocEng 2003, Grenoble, pp.212-221, 2003.

Automatic Assembling of Cadastral Maps Based on Generalized Hough Transformation

Fei Liu, Wataru Ohyama, Tetsushi Wakabayashi, and Fumitaka Kimura

Mie University, Faculty of Engineering,
1577 kurimamachiya-cho, Tsu-shi, Mie, 5148507, Japan
{liufei, ohyama, waka, kimura}@hi.info.mie-u.ac.jp

Abstract. There are numerous cadastral maps generated by past land surveying. The raster digitization of these paper maps is in progress. For effective and efficient use of these maps, we have to assemble the set of maps to make them superimposable on other geographic information in a Geographic Information System. The problem can be seen as a complex jigsaw puzzle where the pieces are the cadastre sections extracted from the map. We present an automatic solution to this geographic jigsaw puzzle, based on the generalized Hough transformation that detects the longest common boundary between every piece and its neighbors. The experiments have been conducted using the map of Mie Prefecture, Japan and the French cadastral map. The results of the experiment with the French cadastral maps show that the proposed method, which consists of extracting an external area and extracting and regularizing the north arrow, is suitable for assembling the cadastral map. The final goal of the process is to integrate every piece of the puzzle into a national geographic reference frame and database.

1 Introduction

In the process of application development of Geographic Information System (GIS), the core issue is the maintenance of national spatial databases. Cadastral maps are always made individually in each district. When the cadastral maps are made in each district, then they are finally combined in correspondence with the connected components of information and the surveyed ground information. The cadastral maps are chiefly assembled according to symbols given to the cadastral map and using prior knowledge available. Automatic map assembling is important because it saves labor power and time. Techniques for treating the separated cadastral maps as one piece of a huge jigsaw puzzle has been proposed by other researchers in the automation of the cadastral map assembling [1],[3],[4]. These techniques are based on the choice of some characteristics on the boundary of each segment [2], and combining segments by the matching results of the characteristics. Though the computational complexity is low because only a number of characteristics are used, when the shape of the segment becomes complex, the characteristic cannot be accurately extracted. Since this problem arises, in this paper, we propose automatic cadastral maps assembling technique based on generalized Hough transformation (GHT). The features of this technique is as follows.

H. Bunke and A.L. Spitz (Eds.): DAS 2006, LNCS 3872, pp. 593–603, 2006.
© Springer-Verlag Berlin Heidelberg 2006

(i)   Because the common longest boundary of two segments is determined based on GHT, segments can be accurately combined.

(ii)   It use all the points on the boundary of the segment, hence the extraction of the characteristics of the boundary becomes unnecessary.

(iii) A smaller error margin of the assembled maps could be realized.

When a feature is detected from an image, the Hough transformation is effective when the feature is expressed by the algebraic equation. In this paper, to detect the curve of arbitrary shape, we propose the method of the common longest boundary detection based on generalized Hough transformation.

This paper is organized as follows. The next section presents the principle of cadastral map assembling. Section 3 describes the assembling process of blank map. In section 4 we present the preprocessing and the assembling by generalized Hough transformation of actual cadastral map. The experiments and the results are given in section 5.

2   Principle of Cadastral Map Assembling

2.1   Longest Common Boundary

When two segments share and parts are connected to each other, the border is called a common boundary. In general there is a possibility that two or more common boundaries exist between two segments. It is necessary to decide the common boundary to connect two segments correctly from these two or more common boundaries. For instance, two or more common boundaries can exist between segment A and segment B as shown in figure 1. A true common boundary is a common boundary shown by the arrow of figure 1 (c). In the proposed technique, a true common boundary was presumed based on the length of the common boundary and the longest common boundary is detected by generalized Hough transformation (GHT), then segments are automatically assembled.

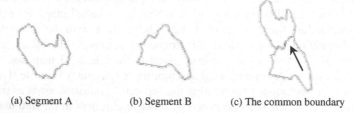

(a) Segment A   (b) Segment B   (c) The common boundary

Fig. 1. Two segments and the common boundary

2.2   The Flow of GHT

The flow of GHT with two segments is shown in figure 2. The longest common boundary detection technique that useing GHT can be described as follows.

(1) The boundary of each segment is traced.

(2) The origin in border B is randomly defined and a symmetrical border B' with the point of origin is generated.

(3) GHT is performed by sweeping the border B' with the origin on border A. Pixel values of GHT are called crossing counts.

(4) The point where the crossing count is the highest is detected by the image of GHT. This point becomes the origin of segment B when each segment is connected by the common longest boundary.

Figure 3 illustrates the GHT between segment A and segment B. In this figure, the gray level is higher as much as the crossing count. The brightest point P in figure 3, at which the crossing count is the largest, becomes the origin of segment B.

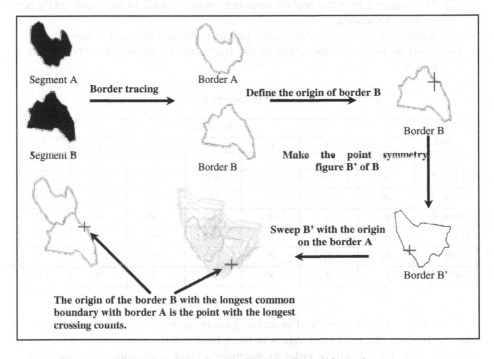

Fig. 2. The flow of generalized Hough transformation

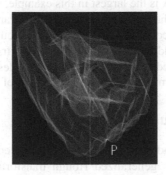

Fig. 3. Generalized Hough transformation image

3 Assembling of a Blank Map

The procedure of assembling two or more segments from the blank map by generalization Hough transformation (GHT) hill climbing is described as follows. The outermost shape when all segments are assembled is assumed to be known and given as a frame.

(1) GHT is done between the frame and each segment, and the highest crossing count of each segment is found.
(2) The segment with the highest crossing count is added to the frame and a new frame is generated.
(3) Same procedure to the new frame and the remaining segment is done.
(4) Until all segments are added to the frame, the procedure described above is repeated.

Table 1. The process of the assembling of the blank map

Crossing count	Segment						
	A	B	C	D	E	F	G
frame 1	502	117	74	38	53	127	93
frame 2	×	190	74	97	53	127	93
frame 3	×	×	93	126	105	127	93
frame 4	×	×	166	126	105	×	93
frame 5	×	×	×	126	207	×	93
frame 6	×	×	×	181	×	×	149
frame 7	×	×	×	×	×	×	149

Table 1 shows the procedure of assembling seven segments and outermost frame 1 of Mie Prefecture. The numerical values in the table show the highest crossing count of each segment. First of all, in order to assemble a blank map using GHT, the highest crossing counts of frame 1 against segment A to G are computed. Because the highest crossing count of segment A is the largest in this example, segment A is added to frame 1 and frame 2 is created. Then, GHT is done between frame 2 and the remaining segment, the highest crossing count of each segment is calculated. The segment with the highest crossing count is added to the frame and a new frame is generated. The white background map is assembled again repeating the above described procedure.

In this example, each segment was assembled in order of A→B→F→C→E→D→G.

4 Assembling of Actual Cadastral Map

In this section, the actual cadastral map assembling procedure, the needed preprocessing and the assembling by generalized Hough transformation (GHT) is described. There are some differences in an actual cadastral map and the blank map.

(1) Various characters and symbols exist together in an actual cadastral map. Especially, the characters and symbols are chiefly included in an internal area of the cadastral map. Because these might become noises in the common boundary detection of the cadastral map, it is important to remove them.

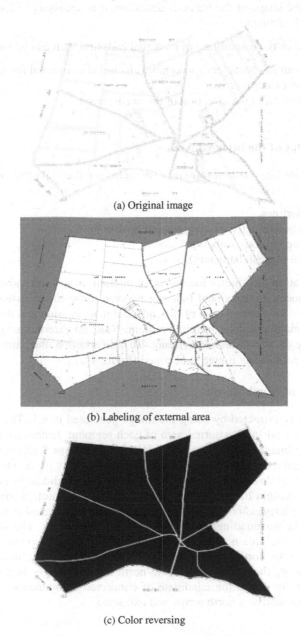

(a) Original image

(b) Labeling of external area

(c) Color reversing

Fig. 4. Painting procedure of internal area

(2) Because each segment was made individually in each district, the direction of the north arrow of each segment is different. Every segment has a north arrow, it is necessary to extract this north arrow, and to regularize direction of the north arrow of each segment.

(3) Because the shape of the frame is unknown, it is necessary to employ GHT between each segment.

The procedure of the assembling of an actual cadastral map can be summaried as:

- Painting out of characters and symbols included in internal area.
- Extraction of north arrow.
- Regularization of the direction of the north arrow.
- GHT.

4.1 Painting Out of the Internal Area

The following are the main information included in the cadastral maps (Refer to figure 4(a)).

- The borderlines.
- Map symbols(chiefly, house sign and broken line).
- Coordinate values(numbers).
- Name of a places(characters).

These information are chiefly located in an internal area of the cadastral maps. Because small connected component that can become noise in the assembling process which included in an external area of the cadastral map, erosion and dilation of pixels of the original image are done to remove them. Next, an external area is painted out with the labeling of 4-neighborhood (figure 4(b)). In addition, the painted background is reversed, and painted out image is obtained (figure 4(c)).

4.2 Extraction of North Arrow

The north arrow is extracted by using the image generated in 4.1. The north arrow is independently located in an external area of each segment. hence, connected components of the map images are detected by the labeling process. The connected components are extracted as a candidate of connected components of the north arrow if its area is between two thresholds that are predefined. The candidate of connected components often is straight lines and curve lines excluding the north arrow. Therefore, a ratio R is given in expression (1). Where S is the area of connected components and C is the length of the surroundings of each connected components. The straight line and the curve, neither the area nor the surroundings length change so much, but because there is a width in the north arrow, the area of north arrow is larger than the surroundings length. That is, the value of R of the north arrow is larger in general than the straight line and the curve, the candidate of connected components with the largest value of R is presumed as a north arrow and extracted.

$$R = S \big/ C \qquad\qquad (1)$$

4.3 Regularization of North Arrow

The direction of north arrow is regularized by using the extracted north arrow. The direction of the principal axis of the north arrow is shown in figure 5, in other words, the angle of the north arrow is obtained as a solution of the expression (2).

$$\tan^2 \theta + \frac{M(2,0) - M(0,2)}{M(1,1)} \tan \theta - 1 = 0 \tag{2}$$

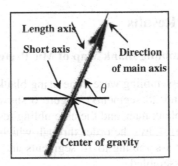

Fig. 5. Angle of north arrow

Here, $M(p,q)$ is a moment feature, and it is defined by the expression (3).

$$M(p,q) = \Sigma (i - i_g)^p (j - j_g)^q f(i,j) \tag{3}$$

Here, $f(i,j)$ is a binary image, and i_g, j_g is center of gravity. When the angle of the north arrow is obtained, the cadastral map is rotated around the center, and each cadastral map was regularized so that the angle of the north arrow is 90 degree.

4.4 Generalized Hough Transformation

After painting out the internal area, the extraction and the regularization of the north arrow, GHT was done. Here, this section explains the process of the map assembling with an example of the cadastral map of France (Fig.7). Table 2 shows the process of map assembling with five segments.

Table 2. The assembling process of the French cadastre map

Crossing count	Segment				
	A	B	C	D	E
A	×	811	888	467	1064
AUE	×	811	886	720	×
AUEUD	×	1033	×	1191	×
AUEUDUB	×	1033	×	×	×

An arbitrary segment (i.e segment A) is selected instead of the frame in the assembling of blank map. GHT is done between segment A and each segment, and the highest crossing count was calculated. The segment with the highest crossing count is connected to segment A and it is assumed to be a new segment. Because the highest crossing count of segment A and segment E is the highest in this example, segment A and segment E are connected. Next, GHT was done between the new segment and the rest of segment. The above procedure is repeated, and the cadastral maps are assembled.

The order of assembling was A→E→C→D→B in this example.

5 Experiments and Results

5.1 Experiment of Assembling Blank Map of Mie Prefecture

The experiments of map assembling were done using blank map of Mie Prefecture (7 segments, 14 segments, and 28 segments). Figure 6 shows the seven segments and frame (figure 6(a)) in the blank map, and the assembling results (figure 6(b)).

The figure in figure 6(b) shows the order through which the assembling was done. Similarly, experiments for assembling to 14 segments and 28 segments show that all segments were correctly assembled.

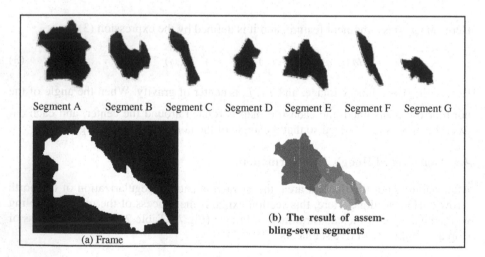

Segment A   Segment B   Segment C   Segment D   Segment E   Segment F   Segment G

(a) Frame

(b) The result of assembling-seven segments

Fig. 6. Seven segments, the frame and the result of assembling

5.2 Experiment of Assembling French Cadastral Map

5.2.1 Experimental Data

The experimental data included images of the cadastral maps generated by a scanner. A total of 51 segments of France were used from ten cities of the cadastral map for the experiments. Table 3 shows the number of segments of each city.

Table 3. The data used in French cadastral map assembling

City	Segment number
Baily	5
Buc	8
Bourg	2
Bios	7
Bougival	5
Boul	3
Carrieres	7
chesnay	5
A	4
Villiers	5
Total	51

5.2.2 Extraction of North Arrow
The extraction experiments of the north arrow were done by using the above-mentioned 51 segments, and all the north arrow were correctly extracted.

5.2.3 Experiments for Map Assembling by Generalized Hough Transformation
The experiments for map assembling were done using cadastral maps of ten cities. Figure 7 shows the experimental results for five segments of Villiers city. Table 4 shows all the experimental results. The success rate in this table was visually judged to be considerably high.

Table 4. The result of the cadastral map assembling

Average success rate		Average processing time
Extraction of the north arrow	Assembling	
100%(51/51)	90.0%(9/10)	720s

In the experiment, the map assembling was failed for a city out of ten cities. It is because the combination of two segments with the longest common boundary found in generalized Hough transformation image was a wrong combination. It is scheduled to introduce mechanisms of error detection and recovery as a topic in the future work.

5.3 Summary of Experiment

Based on the experimental results, it can summaried as follows:

(1) It was possible to automatically assemble the cadastral maps by using generalized Hough transformation.

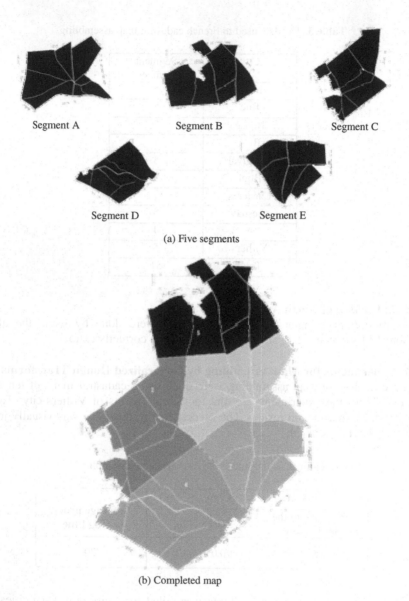

(a) Five segments

(b) Completed map

Fig. 7. The result of map assembling of Villiers city

(2) The assembling of the cadastral maps in which various characters and symbols existed together became possible by painting out an internal area of the segments.

(3) Automatic map assembling was done even when there was an error margin in the segment shape and the shape of the frame was unknown.

6 Conclusion

In this paper, a technique of the cadastral map assembling that uses generalized Hough transformation was proposed, and experiments were done with blank maps of Mie Prefecture, Japan and French cadastral maps. It was shown that generalized Hough transformation is an effective technique for cadastral map assembling.

The following areas might be included in the future work.

(1) Performance evaluation for large amount of cadastral maps. The performance of the proposed technique will be evaluated by using large amount of cadastral map, and practical use will be examined. (2) Introduction of recognition systems of other information included in cadastral maps such as characters and numbers.

References

[1] Jean-Marc Viglino, Laurent Guigues:"Cadastre Map Assembling: a Puzzle Game Resolution ", Sixth International Conference on Document Analysis and Recognition 2001 pp.1235-1239(2001)

[2] Davis,L.S:"Shape matching using relaxation techniques."IEEE-PAMI 1,1,January 1979,60-72 (1979).

[3] L.L.Scarlatos(1999)."Puzzle Piece Topology: Detecting Arrangements in Smart Object Interfaces", Proceedings of the 7th International Conference in Central Europe on Computer Graphics, Visualization and Interactive Digital Media, pp.456-462(1999).

[4] Alex Drogoul and C.Dubreuil."A distributed approach to n-puzzle solving". In Proceeding of the Distributed Artificial Intelligence Workshop (1993).

[5] D.H. Ballard. "Generalizing the Hough transform to detect arbitrary shapes." Pattern Recognition 13, 2, 1981, 111-122

A Few Steps Towards On-the-Fly Symbol Recognition with Relevance Feedback[*]

Jan Rendek[1,2], Bart Lamiroy[1], and Karl Tombre[1]

[1] LORIA–INPL, B.P. 239, 54506 Vandœuvre-lès-Nancy CEDEX, France
[2] France Télécom R&D, Meylan CEDEX, France
Jan.Rendek@loria.fr, Bart.Lamiroy@loria.fr, Karl.Tombre@loria.fr

Abstract. This paper presents some first steps in building an interactive system which allows a user to efficiently browse a large set of scanned documents, without prior knowledge on the content of these documents, and retrieving symbols of interest to him personally, through a relevance feedback mechanism.

1 Introduction

The recognition of graphical symbols has been subject to much effort throughout the years. The methods used include template matching techniques, grammar-based matching techniques, recognition techniques based on structural features or dynamic programming, and a number of stuctural methods based on graph matching.

One of the reasons for which symbol recognition is in many cases a very difficult and ill-defined problem is the large number and variety of symbols to be recognized. Except in strongly context-dependent applications, it may often be impossible to provide a database of all possible symbols. It is also in many cases impossible to assume that symbol recognition can be performed on correctly segmented instances of symbols, as symbols are very often connected to other graphics and/or associated with text. The well-known paradox therefore appears: in order to correctly recognize the symbols, we should be able to segment the input data, but in order to correctly segment them, we need the symbols to be recognized!

The current state of the art makes the following assumption where recognition is concerned: symbols are subject to a number of deformations that need to be taken into account in order to obtain efficient recognition methods. These deformations may have various origins and result in different kinds of visual effects:

1. planar geometric transforms (rotation, translation, scaling) due to general document orientation or lack of a principal reading direction (*e.g.* complex assembly blueprints, annotated drawings, *etc.*),

[*] This work is partially funded by a CIFRE contract between France Télécom R&D and INPL-LORIA.

H. Bunke and A.L. Spitz (Eds.): DAS 2006, LNCS 3872, pp. 604–615, 2006.

2. noise introduced by the physical image production process (speckling, blurs) or by subsequent treatments (rastering, binarization, scaling, numerical instabilities when rotating ...),
3. complex geometric transforms resulting from projecting 3D forms onto 2D images,
4. intra-class object variations when the recognition process is supposed to encompass a certain semantic class of "similar" items.

The classical scenario generally consists in identifying a finite set of *known symbols* in a set of documents. Depending on what type of documents are being considered, the recognition method will integrate the previously mentioned deformations to different degrees in order to produce an as efficient as possible recognition method. The key issue here is that, most of the time, all symbols to be recognized are previously known, and that there exists either a model, or a training set (from which a model can be built) for each symbol. Various efficient techniques have been developed, either using structural pattern description, or statistical pattern recognition techniques [1, 2, 3].

The problem arises when no model nor training set is available or can even be planned (typically in a very open and general application), or when the training set is too poor to derive a usable model. While it is clear that the first three points of the previously mentioned deformation models are rather general and can reasonably well be taken into account for a large range of situations (exception made for extreme scale changes or very distorted acquisition tools, and considering that 3D recognition usually falls into a separate category), it is the intra-class variability that usually calls for an adequately dimensioned training set or a sufficiently complex model. There are, however, situations where there is no *a priori* knowledge allowing for this variability to be captured. In this paper, we present an attempt in addressing a category of these problems.

2   On-the-Fly Symbol Recognition: Proposed Scenario

The scenario we work on is the following: we consider a large set of documents, possibly hand-written or hand-drawn, with very little domain knowledge about the kind of information they embed. A user, not necessarily a specialist, wants to be able to efficiently and interactively navigate in this set of documents, and find information relevant to his needs. These needs are unknown at the time of design of the document analysis system, and can widely vary over time. The scenario simply assumes that the user points out or sketches one or several instances of a symbol of interest to him, asking the system to retrieve all similar items from the set of documents. We insist on the fact that, for the scenario to remain open and generic, no *a priori* knowledge on the symbol, nor on the documents is provided.

Figure 1 presents a typical example from a document set we have used in our first experiments with this concept, and that we will present with more details in § 5. In the present case, we have a set of handwritten notes taken at various meetings, and the user happens to use some symbols such as arrows to indicate tasks to do (another user may use a completely different set of symbols for the same purpose). We absolutely do not plan to try performing handwriting recognition on such notes but only to be able to easily retrieve in the document set those regions where an occurrence of the symbol appears. With the same scenario, we could easily imagine another user browsing through some technical documentation such as a car repair manual.

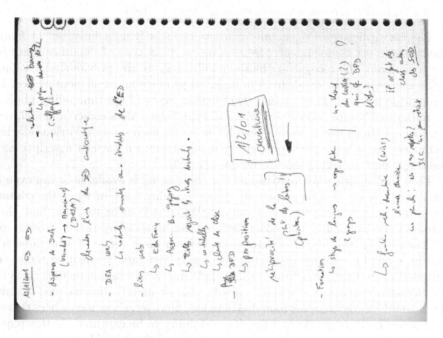

Fig. 1. An example of processed document

The basic idea of our method is to perform a crude segmentation on the documents (as previously mentioned, it is impossible with this scenario to have an exact, reliable segmentation as we do not know in advance what to look for), to extract some features from the candidate symbol, and to define a similarity measure between these features and similar features computed on the regions provided by the segmentation. Unfortunately, finding a descriptor and a metric that maps the user concept of similarity into a distance measure between low level features is nearly impossible since we have no means of determining what intra-class deformation is acceptable to the user. Indeed, depending on the context of use, the same user, using the same documents, may have different retrieval goals, implicitly requiring different intra-class variability. Our idea is therefore to try our best with the provided data, and to interactively prompt the user for extra knowledge to improve the query results until a satisfactory level of symbol identification is achieved.

The user is by no means considered as a pattern recognition expert. He is only asked whether, according to his judgment, a given pattern matches his initial query. Such approaches have initially been introduced in Content Based Image Retrieval [4, 5]. In this paper, we present an attempt in applying such relevance feedback techniques to symbol recognition.

3   Relevance Feedback

Relevance feedback has been an active research subject for the past few years. It has been successfully applied in Content Based Image Retrieval (CBIR) systems [6, 7]. Its purpose is to involve the user in an interactive discussion loop, in order to adapt the similarity measure computed between two patterns to the user similarity concepts, based on their low-level representation.

The core scenario of a relevance feedback system can be summarized as follows. For a given query, the system retrieves an initial set of results, ranked according to a predefined similarity metric. The user provides judgment on the current retrieval, as to whether the proposed samples are correct or wrong, and possibly to what degree. The system learns from the feedback, and provides a new set of results which are then submitted to the user approval. The system loops until the user is satisfied with the result set.

Patterns are represented by a vector of measurements performed on them. With an ideal descriptor, all the samples belonging to the same class would form a cluster in the feature space. The pattern most similar to the query would correspond to the nearest neighbors of the query representation in the feature space. An ideal query would be located right at the center of the space.

Early relevance feedback systems were built using heuristic-based techniques derived from document retrieval [8]. The main idea was to estimate an *ideal query point*, from the given positive samples. Re-weighting the feature space or the metric parameters is also used to maximize the correlation between the user similarity concept and the low level image features. Further developments contributed to formalize the problem by optimization techniques to minimize the total distance between the positive samples to the query [9, 10]. The principal findings were that the optimal query is obtained by averaging the positive samples, and that the Mahalanobis distance is the optimal weighted metric. MindReader [9] and Mars [11] CBIR systems apply these approaches with success.

Parallel work (though somewhat more recent) considers relevance feedback as a two-class classification problem and try to adapt known classification schemes to take into account the supplementary difficulties resulting from the small number of training samples, and the asymmetry in the data set.

Su [12] adapts a bayesian classifier based on the maximum likelihood, estimating the boundary of the relevant items from the positive samples and assigning penalties to unlabeled samples close to a negative one. Zhang [13] and Onada [14] use techniques based on Support Vector Machine, trying to iteratively determine the best hyperplane separating the positive and the negative samples in the projection space.

Other experiments have been carried out, involving decision trees [15, 16], nearest-prototype [17] or Bayesian relevance feedback [18]. According to the experiments reported in the literature, all these adaptive classification based methods outperform the optimization based approaches. It is difficult to determine which is the best, as there is to our knowledge no review reporting on such a comparison.

4   Proposed Prototype System

Our system demonstrates the usefulness of relevance feedback applied to on-the-fly symbol recognition. As described previously, we extract a candidate symbol from a set of handwritten documents and then proceed to finding all relevant representations of the same symbol in the set of documents.

This paper focuses on recognition and relevance feedback. It is clear that a number of preprocessing issues should not be underestimated. They are, however, out of the scope of this paper and we will only briefly summarize our choices.

4.1   Preprocessing

In our case, preprocessing involves two steps: document segmentation, and feature extraction.

Segmentation. Documents are segmented into rectangular regions, each region potentially embedding a symbol. In the first instance of our prototype, we used a very simple and straightforward segmentation technique based on recursive X-Y tree decomposition [19, 20]. While crude and simple, it provides good results on the kind of symbols we aim at in this paper. They consist of manual annotations, most often distinctly separated form the main text. Again, segmentation is not the problem we want to tackle in this experiment. Different application contexts certainly need adapted segmentation approaches. This point will undoubtedly be improved in a near future by implementing more efficient techniques such as connected components analysis [21] or the scale space approach proposed by Manmatha and Rothfeder [22]. Figure 2 shows the kind of segmentation results we currently obtain.

Feature extraction. For each region isolated in the previous step, a feature vector is extracted. In our first experiments, we used Zernike moments as the low level representation of the potential symbols. It is a well-known descriptor, with thoroughly studied performances [23], robust to the different deformation and distortion models cited previously cited , including those induced by hand sketching [24].

It is noteworthy to mention that our system is sufficiently modular to integrate other segmentation methods or different descriptors in a very straightforward manner. Those mentioned here have been implemented in order to prove the validity of our approach and in no way represent our ultimate choices.

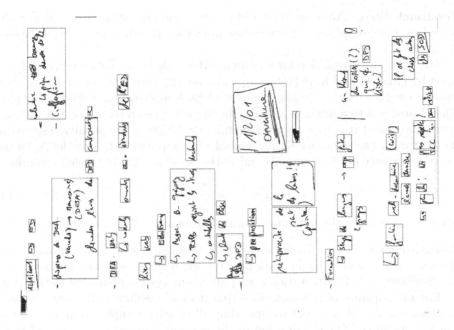

Fig. 2. Example of segmented document

Fig. 3. Initial step: the query and the 20 best matches sorted using the euclidean metric

4.2 Query and Relevance Feedback

Initial Step. The user selects a candidate symbol from the presegmented areas of the document set. From this initial query, the n best matching areas of all documents are retrieved, by computing the Euclidean distance from their representation to the query. A list of candidate areas, ordered in increasing distance from the query is presented to the user. Within this list, the user then selects which samples are relevant and which are irrelevant according to his own perception of similarity between his query and the presented candidates. Figure 3 exhibits a sample query, and the 20 best samples matching the query. This data is taken from the experiment described in section 5.

Feedback Step. From the retrieved positive and the negative samples in the initial step, we compute a relevance measure for all the other remaining unlabeled samples.

The relevance estimation for an unlabeled sample is based on a method developed by Giacinto and Rolli [18] using a nearest neighbor rule. The relevance of a sample depends on its minimal distance to both positive and negative samples. The closest it is to a relevant sample, the highest its own relevance. On the contrary, the closest it is to a negative sample, the bigger is the penalty assigned to its relevance. The relevance R of a symbol s is computed as follows: let $\mathcal{N}$ be the set of negatively labeled symbols and $\mathcal{P}$ the set of positively labeled symbols:

$$R(s) = 1 - e^{-\frac{d_{\min}(\mathcal{N},s)}{d_{\min}(\mathcal{R},s)}} \tag{1}$$

where $d_{\min}(\mathcal{X}, x)$ is the minimum distance from a set $\mathcal{X}$ to a symbol x.

Iteration Step. The areas are sorted by decreasing relevance and submitted to the user, who can then again mark positive and negative samples, and loop over the feedback step. Figure 4 shows the part of our system dedicated to this task.

The main quality of this method is that it locally estimates the relevance of a sample, and that it does not assume that all positive samples form a cluster in the feature space. The distribution of the relevant samples does not need to be Gaussian or have a boundary that can be modeled by a parametric shape. This presents a major advantage over other classification schemes that need these conditions to function properly. Furthermore, the nearest neighbor classifier (1-NN) is known to always yield correct results, provided it iterates over the entire sample set. Implementing a RF method based on the 1-NN rule is an excellent starting point and benchmark for subsequent evaluation of other methods.

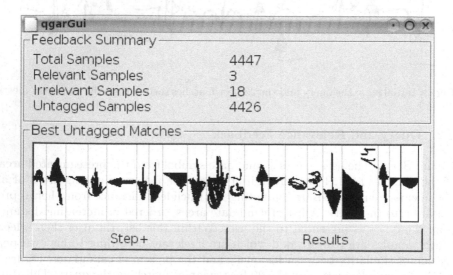

Fig. 4. Unlabeled best matches tagging after one feedback step

5   First Results

5.1   Experiment Setup

To assess the performances of our approach, we built a concrete test case. We extracted 82 A4 pages from a notebook, and used our prototype to retrieve the plain arrows which the notebook owner uses to signal something to be reminded. The pages where scanned at 200 dpi, and segmented using the method previously described. This process yields 4447 regions, that where manually labeled in order to establish a ground truth suitable to our tests. Out of these 4447 regions, 52 were labeled as plain arrows. These regions are shown in Figure 5.

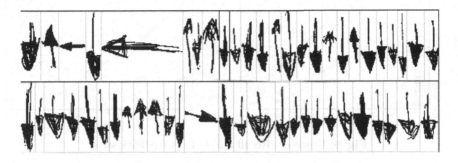

Fig. 5. The 52 positive samples of the corpus

We use *Precision* and *Recall* to evaluate the performance of the proposed approach. *Precision* is defined as the number of retrieved relevant regions over the total number retrieved regions. *Recall* is defined as the number of retrieved relevant regions over the total number of relevant regions (52 in our case).

In order to avoid spurious conclusions based on particular experiments, all measurements are taken on the whole set of arrow symbols. Each relevant symbol is used in its turn as initial query for our system, and 4 feedback iterations are performed, as described in section 4.2. We then plot average *Precision* and *Recall* curves computed over all 52 queries.

Furthermore, to asses the impact of user feedback, the above process is repeated with an increasing number of labeled symbols per feedback step. We performed experiments with 5, 10, 15, and 20 user selected regions per iteration. The *Precision–Recall* curves are shown in Figure 6.

5.2   Results and Observations

A quick analysis of the results in Figure 6 naively implies that the higher the number of user labeled examples per iteration is, the better the final classification results. This, however, needs to be moderated.

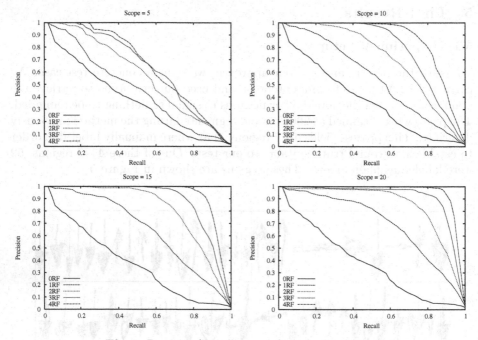

Fig. 6. Precision/Recall curves for 4 feedback steps

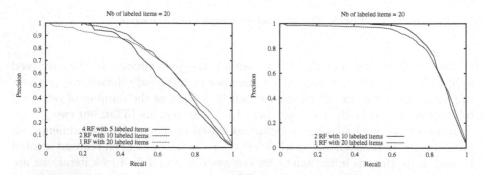

Fig. 7. Precision/Recall curves with identical number of tagged items

The experiment does reveal that:

- User feedback drastically enhances system convergence towards a high recognition rates. Even with very few user-labeled symbols (*e.g.* 10) *P*recision goes up with 30% for a recall of 50%. In other terms, the rank of the median ranked symbol is 37 with 10 labeled symbols, while it is 68 without. Furthermore, in order to retrieve 80% of the 52 searched symbols (*i.e.* 42 items) within 4447 possible candidates, one needs to label 60 to 80 symbols, according to the number of symbols considered at each iteration (15 or 20, in our case).
- Initial convergence speed (*i.e.* enhancement of global recognition quality in the first stages of the relevance feedback loop) is fairly independent of the number of feedback iterations, but rather depends of the total number of la-

beled items. Figure 7 shows that global quality is equivalent for 4 iterations over 5 samples, 2 over 10 or 1 over 20, and similarly for 4 over 10 and 2 over 20.

6   Conclusion and Future Work

We have presented our basic choices in building a framework for quickly browsing a large set of scanned documents without any prior knowledge on their content. This framework allows a user to select a symbol of interest and interactively search for the most relevant symbols, using a relevance feedback mechanism to iteratively reach a satisfactory state. A first noticeable property is that the prototype we have built works and gives us good hope that we are on the right track.

Of course, we are perfectly aware that this represents only the first steps for a full, versatile system able to work on a number of document types. As previously mentioned, we have to provide a choice of segmentation and feature extraction methods, able to robustly cope with various user needs. Indeed, Zernike moments, for instance, worked fine for the arrows used in the example presented in this paper, but are not necessarily the best decriptor in another context.

To extend our system towards the handling of bigger data sets, it will be necessary to work on how to efficiently store, index and access precomputed feature sets combined with various segmentations schemes, so as to provide a quick and efficient feedback to the user in searching and browsing mode.

On the classification front, the 1-NN classifier has also its drawbacks and we need to choose the adequate classifiers which allow user interaction and make it easy to decide when to stop, especially when user feedback starts to degrade the convergence of classification.

Finally, with respect to functionalities of such a system, our goal is that the user should be able to design her *personal dictionary* of symbols of interest, storing information of interest and restoring it for reuse from one session to the other.

At the present time, we are focusing on maximizing the knowledge extracted from the user-provided feedback. Instead of sorting the classification output by relevance, it might be a better idea to guide the user very quickly and efficiently to the "border zone" where his feedback will be most relevant for improving the classification in the next iteration. This may necessitate some "intelligent" analysis of the relevance curve. In the same order of idea, it would be useful to be able to find a correlation between the size of the database, the number of symbols to be found and the scope of the search, in order to minimize the number of iterations with the user and to optimize the convergence and the quality of the recall.

References

1. Chhabra, A.K.: Graphic Symbol Recognition: An Overview. In Tombre, K., Chhabra, A.K., eds.: Graphics Recognition—Algorithms and Systems. Volume 1389 of Lecture Notes in Computer Science. Springer-Verlag (1998) 68–79
2. Cordella, L.P., Vento, M.: Symbol recognition in documents: a collection of techniques? International Journal on Document Analysis and Recognition **3** (2000) 73–88

3. Lladós, J., Valveny, E., Sánchez, G., Martí, E.: Symbol Recognition: Current Advances and Perspectives. In Blostein, D., Kwon, Y.B., eds.: Graphics Recognition – Algorithms and Applications. Volume 2390 of Lecture Notes in Computer Science. Springer-Verlag (2002) 104–127
4. Zhang, L., Lin, F., Zhang, B.: Support vector machine learning for image retrieval. In: Proceedings of IEEE International Conference on Image Processing. (2001) 721–724
5. Zhou, X., Huang, T.S.: Relevance feedback in image retrieval: a comprehensive review. Multimedia Systems 8 (2003) 536–544
6. Smeulders, A.W.M., Worring, M., Santini, S., Gupta, A., Jain, R.: Content-Based Image Retrieval at the End of the Early Years. IEEE Transactions on PAMI 22 (2000) 1349–1380
7. Vasconcelos, N., Lippman, A.: Bayesian Relevance Feedback for Content-Based Image Retrieval. In: Proceedings of IEEE Workshop on Content-based Access of Image and Video Libraries. (2000) 63
8. Doermann, D.: The Indexing and Retrieval of Document Images: A Survey. Computer Vision and Image Understanding 70 (1998) 287–298
9. Ishikawa, Y., Subramanya, R., Faloutsos, C.: MindReader: Query databases through multiple examples. In: Very Large Databases. (1998)
10. Rui, Y., Huang, T.: Optimizing Learning in Image Retrieval. In: Computer Vision and Pattern Recognition. (2000) 1236
11. Rui, Y., Huang, T., Mehrotra, S.: Content-Based Image Retrieval with Relevance Feedback in MARS. In: Proceedings of IEEE International Conference on Image Processing. (1997) 815–818
12. Su, Z., Zhang, H., Ma, S.: Using Bayesian Classifier in Relevant Feedback of Image Retrieval. In: 12th IEEE International Conference on Tools with Artificial Intelligence (ICTAI'00). (2000)
13. Zhang, H.J., Chen, Z., Liu, W.Y., Li, M.: Relevance feedback in content-based image search. World Wide Web 2 (2003) 131–155
14. Onada, T., Murata, M., Yamada, S.: Relevance feedback document retrieval using support vector machines. In: Proceedings of International Joint Conference on Neural Networks (IJCNN-2003). (2003) 1757–1762
15. MacArthur, S.D., Brodley, C.E., Shyu, C.: Relevance Feedback Decision Trees in Content-Based Image Retrieval. In: IEEE Workshop on Content-based Access of Image and Video Libraries. (2000) 68
16. Wang, T., Rui, Y., Hu, S., Sun, J.: Adaptive Tree Similarity for Image Retrieval. Multimedia Systems 9 (2003) 131–143
17. Giacinto, G., Roli, F.: Nearest-prototype relevance feedback for content based image retrieval. In: Proceedings of the 17th International Conference on Pattern Recognition, Cambridge (UK). (2004) 989–992
18. Giacinto, G., Roli, F.: Bayesian relevance feedback for content-based image retrieval. Pattern Recognition 37 (2004) 1499–1508
19. Nagy, G., Seth, S.: Hierarchical Representation of Optically Scanned Documents. In: Proceedings of 7th International Conference on Pattern Recognition, Montréal (Canada). (1984) 347–349
20. Appiani, E., Cesarini, F., Colla, A.M., Diligenti, M., Gori, M., Marinai, S., Soda, G.: Automatic document classification and indexing in high-volume applications. International Journal on Document Analysis and Recognition 4 (2001) 69–83

21. Tombre, K., Tabbone, S., Pélissier, L., Lamiroy, B., Dosch, P.: Text/graphics separation revisited. In Lopresti, D., Hu, J., Kashi, R., eds.: Proceedings of the 5th IAPR International Workshop on Document Analysis Systems, Princeton, NJ (USA). Volume 2423 of Lecture Notes in Computer Science., Springer-Verlag (2002) 200–211
22. Manmatha, R., Rothfeder, J.L.: A Scale Space Approach for Automatically Segmenting Words from Historical Handwritten Documents. IEEE Transactions on PAMI **27** (2005) 1212–1225
23. Liao, S.X., Pawlak, M.: On the Accuracy of Zernike Moments for Image Analysis. IEEE Transactions on PAMI **20** (1998) 1358–1364
24. Hse, H., Newton, A.R.: Sketched Symbol Recognition using Zernike Moments. In: Proceedings of the 17th International Conference on Pattern Recognition, Cambridge (UK). (2004)

The Fuzzy-Spatial Descriptor for the Online Graphic Recognition: Overlapping Matrix Algorithm

Noorazrin Zakaria[1], Jean-Marc Ogier[1], and Josep Llados[2]

[1] L3i, University of La Rochelle, France
{nzakaria, jmogier}@univ-lr.fr
[2] CVC, University Autonoma of Barceleno, Spain
Josep.Lllados@uab.es

Abstract. In this paper we present the algorithm of our fuzzy-spatial descriptor for symbol recognition in on-line sketches. Fuzzy sets are used to enhance this approach to cope with the inherent distortion of freehand drawings. It allows handling some primitive irregularities due to different ways of drawing in complex composite forms. The descriptor provides complete local information of the primitives that consist of only straight lines. This descriptor used the opening angle between primitives and its overlapping properties in 1D projection to describe its local spatial properties. Segmentation by curve and pen-speed properties of each drawing has been used in obtaining our basic primitives. The experiment results show that a part from its rotational-invariant, this descriptor is also robust to multi-scale of segmentation of its primitives.

1 Introduction

With the arrival of tactile platform like TabletPC, the online graphic recognition has to face new problems driven by newly arising applications. The most natural and convenient way to provide graphics in a system is to draw sketches on the tactile platform, just like the drawing freehand graphics on a piece of paper. However the sketchy drawings are usually not neat in appearance, neither compact in representation and storage, nor easy for systems to understand and apprehend.

The recognition of online graphic objects is different from the recognition of online handwritings. For online handwritings, a recognizer should be able to tolerate different writing styles. However rotational invariance is not crucial for online handwriting because direction variations of input characters are small.

On the other hand, a graphic objects recognizer requires more flexibility in orientation of each input object with a robust tolerance of different ways of object drawings that cope with the inherent distortion of freehand drawings. It must be able to handle some primitive irregularities due to different way of drawing in complex composite forms. For this situation, we proposed our method, called Overlapping Matrix, which is based on fuzzy set theory with spatial properties between primitives as the basic classes. We used straight lines as the primitives of our input. From these straight line input, we used the opening angle and the projection overlaps between two primitives to describe the spatial properties of each primitive. In order to improve computational efficiency during the matching of primitives, an approach using global spatial descrip-

H. Bunke and A.L. Spitz (Eds.): DAS 2006, LNCS 3872, pp. 616–627, 2006.
© Springer-Verlag Berlin Heidelberg 2006

tor for every primitive is used. We tested this method using the CVC Barcelona dataset (Graphics Recognition 2003), and it performed at 94% of recognition accuracy.

To begin with, we described few relative works that have been done in Section 2. The details of the algorithm used in this method are developed in Section 3, followed by Section 4 that described the matching process that consists of regrouping all information of descriptors from individual pairs of primitives and classification process. Section 5 showed some experimental results and evaluation. And we conclude with Section 6 with some comments about this contribution.

2 Related Works

A large number of representation and recognition techniques have been proposed for sketch recognition using feature based methods. For example, Rubine [1] defined a gesture characterized by a set of eleven geometric attributes and two dynamic attributes, and constructed a linear discriminate classifier for gesture-based interfaces whose weights are learned from a set of training examples. However, Rubine's method is only applicable to single-stroke sketches and sensitive to drawing direction and orientation.

Fonseca et al[2] proposed a method of symbol recognition using fuzzy logic based on a number of rotational invariant global features, such as the smallest convex hull that can be circumscribed around the shape, the largest triangle that can be inscribed in the hull, and the largest quadrilateral that can be inscribed. Because their classification method relies on aggregate features of pen strokes, it might be difficult to differentiate between similar shapes. A benefit of feature-based approaches is that stroke regrouping is not necessary, while their drawback is that they perform typically in basic shapes recognition, such as rectangle and circles.

In addition, many sketch recognition methods are based on stroke segmentation. Most segmentation techniques in image processing target nicely printed symbols and do not scale well to hand-sketched symbols due to the noise and distortion in sketches. As strokes can be segmented in many different ways, the combinatory approaches based on exhaustive search is clearly infeasible for complex sketchy shapes. Temporal information such as pen speed has been recently explored as a means to uncover users' intentions during sketching. Sezgin[3] and later Calhoun[4], used both curvature and speed information in a stroke to locate breakpoints. Saund[5] uses more perceptual context, including local features such as curvature and intersections, as well as global features such as closed paths. These methods focus on the detection of corner (segment) points, which usually help decompose the original ink into basic geometric components such as lines and arcs. All of them use the empirical thresholds to test the validity of an approximation that ultimately leads to the problem of a threshold being too tight or too loose. Furthermore because of the arbitrariness of the drawing it is hard to manipulate these diverse strokes well. Recently, Heloise et al[6] used Dynamic Programming to approximate recursively a digitized curve with a given number of lines and arc segments based on templates. However, they put emphasis upon stroke segmentation for simple sketchy shapes based on all of the ink points.

In our method, we modified the segmentation of strokes using the approach proposed by Calhoun[4], in order to divide the raw data into straight line segments. In addition to the work, we introduced points of inflexions together with maximum and minimum points in our raw data of our input. From these points, we obtained the straight line primitives for our spatial descriptor. 4 fuzzy membership functions have been used to classify the opening of every pair of primitives, and 6 fuzzy membership functions have been used to describe its overlapping properties in 1 axis of reference. The final step in the matching process is performed by comparing the spatial descriptor of every primitive from a sketched input, with every primitive from the selected models.

3 The Overlapping Matrix Algorithm

The system is composed of three functional units: extraction of graphic primitives, generation of spatial description, indexation and model based matching.

3.1 Straight Line Primitive Extraction

Naturally, users tend to slow the pen when making many kinds of intentional discontinuities in the shape. For example, when drawing a rectangle as a single pen stroke, it is natural to slow down at the corners, which are the segment points. Figure 1 shows the speed profile for a typical square. The corners can be easily identified by the low pen speed.

Once the pen speed has been calculated at each point along the stroke, segment points can be found by thresholding the speed. Any point with a speed below the threshold is a segment point. We specify the threshold as fraction of the average speed along the particular pen stroke. If necessary, the user can adjust the threshold to match his or her particular drawing style.

While many intentional discontinuities occur at low pen speed, others do not. For example, when drawing an "S" shape, there may be no slowdown at the transition from one lobe to the other. Similarly, when drawing a "J" shape, there may be no slowdown at the transition from the line to the arc. We can locate these kinds of segment points by examining the curvature of the pen stroke. Segment points occur at locations where the curvature changes sign.

Firstly a polygonal approximation is used to transform the raw data of online input into straight line primitives. This segmentation is computed based on the speed and curvature properties of the input.

Naturally, users tend to slow the pen when making many kinds of intentional discontinuities in the shape. For example, when drawing a rectangle as a single pen

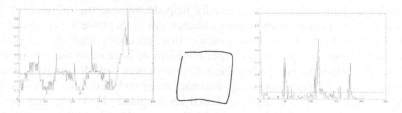

Fig. 1. Speed profile (left) and Curve Profile (right) for a square

stroke, it is natural to slow down at the corners, which are the segment points. Figure 1 shows the speed profile for a typical square. The corners can be easily identified by the low pen speed.

Once the pen speed has been calculated at each point along the stroke, segment points can be found by thresholding the speed. Any point with a speed below the threshold is a segment point. We specify the threshold as fraction of the average speed along the particular pen stroke. If necessary, the user can adjust the threshold to match his or her particular drawing style.

While many intentional discontinuities occur at low pen speed, others do not. For example, when drawing an "S" shape, there may be no slowdown at the transition from one lobe to the other. Similarly, when drawing a "J" shape, there may be no slowdown at the transition from the line to the arc. We can locate these kinds of segment points by examining the curvature of the pen stroke. Segment points occur at locations where the curvature changes sign.

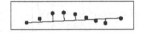

Fig. 2. Window calculating the curvature sign

We consider three distinct signs: positive, negative, and zero. When computing the sign, we examine a window of points on either side of the point in question. We connect the first and last points in the window with a line segment. We then calculate the minimum distance from each point in the window to the line. Distances to the left of the line are positive, while those to the right are negative. Left and right are defined relative to the drawing direction. The signed distances are summed to determine the sign of the curvature.

If the absolute value of the sum is less than a threshold, the curvature is considered to be zero. In the example in Figure 2, the curvature is positive because there are more positive distances than negative ones. (In this example, the drawing direction is from left to right.).

By using a window of points to compute the sign of the curvature, we are able to smooth out noise in the pen signal. Some of the noise comes from minor fluctuations in the drawing, other noise comes from the digitizing error of the input device. The larger the window, the larger the smoothing effect. The size of the window must be tuned to the input device and the user. For mouse input, we have found a window size of 10% of points with respect to the total points in a stroke to be suitable.

The points of inflexion are also detected by localizing the center of zero curvature between pairs of minimum and maximum points.

Once the strokes have been segmented, the next task is to generate spatial descriptions of each primitive.

This Spatial Descriptor provides structural information of every pairs of primitives in of an online symbol. We used the angle formed between 2 segments in each pair of primitives and its degree of overlapping. In practice, the angle formed between 2 segments and its degree of overlapping are sometimes too ambiguous to be identified. Hence we describe them by assigning a membership degree for every possible case in term of fuzzy set theory.

On the other hand, The Sequential Descriptor indicates the neighbouring properties of primitives. This is very helpful to account the penalty for the possible errors from bad segmentation of strokes into straight line primitives.

This leads to the descriptor elaborated here-after.

3.2 Spatial Descriptor

From straight line primitives, we classified every pairs of primitives according to the angle forming between segments (opening angle) and to the overlapping of one segment to another. Four fuzzy classes have been used to classify the opening angles, whilst 6 classes used to identify the type of overlapping of a segment's 1D projection with respect to another segment.

3.2.1 Opening Angle
For every segment Ni, its orientation is defined by,

$$\theta = arctg\left[\frac{(y'_e - y'_s)}{(x'_e - x'_s)}\right] \tag{1}$$

where (x'_s, y'_s) and (x'_e, y'_e) are the coordinates of the initial point and the final point of the segment.

For every pair of primitives (N_a, N_b), we used the first chosen segment, named N_a, as a local reference axis. Figure 3a here-after illustrates this situation.

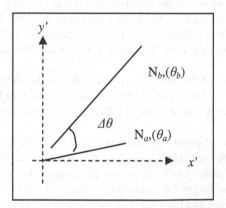

Fig. 3. A pair of primitive

Thus, the angle separating this pair is defined by,

$$\Delta\theta = \theta_b - \theta_a \tag{2}$$

We used 4 classes as fuzzy memberships for this angle. These 4 classes represent 4 possible critical angles for a pair of primitives. They are formulated in a vector,

$$[\mu_1(\Delta\theta), \mu_2(\Delta\theta), \mu_3(\Delta\theta), \mu_4(\Delta\theta)] \tag{3}$$

For every opening angle of one pair of primitives, this vector represents the distribution of belonging of the opening angle into those 4 critical angles [0°, 45°, 90°, 135°].

Table 1. Membership function of the Opening Angles

Type	μ_1	μ_2	μ_3	μ_4
$\Delta\theta(°)$	$0 \pm k180$	$45 \pm k180$	$90 \pm k180$	$135 \pm k180$

In term of fuzzy set theory, the opening angle of a pair of primitives can be regarded as linguistic variable, $\{1, 2, 3, 4\}$ are linguistic terms, each of which corresponds with a fuzzy set, and   is the membership function associated with linguistic
term i, where i=1,2,3,4. The membership function of linguistic term i is defined as,

$$\mu_i(\Delta\theta) = \begin{cases} 1 & \Delta\theta \in [\theta_i - 10°, \theta_i + 10°] \\ 0,5 + 0,5 \times \dfrac{\Delta\theta - (\theta_i - 22,5°)}{12,5°} & \Delta\theta \in [\theta_i - 35°, \theta_i - 10°] \\ 0,5 + 0,5 \times \dfrac{(\theta_i + 22,5°) - \Delta\theta}{12,5°} & \Delta\theta \in [\theta_i + 10°, \theta_i + 35°] \\ 0 & \Delta\theta \notin [\theta_i - 35°, \theta_i + 35°] \end{cases} \quad (4)$$

where i $\in \{1, 2, 3, 4\}$.

3.2.2 Projection Overlapping

In every pair of primitives, one segment, N_b, will be projected into the segment of
reference, N_a. The segment N_a will be considered as the new X co-ordinate. The detailed implementation is as follows.

Firstly, the endpoints of all primitives $\{N_b | b=1,2,\dots,L\}$ are transformed from origi-
nal co-ordinates (x', y') to a new co-ordinates (x, y) via the well known equation

$$\begin{aligned} x &= x'\cos(\Delta\theta) + y'\sin(\Delta\theta) \\ y &= -x'\cos(\Delta\theta) + y'\cos(\Delta\theta) \end{aligned} \quad (5)$$

where $\Delta\theta$ is the opening angle of pair (N_a, N_b) in the old co-ordinates so as to let N_a
act as the X axis of the new co-ordinates. Hence, the overlapping is calculated by
projecting the segment N_a into the new co-ordinate (X axis).

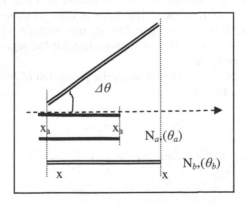

Fig. 4. Projection of segment N_b on N_a

Figure 4 above shows the overlapping of the projection of N_b $[x_{b1}, x_{b2}]$ with Na $[x_{a1}, x_{a2}]$, where $x_{a1} < x_{a2}$ et $x_{b1} < x_{b2}$.

We used 6 fuzzy classes to represent the overlapping of every projection axis of segments. We use a vector

$$\varepsilon_i(N_a, N_b) = \begin{bmatrix} \varepsilon_1(x_{a1}, x_{a2}, x_{b1}, x_{b2}) \\ \varepsilon_2(x_{a1}, x_{a2}, x_{b1}, x_{b2}) \\ \varepsilon_3(x_{a1}, x_{a2}, x_{b1}, x_{b2}) \\ \varepsilon_4(x_{a1}, x_{a2}, x_{b1}, x_{b2}) \\ \varepsilon_5(x_{a1}, x_{a2}, x_{b1}, x_{b2}) \\ \varepsilon_6(x_{a1}, x_{a2}, x_{b1}, x_{b2}) \end{bmatrix} \qquad (6)$$

to describe the possibility that an overlapping belongs to every class. In term of fuzzy set theory, type of overlapping can be regarded as linguistic variable, {1,2,3,4,5,6} are linguistic terms, and $\varepsilon_i(x_{a1}, x_{a2}, x_{b1}, x_{b2})$ is the membership function associated with linguistic term i, where i=1,2,3,4,5,6.

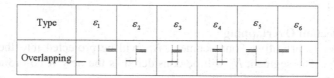

Type	ε_1	ε_2	ε_3	ε_4	ε_5	ε_6
Overlapping						

Fig. 5. Membership functions of the overlapping

As illustrated in Figure 5 above, there are 6 types of overlapping between 2 primitives in an X-axis projection. We used a linear distribution for those 4 fuzzy linguistic terms. Figure 5 also shows us that the overlapping properties of ε_1, ε_2 and ε_3 reflect those of ε_4, ε_5 and ε_6.

To begin with, we describe here-below the overlapping types ε_2 and ε_5. These two classes represent a total separation of each primitive in a pair of segments that projected into a new axis of reference. The limit inferior of these classes is when the primitives in this pair touch each other. During the overlapping, these classes represent the relative length of a fraction of a projection (of the segment N_b for ε_2, and N_a for ε_5.) that is not overlapped.

For the fuzzy membership function of ε_2, the projection of N_a is situated on the left of N_b. This function is defined as:

$$\varepsilon_2 = \begin{cases} 1 - \varepsilon_1 & x_{a2} \leq x_{b1} \\ \dfrac{(x_{b1} - x_{a1})}{a_{\max}} & (x_{b1} < x_{a2}) \wedge (x_{b1} > x_{a1}) \\ 0 & else \end{cases} \qquad (7)$$

On the other hand, for the fuzzy membership function of ε_5, the segment N_b situated on the left of the projection of N_a. Thus, its membership function is defined as:

$$\varepsilon_5 = \begin{cases} 1-\varepsilon_6 & (x_{a1} \geq x_{b2}) \\ \dfrac{(x_{a2}-x_{b2})}{a_{max}} & (x_{a1} < x_{b2}) \wedge (x_{a2} > x_{b2}) \\ 0 & else \end{cases} \tag{8}$$

where $a_{max} = (x_{a2} - x_{a1})$ and $b_{max} = (x_{b2} - x_{b1})$, represent the total length of segment N_a and the projection length of N_b on new x-axis that is parallel with N_a. The first condition in equations (7) and (8) above, represents a total separation of those projections. The second condition shows the relative length of segment of reference (N_a) that is not overlapped. The function returns zero elsewhere.

For the fuzzy membership function of ε_3 and ε_4, a linear distribution is assured by integrating a relative distance of projections' submerge, named ε', together with a distance between the centers of two overlapping projections.

We divided the compute of the relative distance of ε' into 4 situations of overlapping:

1. The first situation consists of a partial overlapping, where one of the extreme points of every projection stay outside the overlapping. During this type of overlapping, the membership functions of ε', represent a ratio between the length of the overlapped projections and the length of segment used as axis of reference, N_a.
2. The second situation is described by a projection that submerges totally in the projection of the segment that used as X-axis. This happens when the projection of N_b is smaller than N_a.
3. The third situation is the opposite of the one that describe in the second. The projection of N_b is longer than N_a.
4. And the forth situation is the complement of the first one. It represents the same ratio as explained in the first situation above.

For the function of ε_3 and ε_4, these 4 situations are represented by:

$$\varepsilon' = \begin{cases} \dfrac{(x_{a2}-x_{b1})}{a_{max}} & (x_{a2} > x_{b1}) \wedge (x_{a2} < x_{b2}) \wedge (x_{a1} < x_{b1}) \\ \dfrac{1}{2} & (x_{a2} > x_{b2}) \wedge (x_{a1} < x_{b1}) \\ \dfrac{1}{4} & (x_{b2} > x_{a2}) \wedge (x_{b1} < x_{a1}) \\ \dfrac{(x_{b2}-x_{a1})}{a_{max}} & (x_{a1} < x_{b2}) \wedge (x_{a2} > x_{b2}) \wedge (x_{a1} > x_{b1}) \\ 0 & else \end{cases} \tag{9}$$

After considering all possibilities of overlapping, we defined the 2 central membership function, ε_3 and ε_4, by multiplying the submergence relative, ε', with the relative distance of centers between 2 overlapping projections.

The relative distance of those centers is defined by:

$$r_{centre} = \frac{2.|m_b - m_a|}{a_{max} + b_{max}}$$
(10)

Hence, we defined our middle membership functions by:

$$\varepsilon_3 = \varepsilon'.(r_{centre} + 1)$$
(11)

$$\varepsilon_4 = \varepsilon'.(1 - r_{centre})$$
(12)

Last but not least, we introduced our last 2 marginal membership functions in order to differentiate between a limit of separation (ε_2 and ε_5) and a total separation within a restricted window of descriptor (ε_1 and ε_6).

Thus, our marginal membership functions are defined by:

$$\varepsilon_1 = \begin{cases} \dfrac{(x_{b1} - x_{a2})}{Dist_{PMS}} & x_{b1} > x_{a2} \\ 0 & else \end{cases}$$
(13)

$$\varepsilon_6 = \begin{cases} \dfrac{(x_{a1} - x_{b2})}{Dist_{PMS}} & x_{a1} > x_{b2} \\ 0 & else \end{cases}$$
(14)

where $Dist_{PMS}$ = window width $- (b_{max}) - (a_{max})$

At the end of this process, we have the overlapping between 2 primitives N_a and N_b in 1 dimentional plan can be obtained by synthesizing their overlapping on X-axis (segment N_a). Here, we let:

$$\varepsilon_{(i)}(N_a, N_b) = \varepsilon_i(x_{a1}, x_{a2}, x_{b1}, x_{b2})$$
(15)

3.3 Reconstruction of Spatial Descriptor

Our spatial descriptor for every pair of primitives is defined by:

$$Ds_{k,(i)}(N_a, N_b) = \mu_k(\Delta\theta) \times \varepsilon_{(i)}(N_a, N_b)$$
(16)

For every pair of primitives, we obtained a matrix of (4x6) elements that describes the spatial properties between them. We applied this descriptor to all possible combination of every pairs of primitives.

4 Matching Process

For every input of online symbols, we have a list of descriptor matrices that describe all possible combination of primitive relationships. In a matching process, we can obtain a very precise description of primitives by comparing all descriptor matrices individually. However, this locally rich information from our descriptor requires lots of time to compute those matrices individually.

4.1 Global Approach

We improved this matching process by regrouping all local information of all pairs according to the segments used as reference axis. To do so, we added all descriptor matrices that belong to the same segment of reference. As a result, we obtained another global spatial descriptor of every primitive. The global spatial descriptor of each primitive N_p is defined by:

$$Ds(N_p) = \frac{\sum_{q=1}^{L} Ds_{k,(i)}(N_p, N_q) \cdot w_{pq}}{\sum_{q=1}^{L} w_{pq}} \tag{17}$$

where L represent the total number of primitives, w_{pq} represent the weigh that used to describe the sequence of 2 primitives.

For 2 consecutive primitives, we reduce the weight of w_{pq} so that the global primitive descriptor is less influenced from them. At the same time, w_{pq}, is also proportional to the relative distance between the reference segment and the projection of its pair. Hence we improved its robustness to noises due to bad segmentation.

4.2 Matching

With the global approach, our primitive descriptor provides information of spatial and relational relationship of each primitive of an online graphic form. The matching between the input and models is to find the correspondence between primitives. This can be done by computing the nearest similarity.

Suppose that an input symbol is composed by line segments $w = \{N_p | p=1,2,...,L\}$ and the model to be compared consists of line segments $w' = \{N'_q | q=1,2,...,L'\}$. The similarity distance between these two line segments N_p and N'_q is defined as:

$$d(N_p, N'_q) = \sum_{k=1}^{4} \sum_{i=1}^{6} \left| Ds_{k,(i)}(N_p) - Ds_{k,(i)}(N'_q) \right| \tag{18}$$

where $Ds_{k,(i)}(N_p)$ and $Ds_{k,(i)}(N'_q)$, defined in equation (18), are the statistical feature associated with each line segment.

Matching two symbols is to find the correspondence between their line segments. This can be done using the nearest neighbour. Following is the computation:

```
for i from 1 to min(L,L')
    for j from 1 to min(L,L')
        d_i = d(N_i, N'_j)
    endfor j
    di = min { d(N_i, N'_j) }
    remove N_i de ω
    remove N'_j de ω'
endfor i
end
```

For every loop of the computation above, we omitted segment from the input, N_p, that similar to the one from the model, N'_p. At the end of these iterations, we obtained min{L,L'} matched pairs and |L-L'| of isolated segments. Thus, the distance between symbols is defined as:

$$D = \frac{\left(1+\frac{|L-L'|}{L+L'}\right) \cdot \sum_{l=1}^{\min\{L,L'\}} (d_l \cdot w_l)}{\sum_{l=1}^{\min\{L,L'\}} w_l} \qquad (19)$$

where $\sum d_l$ is the cost of min{L,L'} matched pairs, $[1+|L-L'|/(L+L')]$ accounts the penalty for |L–L'| unmatched primitives and w_l weighs the similarity distance with respect to the length of the segment.

The objective of fuzzy matrix algorithm is to find the nearest neighbour for an input sketch within selected models. Based on equation (18), the distance between every candidate model and the input symbol can be determined. Then, the model with the minimum distance to the input sketch is selected as the retrieved model.

5   Experimental Results

A dataset collected manually from CVC Barcelona, is used for the comparison. It consists of 50 classes of architectural online and offline symbols, drawn by 40 different people and 20 instances each. Our retrieval is focused in comparing an on-line symbol towards its perfect off-line model of reference.

The matching accuracy of our approach improved up to 94% compared to 88% initially when we did not introduce the sequential factor and segment length in our descriptor. The experimental results also show that this method sustains the same performance of model retrieval with different ways of sketching the strokes.

However, the drawback of our approach is due to its run time of recognition, where it has a tendency of increasing proportionate to the number of primitives. It remains acceptable to isolated symbols that have limited number of segments.

6   Conclusion

In this paper, we propose a complete fuzzy-spatial descriptor in online graphic recognition, proven to be robust in rotational and primitive sequences. The integration of feedbacks in final classification coupled with intelligent matching of structural descriptors is our future endeavour.

References

1. Rubine Dean, Specifying gestures by examples, Computer Graphics, 1991, 25:329-337.
2. Fonseca M. J., Pimentel C. and Jorge J. A., CALI – an online scribble recognizer for calligraphic interfaces. In AAAI Spring Symposium on Sketch Understanding, AAAI Press (2002) 51-58.
3. Sezgin T. M., Stahovich T., Davis R., Sketch based interfaces: early processing for sketch understanding. In Proceedings of the 2001 Workshop on PUI, Orlando, Florida, (2001) 1-8.

4. Calhoun C., Stahovich T. F., Kurtoglu T. and Kara L. B., Recognizing multi-stroke symbols. In Proceddings of 2002 AAAI Spring Symposium – Sketch Understanding, AAAI Press (2002) 15-23.
5. Saund E., Finding Perceptually Closed Paths in Sketches and Drawings. IEEE Transactions on Pattern Analysis and Machine Intelligence. 25(4), (2003) 457-491.
6. Heloise H., Micheal S., and Richard N., Robust Sketched Symbol Fragmentation using Templates. International Conference on Intelligent User Interface, ACM Press 156-160.

Author Index

Agne, Stefan   312
Alimi, Adel M.   25
Alrashed, Saleh A.   449
Alusse, André   437
Ambati, Vamshi   425
Antonacopoulos, A.   302
Arnabat, Jordi   588

Babu, Pavithra   71
Baird, Henry S.   280
Balasubramanian, A.   1, 13
Bapst, Frédéric   529
Beckley, Russell   348
Belaïd, Abdel   117, 437
Bengio, Samy   186
Bloechle, Jean-Luc   141
Bodansky, Eugene   462
Boonstra, Matthew   576
Bortolozzi, Flávio   176
Boto, Fernando   496
Breuel, Thomas M.   368
Bridson, D.   302
Bunke, Horst   186
Busagala, Lazaro S.P.   506

Casey, Matthew R.   280
Chatelain, Clément   564
Chellapilla, Kumar   358
Choi, Nam Sup   62
Collins, Jim   71
Coombs, Jeffrey   348
Cortés, Andoni   496

de Carvalho, João Marques   176
Déjean, Hervé   129
Dengel, Andreas   312
Ding, Xiaoqing   220, 402

Embley, David W.   164
Emptoz, Hubert   25, 38

Facon, Jacques   176
Fadoua, Drira   38
Faini, Stefano   336

Flaster, Michael   291
Fu, Qiang   220

Garg, Saurabh   255
Garofolo, John   576
Goldgof, Dmitry   576
Govindaraju, Venu   106
Gribov, Alexander   462
Gu, Zhimin   390

Hadjar, Karim   141
He, Qinming   474
Heutte, Laurent   564
Hillyer, Bruce   291
Ho, Tin Kam   291
Hotta, Yoshinobu   553
Huang, Weihua   232, 324

Ignácio, Sérgio Aparecido   176
Ingold, Rolf   141, 529
Iwamura, Masakazu   541

Jawahar, C.V.   1, 13, 425
Jiang, Yan   220
Johnsen, Ottar   529
Joshi, Gopal Datt   255

Kang, Gwan Hee   62
Karatzas, D.   302
Kasturi, Rangachar   576
Katsuyama, Yutaka   553
Kawashima, Toshio   413
Keysers, Daniel   368
Kim, Kyoung Min   62
Kimura, Fumitaka   506, 593
Kise, Koichi   541
Klein, Bertin   312
Kumar, K.S. Sesh   13
Kwoh, Leong Keong   268

Lalanne, Denis   141
Lamiroy, Bart   604
LeBourgeois, Frank   25, 38
Lee, Buhm   62
Leedham, Graham   196
Liu, Fei   593

Liwicki, Marcus   186
Llados, Josep   616
Lopresti, Daniel   164
Lu, Shijian   232, 484
Lu, Yue   243

Ma, Junchang   390
Manmatha, R.   84
Manohar, Vasant   576
Mariéthoz, Johnny   186
Marinai, Simone   336
Marino, Emanuele   336
Maruyama, Minoru   96
Meshesha, Million   1, 13
Meunier, Jean-Luc   129
Milewski, Robert   106
Miyao, Hidetoshi   96
Moalla, Ikram   25
Murata, Mayo   506

Nagasaki, Takeshi   413
Nagy, George   164
Nakagawa, Masaki   208
Nakai, Tomohiro   541
Naoi, Satoshi   553
Neves, Luiz Antônio Pereira   176
Nishida, Hirobumi   50

Ogier, Jean-Marc   616
Ohyama, Wataru   506, 593

Paquet, Thierry   564
Park, Joong Jo   62
Pati, Peeta Basa   380
Peng, Liangrui   402
Pervouchine, Vladimir   196
Pratha, Lakshmi   425

Qiang, Qi   474

Raju, Harish   576
Ramakrishnan, A.G.   380
Rangoni, Yves   117
Rath, Toni M.   84
Rawat, Sachin   13
Ren, Zheng   220

Rendek, Jan   604
Richiardi, Jonas   186
Rigamonti, Maurizio   141
Rodríguez, Clemente   496
Rothfeder, Jamie   84

Sankar, K. Pramod   425
Schlapbach, Andreas   186
Shafait, Faisal   368
Shilman, Michael   358
Sikdar, Indraneel Deb   13
Simard, Patrice   358
Simske, Steven J.   588
Sivaswamy, Jayanthi   255
Soda, Giovanni   336
Soundararajan, Padmanabhan   576
Srihari, Rohini   71
Srihari, Sargur   71
Srinivasan, Harish   71
Stotzer, Sylvain   529
Suen, Ching Y.   62
Sun, Jun   553
Suzuki, Masakazu   153

Tabbone, Salvatore   518
Taghva, Kazem   348
Tan, Chew Lim   232, 243, 268, 324, 484
Terasawa, Kengo   413
Tokuno, Junko   208
Tombre, Karl   604
Toyota, Seiichi   153

Uchida, Seiichi   153

Wakabayashi, Tetsushi   506, 593
Wang, Hua   402

Xiu, Pingping   402

Yang, Li   324
Yuan, Bo   268

Zakaria, Noorazrin   616
Zhou, Lijun   243
Zhu, Bilan   208
Zuwala, Daniel   518